Method Infinite

Method Infinite

FREEMASONRY AND THE MORMON RESTORATION

★ CHERYL L. BRUNO ★
★ JOE STEVE SWICK III ★ NICHOLAS S. LITERSKI ★

GREG KOFFORD BOOKS
SALT LAKE CITY, 2022

ISBN: 978-1-58958-689-5 (paperback) 978-1-58958-753-3 (hardcover)
Also available in ebook.

Greg Kofford Books
P.O. Box 1362
Draper, UT 84020
www.gregkofford.com
facebook.com/gkbooks
twitter.com/gkbooks

Library of Congress Cataloging-in-Publication Data

Names: Bruno, Cheryl L., author. | Swick, Joe Steve, III, 1961- author. | Literski, Nicholas S., 1966- author.
Title: Method infinite : Freemasonry and the Mormon Restoration / Cheryl L. Bruno, Joe Steve Swick III, Nicholas S. Literski.
Description: Salt Lake City : Greg Kofford Books, 2022. | Includes bibliographical references and index. | Summary: "While no one thing can entirely explain the rise of The Church of Jesus Christ of Latter-day Saints, the historical influence of Freemasonry on this religious tradition cannot be refuted. Those who study Mormonism have been aware of the impact that Freemasonry had on the founding prophet Joseph Smith during the Nauvoo period, but his involvement in Freemasonry was arguably earlier and broader than many modern historians have admitted. The fact that the most obvious vestiges of Freemasonry are evident only in the more esoteric aspects of the Mormon faith has made it difficult to recognize, let alone fully grasp, the relevant issues. Even those with both Mormon and Masonic experience may not be versed in the nineteenth-century versions of Masonry's rituals, legends, and practices. Without this specialized background, it is easy to miss the Masonic significance of numerous early Mormon ordinances, scripture, and doctrines. Method Infinite: Freemasonry and the Mormon Restoration offers a fresh perspective on the Masonic thread present in Mormonism from its earliest days. Smith's firsthand knowledge of and experience with both Masonry and anti-Masonic currents contributed to the theology, structure, culture, tradition, history, literature, and ritual of the religion he founded"-- Provided by publisher.
Identifiers: LCCN 2021059961 (print) | LCCN 2021059962 (ebook) | ISBN 9781589587533 (hardcover) | ISBN 9781589586895 (paperback) | ISBN 9781589587526 (ebook)
Subjects: LCSH: Church of Jesus Christ of Latter-day Saints--History. | Freemasonry--Religious aspects--Church of Jesus Christ of Latter-day Saints. | Freemasonry--Religious aspects--Mormon Church. | Mormon Church--History.
Classification: LCC HS495 .B884 2022 (print) | LCC HS495 (ebook) | DDC 366/.1--dc23/eng/20220201
LC record available at https://lccn.loc.gov/2021059961
LC ebook record available at https://lccn.loc.gov/2021059962

There is method in Mormonism—method infinite. Mormonism is Masonic.
—Edward Tullidge, *The Women of Mormondom*

CONTENTS

PREFACE

Tis this and 'tis that, They cannot tell what,
Why so many great Men of the Nation,
Should Aprons put on, To make themselves one
With a Free or an Accepted Mason.
                    —Entered Apprentice Song, 1723

Scholars have largely disregarded the tremendous influence exerted by Freemasonry on nineteenth-century American political, social, and religious institutions. As Steven Bullock noted, Masonry seems "too obscure, too unusual to hold much [scholarly or historical] interest." However, he further argued that this "very obscurity" of American "interest and emotional investment in Masonry" can provide "a point of entry that offers a new perspective" for the careful historian. Bullock's study "seeks to understand the appeal of Masonry for eighteenth- and early-nineteenth-century Americans" and "to illuminate the society and culture that first nurtured and then rejected it."[1]

The appeal of Masonry in Joseph Smith's Restoration movement deserves the same careful consideration. Smith was a teenager in a family with strong Masonic ties during the time and the place of the fraternity's greatest upheaval and transformation. His involvement in Freemasonry was arguably earlier and broader than many modern historians have admitted. While no one thing can entirely explain the rise of Mormonism, the historical influence of Freemasonry on this religious tradition cannot be refuted.

This work approaches the subject of Mormonism and Masonry with Bullock's view in mind. It offers a fresh perspective on the relationship between Freemasonry and the Mormon restoration. It asserts that the Mormon prophet's firsthand knowledge of and experience with both Masonry and anti-Masonic currents contributed to the theology, structure, culture, tradition, history, literature, and ritual of the church he founded. There is a Masonic thread in Mormonism from its earliest days.

The topic of Mormonism and Freemasonry has been rife with misunderstanding and misrepresentation, often because scholars have invariably been lacking in one or both relevant perspectives. Few Latter-day Saints who were also Masons have authored book-length treatments of the relationship between the two traditions. The fact that the most obvious vestiges of Freemasonry are

---

1. Steven C. Bullock, *Revolutionary Brotherhood: Freemasonry and the Transformation of the American Social Order, 1730–1840*, 2.

evident only in the more esoteric aspects of the Mormon faith has made it difficult for Masonic authors to recognize, let alone fully grasp, the relevant issues. Even those with both Mormon and Masonic experience may not be versed in the nineteenth-century versions of the rituals, legends, and practices. Without this specialized background, many researchers and writers have missed the Masonic significance of numerous early Mormon statements, doctrines, and practices.

The authors have spent many years researching and wrestling with the subject of Freemasonry's influence upon Mormonism. Nick Literski was the first Mormon Freemason in Hancock County since the Mormon exodus. Nick began the preliminary research and writing of this book in 2002, spending years traveling around the country to examine original records. The resulting expertise became noteworthy in many conferences and online venues. A change in life circumstances led Nick to pass years of research, analysis, and drafts of early chapters on to Joe Swick, a Mormon Freemason and Past Master of Verity Lodge No. 59 in Kent, Washington. Both Joe and Nick approached this project with the benefit of their experiences as Master Masons, Royal Arch Masons, Cryptic Masons, Knights Templar, and Scottish Rite Masons. A student of early Masonic history, Joe amassed a large library of eighteenth- and nineteenth-century Masonic works. His collection, as well as his ideas and insights, have been invaluable to the production of this book. Cheryl Bruno came into the project in 2012. Her interest in esoterica in early Mormonism made Freemasonry a primary research topic, and her writing skills pushed the work to completion. As we researched, we found not just facts, but a fascinating story. The three of us, along with Clinton Bartholemew, Patrick McCleary, Roy Schmidt, Arturo de Hoyos, and Joseph Johnstun (who designed our fabulous book cover) spent hours discussing the evidence and implications of what we had discovered. We thank them, Holly Welker, who provided valuable editing assistance, and many others who have listened to our ideas and offered encouragement. Loyd Isao Ericson, instrumental in the production of *Method Infinite* during the long haul before and through the Covid crisis, has never ceased to believe in us and this project. Throughout our investigation, we have been inspired by the statement Edward Tullidge attributes to Eliza R. Snow: "There is method in Mormonism—method infinite. Mormonism is Masonic."[2] We hope this book will provide the reader a measure of the adventure and insight we found during the many years of its creation.

---

2. Eliza R. Snow in Edward W. Tullidge, *The Women of Mormondom*, 79.

INTRODUCTION

JACHIN AND BOAZ ON THE WOODPILE

In strength I will establish this mine house to stand firm forever.
—Richard Carlile, *Manual of Freemasonry in Three Parts*

Early spring in Salt Lake City is often chilly, though budding vegetation and early flowers saluted the members of the Quorum of the Twelve Apostles of The Church of Jesus Christ of Latter-day Saints as they made their way to the Salt Lake Temple on the morning of April 4, 1899. In this inspiring setting, they held their quarterly meetings in preparation for the Church's upcoming semi-annual general conference. Seated at the front of the room was the quorum's aged president, Elder Franklin Dewey Richards. Throughout the day, each of the apostles spoke to the quorum on various topics pertaining to their ministry, but Richards's words were extraordinary. Elder Rudger Clawson, then the junior member of the quorum, recorded his impressions in his personal diary:

> Pres. Richards . . . said he desired to say a few words about Freemasonry. A Masonic Lodge, he said, was established in Nauvoo and Joseph Smith, Brigham Young, Willard Richards, John Taylor, Lorenzo Snow, Orson Hyde, F. D. Richards, and about 1000 others in all became Masons. Joseph, the Prophet, was aware that there were some things about Masonry which had come down from the beginning and he desired to know what they were, hence the lodge. The Masons admitted some keys of knowledge appertaining to Masonry were lost. Joseph enquired of the Lord concerning the matter and He revealed to the Prophet true Masonry, as we have it in our temples. Owing to the superior knowledge Joseph had received, the Masons became jealous and cut off the Mormon Lodge.[1]

Fellow apostle Elder John Henry Smith, who had served since 1880, was more circumspect in his comments: "All of the Apostles met in their room in the Temple and the day was spent in happy talk and in giving instruction. At our afternoon meeting President F. D. Richards gave some pleasing explanations of Doctrine."[2] Elder Anthon H. Lund, also in attendance, simply wrote, "Meetings were very interesting today. Prest. Richards explained Nauvoo Masonry e.t.c."[3] Other apostles, such as Elder Brigham Young Jr., recorded the meeting without comment on Richards's words.

---

1. Stan Larson, *A Ministry of Meetings: The Apostolic Diaries of Rudger Clawson*, 41.
2. Jean Bickmore White, ed., *Church, State, and Politics: The Diaries of John Henry Smith*, 422.
3. Anthon H. Lund diary, April 4, 1899, in John P. Hatch, ed., *Danish Apostle: The Diaries of Anthon H. Lund, 1890–1921*, 53.

Franklin Richards's diary provides context for his address to the Twelve. Twelve days earlier, he had spent an afternoon consulting the original records of the Nauvoo Lodge.[4] His account of the April 4 meeting states:

> I spoke of the Masonic Organization in Nauvoo & some of the circumstances which led up to the Prophet Joseph asking of the Lord & obtaining promise to restore that which was lost indeed to <u>Restore all things</u> which enraged the high officials of the Mystic Order so that the National Grand conclave expelled or cut off all the Mormon Masonic Order from their fellowship.
>
> The brethren appreciated my explanation highly and I felt reli[e]ved in my Spirit for having accomplished it as it had pressed upon my mind for some time past.[5]

Of the twelve men serving as Apostles in 1899, only Richards had become a Master Mason in Nauvoo. The next senior apostle, Brigham Young Jr., was a child of nine years old when the Latter-day Saints left Illinois under his father's direction. The urgency obvious in Richards's diary reflects his sense that history was already being lost with the passing of the first Mormon generation. With his comments limited by obligations he held sacred, Richards had attempted to convey the nature of "Nauvoo Masonry" to the uninitiated.

Fourteen years earlier, Richards had returned to visit the remnants of Nauvoo, Illinois. The former Masonic Hall received considerable attention in his private diary, where he noted that the building had been repurposed into a private home. In a published account of the 1885 visit, Richards stated:

> Every thing which signified the character of the building has been removed. This spoliation must have been recent, for I saw [Jachin] and Boaz lying upon the wood-pile, accompanied by other emblems and insignia which had been stripped from the building.[6]

The mention by Richards to seeing "Jachin and Boaz lying upon the wood-pile" as a sign of "recent spoliation" would have been a disturbing one for any Mason, and a profoundly distressing symbol for Richards and other Nauvoo Freemasons. In the Bible, Jachin and Boaz are the names of the pillars standing on the porch at the entrance to Solomon's Temple, and they are of great symbolic significance to Masons.[7] *Jachin*, meaning "to establish," was the pillar situated on the south side of the entrance. *Boaz*, meaning "in strength," was located on the north side of the entrance of the Temple. In Masonic tradition, these pillars are said to allude together to the promise of God to King David: "In strength will I establish this mine house and kingdom forever."[8]

---

4. Franklin D. Richards journal, March 23, 1899.

5. Richards journal, April 4, 1899; emphasis in original.

6. Franklin D. Richards, "A Visit to Pueblo, Independence, Carthage, Nauvoo, Richmond, etc.," 471.

7. See 1 Kings 7:15–22 and 2 Chronicles 3:15–17 for the biblical description of these pillars.

8. These precise words are not found in the Bible. However, for their substance, see 1 Chronicles 17:11–14. For early Christian Freemasons, the two pillars alluded to the two

Mystical alchemical diagram of Boaz and Jachin, pillars of the Temple of Jerusalem, 1782.

Pillars representing Jachin and Boaz are placed inside of the entrance to every Masonic lodge, forming a portal through which candidates must pass each time they are admitted for initiation. Because pillars are often the symbol of a covenant, they are intended as a powerful reminder to the Freemason of certain covenants mentioned in the Bible and of his own Masonic obligations:

> And [King Josiah] went up into the house of the LORD, and all the men of Judah and all the inhabitants of Jerusalem with him . . . and he read in their ears all the words of the book of the covenant. . . . And [he] stood by a pillar, and made a covenant before the Lord . . . to perform the words of this covenant . . . written in this book. (2 Kgs. 23:1–3)[9]

What was it that would "press upon" Richards's mind so heavily, leading him to give clarification to the rising group of Church leaders before his death? Perhaps he foresaw just how deeply this part of Mormon history would be buried and forgotten. At the conclusion of the nineteenth century, Richards was speaking to a new generation of Mormons who were not Freemasons. His audience was so widely separated by time and by distance that they had become oblivious to an America that had been entrenched in Freemasonry. Present in the original colonies, Masonry grew and developed along with the new nation. Masonic orations and sermons were published as early as the 1740s and 50s. By the 1800s, it had become a vital part of popular social, political, and religious culture and discourse.

Richards, born in 1821, understood something in Freemasonry that explained and enriched the story of the Church's origins and deepened the significance of Mormonism's own Masonic-inspired rituals—and he wished to pass it on. But those who had turned the corner into a modern era had become far removed from the esoteric system that influenced how Joseph Smith and his colleagues both viewed and understood their work.

While the transformation of the elaborate Nauvoo Lodge into the common dwelling-place that Richards observed in 1885 was literal, he also became witness to a spiritual and historical transformation within Mormonism itself. By the time of his April 1899 meeting with the apostles, Richards had lived to see the transformation of Mormonism's theocratic kingdom into a more conventional American church. Believing it was established by the hand of God through a prophet-heir to David's throne, the Saints of the Great Basin Kingdom had assumed their "religious and civil" order would exist forever.[10] Yet, like the gloriously beautiful Masonic lodge in Nauvoo, the Mormons' own "grand design"

---

covenants: Old (Jewish) and New (Christian).

9. King Josiah is the famed restorer-king of Israel. During his reign, a copy of the lost Book of the Law was discovered by Hilkiah the Priest. The recovery of this book enabled Josiah to restore the worship of the true God to the Israelites. This account is important for Royal Arch Masons and has significant echoes in Mormon tradition as well. See 2 Kings 22, 2 Chronicles 34.

10. "This [the Masonic] society . . . is at once RELIGIOUS AND CIVIL," and in it "great regard has been given to the first knowledge of the GOD OF NATURE, and

Former Nauvoo Masonic Hall, 1885.

lay stripped of the emblems and insignia of its holy and Masonically inspired purpose. Eight months later, the senior apostle would pass on, leaving President Lorenzo Snow as the last surviving Nauvoo Mason.[11] By the time the Nauvoo Masonic Hall was restored in the latter part of the twentieth century, even its original purpose would be masked with a new name, the "Cultural Hall."[12]

Overshadowed by such significant events as the First Vision and the martyrdom of Joseph and Hyrum Smith, one of the most pivotal events in Mormon history has gone largely unappreciated. On March 15 and 16, 1842, in the upper room of his store in Nauvoo, Illinois, Joseph Smith followed the footsteps of his older brother,

---

that acceptable service wherewith he is well pleased." William Hutchinson, *The Spirit of Masonry: in Moral and Elucidatory Lectures*, 9; emphasis in original.

11. Michael W. Homer, "'Similarity of Priesthood in Masonry': The Relationship between Freemasonry and Mormonism," 75.

12. The building's sign does make note that the "Cultural Hall" was used for a variety of purposes, including Masonic meetings. Historian Stanley B. Kimball took exception to the renaming of the building during a conversation with LDS Apostle Mark E. Petersen, who responded, "Why do historians have to tell everything? What is this mania you have for telling everything?" Kimball replied, "Brother Petersen, you can't bottle up truth. Now, would you rather have responsible Mormon historians answer the critics, or should we just abandon the field and let the anti-Mormons run all over it?" Maurine Carr Ward, "The Maverick Historian: A Conversation with Stanley B. Kimball," 109.

receiving the three degrees of Ancient York Freemasonry.[13] Smith's formal induction into the Craft was a ratification and extension of Masonic activity in which he had been immersed since his youth. As an adult, Smith relied on Masonry as one of the primary lenses and means by which he sought to approach God and restore true religion. Yet this aspect of his work has been abandoned by his modern-day followers. Masonry in Mormonism has been placed upon the woodpile.

Just as Joseph Smith's name "should be both good and evil spoken of among all people" (JS—H 1:33), later writers would treat the prophet's participation in Freemasonry with varying degrees of excuses, speculation, and outright denial. From the very beginning, some would suggest that Smith plagiarized Freemasonry in the development of Mormon ritual. In his 1842 *History of the Saints*, John C. Bennett (a former assistant in the First Presidency) indirectly made such an allegation by reporting Mormon practices in specific language familiar to both Freemasons and readers of anti-Masonic exposés.[14] Freemason Samuel Goodwin made the same accusation in 1921.[15]

Largely in response to such charges, modern writers have sought to distance Smith from the Fraternity and have downplayed the significant influence of Freemasonry on the Mormon Prophet's thinking. By the mid-twentieth century, Mormon writer E. Cecil McGavin concluded that Joseph Smith attended only six Masonic meetings during his lifetime. Three of these meetings, McGavin explained, were Smith's initiation under the direction of Illinois Grand Master Abraham Jonas, on March 15 and 16, 1842:

> The Prophet was so busy with Church matters that he never took an active part in lodge work. It seems from the meager records that are extant, that Joseph Smith attended as many meetings on those two days as he did during the rest of his lifetime. . . . In the months that followed, he left the lodge work in the hands of others, never attending more than three subsequent meetings and never receiving a higher degree than the one the Grand Master conferred upon him at the third meeting he attended.[16]

Another Mormon historian wrote in 1992 that "Joseph Smith participated minimally in Freemasonry and, as far as is known, attended the Nauvoo Masonic Lodge on only three occasions."[17]

At the time these writers made their claims, the standard *History of The Church of Jesus Christ of Latter-day Saints* included twelve separate occasions upon which Joseph Smith attended Masonic meetings.[18] Additionally, secretaries

---

13. "History, 1838–1856, volume C-1 [2 November 1838–31 July 1842]," The Joseph Smith Papers, 1289, 1295.

14. John C. Bennett, *History of the Saints, or, An Exposé of Joe Smith and Mormonism*, 265–78.

15. See Samuel H. Goodwin, *Mormonism and Masonry: Origins, Connections and Coincidences between Mason and Mormon Temple/Templar Ritual*, 50–64.

16. E. Cecil McGavin, *Mormonism and Masonry*, 90.

17. Kenneth W. Godfrey, "Freemasonry in Nauvoo," 527–28.

18. Joseph Smith Jr. et al., *History of the Church of Jesus Christ of Latter-day Saints*, 4:550, 552, 588, 589, 594; 5:18, 85, 200, 253, 260, 446; 6:287. Other references are

keeping the minute book of Nauvoo Lodge, despite occasionally missing some attendees, recorded Joseph Smith's attendance at no less than thirty-five Lodge meetings on twenty-seven separate days between March 15, 1842, and June 27, 1844.[19] A comparison of the official minutes with the *History of the Church* indicates that neither provided a complete accounting of the Prophet's approximately forty visits. A typical 1840s Masonic lodge would have met twenty-eight times or fewer during the same period of time. Thus, Smith attended more lodge meetings than members of most Masonic lodges. While some writers appear to have performed inadequate research, resulting in errors which have been carelessly repeated over subsequent decades, others seem to have intentionally minimized the historical record.

Some writers have attempted to explain Smith's involvement in Masonry as a nineteenth-century equivalent of social and political networking.[20] However, to allege that he became a Mason in order to court social connections or political power is defamatory. In his petition to receive the degrees of Freemasonry, Smith would have submitted a written statement that he had no mercenary motive for entering the Fraternity.[21] Thus, to claim that "Joseph Smith and his brethren sought membership in the Masonic lodge" because they "desired the prestige, protection, and power such an alliance should have guaranteed" is to argue against the integrity of the Prophet and his companions.[22] Furthermore, the proceedings of the Nauvoo Lodge under Smith's direction demonstrate his unmitigated lack of concern for making friends and cementing alliances among local Freemasons. Still, this reasoning has been accepted among members of The Church of Jesus Christ of Latter-day Saints to the present day.

In honor of the 150th anniversary of Joseph and Hyrum Smith's martyrdom in 1994, Gary James Joslin produced a tribute volume entitled *Saint Masons: The Divine Restoration and Freemasonry.* Joslin described his own work as "An account of the Restoration from the Heavens to this Planet of the Ancient

---

made to meetings in "the lodge," which are not included here due to lack of clarity.

19. See "Nauvoo Masonic Lodge minutes, 1841–1842."

20. David John Buerger, "The Development of the Mormon Temple Endowment Ceremony," 87–88.

21. "The subscriber, residing in the City of Nauvoo, State of Illinois, of lawful age, and by occupation a [unreadable], begs leave to state that, unbiased by friends, and uninfluenced by mercenary motives, he freely and voluntarily offers himself as a candidate for the mysteries of Masonry, and that he is prompted to solicit this privilege by a favourable opinion conceived of the Institution, a desire of knowledge, and a sincere wish of being serviceable to his fellow creatures. Should his petition be granted, he will cheerfully conform to all the ancient established usages and customs of the Fraternity." See the 1840 Petition of Stephen A. Douglas to Springfield Lodge No. 26 of Free and Accepted Masons, reproduced in Everett R. Turnbull, *The Rise and Progress of Freemasonry in Illinois 1783–1952*, illustration facing page 240.

22. McGavin, *Mormonism and Masonry*, 13.

Science of Righteousness, along with its Brief Contact with and the Testimony to Freemasonry in the Latter Days as a witness and Grand Sign from the Supreme Architect of the Universe."[23] His writing suggested that Mormonism was the fulfillment of Freemasonry, concluding that the Masonic "torch had been passed" to a triumphant Mormonism. To make his case, Joslin points out several of what he interpreted as parallels between the Masonic legend of Hiram Abiff and Hyrum Smith, the Prophet's older brother. Joslin's observations, however, have been taken seriously by only a few Latter-day Saints.

On April 20, 1974, at a meeting of the Mormon History Association, Latter-day Saint educator Reed C. Durham Jr. attempted to objectively examine the relationship between Mormonism and Freemasonry. Unofficial transcripts of his speech, "Is There No Help for the Widow's Son?" spread rapidly through the Mormon historical community. Durham's insightful but controversial lecture reached its climax in stating "that there [were] few significant developments in the Church, that occurred after March 15, 1842, which did not have some Masonic interdependence." Expanding on this theme, Durham noted,

> The parallels of Joseph Smith and the history of Mormonism are so unmistakable, that to explain them only as coincidence would be ridiculous. . . . Aspects of [Masonic] legend seem transformed into the history of Joseph Smith, so much so that . . . it appears to be a kind of symbolic acting out of Masonic lore.[24]

While Durham touched upon some of "these aspects of [Masonic] legend," he focused chiefly on the coming forth of the Book of Mormon and Joseph Smith's assassination, leaving later researchers the task of fully investigating other possible parallels.

The reaction to Durham's lecture was strong and immediate. His suggestions that Freemasonry had influenced Mormon doctrine and practice were interpreted by some Mormon scholars as an attack on the divine origins of the Church. By the following morning, Masonic iconography was removed from the angelic weathervane atop a Nauvoo Temple model in the local LDS Visitor's Center in that city. And, as an employee of the LDS Church Educational System, Durham was required to issue a public "clarification," reaffirming his belief in the prophetic mission of Joseph Smith.

In another controversial treatment, "The Treasure of the Widow's Son," researcher Jack Adamson noted parallels between Masonic legend and the Book of Mormon as well as the history of Joseph Smith. Taking a naturalistic approach, Adamson asserted that Smith had plagiarized Masonic legend and that Mormon scripture was filled with anti-Masonic "clang" (psychologically influenced morphing of words and terms). Still, even Adamson acknowledged certain inexplicable coincidences in the details of Smith's death, in which he reportedly cried,

---

23. Gary James Joslin, *Saint Masons: The Divine Restoration and Freemasonry*, xxvi.
24. Reed C. Durham Jr., "Is There No Help for the Widow's Son?"

"Is there no help for the widow's son?"—an important phrase in Masonic ritual. This final scene constitutes a "symbolic acting out of Masonic lore":

> In this event, symbol is not merely transformed into Joseph's inner history or his sacred writings. Rather, the action goes beyond metaphor and the symbol merges into tragic reality.[25]

The study of Freemasonry and Mormonism has been greatly influenced by the many writings of the late Mervin B. Hogan, a leading light in the Utah Masonic Lodge of Research. Hogan argued strongly against the long-standing prohibition by the Grand Lodge of Utah barring active Latter-day Saints from Masonry in their jurisdiction. His nominal participation in Mormonism during this time allowed him to become a Utah Freemason despite this strictly enforced restriction. As a Mason, he would eventually come to play a critical role, positively influencing a change in the Masonic policy of exclusion. At the same time, the Church's leader, President Spencer W. Kimball, sought to improve relations with the Masonic community by omitting language that discouraged participation in Freemasonry from the Church's official policy book. Hogan's work was undoubtedly groundbreaking and, in his numerous monographs, he frequently discussed the shared history of the two groups. Yet, as one of Hogan's reviewers stated, "A definitive history on the subject of Freemasonry and Mormonism has yet to be written."[26]

In 1994, Michael W. Homer provided what was then the most significant scholarly analysis of Mormon involvement with Freemasonry: "'Similarity of Priesthood in Masonry': The Relationship between Freemasonry and Mormonism." [27] Homer's essay reviewed the oft-tempestuous relationship between the two groups throughout the history of The Church of Jesus Christ of Latter-day Saints. Briefly noting parallels between Joseph Smith's life and Masonic legend, Homer observed that "[t]he mythology associated with Smith's martyrdom also has Masonic undertones" and that certain "images are similar to portions in the legend of Hiram Abiff."[28] In 2014, Homer expanded his article into a book-length treatment titled *Joseph's Temples: The Dynamic Relationship between Freemasonry and Mormonism*. In this work, Homer added a creative but controversial connection between Freemasonry and the LDS Church's position on blacks and the priesthood.

Furthermore, Matthew B. Brown and Jeffrey M. Bradshaw have both compared Mormon temple ritual with the ancient past, and they both downplay the relationship of the Mormon endowment with Masonic rites;[29] Clyde

---

25. Jack Adamson, "The Treasure of the Widow's Son," 11.

26. Kent L. Walgren, "Fast and Loose Masonry," 176.

27. Homer, "Similarity of Priesthood in Masonry," 76.

28. Homer, 95–96.

29. Matthew B. Brown, *Exploring the Connection between Mormons and Masons*, 21–24; Jeffrey M. Bradshaw, "Freemasonry and the Origins of Modern Temple Ordinances," 159–237.

Forsberg has explored esoteric aspects of Mormonism and Freemasonry in two books and several articles;[30] a chapter in Samuel M. Brown's book on the early Mormon conquest of death has included an insightful chapter on Freemasonry in Mormonism;[31] and numerous others have made their own contributions. Yet none of these writers have captured the full scope of the influence of Masonry on the culture in which Joseph Smith lived, nor have they recognized the incorporation of so many aspects of the Fraternity into the early Church.

Official LDS publications have been reticent to discuss the influence Freemasonry had on the Church. In the 2018 church-published volume, *Saints: The Story of the Church of Jesus Christ in the Latter Days: Volume 1: The Standard of Truth: 1815–1846*, despite several chapters covering Nauvoo, Masonry is mentioned only to discount its similarity with the temple endowment.[32] An entry on "Masonry" on the Church official website covers the subject more fully but takes a similar approach. "There are some similarities between Masonic ceremonies and the endowment, but there are also stark differences in their content and intent," the essay states. It also perpetuates the view that Joseph Smith's purpose in becoming a Freemason was to make social and political connections:

> In joining, Joseph may have assumed he would gain a network of allies who could give him access to political influence and protection against persecution. After being betrayed by some of his closest associates in Missouri, Joseph may have found Masonry's emphasis on confidentiality and loyalty appealing.[33]

This book will present evidence that Joseph Smith's actions, in tandem with those of the Mormon Masonic Lodges, were diametrically opposed to what they would have been if the object in joining with Freemasonry was gaining allies. It will demonstrate the strength of Masonry's presence in the culture that surrounded Joseph Smith, from his birth to his death. Throughout his life, Smith was deeply enmeshed in the esoteric tradition that surrounded the Craft, and he developed groups and associations within his new Church organization modeled upon the Fraternity. Masonry would thus influence the Mormon restoration from Vermont to New York, Ohio, Missouri, and Illinois. Believing himself to be a Masonic restorer, Smith called upon God to inspire him to create ritual in the Masonic mold. In doing so, he sought to know the true name of Deity—which in Masonic tradition had been "long lost"—and to bring his followers into the presence of the Divine.

30. Clyde R. Forsberg Jr., *Divine Rite of Kings: Land, Same Sex and Empire in Mormonism and the Esoteric Tradition*; Clyde R. Forsberg Jr., *Equal Rites: The Book of Mormon, Masonry, Gender, and American Culture*.

31. Samuel Morris Brown, *In Heaven as it is on Earth: Joseph Smith and the Early Mormon Conquest of Death*, 170–202.

32. The Church of Jesus Christ of Latter-day Saints, *Saints: The Story of the Church of Jesus Christ in the Latter Days: Volume 1: The Standard of Truth 1815–1846*, 454–55.

33. "Masonry," Church History Topics.

To ground the discussion, we will begin with general background on Freemasonry, then move to an overview of the prevalence of Freemasonry throughout the Northeast United States during Joseph Smith's formative years. We will then provide an explanation of Masonic midrash and the way Joseph used it to produce canonical LDS texts, social structures, and rituals. This Masonic technique affected the way Smith explained his own experiences in restoring "true Masonry" from his first vision to his presidential campaign. We will explore the proliferation of Mormon Masonic Lodges during the Nauvoo period and the Masonic imagery that surrounded the Mormon leader's death. Finally, we will demonstrate how the perpetuation of Masonic elements in numerous sects that succeeded Smith's Mormonism highlights the essential value of Freemasonry in the founding movement.

Opinions in this book are our own and do not attempt to represent the official views of any church organization. However, our approach comes from the perspective of The Church of Jesus Christ of Latter-day Saints headquartered in Salt Lake City. Therefore, the spelling, capitalization, and hyphenation of the phrase "Latter-day Saints" in the name of the Church is used regardless of time period. We do use the words "Mormon" and "Mormonism" for ease of expression and because this convention has been liberally employed throughout the era we are writing about. Furthermore, we have the greatest of respect toward both Latter-day Saint endowment and Masonic rituals, and we have taken great care when discussing the content of these ceremonies. Also with due respect, we generally refer to people by surnames, except when first names are needed to distinguish between family members.

In researching the topic at hand, we have identified both broad ideas and specific items that have been overlooked, misunderstood, or even misrepresented by both Mormons and Masons. In other cases, 160 years have buried the details to the point where conclusions must be reached by circumstantial evidence. Wherever this is the case, we have tried to demonstrate clearly the reasoning behind our conclusions. We believe, as Franklin D. Richards taught, that Joseph Smith's claimed "restoration of all things" contains far more of Freemasonry than either his critics or his supporters have previously imagined.

CHAPTER 1

LEGENDS OF THE CRAFT: THE PHILOSOPHIC SYSTEM OF FREEMASONRY

Of the various modes of communicating instruction to the uninformed, the masonic student is particularly interested in two; namely, the instruction by legends and that by symbols. It is to these two, almost exclusively, that he is indebted for all that he knows, and for all that he can know, of the philosophic system which is taught in the institution.
—Albert G. Mackey, *The Symbolism of Freemasonry*

From its earliest known history, Freemasonry had a rich and colorful legendary tradition, blending truth and fiction in a soup intended to both reinforce its allegorical instruction and give legitimacy and support to its existence. Its historical beginnings were in associations of actual (or "operative") stonemasons who used tokens and signs to distinguish professional Masons from frauds and then safeguarded those hand signals and body positions with keywords. These, in addition to rites and rituals of progression through the craft of stonemasonry, fostered a sense of fraternalism. Members of the trade guilds viewed themselves as successors of the great builders of old, going back to the construction of Solomon's Temple.

During the Medieval period, men who were not stonemasons began to be accepted into the existing network of lodges and guilds relating to the building craft that existed across Europe. These "Accepted Masons"[1] provided financial support through membership fees, placing men who laid stone for a living together with a congregation of educated middle-class and wealthy men who had "an active interest in esotericism, alchemy, Qabala, Hermeticism and utopian ideals."[2] The history of the Craft during this era is shrouded in mystery. Some writers, for example, like to entertain the possibility that Knights Templar fleeing from persecution in France in 1307 came to Scotland and "hid themselves among the

---

1. An account book belonging to "the Company of ffremasons wthin the Citie of London" dated July 1, 1619, contains evidence "that besides the ordinary Freemen and Liverymen of this Company there were other members who are termed in the books the 'Accepted Masons.'" Money was received from these persons "for theyr gratuitie at theyr acceptance into this Lyvery." Albert G. Mackey, William G. Hughan, and Edward L. Hawkins, *An Encyclopaedia of Freemasonry and its Kindred Sciences, Comprising the Whole Range of Arts, Sciences and Literature as Connected with the Institution*, 1:10.

2. Mark Stavish, *Freemasonry: Rituals, Symbols & History of the Secret Society*, 5.

The Baal's Bridge Square, 1507.

stonemasons."[3] Others dismiss this notion. In any case, operative Freemasons were steeped in mystical teachings and magical traditions then associated with the building lore. Some of these ideas were indeed quite ancient. About 280 BCE, for example, the philosopher Mencius taught,

> [M]en should apply the *Square and Compasses* figuratively to their lives, and *the Level* and the *Marking Line* besides, if they would walk the straight and even paths of wisdom and keep themselves within the boundaries of Honour and Virtue.[4]

An early example of an operative Mason moralizing upon his working tools is a brass square excavated from under the foundation of the old Baal's Bridge in Limerick, Ireland, dated 1517 and inscribed with the words "I will strive to live with love and care, Upon the level, by the square."[5]

As Freemasonry transitioned into a speculative rather than a primarily operative institution, it attracted churchmen and antiquarians with a keen interest in history. They combed religious and historical records, embellishing their descriptions of the Masonic past with what they found there. Over time, speculative Masonry developed a significant body of legend and myth. It drew upon legends as old as humanity, tracing the Craft to ancient Egypt, to King Solomon's Temple, and all the way to the biblical Enoch and Adam. Begun as an oral tradition, this body of work appears in written form in various documents known as the "Gothic Constitutions," the earliest of which is dated as far back as the late fifteenth century.[6]

Masonic constitutions and their associated histories were the institutional counterpart of a royal genealogy. Both the monarchs' genealogy and the Masons' books of constitutions connected the present with the mythological past to es-

---

3. Stavish, 5–6. See also W. Kirk MacNulty, *Freemasonry: Symbols, Secrets, Significance*, 21.

4. Quoted in Andrew Sommerville MacBride, *Speculative Masonry: Its Mission, Its Evolution and Its Landmarks*, 140; emphasis in original.

5. Some sketches of the square interpret the date as 1507. See Philip Crossee, "The Baal's Bridge Square."

6. That is, the *Halliwell MS*, otherwise known as the *Regius Manuscript*. For examples of the Old Gothic Constitutions, see Wallace McLeod, ed., *The Old Gothic Constitutions*.

tablish the appearance of long continuity and therefore legitimacy. Further, both genealogy and constitutions provided historical stories, embroidered with rich details intended to illustrate and promote the virtues and chief values of their respected institutions. The literal truthfulness of these accounts was far less important than the ethical lessons they imparted. When a man was made a Mason, the ceremony included a reading of both the moral obligations he was charged with and the legendary history of Freemasonry found in the constitutions. The earliest positively identified speculative Masons were Englishmen Sir Robert Moray (initiated in 1641) and Elias Ashmole (initiated in 1646).[7]

In the year 1717, a date sometimes understood as marking the beginning of organized Freemasonry,[8] four lodges located in London joined together to form the first Masonic Grand Lodge.[9] Six years later, a member of this Grand Lodge, Dr. James Anderson, consulted past and present Grand Masters as well as previously existing regulations to publish *The Constitutions of Freemasonry, Containing the History, Charges, Regulations, &c. of that Most Ancient and Right Worshipful Fraternity*. This definitive work, still in use in the present day, established and formalized the "landmarks" of Masonry.

From the time of Anderson's *Constitutions*, the degree system, based upon mystical and oral traditions, became evident. Framers of the rituals used the tools of operative masonry, such as trowels, hammers, and rules of architecture, to symbolize spiritual truths. The metaphors of stone working were thus transformed into morality plays representing human development and enlightenment.

The Three Degrees of Craft, or Blue Lodge Masonry

In "Craft" or "Blue Lodge" Masonry, an applicant is "initiated" into the first or Entered Apprentice degree. Following a period of time during which he studies and becomes proficient, he is "passed" into the Fellowcraft degree. Finally, he is "raised" a Master Mason. Every Mason is a Master Mason, and the term should not be confused with the Master of a Lodge (or "Worshipful Master") who is the chief of several officers over a group (or "lodge") of men. The principal offices

---

7. "The names of the Brethren present at his initiation are recorded in Ashmole's diary, and that 'casual Lodge' appears to have contained no operative masons." MacNulty, *Freemasonry*, 22.

8. For the existence of speculative Freemasonry, speculative lodges, and Accepted Freemasons in the fifteenth through the seventeenth centuries, see Harry L. Haywood, "How Operative Masonry Changed to Speculative Masonry: The Period of Transition."

9. Additional Grand Lodges were formed in Ireland starting in 1725, the American colonies in 1733, France in 1733, Sweden in 1735, Scotland in 1736, Germany in 1740, Denmark in 1743, and the Netherlands in 1756. In 1751, due to conflicting beliefs, a rival "Antient" Grand Lodge was formed in England. It competed with the existing Grand Lodge for sixty years before differences were resolved by the formation of the United Grand Lodge of England in 1813.

of a lodge are Worshipful Master, Senior Warden, Junior Warden, Secretary, and Treasurer, as well as Senior and Junior Deacon, Steward, and Tyler.

A grand lodge presides over groups of lodges in a similar relationship as that of Mormon stakes over wards. Grand lodges consist of the same officers as lodges, but with a "grand" preceding their title, such as "Grand Master," "Grand Senior Warden," "Grand Secretary," and so forth. In the United States, there is generally one grand lodge in each state, with jurisdiction over all the lodges therein.

Blue Lodge Masonry's three degrees are presented as ritual dramas that are acted out by the initiate and assisted by the lodge brothers. Catechisms and lectures are used to reinforce the lessons taught.

In the Entered Apprentice degree, a candidate is offered "an opportunity to prove himself by his ability to fulfill a solemn obligation and to keep secret those things entrusted to him as such," while being taught moral lessons. Tools formerly used by operative masons to assist them in their work are given allegorical functions that are explained in this degree. The twenty-four inch gauge, once used to measure and lay out the day's work, is now symbolically employed to divide a twenty-four-hour day into equal parts: eight hours set apart for duty to God and one's fellow man, eight for vocational activities, and eight for refreshment and sleep. The common gavel, a tool used to break the rough edges off stones, is presented as a symbol of ridding the mind of vices and the superfluities of life.[10]

In the Fellow Craft degree, the candidate is introduced to the "seven liberal arts and sciences": grammar, rhetoric, logic, arithmetic, geometry, astronomy, and music, which, taken together, are said to represent all human knowledge. Symbolic tools for this degree, the square, the level, and the plumb, are used to test and evaluate one's work. The candidate is instructed in the legendary building of King Solomon's Temple and is given symbolic wages of corn, wine, and oil.[11]

Finally, in the Master Mason degree, the candidate's working tools comprise all the implements of Masonry but most particularly the Trowel. Employed by operative Masons to spread mortar onto bricks, joining them together, it is used symbolically to spread the cement of brotherly love and affection. Through the performance of the ritual drama of this degree, candidates are taught the allegorical legend of Hiram Abiff.[12]

Loss and Recovery: The Legend of Hiram Abiff

The entire Masonic tradition is rife with themes of loss and recovery. This is clearly seen in Masonry's central myth. The Hiramic legend, an expansion of a biblical story, was presented in its early iterations as an historical artifact. At the same time, it emerged as an allegorical telling of the death, burial, and resurrec-

---

10. "Symbolic Ancient Craft Masonry," King Solomon's Lodge.

11. "Symbolic Ancient Craft Masonry." Further information regarding these wages is given in the Capitular degrees in the York Rite.

12. "Symbolic Ancient Craft Masonry."

tion of Jesus Christ. As told in seventeenth- and eighteenth-century Masonic "exposures,"[13] Hiram, the master builder of Solomon's Temple, would not reveal the secret of the Master's Word to three impatient craftsmen before the completion of the Temple. To Freemasons, the Master's Word is a symbol of Divine truth, a word of great value that was known to very few people. Seeking to extort this word so that they could "receive Masters' wages," the craftsmen killed Hiram and buried him on the brow of the hill of Mount Moriah. Searchers were sent out under the direction of King Solomon, and one of them found the body under a sprig of acacia. The body of Hiram Abiff was raised and reinterred in a more suitable place, in or near the *Sanctum Sanctorum* of the Temple, a symbol of the human heart. The three ruffians were found and punished for their crime, but through the death of Hiram, the Master's Word had been lost. Freemasons are now tasked to search for and recover this sacred Word, as demonstrated in this dialogue from Samuel Prichard's 1730 exposé, *Masonry Dissected*:

> Ex. You're an heroick Fellow; from whence came you?
> R. From the East.
> Ex. Where are you a going?
> R. To the West.
> Ex. What are you a going to do there?
> R. To seek for that which was lost and is now found.
> Ex. What was that which was lost and is now found?
> R. The Master-Mason's Word.
> Ex. How was it lost?
> R. By Three Great Knocks, or the Death of our Master *Hiram*.[14]

Through the rest of the eighteenth century, Freemasons expressed desires to learn progressively deeper mysteries. This resulted in the development of additional Masonic degrees and Orders such as York Rite and Scottish Rite Masonry. These supplemental degrees are called "appendant" and are not to be considered superior or higher than the Master Mason degree. They add to the foundations established in the first three degrees by further expounding upon and illustrating the moral lessons taught.

York Rite Masonry

York Rite Masonry consists of three cooperative groups that confer a total of ten degrees: four for the Royal Arch, three for the Cryptic Rite, and three for the Chivalric orders.

---

13. The word "exposure" is a Masonic term for a published exposé. Because Masons are under obligation not to write or reveal certain aspects of their ritual, these exposures are often the best source for reconstructing the complete ritual as it existed at given periods of time.

14. Samuel Prichard, *Masonry Dissected: Being a Universal and Genuine Description of All Its Branches from the Original to this Present Time*, 26; emphasis in original.

Like Craft Freemasonry, the Royal Arch imparts moral lessons through the use of ritual and legend. Its ritualized allegory is based on the Old Testament story of the return of the Jews to Jerusalem following the Babylonian captivity. The Masonic legend portrays three companions who learn certain philosophical lessons on their way to the Holy City to assist in the rebuilding of Solomon's Temple. While clearing the ground of the temple, they make important discoveries that lead them to contemplate man's spiritual nature. These discoveries are meant to both support what the candidate has learned from his own religion and to extend and enhance the practical lessons of the first three degrees.[15] The Royal Arch ritual includes the ceremony of "passing the veils," which had a Christian origin and has been removed from English Masonry in modern times. American Freemasonry, however, has retained the ceremony, during which candidates obtain passwords and signs that enable them to pass successive veils and ultimately be "exalted."[16]

The Scottish Rite

The Scottish Rite is a progressive series of thirty-three degrees that are recognized in the United States as an extension of the three degrees of Craft Masonry. Early "Scott's" degrees, ancestors of the Scottish Rite, were conferred in Bristol, England, from 1733–40. In the United States, a governing body for the nascent Scottish Rite degrees was first constituted in May 1801 at the formation of the Mother Supreme Council at Charleston, South Carolina. During the 1870s, Albert Pike compiled and standardized the modern Scottish Rite degrees, culminating in his extensive book, *Morals and Dogma of the Ancient and Accepted Scottish Rite of Freemasonry*.

Nineteenth-Century Development of Masonic Degrees

While the Blue Lodge degrees had achieved a measure of stability by the 1800s, appendant degrees continued to be formulated and expanded. During Joseph Smith's lifetime, Freemasonry continued to be a developing art, with new rituals springing into form and old rituals being codified and standardized. Smith followed this same tradition by not simply borrowing from the Masons, nor harking back to an earlier tradition, but by creatively adapting Masonic rites. His work was not essentially unlike that of Freemasons John Mitchell, Albert Mackey, or Albert Pike, who were also creating and reworking Masonic rituals throughout the nineteenth century.[17]

---

15. "What is Royal Arch Masonry?," Supreme Grand Chapter of Royal Arch Masons of England.

16. Avery Allyn, *A Ritual of Freemasonry: Illustrated by Numerous Engravings*, 125–26.

17. "The problem of the Scottish Rite(s) as an assortment of competing Constitutions and ritual systems, not to mention Egyptian Rite Masonry with its ninety degrees, ought to suggest that Masonry by its very nature is the epitome of invention and expansion. . . . In the 1820s, when Smith began his 'translation' of the golden plates, American Masonry was still

The Nature of Symbolic Instruction

A basic knowledge of Freemasonry, with its associated ritual and tradition, is necessary to understand how the Craft relates to Mormonism and how Joseph Smith's life and work reflected foundational Masonic myth. A simple and classic definition of the Craft is credited to Dr. Samuel Hemming: "Freemasonry is a system of morality, veiled in allegory, and illustrated by symbols."[18] A more modern definition expands upon this by both emphasizing Masonry's underlying principles and beliefs and recognizing the lodge as its fundamental organizational unit:

> Freemasonry is a system of moral philosophy structured on the principal [sic] of the Brotherhood of Man and a belief in God and immortality, imparted symbolically and allegorically through a coordinated complex of Masonic Lodges.[19]

The symbols populating Masonic ritual are employed in a context giving them the broadest possible range of interpretations, although some specific symbols have relatively fixed traditional meanings. Thus, while ritual elements may have one general signification, it is the privilege of a Freemason to interpret those symbols he has received in a way most genial to his own personal religious views. This may provide some difficulty in making authoritative or definitive statements regarding the meaning of Masonic ritual; however, one can at the very least look at (1) what the rituals themselves suggest, (2) what Freemasons have historically said about their own rituals, and (3) what Masonic critics have said about the shape of the ritual. Of this interpretive complexity, Albert Pike writes,

> All religious expression is symbolism; since we can describe only what we see and the true objects of religion are unseen.[20]

> The ancient symbols and allegories always had more than one interpretation. They always had a *double* meaning, and sometimes *more* than two, one serving as the envelope of the other.[21]

Masonic ritual brings participants together to share in divine mystery and divine power. This forges a brotherhood bound by voluntary oaths, ethical standards, and common moral and spiritual values. The rituals' mystic ties use symbolism to teach Masons to achieve union with the Divine. Furthermore, one of the most exalted and sublime uses of scriptural accounts is to ritualize them, as

---

in its infancy and its 'texts' still gestating. . . . What actually constituted 'orthodox' Masonry was far from resolved." Clyde R. Forsberg, *Divine Rite of Kings: Land, Same Sex and Empire in Mormonism and the Esoteric Tradition*, xli–xliii.

18. Quoted in Albert Gallatin Mackey, *A Lexicon of Freemasonry; Containing a Definition of all its Communicable Terms, Notices of its History, Traditions, and Antiquities, and an Account of all the Rites and Mysteries of the Ancient World*, 109.

19. Masonic Services Association of North America, "What is Freemasonry?"

20. Albert Pike, *Morals and Dogma of the Ancient and Accepted Scottish Rite of Freemasonry*, 512.

21. Pike, 205; emphasis in original.

Masons do, in order to conduct a candidate into sacred time and space. Affiliates thus not only read the stories but ceremonially enter them to become partakers of divine power.[22]

As speculative Masonry developed, symbolism was seen in the following categories (as identified by Masonic author Alex Horne):

a) The Working Tools: which we now moralize upon.

b) Some geometrical patterns: such as the oblong rectangle; the square; the equilateral triangle; the interlaced double-triangle; the circle; the five-pointed star; the point-within-a-circle; etc.

c) Certain numbers having special significance: the 3, 5, and 7, etc.

d) Certain colors: white; blue; and (in the early days) gold; etc.

e) Certain physical objects: the Sun, Moon, and Stars; the Rough and Perfect Ashlars; the Trestle-Board; the Cable-tow; etc.

f) Some architectural features: the Pillars of Solomon; the Winding Staircase; the Mosaic Pavement; the North-East Cornerstone; etc.

g) Symbolic acts: such as Circumambulation;[23] the Rite of Discalceation;[24] Signs and Tokens; the Five Points of Fellowship; the Laying of Cornerstones; and other "acted out symbols."

h) Biblical references: Jacob's Ladder; the Burning Bush; etc.

i) Allegorical legends: the Lost Word; the Hiramic Legend; etc.[25]

Christian Character of Freemasonry

Speculative Masonry, with its historical roots in fourteenth-century England, began as a mystical Christian impulse.[26] Freemasons were tasked with responsibilities that showed clear Christian values, such as caring for widows and the fatherless, an injunction described in the New Testament as distinguishing "religion that is pure and undefiled" (James 1:27). Because the framers of Masonic rituals were devout Christians, Old Testament characters such as Adam, Enoch, and Noah all appear in Masonic legend with their Christian allegorical significances.[27] In Masonry, even Jewish history takes on a decidedly Christian reading. Masonic texts such as the Schaw Statutes,[28] the Old Charges,[29] and the Edinburgh Register

---

22. Mircea Eliade, *Myth and Reality*, 17–18.

23. Walking around an altar or sacred object.

24. Taking off the shoes as a token of respect.

25. Alex Horne, *Sources of Masonic Symbolism*, 16.

26. In fact, "early ritual was also Christian in content—indeed the Premier Grand Lodge met on St. John's Day (24th June)." Michael Barnes, "Spoilt for Choice," 61.

27. Such as John Theophilus Desaguliers, James Anderson, etc.

28. In 1598 William Schaw, believed to have been an Accepted Mason, signed and circulated two sets of Masonic statutes, one for general use by the Craft, and the other for the specific use of the lodge of Kilwinning, Scotland.

29. The "Old Charges" are ancient documents that range in estimated date from 1390 until 1714. They are said to have been used in making Masons during the Operative days of Masonry. Some may have served as constitutions in lodges of that time.

God as Great Architect, fifteenth-century French manuscript.

House Manuscript[30] all show a clear Christian alignment and a requirement for members to be Christians.

According to Masonic author Robert G. Davis, Freemasonry "clearly evolved from a Christian base." As evidence, he points to "eighteenth Century English Masonic ritual [that] was sprinkled throughout with references to the Christian faith."[31] For example, a Masonic pamphlet dated 1722 contains the following statement of belief:

> [B]elieve only in one God the Father Almighty, Maker of Heaven and Earth, and of all Things visible and invisible, the most grand, essential, the prime, eternal, everlasting, fundamental Article of the most holy, catholick [sic], universal, and Christian Faith (of which we are). . . . [A]ll Christians, under whatever other Denomination distinguished . . . cannot . . . take Umbrage at those who believe the prime Article of their (that is, our) holy Faith.[32]

Further, Freemasonry's interior teaching—its very heart—was both Christian and mystical. By 1766, the French ritual exposer M. de Bérage claimed that the "mysteries of Masonry were nothing more in their principle, & are still nothing

---

30. A ritual of admission dated 1696.

31. Robert G. Davis, *The Mason's Words: The History and Evolution of the American Masonic Ritual*, 289.

32. Eugenius Philalethes [Thomas Vaughan], *Long Livers, a Curious History of Such Persons of Both Sexes who Have Liv'd Several Ages, and Grown Young Again*, xi–xii.

more, than those of the Christian religion."[33] However, through the eighteenth and the nineteenth centuries, Christian elements began to be gradually removed from Freemasonry.[34] In 1723, James Anderson's *Constitutions* had theoretically opened lodges to those who could profess belief in the "Great Architect of the Universe":

> A Mason is oblig'd, by his Tenure, to obey the moral Law; and if he rightly understands the Art, he will never be a stupid **Atheist**, nor an irreligious **Libertine**. But though in ancient Times Masons were charg'd in every Country to be of the Religion of that Country or Nation, whatever it was, yet 'tis now thought more expedient only to oblige them to that Religion in which all Men agree, leaving their particular Opinions to themselves.[35]

Thus, men needed only to profess a belief in God to join the Fraternity and were no longer required to be Christian. The order was beginning to be characterized as exemplifying universal moral principles rather than any specific religion. At the union of the "Antient" and the "Modern" Grand Lodges of England in 1813, there was a wave of expansion to open the way for more Jewish members and those of other faiths. The more non-Christians who became Masons, the less Masonry was to be read as a Christian allegory. At the resurgence of Freemasonry in the United States following a steep decline in the 1820s and 1830s, the Craft distanced itself even further from its overt connection with Christian symbolism. This dechristianization was encouraged by those in the anti-Masonic movement who could not bear to think of Masonry as a Christian institution analogous to themselves.

Not all Masons liked this development, however. In his 1767 *A Candid Disquisition*, Wellins Calcott asserted that Freemasonry is "a society *founded* upon wisdom and *cemented* by *morality* and *Christian-love*." Further, he charged his listeners to love one another as Christians love one another in order to "convince the scoffer and slanderer, that we are lovers of Him, who said, *If ye love me keep my commandments*; and, *this is my commandment, that ye love one another as I have loved you*." This, he said, would not only demonstrate that a Mason was "a good Christian," but it would afford Freemasons "a well-grounded hope of

---

33. Arturo de Hoyos and S. Brent Morris, trans. and ed., *The Most Secret Mysteries of the High Degrees of Masonry Unveiled, or The True Rose-Croix, Translated from the English, Followed by Noachite, Translated from the German. From the First Edition of 1766*, xix.

34. David Harrison, *The Genesis of Freemasonry*, 10–11. Masonic scholars generally agree that the trend in Masonry is towards dechristianization, with the first wave occurring following the establishment of the Grand Lodge in 1717, and again at the creation of the United Grand Lodge in 1813. See Neville Barker-Cryer, "The De-Christianizing of the Craft," 34–60; Michel L. Brodsky, "Why was the Craft De-Christianized?," 158.

35. James Anderson, *The Constitutions of the Free-Masons, Containing the History, Charges, Regulations, &c. of that Most Ancient and Right Worshipful Fraternity*, 50; emphasis in original.

admittance into a lodge of everlasting felicity *hereafter*."[36] Likewise, in his popular *The Antiquities of Freemasonry,* George Oliver wrote:

> Who then shall say that Masonry contains no Christianity? Or rather, who shall assert that its illustrations are not principally Christian? For if the virtues and doctrines I have enumerated be Christian virtues and doctrines, they are also Masonic; nay, they contain, with their parallels, the whole system of speculative Masonry; and I do not know, were Masonry minutely analyzed, that it contains a single illustration which does not enforce a Christian doctrine, or recommend a Christian virtue.[37]

Whether or not an individual Mason is Christian, the fact remains that Freemasonry's rituals and legends were framed by Christians in order to appeal to individuals with rational Christian and mystical inclinations, and when seen as Christian allegories, they take on deep meanings. For example, the incorporation of Christian mysticism emphasized the transforming effect of divine grace, and theosis—taking on the divine nature and becoming like God—is apparent in much Masonic symbolism.

While no Freemason is obliged to view the legends as purely Christian allegory, it is important to understand that they were largely seen that way by many nineteenth-century Freemasons who were in fact Christians.[38] Furthermore, although Masons are cautioned to regard their instruction as allegorical and symbolic, many American Freemasons in the 1800s, including early Mormons, accepted the legends portrayed in the degrees as not just allegories but literally true.

Nurtured in the company of cherished companions, a Masonic initiate is admitted to the fellowship of those engaged in building a symbolic edifice—King Solomon's Temple. Symbolically, he is learning the skills he needs to perfect himself and recover the name, or the essence, of Deity. As will be discussed in Chapter 4, the Christian aspect of Freemasonry was profoundly appealing to Joseph Smith Jr. Even as a young man, he found Masonry a fitting vehicle for his spiritual longings. The fact that the continued relevance of Christian Freemasonry was debated by Masons may be one reason Smith saw a need for its restoration,

---

36. Wellins Calcott, *A Candid Disquisition of the Principles and Practices of the Most Ancient and Honorable Society of Free and Accepted Masons,* 161, 169–70; emphasis in original.

37. George Oliver, *The Antiquities of Freemasonry: Comprising Illustrations of the Five Grand Periods of Masonry from the Creation of the World to the Dedication of King Solomon's Temple,* 174.

38. "The symbolic mystery of the death of Hiram Abiff represents to us that of the Messiah; for the three blows which were given to Hiram Abiff, at the three gates of the temple, allude to the three points of condemnation against Christ, at the High Priest's Caiphas, Herod, and Pilate. It was from the last that he was led to that most violent and excruciating death. The said three blows with the square, guage [sic], and gavel, are symbols of the blow on the cheek, the flagellation, and the crown of thorns. The brethren assembled around the tomb of Hiram, is a representation of the disciples lamenting the death of Christ on the cross." David Bernard, *Light on Masonry: A Collection of All the Most Important Documents on the Subject of Speculative Free Masonry,* 299.

and he would make it his life's work to recover what he considered lost and missing aspects of religion and Freemasonry in order to restore them to a prominent place in the lives of his associates.

The First Freemasons

Not wanting to limit the legends to mere Christian allegory or the building of Solomon's Temple, three important Masonic authors, William Hutchinson, Salem Town, and Reverend George Oliver, expounded the belief that the ancient patriarchs and prophets were Masonry's chief promoters in past ages. While these writers were careful to explain that Freemasonry did not exist in its modern organized form, they claimed that Adam, Enoch, Noah, Melchizedek, Abraham, and other holy men were all Masons,[39] in that they taught "geometrical and moral principles" that were fundamental to the establishment of speculative Freemasonry.[40]

Hutchinson, Town, and Oliver, however, went beyond a simple comparison of moral philosophy. Town wrote that "Joseph, the son of Jacob . . . became, in a certain extent, the Grand Master of Egypt,"[41] and Oliver credited Moses as the first to systematically organize Masonic ritual:

> But it was not until the erection of the Tabernacle that our Craft was reduced to the perfect form which it has ever since retained. Moses, when, by the revelation of God, he was dividing the priesthood into three distinct heads, modelled Masonry after the same fashion; himself being grand master.[42]

According to Oliver, following the exodus of the Israelite nation from Egypt, Moses, acting as Grand Master, "opened the FIRST LODGE of which we possess any certain tradition since the time of Joseph."[43] To him, the Israelite priesthood and Freemasonry existed side by side, fully cooperative, and both were presided over by the prophet of God.

The idea that the ancient men of God were also Masonic officials was pervasive enough during the 1820s (and perceived as threatening enough) that it elicited specific responses from anti-Masonic writers. John G. Stearns, another New York clergyman, specifically and repeatedly attacked Salem Town's writings on this topic in his *An Inquiry into the Nature and Tendency of Speculative Free-Masonry*:

---

39. Salem Town, *A System of Speculative Masonry in its Origin, Patronage, Dissemination, Principles, Duties, and Ultimate Designs, Laid Open for the Examination of the Serious and Candid*, 117–20; Oliver, *Antiquities of Freemasonry*; William Hutchinson, *The Spirit of Masonry: In Moral and Elucidatory Lecture*, 169–88.

40. "[M]any principles peculiar to our Institution were understood and patronised by those men. . . . Hence we claim them as ancient patrons, because through their hands have been transmitted those excellent principles which now characterize Speculative Masonry." Salem Town, *A System of Speculative Masonry*, 55–56, fn.

41. Town, *A System of Speculative Masonry*, 121.

42. Oliver, *Antiquities of Freemasonry*, 275.

43. Oliver, 279; emphasis in original.

It is pretended, that masonry originated among the pious men of old, to whom the Lord communicated in a very faint manner, the great mystery of redemption. Mr. Town has told us, that Enoch, Noah, Abraham, Melchizedek, Moses, and all those ancient men were masons, and patrons of the institution. . . . [T]here is not the least shadow of evidence that the system of free-masonry ever entered their hearts. Masons may as well undertake to prove that the inhabitants of Saturn are masons.[44]

A New Dispensation

The notion of Masonic dispensationalism, including both "apostasies" and "restorations," dated back at least to 1775, when William Hutchinson discussed the history of the Craft in his oft-reprinted *The Spirit of Masonry: In Moral and Elucidatory Lecture*. Hutchinson asserted that Adam, as the first Mason, taught his children the philosophical principles contained in Freemasonry:

[W]hen men came to multiply exceedingly upon the face of the earth, and were dispersed to the distant regions of the globe, then the inestimable lessons of KNOWLEDGE and TRUTH, taught by the first men, fell into confusion and corruption with many, and were retained pure and in perfection but by few.[45]

Hutchinson wrote of three successive stages of Freemasonry extending from Adam to Moses, from Moses to Jesus, and from Jesus to the present.[46]

In 1823, George Oliver expanded upon Hutchinson's ideas, writing that the purity of religion was inextricably linked with the purity of Freemasonry; when one deteriorated, so did the other.[47] When false Freemasonry caused a degeneration, a restoration and new dispensation was invariably needed. As a result, Freemasonry had gone through at least five "grand periods," each presided over by the ancient patriarchs and prophets, considered "grand masters" of Masonry in their day.[48] In an 1826 work, Oliver further discussed the distinction between Freemasonry and the "pagan" mystery religions of the world. He applied the term "spurious Masonry" to corruptions of truths first taught by Noah and passed down through his heathen or Gentile line.[49]

The approximately fifty years between Hutchinson's and Oliver's Masonic writings reflects the development of an expectation that was fully ripened by the time of Joseph Smith's early prophetic career. This is the lens through which to see Smith's efforts to translate the Book of Mormon and to "restore" both a church

---

44. John G. Stearns, *An Inquiry into the Nature and Tendency of Speculative Free-Masonry*, 8.

45. Hutchinson, *Spirit of Masonry*, 7; emphasis in original.

46. Hutchinson, 6–22.

47. George Oliver, *Signs and Symbols: Illustrated and Explained in a Course of Twelve Lectures on Freemasonry*, xiii–xiv, 4.

48. Oliver, *Antiquities of Freemasonry*, iv.

49. Oliver, *Signs and Symbols*, 7. See also George Oliver, "On Freemasonry. The Number Three," 356.

and an inspired revision of the Bible.[50] It also influenced the Mormon prophet's own notions of Freemasonry and his behaviors relating thereto. For example, some have seen a great disparity between Smith's earliest expressed opinions and actions regarding the Craft and what he said and did in Nauvoo. It may seem inconsistent for the same man who told his brother to "beware the Freemasons" in 1826 to not only become a Freemason himself but encourage the majority of his adult male followers to do so as well.

However, if Smith held to the view of Town, Hutchinson, and Oliver regarding authentic and spurious Masonry—and his own inspired revisions of the Bible suggest that he did—this might significantly alter our understanding of his recorded statements on Freemasonry. It suggests the possibility that Smith's remarks, behaviors, and perspective on Masonry were consistent and fundamentally unchanged throughout his prophetic ministry. With such views, Smith could have condemned what he saw as false or spurious Masonry while championing a pure and restored version of the Craft—just as he did of Christianity as a whole.

Throughout the 1820s, particularly in upstate New York, both Masons and anti-Masons publicly debated the ideas of Masonic dispensationalism and ancient prophetic connections. That these ideas were current in and around Palmyra is demonstrated by a Masonic discourse given at a St. John's Day celebration in Palmyra's Mount Moriah Lodge No. 112 in 1822. Extolling the example of John the Baptist, one of the two "ancient Christian patrons of Masonry," the speaker summarized:

> It may not, indeed, fall to our lot to engage in the office of a public reformer; nor shall we be summoned to the high vocation of ushering in a new dispensation of religion, or of promulgating a new code of morals. . . . But each man may, in private life, however low, or exalted, be his condition, and in his own domestic sphere, become a reformer. [51]

Thus, it was once again the "pious men of old" who were revered as examples of Masonic philosophy, even in young Joseph Smith's backyard. It is ironic that, despite the last speaker's words, a new prophet from Palmyra would indeed declare himself to be "summoned to the high vocation of ushering in a new dispensation of religion."

---

50. See 2 Nephi 26:22; Ether 8:15, 21, 25; Helaman 2:13–14, 6:22–24; 3 Nephi 6:27–30; and Moses 5:29–33, 47–52. These scriptures are discussed in light of spurious Masonry in Chapter 6 of this book.

51. Orville Luther Holley, *An Address Delivered at the Request of the Mount Moriah Lodge at Palmyra*, 12–13.

CHAPTER 2

THE ENCHANTED LAND: THE SMITH FAMILY'S MASONIC ENVIRONS

Thou land of milk and honey, land of corn and oil and wine,
How longs my hungry spirit to enjoy thy food divine!
I hunger and I thirst afar, the Jordan rolls between,
I faintly see thy paradise all clothed in living green.
　　　　　　　—Rob Morris, *Masonic Odes and Poems*

In its formative years, the United States was wild and green, its rural communities imbued with the spirit of Masonry. The fragrance of philosophical, ethical, moral, and social progress permeated American lodges, and these ideals were broadly disseminated to the public by individual members. Then, Freemasonry had a dynamic role in revolutionary and post-revolutionary America, with the leading lights in the struggle for American independence being attracted to the Masonic brotherhood. These founding fathers saw Masonry's endeavors to bring together men from different regions and backgrounds in an increasingly republican and Christian framework as a "harbinger of the new American society."[1] Until the early 1800s, Freemasons could be found among America's socially privileged—its political, religious, and business leaders. "[T]he period of Masonry's greatest power and prestige," notes historian Stephen Bullock, were "the years from 1790 to 1826, when Americans used Masonry to respond to a wide range of needs, including their hopes for an enlightened Republic, their attempts to adapt to . . . [a rapidly changing] society, and their desire to create a separate refuge from this confusing outside world."[2]

For its disciples, Freemasonry's mythic connection with the ancient past provided a vision in which unsettling social disruptions were understood as natural developments. The turmoil accompanying advances in Enlightenment thinking could optimistically be seen as the birth-pangs of a coming Christian utopia, firmly rooted in the Christian past. Historian David Hackett observed that the "growing convergence of Christianity and Freemasonry around Enlightenment ideals marked the first quarter of the nineteenth century." Masonry "avoid[ed]

---

1. David G. Hackett, *That Religion in Which All Men Agree: Freemasonry in American Culture*, 56.
2. Steven C. Bullock, *Revolutionary Brotherhood: Freemasonry and the Transformation of the American Social Order, 1730–1840*, 2.

the extremes of both sectarianism and nonbiblical rationalism," and it thus attracted ministers and members of liberal denominations such as Episcopalians, Congregationalists, and Unitarians as its leaders. Until the social unravelling of Freemasonry during a scandal known as "the Morgan affair,"[3] the fraternity served as a kind of secular priesthood.[4]

The doctrine of this secular priesthood was well known and well appreciated by the average American. The twenty-first-century mind can scarcely comprehend the influence Freemasonry once held over every aspect of society. Books elucidating the legends of the Craft and relating its many virtues were eagerly read and enthusiastically circulated to a public hungry for what Freemasonry promised to provide. For example, William Hutchinson's wildly popular *The Spirit of Masonry*, first published in 1775, opened to the general reader the world of Masonry and its purported connection with the ancient past.[5] Masonic articles and poetry appeared in local newspapers,[6] while by the late 1820s the content of Masonic ritual was detailed with some regularity in the press.[7]

Vermont served as a crucible for this fertile mix of social idealism, political independence, and religious exuberance. One of the unanticipated byproducts was a new American hybrid religion whose roots were firmly established in the soil of Vermont Freemasonry.

This potent atmosphere provided the context for many key activities of the Smith family. Joseph Smith Sr., the father of the Mormon prophet, was born at the cusp of the American Revolution, on July 12, 1771, in Topsfield, Essex County, Massachusetts. Soon after, the Smiths located close to Vermont's border, a disputed region hotly contested by New Hampshire and New York, both of which made liberal land grants in the area. In July 1777, an assembly convened and declared Vermont to be a territory independent of both New York and New Hampshire and thus effectively a sovereign entity. Vermonters and some historians refer to the territory in the period between 1777 and 1791, when Vermont finally ratified the Constitution and joined the United States, as the "Republic of Vermont." During this period, residents established an autonomous postal system and state currency. Freemasonry went hand in hand with Vermonters'

---

3. The kidnapping of William Morgan in 1826 triggered the anti-Masonic movement in the United States. It and its repercussions are covered thoroughly in Chapter 3.

4. Hackett, *That Religion*, 56.

5. See also Joshua Bradley, *Some of the Beauties of Free-masonry*. Note the author's preface with "introductory remarks designed to remove the various objections made against the order."

6. As an example, see nearby Randolph, Vermont's *Weekly Wanderer*, operated by Freemason Sereno Wright.

7. See David Bernard's 1829 *Light on Masonry: A Collection of All the Most Important Documents on the Subject of Speculative Free Masonry*; John G. Stearns's 1829 *An Inquiry into the Nature and Tendency of Speculative Free-Masonry*; and Henry Dana Ward's 1828 *Free Masonry: Its Pretensions Exposed in Faithful Extracts of Its Standard Authors* as examples of readily available anti-Masonic exposés.

Coins from the Republic of Vermont, 1785.
Images courtesy of US Mint.

independent ideals, as seen by their locally minted coins replete with Masonic symbolism.[8]

During Joseph Smith Sr.'s growing up years—between the ages of six and twenty—he would have been regaled with stories of the rugged independence of Vermont's "Green Mountain Boys." This group, headed by Ethan Allen and members of his extended family, and largely consisting of Freemasons,[9] fiercely resisted both New York's and New Hampshire's attempts to control the territory.

Quaker poet John Greenleaf Whittier penned a ballad called "The Song of the Vermonters" to describe the temperament of the period. The last stanza was so successful in imitating Ethan Allan's activist prose that it was attributed to him for almost sixty years:

> Come York or come Hampshire, come traitors or knaves,
> If ye rule o'er our land ye shall rule o'er our graves;
> Our vow is recorded—our banner unfurled,
> In the name of Vermont we defy all the world![10]

Another illustration of Vermont-style experimentation with Masonic ideals to form a brotherhood may be seen in the Nathaniel Wood group, a quasi-religious association organized around the nucleus of Wood's large family. The family patriarch was a would-be preacher and excommunicate of the Congregational church.

---

8. The first coins issued from Reuben Harmon's mint in Rupert, Vermont, were of the following description: "Obverse, a sun rising from behind the hills and a plough in the foreground; legend, [one of three variations of the motto] VERMONTENSIUM RES PUBLICA, 1786. Reverse, a radiated eye, surrounded by thirteen stars; legend, QUARTA DECIMA STELLA [the fourteenth star]." Henry Sheldon, "Rupert," 226.

9. For example, Green Mountain Boys Ira Allen and Thomas Chittenden were both initiated in Vermont Lodge No. 1 on the same day, June 26, 1782. John Stark was a member of Masters Lodge No. 2, Albany, New York. Seth Warner was initiated, passed, and raised as a first-degree Mason during a visit to the New York Legislature during the summer of 1775. He was listed as the ninety-sixth signer on the bylaws of the old Union Lodge No. 1 in New York.

10. See "Song of the Vermonters; the Ode Attributed to Ethan Allen," 2.

The group was located in Middletown, Rutland County,[11] not far from the Smith family homestead. Known as the "Fraternity of Rodsmen,"[12] this "band of mystics" held several beliefs derived from Masonry, especially the Craft's Royal Arch tradition. Wood's followers began using divining rods to ascertain the mind of God, and Wood received a revelation that they "must build a temple,"[13] an esoteric practice rooted both in the Bible and in Masonic tradition and allegory. As a religious exercise, the Wood group also made excavations in local mountains from which valuable ore was to be taken, recalling the subterranean cavern of Masonic legend wherein lay the gold plate of Enoch.[14] Also reminiscent of the Royal Arch tradition, Wood instructed his followers that they were "descendants of the ancient Jews, and lawful inheritors of the whole country,"[15] and that the "divining rods would designate who they were."[16] Jacob Wood, one of

Ethan Allan, leader of Vermont's Green Mountain Boys. From S. G. Goodrich, *A Pictorial History of the United States*, 1883.

the sons of Nathaniel Wood, prophesied by means of one of these divining rods that he named "St. John's rod." In Royal Arch Masonry, Aaron's rod—which budded, blossomed, and brought forth flowers in a single day—is connected with the concept of restoration, and the figure of Saint John has an important role. Overall, the Wood congregation was a remarkable manifestation of increasing religious pluralism and the fracturing of traditional religious constructs. The group called themselves "Latter Day

11. For a Masonic history of Rutland County, see John L. Brooke, *The Refiner's Fire: The Making of Mormon Cosmology, 1644–1844*, 140–42. Here, Royal Arch chapters were formed by 1800 in Granville, Rutland, and Poultney.

12. Ovid Miner, "The Rodsmen," 2.

13. Barnes Frisbie, *The History of Middletown, Vermont, In Three Discourses Delivered Before the Citizens of That Town, February 7 and 21, and March 30, 1867*, 52. See also Dan Vogel, ed., *Early Mormon Documents*, 1:599–621.

14. "I wrought in the ruins of the ancient temple of Enoch; I penetrated . . . under ground and finally found the Delta, containing the name which God had pronounced to the patriarchs. . . . [That Delta was a triangular plate] of gold, enriched with precious stones and affording great light, and upon which was engraved by Enoch that great and mysterious name, Jehovah." Bernard, *Light on Masonry*, 425 [205].

15. "We are your own brethren and kindred . . . descendants of those noble families of Giblimites, who wrought so hard at the building of the first temple, were present at its destruction by Nebuchadnezzar, by him carried away captive to Babylon, where we remained servants . . . till the first year of Cyrus, king of Persia, by whose order we were liberated, and are now returned to assist in rebuilding the house of the Lord." De Hoyos, 355 [135].

16. Miner, "The Rodsmen," 2.

saints" and made liberal use of Masonic millennialism.[17] However, their misplaced belief in an imminent apocalyptic event on January 14, 1802, combined with their militant fervor, led to an embarrassing incident known as the "Wood Scrape" and the eventual decline of the movement.[18]

The furor surrounding their pronouncements became so intense that it is unfeasible to maintain that the Smiths were not aware of it. Indeed, it has been suggested that both Joseph Smith Sr. and William Cowdery—fathers of two of the founders of the Latter-day Saint movement—were directly involved with the Wood group. Vermont historian Barnes Frisbie presented a series of lectures in 1867 in which he detailed these men's involvement.[19] Of Joseph Sr. he asserted, "I have been told that Joe Smith's father resided in Poultney at the time of the Wood movement here, and that he was in it, and one of the leading rods-men."[20] Frisbie also placed William Cowdery with the Wood group both when Cowdery lived in nearby Wells, Vermont, and after he moved even closer to the Woods' home in Middletown. Because of this, D. Michael Quinn has theorized that "a connection between William Cowdery and the Wood Scrape would help explain why his son Oliver had a rod through which he received revelations."[21]

Whether or not the Smiths and the Cowderys participated personally in the Nathaniel Wood group, the Woods' brand of Masonic religious ardor was thought by contemporaries to have been replicated in early Mormonism. Methodist circuit rider Laban Clark recalled that about the year 1840 he had heard two Mormon preachers in Connecticut who held to the "same or much the same doctrines which the Woods did in Middletown." Clark firmly testified, "I have no doubt that their movement gave origin to the Mormons."[22] Frisbie claimed

---

17. Daniel Dorchester, "St. John's Rod," 235.

18. "Scrape" was used here in its archaic meaning of a difficult predicament caused by one's own unwise behavior.

19. Frisbie, *History of Middletown*, 43–64. Frisbie based his information on interviews with "more than thirty old men and women who were living here in 1800." Additionally, as noted by D. Michael Quinn, subsequent historians received independent verification of Frisbie's account. Nancy F. Glass, a school friend of Oliver's brother Warren Cowdery, wrote that she thought his father was one of the Rutland County rodsmen. The information was also verified by Joseph Parks and Mrs. Charles Garner. See Quinn, *Early Mormonism*, 36. For an opposing view, see Larry E. Morris, "Oliver Cowdery's Vermont Years and the Origins of Mormonism," 107–18.

20. Frisbie, *The History of Middletown*, 62.

21. Quinn, *Early Mormonism*, 36. See also the manuscript and first published versions of what is now Doctrine & Covenants 8:6–8, where Oliver is told that he has the gift of working with the rod and that God's power causes the "rod of nature" (later replaced with "the gift of Aaron") to work in his hands.

22. Frisbie, *History of Middletown*, 60, 57. Rev. Laban Clark, D. D., was a Methodist circuit rider in Vermont and founder of the Wesleyan University. On November 1, 1801, he attended a quarterly meeting of the "rod men" in Salisbury, Vermont. Sometime in December, he visited Poultney and Middletown, Vermont, where he further inquired

that the "system of religion inaugurated by the Woods was transmitted to the Mormons" and that Mormonism could indeed be traced back to Middletown.[23]

This allegation is strengthened by the migration of many of the group's principal leaders and followers into the same area in upstate New York where the Smiths would later relocate and where would become the cradle of the Restoration. In 1881, the Reverend Osborne Myrick called Wood "the virtual father of Mormonism," since among his followers "were the fathers of Joe Smith, of Oliver Cowdery and of A. M. Pratt . . . [who] practise there the same experiments with the hazel rod and advocate the same doctrines as here until 1830, Joe Smith's time, when he vitalized Woodism into Mormonism."[24]

Asael Smith and Freemasonry Arrive in Vermont

Still fiercely independent, the Republic of Vermont became the fourteenth of the United States in 1791, and the border between New Hampshire and the Green Mountain country was set at the Connecticut River in that same year. Between 1763 and 1791, the non-indigenous population of Vermont rose from 300 to 85,000.[25] Along with this expansion, the first two Masonic lodges in Vermont were chartered in 1781 and 1785,[26] under the authority of the St. Andrews Grand Lodge of Massachusetts.[27] Each of their charters bear the signature of Paul

---

into the strange affair. In January, he spent the evening of the apocalypse with the Wood group. He spoke often of his experiences and wrote of them in a manuscript sketch from which was taken a newspaper article in the *Boston Advertiser* by his nephew, the Reverend Daniel Dorchester. See Dorchester, "St. John's Rod," 235. Dorchester also wrote an affidavit which was included in Frisbie's *History of Middletown*.

23. Frisbie, 61.

24. Osborne Myrick, "A Historical Discourse delivered at the Centennial Celebration of the Congregational Church in Middletown, Vt., June 22, 1881." See Edgar C. Emerson, ed., *Our County and Its People: A Descriptive Work on Jefferson County New York*, 585, 610–11, for information on Woodville, a 754-acre tract in New York purchased by the Woods and settled by Nathaniel Sr.; sons Ebenezer, Ephraim, Jacob, Nathaniel Jr., and Mosley; and Oramel Brewster, Simeon Titus, Hezekiah Leffingwell, Obadiah Kingsbury, Oliver Scott, and Samuel Truesdale. They conducted explorations with their divining rods and dug for buried treasure in nearby Ellisburg and an area which was later named "Rodman." These were the sites of ancient aboriginal encampments.

25. Charles W. Johnson, *The Nature of Vermont: Introduction and Guide to a New England Environment*, 50.

26. While the petition for Vermont Lodge No. 1 was dated at Cornish, Vermont, and was chartered to meet in Springfield, local Masons found it more convenient to meet across the Connecticut River in Charlestown, New Hampshire. At the time, both sides of the river were to some extent common territory. No lodge actually met within the future State of Vermont until 1785, when a lodge was chartered at Manchester.

27. Provincial Grand Lodges authorized by the Grand Lodge of England were chartered in the United States beginning in 1733. These included St. John's Grand Lodge in Boston, as well as bodies in Charleston, Philadelphia, Virginia, and New York. See Bullock, *Revolutionary*

Revere. The third Vermont lodge was chartered by the Provincial Grand Lodge of Canada, and the fourth and fifth by the Grand Lodge of Connecticut. Finally, a Grand Lodge of Vermont was formed in Rutland in 1794, enabling forthcoming lodges to be approved within their own state.[28] A Grand Chapter of Royal Arch Masons was formed in Vermont on December 20, 1804, at Rutland.[29]

In 1791, Asael Smith, grandfather of Joseph Smith Jr., moved his family to Tunbridge in Vermont. No regular lodge existed within reasonable travel distance until October of 1798. In that year, when Joseph Sr. was twenty-seven years old,[30] Federal Lodge No. 15 was constituted in Randolph, located roughly seven miles from Tunbridge.[31] Joseph Sr.'s brother-in-law John Curtis Waller had joined the Smith family in Tunbridge in 1798 or 1799, just as this lodge was established.[32] Waller petitioned for membership and received the first or Entered Apprentice degree in 1801.[33] By 1804 at age forty-two, Waller was serving as Senior Warden (second in the lodge hierarchy).[34] It is possible that several of the Smith brothers

---

Brotherhood, 47. A number of American Masons who had been active in the "Antients" style of Freemasonry (a rival tradition) grouped together and petitioned the Grand Lodge of Scotland for a warrant, which was given to "The Lodge of St Andrew" under a Scottish Provincial Grand Lodge in 1756. A Royal Arch Chapter also functioned as part of this lodge. Due to the Revolution and based on the state of affairs between the United States and Great Britain, this Scottish Provincial Grand Lodge broke from the Grand Lodge of Scotland and became Massachusetts Grand Lodge in 1782. There was a growing rift in the Lodge of St Andrew regarding this decision to separate, and eventually those voting for membership in the Massachusetts Grand Lodge were expelled from the Lodge of St. Andrew. However, they formed their own Lodge of St. Andrew under the new Massachusetts Grand Lodge, which caused confusion for some time, until it was renamed Rising States Lodge.

28. Lee S. Tillotson, *Ancient Craft Masonry in Vermont*, 50.

29. In 1806, Jonathan Nye is recorded as a member of Union M. M. Lodge. See *Early Records of the Grand Chapter of the State of Vermont - 1804 to 1850 Inclusive*, 9, 32.

30. The minimum age at which one could regularly petition a Masonic lodge for initiation was twenty-one. Joseph Smith Sr.'s brothers Jesse and Asael were twenty-nine and twenty-four, respectively; Samuel would turn twenty-one within a month; Silas became eligible to petition for membership in 1800; and John, the youngest brother to live to adulthood, was eligible in 1802.

31. Tillotson, *Ancient Craft Masonry*, 71; *Early Records of the Grand Lodge of Vermont, F. & A. M., From 1794 to 1846 Inclusive*, 77. After 1800, this lodge met alternately between Randolph and the neighboring town of Chelsea, each less than ten miles from the Smith homestead in Tunbridge.

32. Waller married Priscilla Smith in 1796 at Royalton, Vermont. *Vermont Vital Records through 1870, Index*, s.v. "Priscilla Smith." The Wallers named their newborn son Dudley Chase Waller, evidently in honor of Dudley Chase Jr., who had served three years as Worshipful Master of Federal Lodge No. 15. See *Early Records of the Grand Lodge of Vermont*, 82 (1800), 86 (1801), 91 (1802).

33. *Register of the Grand Lodge of Vermont, 1794 to 1846*.

34. *Records of the Grand Lodge of Free and Accepted Masons of the State of Vermont from 1794 to 1846 Inclusive*, 99.

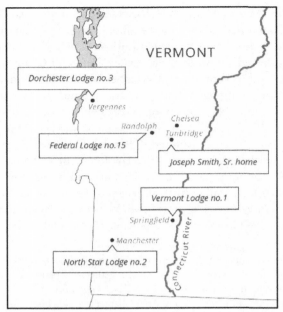

Masonic Lodges near the Joseph Smith Sr. home in
Vermont, 1798. Map by Sariah Swick.

were members of this lodge as well. Unfortunately, the existing abstract of members of the Grand Lodge of Vermont is an incomplete record.[35]

Despite its shortcomings, the *Register of the Grand Lodge of Vermont, 1794 to 1846* contains additional important information pertaining to the Smith family. In November of 1801, the year John Waller joined Federal Lodge, the register records the rejection of a "Joseph Smith" who petitioned for membership.[36] While

---

35. *Register of the Grand Lodge of Vermont, 1794 to 1846.* While it is dated 1794 to 1846, this record is an alphabetical index that seems to have been compiled at a later date. In the case of John Curtis Waller, only the first degree is recorded, although he could not have served as an officer in 1804 without previously receiving all three degrees of craft Masonry. Samuel Smith does not appear in the register, making his membership in a Vermont lodge prior to moving to New York inconclusive. According to this index, an individual by the name of "John Smith" was initiated as an Entered Apprentice in Federal Lodge on September 2, 1805, passed to the degree of Fellow Craft on October 7, 1805, and raised to the degree of Master Mason on January 28, 1806. We cannot assume that this man was the brother of Joseph Smith Sr., for at least one other man by the name of "John Smith" lived in the area. Furthermore, "John Smith" served as Senior Warden of Federal Lodge in 1813 and Junior Warden in 1815. John Smith, the future Mormon, first appeared on official New York lodge records during that same time, namely the 1814–1817 reporting period. While not impossible, it seems unlikely that he would have been retained as Junior Warden while living out of state.

36. *Register of the Grand Lodge of Vermont, 1794 to 1846.*

one other "Joseph Smith" lived in Tunbridge at the time,[37] the involvement of a close relative in the lodge suggests that this record may pertain to the Joseph Smith whose son would eventually found the Latter-day Saint movement. When this Joseph Smith petitioned Federal Lodge for admission, his request would have been submitted to an investigating committee to verify his reputation and suitability for the lodge. Then a balloting would have taken place. Masonic literature often refers to the "sanctity of the ballot box," whereby each Freemason has an unquestioned and anonymous right to determine by ballot who shall or shall not become a member of his lodge. A single negative vote from a member is enough to block admission. Except in the most unusual circumstances, Masonic law forbids asking any member of the lodge how he voted—let alone his reasons—making it nearly impossible to clearly identify the cause of this man's failure to pass the ballot. However, assuming for the sake of argument that this Joseph Smith was the son of Asael Smith, it is possible to hazard a guess as to several potential reasons one or more members of Federal Lodge rejected this petition.

In a day when Freemasons were deliberately escaping from early reputations of revelry, the abuse of alcohol was particularly frowned upon. It appears that at some point in his life, Joseph Smith Sr. overindulged.[38] Habitual drunkenness was a fairly common cause for expulsion of members from the Fraternity and would have been considered firm grounds to prevent admission.

Another possible reason for rejection arose out of Joseph Sr.'s mercantile activities. Sometime between February and August of 1800, the family left Tunbridge, relocating in Randolph well in advance of the November 1801 rejection.[39] Soon after, Joseph Sr. began to raise ginseng as a cash crop. According to recollections of Lucy Mack Smith, her husband had accumulated a quantity of ginseng worth at least $4,500 (about $108,000 in today's dollars) by 1802. Joseph Sr.'s plans to market ginseng would have been known well before November 1801, when Federal Lodge voted on his petition. Lucy's record indicates that another local merchant by the name of "Stevens" was also involved in ginseng cultivation with unfortunate results for the Smith family. While it is no longer possible to precisely identify the

---

37. Vogel, *Early Mormon Documents*, 1:639.

38. Richard L. Bushman, *Joseph Smith—Rough Stone Rolling: A Cultural Biography of Mormonism's Founder*, 42. For an extensive discussion of claims regarding Joseph Smith Sr.'s drinking, see also Lavina Fielding Anderson, ed., *Lucy's Book: A Critical Edition of Lucy Mack Smith's Family Memoir*, 24–27.

39. See Vogel, *Early Mormon Documents*, 1:638. Vogel speculates on the timeline as follows: "While both Hyrum and Sophronia were born in Tunbridge, on 9 February 1800 and 17 May 1803, respectively, Lucy Smith says that between their births the family lived a short time in Randolph, Vermont. In her published History, Lucy dates the move to Randolph in 1802. But the Smiths' absence from the 1800 Tunbridge census suggests the move may have occurred earlier than Lucy remembered. An early 1800 removal from Tunbridge may also explain why Hyrum's birth was not recorded until 1803 when the town clerk made the entry for Sophronia's birth."

"Stevens" mentioned, at least one Stevens was a member of Federal Lodge. If, as appears likely, the merchant Stevens (or one of his relatives) was involved with the local lodge, he may have resented Joseph Sr.'s venture as undesirable competition, leading to a questionably motivated blackball. In any event, the "Stevens" described by Lucy maneuvered to take possession of the proceeds of the Smiths' crop, leaving them nearly four thousand dollars in debt. Joseph Sr.'s resulting insolvency, albeit due to another man's dishonesty, would have presented a further barrier to admission.

A third possible reason for lodge members to vote against Joseph Smith Sr.'s admission to Federal Lodge appears from his reputation as a youth. The collections of the Chicago Historical Society contain an affidavit signed in 1884 by Moses Thompson, of Perry, Ohio. According to Thompson,

> Joseph Smith, the father of the Mormon Prophet, lived with my parents when I <he> w<a>s a boy. Mother said she was afraid of him,—he had such a violent temper, and was so malicious. Some=time after he was discharged<,> he was overtaken in Cornish [a New Hampshire town 25 miles from Royalton, Vermont] with a horse he had stolen. He sent a messenger to [father] to co[m]e and help him out of his trouble.[40]

Historian Dan Vogel has shown that Moses Thompson confused Smith with another man who also had a son named Joseph.[41] However, this same mistake could have been made by others or promulgated among members of Federal Lodge. Dudley Chase Jr. was born in Cornish in 1771, making him the same age as Joseph Sr. Chase subsequently moved to Randolph, Vermont, where he served as Worshipful Master of Federal Lodge at the time Joseph Sr. was rejected. If he or other members of the Lodge believed that the senior Smith had a poor reputation for honesty in Cornish, it might have prompted a negative ballot, assuring that he would not join the Lodge.

Joseph Sr.'s drinking, frequent moves, and penurious condition all could have been reasons why he never became a Freemason in Vermont. The bylaws of the Grand Lodge of Vermont, which were typical of other grand lodges in the United States, indicate that brothers could be suspended or expelled for failing to attend three or more monthly meetings, or for falling behind in annual dues. Restoration to full membership required a unanimous vote of the members of the lodge, and Masonic practice generally required that past dues be either paid or remitted before any restoration to membership. A man might be turned down for lodge membership if there was a concern that he would be suspended or expelled as the family struggled with meeting basic needs. The Smith family moved many

---

40. "Moses Thompson affidavit, 1886," in Vogel, *Early Mormon Documents*, 1:627. Moses Thompson was born just one year before Joseph Smith Sr. was rejected by Federal Lodge No. 15 and clearly well after Joseph Sr. had allegedly lived with the Thompson family. At best, Moses Thompson is reporting information supplied to him by his mother.

41. Vogel, *Early Mormon Documents*, 1:627–28. Vogel points out that Moses Thompson described Joseph Smith as having a brother Jacob who lived in Plainfield, New Hampshire. The 1800 census of Plainfield lists a Jacob, a Joseph Smith (over forty-five years of age), and a Joseph Jr. (between twenty-six and forty-five years of age).

times in the short space of fifteen years. Particularly during the latter part of this period, it would have become difficult for Joseph Sr. to maintain membership in any lodge, even had his petition not been rejected by Federal Lodge.

Despite these obstacles, Joseph Sr. had ample opportunities to become familiar with Masonic legend via family members, Universalist ties, and local newspapers. This familiarity would color the family's destiny throughout the decades to come.

The Mystic Word Encounters Enlightenment Ideas

Freemasonry had a genial relationship with the Deist, Rationalist, and Universalist trends of the day. Its unique ability to merge mystic ritual with rational thought was attractive to men at all levels of society. A certain tension between folk magic, mysticism, and scientific enlightenment can be noted in the proceedings of Federal Lodge. At the St. John's Day festival of 1804, the brothers sang a "Masonic song" that included lines specifically referring to Royal Arch Masonry:

> When orient wisdom beam'd serene,
>   And pillar'd strength arose;
> When beauty ting'd the glowing scene,
>   And faith her mansion chose,
> Exulting hands the fabric view'd;
>   Mysterious powers ador'd;
> And high the Triple Union stood,
>   That gave the Mystic Word.
>
> Pale envy wither'd at the sight,
>   And frowning o'er the pile,
> Call'd murder up from realms of night,
>   To blast the glorious toil.
> With ruffian outrage join'd in woe,
>   They form the league ahhorr'd;
> And wounded science felt the blow,
>   That crush'd the Mystic Word.
>
>   . . .
>
> To depths obscure, the favour'd Trine,
>   A dreary course engage,
> 'Till through the arch, the ray divine,
>   Illumes the sacred page!
> From the wide wonders of this blaze,
>   Our ancient Sign's restor'd;
> The Royal Arch alone displays,
>   The long lost Mystic Word.[42]

---

42. "Royal Arch," 4.

Published in a local newspaper, this hymn celebrated once-secretive legends now squarely placed in public view. Masonic legend told of certain inscriptions whereby the sacred name of God—Freemasonry's "Lost Word"—was preserved. Here, non-Masonic readers such as Joseph Smith Sr. would have understood the author's basic concept of a "mystic word" long buried in "depths obscure" and crushed by the blow of faithlessness. Simultaneously, Enlightenment thinkers would celebrate the new knowledge and truth that a modern understanding of science would "restore" to the Craft.

Struggling for respectability in a rational society that distrusted "antiquated" mysticism, Freemasons nonetheless regarded the legends undergirding Masonic ritual as valuable allegories. Masons began to take a modern, scholarly approach to lore that was traditionally infused with folk magic and mysticism. Freemasonry advocated an enlightened, rational esoterica. As such, it was believed by many American brothers to be the mechanism that would bring about the Millennium.

Federal Lodge, with its appreciation of these principles, was remarkably cosmopolitan for its time and place, with members among the educated class of society. The Reverend Hosea Ballou held the Lodge's most enduring legacy. Born in 1771, the same year as Joseph Smith Sr., Ballou became the central figure in Orange County and other New England Universalist congregations. In the course of his preaching, he found himself profoundly affected by Ethan Allen's 1784 *Reason: The Only Oracle of Man* and Thomas Paine's 1794 *Age of Reason*. Adopting their message that religious faith must be consistent with logic and reason, Ballou soon changed the face of Universalism. His teachings were both applauded and reviled, and Ballou rose to local Masonic prominence amid Vermont's volatile atmosphere. In 1803 he served as Senior Warden of Federal Lodge, and in 1807 he served as Worshipful Master of Warren Lodge No. 23 in Woodstock, Vermont. As both a reverend and a Mason, Ballou promoted both Universalism and Freemasonry among the inhabitants of central Vermont, having what appears to have been a direct and significant impact on the extended Smith family.[43]

---

43. Ballou's influence on the Smith family went well beyond the ideas of Thomas Paine. Along with books and newspaper articles featuring Ballou, Sereno Wright was instrumental in publishing several sermons reflecting Ballou's Universalist and Masonic teachings. These contained numerous ideas that foreshadow the later teachings of Joseph Smith Jr. Speaking just six months before the birth of young Joseph, Reverend Ballou repudiated creation *ex nihilo* and affirmed that mankind were literally the children of deity, both of which later became familiar themes of Mormonism. See Hosea Ballou, *A Sermon, Delivered at Wilmington, Before the Mount Moriah Lodge of Free and Accepted Masons, at their Celebration of the Festival of St. John, the Baptist, June 24th, A.L. 5805*, 5. Other authors have noted the many parallels between Ballou's "Treatise on Atonement" and the teachings and writings of Joseph Smith, including a rejection of idea that "eternal punishment" is endless in duration, a belief in dualistic (spiritual vs. physical) creation, and the concept of an "infinite" Atonement. See Rick Grunder, *Mormon Parallels: A Bibliographic Source*, 172–77. Another of Ballou's published Masonic sermons, given just

Despite dearly held folk magic beliefs, Joseph Sr. was strongly drawn to such Enlightenment ideas. In late 1797, he joined his father Asael, his brother Jesse, and fourteen others in the formation of a Universalist Society in Tunbridge.[44] Following the birth of Hyrum in 1800, the Joseph Smith Sr. family moved seven miles from Tunbridge to Randolph, Vermont, the seat of Federal Lodge. Like seventy-one other Randolph heads of the household at the time, Joseph Sr. took advantage of an 1801 Vermont law to object to the local Congregationalist tax. His oath that he did "not agree in Religious opinions With a Majority of the Inhabitants of the Town" was attested to on July 1, 1802, by town clerk John Woodward Jr.[45] Joseph Sr. was said to have frequently declared "that the whole bible was the work of priestcraft . . . that Voltair[e']s writings [were] the best bible then extant, and Thomas Paines age of reason, the best commentary."[46] His spiritual struggles reflected some of the same tensions apparent in Masonry.

When the Smith family returned to Tunbridge after a short stay in Randolph and the ginseng debacle, Lucy felt in need of religious comfort. She began to attend the Methodist church and prevailed upon her husband to join her. Apparently worried that he was abandoning his enlightened principles, Joseph Sr.'s father and his brother Jesse paid him a visit, carrying Paine's *Age of Reason* with them. Throwing the book into the house, they suggested he should read it until he believed it and to keep his wife away from church meetings.[47]

Lucy later reflected that her husband was "more pliant and flexible" to "the breath of heaven" than Asael or Jesse. She hoped that "when Joseph should be more advanced in life," he would hear and respond to "the pure and undefiled Gospel of the Son of God."[48] Whether consciously or unknowingly, his attempts to do so retained a strong flavor of Freemasonry.

---

four days after the birth of Joseph Smith Jr., reveals similarities to the latter's 1834–35 Lectures on Faith. Speaking to the members of Vermont's Aurora Lodge on December 27, 1805, Ballou cited seven characteristics of deity, which he believed mankind must adopt in order to be prepared for salvation. Twenty-nine years later, Joseph Smith Jr. detailed six characteristics of deity, which he believed mankind must understand in order to exercise sufficient faith for salvation. See Hosea Ballou, *A Sermon, Delivered at Montpelier, Before the Aurora Lodge of Free and Accepted Masons, at their Celebration of the Festival of St. John, the Evangelist, December 27th, A.L. 5805*, 5–11. What amounted to an early 1800s Masonic "media blitz" by Sereno Wright and others had a cultural effect on the surrounding population. One might say that young Joseph had been providentially placed to absorb ideas which would later contribute to the vitality of Mormonism.

44. Tunbridge Town Record, December 6, 1797, in Vogel, *Early Mormon Documents*, 1:633.

45. Randolph Miscellaneous Records, 1790–1805, in Vogel, *Early Mormon Documents*, 1:641. At the time, Woodward was an active Freemason, serving the following four years as Worshipful Master of Federal Lodge No. 15, along with various other positions in both Federal Lodge No. 15 and the Grand Lodge of Vermont.

46. "Green Mountain Boys to Thomas C. Sharp," in Vogel, *Early Mormon Documents*, 1:597.

47. Anderson, *Lucy's Book*, 291.

48. Anderson, 293–94n28.

A Masonic Name

The word "mason" is one of the many French words imported into English after French Normans invaded England in 1066 CE; it replaced terms like "stone-cutter" or "stoneworker." And although there is little historical record for the term "stonesmith," it is sometimes used today by masons as a business name. Thus, while unquestionably common, the surname "Smith" is particularly appropriate to Freemasonry. Webster's 1828 dictionary defined "smith" as

> Literally, the striker, the beater; hence, one who forges with the hammer; one who works in metals. . . . He that makes or effects any thing. . . . The name Smith, which, from the number of workmen employed in working metals in early ages, is supposed to be more common than any other.[49]

The central figure in Freemasonry, Hiram Abiff, was thus a smith, as he is described in the bible as "a worker in brass: and he was filled with wisdom, and understanding, and cunning to work all works in brass" (1 Kgs. 7:14).[50]

Joseph Smith Jr.'s older brother was named "Hiram" during a time when the name was extremely popular in the Smith family's environs (though, as was common with names in the early nineteenth century, no one minded much if it was subsequently spelled Hyram or Hyrum or some variation thereon).[51] In Windsor and Orange counties, where the Smith family variously lived, the name "Hiram" was very rarely given to newborns prior to 1794 when the Grand Lodge of Vermont was formed. But between 1795 and 1834, in the Vermont counties of Orange and Windsor where Hyrum and Joseph Jr. were born, at least 357 male children were given the name "Hiram." The largest increase in the name's use occurred in 1798—the year in which Federal Lodge was installed—and peak usage came in 1806. A comparison with other male biblical names demonstrates that this was not part of an ecclesiastical trend. Rather, as Freemasonry became more popular and established in the Smith family's immediate vicinity, numer-

---

49. Noah Webster, *An American Dictionary of the English Language*, s.v. "smith."

50. Smiths are of particular interest to Freemasons. Not only was the central figure of the Third Degree a master craftsman and worker in metal and brass, but that degree also honors Tubalcain, the first worker in iron and brass mentioned in the Bible. In fact, Tubalcain and Hiram Abiff are both described as workers in brass (Gen. 4:22; 1 Kgs. 7:14). See Harry Carr, *The Freemason at Work*, 162–63. The name "Tubalcain" may also suggest a stonemason. Similarly, the Royal Arch Degree memorializes Moses's master craftsman, Bezaleel. This individual was the metal-worker responsible for the construction of the Ark of the Covenant, and the chief artificer of the Tabernacle (Ex. 36: 1–3; Ex. 37–39).

51. Jeffrey O'Driscoll, biographer of Hyrum Smith, notes that the earliest known document using the "Hyrum" spelling was the 1830 testimonial in *The Book of Mormon*. Beginning in 1831, Hyrum Smith's personal writings consistently used "Hyrum." Either spelling fits within the observed Masonic naming trend described above and may indicate Joseph Smith Sr. had an interest in Masonic legend even prior to his apparent 1801 petition to the lodge. Jeffery O'Driscoll, Email to Nicholas S. Literski, October 23, 2005.

ous locals named their sons after one of the central figures in Masonic legend. In some cases, the clear Masonic intent of these names is demonstrated by the use of middle names such as "Hiram Abiff Morgan,"[52] "Hiram Mason Fisher,"[53] "Hiram Mason Chafee," "Hiram King Wiles,"[54] "Hiram King Noyes,"[55] and "Hiram Solomon Morse."[56] The decline in the name's usage likewise followed the rising influence of anti-Masonry in Vermont.

Treasures Hidden in the Earth and a Son to Find Them

While yet in Vermont, Joseph Smith Sr., who would later be described as "prone to the marvelous,"[57] became a treasure digger.[58] At the time, this activity was a relatively common folk practice, and Joseph Sr.'s surroundings would have uniquely encouraged his quests. Historian Mark Ashurst-McGee has provided a view of this folkway in early America:

> Many believed that treasures had been secreted in the earth by the ancient inhabitants of the continent, Spanish explorers, pirates, or even the dwarves of European mythology. Treasure hunters usually looked to hills, caves, lost mines, and Native American mounds as places to find these hidden deposits. A legend, a map, or a dream of buried wealth initiated the treasure quest. Local specialists were enlisted to use their divining rods or seer stones to locate the treasure.[59]

As a tenant on the Solomon Mack farm, Joseph Sr. was surrounded by stone curiosities, including seven-foot-tall monoliths, man-made stone chambers, and fragments uncovered by farmers' plows. On the adjacent Macintosh farm, numerous saucer-shaped stones stood in parallel arrangements. In the early twentieth century, a Macintosh descendant discovered a stone chamber on the property—one of at least six in the immediate vicinity. Excavations of the site revealed a variety of Native American artifacts. With the annual frost-heave cycle, "an abundance" of inscribed stones were plowed up in nearby fields. A modern investigator of "strange sites" speculated on the effect these ubiquitous curiosities could have had on young Joseph Smith Jr. (and, by extension, his father and brothers):

---

52. Born 1809, Cambridge, Vermont.

53. Born 1817, Danville, Vermont.

54. Born 1822, Topsham, Vermont.

55. Born 1816, Tunbridge, Vermont.

56. Born 1806, Pomfret, Vermont.

57. M. A., "A Swindling Saint," 5.

58. "In Kirtland, Joseph Smith sen'r, the Prophet's father, said in Council: 'I know more about money digging, than any man in this generation, for I have been in the business more than thirty years.'" James Colin Brewster, *Very Important! To the Mormon Money Diggers*, 4. By his own accounting, then, Smith Sr. had been a treasure seeker since his Vermont days.

59. Mark Ashurst-McGee, "A Pathway to Prophethood: Joseph Smith Junior as Rodsman, Village Seer, and Judeo-Christian Prophet," 63.

Smith spent his boyhood in a part of central Vermont that's filled with strange lithic remains—from inexplicable stone chambers to boulders etched with curious markings and grooves (see South Royalton, Vermont). Records indicate that the young Smith was quite curious. He supposedly roamed around Vermont's hillsides searching for unusual things, including buried treasure. Given his surroundings, it's impossible that Smith missed all of the weird underground stone rooms found within walking distance of the many places where he lived.[60]

Joseph Sr. reportedly found an allure in the legendary Captain Kidd's pirate treasure,[61] and he passed his interest on to his sons. Under the influence of Masonic legend and physical environment, there is little wonder that the Smiths would take an active interest in treasure digging. There was an overt Masonic quality to this activity, because Masons are interested in the recovery of a lost sacred word, once engraved upon a triangular plate of gold. Thus, the Smiths' treasure seeking was connected with a sacred holy meaning from the beginning. Much as the true alchemist's search to transmute lead into gold symbolized his spiritual effort to purify the human soul, the family became involved in seeking for a literal but equally important spiritual "treasure" buried in the earth of New England. The activity included special rituals and ceremonies that were performed for the purpose of obtaining buried items thought to be guarded by evil spirits.

It was during the family's time in Sharon, Windsor County, Vermont, that the Smiths' third son was born on December 23, 1805. The attending physician, Dr. Joseph A. Denison, was a member of Federal Lodge, having joined the Fraternity in September of 1800.[62] The birth of Joseph Jr. appears to have been fraught with meaning for his father, who apparently saw great spiritual importance in his son's birth. Joseph Jr. was born four days before the feast day of Saint John the Evangelist, one of the two patron saints of Masonry. Traditionally, this day is chosen for the installation of a new master within an established Masonic lodge. His birth also came one day following the winter solstice, a time representing the rebirth and the restoration of light to the world.

In addition, Joseph Jr. was born in a caul, or with a portion of the placenta over his head, so that he appeared, like Moses, to have "a veil over [his] face" (2 Cor. 3:13). As with many cultures to this day, New Englanders often believed that being born in the unbroken amniotic sack portended the gifts of prophecy and seership.[63] The Masonic timing and prophetic nature of Joseph Jr.'s birth may

60. Salvatore Michael Trento, *Field Guide to Mysterious Places of Eastern North America*, 96.

61. This interest is mentioned in the "Green Mountain Boys to Thomas C. Sharp" and is also found in a reprint of Daniel Woodward's 1870 letter to the *Boston Transcript*. Dan Vogel, *Early Mormon Documents*, 1:597, 624–25.

62. *Register of the Grand Lodge of Vermont, 1794 to 1846.*

63. Various legends told of the biblical Noah, a special child of promise, being born with a veil over his face. The concept of a veil over the face could also have been readily found by Joseph Sr. in the Bible account of Moses veiling his face in order to speak to the people after he had stood in the presence of Deity.

have led his family to believe him to be the fulfillment of a legendary Masonic restorer who would aid in their search for the Lost Word. It was later recalled that Joseph Sr. intended to provide his son a seer stone.[64] From this evidence, historian Dan Vogel drew the conclusion that "Joseph Sr. evidently intended to pass his gifts as a dreamer and treasure-seeker to his namesake. . . . Like the biblical Jacob, Joseph Sr. would bypass the tradition of first-born inheritance and give his greatest blessing—the only blessing he had to impart—to a younger son."[65]

While it cannot be proven what Joseph Sr. had in mind while naming his sons, circumstances render it quite possible that, having named one son Hiram/Hyrum, he chose to make another son his namesake. The importance of this would be referenced in LDS scripture when the Mormon prophet was identified specifically with Joseph of Egypt and as a "Joseph" named after his own father (2 Ne. 3:15).

Residences and Relocations of the Smith Family

After Joseph Smith Sr. lost his potential fortune in the ginseng trade, the young father sold his Tunbridge farm to settle resulting debts and began renting farmland owned by his father-in-law, Solomon Mack, ten miles away on the border between South Royalton and Sharon, Vermont. Though they moved frequently during the following years, the family stayed within a comfort zone of three counties clustered around the Connecticut River. All these residences were well within a twenty-mile circumference of the homestead in Sharon.[66]

Perhaps hopeful that migration to another state would allow him to escape the obstacles he faced in Vermont, Joseph Sr. moved his family to Lebanon, New Hampshire, in 1812. Lucy Mack Smith's history does not seem to detail how the family supported themselves in Lebanon, but their efforts "met with success on every hand."[67] After two years of prosperity, however, the family was afflicted by an epidemic of typhus fever. The disease interrupted the academic career of Hyrum, who came home ill from Moor's Academy. It then spread to all the Smith children, nearly killing young Sophronia. The illness eventually settled in the leg of Joseph Jr. Had the family not had connections to prominent doctors in the area (many of whom were Masons), who were able to provide an experimental treatment, it is likely that the leg would have required amputation to save the young Joseph's life.

---

64. "Green Mountain Boys to Thomas C. Sharp."

65. Dan Vogel, *Joseph Smith: The Making of a Prophet*, 12–13.

66. By 1809, Rising Sun Lodge No. 28 (renumbered in 1849 as No. 7) had been established in Royalton for three years, with the Smiths' former associate, John Woodward, as its first Worshipful Master. Having once been rejected by a Vermont lodge, however, Joseph Sr. could not join Rising Sun Lodge without the prior approval of Federal Lodge No. 15. No record survives to demonstrate such an attempt.

67. Anderson, *Lucy's Book*, 300.

This year of sickness, with its attendant expenses, devastated the family's finances and necessitated yet another move.[68] The Smiths found a home and farm to rent across the river in Norwich, Vermont, where they eked out a meager living, aided by the proceeds of a small orchard and Lucy's in-home industry.[69] The new location was within the seat of Franklin Lodge, and several members of the Lodge lived there. While Hyrum was able to attend an additional year at Moor's Academy, unfortunately the next three years' harvests were so poor that the family was never able to regain their financial footing in New England.

In the fall of 1816, Joseph Sr. again relocated, this time to Palmyra, New York. After a journey that exhausted nearly all their means, Lucy and her children joined him there in January 1817.[70] Lucy made a business of painting oilcloths for decorative use, by which she gathered "an abundance of good and wholesome provision" and even began to replace the "fine" furnishings lost in making the journey from Vermont.[71] Palmyra resident Pomeroy Tucker noted that soon after the Smiths' move to New York, Joseph Sr. "opened a cake and beer shop" in their rented home, situated at the end of Palmyra's Main Street.[72] From here, the family sold "gingerbread, pies, boiled eggs, root-beer and other like notions of traffic." The family establishment was popular with the youth, and sales were particularly brisk during holidays. Such income generated from the family store was supplemented by Joseph Sr. and his elder sons hiring out as common laborers, engaging in "gardening, harvesting, well-digging," and the like.[73] Additionally, Joseph Sr. and his son Hyrum worked at the cooper's trade. Given that cargo for the upcoming Erie Canal would be shipped via the casks, barrels, and tubs fashioned by coopers, this was a wise decision, as the occupation would provide relatively stable and profitable work. As noted by historian Richard L. Bushman, the Smith family was "in a better position by 1818 than they had occupied for fifteen years."[74]

The improvement in the family's economic circumstances may have helped pave the way for Joseph Sr.'s long-awaited initiation into Freemasonry. After his apparent rejection by Federal Lodge in 1801, Joseph Sr. would not have been allowed to join any lodge within the jurisdiction of the Grand Lodge of Vermont without the express and unanimous approval of Federal Lodge No. 15.

---

68. Anderson, *Lucy's Book*, 310–11.

69. The Connecticut River had been bridged between Norwich and Hanover since 1796, allowing easy passage. M. E. Goddard and Henry V. Partridge, *A History of Norwich Vermont*, 59.

70. Anderson, *Lucy's Book*, 169–70. This is consistent with his having arrived in the latter part of 1816.

71. Anderson, 318.

72. H. Michael Marquardt, *The Rise of Mormonism: 1816–1844*, 2–3. Joseph Smith Sr. appears as a resident on Palmyra's Main Street in April 1817.

73. Pomeroy Tucker, *Origin, Rise, and Progress of Mormonism: Biography of its Founders and History of its Church*, 12.

74. Richard L. Bushman, *Joseph Smith and the Beginnings of Mormonism*, 47.

Most of the Smith family's Vermont residences were located relatively close to Federal Lodge, making it exceedingly difficult to circumvent this rule. However, the move to New York provided a new start in a different Masonic jurisdiction. The village of Palmyra had been home to Mount Moriah Lodge No. 112 since October of 1804, and Masons in the adjacent village of Farmington (later called Manchester) had only recently formed Manchester Lodge No. 269. Both lodges were preceded by the 1791 formation of Ontario Lodge No. 23, thirteen miles south at Canandaigua.

During this time, Freemasons were held in high esteem by the American public, and the Fraternity labored to maintain the public trust. While recognizing that not every Mason lived his profession, they made efforts to ensure that applicants were worthy of initiation.[75] Candidates for membership were required to have lived in the area for at least a year, and they were expected to be industrious, stable, trustworthy, and not addicted to vicious habits. Moral integrity was a prerequisite, and it was a requirement that a man petitioning a lodge be vouched for by a Mason who had opportunity to observe his behavior. In this way, a brother could first verify to his own satisfaction the qualifications of an individual before signing his petition to the Lodge. It was hoped that new members would live in the area for many years thereafter, contributing to the annual dues and assisting with initiation of those who followed in their footsteps looking for light in Masonry.

Freemasons generally looked with favor upon a recommendation from a family member who was already a Freemason. The elder Joseph Smith's brother-in-law, John Curtis Waller, had served as a lodge officer. His brothers, John and Samuel Smith, and nephew, Calvin Waller, were Masons in Potsdam and could also vouch for him. Thus, it would have been relatively easy for Joseph Smith Sr. to successfully petition a lodge for membership, as long as his overall personal behavior was viewed favorably by other members of the lodge.

The only question was which lodge Joseph Sr. would join. Two lodges were within easy traveling distance—Palmyra's Mount Moriah Lodge No. 112 and nearby Canandaigua's Ontario Lodge No. 23. Formed in 1804, Mount Moriah was the newer lodge, and it had less time to accumulate the paraphernalia that added luster to the degrees. The Lodge was created in response to a joint petition from brothers in two townships: Palmyra and Phelps (twelve miles southeast of Palmyra and thirteen miles from Canandaigua). For the first few years of its existence, the Lodge met alternately in the two towns. Had he petitioned this lodge, Joseph Sr. would have needed the unanimous affirmative vote of members from two communities for admission.

Although Ontario Lodge was located approximately twelve miles from the Smith home on the Palmyra-Manchester border, it was clearly the older and more prestigious of the two. It had been founded in 1792 by some of Canandaigua's finest citizens. With the Erie Canal only beginning construction in 1817,

---

75. Bradley, *Some of the Beauties of Freemasonry*, xv–xvi, 47–8.

Canandaigua was still a primary commercial center in the region. Other conditions, such as personal friendships or business interests, influenced which lodge a candidate might petition. Joseph Sr. would likely have been required to make periodic trips to the county center to sell crops and deal with land brokers. Since many brothers also farmed, lodge meetings were a chance to travel into town, take care of Masonic business, perform the rituals to induct new members, and afterward enjoy a sumptuous meal accompanied by a few pints and the company of Masonic brothers. Many lodges met in the evening, and the men would stay the night and take care of business in town the next morning. It was not uncommon for brothers to travel ten to fifteen miles to lodge, which was usually only held once a month.

A search of Mount Moriah Lodge's records has not revealed the induction of Joseph Sr., but he does appear on the records of Ontario Lodge No. 23. The Lodge's 1818 annual report of newly initiated Masons indicates that a "Joseph Smith" was initiated as an Entered Apprentice on December 26, 1817, passed to the degree of Fellowcraft on May 2, 1818, and raised to the degree of Master Mason on May 7, 1818.[76] The date of December 26 indicates that he was initiated on the day Ontario Lodge was celebrating St. John the Evangelist's Day,[77] one of two Masonic feasts held at the Summer and Winter Solstices.

The "Joseph Smith" who was initiated on December 26, 1817, would have had to petition the lodge for degrees at least thirty days prior, thus placing his request in late November—just over one year from the arrival of Joseph Sr. in New York. A comparison of the records of Palmyra's Mount Moriah Lodge No. 112 with 1820 census records demonstrates that the Lodge included members residing in not only Palmyra but also in over a dozen nearby towns, including even Canandaigua itself. Some of these towns, such as Lyons, were further from Palmyra than Palmyra was from Canandaigua.

Some historians have questioned if this is our Joseph Smith Sr. or some other person with that name, because Ontario Lodge record lists Canandaigua as the residence of the "Joseph Smith" initiate. The same record indicates Canandaigua as the residence of every listed member, with all but the first being mere ditto marks. The 1820 census, however, lists two of these men as living in nearby Gorham, with others of unclear residence. This would indicate that the secretary was less than careful in specifying the precise residence of each member.

---

76. See "Persons Who Have Been Initiated, Passed, Raised, or Admitted as Adjoining Members of Ontario Lodge No 23, held at Canandaigua, Ontario County, State of New York, From December 27, 1817, to December 27, 1818." Dan Vogel has argued that this "Joseph Smith" was unlikely to be the father of the Mormon prophet. He points out that the Ontario Lodge record lists the initiate as living in Canandaigua, that Joseph Sr. would more likely have joined the lodge in Palmyra, and that there were nine men with the same name in Ontario County. See Dan Vogel, *Early Mormon Documents*, 3:456. Vogel also notes, however, that the 1820 federal census does not list any person by that name living in Canandaigua, suggesting to his mind that the initiated Smith moved from the area prior to 1820.

77. St. John the Evangelist's Day is December 27.

Joseph Smiths Living in Ontario County		
Location	Distance From Ontario Lodge	Closest Lodge
Farmington	8 miles	Palmyra—Mount Moriah Lodge No. 123
Seneca	11 miles	Seneca—Meridian Lodge No. 184
Mendon	15 miles	Victor—Milnor Lodge No. 303
Richmond	15 miles	Richmond—Richland Lodge No. 138
Benton	16 miles	Benton—Vernon Lodge No. 190
Benton	16 miles	Benton—Vernon Lodge No. 190
Jerusalem	19 miles	Benton—Vernon Lodge No. 190
Penfield	21 miles	Ontario—Rising Virtue Lodge No. 321
Avon	24 miles	Avon—Genesee Lodge No. 130

Additionally, there is some ambiguity as to whether this column meant where the brother was currently residing, where the brother legally kept a permanent homestead or business, or if there was a declared intention to reside at that location.

The Road Census in April of 1817 and 1818 does list Joseph Smith Sr. as living in Palmyra. However, was there another Joseph Smith living in Canandaigua at the time who was of legal age and properly vouched for? The 1820 census shows that there was no Joseph Smith living in Canandaigua in 1820, but there were nine Joseph Smiths listed in Ontario County.

Since Masonic lodges did not initiate transients and would likely not have raised a brother who did not plan a long-term residence in the area, we are left with the residents listed. While strictly speaking, residence did not determine which lodge a man must attend, the most obvious feature of the list is that in 1820 the closest man to Ontario Lodge No. 23 was none other than our Joseph Smith Sr., who was enumerated in Farmington.

The one-hundred-acre parcel of land that Joseph Sr. and his son Alvin "articled" in 1820 was purchased from Zachariah Seymour, a Canandaigua land broker. According to historian Michael Marquardt, "Seymour had long been a land agent in the area and was a close associate of Oliver Phelps, who with his partner Nathaniel Gorham had opened a land office in Canandaigua and had instituted the practice of 'articling' for real estate."[78] Thus, Joseph Sr. would have necessarily travelled to Canandaigua on occasion to contract for his 1820 land purchase. One notable member of Ontario Lodge from at least 1815 was Harris Seymour, son of Zachariah Seymour, indicating a possible fraternal connection that allowed the Smiths to purchase their property.

---

78. Marquardt, *The Rise of Mormonism*, 4. Marquardt writes, "Articling was a way for hard working but cash-poor pioneers to obtain possession of land by buying on the installment plan. . . . It was by this method that the Smiths worked to become property owners."

The Smith family quickly established business and personal relationships with local Freemasons. A search of extant local records indicates at least 314 known Masons in the community during their residence.[79] The Smith family physician, the owner of the local drugstore patronized by the family, and even their next-door neighbors were members of the local lodges. Among the values of Freemasonry was education in the liberal arts and sciences, and thus it was no surprise that local Masons would take the lead in those fields.[80] Many local public officials, physicians, and businessmen took their places in lodge meetings alongside farmers. Furthermore, the two lodges included veterans of both the Revolutionary War and the War of 1812. With so many Masonic connections, and with relatively ample access to libraries, bookstores, and newspapers, the Smith family was surrounded by opportunities to be exposed to Masonic ritual, literature, and thought. As one author has suggested, Palmyra became known as "a strong Masonic Town."[81]

Affiliations of Alvin and Hyrum

During the family's Palmyra years, Joseph Smith Sr.'s two eldest sons, Alvin and Hyrum, reached the proper age for initiation. While no documentary evidence has appeared that Alvin was a Freemason, hints of this possibility lie in the chest later used to store the gold plates of the Book of Mormon. Prior to building the Smith family's wood frame house on the Palmyra/Manchester farm, Alvin built a lap desk from tulip poplar and walnut. Family lore indicates that Alvin used this lap desk in designing the home and that he kept his architectural tools inside. When Alvin passed away, the lap desk came into the possession of his brother Hyrum, who supplied it to Joseph Jr. to serve as a temporary chest for the plates, breastplate, and Urim and Thummim. There is no indication that any member of the Smith family may have possessed architectural skills, and such would not be particularly necessary for planning a standard frame house. No information supplies the eventual fate of these architectural tools; however, it is possible that they may actually have been the symbolic "working tools" used in Freemasonry, such as the square, compasses, plumb, and level. If so,

---

79. See Records of Mount Moriah Lodge #112; and Records of Manchester Lodge #269.

80. Addison N. Buck, a member of Manchester Lodge No. 269 and the first Excellent High Priest of Palmyra Eagle (Royal Arch) Chapter, served as librarian of the Farmington/Manchester Public Library during its initial years, only to be replaced in 1818 by fellow lodge member John Pratt, who served until his death in 1865. Local Freemasons Pomeroy Tucker and Egbert B. Grandin owned newspapers and a bookstore, as well as a small lending library in Palmyra. See Robert Paul, "Joseph Smith and the Manchester (New York) Library," 334, 340. Polydore Wisner, a member of Mount Moriah Lodge No. 112, helped to found both the Geneva Public Library in 1798 and the Geneva Academy in 1807. See Ted Deci, "The Short But Eventful Story of Mt. Moriah Lodge No. 112 F.A.M.," 6. Regarding Grandin's published pro-Masonic stance, see Bullock, *Revolutionary Brotherhood*, 303.

81. Deci, "Short But Eventful Story of Mt. Moriah Lodge," 3.

this adds significance to the lap desk or chest, with its contents, being passed directly to Hyrum, the only active Freemason in the family.[82]

Hyrum Smith's Masonic affiliation is more certain, for in the later Nauvoo Lodge records he identified his preceding lodge as Mount Moriah No. 112 in Palmyra. It is easy to imagine why a young man would find the Palmyra Lodge more appealing than the staid Ontario Lodge: construction of the Palmyra portion of the Erie Canal, which passed through Palmyra's village center, was completed in 1822, increasing the community's importance and the opportunities available to its citizens. By 1824, the town boasted of three gristmills, eight sawmills, one fulling mill, an iron works, five distilleries, two asheries, and two tanneries.[83]

While it is entirely possible that Hyrum first received his degrees in a different lodge, the earliest known record of his membership is his quarterly dues on Mount Moriah's financial report dated June 4, 1827, through June 4, 1828.[84] Because he does not appear with those being initiated or admitted that year, we can know that he was initiated prior to June of 1827; however, the exact date of his initiation remains unknown. The earliest he could have been able to petition the Lodge for membership was following his twenty-first birthday on February 9, 1821. According to Heber C. Kimball, "Hyrum Smith received the first three degrees of masonry in Ontario County, New York." This points to Hyrum becoming a Mason before 1823, since county lines shifted in that year and Palmyra became part of Wayne County.[85]

Under normal circumstances, if he had not been raised in the Lodge, he would have been listed as paying an "adjoining" fee for transferring from another lodge. At least in Hyrum's case, the records are incomplete, and the correct explanation may be lost as a result. The Lodge's next existing return, prepared on June 1, 1831, no longer listed Hyrum as a member. This is consistent with Hyrum having moved his family to Colesville, New York, in September or October of 1830.[86]

"By Which He Could Discern Things Invisible to the Natural Eye"

In towns where Rationalism and Universalism coexisted with Methodists and Freewill Baptists—especially when alchemy, treasure digging, and other forms of hermeticism were in operation—one was likely to find a Masonic presence. The

---

82. Eldred Smith, Presentation given at the Joseph Smith Academy in Nauvoo, Illinois, December 31, 2003.

83. Bushman, *Joseph Smith and the Beginnings of Mormonism*, 45.

84. Records of Mount Moriah Lodge No. 112. The financial report lists the quarterly dues, initiation fees, and admission fees (fees charged to Masons joining the lodge from another prior lodge affiliation) during the year.

85. Orson F. Whitney, *Life of Heber C. Kimball, An Apostle: The Father and Founder of the British Mission*, 27; Vogel, *Early Mormon Documents*, 3:452–53. Records of Mount Moriah Lodge are missing for June 1820–June 1821 and December 1822–December 1823.

86. Jeffrey S. O'Driscoll, *Hyrum Smith: A Life of Integrity*, 41, 396.

Craft congenially brought together antipodes like treasure seeking and rationalism. In these New England towns, as well as in the state of New York, there was a
high concentration of individuals who would eventually be amenable to the new
Mormon message. Historian John L. Brooke recognized that it was "the *combination* of sectarian and hermetic influences in a given town" that would eventually
correlate with conversions to the new faith.[87] According to Lance Ownes, "the
treasure sought by the alchemist was often termed the 'philosopher's stone,'" while
the alchemist himself was considered a "priest in a hallowed, ancient priesthood,"
"a knower of creation's ancient secret," and "a digger after hidden treasure."[88]
Freemasons believed that this hidden treasure was no more nor less than divine
knowledge—the very secrets of Nature and Nature's God. Like the Nathaniel
Wood group before them, the Smiths would eventually mix these powerful elements into a potent new faith centered upon a long-lost, newly found holy relic.

Not long after their arrival in Palmyra, the Smith family resumed their quest
for hidden treasure in earnest. Even before leaving Vermont, Joseph Sr. had told
others that he "intended to procure a stone for [Joseph Jr.] to see all over the
world with."[89] Father Smith believed there was "a stone of this quality, some-
where, for every one."[90]

At an 1826 trial in which Joseph Jr. was accused of being a "disorderly person," a court scribe recalled writing the young man's words as he regaled the court
with his seeric adventures. In this telling, Joseph Jr. heard of a neighbor girl's
"glass," went to visit her, and was permitted to look into the seer stone. After it
was placed in a hat to exclude the light,

> He was greatly surprised to see but one thing, which was a small stone, a great way
> off. It soon became luminous, and dazzled his eyes, and after a short time it became as
> intense as the mid-day sun. . . . This singular circumstance occupied his mind for some
> years, when he left his father's house, and with his youthful zeal traveled [some one
> hundred and fifty miles] west in search of this luminous stone. . . . With some labor
> and exertion he found the stone, carried it to the creek, washed and wiped it dry, sat
> down on the bank, placed it in his hat, and discovered that time, place, and distance

---

87. Brooke, *The Refiner's Fire*, 144; emphasis in original. Brooke continues: "Any
sectarian-hermetic combination of Methodists, Freewill Baptists, Masonic societies,
and counterfeiting petitions correlated with Mormon conversion. The combination of
divining, Freemasonry, and Mormon conversion was a relative rarity, but the four towns
where this combination pertained—Milton, Poultney, Rutland, and Rockingham—
together produced fifteen converts, the largest concentration of Mormon conversion of any
category in this analysis. Tunbridge, Royalton, and nearby towns in Orange and Windsor
counties producing Mormon converts were notable for their combination of hermetic and
sectarian influences, whereas the towns around Poultney in Rutland County accounted for
most of the localities where two hermetic influences converged" (pp. 144–45).

88. Lance S. Owens, "Joseph Smith and Kabbalah: The Occult Connection," 136, 138.

89. "Letter from the Green Mountain Boys," in Vogel, *Early Mormon Documents*, 1:597.

90. "1830 Interview with Fayette Lapham," in Vogel, *Early Mormon Documents*, 1:457.

were annihilated; that all intervening obstacles were removed, and that he possessed one of the attributes of Deity, an All-Seeing Eye.[91]

The object Joseph Jr. had found was described as a hard, smooth stone about the size of a small hen's egg and shaped like a "high-instepped shoe." It was "composed of layers of different colors passing diagonally through it."[92] Such stones, hermetic symbols of transformation and change, were of interest to Freemasons, as was the attribute of the "All-Seeing Eye."

Later stories of Joseph Jr.'s seer stones contain common elements but are difficult to harmonize.[93] In the fall of 1819, Joseph Sr. and his three older sons were apparently hired to help dig a well on the Chase property.[94] In an 1830 conversation with the senior Smith, Palmyra resident Fayette Lapham claimed that the "pretense of digging a well" was subterfuge for money digging. The group found water and a "dark stone" at a depth of twenty or twenty-two feet.[95] Willard Chase excitedly brought it to the top of the well, and "as we were examining it, Joseph [Jr.] put it into his hat, and then his face into the top of his hat."[96] Pomeroy Tucker, a member of Mount Moriah Lodge, gave further details in a later account:

> This stone attracted particular notice on account of its peculiar shape, resembling that of a child's foot. It was of a whitish glassy appearance, though opaque, resembling quartz. . . . Joseph Jr. . . . manifested a special fancy for this geological curiosity; and he carried it home with him, though this act of plunder was against the strenuous protestations of Mr. Chase's children, who claimed to be its rightful owners. Joseph kept this stone, and ever afterward refused its restoration to the claimants. Very soon the pretension transpired that he could see wonderful things by its aid. This idea was rapidly enlarged upon from day to day, and in a short time his spiritual endowment

---

91. "William D. Purple Reminiscence, 28 April 1877," in Vogel, *Early Mormon Documents*, 4:133–34.

92. "William D. Purple Reminiscence, 28 April 1877." William Purple, a Royal Arch Mason and physician, was asked by the presiding judge (also a Mason) to take bystander notes during a court hearing, wherein Joseph Jr. was tried as a "disorderly person and imposter."

93. See D. Michael Quinn's commentary on the several accounts involving three different stones: "He obtained the first by digging for it himself after seeing its location in a stone he had borrowed from a neighbor. Someone claimed to give him a second stone. He used most extensively a third stone obtained while he and his brother Alvin were well-digging on a neighbor's property in Palmyra." Quinn, *Early Mormonism*, 42–44. Vogel notes the discrepancies with such a view: "Purple believed that the story Smith related to the court pertained to a dark-colored stone. . . . While Quinn believes Purple was mistaken, it is also possible that Smith told different stories about the origin of his brown stone." Vogel, *Early Mormon Documents*, 4:134n18.

94. Tucker, *Origin, Rise, and Progress of Mormonism*, 19–20; "Willard Chase Statement," in Vogel, *Early Mormon Documents*, 2:65. Tucker gives a date of September 1819, while the Willard Chase account dates the episode to 1822.

95. "1830 Interview with Fayette Lapham."

96. "Willard Chase Statement," in Vogel, *Early Mormon Documents*, 2:65.

was so developed that he asserted the gift and power (with the stone at his eyes) of revealing both things existing and things to come.[97]

With the discovery of a seer stone, it appeared that his father's expectations were on their way to being fulfilled. Young Joseph's 1819–20 discovery of his own seer stone allowed him to take an active part in the family's treasure quest. Joshua Stafford, a treasure digger who lived two miles south of the Smiths, reported that the family "commenced digging for hidden treasures" soon after moving to the farm.[98] Once again, the family found themselves surrounded by the remnants of Native American burial mounds and other relics. At least one source claimed that Joseph Sr. told him the local hills were "nearly all erected by human hands" and that the family was not digging for money but rather "for the obtaining of a Gold Bible."[99] For this reason, Alan Taylor, noting the spiritual dimension of the search, prefers to "call them treasure-seekers rather than the more sordid-sounding money-diggers."[100]

Joseph Sr. was said to have declared that "his son Jo" had seen "the spirit, (which he then described as a little old man with a long beard,)" who would help the young man obtain great treasures.[101] In a paean to Masonic legend, the elder Smith prophesied that his son would bring forth a book telling the account of the antediluvians who, at the approach of the great Flood, had deposited their substance in large and spacious underground chambers.[102] This later account, which foretells the coming forth of the Book of Mormon, was doubtless influenced by later events. But its connection with Masonic lore is further evidence that local residents viewed Father Smith as having promoted his son as a Masonic restorer.

In the meantime, Joseph Jr.'s reputation as a treasure seer was spreading. His introduction to Josiah Stowell occurred within a month of his 1825 visit to Cumorah. Stowell, a native of Vermont, had received land grants in Bainbridge (now Afton), New York, after the 1791 settlement of longstanding border disputes. A deacon in the local Presbyterian Church, Stowell gained respect as an industrious and frugal pillar of the community. Based on his good character, he was initiated in Friendship Lodge No. 129, of Bainbridge, between April and June of 1816.[103] After spending considerable time in search of a lost Spanish mine, Stowell made a visit to his son, Simpson Stowell, in Manchester, where he met

---

97. Tucker, *Origin, Rise, and Progress of Mormonism*, 19–20.

98. "Joshua Stafford Statement, 15 November 1833," in Vogel, *Early Mormon Documents*, 2:27.

99. "Roswell Nichols Statement, 1 December 1833," in Vogel, 2:38.

100. Alan Taylor, "Rediscovering the Context of Joseph Smith's Treasure Seeking," 23.

101. "Gold Bible, No. 4," 100–101.

102. Fawn McKay Brodie, *No Man Knows My History: The Life of Joseph Smith*, 430. The legend of Enoch, more fully covered in chapter 5 in this book, tells of this biblical prophet and his son building a system of nine brick vaults in the bosom of Mount Moriah. Inside, they placed a triangular plate of gold, engraved with the ineffable Name of God.

103. Returns of Friendship Lodge No. 129, 1814–1816.

young Joseph Smith Jr.[104] According to Lucy Mack Smith, Josiah Stowell "came for Joseph on account of having heard that he possessed certain keys, by which he could discern things invisible to the natural eye."[105] The suggestion of "certain keys" is an important piece of information as to Stowell's motivations. The idea of "keys" by which certain hidden information could be discerned was important within Freemasonry, particularly in the Royal Arch rituals. Notably, later editors of Lucy Mack Smith's record uniformly substituted "means" for "keys" in published versions of her memoirs, thus obscuring the Masonic connotations of Lucy's words.[106]

Stowell offered "high wages" for Joseph Jr.'s labor, but according to his mother, the boy was reticent in accepting employment. This reluctance on young Joseph's part became even more evident during a trial in 1826, when the sons of Josiah Stowell, fearing their father was being cheated of their future inheritance, had Joseph Jr. arrested as a "disorderly person and an Imposter" for "pretending" to find hidden things in the earth.[107] This trial was remarkable, if for no other reason than the number of lodge members who became involved. Peter Goff Bridgeman, the son and half-brother of lodge members Reuben Bridgeman and Adna Bridgeman, formally brought charges. Local constable Philip M. DeZeng, another member of Friendship No. 129, took Joseph into custody, spending two days and one night with him before delivering him to trial.[108] Arad Stowell, another lodge member, testified for the prosecution. Justice Albert Neely, who presided over the hearing, was a Mason, as were the other two South Bainbridge judges, Levi Bigelow and Zechariah Tarble.[109]

William D. Purple, of Greene, New York, was secretary of the local lodge.[110] Justice Neely assigned Purple to keep minutes of the trial, in keeping with his experience in taking secretarial minutes. According to his written notes, Joseph Sr. testified regarding his son's gifts of seership, and that

> both he and his son were mortified that this wonderful power which God had so miraculously given him should be used only in search of filthy lucre, or its equivalent

---

104. Vogel, *Joseph Smith*, 70.

105. Anderson, *Lucy's Book*, 360.

106. Anderson, 360.

107. Bainbridge New York Court Record, March 20, 1826, in Vogel, *Early Mormon Documents*, 4:248–49.

108. Philip DeZeng Bill of Costs, 1826, in Vogel, *Early Mormon Documents*, 4:265.

109. Vogel, *Joseph Smith*, 638n17. Albert Neely, the other three justices for South Bainbridge (Zechariah Tarbell, Levi Bigelow, and James H. Humphrey), and constable Philip DeZang appear on the Returns for Friendship Lodge No. 129.

110. As Warden of Friendship Lodge, Purple "was representative in Grand Lodge in June, 1827." William D. Purple, *Historical Reminiscences of Eastern Light Lodge, No. 126, F. & A. M., of Greene, Chenango County, N.Y., From 5811 [1811] To 5897 [1897], with Biographical Sketches*, revised and published by the Lodge, 189, 40.

in earthly treasures . . . [and that] his constant prayer to his Heavenly Father was to manifest His will concerning this marvelous power.[111]

Joseph Jr. would later downplay his involvement in the Josiah Stowell diggings:

> In the month of October Eighteen hundred and twenty five I hired with an old Gentleman, by name of Josiah Stoal who lived in Chenango County, State of New York. He had heard something of a silver mine having been opened by the Spaniards in Harmony, Susquahanah County, State of Pensylvania, and had previous to my hiring with him been digging in order if possible to discover the mine. After I went to live with <him> he took me among the rest of his hands to dig for the silver mine, at which I continued to work for nearly a month without success in our undertaking, and finally I prevailed with the old gentleman to cease digging after it. Hence arose the very prevalent story of my ~~have~~ <having> been a money digger.[112]

On another occasion, Joseph Jr. answered the question of "Was not Jo Smith a money digger?" with, "Yes, but it was never a very profitable job to him, as he only got fourteen dollars a month for it."[113] It seems that both father and son believed that there was a higher purpose to their treasure seeking, which they didn't always achieve.

Nineteenth-century Latter-day Saints saw the Smiths' treasure seeking activities at least in part as allegorical, similar to how they appear in Masonic ritual. This is admitted in an 1875 newspaper article:

> The father had one favorite speculation: that of buried money—vast fortunes hidden with incantations and only to be exhumed with exorcising. This passion he indulged, and many were the pits dug by him in the search for the concealed treasures. . . . Believers in the faith see in this profession an allegory practically expressed of a searcher after truth in the locality where that virtue is proverbally placed.[114]

Thus, the Smiths were physically expressing an allegorical activity. Mormon writer Alan Taylor observed, "We cannot fully understand the treasure seekers if we continue to think of them as simple anachronisms, as practitioners of the timeless occult who were oblivious to, or rebellious against, the larger, cosmopolitan culture's trend toward empirical rationalism."[115]

Winning the Faculty of Abrac

Throughout these years, the Smith family continued their involvement with the legends and quests associated with the Fraternity. In her retrospective family history, written around 1845, Lucy Mack Smith defended the family from ac-

---

111. Vogel, *Early Mormon Documents*, 4:135.

112. "History, 1838–1856, volume A-1 [23 December 1805–30 August 1834]," The Joseph Smith Papers, 7–8.

113. Joseph Smith Jr., "In Obedience to Our Promise," 43.

114. M. A., "A Swindling Saint," 5.

115. Taylor, "Rediscovering the Context of Joseph Smith's Treasure Seeking," 20.

cusations of slothfulness by insisting that these pursuits did not cause them to disregard their obligations:

> I shall change my theme for the present but let not my reader suppose that because I shall pursue another topic for a season that we stopt our labor and went <at> trying to win the faculty of Abrac drawing Magic circles or sooth saying to the neglect of all kinds of buisness we never during our lives suffered one important interest to swallow up every other obligation but whilst we worked with our hands we endeavored to remmember the service of & the welfare of our souls.[116]

Lucy's intended audience would have included over one thousand male Mormons who had been initiated by that time into the Masonic fraternity. Surely, therefore, she knew the implications that her words would carry.

Freemasons had long made use of the "Leland Manuscript," a document containing questions and answers about Freemasonry. It is important for its accurate reflection of the traditions surrounding the Fraternity during that time period.[117] One of the most widely distributed publications of the Leland Manuscript was in William Hutchinson's *The Spirit of Masonry*, which is quoted as follows:

> Q. What dothe the Maconnes [Masons] concele and hyde?
>
> A. They concelethe the arte of ffyndyng neue artes, and thattys for here own proffyte and preise, they concelethe the arte of kypynge secrettes, thatt so the worlde mayeth nothinge concele from them. Thay concelethe the art of wunderwerckynge, and of foresaynge thynges to comme, that so thay same artes may not be usedde of the wyckedde to an euyell [evil] ende; they also concelethe the arte of chaunges, the way of wynnynge the facultye of Abrac, the skill of becommyng gude and parfyghte wythouten the holpynges of fere and hope; and the universelle longage [language] of Maconnes.[118]

It is noteworthy that Lucy used the precise wording of the Leland Manuscript, "winning the faculty of Abrac." Unfortunately, Mormon authors have generally dismissed the Masonic significance of Lucy's words. Concentrating on folk magic, these historians have focused on "Abrac" as a reference to healing or protective amulets. Many representations exist showing the word "ABRACADABRA" at the top of a descending triangle, with the word repeated on each line, minus one letter, as follows:

---

116. Anderson, *Lucy's Book*, 323.

117. This document was allegedly copied by John Leland from an earlier manuscript in the hand of King Henry VI of England. The first known publication was in 1753, in the *Gentlemen's Magazine*, but an even earlier printing has been claimed. While its authenticity has been largely discredited, it was contained in various widely read Masonic texts throughout the late eighteenth and early nineteenth centuries.

118. William Hutchinson, *The Spirit of Masonry: in Moral and Elucidatory Lectures*, 267–68. See also Henry Dana Ward, *Free Masonry: Its Pretensions Exposed in Faithful Extracts of Its Standard Authors*, 47, 104–5, an 1828 exposé ridiculing the Craft: "This is truly Free Masonry; the art of finding new arts, and the way of winning the faculty of Abrac."

ABRACADABRA
ABRACADABR
ABRACADAB
ABRACADA
ABRACAD
ABRACA
ABRAC
ABRA
ABR
AB
A

Just as each line of the charm was diminished by one letter, so the wearer's malady was expected to diminish. This usage was exoteric, and in some Masonic circles it functioned as a convenient way to deflect inquiries from the deeper import of the faculty of Abrac. Hutchinson wrote that he could hardly expect a non-Mason to be anything but "in the dark" as to the meaning of the faculty of Abrac—yet he provided a notably evasive answer:

> Abrac is an abbreviation of the word Abracadabra. In the days of ignorance and superstition, that word had a magical signification, and was written in a certain form peculiar to the craft. The explanation of it is now lost.[119]

Likewise, Christian Freemason George Oliver wrote of this talismanic use of Abrac as bringing "perpetual health and happiness, and protection from temporal dangers."[120]

Notably, no evidence has been found that any member of the Smith family carried a version of the "Abracadabra" parchment amulet.[121] Instead, they were

---

119. Hutchinson, *The Spirit of Masonry*, 280.

120. George Oliver, *The Antiquities of Freemasonry; Comprising Illustrations of the Five Grand Periods of Masonry from the Creation of the World to the Dedication of King Solomon's Temple*, 123.

121. However, W. W. Phelps used a similar device. He wrote, "John's definition of God is the nearest to perfection of any that we know of. It is like the 'pearl of great price, or the diamond of all worth.' By beginning at the letter G, in the middle of the table below, the reader may read till he is satisfied, up, down, and each side, and continually learn that God is love."

E
EVE
EVOVE
EVOLOVE
EVOLSLOVE
EVOLSISLOVE
EVOLSIDISLOVE
EVOLSIDODISLOVE
EVOLSIDOGODISLOVE
EVOLSIDODISLOVE

likely to have understood the faculty of Abrac in light of esoteric writings of Freemasons such as Albert Pike and George F. Fort. These writers interpreted these workings as the obtaining of a divine name—the "Lost Word" referred to repeatedly in Masonic ritual. Discussing the nature of this quest, Pike wrote:

> The True Word of a Mason is to be found in the concealed and profound meaning of the Ineffable Name of Deity, communicated by God to Moses; and which meaning was long lost by the very precautions taken to conceal it. The true pronunciation of that name was in truth a secret, in which, however, was involved the far more profound secret of its meaning. In that meaning is included all the truth that can be known by us, in regard to the nature of God.[122]

Fort, writing in the mid-nineteenth century, acknowledged the talismanic use of "Abracadabra" as an "irresistible charm to avert evil, cure fevers, and dispel diseases, particularly if written in the shape of a triad," even to the point of early duelists being required to swear that they were not carrying such a charm. He went further, however, to claim that Jews believed that arrangements of the word "Abrac" were "all-powerful and profound in mystical lore." Moses, he said, used the name "Jehovah," or a substitute, "Schemhamphorasch," to perform the miracles that astounded the wizards of Egypt. Likewise, he claimed that "Jews, in the time of Christ, boldly charged that the wonder workings of our Savior were accomplished by means of the sacred word or name."[123]

Having suggested the power of the Divine Name, Fort proceeded to explain the role of the faculty of Abrac therein:

> After the correct pronunciation of the word, Jehovah, had become lost, substitutes seem to have been employed for purposes of magic and amulets. . . . Abrak, or abraksax, signifies also, according to Bellerman, "the adorable, blessed name," and . . . corresponds exactly with . . . the unspeakable, omnific, and ineffable Tetragrammaton, the Jehovah of the Jews, both of which are engraven on abraxas stones. The word . . . has descended as an elemental portion of Freemasonry to the fifteenth century, and as representative of a lost name.
>
> The "way of winning the faculty of abrac," thus understood, signifies the means by which the lost word may be recovered, or, at least, substituted. . . . When

---

EVOLSIDISLOVE
EVOLSISLOVE
EVOLSLOVE
EVOLOVE
EVOVE
EVE
E

W. W. Phelps, "God is Love," 144.

122. Albert Pike, *Morals and Dogma of the Ancient and Accepted Scottish Rite of Freemasonry*, 697.

123. George F. Fort, *The Early History and Antiquities of Freemasonry, as Connected with Ancient Norse Guilds, and the Oriental and Medieval Building Fraternities*, 420–21.

the faculty of acquiring [Abrac] had been gained by an investiture with [Masonic] craft secrets, a specific magical power was attributed.[124]

In other words, from the fifteenth through the nineteenth century, Freemasons were understood to conceal, and reveal to initiates, the means by which the sacred name of deity—the "lost word"—may be discovered. This ability is suggested in a biblical passage quoted in the Royal Arch degree: "To him that overcometh will I give to eat of the hidden manna, and will give him a white stone, and in the stone a new name written, which no man knoweth saving he that receiveth it" (Rev. 2:17). Joseph Jr. would later expand upon this idea, teaching that after the earth was purified,

> Then the white stone mentioned in Rev. c 2 v 17 is the Urim & Thummim whereby all things pertaining to an higher order of kingdoms even all kingdoms will be made known and the a white stone is given to each of those who come into this the celestial kingdom, whereon is a new name written which no man knoweth save he that receiveth it. The new name is the key word.[125]

Thus, Joseph Jr. combined the ideas of a seer stone (Urim & Thummim) and the discovery of a sacred divine name. The Smith family's practice of "folk magic" was ultimately a means to one end—that of winning the faculty of Abrac, or in other words, obtaining the sacred lost name of God. Not only is this far from the supposition that the Smiths were employing magic healing charms, but it is also essential to understanding the treasure hunting activities of the family.

Researcher Clinton Bartholemew has noted three important Smith family heirlooms that date to this period: a knife, a Jupiter talisman, and a magical papyrus. The making of these esoteric items was outlined in the occult writings of Henry Cornelius Agrippa:

> According to D. Michael Quinn Agrippa's book *The Three Books of Occult Philosophy* (DOP) was available in Palmyra. Why in particular was the Smith family interested in Agrippa's work? As it turns out both Masons and Anti-Masons claimed that Agrippa had been one of the key founders of Masonry in Europe; and Masons contemporary with Joseph Smith spoke highly of Agrippa. Intriguingly, DOP also contains a cipher called the [aiq beker] cipher which resembles the Royal Arch cipher, but it uses the Hebrew language.[126]

Rational Mysticism—Smith Style

The early American Republic was a heady brew of Enlightenment philosophy, combined with measured doses of political, social, and religious experimentation. During the period when Joseph Smith Jr. came of age, the old

---

124. Fort, 425–26.

125. "Appendix 2: William Clayton, Journal Excerpt, 1–4 April 1843," The Joseph Smith Papers, 69–70.

126. Clinton Bartholomew, "Cipher in the Kirtland Snow: The Royal Arch Cipher and Joseph Smith's Conception of Ancient Languages."

folkways persisted in the cultural backwaters of Vermont and New York State. Simultaneously, the rising tide of rationalism dominated most of the educated population.[127] Adding to this mix were the many Protestant sects grown out of the Reformation. Though supernatural elements remained, and progressive ideas were often resisted, the churches of the Smiths' day deliberately attempted to purge magic from religion.

Freemasonry provided gentlemen with a means of engaging the "religious pluralism and the social disorder of the early nineteenth century,"[128] seeking to blend and harmonize Enlightenment ideals with religious belief into a kind of rational mysticism. David G. Hackett notes that "in its emphasis on the recovery and restoration of ancient truth, postwar Masonry resembled Protestant primitivism," and that Masonry's rituals "paralleled . . . forward-pointing tendencies in Evangelicalism."[129]

The Smith family was immersed in the full spectrum of social issues of the day. Asael Smith (Joseph Sr.'s father) and his eldest son Jesse laid down the gauntlet on the side of Enlightenment philosophical notions. They dismissed what they saw as the vagaries of revealed religion and the irrational emotionalism of the organized churches of the day. They held to reason as the ruling principle, where individuals obtain truth through the rational power of the human mind. Yet, other members of the extended family—including Joseph Sr.—sought to find a genial meeting place between extremes. The spiritual significance of Joseph Sr.'s treasure seeking and his belief in both the Bible and the need for salvation suggest a reliance upon intuitive wisdom rather than strict rationality. The appeal of Masonry as "a way of common men to God"[130] may have encouraged members of the Smith family who wrestled with the issue of the relevance of institutional religion in an increasingly rational age.

Throughout the post-Revolutionary period of Joseph Sr.'s lifetime and during the childhood of his children, Freemasonry's mythical history saturated the collective unconscious of the nation. It provided a sense of continuity with the past, appealing to the primitivist yearnings of many men who intuitively felt that something—perhaps spiritual, political, or personal innocence—had been lost. Masonic tradition and ritual made measured use of non-rational methods in order to help the individual transcend his conventional way of thinking about and experiencing the world. Masonry provided an allegorical background that spiritualized the physical act of treasure seeking. Prevalent in the communities in which the Smiths lived, "digging in the earth" represented an exteriorization of the desire to recover something buried deep within. Like many men in ages of

---

127. Ronald W. Walker, "Joseph Smith, the Palmyra Seer," 465.
128. Hackett, *That Religion*, 84.
129. Hackett, 84–5.
130. Carl H. Claudy, *Introduction to Freemasonry*, 3:iv.

uncertainty, Joseph Smith Sr. certainly felt the sting of "That Which Was Lost" and sought to restore it through the Masonic "working of the Faculty of Abrac."

The enchantment of the land where Joseph Smith Jr. was reared was no common magic. It was the enchantment of the imagination: the belief that humans lived in a world of endless spiritual possibility—the belief that they could speak directly with God and with angels. America was a new order for the ages; the hand of Providence had given Americans a special role in history. Theirs was a new land of treasures lying just beneath the earth, a land of ideas springing to life from human hearts, a land in which dreams and allegories gained objective reality.

CHAPTER 3

A GATHERING OF CROWS:
WILLIAM MORGAN, MASONRY,
AND DEATH

I conceive [of Freemasonry] to be founded on benevolence and to be exercised
for the good of mankind. If it has been a Cloak to promote improper or
nefarious objects it is a melacholly proof that in unworthy hands, the best
institutions may be made use of to promote the worst designs.
—Attributed to George Washington

The deposition of Mary W. Hall, wife of the keeper of the Canandaigua jail, was splashed over every Ontario County newspaper. Her husband was away when a group of Freemasons made an evening call to collect one of the prisoners, she testified. After negotiating the payment of his trifling debt, the men convinced her to discharge the inmate. Hall heard a signal whistle and watched as they hauled their quarry out the door, two of them having hold under his arms on either side. The prisoner struggled and cried out in the most distressing manner, but it was to no avail. One of the men struck a violent warning blow to the curb with a stick, a carriage drew up, and under a full, late autumn moon, William Morgan was unceremoniously tossed inside.[1]

The Smith family was located at the epicenter of the greatest excitement concerning Masonry in American history. As long as they were able to hear a conversation or read a newspaper, they would have known of the episode. The shocking events involving infamous Freemason William Morgan scandalized the nation and powerfully shaped the environment in which Mormonism first appeared.

Although he was destined to shake American society at its roots, Morgan was born in virtual obscurity on what many writers have accepted as August 7, 1774. His service as an army private in the War of 1812 led him to self-importantly title himself "Captain" Morgan. A few years following the end of the war, he married Lucinda Pendleton, the petite, blue-eyed daughter of a Methodist minister who was twenty-six years her husband's junior.[2] Following the death of a baby daughter, Morgan moved his family to Batavia, New York, where they obtained lodging above the jewelry shop of Freemason George Washington Harris.

While he may have cut a handsome figure when he courted the fair Lucinda, Morgan did not age well. He was short and balding with a set of supernumer-

---

1. Mary W. Hall affidavit in "Outrages at Batavia," 1.
2. Todd M. Compton, *In Sacred Loneliness: The Plural Wives of Joseph Smith*, 44.

ary teeth conspicuous enough as to be described as "double teeth all around."[3] Despite his somewhat odd appearance, Morgan was adroit enough to win a respected place among New York Masons for some time.

Morgan the Mason

Morgan's Masonic career is as uncertain as his birth. Though he was undoubtedly an operative Mason, historians have repeatedly noted that no proof exists to demonstrate that Morgan received the three degrees of Speculative, or Craft, Masonry. Masonic records of the period, however, are notoriously incomplete. The first documented evidence of Morgan's involvement with the Fraternity appears at Rochester, where, according to Judge Ebenezer Mix, Morgan claimed to have received his three degrees in a lodge in Canada.[4] If Morgan made any errors when being examined at the door of the lodge by New York Masons, it could easily be explained by the fact that Canadian ritual was somewhat different than the American.[5]

Under the tutelage of Blanchard Powers, a Masonic "Grand Lecturer" of the time, Morgan developed a reputation among nearby Masons for his ritual skills, and he participated actively in degree work for various lodges. He was considered a "bright Mason," meaning he had a great deal of skill and natural facility for ritual work.[6] Samuel D. Greene stated that when he became a member of Batavia Lodge No. 433 in December 1825, Morgan was not only an active lecturer in the Lodge but also his coach in learning the necessary catechism.[7]

Whether or not Morgan had been legitimately made a Mason, his skill persuaded local Royal Arch Masons that he was not only a Master Mason in good standing but that he had received the additional degrees of Mark Master, Past Master, and Most Excellent Master. As such, he was considered qualified as a candidate for Royal Arch Masonry and was subsequently exalted (the Masonic term for receiving the Royal Arch degree) on May 31, 1825, in Western Star Chapter No. 35 at nearby LeRoy, New York.[8]

---

3. Lewiston Committee, *A Narrative of the Facts and Circumstances Related to the Kidnapping and Murder of William Morgan*, 88.

4. Rob Morris, *William Morgan; Or, Political Anti-Masonry, Its Rise, Growth and Decadence*, 60–61.

5. John C. Palmer, *The Morgan Affair and Anti-Masonry*, 17; Henry Leonard Stillson and William James Hughan, *History of the Ancient and Honorable Fraternity of Free and Accepted Masons and Concordant Orders*, 508.

6. Robert Berry, *The Bright Mason: An American Mystery*, 13.

7. Samuel D. Greene, *The Broken Seal: or, Personal Reminisces of the Morgan Abduction and Murder*, 33.

8. David Seaver, *Freemasonry at Batavia*, 47.

Yet, Morgan's signature was quietly dropped from a petition by Royal Arch Masons requesting a charter for a new Royal Arch chapter in Batavia.[9] When the charter was granted, Morgan was surprised to find that he was not included as a member and harsh feelings ensued.[10] Stung by this rejection, Morgan began plotting to avenge himself by exposing the Masonic fraternity. Perhaps intentionally, he was overheard in public places sharing his plans, and word soon spread throughout the area. At first, many Masons were indifferent to Morgan's threats. He was not, after all, the first to publish an account of the three degrees of Ancient Craft Masonry.[11] As the winter snows began to melt in 1826, Morgan filed an application for copyright on a work to be entitled *Illustrations of Masonry*, intentionally mimicking and mocking two standard Masonic monitors of the same title. Preston's *Illustrations of Masonry*, popular in the United Kingdom, was an *aide de memoire* for the lectures of the first three degrees. In the United States, Thomas Smith Webb's was another popular book so named. A "monitor" such as Preston's and Webb's includes only the non-secret parts of a ritual. By contrast, Morgan's version was an exposé. Freemasons in the United States were shocked and disturbed to learn that he planned to make public for the first time in this country the ritual of the Holy Royal Arch—including the carefully guarded "Omnific Word" and its "Covering Word"—that he had promised never to reveal.

On March 13 of that year, Morgan contracted printer David C. Miller and others to produce the work. Some twenty years earlier, Miller had taken the first degree of Freemasonry (Entered Apprentice) and failed a ballot within his lodge to receive further degrees.[12]

---

9. In an effort to account for Morgan's name having been dropped, later writers attempted to blame it on rumors of Morgan's intemperance and unsatisfied debts. More likely, suspicions had been aroused regarding the legitimacy of his Masonic membership.

10. Palmer, *The Morgan Affair and Anti-Masonry*, 18.

11. As early as 1730, the degrees were published in *Masonry Dissected*, a popular exposé printed in England. Its alleged author, Samuel Prichard, followed up with *Jachin and Boaz*, a 1760 booklet that enjoyed success in both Europe and the United States. As recently as 1825, Richard Carlile's Masonic exposure was printed in *The Republican*, a London newspaper.

12. Palmer, *The Morgan Affair and Anti-Masonry*, 19; Greene, *The Broken Seal*, 45–46. Greene, a contemporary of Miller, explains that when the printer lived in Saratoga, he planned to publish the "Jachin and Boaz" exposure. Local Masons solicited him to join the Lodge thinking this would stop his work. He took the first degree in Albany, saw it was the same as the exposure, and became "disgusted" with the whole business. See also David Bernard, *Light on Masonry: A Collection of All the Most Important Documents on the Subject of Speculative Free Masonry*, 449, where Miller is listed as having held one degree. Other authors note that Miller petitioned for further degrees at a later date in the lodge at Stafford, New York, but "did not receive them due to lack of proper vouchers." See the *Masonic Intelligencer* (March 14, 1827), cited in Stephen Dafoe, *Morgan: The Scandal that Shook Freemasonry*, 41n35.

The activities of Morgan immediately after filing for his copyright are some-what unclear, though it can be assumed he was working on his manuscript.[13] A Batavia pro-Masonic newspaper holds a key to Morgan's whereabouts at the time:

> In the spring of 1826, he [Morgan] was absent, and the general impression among his acquaintance was, that he had absconded—at least he had gone to parts un-known.—During Morgan's absence, his wife had her second child, and claimed as-sistance from Masons for the necessaries of life, as she said Morgan was a Royal Arch Mason. . . . During this period, it since appears that Morgan was in Ontario county, writing his "Book."[14]

The seat of Ontario County was Canandaigua, the same town where Joseph Smith Sr. had become a member of Ontario Lodge No. 23. While one newspaper advertisement confirms Morgan spent at least part of May 1826 in Canandaigua, the busy commercial and social hub would have been a difficult place to remain hidden while writing a manuscript.

Interestingly, Ontario County also included the village of Manchester, loca-tion of the Smith family farm. John Whitney, one of the principal conspirators in the Morgan disappearance (and relative of prominent early Mormon, Newel K. Whitney), reported in later years that Morgan "had been a half way convert of Joe Smith, the Mormon, and had learned from him to see visions and dream dreams."[15] LDS scholars have generally dismissed this claim, but surrounding circumstances suggest that Morgan may indeed have had connections with the Smith family. If Morgan spent the spring of 1826 in Ontario County, he may have had a rare opportunity to become acquainted with Joseph Smith Jr. After being employed by Josiah Stowell to search for a rumored Spanish silver mine near South Bainbridge, Joseph Jr. had been brought up on charges of being a fraudulent "glass looker" in March of 1826. According to some sources, the twenty-year-old treasure seer had been allowed to escape conviction by leaving

---

13. In an interview published in the *Saints' Herald* of June 1, 1881, William Bryant, a former neighbor of Oliver Cowdery in western New York, recalled, "He (Cowdery), was strong against the Masons; he helped to write Morgan's book, they said." William H. Kelley, "The Hill Cumorah, and the Book of Mormon," 162. Other evidence shows that Cowdery was pro-Masonic in accord with other members of his family. He may have been living in his brother Warren's home in LeRoy from 1823–26. This makes the claim that he helped write Morgan's book possible. The argument is strengthened by Lucinda Morgan's sworn statement dated September 22, 1826: "That the papers [of her husband William Morgan]. . . were numerous, and formed a very large bundle; they were written in the handwriting of [her] husband, excepting a few, which were written by a person who sometimes assisted her husband by copying, or taking down as he dictated to him." See Greene, *The Broken Seal*, 89–90. Such a description corresponds with the task of dictation that Oliver Cowdery later carried out for Joseph Smith Jr.

14. *Masonic Intelligencer*, Batavia (March 14, 1827): 23.

15. Morris, *William Morgan*, 196.

the area for at least six months.[16] Assuming Joseph Jr. spent those six months back at home, he was present in Ontario County at the same time as Morgan.

Another possibility is that "Joe Smith, the Mormon" referred to Joseph Sr., who was a Masonic peer of John Whitney and closer in age to Morgan. Lucy Mack Smith's narrative demonstrates that Joseph Sr. was a "dreamer of dreams," while the Smith family's interest in "working the faculty of Abrac" may have held the interest of a spiritually minded "bright" Mason. Joseph Sr.'s later actions as a patriarch in Missouri would reveal his sympathies for the deceased anti-Masonic martyr (see the end of this chapter).

Whisperings and Warnings

Once he returned to Batavia, Morgan's efforts were met with prompt opposition. On August 9, 1826, the following unsigned notice appeared in Canandaigua and other nearby newspapers:

NOTICE AND CAUTION

If a man calling himself William Morgan should intrude himself on the community, they should be on their guard, particularly the MASONIC FRATERNITY. Morgan was in this village in May last, and his conduct while here and elsewhere, calls forth this notice. Any information in relation to Morgan can be obtained by calling at the MASONIC HALL in this village. *Brethren and Companions* are particularly requested to *observe, mark and govern* themselves accordingly.

—Morgan is considered a swindler and a dangerous man.

—There are people in this village who would be happy to see this Capt. Morgan.[17]

Samuel Greene, a nominal Mason at the time, was disturbed by the call upon "brethren and companions," in the language of the ritual, to "observe, mark, and govern themselves accordingly." Even to a man of his limited inside understanding, this seemed a "distinct summons to acts of violence, and to spread the intelligence far and wide."[18] A "whispering campaign" began to disseminate reports of Morgan and Miller's poor character. Word spread among local Masons that Morgan's publication must be stopped.[19] Using their positions as law enforcement officers, they arrested their quarry on charges of nonpayment of debts and searched his lodgings for the offending manuscript. Feelings among the brethren became so heated that an effort was organized to burn Miller's printing office. By his own heroic account, Greene could no longer remain silent. He wrote a note of warning that he delivered to George W. Harris: "Compressing this paper into a shapeless wad, as small that it might be crowded into a thimble, I called at Mr.

---

16. Dan Vogel, *Early Mormon Documents*, 4:96, 108.

17. Greene, *The Broken Seal*, 39–40.

18. Greene, 40.

19. Bernard, *Light on Masonry*, 370–71.

Harris's door, and said to him, 'I have important intelligence to communicate . . .' I threw the roll upon his counter, and left him suddenly."[20]

Little is known of silversmith and future Mormon George Harris's part in blocking the arson attempt. But in his shop below the Morgans' apartment, he was well situated to provide warning. Thomas Knight, pro-Masonic writer, avowed that Harris was "keeping track of Morgan's most intimate movements." It is a matter of record that soon after the aborted scheme, at a regular communication of Batavia Lodge on August 15, 1826, Harris was "expelled by a unanimous vote of said lodge, for the enormous depravity of his Masonic conduct." The *Republican Farmers' Free Press* elaborated, stating the "enormity" for which Harris was expelled "consisted in apprizing his friend, Captain Morgan, that the Batavia Lodge was making arrangements to destroy him."[21]

Harris's efforts to protect William Morgan proved to be in vain. On the auspicious date of September 11, 1826, an event occurred that caused repercussions to shake the country and topple the grand edifice of Freemasonry nearly to ground level. Upon the accusation of Freemason Ebenezer Kingsley that Morgan had neglected to return a borrowed shirt and cravat, two men seized the bewildered reprobate in Batavia and brought him to the county jail in Canandaigua. The fifty-mile trip was made necessary due to a series of highly questionable, coordinated actions on the part of a mob of Masons living in several surrounding communities.[22]

Upon his appearance before the justice of the peace in Canandaigua, Morgan was released on the larceny charge. Immediately, however, he was rearrested on an uncollected debt of $2.68. Unable to satisfy the debt on the spot, Morgan was held in the Canandaigua Jail. From here, he was whisked away in the jailer's absence.[23] Following his removal, little is certain as to Morgan's fate. Most witnesses agree that he was taken to a series of towns along the route from Canandaigua to the United States fort at Niagara, with a change of horses and escorts at each location.

---

20. Greene, *The Broken Seal*, 65.

21. "We Want Our Mystic Brethren," 2.

22. Dafoe, *Morgan*, 97–103; Constable Halloway Hayward and his cohort Nicholas Chesebro had procured a warrant for Morgan's arrest from the justice of the peace in Canandaigua. In order to get the warrant, they persuaded the officer that Morgan was within six miles of the village and could be easily captured. On the way back to Batavia, the two stopped in LeRoy to have Squire Foster endorse the warrant and make it enforceable in Genesee County. By the time they reached their next stop, Stafford, they'd acquired a posse of Masons. At James Ganson's supper table, they were joined by additional men, making up, according to different accounts, "two carriages full" of Freemasons, or "between forty and fifty men." A member of Batavia Lodge was sent ahead to tell his Worshipful Master they were on their way. After Morgan was apprehended, Hayward took him back to Canandaigua to appear before the justice of the peace. Greene observes that "one of the noticeable things about all these proceedings of the Masons at this time, was their care to keep within the semblance and forms of law, while they were breaking through all law and that, too, on the largest scale." Greene, *The Broken Seal*, 78–79.

23. Deposition of Mrs. Hall, in Greene, 95–96.

The Abduction of William Morgan. From Edmund Ollier, *Cassells History of the United States*, 1874.

The first change took place at the tiny village of Victor, New York, home to Milnor Lodge No. 303. Located less than twelve miles from Canandaigua, Milnor Lodge was deeply affected by the Morgan kidnapping. Depositions in the case described the abductors' tempestuous passage through western New York, including details such as the exchange of horses with other Masons in villages along the way beginning at Victor.[24] At least four members of Milnor Lodge were later identified as principals in the kidnapping: James Gillis, Loton Lawson, John Sheldon, and John Whitney.[25] Another young and recent member of the Lodge, however, would later figure prominently in Mormon history. A newly established local potter, Heber C. Kimball had been a Master Mason in Milnor Lodge for less than a year. As a relatively new member of the lodge, he may well have been involved in providing the change of horses at Victor. Whatever information Kimball knew of the circumstances he never revealed. He would later testify to his strict faithfulness to Masonic obligations, including keeping a brother Master Mason's vouchsafed secrets: "I have been as true as an angel from the heavens to the covenants I made in the lodge at Victor."[26] After enduring several additional changes of horses and drivers, Morgan was handed over to Niagara County

---

24. *A Narrative of the Facts and Circumstances Relating to the Kidnapping and Presumed Murder of William Morgan*, 21, 47–50.

25. John H. Stelter, "History of Freemasonry in Ontario County, New York," 385.

26. Orson Whitney, *Life of Heber C. Kimball, An Apostle: The Father and Founder of the British Mission*, 27.

Sheriff Eli Bruce, who held him prisoner in the powder room at Fort Niagara for a short time. It is the last place Morgan was seen alive.

David C. Miller, Morgan's printer, claimed to have been falsely arrested on a civil warrant, released by the justice of the peace, then harassed by his captors, all in an effort to keep him from his printing office while it was being vandalized.[27] This commotion, however, did nothing to prevent the publication of an exposé he attributed to Morgan. On December 15, 1826, Miller published the following notice:

Just published

And for Sale at The Advocate Office.

The First Part of Masonry Unveiled,

containing a full Exposition of the Secrets and Ceremonies of that 'Ancient and Honorable' Order.

FREE MASONRY

And God Said, *"Let there be Light and there was light."*

The remaining part is now in press, and will shortly be published.[28]

Due to repeated invasions of Morgan's and Miller's offices, it is difficult to say how much of Miller's publication was actually prepared by William Morgan. Distinct similarities were drawn to the earlier *Jachin and Boaz*, suggesting that Miller may have cribbed the manuscript and attributed it to his lost partner.[29] More importantly, this "first part" included only the three Craft Lodge degrees with nothing from Royal Arch Masonry. No "second part" was ever published.

A Growing Mystery

Because William Morgan was never seen again after September 1826, a great mystery grew up around the event. Several speculations as to his fate appeared in the press of the day. One writer suggested that as part of the acknowledged negotiations between Morgan and local Masons, he was handed off to Canadian Masons with a sum of cash under promise to start a new, anonymous life. Some Masonic sympathizers claimed sightings of Morgan as a simple farmer in Upper Canada, "the first honest work he ever voluntarily engaged in."[30] Various other fanciful stories circulated, such as Morgan being hanged as a pirate in 1838, fleeing to Turkey, or living on the "Island of Deseret" in St. Lawrence Bay.[31]

---

27. Bernard, *Light on Masonry*, 376.

28. Palmer, *The Morgan Affair and Anti-Masonry*, 29; emphasis in original.

29. Palmer, 29.

30. Nancy McCain, "Recollections of Nancy McCain."

31. Harold Van Buren Voorhis, "What Really Happened to William Morgan? A Plausible 'Story,'" 261. "Deseret," an interesting correspondence with a Book of Mormon word, was probably a misspelling of "Desert Island" (off the coast of Maine) by Ezra Sturges Anderson, who published a statement in July 1829 that he had there met with

Others, however, were not so optimistic about Morgan's fate. Accusations of murder flew through the countryside assuming Morgan to have been drowned in the Niagara River. He had been kidnapped by Royal Arch Freemasons and never seen again. It was as though a gathering of crows had settled upon him and carried him away without a trace.

In October 1827—nearly thirteen months after Morgan's disappearance—an unidentified body was recovered from Oak Orchard Creek, a tributary of Lake Ontario. One week after the local coroner, Robert Brown, buried the body, he was approached by Thurlow Weed, an anti-Masonic newspaperman from Rochester, and others who suspected the body might be the remains of William Morgan. Weed orchestrated a public exhumation attended by nearly two hundred onlookers. Two medical professionals expressed doubts that the corpse was in the advanced state of decay expected from one who had been dead so long. But many of Morgan's acquaintances stepped up to positively identify the body down to the double row of teeth. Included in this group were the widow of the deceased and his neighbor, George W. Harris. No sooner was the body released to the family and reburied in Batavia that another claim was made concerning the identity of the corpse. The wife of Timothy Munro of Canada, who had drowned in the Niagara River a month before, was brought forward by a group of Masons to present an alternative claim. Thurlow Weed found it disturbing that she was able to describe minute details of the clothing worn by the victim, but that the features of the body she described differed substantially from the coroner's report.[32] Once again, the body was raised from the grave before a crowd of onlookers. This time, Weed's politically motivated anti-Masonic attempt to demonstrate that a murder had indeed taken place was foiled. A jury at the scene was unable to unequivocally decide that the remains were those of Morgan. With no body, Freemasons were exonerated from the charge of murder, kidnapping now being the most serious crime that could be charged.

The coincidental correspondence to the three burials of Hiram Abiff (see Chapters 1 and 17) could not have escaped the Masons when the corpse was buried a third and final time.

Convention of Seceding Masons

The disappearance of Morgan became a national obsession, focused on the vicinities of Le Roy and Batavia, fifty miles from Palmyra. New York Governor DeWitt Clinton, a prominent Masonic leader in the country, issued two proc-

William Morgan several months earlier. See A. P. Bentley, *History of the Abduction of William Morgan, and the Anti-Masonic Excitement of 1826–30*, 22.

32. "The question . . . seemed to involve the contradiction, if not the absurdity, of proving that Munroe's clothes were found upon the body either of Morgan or of some unknown person." See Thurlow Weed, *Life of Thurlow Weed Including His Autobiography and a Memoir*, 1:318.

lamations seeking information on Morgan's true whereabouts. Throughout the region, citizens banded into anti-Masonic groups, having both spiritual and political motives.

One such citizen group styled itself the "Convention of Seceding Masons." At a meeting on July 4, 1828, the group drafted a widely circulated "Declaration of Independence from the Masonic Institution."[33] While reasons listed for separation from the Fraternity echoed claims made in a variety of anti-Masonic publications, the declaration illustrates how close to home (figuratively and literally) the anti-Masonic movement was for the Smith family. Signers included prominent authors of anti-Masonic books, including David Bernard, David C. Miller, Solomon Southwick, and John G. Stearns. Others were more directly connected with the Smiths. One signer of the declaration, Timothy C. Strong, had been a member of Mount Moriah Lodge No. 112 at Palmyra. He was a newspaper publisher in Middlebury, Vermont, before moving to Palmyra, New York, in September 1817. In 1823, he sold his Palmyra newspaper to fellow Masons Egbert B. Grandin (soon to become printer of the Book of Mormon) and Pomeroy Tucker.[34] Furthermore, six of the signers had recently been expelled from Federal Lodge No. 15, the lodge to which Smith family members had belonged.[35] Traveling approximately three hundred and fifty miles, the party would have passed close by the Palmyra area on their way to the convention.

The timing of the Convention of Seceding Masons at Batavia coincided with notable events in Mormon history. From April to June, Joseph Smith Jr. worked on his translation of the Book of Mormon with Martin Harris as his scribe. Harris, a mature, bearded veteran of the War of 1812, was politically active on an anti-Mason vigilance committee near Palmyra, and his farm was situated close to the course of the Erie Canal. In the summer of 1828, Harris had just returned from his visits to Utica, Albany, and New York City in an attempt to obtain endorsements of translations of the Book of Mormon characters from noted scholars. The endeavor was beginning to be publicized far and wide and would surely have been known and discussed by at least the journalists in the group. In mid-June, Smith allowed Harris to take the translated pages to his farm to show his skeptical family. Harris would have had the manuscript in his possession during the last two weeks of June, just at the time that any seceding Masons would have been passing through the area on their way to the conference held July 4 and 5. Whether any of those who were disaffiliating with Freemasonry were able to view the pages of what Harris would term "the anti-Masonic Bible,"[36] or if they had anything to do with the manuscript's coincident disappearance, is unknown but physically possible.

33. Bernard, *Light on Masonry*, 445–51.

34. The Woman's Society of the Western Presbyterian Church, comp., *Palmyra, Wayne County, New York*, 28.

35. *Records of the Grand Lodge of Free and Accepted Masons of the State of Vermont from 1794 to 1846 Inclusive*, 78, 95.

36. William Perkins, "Antimasonic Religion," 1.

The declaration's third signer was William Wines Phelps, former editor of Tompkins County's anti-Masonic newspaper *Lake Light*. The first issue had been published on October 10, 1827, and Phelps announced his formal renunciation of Masonry three months later on January 14:

> Considering secret societies incompatible with the principles and derogatory to the constitution of a free government; living in a land of liberty;—being engaged in conducting a paper devoted to "equality to all,"—and having been regularly initiated, passed and raised to the degree of Master Mason, I hereby withdraw myself from any connexion with masonic lodges, and renounce the self-organized institution of free masonry. . . . W. W. PHELPS.[37]

Shortly thereafter, Phelps moved to Canandaigua, where he published a similarly critical newspaper, *The Ontario Phoenix*, and involved himself heavily with the Anti-Masonic Convention in LeRoy. Phelps converted to Mormonism within the next three years.

The Question of Freemasonry

At the Morgan trial in January of 1827, Judge Throop sentenced several men accused in the kidnapping of William Morgan.[38] Of the handful of people who were tried and convicted, Eli Bruce received the harshest sentence. Bruce was the sheriff of Niagara County, New York, and Worshipful Master of the lodge in Lockport, located on the shores of Lake Ontario. This county official apparently used his office to arrange the location for Morgan's imprisonment in the battery of Fort Niagara. Bruce spent a scant twenty-eight months in jail for his part in the affair. During that time, he shared a cell with Joseph Smith Sr., who was in prison for debts.[39] Lucy Smith's comments that her husband shared a cell with "a man committed for murder" may provide insight into the Smith family's opinions on Freemasonry at the time.[40] Eli Bruce, of course, had not been imprisoned for the

---

37. W. W. Phelps, "Renunciation."

38. "No. 11, Address of Judge Throop," in Arturo de Hoyos, *Light on Masonry: The History and Rituals of America's Most Important Masonic Exposé*, 764.

39. *"November 5th* [1830]—Not so much pain in my head as yesterday. Had a long talk with the father of *the Smith*, (Joseph Smith,) who, according to the old man's account, is the particular favorite of Heaven! To him Heaven has vouchsafed to reveal its mysteries; he is the herald of the latter-day glory. The old man avers that he is commissioned by God to baptize and preach this new doctrine. He says that our Bible is much abridged and deficient; that soon the Divine will is to be made known to all, as written in the *new Bible*, or *Book of Mormon*." See Rob Morris, *The Masonic Martyr: The Biography of Eli Bruce, Sheriff of Niagara County, New York, Who, For His Attachment to the Principles of Masonry, and his Fidelity to His Trust, was Imprisoned Twenty-Eight Months in the Canandaigua Jail*, 266–67; emphasis in original.

40. Lavina Anderson, ed., *Lucy's Book: A Critical Edition of Lucy Mack Smith's Family Memoir*, 495.

crime of murder, since the body of William Morgan had never been found. Lucy's words, however, reflect her opinion on whether the Masons had killed Morgan.

As the Smiths were close to the participants and events of the Morgan affair, it is natural that they would wrestle with the "question of Freemasonry." How could an institution like Freemasonry—believed by many to be of divine origin and claiming stewardship of sacred Christian mysteries—be engaged in such behavior as kidnapping, murder, and conspiracy? The information that Hyrum Smith was a dues-paying member of Mount Moriah Lodge in 1826 demonstrates that they may have believed something remained in Freemasonry worth preserving. His brother Joseph's own answer to that question unfolded over time, culminating in the theological developments in Nauvoo, Illinois, over a decade later.

The appearance of a broad Masonic conspiracy among different locations and lodges, the seeming obstruction of justice by well-placed Masons in the court system, and the refusal of Masonic witnesses to testify set off a great anti-Masonic furor in the United States. Citizens became aroused by the apparent effort of leaders of the Masonic order to shield, if not exonerate, the abductors of Morgan.

Presses were mobilized both for and against the Masons. The country became flooded with almanacs containing ritual scenes, books with ritual exposés, and travelling troupes publicly performing burlesques of the degrees. Bernard's *Light on Masonry*, published in 1829 in Albany, New York, included over forty rituals, representing the single largest exposure of Masonic degrees to that date. Between 1827 and 1830, Masonic bibliographer Kent L. Walgren cites the publication of nineteen anti-Masonic Almanacs, six proceedings of New York anti-Masonic conventions, and no less than 365 American publications on the subject of William Morgan.[41] One author noted that between December 1826 and September 1827, twenty anti-Masonic conventions were held in New York State, half of which were within a short distance of the Smith farm at Manchester.[42] And in December 1827, two to three thousand protestors confronted about two hundred Masons participating in their annual St. John's Day festival in Batavia.[43] So strong was this new opposition to Masonry that the nation's first plausible third political party, the Anti-Masonic Party, formed over the loudly proclaimed threat of American Freemasonry and elected large numbers of its candidates to office. It was within this charged atmosphere that Joseph Smith Jr. matured from diviner to prophet.

It would be difficult to overstate the excitement and outcry transpiring during this time. Anti-Masonry was ubiquitous in Joseph Smith's New York, making information regarding the Craft both directly and indirectly available to the enquiring mind. Public opinion came down largely against the fraternity, and scores of Freemasons renounced their membership. This led to hundreds of

---

41. For more information on this topic, see Kent L. Walgren, *Freemasonry, Anti-Masonry and Illuminism in the United States, 1734-1850: A Bibliography*.

42. John E. Thompson, *The Masons, the Mormons and the Morgan Incident*, 9–10.

43. Steven C. Bullock, *Revolutionary Brotherhood: Freemasonry and the Transformation of the American Social Order*, 289.

lodges throughout the country being forced to close, decimating Masonry in the United States for decades.

For many, Masonry as a social institution was dead.[44] Freemasons were chagrined over the resulting losses in both membership and in public trust. They bemoaned what they perceived as the hypocrisy of the anti-Masons, pointing out that it was anti-Masonry itself that had almost overnight become a political juggernaut, grinding to dust a harmless society dedicated to Christian principles. For anti-Masons, the conspirators who killed Morgan brought upon themselves the just condemnation of all good men of conscience. Anti-Masonic jeremiads trumpeted the evils of the Fraternity and warned against the imminent destruction it would surely bring upon the nation:

> The disclosures made by Capt. Morgan, and the atrocious act of violence in consequence thereof which deprived him of liberty and life, instigated by high dignitaries of the order far and near, executed by an extensive band of Masonic conspirators, and since, very frequently *justified* by Masons . . . confirmed the truth of those disclosures, and evinced the deep depravity of speculative Masonry; –these circumstances opened my eyes. . . . My own reflections, and the facts and arguments which have since come in my way, have convinced me of the utter depravity, the absurdity, and dangerous and pernicious tendency of the institution. . . . It truly pains me to know, that Free Masonry is not the noble and beautiful system I vainly fancied it to be.[45]

With near-evangelical zeal, anti-Masonic societies published books, papers, tracts, and almanacs, all devoted to the proposition that Freemasonry was fundamentally demoralizing and harmful to American liberties. In the worst telling, the institution of Freemasonry was little more than a murderous gang, seeking political and social power through covert means and combining to shield "wicked and designing men" harboring murderous designs. [46] Anti-Masons opined Masonry deserved to be utterly destroyed as a just and necessary defense of the common good.[47]

---

44. For instance, in his 1869 work, evangelical minister and renounced Mason Charles Finney stated: "Forty years ago [i.e., 1829], we supposed that [Freemasonry] was dead, and had no idea that it could ever revive." See Charles G. Finney, *The Character, Claims, and Practical Workings of Freemasonry*, v.

45. A Citizen of Massachusetts, *Free Masonry: A Poem. In Three Cantos*, v–vi; emphasis in original.

46. In fact, the lengthy full title of A Citizen of Massachusetts, *Free Masonry: A Poem. In Three Cantos*, includes these words as a description: "[T]he Masonic Institution . . . is a dangerous and deadly foe to equal liberty, and a formidable engine in the hands of wicked and designing men; and, also, tends to corrupt christianity, and the public morals."

47. "All pretensions that this institution is of itself a *science*, or that it is the depository of valuable information, are a mere gratuitous assumption. Indeed if speculative Free Masonry were to perish to-day, and all knowledge of its forms, rites, ceremonies, proceedings, and secrets, were at once obliterated from the memory of mankind, I know of no useful or desirable fact, or doctrine, or theory that would be lost to the world." A Citizen of Massachusetts, 41.

Both in and out of the Fraternity were those who were pained that Freemasonry, once held in "the highest regard," failed to live up to its reputation as a "noble and beautiful system" based as it was "on the immutable principles of the purest morality; as having existed from time immemorial, and been patronized by the wise and good in all enlightened and civilized nations."[48] It was an astounding turn that an organization believed by many to have existed since the creation of the world, and to be of divine origin, could be brought low in the matter of a few short years.[49] How could this be true of an institution that professed that its principles shared "the same co-eternal and unshaken foundation," contained and inculcated "in substance, the same truths," and proposed "the same ultimate end, as the doctrines of Christianity"?[50] Freemasons claimed that Cain and his offspring did not share in the secrets of Masonry, yet Masons apparently shared in the sins of Cain.[51] Not only did they combine to destroy William Morgan, they also conspired to cover it up.

To one who sought a reason for such betrayal of principle, it may have seemed that Freemasonry had its origins with Cain, after all. Or perhaps Masonry had begun pure, but had since fallen into sin and error. Perhaps like their Tyrian predecessors, Masons had allowed their Craft to degenerate into a spurious imitation of the pure, authentic tradition.

The False and the True

William Morgan may have disappeared, but Lucinda had not. While the late turncoat was eulogized, his young widow was the darling of the presses and an object of national pity and charity for both Masons and anti-Masons. On several occasions, the Fraternity offered Mrs. Morgan money, accommodations, and assistance. However, Lucinda would not accept their aid, as she looked upon them as "the guilty authors of all her troubles."[52] On February 1, 1830, Lucinda wrote to an anti-Masonic charity group acknowledging receipt of their gift of fifty dollars, which had been presented to her by George W. Harris. She wrote of the comfort their thoughtful gesture had afforded her "though [she was] destitute of property and bereaved of him to whom [she] was accustomed to look for support for [herself] and [her] infant children, by a merciless and cruel institution."

---

48. A Citizen of Massachusetts, iv–v.

49. "Certain it is . . . that free-masonry has been from the creation (though not under that name); that it was a divine gift from God." Laurence Dermott, *Ahiman Rezon, Or a Help to All that are (or Would Be) Free and Accepted Masons*, xiii.

50. Salem Town, *A System of Speculative Masonry in its Origin, Patronage, Dissemination, Principles, Duties, and Ultimate Desings, Laid Open for the Examonaiton of the Serious and Candid*, 2.

51. "Cain and the builders of his city were strangers to the secret mystery of masonry." Dermott, *Ahiman Rezon*, xiii.

52. Greene, *The Broken Seal*, 92.

Readers of Lucinda's thank-you letter may discover she had a similar perspective on the institution of Freemasonry as some of the other seceding Masons. "My bereavement," she wrote, "will contribute to the happiness of the present, as well as future generations, in the total eradication of *false Free Masonry.*"[53] Her words seem indicative of a belief in spurious Masonry, which had become corrupted and needed to be eradicated, while leaving open the possibility of a true and restored form of the Craft.

In the shakeup of Freemasonry following the Morgan affair, some Masons held fast to their views while others renounced the institution, many suspending their membership. This last group of men agreed with criticisms that Masonry had become tainted, and they desired to find a mechanism to bring about the restoration of the ancient and pure form. Such a restoration, they knew, would require a prophet equal to Solomon, Hiram of Tyre, and Hiram Abiff.

George Washington Harris was one who would find such a prophet. He joined the ranks of signers of the "Declaration of Independence from the Masonic Institution" at the Convention of Seceding Masons at Batavia. Sixteen months later, on November 23, 1830, he married William Morgan's widow.[54] This union agitated Masons and anti-Masons alike. Fifty-four-year-old George and his still-young wife and her children moved to Indiana in an attempt to remove themselves from the center of the Morgan controversy.

In the fall of 1834, Orson Pratt came to Terre Haute, Indiana, as a missionary. Pratt "preached a few times, and baptized George W. Harris and his wife."[55] In late 1837, the Harris family abandoned their home and silkworm farm in Indiana and gathered to "Zion" in the state of Missouri with a group of Latter-day Saints. Here, Harris owned one of the more substantial houses in Far West and became a church leader serving on the high council. He would also meet the Joseph Smith Jr. family as they fled to Missouri amid growing dissent and legal problems in Ohio. Harris hospitably offered a portion of the building to Smith for his living quarters and office, and he provided for the Smiths during the first two months of their sojourn in Missouri.[56] Some historians believe that it was here that Smith introduced the principle of plural marriage to the Harrises and married Lucinda in a polyandrous union.[57]

During this period, on September 2, 1838, Joseph Smith Sr., patriarch of the Church, took the opportunity to give a patriarchal blessing to both George and Lucinda. Such a blessing contained a declaration of sacred lineage coupled

---

53. Lucinda Morgan, "Letter from the Bereaved Widow," 1; emphasis in original.

54. Harris's first wife, Margaret, died in 1828.

55. Milando Pratt, "The Life and Labors of Orson Pratt," 84.

56. "We were immediately received under the hospitable roof of George W. Harris who treated us with all possible kindness, and we refreshed ourselves with much satisfaction after our long and tedious journey." See "History, 1838–1856, volume B-1 [1 September 1834–2 November 1838]," The Joseph Smith Papers, 784.

57. For example, see Brian C. Hales, *Joseph Smith's Polygamy*, 2:328.

with individualized prophecy. The ritual prayers were transcribed by Ebenezer Robinson, scribe and recorder. Lucinda's blessing identified her as "Daughter of Joseph Pendleton, and wife of George Washington Harris, and formerly wife of William Morgan."

Joseph Sr. promised Lucinda that she had been cleansed of sin: "Thy name is written in heaven the Lamb's Book of life, thy sins are forgiven thee, and there is no stain upon thee." Additionally, he added words of comfort concerning her deceased husband:

> I feel to say thy husband is in the Paradise of God, thou shalt strike hands with him in the Celestial Kingdom, and sing a song of Zion. Thy children shall be blessed with thee, and I seal the seal of God upon thee, and I bless thee with the blessings of God; and I seal thee up unto Eternal life in the name of Jesus Christ, even so, Amen.[58]

While many Masons saw William Morgan as a deceitful traitor, Joseph Sr. saw him as destined to inherit the highest glory within Mormon theology. In 1841, when the practice of baptism for the dead was revealed, Morgan was one of the first to receive the vicarious ordinance.

---

58. Lucinda Morgan Harris Patriarchal Blessing.

CHAPTER 4

FROM DARKNESS TO LIGHT:
THE PROPHET'S MASONIC INITIATION

Brother, to you the secrets of Masonry are about to be unveiled, and a brighter sun never shone lustre on your eyes.
—Master's observations to the newly obligated Entered Apprentice,
in William Morgan, *Illustrations of Masonry*

People in all societies through all ages have engaged in the making and performing of ritual. It helps to ground them in the world, find meaning in their personal and collective experiences, and discover the significance of their lives. Rituals fulfill human desire for order, creativity, and what theologian Tom F. Driver calls *communitas*. "Their business in society," he writes, "is to effect transformations that cannot otherwise be brought about." Driver explains that the performance of a ritual "articulates something" difficult to put into words and brings myths and symbols into being.[1] Ritual contains an innate power that, when enacted, triggers internal change. When these rituals are shared, the resulting transformation builds a sense of community spirit.

In both Freemasonry and in Christianity, this potent change is known as "illumination" or "enlightenment." Both traditions are premised upon the notion that men are asleep to the innate truth of the nature of the world. Without the regeneration of consciousness brought about by true initiation, they cannot perceive the relationship between themselves and the outer manifest world. Enlightenment, initiated by ritual, provides that fundamental shift in perception that transforms faulty understandings. Ritual helps bridge the gap between the ordinary world of human experience and the innate holiness concealed in everyday objects.

The Masonic Rite of Illumination

As its ceremonies are largely based upon mystical Christian tradition, it is perhaps unsurprising that Freemasonry is largely an exercise in spiritual transformation, initiated by the Rite of Illumination. This rite, in which the candidate is symbolically "brought to light," is a fundamental aspect of the Ancient Craft Degrees. Without it, the candidate is unable to successfully recover what Masonry describes as "That Which Was Lost."

The Masonic candidate is sent on a symbolic search for light (i.e., truth) in the darkness of a fallen world. To convey this emblematically, he is blindfolded

---

1. Tom F. Driver, *Liberating Rites: Understanding the Transformative Power of Ritual*, 91–92.

and bound with a cable-tow, symbolizing the darkness and impotence of ignorance. The seeker is then brought to the door of the lodge, where he knocks and
asks for light. Once admitted, the candidate's first ritual act is to "kneel for the
benefit of prayer" as a token of his trust in God's power to lead him through the
darkness of an unregenerate world. Alluding to this mortal sojourn, the candidate is led in a circumambulation of the lodge. At the apex of his journey, he
finds himself at the altar of Masonry, where he is placed under covenant and
"brought to light."[2] He then receives the symbolic "secrets" of the degree: the
light or knowledge that he came to the door seeking.

The purpose of this ritual in the first degree (Entered Apprentice) is to provide
a "shock" that wakes an initiate to his true condition and the condition of the
world. The fundamental premise is that the mind is dark, confused, and even chaotic. Illuminating light dispels that darkness, allowing a person to act in a rational
and spiritually informed manner. Ritual forms are useful in exteriorizing internal
landscapes and objects, allowing participants to see and work with them. Masons
recognize the difference between *ordinal* initiation (found in ordinance and ritual)
and *real* initiation (grounded in experience).[3] Ordinal initiation plants a seed in
the subconscious mind, which, nourished by water and warmed by the sun of life's
experiences, is intended to blossom and grow into a tangible and real event.

An example of this is found in the conversion experience of Charles Grandison
Finney, a Master Mason who became a well-known nineteenth-century evangelist.
Writer Mark Carnes has shown how Finney used the ordinal ritual of Masonry to
describe his religious conversion experience:

> Much as the initiate circumambulated the temple, Finney set himself in motion to
> find places to pray, traveling first to a "kind of closet" in the woods and going later
> into a back room in his house. Masons, after journeying around the lodge, searched
> for their departed master, Hiram Abiff; Finney received as revelation a passage of
> Scripture concerning a similar quest: "Then shall ye seek me and find me, when ye
> shall search for me with all your heart."[4]

Carnes continues by comparing the metaphysical journey of a Mason to-
ward "more light" with Finney's preoccupation with light and secrecy. He saw
Jesus Christ in a darkened back room that nonetheless appeared "perfectly light."
When he confided his vision to a church elder, the man laughed at him, and a

---

2. That is, "in the middle of life's journey," where the straightway has been lost to a *selva
oscura*—a dark and savage wood. See Dante, *Inferno*, 1.2. A similar theme is found in LDS
temple ritual, where the initiate is found in the "Lone and Dreary World."

3. W. Kirk MacNulty, *The Way of the Craftsman: A Search for the Spiritual Essence of
Craft Freemasonry*, 55. The transformations "do not usually occur at the time the degrees
are conferred." Rather, "the individual Mason who chooses to do so [later] works through
the degrees again, this time actually in the process of living." "This latter process," notes
MacNulty, "may require an entire lifetime."

4. Mark C. Carnes, *Secret Ritual and Manhood in Victorian America*, 71.

darkness came over Finney. This was dispelled the following morning when he awakened to the sun "pouring a clear light" into the room.

Later in his life, Finney came to believe that fraternal ritual provided a kind of "counterfeit salvation." Nonetheless, Finney's experience was a materialization of what he learned in the Rite of Illumination, and the rite provided a framework to grasp the significance of his vision.[5]

Accounts of the First Vision

The foundational myth of the Latter-day Saint movement is Joseph Smith Jr.'s "First Vision" account of seeing God the Father and Jesus Christ, with the earliest surviving record of his vision being a handwritten account of his early life written in 1832.[6] Other extant first-person accounts of Smith's vision were histories he dictated to his scribes in 1835[7] and 1838,[8] a historical sketch solicited by journalist John Wentworth in 1842,[9] and an interview with David Nye White (editor of the *Pittsburgh Weekly Gazette*) in 1843.[10] Four additional accounts were written previous to Smith's death by contemporaries who heard him speak about the vision. These include Orson Pratt's 1840 account, published as a pamphlet in Scotland;[11] Orson Hyde's 1842 account, translated into German for publication in Frankfurt;[12] Levi Richards's diary account of an 1843 public church meeting;[13] and Alexander Neibaur's 1844 journal account of a visit to the Smith home, where Joseph related the circumstances of his experience.[14]

These various accounts were written twelve to twenty-four years after the vision was said to have occurred. By the time of the earliest 1832 telling, it appears the story had developed a fixed structure. In each of the accounts, the elements are arranged in precisely the same order, an order mirroring the Masonic Rite of Illumination. As in Charles Finney's case, Smith chose to clothe his experience in Masonic garb, implying his exposure to the ritual from an early date.

In the several accounts of the First Vision, Smith described his confusion "in matters that involve eternal consequences."[15] As described in early nineteenth-century sources, the Rite of Initiation of an Entered Apprentice into a Masonic lodge is

5. Carnes, 71.

6. "History, circa Summer 1832," The Joseph Smith Papers, 1–6.

7. "Journal, 1835–1836," The Joseph Smith Papers, 23–26.

8. "History, circa June 1839–circa 1841 [Draft 2]," The Joseph Smith Papers, [1–5].

9. "'Church History,' 1 March 1842," The Joseph Smith Papers, 706–7.

10. "Interview, 29 August 1843, Extract," The Joseph Smith Papers, [3].

11. Orson Pratt, *A[n] Interesting Account of Several Remarkable Visions, and of the Late Discovery of Ancient American Records*, 3–5.

12. Orson Hyde, *Ein Ruf aus der Wüste (A Cry out of the Wilderness)*, 13–15.

13. "Levi Richards, Journal, 11 June 1843, extract," The Joseph Smith Papers, [16].

14. "Alexander Neibaur, Journal, 24 May 1844, extract," The Joseph Smith Papers, [23–24].

15. "Journal, 1835–1836," 23.

symbolic of the individual search for knowledge and understanding. This provides a perfect structure for transmitting Smith's encounter with the Divine. What a Mason receives through types, figures, and allegory was literalized in Smith's experience, and then re-ritualized for his followers; not only did the First Vision story develop into a ritualistic narrative, but the Mormon prophet later developed the initiation experience into temple ritual in Kirtland and finally in Nauvoo.

Setting

Each account of the First Vision begins with prefatory remarks discussing the reason for the telling, as well as explanatory details that lead to the heavenly vision. In an early version, Joseph Smith states his intention to provide a "brief history of the establishment of the Church of Christ in these last days."[16] In doing so, he expresses a concern with the skepticism of the public and a desire that true and honest seekers will receive correct information. Three years later, in what became the official account of his vision, he elaborated:

> Owing to the many reports which have been put in circulation by evil disposed and designing persons in relation to the rise and progress of the Church of Latter day Saints, all of which have been designed by the authors thereof to militate against its character as a church, and its progress in the world; I have been induced to write this history so as to disabuse the publick mind, and put all enquirers after truth into possession of the facts as they have transpired in relation both to myself and the Church.[17]

After establishing the setting for his story, Smith gave the details of his birth and family background. His experiences in his immediate environment had prepared him in a significant way for his visionary encounter. As an Entered Apprentice Mason is examined to ensure he is worthy and prepared, Smith presented the reader with his own proven qualifications. Masonic lodges generally require that candidates come of their own free will, believe in a Supreme Being, and be of good morals and good reputation. Additionally, lodges have age and residence requirements. Notably, Smith mentioned all these conditions. He wrote that he was the child "of goodly Parents who spared no pains to instruct me in <the> christian religion,"[18] satisfying the Masonic requirement that an applicant be "worthy and well qualified."[19] Anderson's Constitutions specified that "a Mason is oblig'd, by his Tenure, to obey the moral Law; and if he rightly understands the Art, he will never be a stupid Atheist, nor an irreligious Libertine."[20] Besides declaring his up-

---

16. "Journal, 1835–1836," 22.

17. "History, circa June 1839–circa 1841 [Draft 2]," 1.

18. "History, circa Summer 1832," 1.

19. William Morgan, *Illustrations of Masonry by One of the Fraternity Who has Devoted Thirty Years to the Subject*, 18.

20. James Anderson, *The Constitutions of the Free-Masons, Containing the History, Charges, Regulations, &c. of that Most Ancient and Rightful Worshipful Fraternity*, 50. See also Emory Osgood, "Masonic Sermon," 1: "Take from Masonry the validity of the Bible

bringing as a Christian, Smith identified his various residences: "When ten years old my parents removed to Palmyra New York, where we resided about four years, and from thence we removed to the town of Manchester."[21] His experience took place "sometime in the second year after our removal to Manchester."[22] The accounts vary with regard to Smith's exact age at the time of the vision: he was about fourteen years old,[23] which was his "fifteenth year,"[24] or "in the sixteenth year of my age."[25] The age of fourteen hearkened back to the days of Craft Masonry, when a boy was required to work as an apprentice for seven years until he reached his majority at twenty-one and became a craftsman.

In William Morgan's exposure of the Entered Apprentice degree, the Senior Deacon asks a question before the Candidate is presented at the door of the lodge: "Is he duly and truly prepared?"[26] In order for the ritual to be of most effect, a man must be in a ready state to absorb the teaching which will be presented: "Except a man's mood be right, except his will be in the appropriate attitude, except he act from true motives, and in a reverent prayerful frame of mind, the 'work' will be to him as meaningless as an old wives' tale."[27] The first Degree of Speculative Freemasonry emphasized preparation and worthiness, test and probation. From the very beginning, the future prophet stepped into this Masonic pattern. The various accounts of Smith's First Vision commenced with a verification of his qualifications and then proceeded to demonstrate how his heart and mind were prepared for the illumination he was to receive.

Hoodwinked

Between 1819 and 1820, young Joseph Smith attended various church meetings in search of truth. Each First Vision account details the clash among the different sects that the Smiths encountered in the upper western New York area:

> There was in the place where we lived an unusual excitement on the subject of religion. It commenced with the Methodist, but soon became general among all the sects in that region of country, indeed, the whole district of Country seemed affected by it, and great multitudes united themselves to the different religious parties, which created no small stir and division amongst the people, some Crying, "Lo, here" and

---

... and total darkness will ensue. . . . No DEIST OR STUPID LIBERTINE CAN BE A MASON." Debates about the "question of Freemasonry" and whether it was compatible with Christianity were rampant in the Palmyra area as Joseph Smith was growing up, as Freemasonry was seen as an attempt to mitigate the skepticism of the day.

21. "'Church History,' 1 March 1842," 706.

22. "History, circa June 1839–circa 1841 [Draft 2]," 1.

23. "Journal, 1835–1836," 24; "'Church History,' 1 March 1842," 706; "Interview, 29 August 1843, extract," 3.

24. "History, circa June 1839–circa 1841 [Draft 2]," 2.

25. "History, circa Summer 1832," 3.

26. Morgan, *Illustrations of Masonry*, 18.

27. Harry L. Haywood, *Symbolical Masonry: an Interpretation of the Three Degrees*, 71.

others, "Lo, there." Some were contending for the Methodist faith, Some for the Presbyterian, and some for the Baptist.[28]

Upon enquiring each of their views of the plan of salvation, he found "a great clash in religious sentiment."[29] Smith called "the contentions and divi[si]ons[,] the wicke[d]ness and abominations and the darkness which pervaded the minds of mankind" a "grief to my soul."[30] The action planted the seed of religious change out of which the Restoration would grow.

Smith reported that "[s]o great was the confusion and strife amongst the different denominations" that he found it "impossible for a person young as [he] was and so unacquainted with men and things to come to any certain conclusion who was right and who was wrong."[31] "If God had a church," he reasoned, "it would not be split up into factions. . . . God could not be the author of so much confusion."[32] The young man became "wrought up" in his mind, "concidering it of the first importance that [he] should be right, in matters that involve eternal consequences."[33] Orson Pratt's account described his conundrum thus:

> [T]he thought of resting his hopes of eternal life upon chance, or uncertainties, was more than he could endure. . . . He then reflected upon the immense number of doctrines, now, in the world, which had given rise to many hundreds of different denominations. The great question to be decided in his mind, was—if any one of these denominations be the Church of Christ, which one is it? Until he could become satisfied, in relation to this question, he could not rest contented.[34]

This situation was described in terms of "darkness," which "covered the earth and gross darkness the nations."[35]

Masonic allegory similarly traces man's initial spiritual darkness and subsequent search for illumination. William Morgan's exposure portrayed the initial state of the applicant after he had been recommended, investigated, and accepted as a candidate:

> The candidate is then blindfolded, his left foot bare, his right in a slipper, his left breast and arm naked, and a rope called a Cable-tow round his neck and left arm.[36]

This condition symbolizes the darkness and impotence of ignorance. The "hood-wink" of cloth or leather that is placed over the candidate's eyes is not intended to conceal information. Instead, it symbolizes the fact that he is yet in darkness.

---

28. "History, circa June 1839–circa 1841 [Draft 2]," 2.
29. "'Church History,' 1 March 1842," 706.
30. "History, circa Summer 1832," 2.
31. "History, circa June 1839–circa 1841 [Draft 2]," 2.
32. "'Church History,' 1 March 1842," 706.
33. "Journal, 1835–1836," 23.
34. Pratt, *Interesting Account*, 4.
35. Hyde, *Ein Ruf aus der Wüste*, 15.
36. Morgan, *Illustrations of Masonry*, 18.

The real hoodwink, that which Freemasonry undertakes to remove, is human unawareness of spiritual truth.

Smith's 1835 account depicts the fourteen-year-old as being "wrought up" in his mind respecting religion and the different denominations that taught such differing paths to salvation. His wording that he was "perplexed in mind"[37] over the issue is remarkably similar to a widely circulated exposure of the day, where the candidate's blindfolding is said to cause him "Uncertainty" and to "throw his mind into great Perplexity."[38] Later First Vision accounts make it clear that this condition of "blind uncertainty"[39] caused the poison of contention, resentment, and anger among the various systems of religion.

Like Smith in his tender years, Freemasonry had been wrestling with the issue of religious pluralism since the early eighteenth century. The 1723 Masonic *Constitutions* addressed the controversy in this way:

Masonic candidate as portrayed in *Duncan's Masonic Ritual and Monitor*, 1866.

> Though in ancient Times Masons were charg'd in every Country to be of the Religion of that Country or Nation, whatever it was, yet 'tis now thought more expedient only to oblige them to that Religion in which all Men agree, leaving their particular Opinions to themselves; that is, to be *good men and true . . .* by whatever Denominations or Persuasions they may be distinguish'd.[40]

Thus, Masonry was considered "a Sanctuary in which are garnered all dogmas and all traditions of [the Christian] religion."[41] Smith struggled with the same issue, but he was to be instructed by his encounter with Deity to handle pluralism differently. While Masonry compromised on this point by saying all religious traditions should be respected, he would conclude that the point of union should be one Truth, authored by God.[42]

---

37. "Journal, 1835–1836," 23.

38. *Jachin and Boaz: or, an Authentic Key to the Door of Free-Masonry*, 9.

39. Hyde, *Ein Ruf aus der Wüste*, 14.

40. Anderson, *Constitutions*, 50; emphasis in original.

41. Arthur Edward Waite, *A New Encyclopaedia of Freemasonry (Ars Magna Latomorum) And of Cognate Instituted Mysteries: Their Rites, Literature and History*, 1:180.

42. Later in his career, Smith would reflect a more Masonic view on religious pluralism. "The Mussulman condemns the Heathen, the Jew, and the Christian, and the whole world of mankind that reject his Koran, as infidels, and consigns the whole of them to perdition. The Jew believes that the whole world that rejects his faith, and are not circumcised, are Gentile

Petition

As the future prophet attended meetings of various Christian denominations, he determined by an appeal to scripture to resolve his conviction of personal sin and his uncertainty over which church was right. Several scriptures are mentioned in the various First Vision accounts as having been significant in Joseph Smith's decision to pray directly to God for an answer. The earliest account shows the influence of no fewer than eight well-known Bible verses, all strung together in one emotional composition:[43]

- [F]or I learned in the scriptures that God was the same yesterday today and forever [Heb. 13:8],[44]
- that he was no respecter to persons for he was God [Acts 10:34],[45]
- for I looked upon [the sun, moon, stars, earth, beasts, fowls, fish, etc.] and when I considered upon these things my heart exclaimed well hath the wise man said it is a fool that saith in his heart there is no God [Ps. 14:1].[46]
- [M]y heart exclaimed all these bear testimony and bespeak an omnipotent and omnipresent power [Ps. 19:1],[47]
- a being who maketh Laws and decreeeth and bindeth all things in their bounds [Acts 17: 24-26],[48]

---

dogs, and will be damned. The Heathen are equally as tenacious about their principles, and the Christian consigns all to perdition who cannot bow to his creed, and submit to his ipse dixit. But while one portion of the human race are judging and condemning the other without mercy, the great parent of the universe looks upon the whole human family with a fatherly care, and paternal regard; he views them as his offspring." See "History, 1838–1856, volume C-1 [2 November 1838–31 July 1842]," The Joseph Smith Papers, 1321.

43. "History, circa Summer 1832," 2–3; spelling and punctuation corrected.

44. KJV: "Jesus Christ the same yesterday, and to day, and for ever."

45. KJV: "Then Peter opened his mouth, and said, Of a truth I perceive that God is no respecter of persons: But in every nation he that feareth him, and worketh righteousness, is accepted with him."

46. KJV: "The fool hath said in his heart, There is no God." See Daniel Sickels, *The General Ahiman Rezon and Freemason's Guide*, 155: "By it [geometry] we discover the power, wisdom, and goodness of the Grand Artificer of the Universe, and view with delight the proportions which connect this vast machine. By it we discover how the planets move in their respective orbits, and demonstrate their various revolutions. By it we account for the return of seasons, and the variety of scenes which each season displays to the discerning eye. Numberless worlds are around us, all framed by the same Divine Artist, which roll through the vast expanse and are conducted by the same unerring law of nature."

47. KJV: "The heavens declare the glory of God; and the firmament sheweth his handywork."

48. KJV: "God that made the world and all things therein, . . . And hath made of one blood all nations of men for to dwell on all the face of the earth, and hath determined the times before appointed, and the bounds of their habitation."

- who filleth Eternity who was and is and will be from all Eternity to Eternity [Ps. 90:2].[49]
- [A]nd when I considered all these things and that that being seeketh such to worship him as worship him in spirit and in truth [John 4:24].[50]
- [T]herefore I cried unto the Lord for mercy for there was none else to whom I could go and to obtain mercy [Ps. 27:7].[51]

Many of these scriptures underscore Masonic issues and concerns, and the language used in Smith's History is similar to what one finds in Masonic discourse.

Historian Richard Bushman has speculated that Smith may have considered the Deist question of "how to know of God's existence" in context of the Palmyra debating club of which he was a member.[52] Other club members would later remark of Smith's able skill in public speaking. Significantly, however, the rationalist response provided by Smith to this particular Deist question is framed in language regularly used by Freemasons. In answer to the qualifying Masonic question of whether he believed in a "Supreme being," Smith gave the appropriate reply. After describing the planetary motions of sun, moon, and stars as bespeaking "a being who maketh laws and decreeth and bindeth all things in their bounds,"[53] he concluded, quoting Psalm 14:1: "It is a fool that saith in his heart, 'there is no God.'"[54] In Masonry, the heavenly constellations are foundational for providing a source for belief in a Divine being. These celestial lights are intended to impress on the memory "that All Seeing Eye! whom the sun, moon, and stars obey, and under whose watchful care even comets perform their stupendous revolutions, beholds the inmost recesses of the human heart, and will reward us according to our works."[55]

In his 1835 telling, Smith cited just two scriptures that influenced him as he considered the different systems of religion:[56]

---

49. KJV: "Before the mountains were brought forth, or ever thou hadst formed the earth and the world, even from everlasting to everlasting, thou art God."

50. KJV: "They that worship him must worship him in spirit and in truth."

51. KJV: "Hear, O Lord, when I cry with my voice: have mercy also upon me, and answer me."

52. Richard L. Bushman, *Joseph Smith—Rough Stone Rolling*, 38.

53. "I looked upon the sun the glorious luminary of the earth and also the moon rolling in their magesty through the heavens and also the stars shining in their courses." "History, circa Summer 1832," 2. In Masonry, the sun, moon, and stars perform an important symbolic function. In the initiation ritual, a candidate is told when he is brought to light, that the three lesser lights of the lodge, represented by the three tapers, are the sun, moon, and the Master of the Lodge. The stars are symbols in the high degrees.

54. "History, circa Summer 1832," 3; spelling and punctuation corrected.

55. Malcom C. Duncan, *Duncan's Masonic Ritual and Monitor or Guide to the Three Symbolic Degrees of the Ancient York Rite and to the Degrees of Mark Master, Past Master, Most Excellent Master, and the Royal Arch*, 36, 129.

56. "Journal, 1835–1836," 23.

[B]eing thus perplexed in mind I retired to the silent grove and bow[e]d down before the Lord, under a realising sense that he had said (if the bible be true) ask and you shall receive knock and it shall be opened seek and you shall find. [Matt. 7:7; Luke 11:9][57]

[A]nd again, if any man lack wisdom let him ask of God who giveth to all men libarally and upbradeth not. [James 1:5][58]

The first of these, "ask, seek, and knock," is also cited in the Entered Apprentice Degree. Three distinct knocks at the door of a Lodge are the beginnings of every Mason's adventure. As described in Morgan's exposé, a candidate approaches the entrance of the Lodge for the first time, "hoodwinked, slipshod and awry."[59] He is instructed to give "three distinct knocks" at the door, "which are answered by three from within."[60] Among other things, these knocks allude to Jesus's promise in Matthew 7 and Luke 11.[61] One early (1795) exposure quotes the Entered Apprentice catechism at the end of the degree thus:

> Mas. Brother, you told me you gave Three distinct Knocks at the Door: Pray what do they signify?
>
> Ans. A certain Text in Scripture.
>
> Mas. What is that Text, Brother?
>
> Ans. Ask, and you shall have; seek, and you shall find; knock, and it shall be open'd unto you.
>
> Mas. How do you apply this Text in Masonry?
>
> Ans. I sought in my Mind; I ask'd of my Friend;[62] I knock'd, and the Door of Masonry became open unto me.[63]

Masonic ritual often involves a three-times-three pattern. Thus, there is a three-fold repetition of the three knocks at the door; they are repeated while the initiate kneels in prayer, and then again at the altar.

---

57. KJV: "Ask, and it shall be given you; seek, and ye shall find; knock, and it shall be opened unto you."

58. KJV: "If any of you lack wisdom, let him ask of God, that giveth to all men liberally, and upbraideth not."

59. "'Tis scarcely true that souls come naked down / To take abode up in this earthly town, / Or naked pass, of all they wear denied. / We enter slipshod and with clothes awry, / And we take with us much that by-and-bye / May prove no easy task to put aside." Arthur Edward Waite, *Strange Houses of Sleep*, 231.

60. Morgan, *Illustrations of Masonry*, 18.

61. Three distinct knocks are also representative of death. See also MacNulty, *The Way of the Craftsman*, 56.

62. "I ask'd of my Friend": the petitioner must be recommended by another Freemason in order to qualify for initiation.

63. W. O. Vn, *The Three Distinct Knocks, Or the Door of the most Antient Free-Masonry, Opening to all Men, Neither Naked nor Cloath'd, Bare-foot nor Shod, &c.*, 25.

By 1838 (and in every subsequent version), the telling of the First Vision mentions James 1:5 exclusively as the stimulus for Smith's determination to ask of God.[64] Yet, this scripture had Masonic implications as well:

> While I was laboring under the extreme difficulties caused by the contests of these parties of religionists, I was one day reading the Epistle of James, First Chapter and fifth verse which reads, "If any of you lack wisdom, let him ask of God, that giveth to all men liberally and upbraideth not, and it shall be given him.["] . . . At length I came to the conclusion that I must either remain in darkness and confusion or else I must do as James directs, that is, Ask of God.[65]

From the promise in James, Smith learned "that it was the privilege of all men to ask God for wisdom, with the sure and certain expectation of receiving."[66] Orson Hyde stated, "He [Smith] considered this scripture an authorization for him to solemnly call upon his creator to present his needs before him with the certain expectation of some success."[67] Likewise, Orson Pratt wrote that this "was cheering information to him: tidings that gave him great joy." And in terms a Mason would approve, Pratt continued, writing, "It was like a light shining forth in a dark place, to guide him to the path in which he should walk. He, now, saw that if he inquired of God, there was, not only, a possibility, but a probability; yea, more, a certainty, that he should obtain a knowledge."[68]

Reflection

Joseph Smith meditated carefully upon his situation and upon the scriptures he had read. From the age of twelve to fifteen, the time of religious revival in the area, he "pondered these things in [his] heart."[69] Especially compelling is his depiction of the effect that James 1:5 had upon him:

---

64. J. W. Peterson, "Another Testimony," 11; Larry C. Porter, "Reverend George Lane—Good 'Gifts,' Much 'Grace,' and Marked 'Usefulness,'" 330–36. In an 1893 interview, William Smith identified Reverend George Lane as one who was directly responsible for Joseph's prayerful inquiry. Latter-day Saint religion instructor, Larry Porter, places Reverend Lane in the geographical proximity of Joseph Smith on a number of occasions between the years 1819 and 1825—at a time when Joseph Smith was aware of "an unusual excitement on the subject of religion."

65. "History, circa June 1839–circa 1841 [Draft 2]," 2–3.

66. Pratt, *Interesting Account*, 4.

67. Hyde, *Ein Ruf aus der Wüste*, 15.

68. Pratt, *Interesting Account*, 4–5. James 1:5 is used in the Knights Templar degree. See Robert McCoy, *The Masonic Manual, A Pocket Companion for the Initiated: Containing the Rituals of Freemasonry Embraced in the Degrees of the Lodge Chapter and Encampment*, 255.

69. "History, circa Summer 1832," 2.

Never did any passage of scripture come with more power to the heart of man that this did at this time to mine. It seemed to enter with great force into every feeling of my heart. I reflected on it again and again.[70]

The heart is noted in the Fraternity as "that place where a man is first made a Mason." From the Lecture on the First Degree of Masonry, in Morgan's exposé:

Q. Where were you first prepared to be made a Mason?

A. In my heart.[71]

The darkened human heart is the setting for spiritual illumination.[72] The subsequent interior radiance—referenced in both Christian and Masonic tradition as the "daystar" or "[the bright] morning star"—bestowed certain blessings.[73]

A Secret Place in the Woods

So in accordance with this my determination to ask of God, I retired to the woods to make the attempt. It was on the morning of a beautiful clear day early in the spring of Eightteen hundred and twenty.[74]

Joseph Smith's description of his First Vision is deeply moving and spiritually persuasive, as it is clothed in the language of archetype and symbol. First, the confused young innocent stepped deep into a wooded spot—entering nature to commune directly with "Nature's God."[75] The woods to which he retired was already known to him: he described it as a place where he had been with his father. "I immediately went out into the woods where my father had a clearing,"

---

70. "History, circa June 1839–circa 1841 [Draft 2]," 2.

71. Morgan, *Illustrations of Masonry*, 34.

72. As noted by Albert G. Mackey, "In the Ancient Mysteries, the aspirant was always shrouded in darkness, as a preparatory step to the reception of the full light of knowledge." Albert G. Mackey, William G. Hughan, and Edward L. Hawkins, *An Encyclopedia of Freemasonry and Its Kindred Sciences, Comprising the Whole Range of Arts, Sciences and Literature as Connected with the Institution*, 1:196.

73. The phrases "light shining in a dark place" and "Day Star arising in your hearts" are found in 2 Peter 1:19. The promise of the "morning star" is located in Revelation 2:28. Identification of the bright and morning star with Jesus is found in Revelation 22:16. While all these passages are related, it is this latter verse that is found in some versions of the Master Mason degree. For a discussion of the use of Revelation 22:16 in Masonry, see Harry Carr, *The Freemason at Work*, 2–3.

74. "History, circa June 1839–circa 1841 [Draft 2]," 3.

75. For Masonic use of the term, see, for example, Robert Ramsay, "Rambling Jottings," 8: "The grand and ennobling principles of Freemasonry stand forth in bold relief in whatever direction the Hiramite turns his eyes. He regards, as has often been truly said, all things as the handiwork of the Creator, and in contemplating their looks from Nature up to Nature's God, Freemasonry teaches her followers the most divine precepts of 'moral law.'"

he affirmed, "and went to the stump where I had stuck my axe when I had quit work, and I kneeled down, and prayed."[76]

Masonic author Kirk MacNulty describes the lodge as "a model of the psyche," and its workings as an interior psychological process.[77] Smith's grove is such a place. Designated in two of the First Vision accounts as "a secret place," the setting for the vision suggests the interior, sacred space of the human heart. In this private psychological landscape, the individual performs an "interior work," integrating the outside world with his inner reality.[78] Smith set forth into his "wood" in private response to the confusion brought about by the preachers of the day. There he sought an inner reality among the trees of the forest. In his own recitation, the young Smith was spiritually lost as he entered the grove to face a challenge: having "departed the path," he was concerned about his sins and eventually received a remission via Jesus Christ.

Similarly, the Masonic candidate is challenged as he circumambulates the lodge (representing the world). He is led to kneel in prayer, following which he is presented with a lambskin apron. Described as an "emblem of innocence," the apron symbolizes covering for sin, typifying the Atonement of Christ, and suggests to the Christian Freemason the equally symbolic "coats of skins" provided Adam and Eve in the Garden.[79]

Kneeling for Prayer

The First Vision narrative speaks of Joseph Smith's response to scripture as the first time in his life he had endeavored to pray out loud: "[F]or amidst all <my> anxieties I had never as yet made the attempt to pray vocally."[80] With "a fixed determination" to obtain information, he "called upon the Lord for the first time."[81] "And so," wrote Orson Hyde, "he began to pour out to the Lord with fervent determination the earnest desires of his soul."[82] Some of the accounts link the desire of his soul with his question, "[W]hich of all the sects were right[?]"[83] The 1835, 1838, and 1843 accounts, as well as accounts by Pratt, Hyde, and Neibaur, include the detail that Smith knelt as he prayed.

---

76. "Interview, 29 August 1843, extract," 3.

77. MacNulty, *Way of the Craftsman*, 100–4.

78. Pratt, *Interesting Account*, 5; "'Church History,' 1 March 1842," 706. Both the Pratt and the 1842 Wentworth accounts describe the First Vision as occurring in "a secret place in a grove."

79. Morgan, *Illustrations of Masonry*, 24; David Bernard, *Light on Masonry: A Collection of All the Most Important Documents on the Subject of Speculative Free Masonry*, 23.

80. "History, circa June 1839–circa 1841 [Draft 2]," 3.

81. "Journal, 1835–1836," 23.

82. Hyde, *Ein Ruf aus der Wüste*, 15.

83. "Levi Richards, Journal, 11 June 1843, Extract," The Joseph Smith Papers, 16.

In Morgan's exposure of the Entered Apprentice degree, the door of the lodge is opened to the blindfolded candidate, and he is warned not to "attempt to reveal the secrets of Masonry unlawfully."[84]

> Q. How were you then disposed of?
>
> A. I was conducted to the center of the Lodge and there caused to kneel for the benefit of a prayer.[85]
>
> Q. After prayer what was said to you?
>
> A. I was asked in whom I put my trust.
>
> Q. Your answer?
>
> A. In God.[86]

Upon giving the correct answer, the candidate is told to rise and is conducted around the lodge three times. He is then instructed in the proper kneeling posture in which he will take his obligation.

Another early catechism reviewing this sequence in the Entered Apprentice degree underscores the importance of the initiate's kneeling position during this prayer:

> Q.—What is the first point in Masonry?
>
> A.—Left knee bare and bent.
>
> Q.—Wherein is that the first point?
>
> In a kneeling posture I was first taught to adore my Creator and on my left knee bare and bent I was initiated into Masonry.[87]

In the first degrees of Masonry, the candidate does not pray himself; rather, others pray in his behalf until he is raised to the Master Mason degree. At that point, the candidate is required to make a personal oblation, either silently or vocally, as he prefers. This is reminiscent of Smith's confession that his experience in the grove was the first time he had attempted to pray vocally.[88]

---

84. Morgan, *Illustrations of Masonry*, 19.

85. The prayer, which is offered by the Senior Deacon, is exposed by Morgan as follows: "'Vouchsafe thine aid, Almighty Father of the universe, to this our present convention; and grant that this candidate for Masonry may dedicate and devote his life to thy service, and become a true and faithful brother among us. Endue him with a competency of thy divine wisdom, that by the secrets of our art he may be the better enabled to display the beauties of holiness, to the honor of thy holy name.' So mote it be—Amen!" Morgan, 19.

86. Morgan, 34.

87. A Retired Member of the Craft, *The Text Book of Freemasonry: A Complete Handbook of Instruction to All the Workings in the Various Mysteries and Ceremonies of Craft Masonry*, 69.

88. Orson Hyde's 1842 account seems to vary with other tellings on the point that this was Smith's first vocal prayer: "And so he began to pour out to the Lord with fervent determination the earnest desires of his soul. On one occasion, he went to a small grove of trees near his father's home and knelt down before God in solemn prayer." Hyde, *Ein Ruf aus der Wüste*, 15. Another early account in this vein comes from William Appleby's autobiography and journal, in which he reminisced on hearing Orson Pratt speak about

Bound by an Unseen Power

Initially, Joseph Smith's effort to pray had a strange result. In some of the accounts, he explained that as he attempted to pray, darkness gathered around him, and he was overcome by an evil influence. The official history of the Church attributes the incident to "some actual being from the unseen world who had such a marvelous power as [he] had never before felt in any being." For a time, it seemed as if he were "doomed to sudden destruction."[89] Hyde's account expands upon the notion of an unseen being's effect upon the boy:

> On one occasion, he went to a small grove of trees near his father's home and knelt down before God in solemn prayer. The adversary then made several strenuous efforts to cool his ardent soul. He filled his mind with doubts and brought to mind all manner of inappropriate images to prevent him from obtaining the object of his endeavors; but the overflowing mercy of God came to buoy him up and gave new impetus to his failing strength. However, the dark cloud soon parted and light and peace filled his frightened heart.[90]

Smith's 1835 account describes the endeavor to pray as initially "fruitless." He wrote, "[My tongue] seemed to be swol[l]en in my mouth, so that I could not utter."[91] He explained the unseen power had "such astonishing influence over me as to bind my tongue so that I could not speak."[92] The binding effect described is reminiscent of the condition of the Masonic candidate who is similarly fettered as he makes his way to the altar in search of light. He is "hoodwinked" with a blindfold, and a "cable-tow" is wrapped around his neck. In the initiation, the cable-tow "is to prevent any attempt at retreat."[93] Occultist Arthur Edward Waite sees in the rope "a representation of the gross earthly ties that hold unregenerated men to their appetites and passions."[94]

To a Freemason, the cable-tow additionally refers to his obligation: his tongue is bound from discussing what he has seen. Two questions found in the *Dumfries Manuscript* of 1710 mention this piece of equipment:

Joseph Smith in 1839: "[H]e retired to a secret grove, not far from his Fathrs house; and there ~~day after day~~, did this youth pour out his soul to God to know which of the sects was right, and had the true doctrine that he might obey the same, and become a member of the Church. One day while praying a glorious light encircled him." See William I. Appleby, Autobiography and Journal, 1848–1856, 30.

89. "History, circa June 1839–circa 1841 [Draft 2]," 3. See also Pratt, *Interesting Account*, 5: "At first, he was severely tempted by the powers of darkness, which endeavoured to overcome him; but he continued to seek for deliverance, until darkness gave way from his mind."

90. Hyde, *Ein Ruf aus der Wüste*, 15–16.

91. "Journal, 1835–1836," 23.

92. "History, circa June 1839–circa 1841 [Draft 2]," 3.

93. Carr, *The Freemason at Work*, 223.

94. Arthur Edward Waite, quoted in Haywood, *Symbolical Masonry*, 78.

Q. hou were you brought in

A. sham[e]fully w' a rope about my neck . . .

Q. whay a rop[e] about your neck

A. to hang me if I should Betr[a]y may trust[95]

At the beginning of the degree, the rope is placed upon the candidate as a symbol of those forces that regulate a man's conduct from without. When he takes the obligation, he shows he is now able to control and govern himself from within, and thus the cable-tow is no longer needed. In the Third Degree obligation,[96] the initiate promises to obey signs and summons "if within the length of [his] Cable-tow."[97] As clarified by the Baltimore Convention of 1843, the length of a cable-tow represents the scope of a man's reasonable ability to perform.[98]

The cable-tow can also be compared with the Mystic Tie in Masonry, which author Albert Mackey explains thus:

> The cable tow is emblematic of the cord or band of affection which should unite the whole fraternity, as in Hosea xi. 4, "I drew them with cords of a man, with bands of love."[99]

The Cabletow, as portayed in *Duncan's Masonic Ritual and Monitor*, 1866.

Masonic writer Samuel Lawrence sees it as "the Mystic Tie binding the initiate to God, to the Order, and to Righteousness; a tie which both binds and draws, and which holds a man fast, lest he drift like a ship at sea."[100] When Smith entered the grove, he was bound to worldly passions and earthly foibles. By the time the vision closed, he was bound to God.

---

95. Carr, *The Freemason at Work*, 224.

96. In American lodges, the cable-tow appears in the Second and Third Degrees with additional symbolic meanings.

97. The phrase "the length of my Cable-tow" is an allusion to the regulations which required ancient operative Masons to attend their assemblies if they were held within a specified distance.

98. Henry Wilson Coil, *Coil's Masonic Encyclopedia*, 115.

99. Albert Gallatin Mackey, *A Lexicon of Freemasonry; Containing a Definition of all its Communicable Terms, Notices of its History, Traditions, and Antiquities, and an Account of all the Rites and Mysteries of the Ancient World*, 45.

100. Samuel Lawrence, *Practical Masonic Lectures*, quoted in Haywood, *Symbolical Masonry*, 78.

Brought to Light

The zenith of Joseph Smith's visionary experience was the interior illumination he received as he was brought into the presence of Deity. He was released from the enemy who held him bound, his "mouth was opened," and his "[tongue] liberated."[101] As Smith renewed his efforts to call on the Lord "in mighty prayer,"[102] he was filled with the Spirit, and "the Lord opened the heavens" unto him.[103]

Smith's description of the light that appeared in the process of illumination is similar in all the accounts. He emphasized its brightness, shape, and mystical effect. In his 1832 entry, he records: "[A] piller of fire light above the brightness of the sun at noon day come down from above and rested upon me."[104] The 1835 journal account reports: "[A] pillar of fire appeared above my head, it presently rested down upon my head, and filled me with joy unspeakable. . . . [T]his pillar of flame . . . was spread all around, and yet nothing consumed."[105] The familiar 1838 account goes: "I saw a pillar <of> light exactly over my head above the brightness of the sun, which descended gradually untill it fell upon me."[106] In 1842, Joseph explained his mind was taken away from the objects with which he was surrounded, and he was "enwrapped in a heavenly vision."[107]

The two published apostolic accounts add details that augment Smith's experience with the mystical tradition. Orson Pratt writes:

> He, at length, saw a very bright and glorious light in the heavens above; which, at first, seemed to be at a considerable distance. He continued praying, while the light appeared to be gradually descending towards him; and, as it drew nearer, it increased in brightness, and magnitude, so that, by the time that it reached the tops of the trees, the whole wilderness, for some distance around, was illuminated in a most glorious and brilliant manner. He expected to have seen the leaves and boughs of the trees consumed, as soon as the light came in contact with them; but, perceiving that it did not produce that effect, he was encouraged with the hopes of being able to endure its presence. It continued descending, slowly, until it rested upon the earth, and he was enveloped in the midst of it. When it first came upon him, it produced a peculiar sensation throughout his whole system; and, immediately, his mind was caught away, from the natural objects with which he was surrounded; and he was enwrapped in a heavenly vision.[108]

---

101. "History, circa June 1839–circa 1841 [Draft 2]," 3; "Journal, 1835–1836," 24.

102. "Journal, 1835–1836," 24.

103. "History, circa Summer 1832," 3.

104. "History, circa Summer 1832," 3.

105. "Journal, 1835–1836," 24; see also Exodus 3:2.

106. "History, circa June 1839–circa 1841 [Draft 2]," 3.

107. "'Church History,' 1 March 1842," 706–7.

108. Pratt, *Interesting Account*, 5. This specific language suggests interior illumination.

Orson Hyde elaborated on this last point: "At this sacred moment, the natural world around him was excluded from his view, so that he would be open to the presentation of heavenly and spiritual things."[109]

The language of these accounts calls to mind the Hebrew description of the *Shekinah*, which served as the physical manifestation of the Divine Presence for the ancient Israelites. Resting upon the ancient Tabernacle, the *Shekinah* appeared in the form of a fiery pillar—a powerful symbol of the light and glory of God. Masonic writers in Smith's day were preoccupied with this concept in both its ancient Hebrew and later Christian iterations. Nineteenth-century Masonic writer and lecturer George Oliver wrote, "[T]he divine Shekinah vouchsafed to the prophet Isaiah, is declared by St. John to be the actual glory of Jesus Christ the Saviour of mankind."[110] This was known to some of the faithful ancients who knew the secret and true form and worship of God, Oliver claimed. They "transmitted the sublime science of Lux [Light]; and it has descended to our times pure and unadulterated."[111] Wherever light appeared in a Masonic lodge, it was emblematic of divine truth—an expressive symbol of the manifested glory of God.

As the visible sign of the presence of Deity, the *Shekinah* was coupled with the Masonic Rite of Illumination. Masonic exposures of the day explain how the candidate was ceremonially "brought to light" in the Rite of Illumination. There, the darkness was suddenly removed from his eyes. In a column of light, the Master of the Lodge, dressed in glittering finery, stepped down from his Throne in the East to stand before the newly enlightened candidate. For Christian Freemasons, this Master of the Lodge was a representation of the Lord of the Universe's condescension from his divine throne to instruct individuals on earth.

William Morgan described this transition from darkness to light as the "shock of illumination" in his 1826 Masonic exposure: "After having been so long blind, and full of fearful apprehensions all the time, this great and sudden transition from perfect darkness to a brighter [if possible] than the meridian sun in a mid-summer day, sometimes produces an alarming effect." Morgan added that he "once knew a man to faint on being brought to light."[112]

When the blindfold is taken from the initiate's eyes, he perceives a different arrangement of things, opening his mind to a new perspective.

> "Let him see the Light;" says the Master; they then take the Handkerchief from his Eyes, and whilst they are so doing, the Brethren form a Circle round him with their Swords drawn in their Hands, the Points of which are presented to his Breast. The

---

109. Hyde, *Ein Ruf aus der Wüste*, 16.

110. George Oliver, *Signs and Symbols: Illustrated and Explained in a Course of Twelve Lectures on Freemasonry*, 75. As a symbol of the Divine Presence, Christians associated the *Shekinah* with Jesus Christ, whose name *Immanuel* means "God with Us." See Isaiah 7:14 and Matthew 1:22–23. Here Oliver introduces the concept of pre-Christian Christianity, which will later be a hallmark of Mormonism.

111. Oliver, 71.

112. Morgan, *Illustrations of Masonry*, 22.

Ornaments borne by the Officers, the glittering of the Swords, and the fantastic Appearance of the Brethren in White Aprons, all together, creates great Surprise, especially to a Person, who for above an Hour has been fatigued with the Bandage over his Eyes.[113]

The "pillar of light above the brightness of the sun" resting upon young Smith, his subsequent vision of God, and his receiving of instruction are impressively reminiscent of the Masonic ceremony. Smith entered the grove to recover the secret of the true form and worship of Deity. Even before he penned the earliest surviving history of the First Vision in 1832, a description of such an experience appeared within the verses of the Book of Mormon. The narrative of Lehi's vision includes some of the same Masonic aspects that were present in Smith's:

> And it came to pass as he prayed unto the Lord, there came a pillar of fire and dwelt upon a rock before him. . . . And being thus overcome with the Spirit, he was carried away in a vision. . . . [H]e saw God sitting upon his throne, surrounded with numberless concourses of angels in the attitude of singing and praising their God. And it came to pass that he saw One descending out of the midst of heaven, and he beheld that his luster was above that of the sun at noon-day. (1 Ne. 1:6–9)

Smith later expounded to his followers that only by understanding the true character of God can He be properly worshipped.[114] As Smith's doctrine on the nature of Deity further developed, he disclosed additional details about the vision, including the presence of two figures who appeared in the grove. While the earliest account does not specify more than one personage having appeared ("I saw the Lord"), each of the others clearly state that both the Father and the Son were present.[115] The young seeker "saw a personage in the fire[:] light complexion[,] blue eyes[,] a piece of white cloth drawn over his shoulders[,] his right arm bear [bare.] [A]fter a w[h]ile a[n] other person came to the side of the first."[116] The two beings "exactly resembled each other in their features or likeness."[117]

One may see Smith going to the grove in terms of the individual search for light. Any Entered Apprentice at the altar similarly asks for light.[118] The one who gives him that light—the Worshipful Master in the East—represents God. Additionally, the ceremony has the Junior Warden representing Christ. In the opening ritual of a Masonic lodge, one is told "as the sun in the south, at high meridian, is the beauty and the glory of the day, so stands the Junior Warden in the South."[119]

---

113. *Jachin and Boaz*, 9.

114. "Lecture Third of Faith," in "Doctrine and Covenants, 1835," The Joseph Smith Papers, 39.

115. "History, circa Summer 1832," 3.

116. "Alexander Neibaur, Journal, 24 May 1844, extract," The Joseph Smith Papers, 23.

117. Pratt, *Interesting Account*, 5.

118. "Q. After you had taken your obligation, what was said to you? A. I was asked what I most desired. Q. Your answer? A. Light." Bernard, *Light on Masonry*, 32.

119. Morgan, *Illustrations of Masonry*, 30.

"Inception Of Mormonism—Joseph Smith's First Vision." From T B. Stenhouse, *The Rocky Mountain Saints*, 1874.

At the close of his vision, after regaining consciousness, Smith found himself in the position of a Mason in the Third Degree: "lying on <my> back looking up into Heaven."[120]

Instruction by Degrees

The Masonic initiate is instructed in the progressive science of Masonry by degrees. Initially, he is entrusted with a small portion until he has proven himself true and faithful, and then the full light of Masonry is unveiled. According to one exposure, "One was extremely scrupulous to entrust these important secrets only to those whose discretion was proven & of whom one was sure. This is why degrees were made, to test those to whom they would be given."[121]

Several aspects of the First Vision experience were evocative of the Freemasons' reception of ritual and knowledge by degrees. A compelling visual illustration of this principle is the light that "descended gradually untill it fell upon [him]."[122] Further, the young boy was told to join none of the churches, while "at the same time receiving a promise that the fulness of the gospel should at some future time be made known."[123] Not only was the future prophet given keys of knowledge by degrees, but he would also be given priesthood authority and power dispensed in the same manner. The preface to Joseph Smith's 1832 history, written by his scribe, Frederick G. Williams, set forth what was to be covered in the history, beginning with his First Vision:

firstly he receiving the testamony from on high

seccondly the ministering of Angels

thirdly the reception of the holy Priesthood . . .

forthly a confirmation and reception of the high Priesthood after the holy order of the son of the living God power and ordinence from on high to preach the Gospel in the administration and demonstration of the spirit

the Kees of the Kingdom of God confer[r]ed upon him and the continuation of the blessings of God to him &c——— .[124]

From this preface, it is evident that the idea of a "high Priesthood," a concept that can be found in the Royal Arch Degree, was being discussed in the Church as early as 1832. Jeremy Cross's Masonic Chart outlines the Order of High Priesthood, which "appertains to the office of High Priest of a Royal Arch

---

120. "History, circa June 1839–circa 1841 [Draft 2]," 3.

121. Arturo de Hoyos and S. Brent Morris, trans. and ed., *The Most Secret Mysteries of the High Degrees of Masonry Unveiled, or The True Rose-Croix*, xix–xx.

122. "History, circa June 1839–circa 1841 [Draft 2]," 3.

123. "'Church History,' 1 March 1842," 707.

124. "History, circa Summer 1832," 1.

Chapter."[125] Cross describes it as "a station highly honorable to all those, who diligently perform the important duties annexed to it."[126]

Ritualizing the First Vision

Joseph Smith's First Vision was a literal manifestation of the Masonic initiation ritual. The purpose of ritual is to prepare the mind in an ordinal way to experience the encounter in a real way. Smith, having attained this state, took steps to provide a similar opportunity to his followers. According to Masonic writer Colin Dyer, Masonry is based on progression to the "ultimate perfection." He postulates that "the proliferation of masonic degrees in the eighteenth century was perhaps caused by the realization that perfection is unattainable" and that there always remains further progress to be made. Thus, the "keen Mason" continued to "hive off" new degrees from the basic three, utilizing Bible stories to formulate new ceremonies and instruction.[127]

Similar to this development of new degrees in Masonry, Smith acted as a "keen Mason" when he ritualized his divine initiation experience and created new, Masonic-like degrees in Kirtland and Nauvoo. An early form of the Kirtland temple endowment took place in the School of the Prophets located in an upper room in Newel K. Whitney's general store. The brethren who participated arrived in a state of preparation, having fasted, washed themselves, and put on clean linen. A ritual greeting was then given, drawing the brothers into fraternal comradery.[128] Following the Masonic example of "hiving off" new degrees with biblical underpinnings, the prophet drew upon two New Testament events to create a sacramental ceremony. The washing of feet and partaking of bread and wine were already used in an ordinal way by many Christian sects of the day. Smith, however, gave them the Masonic term "endowments."[129] The meaning he applied to these ritual acts prepared the brethren to enter into the presence of Deity and be "sealed . . . up" unto eternal life.[130]

---

125. Jeremy L. Cross, *The True Masonic Chart, or Hieroglyphic Monitor*, 122.

126. Cross, 136.

127. Colin Dyer, *Symbolism in Craft Freemasonry*, 122.

128. "[W]hen any shall come in after him let the teacher arise & with uplifted hands to heaven yea even directly & salute his brother or brethren with these words saying art thou a brother or brethren I salute you in the name of the Lord Jesus Christ in token of the everlasting covenant in which covenant I receive you to fellowship." "Revelation Book 1," The Joseph Smith Papers, 166.

129. "School of the Prophets Salt Lake City Meeting Minutes, 1883, August–December," 12.

130. "Doctrine and Covenants, 1835," 108. See also Doctrine and Covenants 88:138–39: "And ye shall not receive any among you into this school save he is clean from the blood of this generation; And he shall be received by the ordinance of the washing of feet, for unto this end was the ordinance of the washing of feet instituted."

The rite began with each Elder washing his own feet first. The prophet then draped a towel over his shoulder in imitation of the Savior's actions described in John 13 and ceremonially washed the feet of each of his brethren, wiping them with the towel. He then said to the Elders:

> "As I have done so do ye:" Wash ye, therefore, one another's feet: and by the power of the Holy Ghost I pronounced them all clean from the blood of this generation; but if any of them should sin willfully after they were thus cleansed, and sealed up unto eternal life, they should be given over unto the buffetings of Satan until the day of redemption.[131]

Remarks by Smith published in the *Millennial Star* shortly before the completion of the Kirtland Temple connected the washing of feet with fraternal unity and with an "endowment" consisting of a heavenly manifestation:

> [T]he ordinance of washing of feet . . . is calculated to unite our hearts, that we may be one in feeling and sentiment, and that our faith may be strong, so that Satan cannot overthrow us, nor have any power over us. . . .
> [W]e must be clean every whit. . . .
> All who are prepared, and are sufficiently pure to abide the presence of the Saviour, will see him in the solemn assembly.[132]

Indeed, as early as December 1832, the year of the first extant First Vision account, Smith had penned a revelation promising the faithful that if they would sanctify themselves and place their thoughts upon God, "the days will come that you shall see him, for he will unveil his face unto you" (D&C 88:68).

Zebedee Coltrin described an instance of real initiation such as this that took place during a meeting of the Kirtland School of the Prophets. According to Coltrin, Smith instructed the brethren to kneel in silent prayer with hands uplifted. While praying, Coltrin and others in the room saw a personage who "walked through the room from east to west." Smith told the company that they had just seen Jesus, the Son of God, and asked them to resume their former position in prayer. When they all had knelt, another personage, identified by Smith as "the Father," came through the room "surrounded as with a flame of fire." Coltrin's detail of the progress of Jesus through the room from east to west connects this event more closely with a Masonic ceremony than a Christian service. He described his experience of real initiation as "a sensation that it might destroy the tabernacle as it was of consuming fire of great brightness. . . . This appearance was so grand and overwhelming that it seemed I should melt down in his pres-

---

131. "History, 1838–1856, volume A-1 [23 December 1805–30 August 1834]," The Joseph Smith Papers, 271. This procedure was instituted in the Kirtland School of the Prophets and continued as a temple ordinance after the Kirtland Temple was completed.
132. "History of Joseph Smith. Tuesday 10th," 423–24.

ence." Coltrin shook with a powerful thrill that he felt "in the marrow of [his] bones."[133] The phrasing is a strong Masonic identifier.[134]

Real initiation continued to be described in Masonic terms as it was experienced by many of the Latter-day Saints in the Kirtland Temple following its completion. Visions of God and angels surrounded in light were reported. Many felt the Holy Ghost "like fire in their bones."[135] During solemn assembly services in March of 1836, Joseph Smith instructed the priesthood quorums on the ordinance of washing of feet and the spirit of prophecy. George A. Smith then "arose, and began to prophesy, when a noise was heard like the sound of a rushing mighty wind, which filled the temple." The entire congregation stood up together, "being moved upon by an invisible power; many began to speak in tongues, and prophesy; others saw glorious visions." Even people of the neighborhood gathered around the temple and were said to have heard "an unusual sound within" and seen "a bright light like a piller of Fire resting upon—the Temple."[136]

The First Vision: A Masonic Allegory Made Literal

The story of Joseph Smith's First Vision was not widely circulated during the early years of the Restoration. However, by 1832 Smith found it important enough to be included as a vital feature of the history of the Church. His experience was an archetypal event, but the elements of the archetype that he used to share the experience came from his exposure to Freemasonry. The first account of his vision dates to within six years and fifty miles of the Morgan affair with all its publicity and excitement regarding the Fraternity. The Craft was being discussed and grappled with by the Christian ministers in the New York area and warned against in their revivals. It was Masonry, all-pervasive in Smith's family and his environment, that supplied the particular wording and images Smith used as he recounted his vision. From there, the First Vision story developed into a ritual retelling, containing expected elements in a rote order, including each component that makes Masonic initiation potent and powerful.

Masonic parallels in Smith's recounting of the vision cannot be overlooked or easily attributed to other factors; this is because they occur together, using specific language. Similar theophanies among young seekers were common during the revivals in early America, but they did not include such depth of Masonic imagery. Smith's drawing upon Masonry in his recounting of his First Vision was a tacit approval of its content. It indicated that, rather than being anti-Masonic, Smith had found something authentic in the ritual early in his life. At a time

---

133. "School of the Prophets Salt Lake City Meeting Minutes, 1883, August–December," 58–60.

134. Morgan, *Illustrations of Masonry*, 76.

135. "Journal, 1835–1836," 151b.

136. "History, 1838–1856, volume B-1 [1 September 1834–2 November 1838]," The Joseph Smith Papers, 4 [addenda].

when Masonry was not received favorably in many places, Smith had the aptitude to use its transformative potential.

The Fraternity offers a set of ritual actions that draw its participants into the presence of the Divine. Ideally, a Masonic initiate enters the lodge and, within a few brief hours, a seed is planted. When fully grown, this plant will fundamentally change and transform the initiate with the fruit of personal gnosis. What a Mason receives through types, figures, and allegory was literalized in Smith's description of his initiating experience. He was physically brought into the presence of God; he had been illuminated in the light of the Divine; he had seen a vision. "I knew it, and I knew that God knew it, and I could not deny it," he insisted.[137] Those few brief hours in the grove changed Smith, imparted confidence, and set his future course. He received answers to his questions about religion. His tongue was loosed as a sign of his prophetic office. He stepped out of the grove transformed, initiated into a calling as the anticipated restorer of both true religion and its spiritual handmaiden, Freemasonry.

Devotional readers of Smith's story are invited to recognize their internal spiritual darkness and ignorance. In a search for knowledge and understanding, they are summoned to enter the deep forest of their inner being and "come to light" in their own experience with the Divine. For those acquainted with Freemasonry, the accounts have an additional layer of significance. Familiar rituals of illumination and ascent are slightly modified. They remain similar enough to be recognizable but are altered enough to strike the mind. The framing of the First Vision in Masonic language reveals divine secrets to those who are worthy and well qualified. Smith's story, then, reminds these readers of one of the Masonic axioms—that God continues to reveal his secrets to men.

---

137. "History, circa June 1839–circa 1841 [Draft 2]," 4.

CHAPTER 5

THE BOOK OF THE LAW,
LONG LOST, NOW FOUND

'Twas there, impressed with holy awe,
A gold engraven plate I saw
With dazzling splendor shine.
To us, the "Grand Elect" alone,
Its secret characters are known,
Ineffable-divine.

—"Ode for a Grand Elect Perfect and
Sublime Mason," 1823.[1]

In his 1992 book, *Joseph Smith's Response to Skepticism*, author Robert N. Hullinger rightly observed that many elements in Joseph Smith's history were familiar to Freemasons.[2] However, he also assumed that Smith invented his accounts from whole cloth. This need not be the case, as it is also possible that Smith was describing genuine experiences, informed by his familial and cultural exposure to Masonry.

The story of Joseph Smith and the coming forth of the Book of Mormon is archetypally Masonic. Accounts of the recovery of the golden plates are intimately connected with the backstory of the Royal Arch Degree and its discussion of the discovery of the Book of the Law and the restoration of true religion. The symbolic nature of these elements fits into Smith's witness of this uniquely American book of scripture. The use of Masonic language in his history demonstrates that the coming forth of the Book of Mormon was seen as a fulfillment of Masonic expectations. The elements of the tale—a delving into the depths by means of interior illumination to recover something long lost—are described in Richard Carlisle's *Manual of Freemasonry* as "moral similitudes of material things."[3] The young prophet brought Freemasonry's internal spiritual quest into physical reality through the medium of the folk practice of treasure-seeking.

Later accounts written by Smith's family members and close associates perpetuated the Masonic elements, often extending and intensifying them. The fact

---

1. Charles Thompson McClenachan, *The Book of the Ancient and Accepted Scottish Rite of Freemasonry: Containing Instructions in all the Degrees from the Third to the Thirty-third, and Last Degree of the Rite*, 176.

2. Robert N. Hullinger, *Joseph Smith's Response to Skepticism*, 106.

3. Richard Carlile, *Manual of Freemasonry: In Three Parts. With an Explanatory Introduction to the Science, and a Free Translation of some of the Sacred Scripture Names*, 2:17.

that later writers put the story in Masonic terms, without prompting from their deceased leader, suggests that they, too, understood the cosmological significance inherent in the Craft. Smith and his nineteenth-century followers saw ideas in Freemasonry that expanded the mind and prepared it for religious salvation.

The chronicle of the coming forth of the Book of Mormon derives from many sources, some written years after the actual events. In his tellings, Joseph Smith freely recast events, continuing to add material and introduce concepts in order to meet later needs.[4] Despite his accounts and those of his family and friends often displaying certain disparities, it is nonetheless interesting to note correspondences in these accounts with Masonic legends.

The culmination of Smith's treasure-seeking efforts was the discovery of the golden plates from which he would later claim to translate the Book of Mormon. Early accounts describe the young seer using a stone to determine the precise location of the plates, concealed in a coffer buried in a nearby hill on neighbor Randall Robinson's property.[5] This sacred record was inscribed with mysterious characters, requiring a special key to translate. Just as Smith's retellings of his First Vision share similarities with Masonic initiation rites, from the beginning, narratives of the discovery of the plates share similarities with the legends of Freemasonry, most especially that of the Holy Royal Arch. By 1833, a Masonic connection with these events was conclusively forged, with later narratives augmenting the relationship.

Together with the Hiramic legend, the story of Enoch's recovery and preservation of the Sacred Word and that of the Foundation Stone comprise the central and most significant legends associated with Freemasonry. Nearly every Masonic story is an embellishment or an expansion upon these themes, especially as they relate to the construction of Solomon's Temple. Those familiar with Freemasonry could not fail to see the resemblance between the Royal Arch allegories and the developing tradition in the early Church.

An Ancient American Angel

In an account used in the *History of the Church*, Joseph Smith described a vision he had on the evening of the twenty-first of September 1823. While calling upon God for forgiveness of his sins, a light appeared, growing brighter until "the room was lighter than at noonday." A personage appeared at his bedside, "standing in the air for his feet did not touch the floor." The messenger told Smith of

---

4. Dan Vogel, *Joseph Smith: The Making of a Prophet*, 44.

5. Dan Vogel, "The Locations of Joseph Smith's Early Treasure Quests," 209–13; "Martin Harris Interview with Joel Tiffany, 1859," in Dan Vogel, ed., *Early Mormon Documents*, 2:302. See also "Henry Harris Statement," in Vogel, *Early Mormon Documents*, 2:76. Harris recounted, "Joseph had a stone which was dug from the well of Mason Chase, twenty-four feet from the surface. In this stone he could see many things to my certain knowledge. It was by means of this stone he first discovered these plates."

a book written on golden plates "giving an account of the former inhabitants of this continent and the source from whence they sprang."[6] In 1840, Orson Pratt wrote of this event, explaining that the angel made manifest to Smith "that the 'American Indians' were a remnant of Israel; that when they first immigrated to America, they were an enlightened people, possessing a knowledge of the true God." Inspired writers among these Native Americans—Smith's angel being one of them—"were required to keep a sacred history of the most important events transpiring among them: which history was handed down for many generations."[7]

Numerous printed works in Smith's milieu suggested that Native Americans were of Israelite descent.[8] But more accessible to the young Smith than these printed works were contemporary Freemasons who were fascinated with Native American antiquities, as many of Masonry's rituals were patterned on Native American customs and terminology. In the first years of the Republic, Masons adopted the Indian mystique and made it part of their culture, using its unique traditions and noble qualities to embellish their activities, name their lodges, and dress up at events.[9] Authors of an 1824 New York state history John Van Ness Yates and Joseph W. Moulten asserted that some Native American groups had private societies resembling Freemasonry, including rites of initiation, degrees, and secret signs.[10] Claims of ancient inscriptions and Israelite origins captured the attention of New Englanders versed in Masonic legend, and some were led to theorize that a record or artifact containing the Lost Word may have been carried by displaced Israelites and deposited among their ruins in North America.

The angel who appeared to Joseph Smith that Sunday evening in September quoted several scriptural passages, among them Malachi 3 and 4, Isaiah 11, Acts 3:22–23, and Joel 2:28–32. In Masonic fashion, the angel imparted confidential instruction to the young man, "many explanations which cannot be mentioned here."[11] The secret of the plates came with a penalty for disclosing it. "I should not show <them> to any person," Smith was told. "If I did I should be destroyed."[12] At

---

6. "History, circa June 1839–circa 1841 [Draft 2]," The Joseph Smith Papers, 5.

7. Orson Pratt, A[n] Interesting Account of Several Remarkable Visions, and of the Late Discovery of Ancient American Records, 6–7.

8. Dan Vogel, Indian Origins and the Book of Mormon: Religious Solutions from Columbus to Joseph Smith, 8. James Adair, for example, endeavored to prove this theory through a variety of parallels between Israelite and Native American culture. See James Adair, History of the American Indians; Particularly those Nations Adjoining to the Mississippi, East and West Florida, Georgia, South and North Carolina, and Virginia, 15–220.

9. In 1834, the "Improved Order of Red Men" revived an earlier fraternal society, the "Society of Red Men." Its constitution and membership requirements utilized pseudo-Native American jargon (for example, the treasurer was named "collector of wampum") while accepting into the order only free white males of means.

10. John V. N. Yates and Joseph W. Moulton, History of the State of New-York, Including its Aboriginal and Colonial Annals, 1:55–56.

11. "History, circa June 1839–circa 1841 [Draft 2]," 6.

12. "History, circa June 1839–circa 1841 [Draft 2]," 6.

the close of the vision, the angelic visitor ascended through a conduit leading into heaven, but Smith's miraculous experience wasn't over yet. Masonic instruction is often given in groups of three, and so were the teachings of the angel that night. Twice more he appeared to the boy prophet, repeating the same words with a few additions. At the conclusion of that final visit, a vision of the exact place where the plates were deposited was opened to Smith's mind, with the clarity of detail such that he would know the place without question when he found it.[13]

On the road between Palmyra and Canandaigua was a drumlin of considerable size and elevation that would eventually be called Cumorah by Smith's followers, after the name of the plates' resting place in the Book of Mormon. It was heavily forested and a popular destination among treasure-seekers, and it was to the west side of this hill, not far from the top, that the angel directed Smith to find the golden plates. While Smith was fairly restrained with his rehearsals of his First Vision, keeping most details private, he was much more open and willing to share his experience of finding these plates. Upon examination we can readily see how aspects of Smith's story of the discovery of these plates bear striking resemblance to the legend of the golden plate of Enoch, long part of the Masonic Royal Arch tradition.

The Masonic legend of Enoch—the account of that prophet's vision and restoration of the Sacred Word, and its subsequent various burials, losses, and recoveries—has significant variations in its renderings. Yet, for Freemasons, these tales do not demand absolute consistency. When Smith added his account of the Sacred Word being buried and rediscovered, he made the same kinds of changes and embellishments we would expect to see in Freemasons' own expansions of their traditions.[14]

Joseph Smith's Visits to the Hill

In 1817, Freemason Samuel Cole, speaking figuratively of his experience performing one of the Masonic degrees, wrote, "I dug deep for hidden treasures, found them, and regained the omnific word."[15] Joseph Smith transformed this symbolic passage into literal reality.

After his initial visit to the mound in 1823, Smith returned four additional times before he was able to obtain the plates and begin the work of translation.

---

13. "History, circa June 1839–circa 1841 [Draft 2]," 6. The vision mentioned in this account does not mention the seer stone.

14. Rabbinic explorations of existing legends often add conflicting details, as well. These rabbinic expansions, as well as the fluid Mormon accounts, can seem problematic to the Christian view, since such religious tellings are often expected to harmonize into one seamless narrative that is literally true.

15. Samuel Cole, *The Freemasons' Library and General Ahiman Rezon: Containing a Delineation of the True Principles of Freemasonry, Speculative and Operative, Religious and Moral*, vii.

The Hill Cumorah, ca. 1910.

The most complete accounts of these five visits contain a mélange of folk magic elements and Masonic language and symbolism. In addition, contemporary witnesses of the events, many of whom had assisted Smith in his treasure-seeking quests, were steeped in the Masonic legends of the day.[16] Their narratives seem to assume a familiarity with mystical practices and an acumen for symbolism. In order to analyze Smith's and his contemporaries' accounts of the plates' discovery, each of many early and late statements will be used as they were given, with accuracy and harmonization being a secondary concern. As will be seen, the magical and Masonic elements included in these stories demonstrate important perceptions regarding the coming forth of the record.

The accompanying table shows one reconstruction of Smith's first visit and each of the four returns to Cumorah between 1823 and 1827. At all but one of these visits, he found the same messenger there. Just as a Mason enters the Lodge for more light and learns "by degrees," Smith did not obtain the plates right away; instead, he returned year after year for further tutoring. And each time, he "received instruction and intelligence . . . respecting what the Lord was going to do, and how and in what manner his kingdom was to be conducted in the last days."[17]

---

16. These include Willard Chase, Joseph Knight, Fayette Lapham, Lorenzo Saunders, and John Corrill.

17. "History, 1838–1856, volume A-1 [23 December 1805–30 August 1834]," The Joseph Smith Papers, 7.

1823 Visit: Pursuing the Plates

In 1823, Joseph Smith was directed to go to the hill and ask for the book "in a certain name."[18] This is reminiscent of a Masonic practice of giving a certain sign or name to demonstrate one's qualifications.[19] Until the candidate recovers the real name that was lost, he is required to give a substitute. Assuming that the Book of Mormon represented the lost book of the Law, or lost Word of God, then, like all Masons, Smith would be obliged to supply a substitute name prior to learning the real one.

According to Willard Chase, after obtaining the record, Smith was instructed to "go directly away, and neither lay it down nor look behind him." Chase's articulation of Smith's experience exemplifies myth-like telling, melding Masonic elements with treasure-seeking lore. Chase said that Smith "demanded the book" from the spirit that had charge of it. He removed the book of gold from the unsealed stone box, and "fearing some one might discover where he got it, he laid it down to place back the top stone." To his surprise, when he turned around, "there was no book in sight." Opening the box again, he saw the holy record but was "hindered" in taking it out. In the box was "something like a toad, which soon assumed the appearance of a man, and struck him on the side of his head."

Chase said that Smith was unfazed by a "trifle" such as this. Treasure-seekers of the day often encountered spirits or familiars who endeavored to obstruct the acquisition of the treasure. When he stooped down and tried to take the book once more, "the spirit struck him again, and knocked him three or four rods, and hurt him prodigiously. After recovering from his fright, he enquired why he could not obtain the plates; to which the spirit made reply, because you have not obeyed your orders."[20]

Other accounts of this first visit to the Hill Cumorah contain similar features. In Joseph Knight's 1833 account, Smith lay the book down, and it disappeared back into the box just as above.[21] According to historian Michael Quinn, the term "slippery treasures" was used in the eastern United States in the early 1800s before the phrase appeared in the pages of the Book of Mormon (see Hel. 13:35; Morm. 1:18).[22] The term describes buried valuables that move away

---

18. Willard Chase Statement, 1833, in Vogel, *Early Mormon Documents*, 2:67.

19. Later Mormon traditions developed from this, such as determining angelic messengers, temple names, and so on.

20. Willard Chase Statement, 1833, in Vogel, *Early Mormon Documents*, 2:66–67. According to Chase, he spoke with Joseph Smith Sr. in the month of June 1827. If so, this conversation would have occurred several months before his son's final visit to Cumorah. Quinn places these events with Joseph Jr.'s final visit to the hill in 1827. However, the specific dating of the account as well as the many elements which accord with the 1823 visit make this placement questionable.

21. Dean C. Jessee, "Joseph Knight's Recollection of Early Mormon History," 30–31.

22. D. Michael Quinn, *Early Mormonism and the Magic World View*, 196.

Returns to Cumorah 1823–1827

	Initial Visit	First Return	Second Return	Third Return	Fourth Return
Date	September 22, 1823 Autumn Equinox	September 22, 1824 Autumn Equinox, New Moon	September 22, 1825 Autumn Equinox, Yom Kippur	September 22, 1826 Autumn Equinox	September 22, 1827 Autumn Equinox, New Moon, Rosh Ha-shanah
Age	17	18	19	20	21
Accompanied by	Alone	Alone	Samuel Lawrence or Hyrum Smith	Alone	Emma Hale Smith
Events	Moroni shows Joseph a vision of the hill and the plates and tells him Satan would try to tempt him. He is instructed to demand the book in a certain name. He puts the plates down, thinking of a treasure which might be hidden with them. He is struck on the side of the head by a toad/man.	Alvin dies on Nov. 19, 1823. Joseph goes to the hill alone and tells the spirit his brother is dead. Freemasons assume that Joseph would have had to raise Alvin's body to fulfill the instructions. They make accusations that he has dug up the body.	Joseph and Hyrum obtain a stone with which they plan to locate the plates. Hyrum is 25 years old and a Master Mason. Samuel Lawrence accompanies Joseph to the hill, perhaps shortly before the appointed date.	The angel tells Joseph if he will do right, he will obtain the plates the next year. He cannot get the plates until he is married. Emma must come with him to obtain the plates and is designated as a "key."	Joseph is finally old enough for masonic initiation. He brings Emma, who sits at the bottom of the hill in Joseph Knight's carriage. Joseph is up on the hill all night long. He obtains the plates and is attacked by three ruffians. Lights are seen in the heavens.
Instructions	Come back in one year and bring your oldest brother.	Bring a man with you, and you will know him when you see him.		Bring Emma, and you will obtain the plates if faithful.	

from the seeker when his search does not go in exactly the prescribed manner. When the young Smith attempted to grasp the plates, Knight reports: "Behold he Could not stur the Book any more then he Could the mountin. He exclaimed 'why Cant I stur this Book?' And he was answered, 'you cant have it now.'"[23]

In his official history, Smith stated that he made three attempts to get the plates before he "cried unto the Lord in the agony of [his] soul why can [he] not obtain them."[24] Adding to this, his mother Lucy Mack Smith detailed why her son may have been unable to procure the record:

> He put forth his hand <and> took them up <but> when he lifted them from their place the thought flashed across his mind that there might be something more in the box that might would be a benefit to him in a pecuniary point of view in the excitement of the moment he laid the record down in order to cover up the box least some one should come along and take away whatever else might be deposited there When he turned again to take up the record it was gone but where he knew not.[25]

John Corrill's account agrees with Lucy Smith's. After Joseph obtained the plates, Corrill says that he "began to contemplate the vast riches that he would acquire by their means." Because of his mercenary thoughts, "the Angel hid the plates from his view, and chastised him for his wickedness in acting contrary to the commandment" when the plates were "for the bringing about of God's purposes in the salvation of his people."[26] According to Oliver Cowdery, the angel told Smith the plates were "not deposited here for the sake of accumulating gain and wealth for the glory of this world." Instead, they were sealed by the prayer of faith and were of no worth to the children of men except for the knowledge which they contained.[27] Perhaps not without coincidence, Masonic writer George Oliver expressed this same apprehension in connection with Enoch's golden plate: if it had fallen into the wrong hands, Oliver remarked, they might have treasured it merely for its monetary worth and not for its intrinsic spiritual significance.[28] At a certain place in the Royal Arch Degree, the Master of the Lodge places Enoch's gold plate on the Bible on the altar and tells the brethren that its recovery has been fortuitous: "If it had fallen into improper hands, they might have prized it

---

23. Jessee, "Joseph Knight's Recollection," 31.

24. "History, circa Summer 1832," The Joseph Smith Papers, 4.

25. Lavina Fielding Anderson, ed., *Lucy's Book: A Critical Edition of Lucy Mack Smith's Family Memoir*, 346. Joseph Smith's 1832 history accords with Lucy's explanation: "[F]or now I had been tempted of the advisary and saught the Plates to obtain riches and kept not the commandme[n]t that I should have an eye single to the Glory of God." See "History, circa Summer 1832," 5.

26. John Corrill, *A Brief History of the Church of Christ of Latter Day Saints (Commonly Called Mormons) Including an Account of Their Doctrine and Discipline, with the Reasons of the Author for Leaving the Church*, 12.

27. Oliver Cowdery, "Letter to W. W. Phelps," 198.

28. George Oliver, *The Origin of the Royal Arch Order of Masonry, Historically Considered*, 93–94.

for its metallic value, but they would not have understood its symbolical worth. These four letters [engraved on the plate] compose the Tetragrammaton, or sacred name of the only true and living God."[29]

Joseph Smith was seventeen years old during his first attempt to retrieve the record from the Hill Cumorah. He was not allowed to take the plates at that time but was instructed instead to return one year later, accompanied this time by his "older brother."[30]

1824 Visit: Raising the Dead

Notably, all these accounts present the angelic messenger as referring to Joseph Smith's "oldest brother" rather than mentioning Alvin Smith by name.[31] However, scarcely two months after Joseph's first visit to Cumorah, his brother Alvin succumbed to an overdose of calomel given to him by a country physician. The idea that Alvin was to accompany Joseph to the hill nevertheless spread throughout the community, and Alvin's absence during that second visit to Cumorah was assumed to be the reason why Joseph was unable to acquire the plates at that time.[32]

As discussed by Michael Quinn, rumor that Alvin was to accompany Joseph may have given rise to rumors that Alvin's corpse had been exhumed to fill the angel's directive.[33] Joseph's treasure-seeking companions would have recognized the necessity of following their spiritual guide's instructions exactly, even to the point of bringing his oldest brother's dead body to the digging site. In addition, Freemasons also had a legend that would match such a seemingly grisly action. The 1726 Graham manuscript details a tradition that Noah's sons, Shem, Ham, and Japheth, went to their father's grave to try to find something that would lead them to "the vertuable secret." Finding nothing but the dead body, they "took a

---

29. Oliver, 93–94.

30. "History, circa June 1839–circa 1841 [Draft 2]," 7. See also Eber D. Howe, *Mormonism Unvailed: Or, a Faithful Account of that Singular Imposition and Delusion, from Its Rise to the Present Time*, 242. "He then enquired when he *could* have them, and was answered thus: come one year from this day, and bring with you your oldest brother, and you shall have them." Willard Chase Statement, 1833, in Vogel, *Early Mormon Documents*, 2:67; Fayette Lapham Interview, in Vogel, *Early Mormon Documents*, 1:460; and Lorenzo Saunders Interview, in Vogel, *Early Mormon Documents*, 2:159.

31. Both Joseph and Alvin had an "oldest brother," a son of Joseph Smith Sr. and Lucy Mack, who had died in infancy.

32. "[I]t was not at that time made known to him but he must take his oldest brother & go <to> the spot & he could obtain them." Lorenzo Saunders Interview, in Vogel, *Early Mormon Documents*, 2:159. See also Jessee, "Joseph Knight's Recollection," 30: "Joseph says, 'when can I have it?' The answer was the 22nt Day of September next if you Bring the right person with you. Joseph says, 'who is the right Person?' The answer was 'your oldest Brother.' But before September came his oldest brother died. Then he was disappointed and did not know what to do."

33. Quinn, *Early Mormonism and the Magic World View*, 160–61.

grip at a finger," which came away from joint to joint, wrist to elbow. They next "reared up the body," and took it upon the five points of fellowship:

> setting foot to foot knee to knee Breast to breast Cheeck to cheeck and hand to back and cryed out help o father as if they had said o father of heaven help us now for our earthly father cannot so Laid down the dead body again and not knowing what to do—so one said here is yet mar[r]ow in this bone and the second said but a dry bone and the third said it stinketh.[34]

From this experience, the three were said to have formulated a secret name as a stand-in for the true name they were unable to recover. This legend parallels the Master Mason degree when the initiate, imitating Hiram Abiff, is symbolically raised from the grave in an attempt to gain a secret name or word. In combination with esoteric practices, it resulted in early speculative Masonry exhibiting a strain of necromancy.[35] Thus, Freemasons in New York, hearing that Joseph Smith Jr. had been told by an angel to bring his oldest brother to their next meeting, might have assumed that he would dig up the body either to perform a ritual or obtain a token.

Within one week of Joseph Jr.'s 1824 visit to the hill, his father found it necessary to publish a public announcement denying Alvin's body had been disinterred. It ran for six weeks in the local newspaper:

> TO THE PUBLIC: Whereas reports have been industriously put in circulation, that my son *Alvin* had been removed from the place of his internment and dissected, which reports, every person possessed of human sensibility must know, are peculiarly calculated to harrow up the mind of a parent and deeply wound the feelings of relations—therefore, for the purpose of ascertaining the truth of such reports, I, with some of my neighbors, this morning repaired to the grave, and removing the earth, found the body which had not been disturbed. This method is taken for the purpose of satisfying the minds of those who may have heard the report, and of informing those who have put it in circulation, that it is earnestly requested they would desist therefrom; and that it is believed by some, that they have been stimulated more by a desire to injure th[e] reputation of certain persons than a philanthropy for the peace and welfare of myself and friends. JOSEPH SMITH. Palmyra, Sept. 25th, 1824.[36]

Despite his death, Alvin still played an important part in the recovery of the plates. As the eldest of the Smith sons, Alvin had also participated in treasure-seeking and demonstrated a great concern for obtaining the plates.[37] His last words to Joseph Jr., according to their mother, were telling him to "do everything that lays in your power to obtain the records" and to "be faithful in receiving instruction and keeping every commandment that is given you."[38] For a time after Alvin's death, the

---

34. Harry Carr, *The Early Masonic Catechisms*, 93.

35. Harry Carr, *The Freemason at Work*, 384–85.

36. Joseph Smith [Sr.], "To the Public," 3.

37. See, for example, Lorenzo Saunders Interview, 12 Nov. 1884, in Vogel, *Early Mormon Documents*, 2:153–54.

38. Anderson, *Lucy's Book*, 352–53.

family could scarcely bear speaking about the plates;[39] however, the time eventually came to move forward with what was required of them. In no case did Lucy express concern that the plates would be unobtainable following the death of Alvin.

Joseph returned to the hill on the autumn equinox, September 22, 1824, exactly one year after the angel had first directed him to that location.[40] In Masonry, the equinox is observed as a day of waning light and the descent of the soul from its spiritual home into incarnation. As Willard Chase describes the meeting, when Joseph demanded the book, the "spirit of the prophet who wrote the book" enquired for his brother. Joseph replied that he was dead. Chase continues: "The spirit then commanded him to come again, in just one year, and bring a man with him. On asking who the man might be, he was answered that he would know him when he saw him."[41] With only a few obvious options before him, Joseph may have believed that Samuel T. Lawrence, his treasure-seeking partner and benefactor, was the man alluded to by the spirit.

1825 Visit: Treasure Seeing

In 1825, Joseph Smith was still immersed in many of his treasure-seeking expeditions, including his stint with local Freemason, Josiah Stowell, who had been digging to discover a silver mine. Though official church history, including that of Smith's, would come to downplay it, the "magical world view" permeated the minds of Smith, his family, neighbors, and associates.[42] Porter Rockwell, a childhood friend of Smith, was still telling colorful tales of his associations with the Smiths when he lived in Utah at age 79.[43] There, Rockwell told stories of the

---

39. Anderson, 356.

40. The autumnal equinox for 1825, 1826, and 1827 was actually on 23 September, but almanacs of the day had the date as 22 September.

41. Willard Chase Statement, 1833, in Vogel, *Early Mormon Documents*, 2:67–68. Lorenzo Saunders said that Smith was told another would be appointed to replace Alvin and accompany him to the hill and that Smith chose Samuel Lawrence. See also Lorenzo Saunders Interview, 1884, in Vogel, *Early Mormon Documents*, 2:132. Joseph Knight recounted that the "personage" told Joseph that "the 22nt Day of September nex he mite have the Book if he Brot with him the right person. Joseph says, 'who is the right Person?' The answer was you will know. Then he looked in his glass and found it was Emma Hale, Daughter of old Mr Hail of Pensylvany, a girl that he had seen Before, for he had Bin Down there Before with me." Knight makes it clear that Joseph and Emma married several months later. Thus, his account combines the events of the 1824 visit those of 1826. Joseph and Emma did not marry until January of 1827. See Jessee, "Joseph Knight's Recollection of Early Mormon History," 31.

42. See Quinn's excellent discussion of Smith's visits to Cumorah between 1823 and 1827 in Quinn, *Early Mormonism and the Magical World View*, 158–67.

43. At this age, Rockwell was described as "a bronzed seafaring looking man, with long hair tucked behind his ears, in which he wears little gold rings." Norman R. Bowen, *A Gentile Account of Life in Utah's Dixie: Elizabeth Kane's St. George Journal*, 73.

failures and ultimate success in obtaining the plates in images that "sounded like the German legends of the demons of the Harz Mountains." Elizabeth Kane, chronicler of Rockwell's narrative, mused that religious excitement coexisted with searches for "the phantom treasures of Captain Kidd." She said, "Even in places like Cumorah where the primeval forest still grew undisturbed . . . the most sober settlers of the district . . . stole out to dig of moonlight nights, carefully effacing the traces of their ineffectual work before creeping home to bed." As a boy of twelve, Rockwell frequently heard his mother and Lucy Mack Smith comparing notes on treasure-seeking expeditions, telling "how the spades often struck the iron sides of the treasure chest, and how it was charmed away, now six inches this side, now four feet deeper, and again completely out of reach."[44]

There is some confusion as to whom Smith brought with him on this second return to the hill. It stands to reason that he would choose a fellow treasure seer to assist him in the endeavor that had twice been unsuccessful. In a near-contemporary account, Willard Chase proposed that Samuel T. Lawrence, one of the members of the Smith's company of money-diggers,[45] accompanied Smith to the hill. The somewhat garbled recitation leaves some doubt as to whether it was Lawrence who told Smith to look into his seer stone and "see if there was not a large pair of specks with the plates." Another reading could portray Smith as planting the suggestion in Lawrence's mind that there might be a pair of spectacles under the ground, suitable for translating the Book of Mormon. Regardless, Lawrence cautioned Smith not "to let these plates be seen for about two years, as it would make a great disturbance in the neighborhood."[46]

Several sources confirm this choice of escort. Joseph Knight Sr. intimated that Lawrence "had Bin to the hill and knew about the things in the hill."[47] While these witnesses suggest that Lawrence accompanied Smith to Cumorah in 1825, other accounts leave it in question. Lorenzo Saunders remembered that "Joseph chose Samuel Lawrence. But he did not go." Michael Quinn reconciles these statements by suggesting that Smith took Lawrence to the hill at an earlier date than September 22 of that year.[48]

---

44. Bowen, 74.

45. See Henry Harris Statement, 1833, in Vogel, *Early Mormon Documents*, 2:76, for an example of a description of this group. Harris calls them Joseph's "Gold Bible Company" and intimates that they were called by this name before the discovery of the Book of Mormon plates. Most, if not all, of this group were also Freemasons.

46. "Lawrence asked him if he had ever discovered any thing with the plates of gold; he said no: he then asked him to look in his stone, to see if there was any thing with them. He looked, and said there was nothing; he told him to look again, and see if there was not a large pair of specks with the plates; he looked and soon saw a pair of spectacles, the same with which Joseph says he translated the Book of Mormon." Willard Chase Statement, 1833, in Vogel, *Early Mormon Documents*, 2:68.

47. Jessee, "Joseph Knight's Recollection of Early Mormon History," 32.

48. Quinn, *Early Mormonism and the Magic World View*, 162.

Chase's recollection may reinforce this possibility, and it suggests that Smith may have brought another older brother to the hill as a replacement for Alvin:

> I believe, some time in 1825, Hiram Smith (brother of Joseph Smith) came to me, and wished to borrow the same stone [the seer stone from the Chase well], alledging that they wanted to accomplish some business of importance, which could not very well be done without the aid of the stone.[49]

The "business of importance" was almost certainly again locating the plates' hillside repository. In his 1859 interview, Martin Harris said that the Smith family had all witnessed that he had found the plates by means of the "stone which was dug from the well of Mason Chase, twenty-four feet from the surface."[50]

The Masonic characteristics of the record's depository may have been tied to the angel's directive to bring an older companion. At the 1824 visit, Smith was only eighteen years old, three years short of being able to be initiated into the mysteries of Freemasonry. His brother Alvin, on the other hand, could have become a Mason as early as February of 1819. Hyrum, the only "older brother" remaining by 1824, was likely initiated that year, three years after he became eligible. It may be that the underground hiding place, with its stone masonry and pillars, presented a message in itself that would be communicated to a worthy Master Mason.[51]

Thus, it is possible that Joseph and Hyrum Smith, with the Chase seer stone in hand, made the third annual visit to Cumorah as required by the angel. Further details of this visit remain unknown, other than that the young seer was again deferred to the following year's visit. Still lacking the longed-for record, the Smith family's attention began to focus on raising the final payment for their Manchester farm, which was nearly due.

1826 Visit: Finding a Wife

Joseph Smith first met his future wife, Emma Hale, in the month following his 1825 visit to Cumorah while engaged in treasure-seeking activities in Harmony, Pennsylvania. The next year he made his third return to the hill alone and was probably a bit despondent. According to Joseph Knight, the angelic keeper of the sacred record told Smith that if he would "do right," he would obtain the plates the next year.[52] However, the angel told Smith that in order to acquire them he must first be married.[53]

---

49. Willard Chase Statement, 1833, in Vogel, *Early Mormon Documents*, 2:66.

50. Martin Harris Interview with Joel Tiffany, 1859, in Vogel, *Early Mormon Documents*, 2:302.

51. At this point, it is unknown if Samuel Lawrence was a Master Mason. However, he was married to the sister of a Mason, Abner Cole, and many of his treasure-seeking associates were also Freemasons.

52. Jessee, "Joseph Knight's Recollection of Early Mormon History," 32.

53. "[A]n angel appeared and told him he could not get the plates until he was married, and that when he saw the woman that was to be his wife, he should know her, and she would know

Emma Hale's cousins Joseph and Hiel Lewis attested that "when Smith saw Miss Emma Hale, he knew that she was the person" who must come with him. She had been designated a "key" who would later help him make sense of his experiences in a religious context. The cousins scandalized readers with a lurid tale of a bleeding ghost with a long beard who told Smith that he could not get the plates by himself.[54] The ghost's throat was cut "ear to ear" in a parody of a Masonic penalty, perhaps indicating that what the spirit was teaching must not be revealed. The two cousins defamed Smith as lacking spiritual motivation during his quest to obtain the golden plates, but they did say that the "embryo prophet . . . claimed to possess the supernatural power of second sight."[55] Second sight was an ability claimed by magicians, but toward the beginning of the seventeenth century, it began to increasingly be identified with Freemasonry. Early Rosicrucian Henry Adamson wrote of this prophetic gift:

> For we be brethren of the rosie cross;
> We have the mason-word and second sight,
> Things for to come we can foretell aright.[56]

The Mason word, second sight, and prophecy are firmly related in the person of Joseph Smith.

Smith's official account describes the persecution that followed him due to his assertion that he had seen a vision. Thus, he said, "my wife's father's family were very much opposed to our being married. I was therefore under the necessity of taking her elsewhere, so we went and were married at the house of Squire Tarbill, in South Bainbridge, Chenango County, New York."[57] The marriage took place on January 18, 1827, and the young couple proceeded to the home of Smith's parents to set up housekeeping.

1827 Visit: The Three Ruffians

In 1827, the year that Joseph Smith was finally able to recover the plates, he was an adult of twenty-one, the age of majority when a man may join the Masonic

him." Henry Harris Statement, 1833, in Vogel, *Early Mormon Documents*, 2:76. Harris does not distinguish between the visits to Cumorah in his statement. See also Lorenzo Saunders Interview, 1884, in Vogel, *Early Mormon Documents*, 2:132: "Joe said in our house to my mother, the angel said he must get him a wife and take her and go and get the plates."

54. Joseph and Hiel Lewis Statements, 1879, in Vogel, *Early Mormon Documents*, 4:304. This account was published on the exact death date of their cousin, Emma Smith. According to another late source, Joseph Smith Sr. described the guardian of the treasure in similar terms: he was "a very large and tall man . . . dressed in an ancient suit of clothes, and the clothes were bloody." Fayette Lapham Interview, in Vogel, *Early Mormon Documents*, 1:458.

55. Hiel Lewis Rejoinder, June 4, 1879, in Vogel, *Early Mormon Documents*, 4:308.

56. Henry Adamson, *The Muses Threnodie; or Mirthful Mournings on the Death of Master Gall*, 84.

57. "History, 1838–1856, volume A-1 [23 December 1805–30 August 1834]," 8.

fraternity. September 22 was both the autumnal equinox and the night of a full moon. The esoteric significance of these coincidences, as well as the celebration of a Jewish holy day, the feast of Rosh Hashanah,[58] were equally important to Freemasons. Brigham Young later declared that the night Smith found the plates "there was a wonderful light in the heavens." Living about seventy miles distance from Cumorah, Young had observed the celestial display directly for hours:

> There were lances darting and the sound of cannon and armies just at hand, and flashes of light, though there were no clouds. Joseph's discovery was in the papers directly, and everywhere people remarked the coincidence, because for hundreds of miles they had been out watching like myself.[59]

Heber C. Kimball also claimed to have witnessed the miraculous event: according to his autobiography, it involved "a white smoke" arising on the horizon, growing "clear and transparent of a bluish cast" to reveal an army on the move "in platoons."[60]

Joseph Knight Sr. recalled that "Joseph was some afraid of Samuel Lawrence that he might be a trouble to him." For several reasons, Lawrence felt he should have a share in any financial gains the golden plates might bring. Therefore, prior to his trip to the hill, Smith sent his father to Lawrence's residence "to see if there was any signs of his going away that night."[61] In her 1853 memoir, Lucy Mack Smith recalled her husband's visit to the Lawrence house. Members of the "Gold Bible Company," a band of treasure-seekers who had been involved with Smith in the past, were present. They had sent for a "conjurer," probably Luman Walters, to help them discover where the plates were buried. Lucy wrote that her husband "could overhear their conversation," and they were "devising many plans and schemes to find 'Joe Smith's gold bible.'" Reportedly, Lawrence's wife warned her husband that the elder Smith was listening. "'Sam, Sam' said she. 'You are cutting your own throat.' At this, the conjuror bawled out at the top of his voice, 'I am not afraid of anybody—we will have them plates in spite of Joe Smith, or all the devils in hell.'"[62]

As well as bringing his wife, Smith was given specific instruction on how he should be dressed. He was to wear an "old-fashioned" suit of black clothing and procure a black horse with which to appear at the hill.[63] This attire seems more suited to a man attending a Masonic event than one who is to be out treasure-digging. Michael Quinn identifies it as a style popularized when US President

---

58. This Jewish feast commemorates Moses's reception of the Law from Mt. Sinai.

59. Bowen, *Elizabeth Kane's Journal*, 75.

60. Heber C. Kimball journal, quoted in "History of Brigham Young," 472.

61. Jessee, "Joseph Knight's Recollection of Early Mormon History," 33.

62. Anderson, *Lucy's Book*, 380–81.

63. Lorenzo Saunders Interview, 1884, in Vogel, *Early Mormon Documents*, 2:132; See also Willard Chase Statement, 1833, in Vogel, *Early Mormon Documents*, 2:66–67. Chase specifies that the clothes and horse must be black; however, he locates this information with his description of the 1823 visit.

James Madison attended his inauguration "dressed in a plain suit of black broad-cloth with a single-breasted coat and waistcoat with flaps, in the old fashion."[64]

Following directions he had been given, Smith "arose early in the morning, and took a one horse wagon . . . and, together with his wife, repaired to the hill which contained the book." Leaving Emma by the road in the wagon, he walked about 600 feet up the hill.[65]

Smith's history says that the heavenly messenger delivered the plates to him with a charge that he "should be responsible for them" and "use all [his] endeavours to preserve them." He soon discovered the reason why he had received such strict instructions: "[F]or no sooner was it known that I had them than the most strenious [sic] exertions were used to get them from me. Every stratagem that could be invented was resorted to for that purpose."[66]

To keep the book safe after he had removed it from the ground, Smith wrapped it up and placed it in "a cavity in a birch log" about two or three miles from his home.[67] He then went to the town of Macedon to work. After about ten days, he "became concerned about the plates." Willard Chase reported, "He hired a horse, and went home in the afternoon, staid long enough to drink one cup of tea, and then went for his book, found it safe, took off his frock, wrapt it round it, put it under his arm and run all the way home, a distance of about two miles."[68] On his return home, carrying the forty- to sixty-pound plates under his arm, Smith was attacked in the woods. Expressed in a manner reminiscent of the Hiram Abiff legend, his mother's telling of the encounter has him given three blows by a set of ruffians who came after the treasure. In the Masonic legend, as the construction of Solomon's Temple was nearing completion, three fellowcraft Masons from the workforce ambushed Hiram, the master craftsman, one evening. Each challenged him in turn, demanding the secrets of a Master Mason. At each refusal to divulge the information, his assailant struck him with a Mason's tool.[69]

The first blow to Smith took place as he "struck through the timber where there was a large windfall to cross." As he jumped over a fallen log, "a man spran[g] up and gave him a heavy blow with a gun." Being a young and sturdy fellow, Smith soon leveled the attacker to the ground. At the top of his speed, he ran about a half mile farther, where he was struck a second blow by another man. He was able to bring this foe down as well, and he ran on. But before he arrived home, "he was accosted the 3 time with a severe stroke with a gun." As he

64. Quinn, *Early Mormonism and the Magic World View*, 166.

65. Willard Chase Statement, 1833, in Vogel, *Early Mormon Documents*, 2:71.

66. "History, circa June 1839–circa 1841 [Draft 2]," 8.

67. Anderson, *Lucy's Book*, 385.

68. Willard Chase Statement, 1833, in Vogel, *Early Mormon Documents*, 2:71.

69. These tools often differ according to the jurisdiction, but in William Morgan's exposure they were "the twenty-four-inch gauge," "the square," and "the common gavel." See William Morgan, *Illustrations of Masonry by One of the Fraternity Who has Devoted Thirty Years to the Subject*, 72.

defended himself with his fists, he dislocated his thumb. When he finally came within sight of home, "he threw himself down in the a corner of the fence to recover his breath and as soon as he could get on he rose and finished his race for the house—where he arrived altogether speechless from fright and exhaustion."[70]

Now that they had been recovered, Smith set about translating the plates' contents into English, with the assistance of his wife and other scribes, "who wrote as he dictated." One of his followers noted that "through much difficulty, on account of persecution and poverty, he translated it by degrees."[71]

Truth from the Earth

In what would later become the official church history, Joseph Smith described the discovery he made on the Hill Cumorah. The plates lay deposited in a stone box, he said, under a stone of considerable size. "This stone was thick and rounding in the middle on the upper side, and thinner towards the edges, so that the middle part of it was visible above the ground, but the edge all round was covered with earth." Clearing away the remaining accumulated debris, the young Smith "obtained a lever," which he "fixed under the edge of the stone, and with a little exertion raised it up."[72]

The Royal Arch Degree is in part a matching story of the recovery of a holy treasure. As recounted in exposures of the day, three Mason companions of noble lineage return from Babylonian captivity for the express purpose of rebuilding the holy city and restoring its sacred temple. The three are sent to Mount Moriah to begin the work of "removing the rubbish"[73] preparatory to the work of restoration, and they are tasked by the Grand Council at Jerusalem to observe and preserve anything of significance relating to Solomon's original temple. After days of fruitless efforts, the companions discover "what seemed to be a rock, but on striking it with a crow, it gave a hollow sound."[74] Redoubling their efforts, they remove the rubbish from around the stone and discover that it is an arch with a curiously wrought stone at its crown.[75] Using the crow, the companions "with great difficulty . . . succeeded in removing" the stone, the keystone of the arch.[76] Beneath it, the workmen find a sacred treasure—Enoch's gold plate upon which was inscribed the Lost Word. Knowledge of this Masonic legend was ubiquitous

---

70. Anderson, *Lucy's Book*, 385–86.

71. Corrill, *A Brief History of the Church of Christ of Latter Day Saints*, 12. Note that the Book of Abraham was also translated "by degrees" (see Chapter 7).

72. "History, circa June 1839–circa 1841 [Draft 2]," 7.

73. David Bernard, *Light on Masonry: A Collection of All the Most Important Documents on the Subject of Speculative Free Masonry*, 136.

74. Bernard, 136.

75. Carlile, *Manual of Freemasonry*, 2:16.

76. F. de P. Castells, *Historical Analysis of the Holy Royal Arch Ritual*, 47. See also Carlile, *Manual of Freemasonry*, 2:17.

both within and without Masonry. Its details were especially well known in the United States, where its strong Christian character was particularly cherished.

In common with the Royal Arch tradition that it echoes,[77] one perceives elements of Smith's own struggles to "remove the dirt and rubbish" in his life, to confront those flaws he felt marred his own character, and to bring forth truth from the earth—in other words, to recover from deep within himself something true, authentic, and holy. John Sheville and James Gould's monitorial *Guide to the Royal Arch Chapter* uses language that Mormons would later claim as their own in referring to truth from the Book of Mormon being buried in the earth:

> The Royal Arch Mason cannot fail to learn further from the diligent use of these implements, that he must search to the very foundations which underlie all human knowledge if he would find that great object of all his earthly pilgrimage—the end of his labors. Truth may be buried for a time under a cumbrous mass of error; the ruins of a better civilization may have been thrown down upon it; its very existence may be forgotten, but the diligent seeker after it will surely find it.
>
> > "Truth crushed to earth shall rise again,
> > Th' eternal years of GOD are here."[78]

Reports by others of the recovery of the stone box that contained the Book of Mormon deepen and expand the tale to include additional elements from the Masonic legend. Smith depicted the box as being "formed by laying stones together in some kind of cement." In the bottom of the box, two stones were laid "crossways . . . and on these stones lay the plates and the other things with them."[79] In the pages of the *Latter Day Saints Messenger and Advocate*, Oliver Cowdery described an arched stone that overlaid the cemented box. The box was large enough to hold a breastplate, from which "arose three small pillars, composed of the same description of cement used on the edges; and upon these three pillars were placed the record."[80] Writing in 1839, Apostle Orson Pratt provided an account similar to that published by Cowdery, mentioning the cement, breastplate, and pillars. The whole was overlaid with "a crowning stone, a small part of which was visible when he first visited the spot."[81]

---

77. In fact, the story of the recovery of the Book of Mormon may be appreciated not only as an echo of Masonic tradition but also as Smith's own expansion and reenvisioning of the Masonic allegory of the "recovery of That Which Was Lost" as expressed in Royal Arch Masonry.

78. John Sheville and James L. Gould, *Guide to the Royal Arch Chapter: A Complete Monitor for Royal Arch Masonry*, 168.

79. "History, circa June 1839–circa 1841 [Draft 2]," 7.

80. Cowdery, "Letter to W. W. Phelps," 196–97.

81. Orson Pratt Statement, in Vogel, *Early Mormon Documents*, 1:148. Joseph Smith's mother provided a comparable account. She recalled that the angel instructed, "[T]he record is on a side hill on the Hill of Cumorah 3 miles from this place[;] remove the Grass and moss and you will find a large flat stone[;] pry that up and you will find the record under it laying on 4 pillars <of cement>—then the angel left him." Anderson, *Lucy's Book*, 336.

Smith's description of the plates' hiding place featured certain elements that clearly stood out in the minds of his family and close associates. These details were striking and powerful for those familiar with Masonic lore: the recovery of a golden treasure or long-lost sacred book concealed by an ancient prophet on a holy mount, deposited beneath an arched stone, and resting upon pillars. Each of these elements skillfully enhances and amplifies the Masonic themes of loss and restoration inherent in the legendary history of the Craft. At once, pillars suggest a divine repository and remind Freemasons of the expression "in strength He shall establish His kingdom forever." The threefold pillars—representative of the Trinity—additionally hint at the idea that God himself has preserved the record and provided the means of translation. The perfect cubic stone, finished with cement, alludes to the divine nature of both what that stone contains[82] and the love of God which preserved it.[83]

The keystone in Masonry suggests the Word of God, both in the sense of the person of Jesus and the scriptural record he embodies. These elements, and the Masonic legend behind them, pointed to themes of recovery and restoration, and they strongly hinted at precisely what that restoration would entail. "I told the brethren," Smith later declared, "that the Book of Mormon was the most correct of any book on earth, and the key stone of our religion, and a man would get nearer to God by abiding by its precepts, than by any other book."[84] Duncan Moore explained the keystone's significance to Freemasonry similarly:

> The keystone is important both in architectural terms because it is locking the other stones together to support the weight above it and in symbolic terms because it is, in the words of the Mark Degree, '*The most important stone in the building*.'[85]

Masonic illustrations have preserved this symbolism by placing a book—representing the Book of the Law—above the keystone of an arch. Another well-known image shows Craft Masonry's conception of the vertex of an arch: the point within a circle bounded by two straight lines. This allegorical concept is flanked by the two "Saints John" and surmounted by the Book of the Law.

---

82. "The *Rough Ashler* is a stone as taken from the quarry in its rude and natural state. The *Perfect Ashler* is a stone made ready for the hands of the workman, to be adjusted by the tools of the Fellow Craft. . . . By the *Rough Ashler* we are reminded of our rude and imperfect state by nature; by the *Perfect Ashler*, that state of perfection at which we hope to arrive, by a virtuous education, our own endeavors, and the blessing of God." Joshua Bradley, *Some of the Beauties of Free-masonry*, 58; emphasis in original.

83. In speculative Freemasonry, cement is important as a representation of charity, or the love of God.

84. "History, 1838–1856, volume C-1 [2 November 1838–31 July 1842]," The Joseph Smith Papers, 1255.

85. Duncan Moore, *In Search of That Which Was Lost: True Symbolism of the Royal Arch*, 57; emphasis in original.

The Book of the Law and the Golden Plates

Masonic legend teaches that deity appeared to the prophet Enoch "in the shape of a bright, golden triangle" and said to him, "Enoch, thou hast longed to know my true name. Arise and follow me, and thou shalt know it." The golden triangle had bright rays of the sun coming from it and was thenceforth known as the Delta of Enoch.[86] In commemoration of this vision, the Masonic Enoch and his son Methuselah built a temple underground and dedicated it to God. This temple consisted of nine brick vaults, situated perpendicularly beneath each other. In the crown of each arch, he left a narrow aperture, closed with a square stone. Modeled upon the vision that he had, Enoch created a triangle made out of pure gold. Placing it on a cubical pedestal of white marble, known thereafter as the "stone of foundation," he deposited the whole within the deepest arch. When this subterranean building was completed, he made a door of stone and attached to it a ring of iron by which it might be occasionally raised. He then placed it over the opening of the uppermost arch and covered it over so that the aperture could not be discovered. Enoch himself was only permitted to enter it once a year. Upon the death of Enoch, Methuselah, and Lamech, and the destruction of the world by the deluge, all knowledge of this temple and the sacred treasure that it contained was lost. In later times, it would be accidentally discovered when King Solomon was engaged in the erection of a temple on the same spot.[87]

According to George Oliver, the plate of gold was "in the form of an equilateral triangle, each of whose sides was eighteen inches." Enoch had also enriched it "with precious stones, and encrusted it on a triangular agate of the same dimensions. On this plate he engraved the ineffable characters he had seen in his vision."[88] A similar description is offered in David Bernard's exposé of the Knights of the Ninth Arch degree, where the initiate is asked:

Q. What is the Delta?

---

86. Masonic author F. de P. Castells described early Royal Arch ritual and its use of Enoch's triangle to represent the Word of God—Jesus—or the scriptures incarnate. "The Triangle of Light," he explains, "has its counterpart on a plate of pure gold; but while on the latter it is enclosed in a circle, the Greater Triangle itself is conceived as surrounded by the Companions in the Chapter." These brothers arrayed themselves into a circle representing "the Sphere of the Universe" and "a type of God." He continues: "On the plate of gold there is an upright Triangle; a second Triangle is needed to form the Star and Seal of Solomon, but this is outside the Triangle of Light. The two form an antithesis, one pointing downwards the other upwards, the two being harmoniously interlaced." F. de P. Castells, *Antiquity of the Holy Royal Arch: The Supreme Degree in Freemasonry*, 142–43.

87. Moore, *In Search of That Which Was Lost*, 139–43.

88. George Oliver, *The Antiquities of Freemasonry; Comprising Illustrations of the Five Grand Periods of Masonry from the Creation of the World to the Dedication of King Solomon's Temple*, 89–90.

A. The triangle of gold, enriched with precious stones and affording great light, and upon which was engraved by Enoch that great and mysterious name, Jehovah.[89]

Masonic authors' descriptions of the golden plate of Enoch bore similarities to the appearance, unearthing, repository, and purpose of Joseph Smith's golden plates, as described by his contemporaries. Masonic features in accounts describing the coming forth of the Book of Mormon continued to appear years later, such as in a magazine article by Fayette Lapham. Ostensibly an 1830 interview with Joseph Smith Sr., it was published forty years after the fact. This source is notable for its overt masonic connection. According to Lapham, Joseph Sr. told him that under the first golden plate (or "lid") lay the stone spectacles that would later be named the Urim and Thummim, and "on the next page were representations of all the masonic implements, as used by masons at the present day."[90]

Another secondhand account describes a "large iron ring" in the center of the stone box's lid, "into which a man could comfortably put his hand." Smith pulled upon this ring in an attempt to retrieve the plates on his first visit to the Hill Cumorah.[91] This, of course, calls to mind the aforementioned keystone in the uppermost arch of Enoch's underground temple that could be lifted by means of the ring of iron to uncover Enoch's triangular plate.

Similarities between the golden plate of Enoch and Joseph Smith's golden plates go far beyond simple physical correspondences; namely, they were both made of gold and found in stone enclosures under elevated mounts named, respectively, Moriah and Cumorah. On the one hand, Enoch's mountaintop vision of a triangular plate of gold is a veiled allusion to the *visio dei*—that beatific vision of God, which is both the end and summit of the Christian's journey and the promised reward of divine transformation and glorification.[92] On the other, it is a symbolic representation of the Word of God—both the written scripture restored to mankind and the glorious Person of Jesus Christ, the Living Word, restored to each believer. For Latter-day Saints, the story Joseph Smith related of his own experience on a mysterious mountaintop in upstate New York mirrors this Masonic legend. The Restoration is a symbol of the recovery of the God of Heaven's personal association with humankind—the long-lost Word of God in all its purity and power restored to the earth. In both cases, God demonstrated his approval of the prophet by bestowing upon him a peculiar revelation and the restoration of the Word.

---

89. Bernard, *Light on Masonry*, 205.

90. Fayette Lapham Interview, in Vogel, *Early Mormon Documents*, 1:462–63.

91. "Joe lay hold of the ring to pull it out and get it up; but there was no moving to it." John Murdock's Sidney Rigdon Account, in Vogel, *Early Mormon Documents*, 1:49.

92. "Beloved, now are we the sons of God, and it doth not yet appear what we shall be: but we know that, when he shall appear, we shall be like him; for we shall see him as he is. And every man that hath this hope in him purifieth himself, even as he is pure" (1 Jn. 3:2–3).

Urim and Thummim: A Masonic Key

In his history, Joseph Smith recounted the angel's prophecy given
to him during his evening vision in
September 1823. God had prepared
a means of translating this restored
scriptural record: "[T]here were two
stones in silver bows and these put into
a breast plate . . . deposited with the
plates, and that was what constituted
seers in ancient or former times."[93]
Described as "interpreters" in the Book
of Mormon record, the Prophet would
come to call this divine key the "Urim
and Thummim." Joseph's brother
William Smith explained that when
wearing the breast plate and "by press-
ing the head a little forward, the rod
held the Urim and Thummim before
the eyes much like a pair of spectacles."
Because the instrument was too large
for Joseph's eyes, he sometimes resorted
to removing them from the breastplate
and "covering his eyes with a hat to exclude the light in part to prevent eye
strain."[94] Joseph continued this practice when he later used his seer stone
for translation.

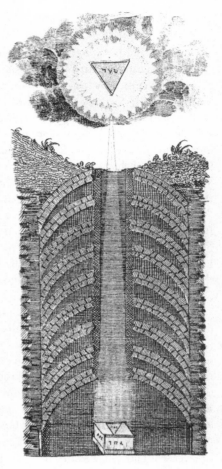

Enoch's Vision and Burial of the Golden
Plate, from Jeremy Cross, *True Masonic
Chart and Hieroglyphic Monitor*, 1820.

One of the most detailed descriptions of the interpreters was given by
Martin Harris. In 1859, Harris recalled
the object as "two stones set in a bow of silver . . . the stones were white, like
polished marble, with a few gray streaks." He provided the precise measurements
of "two inches in diameter, perfectly round, and about five-eighths of an inch
thick at the centre; but not so thick at the edges where they came into the bow."
The round bar of silver joining them was "about three-eighths of an inch in diameter, and about four inches long, which, with the two stones, would make eight
inches." Harris further cautioned that only those selected by God were allowed
to use the interpreters:

93. "History, circa June 1839–circa 1841 [Draft 2]," 5.
94. Interview with William Smith in J. W. A. Bailey, "The Urim and Thummim," 238.

I never dared to look into them by placing them in the hat, because Moses said that "no man could see God and live," and we could see anything we wished by looking into them; and I could not keep the desire to see God out of my mind. And beside, we had a command to let no man look into them, except by the command of God, lest he should "look aught and perish."[95]

Harris makes it clear that Joseph Smith used the Urim and Thummim to do more than translate the plates. For example, Harris says that Smith was told by the angel to look in the spectacles to be shown the man who would assist him. "That he did so, and he saw myself, Martin Harris, standing before him. That struck me with surprise," Harris recalled. "I told him I wished him to be very careful about these things. 'Well,' said he, 'I saw you standing before me as plainly as I do now.'"[96]

The objects constituting the Urim and Thummim are depicted slightly differently in these accounts. They are variously described as "crystal stones,"[97] "transparent stones, clear as crystal,"[98] white stones "like polished marble,"[99] "glasses,"[100] or simply "stones."[101] Smith's mother, Lucy Mack Smith, described them as "two smooth three-cornered diamonds set in glass, and the glasses were set in silver bows, which were connected with each other in much the same way as old fashioned spectacles."[102] The variation may be due to contemporary folklore surrounding seer stones. The words "diamond" or "glass" were local colloquialisms for seer stones, regardless of their appearance.[103]

After Harris's loss of the first group of translated manuscript pages, the "spectacles" were taken, and Smith began to use his chocolate-colored seer stone to translate the record (D&C 10:1).[104] He legitimized and biblically inflected this relic of folk magic by renaming it a "Urim and Thummim" as well, making it clear that the term was not reserved for the relics in the Israelite temple or the stone

---

95. Martin Harris Interview with Joel Tiffany, in Vogel, *Early Mormon Documents*, 2:305.

96. Martin Harris Interview with Joel Tiffany, in Vogel, *Early Mormon Documents*, 2:309.

97. "Questions Proposed to the Mormonite Preachers and Their Answers Obtained before the Whole Assembly at Julian Hall, Sunday Evening, August 5, 1832," 2.

98. Pratt, *A Interesting Account of Several Remarkable Visions, 1840*, 13.

99. Martin Harris Interview with Joel Tiffany, in Vogel, *Early Mormon Documents*, 2:305.

100. Jessee, "Joseph Knight's Recollection of Early Mormon History," 33.

101. Joseph Lewis and Hiel Lewis, "Mormon History: A New Chapter, About to be Published," 1.

102. Anderson, *Lucy's Book*, 379; Vogel, *Early Mormon Documents*, 1:328–29; Quinn, *Early Mormonism and the Magic World View*, 171. Fayette Lapham also described the eyes of the "spectacles" as being made "not of glass, but of diamond." See Vogel, *Early Mormon Documents*, 1:462.

103. Quinn, *Early Mormonism and the Magic World View*, 171.

104. Don Bradley has persuasively argued that the lost pages likely numbered more than 116 and that the figure was simply the number of pages that replaced them. Don Bradley, *The Lost 116 Pages: Reconstructing the Book of Mormon's Missing Stories*, 84–85.

Depiction of the Urim and Thummim by W. A. Bailey, early Mormon pioneer and first photographer in the Salt Lake Valley.

spectacles accompanying the plates.[105] Noting the inclusivity of the term, Orson Pratt later elaborated: "The Urim and Thummim is a stone or other substance sanctified and illuminated by the Spirit of the living God."[106] Metaphorically, anything that God touches is spiritually transformed. While Smith continued to receive revelation through the Urim and Thummim, he would eventually lay aside all tools of translation, because he himself had become the illuminated object through which revelation came. This process of divine alchemy is what the symbols of Freemasonry are meant to elucidate.

Religious reference books from the 1820s and 1830s contained comments about the biblical Urim and Thummim, but as Michael Quinn notes, "Joseph

---

105. Catherine L. Albanese, "The Metaphysical Joseph Smith," 70. See also Doctrine and Covenants 130:10–11: "Then the white stone mentioned in Revelation 2:17, will become a Urim and Thummim to each individual who receives one, whereby things pertaining to a higher order of kingdoms will be made known; and a white stone is given to each of those who come into the celestial kingdom, whereon is a new name written, which no man knoweth save he that receiveth it. The new name is the key word."

106. Orson Pratt, [Eight Pamphlets on the First Principles of the Gospel], 72.

Smith's description of the Urim and Thummim's revelations to him was inconsistent with the scholarship of his time."[107] Instead, his portrayal of the translation process is more Masonic than ancient Hebrew. Contemporary Masonic writings show an interest in this biblical item and illuminate Smith's use of the implement. In New York City in 1820, the Reverend John Stanford's 1801 "Discourse on the Urim and Thummim" was in sufficient demand by Freemasons to justify an enlarged reprint.[108] Stanford, not a mason, reviewed for the members of Hiram Lodge No. 72 the various theories then current in regard to the composition and use of the Urim and Thummim, noting his personal disagreement with each. In particular, Stanford disagreed with the opinion that the Urim and Thummim were one and the same with the twelve jewels on the breastplate of Aaron.[109] This accords with Smith's description of the Urim and Thummim as separate and distinct from the breastplate. Stanford began by analyzing the name:

> By the Septuagint they are called "Manifestation and Truth." Jerom calls them "Doctrine and Judgment." The Seventy, "Declaration," nearly following the Septuagint. The Vulgate, "Doctrine and Truth," that is, instruction proceeding from the perfection of wisdom and truth. An excellent Hebrewist of the last century says, Urim is clear, lucid, transparent; Thummim, perfect, complete. But, to me, the best and most critical interpretation of these two Hebrew nouns, which are of the plural number, are "Lights and Perfections."[110]

As for usage, the reverend indicated "the specified use of the Urim and the Thummim was, *to inquire before the Lord.*"[111]

A few years later, George Oliver discussed the Urim and Thummim in his 1823 *Antiquities of Freemasonry*. Here, Oliver included this "mysterious power" as part of the "five distinguishing particulars" that made up the "principal excellence"

107. Quinn, *Early Mormonism and the Magic World View*, 170.

108. Kent L. Walgren, *Freemasonry, Anti-Masonry and Illuminism in the United States, 1734-1850: A Bibliography*, 1:373.

109. "[W]hatever they [the Urim and Thummim] were, they must have been entirely distinct from the twelve jewels. Besides, these could not have been placed *upon* the breastplate; for, the position of the twelve jewels set therein, formed twelve squares, which could not possibly admit either of a centre, or any space for their reception. The 15th and 16th verses of this chapter [Leviticus 8], will inform you of the materials, the size, and the construction of the breast-plate. It was not to be made of gold, or any other metal, but of *fine twined linen, embroidered work of fine colors*; and therefore might properly be called a breast-piece. *Four square it shall be, being doubled, a span shall be the length thereof, and a span shall be the breadth thereof.* A span is 10 inches, which is the estimated size of the breast of a man of an ordinary stature. The length was double; so that being folded, in the interior, it formed a sort of purse, or pocket, into which the Urim and the Thummim might be deposited; and, as easily taken out for the purposes intended." John Stafford, *A Discourse on the Urim and Thummim, Delivered Before Hiram Lodge, No. 72, at Mount Pleasant, Westchester County, on St. John's Day, Dec. 27*, 8; emphasis in original.

110. Stafford, 9.

111. Stafford, 13; emphasis in original.

of the Solomonic Temple. "It is clear," wrote Oliver, "that oracles were delivered by them." This information thus obtained "led the Israelites safely though so many dangers, and placed them at length in undisturbed possession of the Promised Land."[112] Oliver's discussion adds a possible reason for Smith's interest in the Urim and Thummim—its widely recognized Masonic conception as a power to deliver oracles would legitimize the Mormon scripture he was producing.

Further Masonic interest can be seen in William Hutchinson's *The Spirit of Masonry*. First published in 1775, its 1800 and 1810 New York editions enjoyed robust circulation among Masons and non-Masons in Smith's early environs.[113] In a chapter titled "The Secrecy of Masons," Hutchinson spoke of an ancient Jewish legend in which the Savior had taken the Urim and Thummim, containing "the mystic words, the TETRAGRAMMATON," from the foundation of the temple, and was said to carry it "concealed about him, whereby he was enabled to work his miracles."[114]

Later teachings by Latter-day Saint leaders on the Urim and Thummim show a clear Masonic influence. For example, in the *Times and Seasons*, W. W. Phelps speculated that Aaron's Urim and Thummim "was as old as Adam."[115] Likewise, Orson Pratt taught that Noah "had a Urim and Thummim by which he was enabled to discern all things pertaining to the ark, and its pattern."[116]

More important than any discussion of the biblical Urim and Thummim was the Royal Arch Masonic tradition of the "key" found with the stone box containing Enoch's gold plate. This key, subject of many Masonic lectures, is both literal and symbolic. Not only could it open the box, but it was also the means whereby the mysterious characters on the plate of gold might be read. In this Degree, the High Priest examines the box and finds a key with which he is able to read the words of the book inside. It is discovered to be the Book of the Law: "Long lost, now found, Holiness to the Lord."[117]

For Smith, that key was the Urim and Thummim—a revelatory device and a creative expansion upon a Masonic theme. Like the key in Masonry, it is found

112. Oliver, *Antiquities of Freemasonry*, 351–54.

113. The introduction to the 1987 edition of *The Spirit of Masonry* details its circulation in the United States and concludes that "clearly Hutchinson's readership was not restricted to just New York Freemasons" but to the general public as well. Trevor Stewart, introduction to *The Spirit of Masonry: In Moral and Elucidatory Lectures*, xxix.

114. William Hutchinson, *The Spirit of Masonry: In Moral and Elucidatory Lectures*, 179–80. See also George Oliver, *Signs and Symbols: Illustrated and Explained in a Course of Twelve Lectures on Freemasonry*, 30: "The modern Jews say that this word was engraven on the Rod of Moses, and thus he was enabled to work his miracles; and they add, that Jesus Christ stole the same word out of the Temple, and inserted it in his thigh, between the skin and the flesh, and by its sovereign potency performed all his wonders in Judea."

115. W. W. Phelps, "Despise not Prophesyings," 298.

116. Orson Pratt, May 18, 1873, *Journal of Discourses*, 16:50.

117. Bernard, *Light on Masonry*, 137–38.

within the box together with the mysterious characters upon the golden plates. His identification of the interpreters with that Masonic key is seen in Lucy Mack Smith's account of the discovery:

> "Mother," said [Joseph] "do not be uneasy. All is right. See here: I have got the key."
> . . . The thing which [I] spoke of that Joseph termed a Key was indeed nothing more nor less than a Urim and Thummim, by which the angel manifested those things to him that were shown him in vision, [and] by the which he could also at any time ascertain the approach of danger either to himself or the record and for this cause he kept these things constantly about his person.[118]

Masonry, Anti-Masonry, and the Book of Mormon

Some have wondered why, if the discovery of the golden plates was associated so closely with Masonry, there are elements in the Book of Mormon that seem anti-Masonic. For example, the phrase "secret combinations"—a pejorative commonly applied to nineteenth-century Freemasons, especially in the wake of the William Morgan affair—is used to describe secretive groups within the Book of Mormon that show marked similarities to popular images of the Masonic fraternity (Ether 8:18–25).[119] Their clandestine nature, claims of ancient origin, oaths to protect one another in iniquity, and commandeering of high offices are roundly condemned in the narrative, leading contemporaries to describe the book as anti-Masonic. However, those who promote this view seem not to have noticed the other positive Masonic correspondences throughout the book.[120] Conversely, those who discredit anti-Masonry in the Book of Mormon because of its implications of anachronisms in the narrative attempt to distance the work from any Masonic influence whatsoever.[121]

Both of those responses fail to recognize that the Book of Mormon "combinations" are put in their proper perspective when seen as textual evidence of "spurious Masons"—those who use their power as members of an oath-bound community for immoral purposes. As discussed in Chapter 1, the idea of a degenerated or spurious Freemasonry requiring purification and restoration came

---

118. Anderson, *Lucy's Book:* 378–79, 389; spelling and grammar regularized.

119. See Dan Vogel, "Mormonism's Anti-Masonick Bible," 18. Vogel points out that at the time of the Book of Mormon's publication, the term "secret combinations" referred almost exclusively to the Masonic fraternity. To illustrate, he uses a quotation from the Batavia, NY *Morgan Investigator* published on March 29, 1827: "BEWARE OF SECRET COMBINATIONS. These are the words of General George Washington. . . . Do not these words . . . point with an index that cannot be mistaken, to the society of Freemasons?"

120. Vogel, *Joseph Smith,* 242–43, 260, 270–72, 276–77, 280, 295–99, 350–52, 434–35, 552; Vogel, "Mormonism's 'Anti-Masonick Bible,'" 17–30; Dan Vogel, "Echoes of Anti-Masonry: A Rejoinder to Critics of the Anti-Masonic Thesis," 275–320.

121. See Nathan Oman, "'Secret Combinations': A Legal Analysis," 70; and Gregory L. Smith, "Cracking the Book of Mormon's 'Secret Combinations'?" 63–109.

to characterize Smith's own theological perspective. Rather than being merely anti-Masonic, the Book of Mormon presents a comprehensive view of two rival groups: the *authentic Masons* and the *spurious Masons*. Nephites—the followers and descendants of the founding prophet Lehi and his son Nephi—correspond with authentic Masons as described by Masonic writer George Oliver (see Chapter 1). They descend from a patriarchal priesthood line connected to Adam, Enoch, Noah, Abraham, and Moses, and they possess skills of metalworking, woodcraft, shipbuilding, and so on. In a symbolic act of true religion, they marked their arrival in their promised land by building a Solomonic Temple in the Masonic tradition (2 Ne. 5:16).

Throughout the Book of Mormon, the reader also encounters those who contend against the pure and righteous strain of Priesthood. These peoples are a corrupt version of the Nephites. They take oaths, form clandestine conspiracies, and cover the iniquity of their fellows. At their place of worship, they build a Babel-like tower, the Rameumptom, which for Latter-day Saint readers has long stood as a symbol of priestcraft (Alma 31:13–22).[122] Gadianton, leader of one of these secret societies, exemplifies political corruption and conspiracy, becoming a foil to the more righteous political and ecclesiastical leaders like Mosiah and Alma (Hel. 2:4–5).

In addition to these narrative parallels, several small references indicate the Masonic connection of these secret combinations. In one passage, Satan leads them by the neck with a "flaxen cord" into works of darkness "until he bindeth them with his strong cords forever" (2 Ne. 26:22). This implement is similar to the Masonic cable-tow. In a later passage, the Gadianton robbers are described as having "a lamb-skin about their loins" (paralleling the lamb-skin aprons worn by Masons) and being "dyed in blood" as they come forth in battle against the Nephites (3 Ne. 4:7). George Oliver's description of spurious Masons fits the actions of these groups: "Their rites of divine worship became fierce and bloody, implacable and severe; and this produced a corresponding change in the disposition of the heart."[123] Just as the spurious Masons are "a retrograde movement from original purity,"[124] the secret combinations of the Book of Mormon are a corruption of the Nephite priesthood order and act as a modern warning against spurious Masonry and a prefiguration that Smith would overcome the apostate Masonry of his day. Such a split between the true and spurious is acknowledged by Mormon apologist Stephen Smoot, who frames the Gadianton robbers of the Book of Mormon as a corruption of the temple priesthood:

> To summarize, Mormon found the Gadianton Robbers such a grave threat to the Nephites precisely because he saw them as reviving an ancient counterfeit temple

---

122. In the Book of Mormon narrative the Zoramites, who built the Rameumptom, later encouraged others to join with Gadianton's secret combination (3 Ne. 1:29).

123. Oliver, *Signs and Symbols*, viii.

124. Oliver, viii.

priesthood. They were more than political insurrectionists. To Mormon, they were no less than false priests of Satan who were fundamentally perverting the Nephite sense of holiness.[125]

In an environment ripe with debates over the value of Freemasonry, the Masonic elements in the Book of Mormon were immediately pointed to by both believers and critics of the new religion. In an article in the *Geauga Gazette* appearing in March of 1831, editor Billy Perkins wrote:

> The Mormon Bible is anti-masonic, and it is a singular truth that every one of its followers, so far as we are able to ascertain, are anti-masons. . . . Martin Harris is quoted as saying The Book of Mormon is "the Anti-masonick Bible," and that all who do not believe in it will be damned.[126]

However, the following week, Eber D. Howe, editor of the nearby *Painesville Telegraph*, took Perkins to task, saying that it was an error to believe that all who had embraced the Book of Mormon were anti-Masons.

> You appear not to be aware that some "zealous masons" and several "republican jacks," have beset Jo Smith for "more light." And perhaps you have yet to learn that the Mormon bible was printed and sent forth to the world, from a masonic printing office,[127] under a masonic, or some other injunction of secrecy. You may also discover a very striking resemblance between masonry and mormonism.[128]

Contemporary descriptions of the circumstances of the Book of Mormon's discovery make it evident that Latter-day Saints and those who wrote about them

---

125. Stephen Owen Smoot, "Gadiantonism as a Counterfeit Temple Priesthood." Citing Helaman 6:26–31, Smoot argues that "the 'secret oaths and covenants' employed by the Gadianton Robbers were as old as Adam and Eve"; "the 'works of darkness and abominations' employed by the Gadianton Robbers were also those of Cain; that is, 'secret murder'"; and that "these works of darkness and murder were the result of conspiracy with Satan." Compare this with George Oliver, who argued: "When men became numerous upon the earth, the evil spirit of darkness was very busily engaged in the corruption of their morals; and succeeded in working up the malevolent passions in the heart of Cain, *until he apostatized from Masonry*, and slew his brother Abel." Oliver, *Antiquities of Freemasonry*, 46; emphasis added.

126. William Perkins, "Antimasonic Religion," 1. See a colorful description of Martin Harris's barroom preaching that inspired this newspaper article in Michael W. Homer, *Joseph's Temples: The Dynamic Relationship Between Freemasonry and Mormonism*, 90–91.

127. The Smith family first chose to market the Book of Mormon to Grandin, a well-known pro-Masonic publisher. Due to Martin Harris's great "anti-Masonic Bible" pitch (March 1831), Grandin properly suggested Thurlow Weed, an anti-Masonic publisher in Rochester. Yet Smith chose to stick with Grandin, even though Weed would have published the book. Grandin had soured on what he then perceived to be an "anti-Masonic" project and required serious persuading to publish. Even then, he had an interest in allowing Obadiah Dogberry access to the Book of Mormon galleys on which he based his anti-Mormon *Book of Pukei*.

128. Eber D. Howe, "Our Neighbor-in-law," 2.

disagreed about whether the Book of Mormon was pro- or anti-Masonic. While Alexander Campbell, writing in 1831, suggested that the Book of Mormon answered all the great controversies of the day, including the "question of Freemasonry,"[129] it is less certain in the early press how the question was resolved. If Smith had indeed "decided" the question of Freemasonry, what conclusion were its readers to make?

In his book *The Refiner's Fire*, John L. Brooke agrees that "Smith's controversy was not with the fundamental ideals of Freemasonry." Instead, Brooke contends that Joseph Smith embraced the pure Masonic tradition but condemned aspects of the brotherhood he believed had fallen into disrepute and apostasy.[130] Smith's teaching and actions suggest a belief that just as there was a spurious and Satanic Masonry that was subverted to evil ends, there was also a true and Celestial Masonry that would be the vehicle for the ushering in of the Christian millennium.[131] Both of these Masonic iterations find space in the Book of Mormon. From this perspective, the newly restored "Book of the Law," long lost in the Americas but now found, was not condemning Freemasonry; instead, it spoke against "spurious Masonry," a corruption of the true Craft, the restoration of which the record itself presaged. This understanding challenges the common assumption that Smith drastically reversed his views of Masonry over time from being "anti-Masonic" during the period of the translation to fully adopting Masonry in the final years of his life. Instead, through the lens of the divisions of authentic and spurious Masonry, we can see that Smith's opinions about Masonry remained consistent.

---

129. According to Campbell, written in the Book of Mormon were "every error and almost every truth discussed in New York for the last ten years. He [Smith] decides all the great controversies—infant baptism, ordination, the trinity, regeneration, repentance, justification, the fall of man, the atonement, transubstantiation, fasting, penance, church government, religious experience, the call of the ministry, the general resurrection, eternal punishment, who may baptize, and *even the question of free masonry*, republican government; and the rights of man." Alexander Campbell, "Delusions," 93; emphasis added.

130. John L. Brooke, *The Refiner's Fire: The Making of Mormon Cosmology, 1644–1844*, 169.

131. This is supported by the fact that later Mormon leaders were fond of referring to the LDS Temple ritual as "Celestial Masonry." J.H. Beadle, *Life in Utah; Or, the Mysteries and Crimes of Mormonism*, 275, 499.

CHAPTER 6

MORMONISM'S MASONIC MIDRASH

Joy! the secret vault is found; full the sunbeam falls within,
Pointing, darkly underground, to the treasure we would win;
They have brought it forth to light, and again it cheers the earth;
All its leaves are purely bright, shining in their newest worth.

—The Royal Arch Song,
or Leaves of the Sacred Treasure Made Bright Again[1]

Like many of the prolific nineteenth-century Freemasons, Joseph Smith was fascinated by the ancient Jewish world. As he began producing his own scriptural texts, he dove into a readily available pool of Jewish antiquity collected by Masonic writers of the day. Much of Smith's oeuvre of religious literature can be described as "Mormon Masonic midrash" because of the simultaneous influence of both Jewish and Masonic writing.

In the Jewish tradition, midrash is an interpretive expansion of a text of scripture that transcends simple analysis of religious, legal, or moral teachings. It fills in gaps left in biblical narratives regarding events and personalities that are only briefly mentioned. The purpose of midrash was to resolve problems in the interpretation or harmonization of difficult passages of the Hebrew Bible. For example, the story of Lilith as Adam's first wife originated as an explanation for the two separate accounts of women being created in Genesis 1:27 and 2:21–23. Midrashic expansions of the biblical text resulted in oral as well as written supplements to the scriptural canon.[2]

Freemasonry borrowed vigorously from Jewish midrash, and the ancient tales were further embellished as they were brought into Masonic lore and ritual. Many of the Masonic degrees employed rewritten and mythologized biblical stories, furnished with layers of allegorical content to teach moral lessons. The Hiram Abiff legend is one such midrash, an expansion of the biblical account of building Solomon's Temple. As in the case of Jewish midrash, literal historicity in Masonic lore was not as important as the lessons supplied.

Following Masonic convention, Smith increasingly functioned as a prophet called to restore lost or corrupted tradition. He used creative textual expansions to fill in gaps in religious understanding, grounded upon his revelations and prophetic authority. His inspired reworking of texts was often intended to establish,

---

1. Robert Macoy, comp., *The Masonic Vocal Manual*, 63 [Hymn 71].
2. See examples in Anthony Hutchinson, "A Mormon Midrash? LDS Creation Narratives Reconsidered," 13–14.

extend, reframe, or legitimize new doctrines and concepts, or to clarify ideas that had been only partially elucidated. In doing so, Smith used the Masonic world-view to provide a mythical backdrop for the emerging LDS ritual tradition and to imbue the religion he was founding with meaning and appeal.

The Book of Mormon

Latter-day Saints accept the Book of Mormon as a prophetic restoration of long-lost ancient scripture. Whether or not one accepts the historicity of the Book of Mormon, the process of bringing forth this book was affected by several factors present in Joseph Smith's environment. While some have noted the presence of "a mixture of New Testament passages and nineteenth-century revivalisms" in the text,[3] it also contains elements included in the Masonic expansion of the Bible story. A mélange of Jewish midrash-like textual expansions and a reliance upon Masonic legendary history is readily observable.

Mormon and Masonic Exoduses

Notably, the Book of Mormon begins at the same period of time as the Royal Arch degree: the reign of biblical Zedekiah and the Babylonian captivity (1 Ne. 1:4). The Mormon narrative relates the adventures of the prophet Lehi, who preached repentance to the people of Zedekiah's Jerusalem and warned them of the desolating scourge and captivity to come. Prior to the arrival of Nebuchadnezzar's armies, Lehi escaped the city into the desert with an extended family group. According to the Book of Mormon, Zedekiah's son Mulek also escaped death and captivity by fleeing across the ocean. In the same Promised Land, he founded a nation that later encountered and merged with Lehi's descendants.

Both the Masonic and the Mormon midrash develop similarly by building a story around the biblical narrative and adding details and figures possessing a great deal of symbolic meaning. In doing so, they introduce new values or provide new settings for familiar tales.

Historically, the Royal Arch degree has utilized the story of Moses and the burning bush (see Exodus 3) to develop the theme of prophetic theophany and the return and recovery of truth. An enactment of the scripture is narrated and led by the Principal Sojourner immediately following the taking of the obligation for Royal Arch Masonry.[4] The Book of Mormon includes its own adaptation of Exodus 3, in which Lehi plays the part of the Principal Sojourner:

> And it came to pass as he [Lehi] prayed unto the Lord, there came a pillar of fire and dwelt upon a rock before him; and he saw and heard much; and because of the things which he saw and heard he did quake and tremble exceedingly. (1 Ne. 1:6)

---

3. Dan Vogel, *Joseph Smith: The Making of a Prophet*, 205.

4. David Bernard, *Light on Masonry: A Collection of All the Most Important Documents on the Subject of Speculative Free Masonry*, 132.

Miniature book fob circa 1919. Seven leaves, each engraved with Masonic implements. From the collection of Wor. Bro. Paul McEvoy of Goulburn Menturia Lodge 3478, England. Made by Joseph Woolfson, of Glasgow, Scotland. Used with permission.

One of the most powerful biblical themes is the Exodus from Egypt, which is recalled throughout the Old and New Testaments, emphasizing the principle of deliverance and Divine guidance. The Royal Arch degree overtly compares the Egyptian Exodus with the escape from Babylon. After the three representative "Most Excellent Masters" symbolically traverse the desert wastes and rugged roads lying between Babylon and Jerusalem, they arrive at the first of several partitioning veils. Here they are told that "none are permitted to engage in this great and glorious work" of rebuilding the temple "except the true descendants of the twelve tribes of Israel"; they must therefore trace their genealogy and state their intentions. "We are of your own brethren and kin," they confidently assert, ". . . true descendants of those noble families of Giblimites who wrought so hard at the building of the first temple."[5] Being liberated by Cyrus, they "are now returned to assist in rebuilding the house of the Lord."[6] Principles taught in this ritual highlight the importance of following a spiritual path and relying upon God over the rough passages of life. Restoration is also a strong leitmotif, through building upon strong foundations laid by others.

In a similar way, the Book of Mormon repeats the themes of escape and deliverance. In his exodus from Jerusalem, Lehi passes through the same Arabian desert to which the Masons refer in their Royal Arch ritual. At one point, Lehi asks his son Nephi to return to Jerusalem to obtain a book of scriptural writings inscribed on brass plates from a relative, the nefarious Laban. Nephi's courageous response to this difficult directive is the ringing declaration, "I will go and do

---

5. Jacob O. Doesburg, *Freemasonry Illustrated. The Complete Ritual of the First Seven Masonic Degree*, 524.

6. Bernard, *Light on Masonry*, 135.

the things which the Lord hath commanded, for I know that the Lord giveth no commandments unto the children of men, save he shall prepare a way for them that they may accomplish the thing which he commandeth them" (1 Ne. 3:7). The statement is strongly evocative of the Royal Arch ritual, wherein the initiates are told they are needed to rebuild the city and Temple: "[W]e will endeavor to overcome every obstacle, endure every hardship, and brave every danger, to accomplish the great and glorious work upon which we have entered."[7] In the Book of Mormon, the Nephites are the genealogical heirs of the true builders of Jerusalem. Lehi's son Nephi leads the group to a promised land in the Americas where they establish a city and a temple of their own "after the manner of the temple of Solomon" (2 Ne. 5:16).

Smiths

Nephi is an important character in the construction of the Mormon and Masonic midrash. His return to Jerusalem composes a mythic reversal of the Masonic legend of Akirop. In the Masonic tale, the protagonist Joabert is sent out of Jerusalem with eight others to avenge the murder of Hiram Abiff. In a cave, Joabert finds one of the assassins, Akirop, asleep with his sword lying by his feet. Joabert takes up the sword and pierces the villain in the head and heart, then decapitates Akirop as bloody retribution for his treachery. With the spoils found in the cave, he and his brothers return to the Holy City.[8] In Masonry, the action of beheading is used in story form as an archetype to represent vengeance. In the Mormon version, the decapitation is performed as a response to divine command. When Nephi finds Laban lying in a drunken stupor, he determines that he must listen to the voice of the Spirit and make the acquisition of the brass plates his priority in order to preserve a scriptural tradition from being lost. Nephi takes Laban "by the hair of the head" and decapitates him with his own sword (1 Ne. 4:8–18). He then assumes Laban's identity by dressing in his clothes.

By impersonating Laban, Nephi is able to convince his servant Zoram to open the treasury. The two make their way outside the gates of the city with the brass plates. When Zoram discovers that Nephi is not his master, he begins to flee, but Nephi binds him fast with the strength of his arms. Zoram takes an oath of secrecy and is promised he will become a "free man" (1 Ne. 4:19–33). The pattern of binding, covenanting, and loosing—or freeing—is common in every degree of Freemasonry. Additionally, the Royal Arch midrashic expansion of the themes of exile, return, and recovery is also a major point of emphasis in Nephi's story.

Nephi is skilled in shipbuilding as well as metallurgy. He forges tools that help his family survive in the wilderness (1 Ne. 17:8–16); he builds a boat

---

7. Doesburg, *Freemasonry Illustrated*, 519. See also a reference to this return to Jerusalem in Bernard, *Light on Masonry*, 133.

8. This degree is found in the "Elu of the Nine Degree" in the Scottish Rite. It was first fully exposed in Bernard's *Light on Masonry*. See Bernard, *Light on Masonry*, 198, 400.

Depiction of the legend of Akirop in David Bernard, *Light on Masonry*, 1829.

that ensures the survival of his people and carries them to the Promised Land (18:1–2); and he engraves a holy record—a sacred artifact—on thin plates of ore (19:1–5). Thus, he calls to mind the Masonic "Legend of the Smith," an iconic figure represented by several characters.[9] First, the biblical Tubal Cain is described as someone who "forged all kinds of tools out of copper and iron" (Gen. 4:22 NIV).[10] His profession is closely connected with the Masons' craft and thoroughly described in Masonic lore. Noah, builder of the ark, is another who fits into this tradition. He is an individual with great mystical significance in Masonry, and his story is prevalent in early Masonic documents.[11] For example, Masonic author Manly Hall connects the Legend of the Smith with Noah and his cosmic ark,[12] and the 1726 Masonic *Graham Manuscript* ties Noah to Hiram Abiff, a later smith who forges the implements for the temple.[13]

The Book of Mormon opens and then closes with Masonic "smiths." In its final pages, the brother of Jared, clearly a smith, comprises aspects of Tubal Cain,

9. "Of all the myths that have prevailed among the peoples of the earth, hardly any has had a greater antiquity or a more extensive existence than that of the *Smith* who worked in metals. . . . Freemasonry . . . has transformed the Scriptural idea of a skillful smith into that of an architect and builder." Albert Gallatin Mackey, *The History of Freemasonry: Its Legendary Origins*, 420–30; emphasis in original.

10. In Masonic legend, Tubal-Cain was the "founder of the smith's craft and of the other crafts of metal." Matthew Cooke, ed., *The History and Articles of Masonry*, 36–37.

11. James Anderson, *The Constitutions of the Free-Masons, Containing the History, Charges, Regulations, &c. of that Most Ancient and Right Worshipful Fraternity*, 3.

12. Manly P. Hall, *A Encyclopedic Outline of Masonic, Hermetic, Qabbalistic and Rosicrucian Symbolical Philosophy, Being an Interpretation of the Secret Teachings Concealed within the Rituals, Allegories, and Mysteries of all Ages*, 127.

13. Harry Carr, ed., *The Early Masonic Catechisms*, 92–93.

Noah, and Hiram Abiff. He builds barges as directed by the Lord, and he melts stones from a rock, which are then touched by the Lord's finger to provide light during his oceanic journey (Ether 3).

Lineage and Language

The Book of Mormon emphasizes the importance of lineage and affirms the tradition of a pure Hebraic language (see 1 Ne. 5:14–16; Morm. 9:33; Omni 1:17–18). Masonic writer Francisco Castells points out that in 1687 the Mason Word was understood to be "a secret Signal"—a Hebrew word coming from "at least the time of Solomon" and perhaps "as old as the Tower of Babel." In those days, it was commonly understood that Hebrew had been the original form of speech.[14] This idea is first mentioned in the Book of Mormon in association with the people of Jared, a family group who, with a few others, "came forth . . . from the great tower, at the time the Lord confounded the language of the people, and swore in his wrath that they should be scattered upon all the face of the earth" (Ether 1:33). Their prophetic leader, the brother of Jared, asked the Lord not to confound their language as he had others (v. 35),[15] and through him the Lord led the Jaredites through the wilderness to the seashore where they built small watertight barges with peaked ends. The barges, which would carry the Jaredites to the Promised Land, are suggestive of the Masonic version of Noah's Ark, built upon the same principles of "true *Geometry*" utilized in the Tower of Babel.[16]

Illuminating Stones

One tracing board—a teaching aid depicting the various emblems and symbols of Freemasonry—used in the mid- to late 1700s includes some interesting elements.[17] This particular board depicts Noah's Ark, the Tower of Babel, and a

---

14. F. de P. Castells, *Genuine Secrets in Freemasonry Prior to AD 1717*, 217.

15. See also Joseph Smith's revision of the Bible, where the "language of Adam" is described as "a language . . . pure and undefiled" (Moses 6:5–6).

16. Anderson, *Constitutions of the Free-Masons*, 3–7, 85. See also James Hardie, *The New Free-Mason's Monitor; Or, Masonic Guide. For the Direction of Members of that Ancient and Honourable Fraternity, as well as for the Information of those, who may be Desirous of Becoming Acquainted with its Principles*, 311.

17. Masonic tracing boards originated as chalk drawings on the floor of the tavern room in which a Masonic Lodge met. Various Masonic symbols of a geometric type, such as circles and pentagrams, were added to the drawing as time progressed. Also included were illustrations or actual physical objects—ladders, beehives, or other symbolic items. By the second half of the eighteenth century, tracing boards were being painted on a variety of materials from canvas to small marble slabs, displaying the Masonic symbols in a more and more decorative and elaborate presentation. They began to reinforce and reflect the ritual instruction of the lodge. In modern times, tracing boards for each of the degrees

rough stone being smoothed by a hammer and fire.[18] It brings to mind the story of the brother of Jared with sixteen stones he fashions, which the Lord touches with his finger so that they would glow and illuminate the darkness of the barges (Ether 3–16; 6:2–3).

The Book of Mormon verses here are similar to Jewish midrash on Genesis 6. In this chapter, God instructs Noah to illuminate the ark by *tzohar taaseh*, meaning "a brightness you will make." Jewish esoteric tradition considers the *tzohar* a luminous gemstone holding the primordial light of creation. Targum Yonatan elaborated: "During the entire twelve months that Noah was in the Ark he did not require the light of the sun by day or the light of the moon by night, but he had a polished stone which he hung up—when it was dim, he knew it was day, when it was bright, he knew it was night."[19]

The *Polychronicon*, an epic fourteenth-century work of world history and theology, contains a similar story. Mormon apologist Hugh Nibley, writing in the 1960s, considered the correspondence between Jaredite

Masonic tracing board pictured in *Le Parfait Maçon*, 1744.

stones and Noah's *tzohar* an indication of Smith's prophetic ability. Nibley insisted the archaic sources could not have been known to Smith in the early 1800s.[20] However, Smith may have been familiar with this curious tale through Freemasonry, which draws upon sources such as Higdon's *Polychronicon* for its legends of Enoch and Noah.[21]

---

have been standardized, as have the degrees themselves. There exist many examples of creatively fashioned tracing boards from the period when this evolution took place.

18. Harry Carr, ed., *Le Parfait Maçon or The Genuine Secrets of the four Grades of Apprentices, Fellows, ordinary & Ecossois Masters of Freemasonry*, 181.

19. Targum Yonatan Genesis 6:16; and Genesis Rabbah 31:11, quoted in Geoffrey Dennis, "Tzohar: Gem of Noah, Light of Heaven."

20. Hugh Nibley, *An Approach to the Book of Mormon*, 348–50.

21. "The writer of the Cooke MS. (1410/1450 CE) had before him an original which may have been written about 1350 A.D. The author of that original frankly acknowledges that many of his historical statements are taken from 'the polycronicon,' a sort of universal history, or *omnium gatherum*, in which were collected scraps and fragments of lore of many kinds, especially about the remote past, and without any attempt to distinguish

Passing through the Veil

The brother of Jared provides an example of a Book of Mormon exile who achieves a Royal Arch-inspired exaltation. In the degree, the candidate is instructed with the knowledge that will allow him to pass through the veils and into the presence of the Divine Council, situated within the Holy of Holies. This passing through veils is a critical part of the Royal Arch "exaltation" of the candidate, where he has the Word restored to him as a reward for his labors and is then crowned as a companion to "those who know." The Book of Mormon describes the brother of Jared thus: "And because of the knowledge of this man he could not be kept from beholding within the veil. . . . Wherefore, having this perfect knowledge of God, he could not be kept from within the veil" (Ether 3:19–20). As in Freemasonry, this instruction was confidential: "Behold, thou shalt not suffer these things which ye have seen and heard to go forth unto the world. . . . [W]herefore, ye shall treasure up the things which ye have seen and heard, and show it to no man" (v. 21).

The brother of Jared was instructed to record these confidential teachings and "seal them up" for a future generation, and to do so in a language that "no one can interpret," that is, "in a language that . . . cannot be read" (v. 22). In order for the writings to be read at a future time, two interpreter stones, which Joseph Smith would call a "key," were divinely created and given to the brother of Jared to include with his record (vv. 23–24).

Swarm of Bees

One of the most enduring early Mormon symbols is the beehive, an emblem which has been described as "link[ing] the Mormon community across time while symbolizing the Mormon pioneer past."[22] Given the many additional symbols of Masonry that appear alongside the beehive in early Mormon art and architecture, it is imprudent to disregard the influence of the Fraternity in association with this iconic symbol. The beehive predates Mormon use and is a conspicuous part of Masonic symbolic teaching. According to Jonathan Swift, writing in the eighteenth century,

> A *bee* has in all ages and nations, been the grand *hieroglyphick* of *masonry*, because it excels all other living creatures in the contrivance and commodiousness of its *habitation* or *comb*. . . . *[M]asonry* or *building*, seemeth to be of the very essence or nature of the *bee*.[23]

---

genuine history from myths, legends, tales, fables." Albert Gallatin Mackey, *Revised Encyclopaedia of Freemasonry and its Kindred Sciences*, 3:152.

22. Richard G. Oman, "Beehive Symbol," 1:99.

23. Jonathan Swift, "A Letter from the Grand Mistress of the Female Free-masons to George Faulkner, Printer," 336–37; italics in original.

Swift explained that what Masons of his day called a lodge was anciently known as "a HIVE of freemasons. . . . [W]hen a dissention happens in a *lodge*, the going off and forming another lodge, is to this day called SWARMING."[24] One of the earliest Mormon appropriations of the bee is found in the Book of Mormon description of what the Jaredites brought with them on their journey to the New World: "And they did also carry with them deseret, which, by interpretation, is a honey bee; and thus they did carry with them *swarms of bees*, and all manner of that which was upon the face of the land, seeds of every kind" (Ether 2:3; emphasis added). This passage expresses to those familiar with the Masonic symbolism of the honeybee that the Jaredites are a remnant of Israel, or a "swarm of bees" separated from the main hive in Jerusalem and brought to the Promised Land to spread true religion. Drawing further similarities between the ark-building Noah and the brother of Jared, George Oliver reports,

> The Beehive . . . teaches us that as we came into the world rational and intelligent beings, so we should ever be industrious ones; never sitting down contented while our fellow creatures around us are in want.[25]

It is thus an appropriate symbol for the prophets who individually saved their families and began new peoples on uninhabited lands after departing from their vessels. Thus, Oliver writes that the swarm of bees "symbolized only *the just man [Noah] and his pious family*, not the incorrigible race which perished beneath the waves of the deluge."[26]

Freemasons have long been fascinated with Jewish Kabbalah, a form of midrash kept secret and hidden from all but a select group initiated into its mysteries. The bee and beehive symbols are a Masonic example of using kabbalah. Outwardly, the bee is presented as a representation of the quality of "industriousness." The hive suggests a harmonious social order brought about by enlightened, transformed individuals who strive to bring about the Grand Design. Yet, there is a secret meaning. Freemason George W. Bullamore postulated that the symbol possesses a meaning that was kept from the Entered Apprentice in many lodges but was more fitted for the third degree: that is, resurrection, or the return of the soul.[27]

It has been suggested that the symbol had a Kabbalistic meaning in Mormonism as well. Fred Collier, compiler of Brigham Young's sermons and teachings, correctly noted that although the beehive is readily recognized as the Utah state emblem, "very few comprehend the essence of its symbolism as it existed in the mind of Brigham Young." Collier explained it was represented to the public as "a capitalistic symbol for industry" but that its inner meaning went far deeper. The beehive, a symbol pertaining to the temple, signified "the order

---

24. Swift, 399.

25. George Oliver, *Signs and Symbols: Illustrated and Explained in a Course of Twelve Lectures on Freemasonry*, 117–18.

26. Oliver, 119; emphasis in original.

27. George W. Bullamore, "The Beehive and Freemasonry," 219–46.

and government of the Kingdom of God as it will exist under the administration of the Royal Priesthood."[28]

Prophet, Priest, and King

In the Royal Arch tradition, the Book of the Law is restored through the prophet Haggai, high priest Jeshua, and king Zerubbabel. The threefold classification "prophet, priest, and king" was symbolically applied to Royal Arch Masons after the passing of the veils. George Oliver considered this threefold office God's perfect system of government, and Royal Arch Freemasons hold that this is the "perfect patriarchal order" exemplified by Adam, Shem, Abraham, Noah, and Moses—each considered a prophet, priest, and king (as well as a Grand Master) in Masonic tradition.

Latter-day Saints applied this *munus triplex* to the Old Testament patriarchs and dispensation heads, including additional prophets of their own. As early as 1830, Alexander Campbell recognized and took issue with the Book of Mormon's portrayal of Nephi as "prophet, priest, and king," a phrase that Christians have reserved solely for Jesus Christ.[29] By 1844 Joseph Smith had assumed these offices in his organization of the Council of Fifty.[30] Additionally, he made it a critical part of his theology that Latter-day Saints, like Royal Arch Masons, could participate in that perfect patriarchal order.

The "Joseph Smith Translation"

As chronicler and developer of Masonic lore, George Oliver amplified his readers' understanding of the prophetic office by elaborating on the lives of the biblical patriarchs and their descendants. Pulling from various legends and lore, he gave these characters vocations and professions, many based on Masonry. For example, Lamech is depicted building a walled city on the principles of operative Masonry, thus forming a society with civil government and social order.[31] Oliver describes Enoch as a scientific researcher, devoting his attention to the investigation of celestial bodies.[32] Abraham was pictured as "eminently distinguished for a competent knowledge" of arithmetic, which he taught to his family and friends, eventually introducing this science into Egypt.[33]

---

28. Fred C. Collier, *The Teachings of President Brigham Young, Vol. 3, 1852-1854*, xxix.

29. Alexander Campbell, "Delusions," 91.

30. See "Council of Fifty, Minutes, March 1844–January 1846; Volume 1, 10 March 1844–1 March 1845," The Joseph Smith Papers, 114.

31. George Oliver, *Antiquities of Freemasonry: Comprising Illustrations of the Five Grand Periods of Masonry from the Creation of the World to the Dedication of King Solomon's Temple*, 49.

32. Oliver, 87.

33. Oliver, 67.

Certainly aware of these extra-biblical narratives of these prophetic characters, from the early 1830s, Joseph Smith was concerned with the Masonic idea that portions of the biblical record had been lost. He observed, "[M]any important points, touching the salvation of man, had been taken from the Bible, or lost before it was compiled."[34] While this theme is developed in the pages of the Book of Mormon (see 3 Ne. 23:6–13; 1 Ne. 13:26, 40), by the time the book was being printed at Egbert Grandin's print shop, Smith determined to directly remedy the shortcomings he saw in the Bible. A large edition of the King James Version that included the Old Testament Apocrypha was obtained from Grandin's bookstore in Palmyra on October 8, 1829, for $3.75.[35] By June of 1830, Smith was using the volume "to restore and clarify vital points of history and doctrine missing from the Bible."[36] Although he called his work a "translation," it was not a literal translation from ancient documents. Rather, it is perhaps described best as an inspired commentary that is clearly midrashic in nature.

Philip Barlow observed that Smith made six basic types of changes from the King James Version in the Joseph Smith Translation. Besides common-sense changes and grammatical corrections, these included four types of revisions that epitomized Jewish scriptural midrash:

- Lengthy revealed additions that had little or no biblical parallel, such as the visions of Moses and Enoch, and the passage on Melchizedek;
- "Interpretive additions," often signaled by the phrase "or in other words," which Smith appended to a passage he wished to clarify;
- "Harmonization," in which Smith reconciled passages that seemed to conflict with other passages;
- "Not easily classifiable": here one can observe only that the meaning of a given text was changed, often idiosyncratically.[37]

Smith appears to have drawn deeply from the well of Masonic legend and tradition to frame his expansions as he worked through the Bible, particularly within the book of Genesis.[38]

---

34. "History, 1838–1856, Volume A-1 [23 December 1805–30 August 1834]," The Joseph Smith Papers, 183.

35. This information comes from a notation in what appears to be Joseph Smith's handwriting. Robert J. Matthews, "Joseph Smith Translation of the Bible (JST)," 2:765.

36. Bruce T. Taylor, "Book of Moses," 1:216–17. There is strong evidence that Smith also used Adam Clarke's Commentary on the Bible, a popular reference work of the day. See Thomas A. Wayment and Haley Wilson-Lemmon, "A Recovered Resource: The Use of Adam Clarke's Bible Commentary in Joseph Smith's Translation, 262-284." Clarke was often quoted by nineteenth-century Freemasons such as Albert Mackey.

37. Philip Barlow, *Mormons and the Bible: The Place of the Latter-day Saints in American Religion*, 55–59.

38. Like Joseph Smith and a number of contemporary Bible scholars, some Masons believed textual errors had crept into the Bible and required correction. For instance, George Oliver felt that the passage "And I appeared unto Abraham, unto Isaac, and unto Jacob, by the

Among Christian churches in the nineteenth century, Latter-day Saints were largely unique in teaching that God created the earth out of preexisting materials.[39] In explaining his rendering of Genesis 1:1, Smith taught,

> Now the word create came from the word baurau, which does not mean to create out of nothing; it means to organize. . . . God had materials to organize the world out of chaos. . . . The pure principles of element are principles which can never be destroyed; they may be organized and re-organized, but not destroyed; they had no beginning, and can have no end.[40]

The principle "order from disorder"—*ordo ab chao*—is one of the oldest mottos of Ancient Craft Masonry. The idea hails back to ancient Near Eastern mythologies and classical Greek creation myths that describe the creation of the world as resulting from the actions of a god or gods upon already-existing primeval matter, or *chaos*. Both John Browne in his 1802 *Masonic Master-Key* and James Hardie in his 1818 *The New Free-Mason's Monitor* spoke of the elements and materials making up the earth as existing "without form or distinction." God commanded the world into being by bringing these resources "from chaos to perfection."[41] Thomas Starr King, Grand Orator of the Grand Lodge of California in 1853, explained:

> The Almighty is *the Organizer*. He creates elements in order to mingle and fraternize them in composition and products. In the original chaos, matter was unorganized. The process of death is disorganization. All the marvels of beauty, all the victories of life, are exhibitions and triumphs of organizing force.[42]

---

name of God Almighty, but by my name Jehovah was I not known to them" (Ex. 6:3 KJV) should be read interrogatively, thus "by my name Jehovah was I not known unto them?" See Oliver, *Antiquities of Freemasonry*, 232. This particular insight is also found in Joseph Smith's inspired revision of the same passage: "I am the Lord God Almighty; the Lord JEHOVAH. And was not my name known unto them?" See Joseph Smith Translation, Exodus 6:3.

39. Many scholars agree that the doctrine of *creatio ex nihilo* was not the original intent of the biblical authors, but instead a change in the *interpretation* of the texts that began to evolve in the mid-second century A.D. in the atmosphere of Hellenistic philosophy. See Gerhard May, *Creatio ex nihilo: The Doctrine of 'Creation out of Nothing' in Early Christian Thought*, 1–3; Frances Young, "'Creatio Ex Nihilo': A Context for the Emergence of the Christian Doctrine of Creation," 139–52.

40. "History, 1838–1856, volume E-1 [1 July 1843–30 April 1844]," The Joseph Smith Papers, 1973.

41. John Browne, *Browne's Masonic Master-Key through the Three Degrees, by way of Polyglot. Under the Sanction of the Craft in General*, 49; and Hardie, *The New Free-Mason's Monitor*, 122–23. The recounting of the Creation Myth as well as the phrases "elements and materials of the creation," "*Chaos* to *Perfection*," and "new-framed matter" are witnessed repeatedly in these and other respectable Masonic sources. In addition to Hardie and Browne, see George Claret, *The Whole Craft of Free-Masonry*, 225; and *The Lectures of the Three Degrees in Craft Masonry, A New and Revised Edition*, 48–50.

42. Thomas Starr King, "Oration delivered before the Grand Lodge of Free and Accepted Masons of California, at its Annual Communication, May 1863," 212; emphasis

The notion of creation out of existing materials (*ordo ab chao*) makes perfect sense for a craftsman or builder who works in precisely this way. Finding it in religion—especially in Christianity, which interprets Genesis 1:1 to be *creatio ex nihilo*—is unusual.

As he continued revising the book of Genesis into what is known to Latter-day Saints as the Book of Moses, Smith crafted an explicitly Masonic tale. In it, Adam and Eve were given commandments to worship God and offer Him "the firstlings of their flocks":

> And after many days an angel of the Lord appeared unto Adam, saying: Why dost thou offer sacrifices unto the Lord? And Adam said unto him: I know not, save the Lord commanded me. And then the angel spake, saying: This thing is a similitude of the sacrifice of the Only Begotten of the Father, which is full of grace and truth. (Moses 5:6–7)

This idea is echoed in George Oliver's analysis of animal sacrifices. He places them as far back as Adam and Eve and explains they must be "typical of the one sacrifice of the Lamb without spot, as a propitiation for the sins of the whole world," so that they may "preserve alive in men's minds the true knowledge of God." He continues,

> Hence Abel's sacrifice was more acceptable than that of Cain, because it was an animal sacrifice, and offered conformably to the divine appointment; while that of Cain, being unbloody, was an abomination, because it did not contain any reference to the atonement of Christ.[43]

In Smith's revision, after the ritual sacrifice by Cain and Abel, the older brother was angry because God rejected his offering while accepting Abel's sacrifice of a sheep carcass. This prompted Cain to make a secret, recognizably Masonic, pact with Satan. "Swear unto me by thy throat," demanded the devil, "and if thou tell it thou shalt die; and swear thy brethren by their heads, and by the living God, that they tell it not; for if they tell it, they shall surely die" (Moses 5:29).

Upon making this oath, Cain exclaimed, "Truly I am Mahan, the master of this great secret, that I may murder and get gain." The arrangement was referred to as a "secret combination," and thereafter Cain became known by the title "Master Mahan" (Moses 5:31, 51). Several commentators have attempted to account for this name. Hugh Nibley has suggested that the term means "great

---

in original. Compare Brigham Young, July 10, 1853, *Journal of Discourses*, 1:349–53.

43. Oliver, *Antiquities of Freemasonry*, 44–45. The idea that sacrificial offerings were first introduced to Adam as a representation of the Lamb of God is in accordance with popular Bible commentaries of the time. For example, see Matthew Henry and Thomas Scott, *A Commentary upon the Holy Bible from Henry and Scott: Genesis to Deuteronomy*, 17: "[W]e may conclude that God commanded Adam, after the fall, to shed the blood of *innocent* animals. . . . He [God] thus . . . prefigured the sufferings of Christ." See also Adam Clarke, *The Holy Bible, Containing the Old and New Testaments. A Commentary and Critical Notes Designed as a Help to a Better Understanding of the Sacred Writings. Volume 1: Genesis to Deuteronomy*, 46.

keeper of secrets," deriving from an Arabic word *Mustirr* (keeper of secret), and a Sanskrit word *Maha* (great).[44] D. Michael Quinn traces "Mahan" to a Scottish name for Satan, *Mahoun* (pronounced "mahan").[45] However, equally plausible as these two proposals is the idea that "Master Mahan" is simply a variation of "Master Mason." Clearly, the word "master" is not at issue, as Cain himself confirms it: "truly I am . . . the master." As he has been initiated into a degenerate or corrupted tradition, the notion that the word *mason* has become corrupted into *mahan*—suggesting a degenerate or spurious form—makes literary sense. Further, Cain not only "swear[s] by his throat," as described in *Light on Masonry's* exposure of the Entered Apprentice degree, he announces "I am free," apparently alluding to the Free-Mason.[46]

The story continues to support a Masonic interpretation as Cain produces a son named Enoch,[47] whose descendants "entered into a covenant with Satan, after the manner of Cain" and also become "Master Mahan, master of that great secret which was administered unto Cain by Satan" (Moses 5:49). In doing so, these cursed children of Enoch act as a foil to the righteous Enoch and offer an illustration of George Oliver's authentic-versus-spurious theory of Freemasonry.[48]

In Oliver's view, God, the "Great Architect of the universe," was the founder of Freemasonry and initiated Adam into the principles of speculative Masonry in the Garden. This authentic form of the Craft was passed down over the generations to Seth, Enoch, Noah, Shem (who Oliver identifies as Melchizedek), Abraham, and down through the Jewish line to Solomon.[49] Then it was passed on through Christianity. In opposition to God, Satan was the author of spurious Masonry, which he taught to Cain. This was then disseminated through Cain's posterity to Lamech, ultimately leading to the Deluge. Following the Flood, spurious Masonry

---

44. Hugh Nibley, *Ancient Documents and the Pearl of Great Price*, 12.

45. D. Michael Quinn, *Early Mormonism and the Magic World View*, 209. Quinn demonstrates that 1830 Palmyra residents had access to books of Scottish poetry describing a satanic pact with *Mahoun*.

46. ". . . binding myself under no less penalty, than to have my throat cut across, my tongue torn out by the roots." Bernard, *Light on Masonry*, 20.

47. From Cain's line also comes "Tubal Cain," a worker in brass and iron. Smith separates the name into two words, where it is either hyphenated (Tubal-cain) or written as one word (Tubalcain) in virtually every version of the Bible. It is found separated in *Antiquities of Freemasonry*. Additionally, the two-word name is found as the Master Mason's password in William Morgan's *Illustrations of Masonry by One of the Fraternity Who has Devoted Thirty Years to the Subject* and David Bernard's *Light on Masonry: A Collection of all the Most Important Documents on the Subject of Speculative Free Masonry*.

48. Homer calls this the "two seed tradition." See Michael W. Homer, *Joseph's Temples: The Dynamic Relationship Between Freemasonry and Mormonism*, 125.

49. Oliver, *Antiquities of Freemasonry*, 4. See also Kenneth Mackenzie, ed., *The Royal Masonic Cyclopaedia of History, Rites, Symbolism, and Biography*, s.v. "Melchizedek."

survived through Noah's son Ham and was eventually passed on to the pharaoh of Egypt who preserved the corrupted secrets of false Masonry.[50]

Smith's revision of the Genesis stories adds a lengthy passage about Cain's descendant Lamech, who learns that "Irad, the son of Enoch, having known their secret, began to reveal it unto the sons of Adam" (Moses 5:49). In response, "Lamech, being angry, slew him, not like unto Cain, his brother Abel, for the sake of getting gain, but *he slew him for the oath's sake*" (v. 50; emphasis added). Such a murder corresponds to the William Morgan abduction in which Morgan was believed to have been killed by Freemasons to enforce the Masonic obligation of secrecy.

Royal Arch Masonry's Enoch: The Authentic Tradition Restored

Just as Freemasonry includes an Enoch midrash, so does Latter-day Saint scripture revealed by Joseph Smith.[51] A lengthy portion of Smith's revision of the Bible is a textual expansion of three short verses in Genesis 5:

> And Enoch walked with God after he begat Methuselah three hundred years, and begat sons and daughters: And all the days of Enoch were three hundred sixty and five years: And Enoch walked with God: and he *was* not; for God took him. (vv. 22–24)

---

50. Oliver, *Antiquities of Freemasonry*, 13, 153–54, 207. Oliver's rewriting of biblical history and his assertion that the early biblical patriarchs were Freemasons was disturbing to non-Masons living in New England and New York; however, amongst Freemasons such a view was common. In 1723, James Anderson wrote that Adam, Noah, Abraham, and his successors were Freemasons. See James Anderson, *The Constitutions of the Free-Masons, Containing the History, Charges, Regulations, &c. of that Most Ancient and Right Worshipful Fraternity*, 7–23.

In New York in 1818, Salem Town argued that Freemasons had secretly preserved the original text of the Old Testament from the time of Moses until its recovery after the Babylonian captivity. See Salem Town, *A System of Speculative Masonry in its Origin, Patronage, Dissemination, Principles, Duties, and Ultimate Designs, Laid Open for the Examination of the Serious and Candid*, 207–38. Thus, New York Masons such as the Smith family would likely not have been surprised at the claims made in *Antiquities*.

51. Brent Metcalfe has outlined the authorship and dating of the manuscript as follows: Joseph Smith dictated the Enochian story to his scribes beginning on "Dec 1rst" 1830 as Emma Smith records in Old Testament manuscript 1, page 11. John Whitmer returned for a brief stint as scribe on page 14. Sidney Rigdon's handwriting begins on page 15 after he was designated as Smith's scribe for the scriptures on December 7, 1830 (see D&C 35:20). Rigdon transcribed the remainder of the Enoch tale. Later in December, Joseph Smith issued a revelation instructing him and Rigdon to stop work on the Bible revision until they had relocated to Ohio (D&C 37:1). Smith's and John Whitmer's histories agree that Smith and Rigdon had already completed "the prophesy of Enoch" by this time. Thus, the ending date can be further tightened to before Smith left Fayette to meet William W. Phelps on December 24, 1830, and possibly even as early as mid-December when Joseph Smith Sr. returned to Fayette after being incarcerated. Brent Lee Metcalfe, correspondence with authors, December 29, 2013.

While recent scholarship has shown that Enoch pseudepigrapha expanding on these passages may have been available on the western frontier by 1830,[52] it seems more plausible that Smith would utilize Masonic tradition rather than other sources for inspiration in his Enoch writings.[53] Not detailed anywhere in the Masonic ritual itself, the theophany and heavenly ascent in the 1 Enoch pseudepigrapha and other ancient sources formed the basis of a legendary background to the culminating Royal Arch degree, created between 1725 and 1730. Here, Enoch was the archetypal seeker who held the ability to uncover and preserve the name of God for future generations.[54] Given the saturation of Masonic discussion, exposés, and resources in the early nineteenth century, a thorough education in the Masonic Enoch legend was readily available to Smith both through Masonic authors Thomas Webb and George Oliver and by way of anti-Masonic activity in the New York area.[55]

Thomas Smith Webb's highly influential monitor of early American Masonic ritual presents Enoch as a righteous man, devotedly studying the seven liberal arts and sciences with special attention to astronomy.[56] In the Masonic telling of the Enoch story, humanity is elevated by the sciences,[57] and Enoch's own studies have such a life-altering effect upon him that God promises him a special revelation according to his desire. He is then transported to the top of a mountain where God appears in a vision. The characters of the Divine name are given upon a triangular plate of gold and restored to mankind. Enoch is then called to preach to the degenerate inhabitants of the world who, he has foreseen, will soon be destroyed in a great flood.

The Masonic legend emphasizes Enoch's acquisition of specialized knowledge (gnosis). To preserve this knowledge, he builds two pillars atop a mountain, and upon these he engraves knowledge of the arts and sciences, as well as direc-

---

52. Colby Townsend, "Revisiting Joseph Smith and the Availability of the Book of Enoch," 41–71.

53. Cheryl L. Bruno, "Congruence and Concatenation in Jewish Mystical Literature, American Freemasonry, and Mormon Enoch Writings," 4–5.

54. These included the biblical book of Jude; writings by Church Fathers Justin Martyr, Minucius Felix, Irenaeus, Origen, Cyprian, Hippolytus, Commodianus, Lactantius and Cassian; and George Syncellus' eighth-century work Chronographia Universalis.

55. Neville Barker Cryer, The Royal Arch Journey, 25. The Enoch legend is found throughout George Oliver's 1823 Antiquities of Freemasonry, as well as Thomas Smith Webb's 1808 The Freemasons Monitor, where the Enoch tradition is associated with "the Degree of Knights of the Ninth Arch."

56. Webb, The Freemason's Monitor, 244–47. See also Oliver, Antiquities of Freemasonry, 87–92.

57. The seven liberal arts and sciences are depicted as seven steps on a winding stair discussed in the second, or Fellowcraft, degree. The candidate ascends the staircase, which leads into the symbolic presence of Deity. Elsewhere, the steps are described as the components of a chariot, taking the initiate to heaven, as Enoch was taken. This connects Freemasonry with Merkabah (chariot) mysticism.

tions on how to find the name of God so it will not be lost to the world in the general destruction. One pillar is made of brass to withstand water; the other is made of marble to withstand fire.

In the ritual, the candidate participates in the appendant story of the revelation of the Divine Name of God to Moses on Mount Horeb. Later, the candidate will make a symbolic ascent to the celestial temple to seek the divine name. Thus, Enoch, Moses, and the candidate are thematically linked in a recurring motif.

The Masonic Enoch tradition, with its esoteric, mystical, and symbolic aspects, provides important spiritual insights to Masons. Enoch's journey represents the apotheosis each Royal Arch Mason seeks to achieve. Through ritual, the initiate, like Enoch, is called by God, experiences a theophany, receives a token of his calling (the divine name), and experiences a heavenly ascent. The candidate sees this dramatic reenactment as a symbolic journey inside himself to discover that which is lost. Having accomplished this task, he is transformed into a companion of the company of heaven. He literally stands beside the throne (i.e., "Metatron") and becomes the reflection of the divine. As a part of the Western mystery tradition, one of the fundamental preoccupations of Masonic ritual and tradition is this same perfection of human personality and subsequent transformation of human society. Of the legend of Enoch, Freemasons say: "We must view it, therefore, as an allegory; but as one which has a profound symbolic character. It was intended to teach the doctrine of Divine Truth."[58] Restored to each Mason by a theological working within the ritual itself, the lost name is recovered by the initiate, and then a crown is symbolically placed upon his head.

Joseph Smith's Enoch experiences a similar theophany and call to preach as in the Masonic legend. On the mount Simeon, he is "clothed upon with glory" and sees the Lord face-to-face. He is then shown the world and all the people in it and is taught about Jesus Christ, the coming Savior (Moses 7:2–11). Here, Enoch is a patriarchal "type," whose experience is mirrored by other key figures. When they receive their commissions, Smith's Enoch, Moses, Abraham, and the Book of Mormon's Nephi and brother of Jared—like the Enoch of Masonic legend—experience reviews of history and visions of the peoples of the earth, followed by cosmic transformation.

In both the Masonic and the Mormon traditions, Enoch works to impart spiritual knowledge to others and bring them with him as he ascends. Thus, divinization occurs only within community, extending from the individual to society at large. Just as radical social transformation was emphasized in eighteenth- and nineteenth-century Masonry, in Smith's revision, Enoch continued his preaching to the people of God and built a city of holiness: "And the Lord called his people Zion, because they were of one heart and one mind, and dwelt in righteousness; and there was no poor among them" (Moses 7:18). In time, Enoch and the entire city were taken up into heaven by the transforming power of divine love.

---

58. Robert Ingham Clegg, *Mackey's The History of Freemasonry*, 2:428.

In light of the probable interface between Mormonism, Freemasonry, and ancient sources, it is unsurprising that many similarities would exist among the three traditions. However, Smith's Enoch most closely resembles that of the Masonic legend. For instance, Smith's version and the Masonic ritual both contain a restoration emphasis, making Enoch an appropriate figure for Smith to associate himself with.[59] Thus, Freemasons and Mormons used the Enoch stories in much the same way by drawing upon threads of mystical tradition that shed light on human spiritual yearnings.[60]

Doctrine and Covenants

In addition to expanding the scriptural canon, Joseph Smith received divine revelation in response to his own concerns or to the questions of his followers. These cherished texts were collected by scribes and historians and published in a book that came to be known as the Doctrine and Covenants.[61] Many of the sections in this book included Masonically inspired midrash delivered as a dynamic response to events occurring in the immediate vicinity, again highlighting Smith's intimate familiarity with Freemasonry.

The Saints John

The Royal Arch Degree is believed to have been fashioned from a tale told by the ancient Greek historian Philostorgius. In his account, when the Roman Emperor Julian ordered the rebuilding of the temple at Jerusalem, a cavern was found built into the rock of the foundation. One of the workmen was lowered down with a long rope. When he was pulled up, he had recovered a scroll containing the Gospel of John. The author of this Gospel and John the Baptist are considered the two patron Saints of Freemasonry. Their feast days are celebrated

---

59. Joseph Smith's habit of using the code word Enoch to identify himself shows that he, too, was capable of placing himself into the prophetic paradigm. Like Enoch, he was destined to purify Masonry and religion from the filth that had accumulated. See Oliver, *Antiquities of Freemasonry*, 88. Smith was recovering that which was lost, restoring it to humanity, connecting with the Divine within himself.

60. An example of one of the ancient traditions that finds its way into Masonic legend and ritual and then into Mormonism is found in the 1 Enoch Apocrypha. Michael the archangel (whose name means "who is like God") takes Enoch (whose name means "initiate") by the right hand, raises him up, and instructs him in the mysteries of the Divine. This image is repeated and placed into a ritual context in both the Master Mason and Royal Arch degrees, and then in the Mormon endowment. Lifting up by the right hand of fellowship is found in the raising of a Master Mason and the subsequent passing of the veils in the Royal Arch Degree's Rite of Exaltation, as well as in Mormonism's ceremony at the veil.

61. An earlier version of this book of scripture was published as the *Book of Commandments*.

yearly in Masonic lodges, and early Masons took their obligations on the Bible opened to the Gospel of John and were known as "St. John's men."[62]

Joseph Smith's writings show a familiarity with the Masonic veneration of the "Saints John." In April 1829, while Smith and Oliver Cowdery were working on the Book of Mormon translation, a question arose regarding the final chapter of the Gospel of John. A common debate among the religions of the day was whether John the Apostle had died or whether he would continue on earth until the second coming of Christ. Through the Urim and Thummim, Smith dictated a revelatory answer that was described as being "Translated from parchment, written *and hid up* by himself [John]."[63] On this hidden parchment seen through a vision, the Lord confirms that John would continue to live until the second coming: "Verily, verily I say unto thee [John], . . . thou shalt tarry till I come in my glory" (D&C 7:1).

When writing of John the Evangelist and John the Baptist, Smith focused on the Masonic theme of restoration. In 1833 he dictated a revelation found in Doctrine and Covenants 84, which describes what happened when Moses was taken out of the midst of Israel and the High Priesthood was lost. The lesser priesthood, which "holdeth the key of the ministering of angels and the preparatory gospel" (D&C 84:25–26), continued with the house of Aaron until the birth of John the Baptist, who Smith described as "being filled with the Holy Ghost from his mother's womb." John was baptized "while he was yet in his childhood" and was "ordained by the angel of God at the time he was eight days old" (D&C 84:27–28).

These two sections of the Doctrine and Covenants provide examples of Joseph Smith's use of the Masonic concepts of a bifurcated Priesthood, restoration, and the Saints John in order to create a distinctive Mormon midrash. Rather than merely copying the Masonic legends, Smith did the imaginative work to provide details on the two biblical characters, giving them their own personal stories. Through them, Smith literalized the view that legitimate Levitical priesthood was restored, gathering together all authority from all dispensations.

Keys

The frequent mention of "keys" in Mormonism is typically connected with priesthood authority. Some passages in the Doctrine and Covenants mentioning keys seem to come from a unique understanding of continuity in Matthew 16 (where Peter is promised the keys of the kingdom), Matthew 17 (where Moses and Elijah appear on the Mount of Transfiguration), and Matthew 18 (where the power to bind and seal is mentioned). Yet, these passages are also infused with the idea of secrecy and confidential instruction by the Savior to his Apostles.

---

62. In Freemasonry, St. John the Evangelist is usually seen as an amalgamation of several Johns in the New Testament, including John the disciple of Christ, John the epistle writer, and John the author of the Book of Revelation.

63. "Book of Commandments, 1833," The Joseph Smith Papers, 18; emphasis added. (Now Doctrine and Covenants 7.)

In Masonic thought, the symbol of a key serves as a hieroglyphic reminding the Mason of the prudence that should afford the sacred mysteries being unfolded.[64] As noted by Albert Mackey, "In the rituals of the First Degree, in the eighteenth century, allusion is made to a key by whose help the secrets of Masonry are to be obtained." The symbol of the key

> is still preserved as a symbol of secrecy in the Royal Arch Degree. . . . In many of the German Lodges a . . . key is . . . part of the Masonic clothing of each Brother, to remind him that he should lock up or conceal the secrets of Freemasonry in his heart. But among the ancients the key was also a symbol of power.[65]

Secrets entrusted to a Freemason by a friend must be kept in confidence, that they may thus be trusted with the weightier secrets and associated power of God.

This is the implication of Joseph Smith's statement that "[t]he secret of Masonry is to keep a secret."[66] He similarly taught that keeping confidences both human and divine is a preliminary virtue without which revelation cannot be imparted to man from God:

> The reason we do not have the secrets of the Lord revealed unto us, is because we do not keep them but reveal them; we do not keep our own secrets, but reveal our difficulties to the world, even to our enemies, then how would we keep the secrets of the Lord? "I can keep a secret till Doomsday."[67]

Degrees of Glory

By the year 1717, Freemasonry included three speculative degrees. In Masonic degrees, heavenly knowledge is increasingly imparted to the initiate as he is brought from darkness to light. The third degree of Masonry specifically engages the idea of resurrection and the perfection of human personality.[68] This Masonic view of degrees is utilized in two separate revelations in the Doctrine and Covenants: sections 76 and 93.

---

64. The key is symbolic of the tongue: "That excellent key, a Freemason's tongue . . . should adopt that excellent virtue of the Craft, which is silence." *Lectures of the Three Degrees in Craft Masonry*, 9.

65. Albert G. Mackey and William G. Hughan, *An Encyclopedia of Freemasonry and Its Kindred Sciences, Comprising the Whole Range of Arts, Sciences and Literature as Connected with the Institution*, s.v. "key."

66. "Journal, December 1842–June 1844; Book 3, 15 July 1843–29 February 1844," 134, The Joseph Smith Papers. Similarly, Brigham Young noted that "the mane [main] part of Masonry is to keep a secret." Wilford Woodruff journal, January 22, 1860.

67. "History, 1838–1856, volume C-1 Addenda," The Joseph Smith Papers, 46; emphasis in original.

68. Masons often privilege sets of threes, capitalizing on Christian themes of the Trinity, the three years of Jesus's ministry, and the three days between his death and resurrection. See Arturo de Hoyos, *Albert Pike's Morals and Dogma of the Ancient and Accepted Scottish Rite of Freemasonry, Annotated Edition*, ch. 26, par. 113–14.

Doctrine and Covenants 76, a vision of three degrees of heavenly glory given to Joseph Smith and Sidney Rigdon in 1832, draws upon 1 Corinthians 15 and relates it to 2 Corinthians 12:2.[69] Each degree is pictured as a separate kingdom governed by its own laws such that

> the glory of the celestial is one, even as the glory of the sun is one. And the glory of the terrestrial is one, even as the glory of the moon is one. And the glory of the telestial is one, even as the glory of the stars is one; for as one star differs from another star in glory, even so differs one from another in glory in the telestial world. (D&C 76:96–98)

Which glory a person attains is determined when "they shall be judged according to their works, and every man shall receive according to his own works, his own dominion, in the mansions which are prepared" (v. 111).

A similar discussion of these biblical passages and the concept of degrees of glory are found in George Oliver's writings:

> If an inspired Apostle speaks of a third heaven: (2 Cor. xii.., 2,) of the righteous differing from each other in glory, as one star differs from another; (1 Cor. xv. 41,) if the plural number be commonly used by Christ and his apostles, when speaking of the place of supreme bliss; (Mark i., 10. Acts vii., 56. Eph. iv., 10. Heb. i., 10. 2 Pet. iii., 5, &c.,) and if the Saviour himself should acknowledge that heaven contains many mansions; (John xiv., 2,) then we may also conclude that as there are many heavens, so there are also degrees of reward proportioned to the measure of man's faith and obedience.[70]

Receiving the Fulness

Doctrine and Covenants 93, a revelation received on May 6, 1833, depicts a vision of the glorified Savior experienced by the Apostle John. In the Doctrine and Covenants expansion, John beheld "the glory of the Only Begotten of the Father" who came and dwelt among humankind in the flesh. He saw that Jesus "received not of the fulness at first, but continued from grace to grace, until he received a fullness" (D&C 93:12).

Just as Masonry is "a progressive moral science taught by degrees only" and is meant to bring men to the truth,[71] enlightening them step by step, the same seasoning process is offered in Smith's revelation: "If you keep my commandments you shall receive of his fulness, and be glorified in me as I am in the Father; there-

---

69. "There are also celestial bodies, and bodies terrestrial: but the glory of the celestial is one, and the glory of the terrestrial is another. There is one glory of the sun, and another glory of the moon, and another glory of the stars: for one star differeth from another star in glory. So also is the resurrection of the dead" (1 Cor. 15:40–42). "I knew a man in Christ above fourteen years ago, (whether in the body, I cannot tell; or whether out of the body, I cannot tell: God knoweth;) such an one caught up to the third heaven" (2 Cor. 12:2).

70. George Oliver, *The History of Initiation, in Twelve Lectures; Comprising a Detailed Account of the Rites and Ceremonies, Doctrines and Discipline, of all the Secret and Mysterious Institutions of the Ancient World,* 40n76.

71. *Proceedings of the Grand Chapter of Royal Arch Masons of the State of California,* 244.

fore, I say unto you, you shall receive grace for grace" (D&C 93:20). This idea is a mystical Christian concept utilized by Freemasons in their Rite of Illumination. There, men are brought to the truth by receiving "light" or knowledge progressively. Symbolically, along with the prophets Adam, Enoch, Noah, Abraham, and Solomon, they discover, learn, and apply the "seven liberal arts and sciences." In the Doctrine and Covenants, followers are similarly urged to "obtain a knowledge of history, and of countries, and of kingdoms, of laws of God and man, and all this for the salvation of Zion" (v. 53), for "the glory of God is intelligence, or, in other words, light and truth" (v. 36).

Celestial Lodges

Partakers of the "fulness" become what is termed "the church of the Firstborn" (D&C 93:22), another concept with a counterpart in Freemasonry. Masonic ritual teaches of a celestial lodge above, "where the supreme architect of the universe presides."[72] The celestial lodge represents heaven and the revolutionary social order—the goal of which is the transformation of society. We see this idea picked up and fleshed out in Smith's revelatory writing. "I shall prepare," announces the Lord, "an Holy City, that my people may gird up their loins, and be looking forth for the time of my coming; for there shall be my tabernacle, and it shall be called Zion, a New Jerusalem" (Moses 7:62). This city would meet the translated city of Enoch, which had been taken up into heaven:

> And the Lord said unto Enoch: Then shalt thou and all thy city meet them there, and we will receive them into our bosom, and they shall see us; and we will fall upon their necks, and they shall fall upon our necks, and we will kiss each other. (vv. 62–63)

Adam-ondi-Ahman

Another closely related example of midrash in the Doctrine and Covenants is found in section 116, received as revelation on May 19, 1838. The revelation identifies a site located in Missouri as "Adam-ondi-Ahman," believed by Latter-day Saints to be the place where Adam and Eve lived after being expelled from the Garden of Eden. The term also inspired a popular Latter-day Saint hymn written by W. W. Phelps and published in 1835 in the *Messenger and Advocate:*

> This earth was once a garden place,
> With all her glories common,
> And men did live a holy race,
> And worship Jesus face to face,
> In Adam-ondi-Ahman.[73]

---

72. Wellins Calcott, *A Candid Disquisition of the Principles and Practices of the Most Ancient and Honorable Society of Free and Accepted Masons*, 168, 175.

73. W. W. Phelps, "This Earth Was Once a Garden Place," in *Hymns of The Church of Jesus Christ of Latter-day Saints*, 49.

The Masonic Enoch legend as described by George Oliver seems a likely source for Mormon teachings surrounding Adam-ondi-Ahman. Because degenerate humankind would not listen to his preaching, the Grand Master Enoch called a special assembly of Masons "in whom he could confide." In the presence of Adam, Seth, Jared (Enoch's father), and Methuselah (Enoch's son), Enoch lamented the wickedness of men on earth and asked for advice and assistance in stemming the torrent of evil. As part of this remarkable meeting, Adam communicated a great and terrible prophecy "that all mankind, except a few just persons, should so far swerve from their allegiance to God, as to cause the destruction of all created things by water and fire."[74]

Mormon scripture includes similar elements. In accord with the Masonic description, revelation from Smith reports that, three years before his death, Adam called his children together, including Enoch and all the faithful down to the generation of Methuselah. In the company of the Lord, Adam "stood up in the midst of the congregation; and, notwithstanding he was bowed down with age, being full of the Holy Ghost, predicted whatsoever should befall his posterity unto the latest generation" (D&C 107:56).

In Mormonism, this teaching is expanded to include restoration and eschatological themes. Latter-day Saints teach that at the Second Coming, a vast meeting will be held at the same place: a spot in Jackson County, Missouri, near where the Garden of Eden was once located. At this time, the city of Enoch, taken up into heaven due to the great righteousness of its inhabitants, will return to the earth. These righteous people and many others will join all the dispensation heads such as Adam, Enoch, Abraham, Moses, and Jesus Christ himself, with Adam again holding a special role at this council.[75]

Eternal Matter

In his popular book, *The Spirit of Masonry*, William Hutchinson described early Christians who had become "infected with the Egyptian philosophy."[76] They held that the Supreme Being "was not the creator of the universe, nor the

---

74. Oliver, *Antiquities of Freemasonry*, 87–92.

75. "I saw Adam in the valley of Ah-dam ondi-ahman—he called together his children & blessed them with a Patriarchal blessing. The Lord appeared in their midst. & he (Adam) blessed them." "Discourse, between circa 26 June and circa 4 August 1839–A, as Reported by Unknown Scribe," The Joseph Smith Papers, 3. See also Joseph Fielding Smith, *The Way to Perfection*, 310: "The City of Enoch with its inhabitants is to return and join in the grand celebration at the coming of Christ to reign, and all the prophets of old and the righteous saints shall be gathered in the grand assembly of rejoicing."

76. Hutchinson's book and its descriptions were well known throughout America. First published in 1775, it was continuously in print for over a hundred years, going through multiple editions in both the United Kingdom and the United States.

alone independent Being: for, according to them, matter too was eternal."[77] This teaching became a core theological notion in Mormonism during the 1830s and 1840s,[78] when declarations on the subject were first formulated in relation to work on the Book of Abraham in Kirtland and found their way into the Doctrine and Covenants: "Man is spirit. The elements are eternal, and spirit and element, inseparably connected, receive a fulness of joy" (D&C 93:33). While imprisoned in Columbia, Missouri, in 1838 and 1839, Apostle Parley P. Pratt wrote a treatise on the "eternal duration of matter," wherein he explained that matter and spirit were the two great principles of all existence:

> Everything animate and inanimate is composed of one or the other, or both of these eternal principles. . . . Matter and spirit are of equal duration; both are self-existent,—they never began to exist, and they never can be annihilated.[79]

> [M]atter as well as spirit is eternal, uncreated, self-existing. However infinite the variety of its changes, forms and shapes . . . , it is there, durable as the throne of Jehevah [*sic*]. ETERNITY is inscribed in indelible characters on every particle.[80]

Expansions upon the doctrine continued to be articulated and formalized throughout the Doctrine and Covenants. In May 1843, Smith declared: "There is no such thing as immaterial matter. All spirit is matter, but it is more fine or pure, and can only be discerned by purer eyes; we cannot see it; but when our bodies are purified we shall see that it is all matter" (D&C 131:7–8). By April 1844 Smith taught from the pulpit that the elements had existed "from the time [God] had. The pure principles of element are principles that can never be destroyed."[81] More specifically, Smith also taught that the mind of man was as immortal as God:

> The spirit of man is not a created being; it existed from eternity, and will exist to eternity. Anything created cannot be eternal; and earth, water, etc., had their existence in an elementary state, from eternity.[82]

This was expressed again in an 1844 discourse, in which Smith utilized a well-known Masonic allegory:

> I take my ring from my finger and liken it unto the mind of man, the immortal spirit, because it has no beginning. Suppose you cut it in two; but as the Lord lives there would be an end. . . . God never did have power to create the spirit of man at all. God himself could not create himself: intelligence exists upon a self existent

---

77. William Hutchinson, *The Spirit of Masonry: in Moral and Elucidatory Lectures*, 61–62.

78. "Matter is eternal" (D&C 93:3); "Man was also in the beginning with God. Intelligence, or the light of truth, was not created or made, neither indeed can be" (v. 29).

79. Parley P. Pratt, "Regeneration and the Eternal Duration of Matter," 105.

80. Pratt, 111.

81. "History, 1838–1856, volume E-1 [1 July 1843–30 April 1844]," The Joseph Smith Papers, 1973.

82. "History, 1838–1856, volume C-1 [2 November 1838–31 July 1842]," The Joseph Smith Papers, 11 [addenda].

principle, it is a spirit from age to age, and there is no creation about it. . . . The first principles of man are self existent with God.[83]

Eternal Bonds

Joseph Smith frequently referred to priesthood ordinances as the "welding link" in a chain to bring together all of humanity.[84] He also referred to the welding bonds of friendship, a more Masonic idea. A well-known 1843 teaching by Smith expounds upon the relationship between God and mortal man as well as the association that humankind will have among themselves in the eternal worlds:

> When he [the Savior] shall appear we shall see him as he is. we shall see that he is a man like ourselves.—And that same sociality, which exists amo[n]g[s]t us here will exist amo[n]g us there only it will be coupled with etern[a]l glory, which glory we do not now enjoy.[85]

Mormon scholar Don Bradley has written about the Masonic ideal of oneness through fellowship influencing Joseph Smith's "Grand Fundamental Principles of Mormonism." In Smith's dexterous hands, the Masonic principles of brotherly love and sacred kinship evolved into the doctrine of eternal union through the priesthood.[86] Samuel Brown's *In Heaven as it is on Earth* contains a discussion that he terms the Mormon "chain of belonging."[87] This phrase owes a debt to Freemasonry both in concept and terminology. For example, George Oliver wrote:

> Our secrets embrace, in a comprehensive manner, human science and divine knowledge; they *link mankind together in the indissoluble chain of sincere affection*; and, which is of far greater import, they incite to the practice of those virtues, which may do much towards securing happiness in a future state.[88]

Masonic writer Rob Morris put this same sentiment into poetry in 1854:

> Hands round! Ye faithful brotherhood, the bright fraternal chain,
> We part upon the Square below and meet in Heaven again;
> And the words of precious meaning, those words Masonic are:
> "We meet upon the Level and we part upon the Square."[89]

---

83. Joseph Smith discourse, April 7, 1844, reported in "Conference Minutes: Continuation of Last April's Conference," 615.

84. See, for example, "Journal, December 1841–December 1842," The Joseph Smith Papers, 199.

85. "Journal, December 1842–June 1844; Book 2, 10 March 1843–14 July 1843," The Joseph Smith Papers, 37. This was later canonized as Doctrine and Covenants 130:2.

86. Don Bradley, "'The Grand Fundamental Principles of Mormonism' Joseph Smith's Unfinished Reformation," 32–41.

87. Samuel Morris Brown, *In Heaven as It Is on Earth: Joseph Smith and the Early Mormon Conquest of Death*, chs. 7–8.

88. Oliver, *Antiquities of Freemasonry*, 11; emphasis added.

89. Rob Morris, "The Level and the Square," in Rob Morris, *The Poetry of Freemasonry*, 11.

In the words of these authors, the bonds of brotherhood form an indissoluble chain forged by the hand of God, each link bright and virtuous.

Joseph Smith recognized the importance of midrash in a vibrant religious tradition, and he utilized it for purposes similar to those found in Judaism and in Freemasonry: as a vehicle for moral instruction and the building of complex theological concepts. It provided both permission and framework to explore, expand, borrow, adapt, and innovate when considering any aspect of religious life or thought. Because the building blocks of his work were typically Masonic beliefs that permeated his environment, Masonic-like expansions are found in every Mormon scripture from the Book of Mormon to Joseph Smith's inspired revision of the Bible, and from the Doctrine and Covenants to the Book of Abraham. Numerous ideas from these works that Latter-day Saints have come to believe are uniquely Mormon have antecedents in popular Masonic sources of Smith's day.

In his work as latter-day prophet, Smith established ideas expressed by such Masonic luminaries as William Hutchinson, George Oliver, Joshua Bradley, and Salem Town as part of Latter-day Saint scriptural tradition. He emphasized elements of Masonic culture to provide a narrative that looked and felt familiar to its audience. Yet, he was not merely appropriating Masonic concepts. Smith reframed foundational myths of Freemasonry in light of his unique understanding of God.

CHAPTER 7

THE BOOK OF ABRAHAM: ADVANCING THE INTERESTS OF TRUE MASONRY

Abraham was born; a man who was destined to impede the rapid progress of idolatry, to reduce the influence of the Cabiric mysteries, and to advance the interests of true Masonry and religion amongst mankind.

—George Oliver

Napoleon Bonaparte's Egyptian campaign of 1798 to 1801 launched the worldwide scientific study of ancient Egyptian remains and culture. In the United States as well as the rest of the world, Egyptian culture spurred conversation on topics ranging from art and architecture to independent nationhood, national identity, race, and slavery. Freemasonry, with its specific interest in the ancient past, was particularly influenced by this nineteenth-century Egyptomania.[1]

By late 1832 or early 1833, the enigmatic Irish American entrepreneur Michael Chandler mysteriously obtained eleven Egyptian mummies from the estate of their deceased Italian discoverer, Antonio Lebolo. Aware of the interest that Freemasons took in Egyptian antiquities, Chandler first displayed the mummies and other curiosities at the Masonic Hall in Philadelphia on April 3 and April 22, 1833. In September of that same year, the exhibit was also shown at the Masonic Hall in Harrisburg, Pennsylvania.[2] Chandler arrived in Ohio by March

---

1. From the time of its official beginnings in 1717, speculative Masonry had exhibited a keen interest in ancient Egypt. See Erik Hornung, *The Secret Lore of Egypt: Its Impact on the West*, trans. David Lorton, 116–27; Manly P. Hall, *Freemasonry of the Ancient Egyptians, to which is added an Interpretation of the Crata Repoa Initiation Rite*, 81–100. By 1728, the seal of a lodge in Naples already displayed a pyramid and sphinx. In 1770, an "Egyptian" initiation path through seven degrees was described in a German Masonic tract. The *pastophoris* (apprentice) was initiated into the sciences and the "common hieroglyphic writing system," and then clad in an "Egyptian" fashion with a pyramid-shaped cap, apron, and collar. In the third degree he passed through the door of death into a room containing embalmed bodies and the coffin of Osiris; here, he learned "hierogrammatic" writing. In the sixth degree, he learned about the stars and the divine. With the password *ibis*, he reached the seventh and last degree, that of a Prophet. Early American Freemasons demonstrated the Egyptian influence as well, adorning the one-dollar bill with a pyramid and all-seeing eye.

2. "Six Egyptian Mummies," *The Harrisburg Chronicle* (September 9, 1833), quoted in H. Donl Peterson, "The History and Significance of the Book of Abraham," 178.

1835 with four remaining mummies. In Painesville, Chandler allowed them to be examined by a phrenologist, who attempted to identify them based on the shape of their heads.[3]

At the end of June 1835, Chandler traveled to Kirtland to meet the controversial Mormon prophet, Joseph Smith. Chandler had heard from believers and skeptics alike the claims of Smith translating a holy book from ancient Egyptian writings engraved on plates of gold, and he believed the Mormon leader would be interested in viewing, and perhaps purchasing, the mummies and Egyptian funeral papyri found with them. Smith soon identified the mummies as a pharaoh and his family, but he was most captivated by the accompanying papyri. The scroll on the oldest woman's chest, Smith declared, was a record kept by the biblical Joseph during his sojourn in Egypt, while the roll discovered on the male's chest comprised the record of Abraham "written by his own hand."[4] The Mormons purchased the four mummies, three papyrus rolls, and a few remaining scraps of papyrus in Chandler's collection. For these items they raised $2,400, the equivalent of the average yearly salaries of five farm families.[5]

To those who believed the legendary history of Freemasonry was literally true, the Kirtland Egyptian papyri must have held an incredible fascination. As Joseph Smith unrolled the scroll that he would believe to be the writings of Abraham, the first figure to catch his eye was what appeared to be the attempted sacrifice of Abraham at the hands of spurious Egyptian priests. A drawing of what he perceived as Abraham in Pharaoh's court teaching the principles of astronomy to the Egyptians was pictured at the end of the scroll. It seems that to the mind of the prophet, God had miraculously delivered the original scriptural stories of the patriarch Abraham into his hands. By rendering the hieroglyphic text on the papyrus into modern language, he took up the role of a Masonic restorer, bringing to light the heretofore concealed Masonic and priestly mysteries.

LDS scholars disagree on precisely how the text of the Book of Abraham was produced. Some have speculated it was translated directly from papyrus that

---

3. See A. Gardner, "Mummies." Phrenology characterized the mummies as an eighty-year-old man with "mild passions," a sixty-year-old female full of "motherly goodness," a woman in her forties, and a twenty-year-old female with a misshapen head that approximated the "form of the Orang Outang" and whom was a "demon of society."

4. "A Translation," 704.

5. Marvin C. Hill, C. Keith Rooker, and Larry T. Wimmer, "The Kirtland Economy Revisited: A Market Critique of Sectarian Economics," 396. Josiah Quincy describes his visit to Nauvoo in 1844, where he was told that Lucy Mack Smith purchased the mummies: "'And now come with me,' said the Prophet, 'and I will show you the curiosities.' So saying, he led the way to a lower room, where sat a venerable and respectable-looking lady. 'This is my mother, gentlemen. The curiosities we shall see belong to her. They were purchased with her own money, at a cost of six thousand dollars.'" Josiah Quincy, *Figures of the Past from the Leaves of Old Journals*, 386.

Reconstructed scroll of the "Breathing Permit" of Hor.

Joseph Smith had in his possession.[6] Others believe the hieroglyphic characters functioned as a mnemonic device.[7] Still others claim that the Egyptian papyri stimulated revelation by which Smith wrote the text.[8] Each of these variations constitutes the creation of a scriptural midrash, and this midrash was influenced by nineteenth-century Freemasonry.

Although some authors exult in pointing out the similarities of Mormon scripture, especially the Book of Abraham, with the ancient past, one must follow the chain of influence from the closest to the furthest out. Masons had been studying and drawing comparisons between their rites and ancient Egyptians for a very long time, providing Joseph Smith and those in his environs with ample and readily available interpretations of the biblical and ancient world. Thus, even where similarities exist between restoration scripture and the ancient past, they are best explained by the long tradition of Masonic interest in that past.

Recovered Text of the Egyptian Papyri

Joseph Smith's Book of Abraham traces the "first government of Egypt," which "was established by Pharaoh, the eldest son of Egyptus, the daughter of Ham, and it was after the manner of the government of Ham, which was patriar-

---

6. John Gee, *An Introduction to the Book of Abraham*, 84–86.

7. John A. Tvedtnes, "The Use of Mnemonic Devices in Oral Traditions, as Exemplified by the Book of Abraham and the Hor Sensen Papyrus," 2–10.

8. Terryl Givens and Brian M. Hauglid, *The Pearl of Greatest Price: Mormonism's Most Controversial*, 121–40, 189–93.

chal" (Abr. 1:25). During Smith's day, there were roughly four streams of thought on Masonic origins, each based more or less on the legends and myths found in the Old Gothic Constitutions.[9] Of significance to Latter-day Saints, each of these legends engages the transmission of Masonic mysteries through ancient Egypt. Freemasons claimed the authentic mysteries had descended to them pure and undefiled over the course of time: first from Adam, then through Noah and his sons to ancient Egypt, then through Solomon and ancient Israel, and eventually to modern times. Mason George Oliver theorized that when Masonry entered Egypt it was corrupted by the magical practices of the Pharaohs:

> It is evident that, before the call of Abraham to restore the true worship along with the purity of Masonry, the efforts of the Cabiri, in conjunction with Thoth and others, had succeeded in substituting their mysteries for truth amongst the posterity of Shem, as well as of Ham and Japheth.[10]

Recovering the Order of the Priesthood

Like the works of prominent eighteenth- and nineteenth-century Masonic writers, the Book of Abraham addresses the use of proper authority when imparting or administering the mysteries. It tells the story of a righteous Pharaoh, a good man who earnestly sought to imitate the true order "established by the Fathers" (Abr. 1:26). Despite his righteous intentions, Pharaoh did not have the proper authority to administer. Through this story, Smith reveals both his attitude toward the contemporary and spurious craft of Masonry and his reliance upon George Oliver's "two traditions" theory. The text of Abraham 1 implies that the heavenly order was patriarchal and therefore could not be passed down any other way. Further, Ham had been cursed by Noah pertaining to priesthood so he could not bequeath legitimate authority to instruct in authentic mysteries, nor administer its related rites and ordinances. At best, he could only imitate that ancient order (vv. 26–27).

Assuming that Smith's midrash is meant to address the issue of Masonic authority, it warns that Freemasons may be righteous and good men, but at best, they can only imitate that ancient order that is the property of the holy priesthood. Theologically, nineteenth-century Freemasonry held no salvific power. Royal Arch Masons replicated the tabernacle in the wilderness, the Ark of the Covenant, and related holy items in order to provide an allegorical recovery of truth.[11] In Smith's

---

9. Andersonian, Prestonian, Hutchinsonian, and Oliverian. These are reviewed in Albert Gallatin Mackey, *The History of Freemasonry: Its Legendary Origins*, 116–50.

10. George Oliver, *The Antiquities of Freemasonry; Comprising Illustrations of the Five Grand Periods of Masonry from the Creation of the World to the Dedication of King Solomon's Temple*, 154.

11. "Brethren, the Grand Council is of the opinion—that this most valuable discover—is an imitation of the Ark of the Covenant . . . a symbol of the Divine Presence with—and protection of the Jewish people—and a pledge of the stability of their nation—as long as they obeyed the commands of God." Stichting Argus, "Ritual for the Royal Arch Degree, Indiana."

view, however, this was all a pale imitation of the real thing he could provide. He thus told his private secretary, Benjamin F. Johnson, that "Freemasonry was the apostate endowment as sectarian religion was the apostate religion."[12]

It is significant that Smith called Masonry the apostate endowment, as the fundamental concern of his Abraham midrash was the issue of legitimate versus spurious Masonry.[13] His translation of the Egyptian papyri tells of Egyptians who "would fain claim [the right of Priesthood] from Noah, through Ham" (Abr. 1:27), alluding to the Masons who claimed to receive their doctrines and "Geometry" pure from Ham through the priesthood of the Egyptians. In nineteenth-century America, Ham was considered the ancestor of Africans, and biblical passages like Genesis 9:25–27 provided justification for those who enslaved them.[14] Although the Book of Abraham was later used to justify denying priesthood ordination to men of African descent, evidence suggests that Smith was favorable toward the ordination of free black men,[15] and he never used the Abraham passages to establish an anti-Negro policy. This is because the central issue of this passage of the Book of Abraham is not one of race except in an incidental way; rather, it describes how legitimate authority is transferred.

Human Intelligences

The pages of the Book of Abraham also contain doctrinal content on celestial bodies and spiritual beings placed in a Masonic framing. Here, Smith presented what he saw as the original cosmology of Abraham, which had been given by the patriarch to the Egyptians in ancient times. Abraham 3 describes the great and governing stars "nearest unto the throne of God" (Abr. 3:2), with the star Kolob being "the greatest of all the Kokaubeam[16] [stars] that thou hast seen, because it is nearest unto [God]" (v. 16).

Masonic writer Will Hutchinson referred to a similar concept in 1775. He described a Supreme Being who produced "other immortal and spiritual natures," some of whom were "placed in the higher regions, others in the lower." Those

---

12. Benjamin F. Johnson, *My Life's Review: The Autobiography of Benjamin F. Johnson*, 85.

13. For another perspective, see Michael W. Homer, *Joseph's Temples: The Dynamic Relationship Between Freemasonry and Mormonism*, 113–37. His chapter "Pharoah's Curse" details Smith's scriptural writings on Cain and the curse of skin color. Homer's writings propose that this idea prompted American Freemasonry's "exclusionary policies" prohibiting anyone with African descent from entering the Lodge and refusing to recognize African American (Prince Hall) Lodges.

14. Larry R. Morrison, "The Religious Defense of American Slavery Before 1830," 16–29.

15. Kyle R. Walker, *William B. Smith: In the Shadow of a Prophet*, 439.

16. Hebrew: *kochavim*, "stars." Smith's spelling betrays the Sephardic pronunciation of Joshua Seixas, Smith's Hebrew teacher in Kirtland. See Louis C. Zucker, "Joseph Smith as a Student of Hebrew," 51.

in the lower regions were "nighest to the place of matter."[17] Thus, Hutchinson described what was later incorporated into Mormonism as a tripartite theory of spirit creation. In this theory, intelligence exists in non-created form until organized into a spirit being by God. The spirit can then inhabit a human body and become a mortal being.

The Book of Abraham compares these "higher and lower" intelligences to the very order of the heavens:

> And thus there shall be the reckoning of the time of one planet above another, until thou come nigh unto Kolob, which . . . is set nigh unto the throne of God, to govern all. . . .
>
> If two things exist, and there be one above the other, there shall be greater things above them. . . .
>
> These two facts do exist, that there are two spirits, one being more intelligent than the other; there shall be another more intelligent than they; I am the Lord thy God, I am more intelligent than they all. (Abr. 3:9, 16, 19)

The scripture also makes clear that "spirits . . . have no beginning; they existed before, they shall have no end, they shall exist after, for they are *gnolaum*, or eternal" (v. 18).[18]

This language imputed to God in the Book of Abraham—particularly the use of the word "intelligent"—suggests a broader thematic argument that spirit and intelligence are eternal. The prophet would later discuss this in some detail:

> The mind or the intelligence which man possesses is co-equal [co-eternal] with God himself. . . . I am dwelling on the immortality of the spirit of man. . . . The intelligence of spirits had no beginning, neither will it have an end. . . . Their [sic] never was a time when there were not spirits; for they are co-equal [co-eternal] with our Father in heaven.[19]

Smith believed that the human spirit was not a "created being"; instead, "the Father called all spirits before him at the creation of man and organized them."[20]

In his 1775 *The Spirit of Masonry*, Hutchinson quotes a "Dr. Prideaux" who comments on analogous aspects of celestial bodies and spiritual beings or "intelligencies." He remarks that in Abraham's day the Egyptians believed:

> [T]he Sun, Moon, and Stars . . . were *Habitations of Intelligencies*, which animated the orbs in the same manner as the soul animates the body of man, and were causes of their motion; and that these intelligencies *were of a middle sort between God and them*: they thought these the properest things to be *Mediators* between God and them; and

---

17. William Hutchinson, *The Spirit of Masonry: In Moral and Elucidatory Lectures*, 61–62n.

18. "Book of Abraham and Facsimiles, 1 March–16 May 1842," The Joseph Smith Papers, 720. *Gnolaum* is a transliteration of the Hebrew word, ʿolam meaning *eternal* or *everlasting*. See Zucker, "Joseph Smith as a Student of Hebrew," 51.

19. "History, 1838–1856, volume E-1 [1 July 1843–30 April 1844]," The Joseph Smith Papers, 1973–74.

20. "History, 1838–1856, volume C-1 [2 November 1838–31 July 1842]," The Joseph Smith Papers, 11 [addenda].

therefore the planets being nearest of all the heavenly bodies, and generally looked on to have the greatest influence on this world, they made choice of them in the first place, as their Gods' mediators, who were to mediate with the Supreme God for them, and to procure mercies and favours, which they prayed for.[21]

Council of Heaven

Freemasons also commented on how the divine creative work was realized. Specifically, the Royal Arch degree alludes to a "Grand Council" that exists eternally in the heavens. It is first mentioned during the preliminary prayer of that degree:

> And finally, O merciful Father, when we shall have passed through the outward *veils* of these earthly *courts*, when the earthly house of this *tabernacle* shall be dissolved, may we be admitted into the *Holy of Holies* above, into the presence of the *Grand Council* of heaven, where the Supreme *High Priest* for ever presides, for ever reigns. Amen. *So mote it be.*[22]

Salem Town, the Grand Chaplain of the Grand Chapter of Royal Arch Masons in New York, mentioned another function of the council: "Such the Grand Council of Eternity, which devised and executed that great plan of man's redemption."[23] To Royal Arch masons, the work of the Grand Council is both creative and redemptive.

Midrash in chapter 3 of the Book of Abraham develops a passage in Psalms in a strikingly similar manner. The Psalm is vague: "God standeth in the congregation of the mighty; he judgeth among the gods" (Psalm 82:1). In the Book of Abraham, the reader is told of a group of premortal souls gathered in the presence of God. In council, they considered the Father's great plan of salvation, including the Creation, Fall, and Atonement:

> Now the Lord had shown unto me, Abraham, the intelligences that were organized before the world was; and among all these there were many of the noble and great ones; . . . And there stood one among them that was like unto God, and he said unto those who were with him: We will go down, for there is space there, and we will take of these materials, and we will make an earth whereon these may dwell; And we will prove them herewith, to see if they will do all things whatsoever the Lord their God shall command them. And they who keep their first estate shall be added upon; and they who keep not their first estate shall not have glory in the same kingdom with those who keep their first estate. (Abr. 3:22–26)

Stimulated by Masonic concepts, Joseph Smith added his own prophetic insight to the biblical record.

---

21. Hutchinson, *The Spirit of Masonry*, 103n.

22. Jeremy L. Cross, *The True Masonic Chart, or Hieroglyphic Monitor*, 103; emphasis in original.

23. Salem Town, *A System of Speculative Masonry in its Origin, Patronage, Dissemination, Principles, Duties and Ultimate Designs, Laid Open for the Examination of the Serious and Candid*, 25.

The Facsimiles: Dating and Descriptions

The Egyptian papyri were adorned with several intriguing drawings Joseph Smith connected with the story of Abraham. In 1841, he commissioned artist Reuben Hedlock to engrave printing blocks of three of the images and accompanied these with keys to explain the figures in each one.[24] Masonic language and symbolism can easily be seen in both the engravings and their accompanying explanations. Because there is no manuscript evidence of any of the facsimiles or their explanations before 1842, some have assumed the Masonic influence in these writings comes from the Nauvoo period. However, much of the material included in the explanations was mentioned in Smith's 1835 translation activities. For example, his journal entry for October 1, 1835, reads: "This after noon labored on the Egyptian alphabet, in company with brsr. O. Cowdery and W. W. Phelps: The system of astronomy was unfolded."[25] This evidently refers to the bound "Grammar and Alphabet," where, on page 24, the subject matter shifts from Abraham, Egypt, and the patriarchal priesthood to astronomy. Additionally, entries in the Grammar document penned by Warren Parrish shortly after October 29, 1835, introduce "Veh Kli flos-isis" (the "fo[u]rth fixed governing star") at the end of the fifth, fourth, and third degrees, and "Kolob" (the "first creation nearer to the Celestial, or the residence of God") at the end of all five degrees. Influence from the above passages can be seen in the explanatory key for Facsimile 2.

Thus, the facsimiles' connection of Abraham with the patriarchal priesthood and with a knowledge of astronomy persuasively derives from Freemasonry and substantially dates from 1835. Even at this early date, Smith and Cowdery would have been intimately familiar with Masonry through their family connections, and Phelps, as a renounced Mason, had been involved with the Fraternity directly.

Facsimile 1: Masonic Initiation

Discussing a ritual designed to prepare an aspirant for initiation into esoteric knowledge, George Oliver mused,

---

24. "23 February 1842. [I] gave Reuben Hedlock instruction concerning the Cut for the Altar and Gods in the Records of Abraham" (Facsimile 1). "1 March 1842. [D]uring the forenoon I was at my Office and the printing Office, correcting the first plate or cut of the Records of Father Abraham, prepared by Reuben Hedlock." "4 March 1842. At my office exhibiting the Book of Abraham in the original To Brother Reuben Hedlock, so that he might take the size of the several plates or Cuts, and prepare the Blocks for the Times and Seasons; and also gave instruction concerning the arrangement of the writing on the large cut, illustrating the principles of Astronomy." (Facsimile 2). See "History, 1838–1856, volume C-1 [2 November 1838–31 July 1842]," 1275–76, 1286.

25. "Journal, 1835–1836," The Joseph Smith Papers, 3.

Book of Abraham Facsimile 1, as published in the *Times and Seasons*.

[T]here is scarcely a single ceremony in Free Masonry, but we find its corresponding rite in one or other of the idolatrous mysteries; and the coincidence can only be accounted for by supposing that these mysteries were derived from Masonry.[26]

Of course, Masonry might have derived from "idolatrous mysteries" instead of the other way around, but it was nonetheless important to establish a link between Masonry and "idolatrous" rites, rituals, and customs: it legitimized the interpretation of any practice similar to Freemasonry through a Masonic lens. For example, Oliver describes an ancient mystical custom an aspirant had to perform before he could participate in the higher secrets: "He was placed within the *Pastos*, or *Bed*, or *Coffin*." Here, he fasted for three days and nights in seclusion and darkness until he reached the proper state of mind to receive certain great and important truths. "I am inclined to think," said Oliver, "that when the aspirant entered into the mystic cell, *he was directed to lay himself down upon the*

---

26. George Oliver, *Signs and Symbols: Illustrated and Explained in a Course of Twelve Lectures on Freemasonry*, 109.

bed, which shadowed out the tomb or coffin of the Great Father." While lying on this "holy couch" in simulation of "*his figurative deceased prototype*," he reproduced first "the deep sleep of death" and then a "*resurrection from the bed . . . his restoration to life,* or his regeneration into a new world."[27]

This could correspond to the scene Smith saw of Abraham on the sacrificial bed in Facsimile 1. The resulting Mormon midrash involved Abraham's forced immolation on the lion couch by the idolatrous Priests of Pharoah. Hands raised in the grand hailing sign of a Master Mason, Abraham was raised from that bed and initiated into the higher mysteries.

Facsimile 2: Cosmology, Key Words, Signs, Tokens, and Penalties

The higher mysteries received by Abraham are laid out in Facsimile 2. Joseph Smith described this in the most Masonic terms of any of the facsimiles, imbued it with religious significance, and used it as allegorical temple instruction.

Smith's explanation of the facsimile suggests he considered the circular hypocephalus[28] to be Abraham's teachings on Egyptian cosmology.[29] The shape of the facsimile calls to mind the "eternal round"—a concept of the universe. Smith understood the figure labelled "No. 1" to be "Kolob, signifying the first creation, nearest to the celestial, or the residence of God," and keeping the same celestial measurement of time. Next to Kolob was No. 2, Oliblish, "holding the key of power" pertaining to other planets. These were said to be "revealed to from God from ^to^ Abraham, as he offered incence Sacrifice upon an alter [sic]."[30] Just as George Oliver did in his Masonic writings, Smith pictured Abraham as the recipient of heavenly instruction concerning astronomy and mathematics. He also possessed a Masonic-like priesthood with its "grand Key words" bestowed by God to him, Adam, Seth, Noah, and Melchizedek.

In Reuben Hedlock's facsimile of the hypocephalus, a stylized figure of God on His throne appears to be giving a Masonic sign. His right arm is "raised to the square," surmounted by a pair of compasses; His other arm is extended at His side.[31] This section labeled No. 7 "represents God sitting upon his throne, reveal-

---

27. Oliver, 112–13; emphasis in original.

28. A disk-shaped amulet placed under the head of the deceased, usually of a priestly family. It was intended to magically preserve and enliven the mummy. James R. Harris, *The Facsimiles of the Book of Abraham: A Study of the Joseph Smith Egyptian Papyri,* 50.

29. Robert K. Ritner, *The Joseph Smith Egyptian Papyri: A Complete Edition, P. JS 1–4 and the Hypocephalus of Sheshonq,* 224.

30. "Explanation to Accompany Facsimile 2, circa 15 March 1842," The Joseph Smith Papers, 1.

31. "Book of Abraham and Facsimiles, 1 March–16 May 1842," The Joseph Smith Papers, insert between 720–21. Compare with the explanation of the hypocephalus in the Willard Richards document, "Explanation to Accompany Facsimile 2, circa 15 March 1842," The Joseph Smith Papers.

Book of Abraham Facsimile 2, as published in the *Times and Seasons*.

ing, through the heavens, the grand Key words of the Priesthood; as, also, the sign of the Holy Ghost unto Abraham, in the form of a dove." Similarly, section No. 3 "[i]s made to represent God, sitting upon his throne, clothed with power & authority; with a crown of Eternal light upon his head." This crown of light would be understood in Masonic terms to represent a fullness of understanding. The section also represents "the grand Key words of the Holy Priesthood, as revealed to Adam in the Garden of Eden, as also to Seth, Noah, Melchisedek Abraham and all to whom the priesthood was revealed."[32]

As shown in the explanatory material, the Grand Key Word is communicated by God and not to be revealed publicly. No. 8 "contains writing that cannot be revealed unto the world; but is to be had in the Holy Temple of God."[33] This confidential instruction pertaining to temples owes a debt to Masonry, where the lodge symbolically represents King Solomon's Temple. The secrets mentioned in Smith's explication of Facsimile 2 are the same kind of secrets to be

---

32. "Book of Abraham and Facsimiles, 1 March–16 May 1842," insert between 720–21.
33. "Book of Abraham and Facsimiles, 1 March–16 May 1842," insert between 720–21.

had in Freemasonry. For Masons as well as Mormons, concealed ritual elements pertaining to key signs and words can only be found in the temple or lodge.

Smith's treatment of secret words around the border of the hypocephalus parallels in interesting ways the writing around the border of the triangular plate in the Royal Arch degree inscribed in the Royal Arch cipher, which represents the golden triangular plate given to Enoch. In some depictions there is a double-bordered circle around the triangle.

Additional evidence may suggest that others besides Smith understood the facsimiles to have Masonic meaning. The earliest extant manuscript of Facsimile 2 is in the handwriting of Willard Richards. It was created in late 1841 to early 1842 in Nauvoo. When recording Smith's explanatory key for Facsimile 2, section no. 11, Richards utilized a well-known expression in Freemasonry that concludes every Masonic prayer: "[A]lso. If the world can find out these n[u]mbers, *So mote it be*, Amen."[34]

Royal Arch cipher on golden plate, "The Mistery of the Royal Arch Word," by Arturo de Hoyos. Courtesy of the Scottish Rite Research Society.

The origin of the phrase "so mote it be" in Freemasonry dates from the Middle Ages in England. It is found in two important Masonic manuscripts, the earliest versions of the *Old Charges*. The Regius Manuscript, dated to 1390, closes with the words "Amen amen so mote it be, So say we all for charity." The Cooke Manuscript, dated to 1410, contains the words "Amen so mote it be."[35] In modern times, groups derived from Masonry (such as Wicca) have adopted the Masonic invocation "so mote it be," but in the nineteenth century, it was an identifying Masonic idiom. When the section was reprinted in the *Times and Seasons*, the phrase "so mote it be" was changed to "so let it be," veiling the Masonic nature of the phrase.

Facsimile 3: Judgment of the Dead

Egyptologists have agreed that the image on Facsimile 3 represents the judgment of the dead before the throne of Osiris. Interestingly, by the beginning of the nineteenth century, this scene informed the ritual in the thirty-first degree of Scottish Rite Masonry.[36] The initiate takes part in an allegorical Egyptian judgment

---

34. "Explanation of Facsimile 2, circa 15 March 1842," 2, The Joseph Smith Papers; emphasis added.

35. Harry Carr, *The Freemason at Work*, 214.

36. This degree was given in the United States by 1801, but all the Scottish Rite degrees were substantially revised by Albert Pike in 1855.

Book of Abraham Facsimile 3, as published in the *Times and Seasons*.

ceremony in which his heart is weighed to determine his character. The Egyptian scene is meaningful to Freemasons because it reinforces universal moral lessons.

Joseph Smith interpreted the scene as "Abraham, sitting upon Pharoah's throne . . . reasoning upon the principles of Astronomy."[37] This parallels Masonic tradition, where Abraham is first tested before the heavens open and he is divinely instructed. In his role as patriarch, he then begins to instruct others in the sciences of astronomy and mathematics.[38]

The Facsimiles as Sacred Instruction

The three facsimiles included with Joseph Smith's Book of Abraham seem to function in a similar fashion to Masonic tracing boards. A tracing board is associated with each of the Blue Lodge degrees, for a total of three. The boards are described as containing "hieroglyphics."[39] They consist of confidential sacred instruction and allow Freemasons to remember important points in a ritual. Smith assigned the figures on the facsimiles with certain meanings that would allow Latter-day Saints who had been instructed in their esoteric significance to progress spiritually. Consequently, the images could function as mnemonic devices for Latter-day Saints, regardless of their original meanings.

---

37. "Book of Abraham and Facsimiles, 1 March–16 May 1842," 783–84.
38. See Oliver, *Antiquities of Freemasonry*, 67.
39. The symbolic pictures on a Masonic apron are also known as "hieroglyphics."

The facsimiles illustrate scenes of universal theological importance. As George Oliver noted, Abraham represents the perfect theocratic type.[40] The first facsimile denotes the principle of sacrifice and initiation. In the Mormon midrash, Abraham is delivered from the attempt of apostate priests to offer him as a sacrificial victim only to face the Lord's baffling request to offer up his own son and heir. Once he has passed his test, the second facsimile illustrates the principle of revelation. The initiate encounters God who gives him the instructions he needs to part the veil. Finally, in the third facsimile, he reasons upon the principles he has mastered, teaching them to others. His position on the throne indicates heavenly ascent and divinization. The vignette emphasizes his role as prophet, priest, and king.

The references to astronomy, grand keywords, square and compasses, signs, tokens and penalties, included together collectively in Joseph Smith's explanatory keys to the facsimiles, demonstrates that Freemasonry had become part of his revelatory process. From the Kirtland to the Nauvoo period, the Mormon prophet was meditating upon Masonic ideas, asking questions about them and receiving his answers. In doing so, Smith actively used Masonic concepts and symbols to build a framework for the Book of Abraham.

Papyrus Fragments

The description of another set of papyrus fragments further shows the influence of Freemasonry in Kirtland. The Joseph Smith Papyrus fragments labeled by Hugh Nibley as V, VI, VII, and VIII were identified by Egyptologist Klaus Baer as "The Book of the Dead belonging to the lady Tshenmîn."[41] Smith taught his followers that they were writings of the biblical Joseph who was sold into Egypt.[42] The set of fragments contains small drawings illustrating the text, and an interpretive exegesis of the drawings was provided by Oliver Cowdery in the *Messenger and Advocate*, published in December of 1835. "Enoch's Pillar, as mentioned by Josephus, is upon the same roll," wrote Cowdery. He noted that our present version of the Bible does not mention this fact but that

> Josephus says that the descendants of Seth were virtuous, and possessed a great knowledge of the heavenly bodies, and, that, in consequence of the prophecy of Adam, that the world should be destroyed once by water and again by fire, Enoch

---

40. George Oliver, *Historical Landmarks and Other Evidences of Freemasonry, Explained; a Series of Practical Lectures, with Copious Notes. Arranged on the System which has been Enjoined by the Grand Lodge of England, as it was Settled by the Lodge of Reconciliation, at the Union in 1813, in Two Volumes*, 214–16.

41. Klaus Baer, "The Breathing Permit of Hôr: A Translation of the Apparent Source of the Book of Abraham," 111.

42. William I. Appleby, *Autobiography and Journal of William I. Appleby*, 71–72; Oliver Cowdery, "Egyptian Mummies—Ancient Records," 234–36; "John Whitmer, History, 1831–circa 1847," The Joseph Smith Papers, 76.

wrote a history or an account of the same, and put into two pillars one of brick and the other of stone; and that the same were in being at his (Josephus') day.[43]

A careful examination of the relevant passage by the first-century Jewish-Roman historian Josephus shows that the antiquarian mentions the children of Seth as the makers of the pillars of brick and stone, not Enoch.[44] The inclusion of Enoch into the myth comes from nineteenth-century Freemasons who instead had Enoch as the maker of the two pillars.[45] Thus, although the writings of Josephus were available to the Latter-day Saints in 1835, it is more likely that Cowdery's reference to Josephus comes through Freemasonry.

The Kirtland Egyptian Papers

Several documents preserved from the Kirtland period show Joseph Smith experimenting with the text of the Book of Abraham and the Egyptian characters on the papyri. During early July of 1842, the Prophet worked in conjunction with his scribes W. W. Phelps and Oliver Cowdery to produce an "Egyptian Alphabet" and, in the latter half of that month, an expanded version of the project called the "Grammar and A[l]phabet of the Egyptian Language." A third "Egyptian Counting" manuscript pictured hieratic characters with corresponding counting numbers. Throughout the twentieth- and twenty-first centuries, Mormon writers believed these to be attempts by Smith's scribes to translate Egyptian characters from the papyri and not necessarily the Prophet himself. More recent LDS scholarship, however, has shown Smith to be personally involved in all aspects of the Book of Abraham project, including the "Alphabet,"

---

43. Oliver Cowdery, "Egyptian Mummies—Ancient Records," 236.

44. "[The children of Seth] . . . were the inventors of that peculiar sort of wisdom which is concerned with the heavenly bodies, and their order. And that their inventions might not be lost before they were sufficiently known, upon Adam's prediction that the world was to be destroyed at one time by the force of fire, and at another time by the violence and quantity of water, they made two pillars, the one of brick, the other of stone: they inscribed their discoveries on them both, that in case the pillar of brick should be destroyed by the flood, the pillar of stone might remain, and exhibit those discoveries to mankind; and also inform them that there was another pillar of brick erected by them. Now this remains in the land of Siriad to this day." Flavius Josephus, *Antiquities of the Jews*, Bk 1, Ch 2.

45. "ENOCH erected *Two* large Pillars, the one of *Stone* and the other of *Brick*, whereon he engraved the Abridgment of the Arts and Sciences, particularly *Geometry* and *Masonry*. . . . Some call them SETH's *Pillars*, but the old *Masons* always call'd them ENOCH's *Pillars*, and firmly believ'd this Tradition: nay *Josephus* (Lib i. cap.2.) affirms the *Stone-Pillar* still remain'd in *Syria* to his Time." James Anderson, *The New Book of Constitutions of the Antient and Honourable Fraternity of Free and Accepted Masons, Containing their History, Charges, Regulations, &c., Collected and Digested by Order of the Grand Lodge from their Old Records, faithful Traditions, and Lodge-Books, for the Use of the Lodges*, 3.

"Grammar," and "Counting" documents.[46] The question still being asked is what Smith was doing in these papers.

In a 2010 conference for Mormon apologetics, Will Schryver postulated that the "Alphabet," "Grammar," and "Counting" documents postdated the reception of the Book of Abraham and were an attempt to put phrases from this and others of Smith's earlier revelations into a Masonic-like cipher.[47] Challenging this thesis are six consecutive figures from the "Alphabet" described by Phelps in an 1835 letter to his wife, which he offers as a specimen of the "pure" Adamic language. This description of Smith's project to uncover the ancient Adamic language was largely extracted from an earlier document titled "A Sample of pure Language," issued by Smith in 1832. This demonstrates that Smith's explorations into "pure language" predate Chandler's arrival in Kirtland with the Egyptian mummies. Additionally, verbiage that would later be associated with the Book of Abraham had been employed by Smith in writings that also predated his reception of the Egyptian papyri.[48]

Brian Hauglid, an emeritus professor of ancient scripture at Brigham Young University, postulates that Phelps's May 1835 "Specimen" letter, containing the same characters in the Egyptian Alphabet documents, "may evidence some kind of an ongoing Egyptian language project occurring before the [July 1835] arrival of the mummies and papyri in Kirtland." Additionally, the Egyptian documents begin with over a page of characters not found on the papyri. According to Hauglid, "it is quite apparent where the unrelated characters end and the papyri characters begin," suggesting that the first part of the Egyptian alphabet documents also predate the arrival of the papyri in Kirtland.[49] While Hauglid attributes this phenomenon to the general "Egyptomania" present in the United States at the time, a more particular type of "Egyptomania" was to be found among American Freemasons who used the term "Egyptian" to reference a par-

---

46. For example, see Dan Vogel, *Book of Abraham Apologetics: A Review and Critique*, xvii, 93, 243–50.

47. William Schryver, "The Meaning and Purpose of the Kirtland Egyptian Papers."

48. For example, in 1834 Oliver Cowdery wrote the following concerning the restoration of the priesthood: "We diligently sought for the right of the fathers and the authority of the holy priesthood, and the power to administer in the same for we desired to be followers of righteousness and the possessors of greater knowledge." Quoted in Joseph Fielding Smith, "The Restoration of the Melchizedek Priesthood," 942. Compare this sentence with Abraham 1:2: "I sought for the blessings of the fathers, and the right whereunto I should be ordained to administer the same; having been myself a follower of righteousness, desiring also to be one who possessed great knowledge."

49. "First, the three Egyptian alphabet documents (EA) employ the same characters as those found in the 'Specimen' letter (albeit with different explanations) and, second, the first page and a half of the EA documents contain characters not associated with the papyri." Brian M. Hauglid, "The Book of Abraham and the Egyptian Project: 'A Knowledge of Hidden Languages,'" 481.

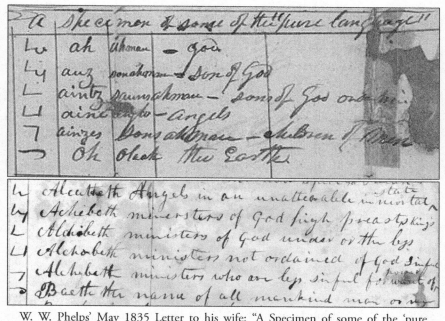

W. W. Phelps' May 1835 Letter to his wife: "A Specimen of some of the 'pure language'" (top). Compare to July 1835 Egyptian Alphabet document (bottom).

ticular form of ancient, legendary Freemasonry, and "hieroglyphs" to mean the pure, Hebraic language of Adam.[50]

---

50. "*Free-masonry* deals in *hieroglyphicks, symbols,* and *allegories,* and to be qualified to reveal their *meaning,* a man must know more than a mere nominal mason. The full interpretation of them, like that of the mysteries of old, is in select hands; . . . Others . . . are not qualified, if willing to betray it. Hence the secrecy, which has so long distinguished the fraternity." James Hardie, *New Free-Mason's Monitor; or, Masonic Guide,* 158; emphasis in original. See also Fabret d'Olivet, *The Hebraic Tongue Restored: And the True Meaning of the Hebrew Words Re-established and Proved by their Radical Analysis,* ix. D'Olivet was not a Freemason himself but was associated with the Martinists and formed his own quasi-Masonic order. His translator states: "Fabret d'Olivet claims the Hebrew contained in Genesis is *the pure idiom of the ancient Egyptians* . . . and has undertaken to restore this tongue lost for twenty-five centuries." The idiom of Hebrew had "become separated from a tongue which had attained its highest perfections [and had fallen] from degeneracy to degeneracy." See also Hutchinson, *The Spirit of Masonry,* 15–17: "Moses was also possessed of knowledge superior to that of his Egyptian teachers, through the revelations and inspirations of the Deity; —he had acquired the comprehension of, and was influenced to decipher all the hieroglyphical characters used by that people in their records:—it was no doubt a part of the original knowledge, to express by characters to the eye, the thoughts and sentiments of the mind—but this was obscured and debased in after ages by symbols and hieroglyphics: yet by the immediate dispensation of heaven, Moses attained the knowledge of those original characters; by which he was enabled to reveal to his people, and preserve

Joseph Smith's personal involvement with these Egyptian documents is further evidenced by several references in his diary to time spent working on the Egyptian Grammar and Alphabet. For example, a July 14, 1835, entry states:

> The remainder of this month, I was continually engaged in translating an alphabet to the Book of Abraham, and arrangeing a grammar of the Egyptian language as practiced by the Ancients.[51]

What was Smith's conception of the grammar "as practiced by the Ancients"? In the same ways mystics expand upon the essential meanings of tarot cards to divine certain things about an individual or situation, perhaps Smith was using a divination technique with the characters. Indeed, certain LDS authors have suggested that the prophet used the Egyptian characters as a springboard to revelation.[52]

Mormon Freemason Clinton Bartholomew has pioneered an investigation into the six consecutive characters of the Adamic written language in Phelps's "Specimen" letter and repeated in the "Alphabet" document. Five out of the six characters come from the Royal Arch. Using both the Royal Arch and the קיא רכב [aiq bkr][53] ciphers, Bartholomew demonstrates a correlation between the definitions Smith gave for the hieroglyphs and their English and Hebrew letters.[54] Additionally, he points to evidence that Smith was taking his conception of the interrelationship between the Adamic, Hebrew, and Egyptian languages directly from Masonic texts. Finally, Bartholomew suggests that Smith was led to believe that the Adamic written language was related to the Royal Arch cipher by Masonic ritual, specifically the Royal Arch degree in which the initiate is shown an artifact produced by Enoch with words written in the Royal Arch cipher.[55] The Royal Arch ritual and tradition ties together themes of ascent, exaltation, and restoration, specifically the restoration of pure language and the true pronunciation of the Divine Name.[56]

---

to posterity, the COMMANDMENTS OF GOD, delivered to him on the mount by inscribing them on tables of stone."

51. "History, 1838–1856, volume B-1 [1 September 1834–2 November 1838]," The Joseph Smith Papers, 597.

52. Harris, *Facsimiles of the Book of Abraham*, 84–85.

53. A Hebrew Kabbalistic cipher upon which the Royal Arch cipher is based.

54. Joseph Smith would have known the רכב קיא cipher from his reading of Henry Cornelius Agrippa's work either from English translations of *De Occulta Philosophia* or through Francis Barrett's *The Magus*. Smith likely had access to Agrippa's work, as it was used to produce the Smith family's Jupiter Talisman, knife, and magical lamens. Note that each of these artifacts was known by the family as Masonic. See D. Michael Quinn, *Early Mormonism and the Magic World View*, 83–84; and Reed C. Durham, Jr., "Is There No Help For The Widow's Son?"

55. Clinton Bartholemew, "Cipher in the Kirtland Snow: The Royal Arch Cipher and Joseph Smith's Conception of Ancient Languages," 6–7.

56. It appears that Joseph Smith attempted to apply the characters in the Kirtland Egyptian papers to the Kinderhook plates. Along with the transcript of the Book of

Despite continuing efforts to explain Smith's involvement in a "translation" project that apparently had little to do with the rendering of the hieroglyphs into the English language, substantial questions remain. Hauglid writes,

This Egyptian project has given rise to questions that generally focus on how much Joseph was involved in the project, and whether or not the Abraham translation and Egyptian projects somehow inform each other. If the Egyptian project can be considered separate from the translation project then the question remains as to what those involved in the Egyptian project were trying to do.[57]

He further points out that modern Egyptologists would find the Mormon Egyptian translations to be "gibberish." However, he stresses,

[I]t must be understood that Joseph Smith and his associates took their language study quite seriously. . . . While approaching the Egyptian documents from a purely Egyptological standpoint yields minimal value, analyzing the systematic nature of the documents themselves can tell us something about those who created them. In doing so it becomes quite clear that Joseph Smith and W.W. Phelps, in particular, developed a complex, if not imaginative, system toward *their* apprehension of the Egyptian language.[58]

It is clear that the Egyptian project was important to the early Latter-day Saints who worked on it, but scholars have been unable to explain exactly what they were doing. Freemasonry may provide a solution that has not yet been considered: the project was an experiment with the creation of a Masonically based Mormon ritual.

Early Development of a Mormon Ritual

Consideration of Joseph Smith's Egyptian project as an effort to prepare a set of rituals for a new temple sheds new light upon these seemingly scattered and disconnected documents. At the time the Egyptian papers were being prepared, plans for several temples were in progress. As part of temple worship, a number of verses in the Book of Commandments promised the Saints an "endowment" similar to the "enduement" of divine wisdom given to Masonic initiates.[59]

Abraham, the Kinderhook plates were placed in the cornerstone of the Masonic hall, thus making a connection with Freemasonry. See Don Bradley and Mark Ashurst-McGee, "Joseph Smith and the Kinderhook Plates," 107–9.

57. Hauglid, "The Book of Abraham and the Egyptian Project," 476.

58. Hauglid, 487.

59. See for example, "Revelation Book 1," The Joseph Smith Papers, 52: "Ye should go to the Ohio & there I will give unto you my law & there you shall be endowed with power from on high" (D&C 38:32); and "Revelation Book 1," 199: "[The redemption of Zion] cannot be brought to pass until mine elders are endowed with power from on high, for behold I have prepared a great endowment and blessing to be poured out upon them" (D&C 105:11–12). See also David Bernard, *Light on Masonry: A Collection of All the Most Important Documents on the Subject of Speculative Free Masonry*, 18: "Endue him with a

Though never completed, work on the Egyptian papers is indicative of what one might do when developing a new Masonic degree or rite. In fact, such development was being done in Europe and America contemporaneously with the advent of Mormonism. For example, the *Crata Repoa*, a series of seven Egyptian-inspired degrees written in German, appeared for the first time in 1770. While nineteenth-century Masonic scholars Pike, Mackey, and Oliver were in general agreement as to its probable Egyptian origin, it is more likely that its creator brought together fragments from many ancient authors into a ritual form. Furthermore, it is not believed that the *Crata Repoa* was ever actually practiced. According to Manly P. Hall, it instead "appear[ed] to belong to the literature and philosophy of the Craft rather than to its working degrees."[60] Other ritualists did, however, develop degrees with Egyptian themes that became working rituals. One such person was Joseph Balsamo (Cagliostro), who founded the Rite of High Egyptian Masonry in 1784. Likewise, the Rite of Memphis was constituted by Jacques Etienne Marconis de Négre in 1838. And slightly later than the Joseph Smith period, the enthusiastic Rob Morris wrote the Eastern Star Degrees, based on French "Adoptive Masonry" (Maconnerie d'Adoption), which enabled women with Masonic relationships by blood or marriage to participate in mixed-sex lodges. Morris drew his inspiration for the ritual, ceremonies, and lectures from five female characters in the Bible, and he conceived and arranged these degrees in 1850, often holding them in his Kentucky home.[61]

Like Morris and the creators of the Egyptian rites, the developer of a Masonic degree would often construct a biblical midrash upon which to base the ritual. In the Royal Arch, this backstory recounts the journey of the liberated Jewish captives in Babylon back to Jerusalem to participate in rebuilding the temple. In the Book of Abraham, Smith develops just such a legend: Abraham's escape from the idolatrous priests of Egypt.[62] Additionally, Abraham's schooling in astronomy provides an opportunity for allegorical instruction of potential candidates in the seven liberal arts and sciences.

The Masonic nature of the Egyptian papers is further made clear by the five "degrees" of understanding for each considered hieroglyph, wherein Smith arranged several word constructions into degrees, demonstrating his understanding of the progressive nature of Freemasonry. For example, the Hebrew *beth* (house) is expanded by degrees in order to draw more narrative meaning. Thus, in the

---

competency of thy divine wisdom, that by the secrets of our art, he may be better enabled to display the beauties of holiness, to the honor of thy holy name."

60. Hall, *Freemasonry of the Ancient Egyptians*, 78–80.

61. Robert Macoy, *Adoptive Rite Ritual: A Book of Instruction in the Organization, Government and Ceremonies of Chapters of the Order of the Eastern Star*, 8–11.

62. Evidence that Smith was constructing a biblical midrash upon which to base a ritual is found in the reliance upon the Book of Abraham backstory in the later Nauvoo Temple endowment.

first degree "the signification of Beth is Man's first residence."[63] In the second degree, *beth* is "a fruitful garden or a great valley or plain filled with fruit trees and flow[er]s."[64] When added to the first degree, the explanation expands the understanding of what man's first residence was like—a fruitful garden. The third degree tells us that *beth* is "good to the taste, pleasing to the eye";[65] the fourth, "sweet and precious to the smell."[66] Each of these degrees describes how the garden is perceived by the senses. In the fifth degree, *beth* is a "place of happiness, purity, holiness, & rest."[67] The five degrees of *beth* in the Joseph Smith Egyptian papers expand the word's meaning from residence to fruitful garden, to a pleasuring of the senses, and finally to joy. This mirrors the Masonic initiate's progression through the degrees to greater light and knowledge approaching the Divine.

Also included in the Alphabet and Grammar is a "second part" of each degree. The degrees are interspersed throughout the pages of the notebook with many blank pages between, as if more were to be added. There, the word *beth* is given a definition in the second part of the fifth degree:

> The place appointed of God for the residence of Adam; Adam ondi=Ahman a ~~fruit~~ garden made to be fruitful, by blessing or promise; great valley or plain given by promise, filled with fruit trees and precious flowers, made for the healing of Man. Good to the taste, pleasing to the eye; sweet and ~~precious~~ ^deligh[t]ful^ to the smell; place of happiness—purity, holiness, and rest: even Zomar—Zion.[68]

This signification is even further expanded and spiritualized. It gives detailed information, including the Hebrew-sounding terms "Adam ondi=Ahman" and "Zomar." Parts of the language in these degrees for the word *beth* are later seen in the Nauvoo Temple endowment.

This pattern of progressive transformation of meaning is also evident in the name of the patriarch, Abraham. In the first degree is his name Abram, or "Ahbroam," which signifies "The Father of the faithful. The first right," and, indicates the priesthood of "The elder." The next several degrees use wording matched in Abraham 1:2:

- Second degree—same sound—"a follower of righteousness"
- Third degree—same sound—"One who possesses great knowle[d]ge"
- Fourth degree—same sound—"a follower of righteousness a possesser of greater knowledge"

---

63. "Grammar and Alphabet of the Egyptian Language, circa July–circa November 1835," The Joseph Smith Papers, 20.

64. "Grammar and Alphabet of the Egyptian Language," 16.

65. "Grammar and Alphabet of the Egyptian Language," 13.

66. "Grammar and Alphabet of the Egyptian Language," 9.

67. "Grammar and Alphabet of the Egyptian Language," 2.

68. "Grammar and Alphabet of the Egyptian Language," 23.

- Fifth degree—"Ah bra-aam—a father of many nations a prince of peace, one who keeps the commandments of God. A patriarch a rightful heir, a highpriest."[69]

As in the biblical account, Abram's name and status are transformed in the fifth degree, where he now holds the patriarchal priesthood of "high priest." Similarly, every Masonic initiate undergoes a transformation connected with a mythic story as the true meaning of their philosophy is revealed to them through allegory.[70] A Mason who advances stage-by-stage through the thirty-three degrees of the Masonic hierarchy learns new meanings for each symbol at every stage. While Smith's attempt at a Kirtland ritual was more condensed, the later Nauvoo Temple practice was more centered on the Masonic concept of transformation by degrees. For Latter-day Saints, the priesthood that transforms them is the priesthood of Abraham in the fifth degree.

The Royal Arch degree concludes with a catechism where the initiate reviews what he has learned in a question-and-answer format. A portion of this catechism exposed by Richard Carlile in 1826 looks like this:

Q. Were you intrusted with the grand word?

A. I was. They gave me the grand movement, taught me the sign, and intrusted me with the sacred word, which is too incomprehensible for an individual to express.

Q. Was that word ever lost?

A. It was.

Q. In what manner?

A. By the untimely death of our Grand Master, Hiram Abiff.[71]

This sample is similar to the catechism in "A Sample of pure Language" issued by Joseph Smith in 1832:

---

69. "Grammar and Alphabet of the Egyptian Language, circa July–circa November 1835," 20, 16, 13, 9, 2. Compare with Abraham 1:2: "I sought for the blessings of the fathers, and the right whereunto I should be ordained to administer the same; having been myself a follower of righteousness, desiring also to be one who possessed great knowledge, and to be a greater follower of righteousness, and to possess a greater knowledge, and to be a father of many nations, a prince of peace, and desiring to receive instructions, and to keep the commandments of God, I became a rightful heir, a High Priest, holding the right belonging to the fathers."

70. "Trismegistus *concealed the mysteries of religion under hieroglyphics and allegories,* and exposed nothing to the eyes of the vulgar but the beauties of his morality. This has been the method of the sages in all times, and of the great legislators in all countries: these divine men were sensible that corrupted minds could have no relish for heavenly truths, till the heart was purified from its passions; for which reason they spread over religion a secret veil, which opens and vanishes when the eyes of the understanding are able to support its brightness." Oliver, *Antiquities of Freemasonry,* 121; emphasis in original.

71. Richard Carlile, *Manual of Freemasonry: in Three Parts. With an Explanatory Introduction to the Science, and a Free Translation of some of the Sacred Scripture Names,* 132.

Question What is the name of God in pure Language
Answer Awmen . . . [72]

Q What is the name of the Son of God.
A Son Awmen . . .

Q What is man.
A This signifies Sons Awmen . . .

Q What are Angels called in pure language.
A Awmen Angls-men[73]

Still later, a catechism of questions and answers is seen near the end of the Nauvoo Temple ceremony when the initiate passes through the veil.

In the Royal Arch, as in other degrees, a Grand Omnific key word is given and broken into three syllables so that it may easily be repeated by the companions. This word is similar to the tri-syllabic words that Smith uses as names of Deity in the Egyptian papers, such as Jah-oh-eh. Perhaps Smith's use of strange names to label places and people of the Restoration has been misunderstood. Rather than concealing their identities, they may be an attempt to transform names and identities into the "pure language" and reveal certain aspects of their true character.

Joseph Smith as Prophetic Restorer

Incipient ritual informed by Freemasonry is evident in Smith's Egyptian workings throughout the 1830s and 1840s. Temple ordinances during this time were progressive and later elaborated in Nauvoo. First, the name of Deity was revealed in the Egyptian papers. Then, in the Kirtland Temple, the name was used with ritual action. In this temple, members of the School of the Prophets dropped to their knees, raised their hands to heaven, and called on the deity "Ahman" who walked through the room. The name they invoked was the secret name found in the Kirtland Egyptian papers. Finally, in Nauvoo, names and ritual action were placed together into a biblically based ritual story—Adam at the altar representing every man on his knees. The development of a Masonically based ritual accounts for all the different parts of the Egyptian project in a way that no other theory has. The Mormon Egyptian papers may not be the product of the translator's craft, but they are certainly the product of imagination, vision, and inspiration.

The arrival of the mummies and papyrus in Kirtland was the closest that Joseph Smith had come to anything from Egypt, and they held great fascination

---

72. Throughout this document, "Awmen" was changed to "Awman," either by John Whitmer at the time of inscription or later by an unidentified scribe.

73. "Sample of Pure Language, between circa 4 and circa 20 March 1832," *The Joseph Smith Papers*, 144. See also Orson Pratt, February 18, 1855, *Journal of Discourses*, 2:342. The document was copied into Revelation Book 1 by John Whitmer between April and March 1832.

among early Mormons. Because of Masonry's Egyptian connection, it was easy for those who were working with the papyri to put them into Masonic terms. They connected the papyri with pure language, higher mysteries, temple instruction and ritual, and the "ancient order of things."

In spite of this, what Smith did was not mere slavish borrowing. While the seeds of Mormon midrash can be observed in Masonry, these concepts were re-contextualized in Mormonism. As demonstrated in this chapter, Smith used an identifiable process to bring Masonic concepts into a uniquely Mormon setting. In his hands, many Masonic traditions were transformed into sacred stories, literalized, and canonized.

Salem Town and others expected that Masonry would be restored to its pristine beauty before the Second Coming of Christ and that it would serve as the means by which Christianity would be purified. Smith conceived of himself as the individual who would both initiate these changes in Masonry and complete the climactic task of purifying and restoring true religion. There were three aspects to the work of this expected restorer.

First, he must create and interpret scripture. Smith fulfilled this prophetic responsibility by producing a unique Mormon midrash rooted in a process familiar to Freemasons. The resulting body of work was different from Jewish midrash, which comes from a number of different perspectives. Smith's work advanced a particular opinion.

Next, the prophetic figure must restore the body of legends to a theologically pure form. Smith selectively took Masonic stories or traditions and made them sacred by virtue of his prophetic office. He used the authority of his priesthood to impart integrity to what he restored. What in Masonry may have been an allegory, encouraging good moral behavior, was thus transformed into literal or factual spiritual history, imposing moral imperatives. Eventually, Smith's Mormon midrash provided a rich font of symbols and allegories from which to draw. In Masonry they existed as a secret tradition, but in Mormonism they became sacred scripture and a backdrop for spiritually powerful religious ceremonies.

Finally, the Masonic restorer, exemplified by King Solomon, must bring forth a purified ritual. In Masonic legend, Solomon created the system of Masonry and ritual that governs the Craft to this day. From the earliest introduction of Mormon scripture, Smith's midrash began to introduce concepts evident in the Kirtland Temple ritual and which continued to blossom into their full form in Nauvoo.

Joseph Smith's midrashic expansions introduced concepts and theology in a decidedly hermetic manner, common to Freemasons of his day. His expansions were scripture in that they were the product of revelation. In nineteenth-century Freemasonry, the scriptural text was dynamic and participatory. Individuals were expected to engage the text and make new discoveries using an established hermeneutic. In today's world, the method Smith used to create midrash is largely obscured from our view.

Modern Latter-day Saint views of how a prophet might approach and interpret scripture are relatively conservative and Protestant in nature. This seems different from Smith's own approach to sacred texts. As in Masonry, absolute consistency in sacred texts was not demanded of early Mormonism. Apparent inconsistencies and variants were presented to engage the mind in what Smith called "the proving of contrarreties."[74] Scriptures were not simply statements of facts; they were a tool to work upon the mind, providing individual insight and personal transformation. In this context, the precise facts of the sacred story are less important than their transformational and revelatory functions. From his scriptural record and ritual workings, Smith demonstrated that he was, with little argument, both a "myth-making genius" and a consummate ritualist.[75]

---

74. "Letter to Israel Daniel Rupp, 5 June 1844," The Joseph Smith Papers, 1.
75. Harold Bloom, The American Religion: The Emergence of the Post-Christian Nation, 97.

CHAPTER 8

THE TROWEL AND THE SWORD

This union was made after the example set by the Israelites when they erected the second Temple who, whilst they handled the trowel and mortar with one hand, in the other held the sword and buckler.
—Chevalier Andrew Michael Ramsay,
Ramsay's Oration of 1737

The biblical book of Nehemiah contains a story both revered and allegorically utilized by Cryptic Masons of the York Rite of Freemasonry.[1] The story is portrayed on English Royal Arch tracing boards and exposed in Bernard's 1829 *Light on Masonry*.[2] As recounted in the Bible, after Nehemiah received permission to gather a group of Jews to rebuild Jerusalem and restore the walls of the temple, the work was greatly hindered by their enemies so that each laborer "with one of his hands wrought in the work, and with the other hand held a weapon" (Neh. 4:17). Freemasons visually depict this scene with an emblem of the temple masons holding the implements of Masonry: a trowel and mortar in one hand, and a sword in the other for defense.[3] Along with a broken triangle symbolizing the Lost Master's Word, these objects are associated with themes of restoration and recovery.[4] They are mentioned in the "old verses" quoted by Joseph Laycock in his lecture delivered March 8, 1736, at the constitution of a new lodge in Gateshead, England:

---

1. A Master Mason may join the York Rite to further enhance his knowledge of Freemasonry. There are three primary bodies of the York Rite: The Royal Arch Masons (including four degrees), the Cryptic Masons (three degrees), and the Commander of Knights Templar (three degrees).

2. "Sov. 'What is your name?'
Can. 'Zerubbabel; the first among my equals, by rank a Mason, by misfortune a captive.'
Sov. 'What is the mercy that you demand of me?'
Can. 'That, under the protection of the G. A. of the universe, the king will restore our liberty and allow us to return and rebuild the temple of our GOD.' . . . When the brethren hear the alarm, they detach the trowel from their aprons, and hold it in the left hand, and the sword in the right."
David Bernard, *Light on Masonry: A Collection of All the Most Important Documents on the Subject of Speculative Free Masonry*, 323, 325.

3. Even earlier, in 1536, the image was portrayed as a Masonic emblem featuring a cloud from which emanated arms holding a sword and trowel. See Henry Green, ed., *Whitney's "Choice of Emblemes," A Fac-simile Reprint*, 66.

4. George Oliver, *Historical Landmarks and Other Evidences of Freemasonry, Explained; a Series of Practical Lectures, with Copious Notes*, 2:353n17.

> When *Sanballat Jerusalem* distress'd
> With sharp Assaults in *Nehemiah's* Time,
> To War and Work the Jews themselves address'd,
> And did repair their Walls with Stone and Lime.
> One Hand the Sword against the Foe did shake
> The other Hand the Trowel up did take.[5]

The first reference to temples in the Latter-day Saint canon shares this biblical legend. Like Nehemiah, Nephi and his people encountered opposition as their numbers increased in the new land. In the tradition of Tubal Cain in Masonic legend, Nephi taught his people smithing skills. Once they were able to forge metal, he armed his people so that they could protect themselves from hostile Lamanites while building a temple. With tools of masonry in one hand and swords in another, Nephi's workmen built a structure "after the manner of King Solomon" (2 Ne. 5:14–16).[6] This Book of Mormon temple story subtly introduces elements suggested in the biblical account but more liberally included in the Masonic sources.

In the early 1830s, Joseph Smith sought to restore keys and authority preparatory to the literal recovery of Masonry's symbolic Lost Word. This endeavor required the construction of temples similar in form and function to those of the Freemasons. From their first efforts to build and develop temples, Latter-day Saints shared the Masonic perception of Old Testament temples, and their encounters with the hostility of the outside world were also framed in terms of the "trowel and the sword."

Hiram, Ohio: "A Hill of Zion"

The Latter-day Saint city and temple-building impulse—with a Masonic flair—can be seen as early as 1831. Late in this year, Joseph Smith visited a small settlement in Hiram, Ohio (also known as Hiram Hill), which had coincidentally been founded at the turn of the century by a group of Freemasons and named for one of their ancient Grand Masters. Daniel Tilden of Lebanon, Connecticut, was one of the original purchasers.

After the first schoolhouse was built in Hiram in 1820, another was begun in the Center District of town. According to a town historian, "A frame building was put up to subserve the purpose of a schoolhouse, and with a Masonic

---

5. William Smith, *The Book M: or, Masonry Triumphant*, 20; emphasis in original. These lines are from the degree of *R.Y.C.S.* (Knight of the Order of the Rosy Cross) from the Royal Order of Scotland, which is likely the oldest high degree system in existence. It may date before 1732, when Joseph Laycock was appointed Provincial Grand Master of the Harodim body in London. The authors wish to thank Arturo de Hoyos for this information and these references.

6. Robert N. Hullinger, *Joseph Smith's Response to Skepticism*, 110.

Foundation of John Johnson home in Hiram, Ohio.
Photo by Nicholas S. Literski.

Hall above, but it was never completed."[7] The mention of a building such as this necessitates a group of Masons living in Hiram or nearby.[8] As was common at the time, local Masons may have met in a large upper room in a private home. The John Johnson farmhouse, where Joseph Smith would later live, was just such a place.[9] It may have even been built with that purpose in mind—with a large upper room suitable for meeting, and the square and compasses, implements of speculative Masonry, etched in two locations on exposed foundation stones.[10]

---

7. Alvah Udall, "Early History of Hiram: A Few Anecdotes Will Serve."

8. Morning Star Lodge at nearby Mantua, Portage County (five miles from Hiram), was granted a charter at the Ohio Grand Lodge meeting of January 1827. This lodge could have been working sporadically for as many as ten years, as "brethren near Mantua" had presented petitions at the Grand Lodge in both 1817 and 1820. After 1827, however, the Lodge was never again represented in meetings of the Grand Lodge of Ohio and was retroactively declared extinct as of 1826. See *The Grand Lodge of the Most Ancient and Honorable Fraternity of Free and Accepted Masons of the State of Ohio at its Several Grand Communications from 1808 to 1847, Inclusive*, 91, 113, 176. Several brothers from this lodge later became founding members of Nauvoo Lodge.

9. A person named John Johnson may have received two of the three craft degrees in 1806, in Olive Branch Lodge No. 11 at Chester, Vermont. This may not have been the same John Johnson, since it is a common name, and this lodge was located about thirty miles from his home in Pomfret, Vermont.

10. Nicholas S. Literski, "Joseph Smith's Masonic Tutors." See also Mark Lyman Staker, *Hearken, O Ye People: The Historical Setting of Joseph Smith's Ohio Revelations*, 274n11. Staker writes that "[the compass and square] marks were a common symbol that

The religious ideas of Alexander Campbell took deep root in this section of the country. Campbellite views on baptism, the Lord's Supper, the necessity of implicit obedience, and the notion of a restoration of strict biblical constructs were adopted by many of the residents of Hiram. They called themselves learners, "Disciples," or "Rigdonites," after one of their most ardent converts, Sidney Rigdon. Well educated in eastern schools, Rigdon became a preacher, and from his cabin home in Mentor made many long preaching tours in every direction.[11] His several congregations included future Mormon converts Newel K. Whitney, Lyman Wight, Isaac Morley, Frederick G. Williams, Titus Billings, Oliver Snow, David Pond, Lucius N. Scovil, Basil Windsor, Walter Carlton, Rufus Edwards, the Reddens, the Beechers, the Careys, and the Richersons, to name a few.[12]

On November 8, 1830, Rigdon was baptized by Oliver Cowdery into Joseph Smith's newly formed church, followed by many of his parishioners in the following year. Two of the leading Methodists in the area, John Johnson and Reverend Ezra Booth, traveled thirty miles north to Kirtland with their wives to visit Smith. A miraculous healing of Elsa Johnson's arm by the Prophet impelled them to baptism in late March 1831.[13] Booth was so roused by his new faith that he returned to Portage County preaching Mormonism to the Methodists, Baptists, and Symonds Ryder's Disciples congregation in Hiram. Large numbers of converts soon filled the small town.

The new Portage County Saints approached Smith with what some said was "the purpose of getting the settlement removed to Hiram."[14] This scenario seems plausible considering the sizeable group of enthusiastic converts gathered in the area. While on his way to survey the possibilities, Smith "had a vision which told him that Hiram Hill was the 'Hill of Zion' for which he had been searching . . . and that the principal office of the church should be here."[15] Because of this,

---

a professional stonemason had worked on the foundations" and not a sign of Johnson's interest in Freemasonry. However, the icon of the joined square and compasses is not used by operative stonemasons but is a symbol used by speculative Freemasons around the world.

11. Charles H. Ryder, "A Hill of Zion: Reminiscences of the Early Days of Mormonism in Ohio," 9. The development of religion in this area was also traced by A. S. Hayden, *Early History of the Disciples in the Western Reserve, Ohio.*

12. Richard McClellan, "Sidney Rigdon's 1820 Ministry: Preparing the Way for Mormonism in Ohio," 156–59.

13. Staker, *Hearken, O Ye People,* 284. Staker places the baptism shortly before Marinda Johnson's baptism in April 1831 and the establishment of an LDS branch in neighboring Nelson by Lyman Wight and John Whitmer on April 9.

14. Ryder, "A Hill of Zion," 9.

15. Ryder, 9; Lucius V. Bierce, "Hiram," 1. Bierce was Ohio Grand Master during the late 1850s and maintained personal relationships with Freemasons throughout the state. He provides the earliest known reference to a proposed Mormon temple at Hiram— the site of which he vaguely locates "on a hill near the 'Hinckley farm.'" It is possible that Bierce obtained his "Mormon" information from John Tilden, whose story of nonparticipation in the 1832 tar and feathering is told in Bierce's work. A 1934 fictional story

many Saints believed Hiram "had been marked to be the Mormon capital instead of Kirtland."[16]

Records indicate the site of the contemplated temple was chosen—a picturesque elevated spot on Symonds Ryder's property "near the Hinckley farm."[17] One local reminiscence states that, as a preparation for the work of building the temple, rows of beautiful maple trees were transplanted along the roadside.[18]

Joseph Smith and his small family relocated to Hiram on September 12, 1831,[19] where they were offered a home with John Johnson. The Whitmers, the eight witnesses of the Book of Mormon, and other leading members and their families arrived during the winter of 1831–32. Many built cabins adjacent to the Johnson property. Meetings were held in local schoolhouses, and men were sent to the surrounding areas on mission assignments. "There was hardly a family in the township which was not wholly or in part converted," one local history indicated. More than sixty people had been baptized, and, along with those who had moved into the area, the Church boasted over two hundred members.[20] In later years, when older residents were questioned about the Mormons, they recalled that "the plan of Smith at this time was to build three Zions—one in Kirtland, one in Hiram and one in the Far West [Missouri]."[21]

Many of the revelations included in the Doctrine and Covenants were received by Smith while he lived in Hiram, and they caused a great stir in the vicinity. According to a close friend, Joseph B. Noble, Smith became convinced of the theological necessity of polygamy "while he was engaged in the work of translation of the Scriptures," evidently a reference to Smith's and Rigdon's early 1830s revision of the Bible.[22] The Prophet's interest in this subject may evidence his seeing himself as a Solomonic figure in many ways.

---

by Abram Garfield relies upon Bierce's article to tell the tale of the Mormons at Hiram. It mentions the proposed Hiram temple and replicates Bierce's misspelling of Whitmer as "Whittemore."

16. James B. Holm, ed., *Portage Heritage*, 77.

17. Bierce, "Hiram," 1; Ryder, "A Hill of Zion," 9.

18. Ryder, 9.

19. "History, 1838–1856, volume A-1 [23 December 1805–30 August 1834]," The Joseph Smith Papers, 153.

20. Ryder, "A Hill of Zion," 9.

21. Ryder, 9.

22. Joseph B. Noble, speech at a quarterly stake conference held at Centerville, Utah, June 11, 1883, quoted in Andrew Jenson, "Plural Marriage," 232–33. See also Michael R. Caldwell, *The John Johnson Family of Hiram, Ohio: For He Is a Descendant of Joseph*, 57–58. Caldwell cites a family recollection that Joseph Smith spoke to Orson Hyde when he was courting Marinda Johnson, saying, "God has given that woman to me. Do not marry her." Caldwell suggests that this statement may have been used as a basis for accusations of early polygamy on the part of Smith. Years later, Joseph F. Smith said "that the women who entered into plural marriage with the Prophet Joseph Smith were shown to him and named to him as early as 1831; when the Prophet Joseph Smith received the revelation in

Another revelation on three heavenly kingdoms resembled one of the Campbellite teachings so closely that Cecil McGavin called it "the last straw—the straw that broke the Campbell back." One opponent, recognizing the Masonic flavor of the revelations, observed that Smith "out masoned King Solomon," but "the 'Campbellites' complained that he had stolen their thunder and was running wild with it."[23] Smith's recasting of several Christian doctrines appeared to his contemporaries to draw from Freemasonry as well as the unique and innovative Campbellite religion. This angered both opponents and adherents to those two traditions.

While the practice of consecration of property into a communal society was not uncommon in 1830s America, Smith's revelation on the subject was the cause of great consternation among his followers.[24] One source states that while Smith was away, his "charts and papers" were examined and found to contain "a plot . . . to take the property of all the converts out of their hands and form a great stock company, with Smith as the head or president." This plan took some members by surprise, and "was far more than they could endure."[25] In consequence of the ensuing outrage, both Smith and Rigdon were tarred and feathered by a group of disgruntled members and townspeople on the night of March 24, 1832.[26]

Over the next year, the Mormons struggled to maintain their presence in Hiram as the leading families began to move on. Within a week of their painful ordeal, Smith and Rigdon left for Missouri to conduct church business and would not permanently return. Emma and her adopted daughter, Julia, remained with the Johnsons for six months after the attack (with the exception of a short stay in Kirtland). They moved to Kirtland on September 12, 1832, and took up quarters in an apartment above Newel K. Whitney's store. The Whitmers and a group of nearly one hundred members from the Hiram branch departed on May 2, 1832,

---

relation to the eternity of the marriage covenant, which includes plural marriage, in 1831, the Lord showed him those women who were to engage with him in the establishment of that principle in the Church, and at that time some of these women were named and given to him, to become his wives when the time should come that this principle should be established." See Joseph F. Smith, "Correction," 2.

23. E. Cecil McGavin, *Historical Background of the Doctrine and Covenants*, 191.

24. See, for example, the Rappites, the Harmony Society, Zoarites, New Philadelphia Colony, Oberlin Colony.

25. Ryder, "A Hill of Zion," 9.

26. A late secondhand witness, Clark Braden, alleged that Eli Johnson led the attack and that its intent was to punish Smith for an improper relationship with John Johnson's daughter Marinda. Fawn McKay Brodie, *No Man Knows My History: The Life of Joseph Smith*, 119. Braden identified Eli as a son of John Johnson, but he was, in fact, John's brother and Marinda's uncle, and he was living with the family at the time. The mob enlisted the services of a physician to castrate Smith, lending credence to the accusation of sexual impropriety.

and traveled to Missouri. There they formed the Whitmer Settlement (or Timber Branch) in Jackson County.[27]

In the face of continued harassment by his neighbors, John Johnson moved to Kirtland in early 1833 and opened an inn next to Whitney's establishment. Many of his adult children and their spouses also obtained property in Kirtland at this time. Father Johnson sold most of his 160 acres the following spring and donated the $3,000 to the Church's United Firm, which managed all financial aspects of the communal order. These proceeds, along with other funds from donations to the United Firm, were used to pay the mortgage on a large piece of acreage upon which the Kirtland temple lot was laid out. Thus, Kirtland, rather than Hiram, became the site for the first Mormon temple.

Kirtland, Ohio:
Masonic Architecture, Appurtenances, and Inner Workings

On June 1, 1833, Joseph Smith received a revelation that the temple in Kirtland should be built "after the manner which I shall show unto three of you" (D&C 95:14)—referring to Smith, Sidney Rigdon, and Frederick G. Williams. This instruction is significant in view of the Masonic tradition that King Solomon's Temple was built under the direction of three principals: Solomon, King of Israel; Hiram, King of Tyre; and Hiram Abiff, skillful artificer. Williams was said to have reported:

> We [Smith, Rigdon, and Williams] went upon our knees, called on the Lord, and the building appeared within viewing distance. I being the first to discover it. Then all of us viewed it together. After we had taken a good look at the exterior, the building seemed to come right over us, and the makeup of this hall seemed to coincide with what I there saw to a minutia.[28]

Mormons were directed to construct the temple with dimensions of 55 feet in width and 65 feet in length with a "lower court," a "higher court," and an attic story.[29] These dimensions were considerably different than the biblical description of Solomon's Temple, which was a rectangular building roughly 30 feet wide, 105 feet long, and 45 feet high.[30]

By the 1830s, "Solomon's Temple, Spiritualized"—that is, the mystical significance of that temple in all its aspects—had been one of the central allegorical concerns of Freemasonry for nearly two centuries, and Masonic lodges were said to symbolically represent that sacred edifice. It makes sense then that the first realized temple of the Latter-day Saints was more closely aligned conceptually

---

27. Levi Jackman, *A Short Sketch of the Life of Levi Jackman*. The move had been planned at a Church Conference the previous November.

28. Truman O. Angell, Autobiography, 14–15.

29. Edward W. Tullidge, *The Women of Mormondom*, 81; See also William S. West, *A Few Interesting Facts Respecting the Mormons*, 4–5.

30. William J. Hamblin and David Rolph Seely, *Solomon's Temple: Myth and History*, 25.

with Masonic temples than any biblical model. An examination of the use of the Kirtland temple, as well as its appurtenances, demonstrates a reliance upon a Masonic rather than an ancient Jewish conception of Solomon's Temple. Instead of being strict imitations of the biblical model, Masonic temples were reconstructions made for allegorical purposes, each aspect being a "type" of Christ.[31]

By the time the Kirtland temple was built, several Mormon insiders were already well acquainted with the signs, symbols, and inner workings of Freemasonry.[32] They participated in and were impacted by Masonic motifs in the rituals and ordinances performed within the lodges, in the architecture and use of ritual space, and in the historical backdrop of the temple's establishment. Even those who were neither Freemasons nor involved in the inner circle of men who had received washings and anointings had sufficient cultural awareness of the Fraternity so that they could recognize Masonic influence as the temple took shape. According to Edward Tullidge,

> There is a grand Masonic consistency in the divine scheme of the Mormon prophet, and the sisters began to comprehend the infinite themes of their religion when they worked in the temple at Kirtland, and beheld in the service the glory of Israel's God.[33]

A significant difference between the Kirtland temple and the Jewish temple is that while ritual space in the Jewish temple was based on animal sacrifice, the organization of the inside of the Kirtland temple was more conducive to Masonic meetings. Although the lower court was to be "dedicated unto me for your sacrament offering, and for your preaching, and your fasting, and your praying, and the offering up of your most holy desires" (D&C 95:16), these offerings were figurative, in the Masonic tradition, rather than literal. Both Masonic and Mormon temples illustrate a theme of restoration and an allegorical ceremony of passing through a veil to come into the presence of God.

The cornerstone of the Kirtland temple was laid on July 23, 1833. At this time in the United States, cornerstone ceremonies of important civil and religious buildings were frequently held by Freemasons, with the cornerstones being most often laid in the northeast corner of the building. Albert Mackey explained the symbolism of this placement: The east, as the source of material light, represents a new day arising, "dissipating the clouds of intellectual darkness and error." The north is the place of darkness and symbol of the profane world. With one surface of the stone facing the north and the other facing the east, it is "neither wholly

---

31. Two major works that were influential in shaping Masonic ritual were Samuel Lee's 1689 *Orbis Miraculum, or, The Temple of Solomon Pourtrayed by Scripture-light*, which describes the temple of Solomon for Christians; and John Bunyan's 1688 *Solomon's Temple Spiritualized, or, Gospel-light Brought out of the Temple at Jerusalem*, which displays its allegorical significance.

32. These included Newel K. Whitney, Orson Hyde, Heber C. Kimball, Hyrum Smith, and Warren Cowdery.

33. Tullidge, *Women of Mormondom*, 79.

in the one part nor wholly in the other, and in so far it is a symbol of initiation not fully developed."[34]

At times, this symbolism did not seem to fit the building being dedicated. The United States Capitol building, for example, was considered the center of the Federal City and of the nation. Its cornerstone was laid in the southwest corner by George Washington, assisted by members of Maryland's Lodge No. 9, Virginia's Alexandria Lodge No. 22, and Federal Lodge No. 15. Brigham Young later explained that the first stone of the Kirtland temple was laid at the southeast corner, the point of greatest light at high noon.[35] This was an overt Masonic reference that followed the example set by Washington and his Masonic companions.

It seems likely that the cornerstone for the Independence, Missouri, temple, designed at the same time as Kirtland but never completed—was also laid at the southeast. On August 3, 1831, Smith and seven other Elders gathered at the site to dedicate the ground and lay the cornerstone. John Whitmer's account of the event mentions the cornerstone was laid at the northeast by Smith, but in 1929, excavations revealed a southeast cornerstone labeled "SECT" (South East Cornerstone Temple) and a "witness marker" on the northeast.[36] The witness marker is etched with a "surveyor 4" (backwards numeral "4") and a zero, referring to it being forty feet from the southeast cornerstone, and thus subordinate to it.

Ezra Booth wrote a picturesque description of the Missouri temple site, directing locals who wished to visit to "walk one half of a mile out of the Town, to a rise of ground, a short distance south of the road." There,

they will be able to ascertain the spot, by the means of a sapling [sapling], distinguished from others by the bark being taken off on the north and on the east side. —On the south side of the sapling will be found the letter, T, which stands for Temple; and on the east side ZOM for Zomar; which Smith says is the original word for Zion. Near the foot of the sapling, they will find a small stone, covered over with bushes, which were cut for that purpose. This is the corner stone for the Temple.[37]

The Kirtland temple was a notable edifice for a small frontier town. From the outside, it didn't look substantially different than many New England chapels of the day.[38] Its inner architecture, however, was unique. Taken separately, these elements might attract little notice, but their concurrent presence suggests a strong reliance upon Freemasonry.

34. Albert Gallatin Mackey, *The Symbolism of Freemasonry: Illustrating and Explaining its Science and Philosophy, its Legends, Myths, and Symbols*, 166, 168.

35. Brigham Young, April 6, 1853, *Journal of Discourses*, 1:133.

36. "John Whitmer, History, 1831–circa 1847," The Joseph Smith Papers, 32.

37. Ezra Booth, letter number 6 to Rev. Ira Eddy, November 14, 1831, quoted in Michael Marquardt, "Ezra Booth on Early Mormonism: A Look at his 1831 Letters," 76. For Zomar, see "Grammar and Alphabet of the Egyptian Language, circa July–circa November 1835," The Joseph Smith Papers, 23.

38. Laurel B. Andrew, *The Early Temples of the Mormons: The Architecture of the Millennial Kingdom in the American West*, 41–53.

First, a set of three pillars frame each side of the seating section. These are reminiscent of the three Masonic pillars, "Wisdom," "Strength," and "Beauty." Many Masonic tracing boards include three pillars representing the three allegorical principles that "support" a lodge. Pulpits in the east and west of both stories of the Kirtland temple suggest the organization of a lodge, with officers located in the sections designated East and West. Gilbert Belnap, a Nauvoo Mason, was impressed by the "poolpit [pulpit] at each end of those rooms ['on the first and second floors'] constructed for the purpose of accommodating those holding different degrees of the holy priesthood."[39] The pulpits are arrayed in a tiered pattern of three by three. This arrangement is related to the Royal Arch and emphasizes the sacred character of the number three, which suggests the presence of divine power.

The front face of each pulpit was engraved with a series of three cryptic gilt letters related to the office of the men who were appointed to each pulpit.[40] Masons characteristically form abbreviations using the first letter of each word. These are widely employed throughout the Masonic system in acronyms, monitors (booklets containing the wording of ceremonies, rituals, and prayers), signets, and so forth. Following the letters in a formal Masonic document are placed three points in a triangular form. These dots indicate a Masonic title or a technical word.[41] The letters P, E, and M carved into the sacrament table in front of the pulpit are also placed in this triangular formation.

On the west end of the building, behind the sacrament table and pulpits, is a magnificent window framed by a double arch and keystone combination, resting upon two pillars. These items were vital to Royal Arch legend and used in nineteenth-century Masonic lodge rooms. Smith's purpose in building a temple was to provide a place for making covenants, encountering the Lord, and being endowed with "power from on high" (D&C 95:8). The architectural components symbolized these objectives. The arch, as represented in some Royal Arch chapters, has three letters (J Z H)[42] engraved upon it representing the three principal

39. Gilbert Belnap Autobiography, 33.

40. "There is a pulpit in the west end for the Melchizedek priesthood, composed of four seats parallel with each other, those in the rear suitably elevated, and each seat calculated for three officers and accommodated with a suitable desk, which is ornamented with a cushion and fringe, and a curve for each occupant, on the front of which is the initials of his office, in gilt letters. The desk of the front seat consists of the leaves of the communion table, upon which are the initials of its occupants, in letters of stain. There is also a pulpit in the east end for the Aaronic priesthood, which is of the same construction." West, *A Few Interesting Facts Respecting the Mormons*, 4–5.

41. "Three points in a triangular form are placed after letters in a Masonic document to indicate that such letters are the initials of a Masonic title of a technical word in Masonry...it is not a symbol, but simply a mark of abbreviation." Albert G. Mackey, William J. Hughan, and Edward L. Hawkins, *An Encyclopaedia of Freemasonry and its Kindred Sciences, Comprising the Whole Range of Arts, Sciences and Literature as Connected with the Institution*, 2:785.

42. JZH: Jerubbabel, Zedekiah, Haggai.

Kirtland Temple Pulpits, ca. 1912.

officers of the chapter. It stands for "the Blue Arch of Heaven and the rainbow which . . . represents God's covenant with mankind after Noah's flood. . . . The legend upon which the ceremony [of the Royal Arch] is based speaks of not one arch but nine [3X3], supporting and enclosing a vault beneath the temple of Solomon."[43] Royal Arch history informs us that "[b]eneath King Solomon's Temple was a vaulted chamber containing nine arches and it was within the ninth of these that the Sacred Name [of Deity] was deposited."[44]

Written on the wall between the men and women's entrance of the Kirtland temple were three Latin phrases: *Laus Deo* (praise God), *Crux Mihi Anchora* (the cross is my anchor), and *Magna Veritas et Prevalebit* (great is truth and it shall prevail). Such Latin mottos are employed by Freemasons on banners or on the heads of documents to express the character and design of different branches or orders.[45] For example, the motto for the Order of the Red Cross is *Magna est Veritas, et praevalabit*. Both it and the slogan *Laus Deo* appeared in Bernard's 1829 *Light on Masonry*.[46]

The phrase "House of the Lord" emblazoned above the main entrance to the Kirtland temple and later temples marked with the phrase "Holiness to the Lord"

43. Duncan Moore, *In Search of That Which Was Lost: True Symbolism of the Royal Arch*, 58–59.

44. Moore, 56.

45. Mackey, Hughan, and Hawkins, *Encyclopaedia of Freemasonry*, s.v. "Motto" (2:495).

46. Bernard, *Light on Masonry*, 154, 296.

continue this use of religious slogans in association with Mormon temple worship. The latter expression is found in the Old Testament, where it was engraved upon the gold plate of a crown worn as part of the priestly garments (Ex. 28:36; 39:30). Freemasons used this biblical axiom since at least 1710 when it appears in the Dumfries manuscript.[47] In the Royal Arch degree, "Holiness to the Lord" is found upon the mitre of the High Priest, is spoken in praise three times by characters who have made a marvelous discovery, and is painted on the central symbol of the arch.[48]

An elegant, narrow spiral staircase in the Kirtland temple curls purposefully from the first to the second floor. According to scripture, a "winding stair" was similarly located within King Solomon's Temple, connecting the ground floor of that structure with the middle chamber of the building (1 Kgs. 6:8). The Freemasons' appropriation of the winding stair contains rich allegorical meaning and is featured prominently on tracing boards and in the design of many lodges, and Royal Arch aprons often depict pillar, arch, and veil behind a staircase consisting of three, five, or seven steps. In the Fellow Craft degree, the winding stair suggests spiritual advancement and the imparting of spiritual knowledge. In the middle chamber of the Lodge, the initiate learns about "the mystery of the Letter G."[49] The figurative goal of the Masonic version of the winding stair is to represent heavenly ascent and to bring one near to God.

In the context of looking for the "Word," the arch and keystone, pillars, three multiples of three, mysterious lettering, inscriptions, winding staircases, and passing through veils are all significant. They are key elements of the Royal Arch ritual, which points to the restoration of King Solomon's Temple and the discovery of "that which was lost." Many of these features are biblical; however, they don't all occur together and in the context of restoration in the Bible as they do in Freemasonry.

Kirtland School of the Prophets

During Mormonism's Kirtland period, Joseph Smith found in Masonry a system of teaching that enabled him to present complex principles to a select group of the leading elders of the Church. The first recorded meeting of the Kirtland

---

47. Dumfries Manuscript No. 4, in Harry Carr, *The Early Masonic Catechisms*, 68.

48. Malcolm C. Duncan, *Duncan's Masonic Ritual and Monitor or Guide to the Three Symbolic Degrees of the Ancient York Rite and to the Degrees of Mark Master, Past Master, Most Excellent Master, and the Royal Arch*, 246–47.

49. In the lower degrees, the initiate is told that the letter G stands for "God" and for "Geometry," which the Supreme Architect of the Universe used to design the cosmos. The mystery of the letter G is that the symbol contains layers of meaning, which the initiate learns as he progresses in knowledge and understanding. See William Morgan, *Illustrations of Masonry*, 50; and Albert Pike, *Morals and Dogma of the Ancient and Accepted Scottish Rite of Freemasonry*, 15.

School of the Prophets was held in the upper room of Newel K. Whitney's store on January 23, 1833, and it was organized in the same tradition as the Masonic Schools of Instruction.[50] The school became a prototype of forthcoming Kirtland temple ritual.

Whitney, a young merchant and businessman, had been a Freemason since July 26, 1819, when, at the age of twenty-four, he was raised to Master Mason in Meridian Orb Lodge No. 10 at Painesville, Ohio. Not content to only receive the three degrees of Craft Masonry, Whitney also received the Royal Arch Degree, taking an active part in the attempted formation of a Royal Arch chapter at Painesville.[51] He would repeat that effort in Hancock County in 1843, after the establishment of craft lodges at Nauvoo and Warsaw.[52]

For a time, Whitney affiliated with the Campbellite, or Disciples of Christ tradition, and he was baptized into Joseph Smith's church in November of 1830. Meetings of Kirtland's leading elders in his respectable dry goods store resembled those of contemporary nineteenth-century lodges that frequently occupied an upper room in an existing building, such as a tavern.

An announcement was soon made that a new edifice was to be built to house the School of the Prophets and to "endow those whom I [the Lord] have chosen with power from on high" (D&C 95:8).[53] Language such as this suggested that, just as the School of the Prophets was an elite and exclusive group, the endowment would also be given to a chosen and selective company whom the Lord would honor with his presence.[54] Not unlike the Masonic Fraternity, the Mormon School of the Prophets was a select body with specific membership requirements (D&C 88:133, 138). Its meetings began with a ritual greeting of uplifted hands between the instructor and class members. Zebedee Coltrin recalled:

> Elder Orson Hyde was the teacher and saluted the brethren with uplifted hands, and they also answered with uplifted hands. . . . The teacher saluted the brethren (one or more) as they came in. This salutation was given every morning when they met.[55]

---

50. For background on the name, see Joseph F. Darowski, "Schools of the Prophets: An Early American Tradition," 1–13.

51. Newel K. Whitney, letter to Painesville, Ohio masonic chapter, March 27, 1827.

52. "Masonic Notice," 2.

53. See David John Buerger, *The Mysteries of Godliness: A History of Mormon Temple Worship*, 6.

54. Joseph Smith spoke of the grand design he had for the School of the Prophets in a letter to W. W. Phelps:

"[Y]ou will see that the Lord commanded us in Kirtland to build an house of God, & establish a school for the Prophets, this is the word of the Lord to us, & we must— yea the Lord helping us we will obey, as on conditions of our obedience, he has promised <us> great things, yea <even> a visit from the heavens to honor us with his own presence." See "Letter to William W. Phelps, 11 January 1833," The Joseph Smith Papers, 19.

55. School of the Prophets Salt Lake City Meeting Minutes, October 3, 1883 [58].

This formality was described as "a salutation to one another in the house of God, in the school of the prophets" (v. 136), connecting the school with the planned temple. In this responsorial greeting, men were received by covenant as brothers "in the bonds of love" (v. 133). This indicated a mystic fraternal tie in which they were bound together by mutual obligations to God.

Masonic tradition identifies prayer with uplifted hands as a Jewish practice. This type of prayer is likewise found in the Book of Mormon's description of the tradition of the apostate Zoramites meeting in their false synagogue. One person at a time would

> go forth and stand upon the top thereof, and stretch forth his hands towards heaven, and cry with a loud voice, saying: Holy, holy God . . . we thank thee . . . that we are a chosen and a holy people. . . . Now the place was called by them Rameumptom, which, being interpreted, is the holy stand. (Alma 31:14, 18, 21)

While the context makes clear it is associated with a false religious form, the action itself is not spoken of disparagingly. Rather, it is the words that accompanied this ritual act that are treated with disapproval. Thus, there was no contradiction when in the School of the Prophets, Joseph Smith himself inaugurated the practice of prayer with uplifted hands.[56]

Following the greeting, class members received confidential instruction. As in Freemasonry, emphasis was placed on learning certain "liberal arts and sciences" such as astronomy, geography, geology, history, languages, and politics (D&C 88:77–79). Those who attended in the winter and early spring of 1833 were instructed in several secular topics as well as church doctrine to prepare them for their ministry. Members of the School of the Prophets were given admonitions concerning their personal habits, spiritual practices, and comportment. But "above all things," they were to "clothe [them]selves with the bond of charity, as with a mantle" (v. 125). This mirrored Masonic injunction: charity is the chief characteristic of the Lodge. From the very first degree, Freemasons are told that such charity is an identifying mark of the individual Freemason, for like the soul itself, it endures forever: "Faith may be lost in sight; Hope ends in fruition; but Charity extends beyond the grave, through the boundless realms of eternity."[57]

One of the courses of study at the School of the Prophets was the *Lectures on Faith*, which contains the earliest articulation of the Mormon doctrine of divinization. As was true of the instruction of candidates in the Masonic degrees, the lectures utilize a catechismal structure. For example, members of the school learned in Lecture 5 that by keeping the commandments they would grow "from grace to grace and become heirs of the heavenly kingdom . . . being transformed into the express image" of God. Referencing John 14, Lecture 7 explains Jesus

---

56. See Eliza R. Snow's description of the Kirtland Temple Dedication in Tullidge, *Women of Mormondom*, 82–95.

57. Mackey, Hughan, and Hawkins, *An Encyclopaedia of Freemasonry and its Kindred Sciences*, 1:260.

"declares to his Father, in language not to be easily mistaken, that he wanted his disciples, even all of them, to be as himself and the Father. . . . [T]he Savior wished his disciples to understand that they were to be partakers with him in all things, not even his glory excepted."[58] The perfectibility of human personality is an idea that was strongly apparent among contemporary Masonic writers such as Hosea Ballou and was seen symbolically in Masonic ritual. The members of the School of the Prophets were to sanctify themselves so that they would become worthy to see the face of God (D&C 88:68). From among the members of the School, the "sons of Jacob" were to "build a holy city" (v. 58). The grand purpose of the school and eventually the temple ritual was to receive the name of God (D&C 109:9, 19, 22).

The Development of Early Temple Rituals

Masonic rites are known for their appropriation and ritualization of scriptural stories. Likewise, the first temple ordinances and proto-rituals seen in the School of the Prophets adapted such biblical precedents. These included the washing of feet, washing and anointing, the Hosanna Shout, and the passing through veils of the temple.

Washing of Feet

A ritual introduced in the School of the Prophets that contained a peculiarly Masonic flavor found its scriptural basis in a scene from the Gospel of John where Jesus washes the feet of his disciples. As in the Bible, Mormon washing of feet had been used in several different circumstances, but in the School of the Prophets it took on a more formal aspect.[59] An 1832 revelation to the School directs:

> And he shall be received by the ordinance of the washing of feet, for unto this end was the ordinance of the washing of feet instituted. And again, the ordinance of washing feet is to be administered by the president, or presiding elder of the church. It is to be commenced with prayer; and after partaking of bread and wine, he is to gird himself according to the pattern given in the thirteenth chapter of John's testimony concerning me. Amen. (D&C 88:139–141)

Here, the action of foot washing is specifically termed an ordinance, ritualizing the practice. In Kirtland temple rites, the washing of feet began as a preparation for the endowment of "power from on high." When the temple was dedicated on March 27, 1836, the hymn "The Spirit of God," written for this occasion by W.W. Phelps, was sung. It included these words:

> We'll wash, and be washed and with oil be anointed,
> Withal not omitting the washing of feet.[60]

---

58. "Doctrine and Covenants, 1844," The Joseph Smith Papers, 62, 80.
59. See Doctrine and Covenants 60:15; 84:92; 99:4.
60. Emma Smith, *A Collection of Sacred Hymns for the Church of the Latter Day Saints*, 121.

Washing of feet took on added significance later in Nauvoo where it was performed as part of the second anointing, an ordinance connected with the receiving
of the High Priesthood.[61] The washing followed the pattern laid out in the Gospel
of John and was accompanied by partaking of bread and wine, which is not present
in the biblical account but is found in the Masonic Order of High Priesthood.[62]

Washing and Anointing

The washing of feet that began in the School of the Prophets would later
be followed up with a similar ritual for the whole body. On Tuesday, January
19, 1836, Joseph Smith noted in his journal history that he spent the day at
the School of the Prophets learning and reading in the Hebrew language of the
Bible: "my prayer is that God will speedily indue us with a knowledge of all
languages and toungs, that his servants may go forth for the last time, to bind
up the law and seal up the testimony."[63] Amid some turmoil among the Church
leadership, Smith invited his followers to prepare themselves for an induement
[endowment]—a bestowal of divine power and knowledge which would be given
in the temple. The promised gift was especially directed toward the Council of
the Twelve and those elders who were performing missionary work in the field.

---

61. An 1883 version of the ritual as performed by President John Taylor was as follows:
"Brother (giving name) in the name of the Lord Jesus Christ and by virtue of the Holy
Priesthood I wash thy feet in accordance with the order instituted by God in his church
and as practised [sic] by our Lord and Savior Jesus Christ when in the flesh upon his
apostles and diciples [sic] and also observed by his servant Joseph Smith the Prophet as
an introductory ordinance into the school of the prophets. I pronounce thee clean from
the blood of this generation, and confer upon thee all the rights, blessings, powers and
privelages [sic] associated with this holy ordinance, and I do it by virtue of the Holy
Priesthood in the name of the Lord Jesus Christ. Amen." Occasionally he inserted "And I
say unto thee thy sins are forgiven thee." School of the Prophets Salt Lake City Meeting
Minutes, October 12, 1883 [86].

62. Thomas Smith Webb, *The Freemasons Monitor*, 178–79. In this degree, Freemasons
receive the High Priesthood in a ceremony based on Genesis 14. Melchizedek brings forth
a sacrament of bread and wine and blesses Abraham with the Priesthood.

63. "Journal, 1835–1836," The Joseph Smith Papers, 131. See also "History, 1834–
1836," The Joseph Smith Papers, 162–63. This prayer was a counterpart of one given
early in the Masonic initiation ritual: "We beseech thee, O Lord God, to bless our present
assembling, and grant that this our new made brother, may prove true and faithful. Endue
him with a competency of thy divine wisdom, that he may, with the secrets of freemasonry, be able to unfold the mysteries of godliness; and may he and we walk in the
light of thy countenance, and when all the trials of our probationary state shall be over,
be admitted into the temple not made with hands, eternal in the heavens. Amen." James
Hardie, *The New Free-Mason's Monitor; or, Masonic Guide. For the Direction of Members
of that Ancient and Honourable Fraternity, as well as for the Information of those, who may
be Desirous of Becoming Acquainted with its Principles*, 218. Of immediate interest to a
Latter-day Saint is the use of the word "endue."

Around this time, Oliver Cowdery and John Corrill met Smith at his home for an unusual ceremony.[64] After preparing a container of pure water, they "called upon the Lord and proceeded to wash each other's bodies, and bathe the same with whiskey, perfumed with cinnamon." Cowdery later recalled how their "minds were filled" with thoughts of "how the priests anciently used to wash always before ministering before the Lord." Before they had finished their observances, Martin Harris arrived "and was also washed."[65] Days later, a similar ritual took place among the members of the First Presidency and other church leaders.[66] Smith's history reports that on January 21, in the attic of the printing office, the presidency, consisting of Smith, Sidney Rigdon, and Frederick G. Williams, as well as Hyrum Smith, David Whitmer, John Whitmer, Oliver Cowdery and John Corrill, "attended to the ordinance of washing our bodies in pure water, [and] we also perfumed our bodies and our heads, in the name of the Lord."[67] In five days, the washing ceremony had become an ordinance with a prescribed pattern. The company of eight then moved to the unfinished temple. Here, they met Smith's scribe Warren Parrish and Joseph Smith Sr.,[68] along with the bishop of Kirtland and his counselors,[69] and the bishop of Zion with his counselors.[70]

A noteworthy detail in Edward Partridge's account of the events at the temple that evening informs us that the meeting was "opened" three successive times, first "by Prest. Joseph Smith, Jun., in behalf of the Presidency," next by "Bishop Whitney in behalf of himself and counsellors," and finally by Bishop Partridge "in behalf of myself & counsellors."[71] This procedure is reminiscent of the opening of a lodge when business is to be conducted for Entered Apprentices, Fellowcrafts, and Master Masons. The lodge must be opened on each degree. Furthermore, the charge used at opening a lodge referred to the Old Testament anointing of Aaron:

---

64. After returning to Ohio with Joseph Smith following the Zion's Camp march in 1834, Corrill was appointed to take charge of the final construction of the Kirtland temple. See Leonard J. Arrington, "Oliver Cowdery's Kirtland, Ohio, 'Sketch Book,'" 416n16.

65. Arrington, 416. ["Postscript" to 16 Jan 1836].

66. Compare Arrington, "Oliver Cowdery's Kirtland, Ohio, 'Sketch Book,'" 418–19 [January 21, 1836]; "Journal, 1835–1836," 135–38 (January 21, 1836); and Edward Partridge, diary, January 21, 1836.

67. "History, 1838–1856, volume B-1 [1 September 1834–2 November 1838]," The Joseph Smith Papers, 695.

68. It is not clear from the records if Joseph Smith Sr. attended the earlier washing ceremony in the printing office. Had he done so, the company would have numbered nine men, the same as at the organization of the Anointed Quorum in 1844, and the number of men necessary to form a Royal Arch Chapter.

69. Newel K. Whitney, Reynolds Cahoon, and Vinson Knight.

70. Edward Partridge, Isaac Morley, and John Corrill.

71. Partridge, diary, January 21, 1836.

Behold! How good and how pleasant it is for brethren to dwell together in unity!

It is like the precious ointment upon the head, that ran down upon the beard, even Aaron's beard, that went down to the skirts of his garment:

As the dew of Hermon, that descended upon the mountains of Zion: for there the Lord commanded a blessing, even life forevermore.[72]

After the meeting was opened, church leaders beginning with Joseph Smith Sr. were anointed with consecrated oil—"the same kind of oil and in the man[ner] that were Moses and Aaron, and those who stood before the Lord in ancient days."[73] Members of the High Councils of Kirtland and Zion, who had been waiting in adjoining rooms, were then anointed in their turn.[74] In his description of these first washings and anointings, historian David Buerger assumes that "these ordinances clearly were patterned after washings and anointings described in the Old and especially New Testaments."[75] Nonetheless, these types of ceremonies had been adopted decades before in Freemasonry and exposed in Webb's *Monitor* and Bernard's *Light on Masonry*. In the degree called "Knights of the East and West," for example, a basin of water and a ewer of perfume and are placed on the east side of the room. At a certain point in the ritual,

The Most Puissant then takes the ewer filled with perfumed ointment, and anoints his head, eyes, mouth, heart, the tip of his right ear, hand, and foot, and says, "You are now, my dear brother, received a member of our society; you will recollect to live up to the precepts of it, and *also remember that those parts of your body, which have the greatest power of assisting you in good or evil, have this day been made holy!*"[76]

On February 22, members of the Council of the Twelve, or "traveling High Council" (D&C 107:33; 124:139), the presidents of the Seventy, and newly called "president of the high priesthood of the Melchisedek priesthood," Don Carlos Smith, were anointed and blessed.[77] Anointings continued throughout February and were accompanied each evening by an endowment of the Spirit. The heavens were opened, and many visions experienced. Quite intentionally, the Prophet was building a fraternity of the first elders of the Church.

The dedication of the temple took place on Sunday, March 27, 1836. On the following Wednesday, Smith declared that "the time that we were required to tarry in Kirtland to be endued would be fulfilled in a few days, and then

---

72. Webb, *Freemason's Monitor*, 25.

73. Arrington, "Oliver Cowdery's Kirtland, Ohio, 'Sketch Book,'" 419 [January 21, 1836].

74. "Hyrum Smith annointed Father John Smith who annointed the rest of the High Council of Kirtland. Br. David Whitmer annointed Br. Simeon Carter, who annointed the High Council from Zion." Partridge, diary, January 21, 1836.

75. Buerger, *The Mysteries of Godliness*, 11.

76. Bernard, *Light on Masonry*, 220; emphasis in original.

77. Arrington, "Oliver Cowdery's Kirtland, Ohio, 'Sketch Book,'" 420 [January 22, 1836]. See also Partridge, diary, January 15, 1836. Partridge states, "Carlos Smith was appointed president over the H[igh] Priests at K[irtland]."

the Elders would go forth."[78] Speaking of the evening's activities of "exhorting, prophesying and speaking in tongues until 5 o clock in the morning," with the Savior appearing to some and angels ministering to others, Smith said that "it was a penticost and enduement indeed, long to be remembered."[79] This remark makes it clear that the Kirtland endowment referred to a manifestation of the Spirit, though accompanied by rites and rituals such as washing and anointing.

Hosanna Shout

Another part of the observances mentioned in accounts of each anointing session was a ritualized cry of "Hosannah" such as is described in Masonic ritual.[80] On January 21, Joseph Smith's journal reports, "We shouted Hosanah to God and the Lamb,"[81] while Edward Partridge recalled, "We shouted Hosanna to the Most High."[82] On January 22, Smith wrote, "The congregation shouted a loud hosanna the gift of toung[ue]s fell upon us in mighty pow[e]r."[83] Partridge elaborated,

> Prest. J.S. Jun., requested Prest. Sidney Rigdon to ask the Lord to accept the performances of the evening, and instructed us, when he was done, to shout Hosannah, Blessed be the name of the Most High God. These things were performed; the shout & speaking in unknown tongues lasted 10 or 15 minutes. During the evening, more especially at the time of shouting, a number saw visions as they disclosed unto us.[84]

On January 28, when members of the Elders quorum, Melchizedek Priesthood quorum, and the Seventies quorum were anointed,[85] Smith instructed the Twelve and the seven presidents of the Seventy "to call upon God with uplifted hands to

---

78. "Journal, 1835–1836," 188. Despite this statement, it is difficult to pinpoint precisely when these types of temple ordinances were first performed. Almost five years earlier, the Painesville Telegraph described a June 1831 conference, in which a group of Elders was chosen to go and preach the gospel in Missouri: "The ceremony of endowing them with miraculous gifts, or supernatural power, was then performed, and they were commanded to take up a line of march; preaching their gospel, (Jo's Bible) raising the dead, healing the sick, casting out devils, &c." See "Mormonism on the Wing."

79. "Journal, 1835–1836," 189.

80. The following is sung in full chorus at the conclusion of the Recitation:

> Lift your head, ye golden gate,
> Jesus comes in royal state;
> Shout Hosanna, shout and sing,
> Jesus Christ, the Lord is King!

See Rob Morris, *The Poetry of Freemasonry*, 24.

81. "Journal, 1835–1836," 135–38 [January 21, 1836].

82. Partridge, diary, January 21, 1836.

83. "Journal, 1835–1836," 141 [January 22, 1836].

84. Partridge, diary, January 22, 1836.

85. The Presidency of the Elders Quorum in Kirtland was Alvah Beaman, Reuben Hedlock, and John Morton.

seal the blessings which had been promised to them by the holy anoint[in]g."[86]
Then Sidney Rigdon was called upon "to seal them with uplifted hands. . . . [W]hen
he had done this & cried hossannah that all congregation should join him & shout
hosanna to God & the Lamb & glory to God in the highest."[87]

The detail of uplifted hands recalls a point in Masonic ritual where prayer is
offered over Hiram Abiff's deceased body. While praying, the brethren raise and
drop their hands three times. This gesture would be carried over into the prayer
circle performance in the Nauvoo temple.

Smith spent several of the following days organizing the different quorums
of the Church. On Saturday, February 6, he called together those who had been
anointed to "receive the seal of all their blessings."[88] He separated the brethren
into three different rooms in the temple; he then went from room to room repeatedly, instructing them in a very specific ritual that God had shown to him:

> first part to be spent in solemn prayer before god without any talking or confusion
> & the conclusion with a sealing prayer by Pres. Sidney Rigdon when all the quorems
> are to shout with one accord a solemn hosanna to God & the Lamb with an Amen—
> amen & amen—& then all take seats & lift up their hearts in silent prayer to God
> & if any obtain a prophecy or vision not to rise & speak that all may be edefied &
> rejoice together.[89]

A solemn assembly celebrating the seventh anniversary of the founding of the
Church was held on April 6, 1837, at which the previous week's anointings were
sealed. Elder Wilford Woodruff related that "with uplifted hand to heaven" those
gathered repeated "HOSANNA, Hosanna, Hosanna, to GOD & the LAMB,
Amen, Amen, & Amen" three times, and that the shout "was repeated by angels
on high & caused the power of God to rest upon us."[90] Thus, the Hosanna Shout
was ritualized and used as a seal for ordinances.[91]

This Hosanna Shout that accompanied the first ordinances was standardized
and more firmly placed into Mormon ritual as part of the dedication of the Kirtland
temple.[92] Eliza R. Snow described the shout at the temple dedication as follows:

> One striking feature of the ceremonies, was the grand shout of hosanna, which was
> given by the whole assembly, in standing position, with uplifted hands. The form of
> the shout is as follows: "Hosanna-hosanna-hosanna-to God and the Lamb-amen-
> amen, and amen." The foregoing was deliberately and emphatically pronounced, and

86. "Journal, 1835–1836," 143 (January 28, 1836).
87. "Journal, 1835–1836," 143 (January 28, 1836).
88. "Journal, 1835–1836," 151a (February 6, 1836).
89. "Journal, 1835–1836," 151a (February 6, 1836).
90. Wilford Woodruff journal, April 6, 1837.
91. Buerger, *The Mysteries of Godliness*, 15, 33.
92. Brigham Young and Heber C. Kimball recognized that Joseph Smith had taught
the "correct order" of shouting Hosanna at Kirtland. James G. Bleak, "Dedication of St.
George Temple Site," 255.

three times repeated, and with such power as seemed almost sufficient to raise the roof from the building.[93]

The three-fold shout has been repeated at every Latter-day Saint temple dedication since that time, as well as other special occasions.[94]

Some authors have recognized possible Hebrew roots of the Hosanna Shout.[95] However, the focus on "God and the Lamb" betrays a more Christian emphasis. A similar ritual, more closely related to the Mormon form of the Hosanna Shout than the biblical version, was developing simultaneously in the same area of the country. The ritual of the Heroines of Jericho, a concordant Masonic body associated with the Royal Arch, was available in upstate New York as early as 1826.[96] A Hosanna Shout is found in several places in the Heroines rituals, and their installation of grand officers is very similar to the Mormon Hosanna Shout. Here, a three-fold shout is performed encircling an altar and accompanied by the clapping of hands and waving of handkerchiefs.[97] As this Heroines shout appears

---

93. Eliza R. Snow, quoted in Tullidge, *Women of Mormondom*, 94.

94. A recent example of the Hosanna Shout being performed outside of temple dedications was during the April 2020 general conference of The Church of Jesus Christ of Latter-day Saints, in which President Russell M. Nelson led Latter-day Saints in the shout for the bicentennial commemoration of the First Vision. Nelson, however, incorrectly stated that the "sacred shout was first given in this dispensation at the dedication of the Kirtland Temple on March 27, 1836." See Russell M. Nelson, "Hosanna Shout."

95. See Steven H. Heath, "The Sacred Shout," 115–23; Jacob W. Olmstead, "From Pentecost to Administration: A Reappraisal of the History of the Hosanna Shout," 7–37. Olmstead notices that the earliest Hosanna Shouts by the followers of Joseph Smith occurred as spontaneous shouts by individuals expressing praise to God at the occurrence of a spiritual manifestation. One example is Heber C. Kimball's account of hearing the gospel with Brigham Young in the fall of 1831: "These things caused such great joy to spring up in our bosoms, that we were hardly able to contain ourselves, and we did shout aloud, Hosannah to God and the Lamb." See Heber C. Kimball, "History of Brigham Young," 504. In a second instance, Seymour B. Young recalled that his father, Joseph Young (a brother of Brigham), had said Hyrum Smith gave the Hosanna Shout during the Zion's Camp March in 1834. Olmstead connects the shout with the Christian Pentecostal revivalist movement of the early nineteenth century. However, at both of these times, a Master Mason was involved in initiating the shout—Heber C. Kimball was a Mason prior to the Morgan Affair, and Hyrum Smith had been a Mason since 1826.

96. S. Brent Morris, "The High Degrees in the United States: 1730–1830." Of the many pre-1830 American side degrees, "only the Heroines of Jericho seems to be an American original. It survived and is worked today by Prince Hall Masons." Morris lists three degrees for women as part of the "Pre-1830 American Masonic Side Degrees." These are "Master Mason's Daughter (for women); True Kindred (for women); Heroine of Jericho (RAMs, wives and widows)." See also Avery Allyn, *A Ritual of Freemasonry: Illustrated by Numerous Engravings*; and William Leigh, *The Ladies' Masonry: Or, Hieroglyphic Monitor*.

97. Moses Dickson, *Revised Landmarks and Ceremonies of Courts of Heroines of Jericho*, 72, 76. Clapping hands during the shout was mentioned in an affidavit against Joseph Smith on the "affairs in Missouri" reprinted in the *Times and Seasons* of July 1843: "They

along with the installing of officers, it compares closely with the endowing of church officials which took place in the Kirtland temple.

Three other notable performances of the triple Hosanna Shout not associated with anointings, temple dedication, groundbreaking, or laying of capstones were evocative of Freemasonry. First, at a Fourth of July celebration in 1838, Sidney Rigdon gave a rousing sermon declaring the Mormons' independence from mobs. One observer reported, "At the conclusion of the oration the vast multitude shouted, Hosanna! Hosanna!! Hosanna!!! three times."[98]

Seven years later, on April 11, 1844, Joseph Smith met with the Council of Fifty in the newly completed Masonic Hall and "had a very interesting time. The Spirit of the Lord was with us and we closed the Council with loud shouts of Hosanna."[99] William Clayton reported, "President Joseph Smith was voted our P[rophet] and K[ing] with loud Hosannas."[100]

Finally, on December 27, 1847, the reorganization of the First Presidency under Brigham Young took place at Winter Quarters.[101] Participants in this event were "striking the right hand into the palm of the left at sound of each word: Hosanah! Hosanah! Hosanah! [sic] To God and the Lamb! Amen! Amen! and Amen!"[102] This occasion is reminiscent of a Masonic installation of officers, a public meeting of grand honors, and a threefold clapping of hands signaling recognition of the authority of the person being honored.

Passing of the Temple Veils

On Thursday, March 23, 1837, nearly a year after the temple dedication, the Saints were asked to set apart the day for prayer and fasting. Future Church President Wilford Woodruff rose early and set off for the temple. As he entered the building, he saw that the three veils separating the pulpits one from another had been lowered. These large canvas sheets were painted white and hung from the ceiling using an intricate system of cords and pulleys.[103] The heavy fabric provided a private area where he and several other elders could gather in the Aaronic stand and offer morning prayer. Later, the congregation took their seats in the main space of the first floor of the temple. Larger veils divided this common area into four compartments, and each section was presided over by church presiden-

---

would slap their hands and shout hosanna, hosanna, glory to God." See Hyrum Smith, "Missouri vs Joseph Smith," 255.

98. Ebenezer Robinson, "Items of Personal History of the Editor, No. 6, Including Some Items of Church History Not Generally Known," 149.

99. "History, 1838–1856, volume E-1 [1 July 1843–30 April 1844]," The Joseph Smith Papers, 2009.

100. George D. Smith, ed., *An Intimate Chronicle, The Journals of William Clayton*, 129.

101. Aaron L. West, "Sustaining a New First Presidency in 1847."

102. Norton Jacob, journal, December 27, 1847.

103. West, *A Few Interesting Facts Respecting the Mormons*, 4–5.

cy leaders, with women in two of the compartments and men in the other two. In the late afternoon, the veils were rolled up, bringing the congregation together, and, according to Woodruff, "the presence of the LORD filled the house."[104]

A similar arrangement of veils was familiar to Freemasons. Four veils are used to divide the ritual space in Masonry's Holy Royal Arch degree for the part of that ceremony known as "the passing of the veils." Tests of knowledge are given at each veil, with the successive passing of the veils of the temple forming an important part of the Royal Arch's Rite of Exaltation.[105] At the end the candidate is crowned.

A miraculous experience that also occurred behind the Kirtland temple veils took place following the temple's dedication on the first Sunday in April 1836. The Twelve were officiating at the sacrament table, and Joseph Smith assisted in administering the bread and wine of the Lord's Supper to the congregation. Following the meeting, Smith and Oliver Cowdery knelt in prayer behind the veils separating the pulpits from the main room. There, they saw a magnificent vision of the Savior, who appeared above them "upon the breastwork of the pulpit" and regarded them with a piercing, fiery gaze. "For behold I have accepted this house," he told them, "and my name shall be here; and I will manifest myself to my people, in mercy, in this House."[106] This promise that the Lord's "name" would be in the temple recalls the Masonic search for the Lost Word—the true name of Deity.

The experience was recorded by Oliver Cowdery's brother, Warren, a Royal Arch Mason from a family of Royal Arch Masons, whose conversion to the Latter-day work is noted in a canonized revelation: "there was joy in heaven when my servant Warren bowed to my scepter, and separated himself from the crafts of men" (D&C 106:6). Aspects of the vision would have held deep significance to a Royal Arch Mason. In the Royal Arch ritual, after passing through the veils and giving the correct passwords, candidates enter the presence of a Divine council consisting of a prophet, priest, and king. Smith's experience, as recorded by Warren Cowdery, followed this pattern. His encounter with Jesus, the "prophet, priest, and king" of the New Testament, was a literal fulfillment of the Royal Arch type. The vision continued with biblical prophets Moses, "Elias," and Elijah conferring keys of the Priesthood.[107] As this bestowal occurred behind veils, it holds a remarkable synchronicity with Royal Arch Masonry, where each of the veils are associated with biblical figures, Moses being one of them.

---

104. Wilford Woodruff journal, March 23, 1837.

105. T. T. Kuruvilla, "The Excellent Masters' Degree (Passing The Veils)- A Link Between The Craft And The Holy Royal Arch."

106. "Visions, 3 April 1836 [D&C 110]," The Joseph Smith Papers, 192.

107. "Visions, 3 April 1836 [D&C 110]," 192.

Joseph Smith as Ritualist

King Solomon was considered by Masons to be a prophetic figure and one of the three Grand Masters of ancient Craft Masonry. At the dedication of the House of the Lord in Jerusalem, the biblical potentate "kneeled down upon his knees before all the congregation of Israel and spread forth his hands toward heaven" (2 Chr. 6:13). Joseph Smith openly stepped into Solomon's role as prophet, priest, and king when he himself offered the dedicatory prayer for the completed Kirtland temple on March 27, 1836.

The dedicatory prayer of the Kirtland temple was modeled on Solomon's words in 1 Kings 8:22–61. Warren Cowdery, a Royal Arch Mason, apparently assisted in its composition, and certain wording in the prayer reveals a Masonic interest.[108] This is best seen in specific reference to ritual that Smith had developed for the School of the Prophets, further linking them to the newly completed House of the Lord (D&C 109:17–19); the Royal Arch emphasis on rebuilding both the temple and the city of Jerusalem (v. 73); and the reference to the Hosanna Shout at the end of the prayer (v. 79). Smith's assumption of King Solomon's role, while only hinted at in Kirtland, would be startlingly expressed in Nauvoo.

For Latter-day Saints, the purpose of temple ordinances is to bind the individual to God and to enable them to come into God's presence. In the esoteric practice of Freemasonry, confidential instruction on this objective was passed down through the oral tradition. Masons believed they possessed a significant oral tradition, one that, when rejoined to Christianity, would revitalize it. In developing the Kirtland temple rites, Smith drew upon the oral tradition and legends of the Freemasons and included all the required components of a Masonic working ritual.[109] These included specific forms such as ritual wording, secret names, ritual gestures, ritual action, and ritualization of biblical passages and stories. As seen in this chapter, Kirtland temple performances included all of these Masonic elements.

First, ritual wording was seen in the Hosanna Shout, from its beginnings in the anointing ceremony, and culminating in a more or less standard form at temple dedications. The brethren also called upon Deity using the sacred name *Ahman*, a secret name found in the Kirtland Egyptian papers. Responding to this call, *Ahman* walked among the members of the School of the Prophets.[110]

---

108. Oliver Cowdery, diary, March 26, 1836: "I met in the presidents room pres J. Smith, jr. S Rigdon, my brother W.A. Cowdery & Elder W. Parrish, and assisted in writing a prayer for the dedication of the house."

109. In the United States there were still local areas who were forming their own traditional practices, and even new workings and side degrees, which were very popular in the early to mid-1800s.

110. Zebedee Coltrin testimony in "School of the Prophets Salt Lake City Meeting Minutes, 1883, August–December," October 3, 1883. To pass from east to west is God passing from east (heavenly realms) to west (the mortal world).

Doctrine and Covenants 82 speaks of code names which were given to some of the brethren. These names were received and related to an oath or covenant with a penalty for its violation.[111]

Next, ritual forms and gestures, including kneeling with uplifted hands to heaven, were performed in the School of the Prophets and continued as a part of ordinances such as washings and anointings. These were also seen at the dedication ceremony of the Kirtland temple.

Finally, ritual action was an important component of incipient ritual at Kirtland. This was seen in the washings and anointings themselves. They began as simple foot washing in the School of the Prophets, and later as part of an endowment of power given in connection with offices in the priesthood. Later still, washings and anointings would be connected to the temple ritual in Nauvoo.

Features of Kirtland temple ritual and structural design were as stones piled one upon the other. As they accumulated, they began more and more to resemble a Mason's arch. Each of the Masonic allegorical associations used gave meaning to the temple's construction and purpose to the ritual that Joseph Smith was inaugurating.

Building the Fane

The building of the Kirtland temple was done under difficult circumstances and at great financial sacrifice. Of the several planned latter-day temples in the 1830s, it was the only one erected, and that amid much persecution. Looking back upon the Kirtland experience, Brigham Young couched the building of the temple in language known to every Cryptic Mason:

> [T]he great Prophet Joseph, in the stone quarry, quarrying rock with his own hands; and the few then in the Church, following his example of obedience and diligence wherever most needed; with laborers on the walls, *holding the sword in one hand to protect themselves from the mob, while they placed the stone and moved the trowel with the other*, the Kirtland temple—the second house of the Lord, that we have any published record of on the earth, was so far completed as to be dedicated. [112]

Brigham Young, a Freemason who used Royal Arch cipher in his journal, employed the illustration of the trowel and the sword to describe workers on the Kirtland temple. Later, he used this same imagery to refer to the Nauvoo temple

> But what of the Temple in Nauvoo? *By aid of sword in one hand, and trowel and hammer in the other*, with fire arms at hand, and a strong band of police, and the blessings of heaven, the Saints, through hunger, and thirst, and weariness, and watchings, and prayings, completed the Temple.[113]

---

111. Code names were removed from the LDS version of the Doctrine and Covenants beginning with the 1981 edition. For more on code names, see pages 224–25.

112. Brigham Young, April 6, 1853, *Journal of Discourses*, 2:31; emphasis added.

113. Young, 2:32; emphasis added.

Thus, Young undeniably connected the Kirtland as well as the Nauvoo temple with Freemasonry. In Ohio, the seeds of Freemasonry that had been planted in Joseph Smith's mind and heart early in his life took root, and his talents as a ritual builder began to take shape. The effect that building a Masonically inspired temple and participating in early Mormon rituals had on Smith's followers would be more clearly seen as they moved into the state of Missouri.

CHAPTER 9

ANGEL AT THE THRESHING-FLOOR

But if any so mean, Thro' avarice or stain,
Shou'd debase himself in this high station
That person so mean, For such cursed gain,
Should be slain by the hand of a mason.
—Laurence Dermott, *Ahiman Rezon*

Following the Morgan affair, most Americans became suspicious of the notion of theocratic kingdom-building, and they feared Masonic oaths and the concomitant penalties involving horrific death. American Baptist preacher John Glazier Stearns warned: "[T]o bind [men] together by solemn oaths secret societies to stand by, and defend, and promote each other, must be regarded as a dangerous procedure, both in relation to church and state."[1] An 1829 exposé of the Royal Arch obligation, widely circulated in the area where Joseph Smith lived, underscores what alarmed many Americans. A portion reads:

> I promise and swear . . . that I will aid and assist a companion Royal Arch Mason, when engaged in any difficulty; and espouse his cause . . . whether he be right or wrong. Also, that I will promote a companion Royal Arch Mason's political prefer- ment in preference to another of equal qualifications. Furthermore . . . a companion Royal Arch Mason's secrets . . . shall remain as secure and inviolable in my breast as in his own, murder and treason not excepted . . . under no less penalty than that of having my skull smote off.[2]

To promise to come to the aid of a brother seems harmless enough, but to take up a brother's cause whether he was right or wrong, or to promote his political aspirations above all others, contradicted the average American's sense of ethics. Furthermore, penalties that Masons generally understood as figurative were seen by outsiders to mean that those who revealed Masonic secrets would be put to death in extralegal bloody and retributive acts of Masonic vengeance.

The events surrounding the abduction and disappearance of William Morgan substantiated the fears of many Americans that penalties mentioned in Masonic ritual were literal and not symbolic. In a series of letters published in 1828 in the

---

1. John G. Stearns, *Letters on Freemasonry: Addressed Chiefly to the Fraternity*, 176.

2. David Bernard, *Light on Masonry: A Collection of All the Most Important Documents on the Subject of Speculative Free Masonry*, 130. In other places (e.g., page 63) he renders this "murder and treason excepted, and they left to my own election." See also *An Abstract of the Proceedings of the Antimasonic State Convention of Massachusetts, Held in Faneuil Hall, Boston, May 19 & 20, 1831*, 30.

LeRoy Gazette of Genesee County, New York, an anonymous author compared Morgan's murder to the allegorical punishment of Akirop, one of the murderers of Hiram Abiff. A candidate for the degree represents Joabert, who severs Akirop's head from his body with his own sword. This degree includes swearing an oath to avenge all who may betray Masonic secrets; receiving a password, *Nekam*, meaning "revenge"; wearing an apron embroidered with a depiction of a bloody hand holding aloft a severed head; and embracing other accoutrements of vengeance.[3]

Depiction of the "Elu of Nine" Degree, from *Richardson's Monitor of Freemasonry*, 1860.

"It is preposterous to suppose," asserts the letter's author,

> that the members of that degree, assembled in their bloody dens, with bloody aprons, and representations of the bloody head of a traitor before them, and seeing VENGEANCE written in capital letters upon the walls of their dark cavern, and knowing Morgan was writing the secrets of Masonry, that they would not, one and all, with the zeal of Joabert and Stokin, arise in their wrath and strike the villain to the heart.[4]

This theme is played out in the opening chapters of the Book of Mormon, when Nephi beheads Laban with his own sword, placing himself outside of the law in obedience to the voice of the Spirit. Such a theocratic ethic would become evident among the Mormons in Missouri where they clashed with locals in violent conflicts now known as the Mormon Wars.[5] By the late 1830s, the Latter-day Saints themselves had formed a secret, oath-bound organization designed to sow terror in the populace—a literal band of "avenging Masons" called the Danites.

In describing the Danite organization, John Whitmer, first official historian of the Church, placed their beginnings in Kirtland. The brethren were organized Masonically

> into a secret Society which they termed the Brother of Gideon, in the which Society they took oaths that they would Support a brother wright [sic] or wrong even to the shed[d]ing of blood. ~~also to~~ thus [those] who belonged tho [to] this society were bound to keep it a profound Secret never to reveal but ever to conceal these abominations from all and every person axcept those who were of the same Craft. But these things could not be kept a secret in consequence of betreyers who fel[l] from their faith, and revealed their Secrets thus things were carried on by secret plots and

---

3. Bernard, 198, 400.

4. Bernard, 400–401; emphasis added.

5. In his attempt to establish the kingdom of God, Joseph Smith embraced a set of what Michael Quinn calls "theocratic ethics" that placed Mormon priesthood authority above civil law. D. Michael Quinn, *The Mormon Hierarchy: Origins of Power*, 88.

midnight machinations, which Society was begin[n]ing to be established in Kirtland Ohio in the fall of 1836.[6]

A December 1833 revelation in Kirtland authorized the first presidency to deal harshly with dissenters. Now Doctrine and Covenants 101, the revelation portrayed the children of Zion as "the salt of the earth and the savor of men." If they transgressed, they were "thenceforth good for nothing only to be cast out and trodden under the feet of men" (D&C 101:40; cf. Matt. 5:13). A subsequent revelation in February 1834, now D&C 103, likewise used the biblical salt metaphor: "inasmuch as they are not the saviors of men, they are as salt that has lost its savor" (v. 10).[7] Included in these two sections was strong language that foreshadowed the Danite purposes in Missouri: "they were found transgressors, therefore they must needs be chastened" (101:41).[8] In Wilford Woodruff's 1836 diary, he termed Kirtland "the strong hold of the daughter of Zion," a biblical name by which Danites were also known.[9]

Additional Danite activity occurred at an October 18, 1837, Kirtland High Council meeting in which the body "concluded that it <was> time to . . . commence the work of reform, by pruning the vine of God in Kirtland, and to follow up the work night after night until it should be thought best to stay the hands."[10] A few weeks later, on November 7, 1836, church leaders and nearly sixty other members threatened non-Mormon justice of the peace Ariel Hanson into leaving the town. Later, in Missouri, a group of dissenters were similarly pressured to leave Caldwell County in what many believe was the first Danite action.[11]

Mormon historian Leland Gentry hypothesized that the several names by which the Danite organization was known correspond to changes and developments in functions over time.[12] Because the group and its purposes evolved quickly, it is dif-

---

6. "John Whitmer, History, 1831–circa 1847," The Joseph Smith Papers, 96. Initiated by Apostle Thomas B. Marsh, oaths of allegiance were demanded of the elders in Far West, MO, in the fall of 1837. Those critical of the prophet were counted disloyal. See also Marvin S. Hill, *Quest For Refuge: The Mormon Flight from American Pluralism*, 72–76; and Alanson Ripley, "To the Elders Abroad," 39. Ripley exhorted the missionaries abroad to rejoice, for "the Lord our God is about to establish a Kingdom, which cannot be thrown down, neither can the gates of hell prevail against it." For more on Danite activity in Kirtland, see Quinn, *The Mormon Hierarchy: Origins of Power*, 91.

7. D. Michael Quinn, "The Culture of Violence in Joseph Smith's Mormonism," 22.

8. See also Doctrine and Covenants 101:58: "And inasmuch as they gather together against you, avenge me of mine enemies, that by and by I may come with the residue of mine house and possess the land"; Doctrine and Covenants 103:15: "the redemption of Zion must needs come by power"; and Doctrine and Covenants 103:26: "and my presence shall be with you even in avenging me of mine enemies."

9. Wilford Woodruff journal, April 6, 1837.

10. "Minute Book 1," The Joseph Smith Papers, 251.

11. Ronald E. Romig, *Eighth Witness: The Biography of John Whitmer*, 309.

12. Leland H. Gentry, "The Danite Band of 1838," 429. According to Gentry, "With the flight of the dissenters on 19 June 1838, the Danites lost their reason for existence. A

ficult to argue for a chronological progression of nomenclature. Additionally, Danite activity can be seen some time earlier than Gentry had supposed. However, the different terms—the Big Fan, Gideonites, Danites, Daughter of Zion—do correlate with the fundamental objectives of the organization and suggest a consistent (and Masonically inspired) purpose from the outset. In a Mormon adaptation of Masonic principles, Danites used biblical allusions to portray their aims and activities.[13]

The Big Fan

One clearly identifiable manifestation of a Danite objective was associated with driving dissenters out of Caldwell County, Missouri, where the Saints had begun to gather. As a depiction of this goal, the group took the name of the "Big Fan,"[14] which John Corrill described as "figurative of their intentions to cleanse the chaff from the wheat."[15] On June 17, 1838, Sidney Rigdon preached an inflammatory address known as the "Salt Sermon," which compared Mormon dissenters to salt which had lost its savor. A threatening letter was soon delivered to the offending parties, which Ebenezer Robinson recalled was "gotten up in the office of the First Presidency."[16] The letter bore the signatures of eighty-three men, all members of a newly formed covert society dedicated to principles espoused by Rigdon. Naming Oliver Cowdery, David Whitmer, John Whitmer, William W. Phelps,[17] and Lyman Johnson as covenant-breakers and apostates, the dispatch warned these men to leave town.[18]

---

new purpose had to be found to justify their continuation" (p. 427). The evidence does not seem to support the conclusion that the Danites needed to find a new purpose beyond that which they originally embraced. Sidney Rigdon himself described this purpose thus: "the Danites were organized for mutual protection against the bands that were forming and threatened to be formed" (p. 428).

13. William Wyl, *Mormon Portraits of the Truth About the Mormon Leaders from 1830 to 1886*, 169.

14. See Matthew 3:12: "Whose fan is in his hand, and he will thoroughly purge his floor, and gather his wheat into the garner; but he will burn up the chaff with unquenchable fire" (cf. Luke 3:17).

15. John Corrill, *A Brief History of the Church of Christ of Latter Day Saints (Commonly Called Mormons) Including an Account of Their Doctrine and Discipline, with the Reasons of the Author for Leaving the Church*, 32.

16. Robinson is quoted in Quinn, *The Mormon Hierarchy: Origins of Power*, 94. Robinson also claimed all the signers were Danites.

17. W. W. Phelps was reconciled with the Church before the letter was delivered and was thus spared the expulsion.

18. According to John Whitmer, the dissidents were threatened with lawsuits to attach their property. David and John Whitmer, Lyman Johnson, and Oliver Cowdery went to Clay County for legal counsel, but on their way back to Far West, they were met by Cowdery's and Johnson's families, who had been driven from the township with only their bedding and clothing. Whitmer charged that, during their absence, Smith, Rigdon,

Rigdon delivered a second incendiary speech two-and-a-half weeks later at a Fourth of July gathering in Far West, Missouri. The event included the laying of the cornerstone of the Far West Temple and was held in a style similar to contemporaneous Masonic cornerstone laying ceremonies. Such observances took place under the jurisdiction of the Grand Lodge with the Grand Master or his representative present. In the Mormon ceremony, the powerfully charismatic Joseph Smith appears to have acted as "Grand Master." Presiding officers were designated and consisted of the First Presidency, a group of marshals, and military officers and generals—all Danites.[19]

As in Masonic cornerstone ceremonies of the period, a procession was formed.[20] Led by a uniformed militia under Colonel George M. Hinkle and accompanied by the music of a small band under the direction of Dimick Huntington, the group of thousands marched to the excavation and formed three large concentric circles. After a prayer by Joseph Smith and a musical number, each of the cornerstones were laid in a precise order. The stones, 7 x 4 x 2 ft. thick, had been quarried by Joseph Holbrook and others and hauled to the spot the day before. Significantly to Masons, Brigham Young later said that the first stone was laid in the southeast, "because there is the most light."[21] This cornerstone was laid by the presidents of the stake, assisted by twelve men. The southwest stone was laid by the presidents of the elders, assisted by twelve men; the northwest cornerstone by the Bishop, again assisted by twelve men; and the northeast by

---

and "the band of gadeantons [Gadiantons] kept up a guard, and watched our houses and abused our families, and threatened them, [that] if they were not gone by morning, they would be drove out & threatened our lives if they ever saw us in Far West." Bruce N. Westergren, ed., *From Historian to Dissident: The Book of John Whitmer*, 184. George W. Robinson presented another view of the event: "These men took warning, and soon they were seen bounding over the prairie like the scape Goat to carry of[f] their own sins [Lev 16:21–22] we have not seen them since, their influence is gone, and they are in a miserable condition, so also it [is] with all who turn from the truth to Lying cheating defrauding & Swindeling." "Journal, March–September 1838," The Joseph Smith Papers, 47; see also Corrill, *A Brief History*, 30.

19. "Celebration of the 4th of July," 60.

20. The order of the procession was as follows: Following the infantry, "1st the patriarchs of the Church; 2nd the President, vice president, and orator, of the day; 3rd the Twelve; 4th the Presidents of the stake, with the high Council; 5th the Bishop and Council; 6th the architects; 7th the ladies, and then the gentleman of the civil procession. Then the Cavalry brought up the rear." The whole company marched to the notes of a small band of music under the direction of Dimick Huntington. "Celebration of the 4th of July," 60.

21. Brigham Young, April 6, 1853, *Journal of Discourses*, 1:133. According to the *Dumfries MS No. 4*, circa 1710, in Harry Carr, *The Early Masonic Catechisms*, 63: "Q[uestion:] who laid the first stone in ye foundation of ye temple A[nswer:] ye above said Hiram [King of Tyre] Q[uestion:] what place did he lay ye first stone A[nswer:] in ye south east corner of ye Temple. . . . Q[uestion:] what was greatest wonder yet seen or heard about the temple A[nswer:] god was man & man was god."

the president of the teachers and twelve men. Rigdon's incendiary oration was then delivered.

Danite Parley P. Pratt described the program in a glowing report. Many thousand people assembled around a liberty pole, surmounted by "the bald eagle, with its stars and stripes."[22] Pratt reports that after the cornerstone laying, Rigdon delivered an address "in which was painted, in lively colors, the oppression which we had long suffered from the hand of our enemies." A declaration to "resist all oppression and to maintain our rights and freedom according to the holy principles of liberty, as guaranteed to every person by the constitution and laws of our government . . . was received with shouts of hosanna to God and the Lamb, and with many and long cheers by the assembled thousands, who were determined to yield their rights no more."[23]

As noted in Chapter 8, the three-fold Hosanna Shout had Masonic roots. Thus, the ceremony drew upon the Saints' tender fraternal feelings of love and loyalty while playing on their nationalistic and religious sympathies. Participants were stirred to a fever pitch all the while presided over by their religious, military, and Danite leaders who were seated above them on a stand of honor.[24] Although some historians have suggested that Rigdon went beyond what the Prophet intended in stirring up the crowd, there are accounts of eyewitnesses to the speech indicating the contrary. Ebenezer Robinson believed that Rigdon's speeches were fully endorsed, if not actually prepared by the entire First Presidency of the Church, including Joseph Smith:

> Let it be distinctly understood that President Rigdon was not alone responsible for the sentiment expressed in his oration, as that was a carefully prepared document, previously written, and well understood by the First Presidency, that Elder Rigdon was the mouth piece to deliver it, as he was a natural orator, and his delivery was powerful and effective.[25]

Days later, over the weekend of July 6–7, 1838, a quarterly conference was held at which Sidney Rigdon, playing upon imagery from operative Masonry, exhorted the priesthood holders to convert the world. He compared the Elders to "quarriers of Stone" who brought the stone from the quarry to the building

---

22. The liberty pole was made of white oak and was sixty feet in length. Dan A. and Janet L. Lisonbee, *Far West Missouri: It Shall Be Called Most Holy*, 98.

23. Parley P. Pratt, *History of the Late Persecution Inflicted by the State of Missouri Upon the Mormons*, 27.

24. "At the end of each sentence, Rigdon was loudly cheered; and when he closed his oration, I believed the Mormons could successfully resist the world." John D. Lee, *Mormonism Unveiled; Or The Life and Confessions of the Late Mormon Bishop, John D. Lee; (Written by Himself)*, 63.

25. Ebenezer Robinson, "Items of Personal History of the Editor, No. 7, Including Some Items of Church History Not Generally Known," 170.

"where the Priests, Teachers, and Deacons, are polishers, whose duty it is to prepare them for the building."[26]

About that time, the liberty pole raised on the Temple grounds was destroyed by lightning, dismaying many of the Saints. Some saw the natural disaster as a foul omen that their liberty was about to end.[27] But in a startling, almost ritualistic action, Joseph Smith turned the symbol to his advantage. Playing the part of Captain Moroni, he identified the cause of the Latter-day Saints as the same as the Nephites' and reaffirmed the covenant nature of the Danite obligations. Striding over the slivers of the pole with a countenance that Oliver Huntington described "shone white as snow," Smith prophesied that as the pole had been "shivered to atoms, so should the Nation be shivered." In the same manner, as he walked over the blackened remains of their title of liberty, so Smith would tread over the ashes of his enemies.[28]

Just as the biblical prophet Isaiah prophesied those who contended with the Lord's people would be destroyed, the "Big Fan" was about to be turned upon the enemies of the Saints:

> Behold, I will make thee a new sharp threshing instrument having teeth: thou shalt thresh the mountains, and beat them small, and shalt make the hills as chaff.
>
> Thou shalt fan them, and the wind shall carry them away, and the whirlwind shall scatter them: and thou shalt rejoice in the Lord, and shalt glory in the Holy One of Israel. (Isa. 41:15–16)

Brother of Gideon

Another early name by which the company was known was the "Brother of Gideon," or "Gideonites."[29] This name demonstrates the intention of the group

---

26. "Minute Book 2," The Joseph Smith Papers, 151–52. This image calls to mind the rough and smooth "ashlars" in a Lodge room. The rough stone represents a man's unrefined state and his need for improvement. The smooth or polished stone is an allegory to a Freemason who, through Masonic education, has diligently worked to achieve an upstanding life and to obtain enlightenment.

27. "Shortly after the Fourth a terrible storm arose; the thunder and lightning were terrific; the liberty pole was struck and shattered by a bolt, foreshadowing coming events, as the sequel proved." Emily D. P. Young, "Autobiography of Emily D. P. Young," 17. See also Pratt, *History of the Late Persecution*, 27: "[A few days after the oration] the thunder rolled in awful majesty over the city of Far West, and the arrows of lightning fell from the clouds and shivered the liberty pole from top to bottom; thus manifesting to many that there was an end to liberty and law in that State."

28. Ebenezer Robinson, "Items of Personal History of the Editor, No. 6," 149; Oliver Huntington, Journal, Volume 13, 1858–1880, 55.

29. "Smith called a counsel of the leaders together in which council he Stated that any person who said a word against the heads of the church should be driven over these prairies as a chaced deer by a pack of hounds, having an allusion to the gideanats [Gideonites] as they were then termed to Justify themselves, in their wicked designes Thus on the 19th

to serve as protectors against outside attack, and members were told that the major purpose of the group was to "be perfectly organized to defend ourselves against mobs."[30] Some claimed they were called Gideonites because they were under the command of Jared Carter, the "terrible Brother of Gideon," but the term had been used much earlier. The men of Zion's Camp, a group that had marched from Kirtland to aid the Saints in Missouri in 1834, thought of themselves as Gideonites. Heber C. Kimball, filled with the Spirit of the Lord which "diffused strength into my body, and into my limbs, until the very hair of my head felt all alive," compared the members of that company with the biblical Gideonites:

> When Brother Brigham and myself and others left Kirtland to go to Missouri with Joseph Smith, was there any fear in us? No. . . . Did they fear us in that upper country? Yes, they ran as though they were never going to stop in the world. We felt perfectly able to clear out that country to Nova Scotia, and we could have done it, with two hundred and five men, if the Lord had commanded us, as the Gideonites in days of old. Yes; two hundred and five men, with the Spirit and power of God upon them and their faces shining like the sun, it cannot be told what they could accomplish, neither can we form any conception of it.[31]

This name was also widely used to suggest a larger company with considerable force. For example, Sidney Rigdon warned that those who would not comply with the law of consecration should be "delivered over to the brother of Gideon and be sent bounding over the Prairies as the dissenters were a few days ago." Indeed, "all matters comprising anything not completely subject to the will of the presidency were to be managed by the terrible brother of Gideon."[32] Additional evidence that the "Brother of Gideon" did not refer solely to Jared Carter is given by W. W. Phelps's description of a series of meetings enforcing the consecration program:

---

of June 1838 they preached a sermon called it the Salt sermon in which these gideonites understood that they should drive the disenters as they termed those who believed that not in their secret bands in fornication adultery of or midnight machinations." See "John Whitmer, History, 1831–circa 1847," 86–87.

30. Reed Peck Testimony, in *Document Containing the Correspondence, Orders, &c. in Relation to the Disturbances With the Mormons*, 116.

31. Orson Whitney, *Life of Heber C. Kimball, An Apostle: The Father and Founder of the British Mission*, 469. See also Dean C. Jessee and David J. Whittaker, "The Last Months of Mormonism in Missouri: The Albert Perry Rockwood Journal Edited," 12–13: "The origin of the [Danite] 'Armies of Israel' predates 1838; in fact, it goes back to Zion's Camp in 1834 (see D&C 105:30–32). Here militia operations in or by the Church were tied to divine injunctions to redeem Zion, a central part in Joseph Smith's mission of establishing the latter-day kingdom of God in Missouri (see D&C 107:72–73). And it has been clearly established that 'Zion's Camp' was a defensive operation, depending solely on the promises of the governor of Missouri."

32. Reed Peck, *The Reed Peck Manuscript*, 10.

It was observd in the meeting that if any person spoke against the presidency they would hand him over in to the hands of the brother of Gideon. I knew not at the time who or what it meant. Shortly after that I was at another meeting where they were trying several, the first presidency being present. Sidney Rigdon was chief spokesman—the object of the meeting seemed to be to make persons confess and repent of their sins to God and the Presidency and arraigned them for giving false accounts of their money and effects they had on hand and they said whenever they found one guilty of these things they were to be handed over to the brother of Gideon. Several were found guilty and handed over as they said—I yet did not know what was meant by this expression 'the brother of Gidion'—Not a great while after this [illegible] of private meetings were held I endevored to find out what they were and I learned from John Corrill and others they were forming a secret Society called Danites formerly called the brother of Gidion.[33]

John C. Bennett suggested the name had a scriptural allusion he was unable to discover.[34] A likely scriptural explanation, however, is found in the book of Judges, which thematically links the group's several objectives with the concept of threshing and grinding:

And there came an angel of the Lord, and sat under an oak which was in Ophrah, that pertained unto Joash the Abi-ezrite: and his son Gideon threshed wheat by the winepress, to hide it from the Midianites. (Judg. 6:11)

The story of Gideon meeting an angel and threshing wheat by the winepress is iconic. The winepress represents the suffering of Israel under Midianite occupation, and Gideon was divinely called to sweep the Midianites from the land God gave them by covenant. Similarly, the Latter-day Saints felt that the Missourians had acted the part of Midianites, disputing the claim of modern Israel to the land God had promised them and bringing upon them great suffering. Gideon's covert threshing suggests the secret nature of the action of the "Brother of Gideon" and links the group's activity with the threshing of the "Big Fan." Gideon is called a "mighty man of valor" (Judg. 6:12), and the Brothers of Gideon may have felt an affinity with this title. In Judges 6, Gideon is urged by God, appearing as an angel, to use his power to deliver the Israelites. Later in a dream, Gideon is told to break down his father's altar erected to Baal and replace it with an altar dedicated to the true and living God. He does so and names the place *Jehovah-shalom* (v. 24). Here, then, are revealed some of the objectives of the Danites: to deliver modern Israel out of the hands of their enemies, within and without; and to break down false religion, replacing it with the worship of the true God. The

---

33. W. W. Phelps, witness statement, November 12, 1838, 1.

34. "This name, however [the 'Big Fan'], did not seem sufficiently dignified for so holy a body, and was soon set aside for a scriptural appellation; they were called the 'Brother of Gideon;' but the *rationale* of this title I have never been able to discover. They are usually styled *Danites*, and sometimes *Daughter of Zion*, for the origin of which names, see Micah iv. 13; read the whole chapter; also Judges xvii. And xviii." John C. Bennett, *History of the Saints, or, An Expose of Joe Smith and Mormonism*, 265.

aim was to bring about the peaceful reign of the King of Peace by establishing his millennial Kingdom. In these verses of Judges, the Mormons found justification for vigilante action.

Danites

John Corrill testified that the organization "afterward grew into a system to carry out the designs of the presidency; and, if necessary to use physical force to upbuild the kingdom of God."[35] He pointed to the group's ultimate plans, which became increasingly apparent in the autumn of 1838. The term "Danites" comes from three usages in the Old Testament. First, the association of the tribe of Dan with judgment and vengeance is ancient and includes the concept of reclaiming the promised land by any means necessary. For example, the name "Dan" itself is derived from the Hebrew word meaning "to contend or judge."[36] And in Jacob's prophetic words to his sons at the end of his life, Dan is given this blessing:

> Dan shall judge his people, as one of the tribes of Israel.
> Dan shall be a serpent by the way,
> an adder in the path, that biteth the horse heels,
> so that his rider shall fall backward.
> (Gen. 49:16–17)[37]

Second, Dan is seen as the warrior tribe of Judges 18 that was sent on a mission to capture new lands. When advance scouts returned, they admonished the Israelites to "be not slothful to go, and to enter to possess the land. When ye go, ye shall come unto a people secure, and to a large land: for God hath given it into your hands" (Judg. 18:9–10). The destructive nature of the tribe of Dan is illustrated as they plunder, spoil, and raze a town to the ground.

Finally, the term Danites was rooted in the book of Daniel. According to Albert Perry Rockwood, this was "because the Prophet Daniel has said they [the Saints] shall take the Kingdom and possess it for ever"—alluding to the prophecy of the great stone that will roll forth and beat into pieces all the nations (Dan. 2:31–45).[38] Parley P. Pratt explained the connection of the Mormon establish-

---

35. John Corrill, in *Document Containing the Correspondence*, 113.

36. James Strong, *A Concise Dictionary of the Words in the Hebrew Bible With Their Renderings in the Authorized English Version*, sv H1835. See the related Hebrew *dîn*, which Strong defines as "a primitive root . . . [meaning] to *rule*; by implication to *judge* . . . also to *strive* . . . contend, execute (judgment), judge, minister judgment, plead." Strong, s.v. H1777.

37. "The Mormons indulged in many Bible quotations, and any ignorant fanatical Mormon could quote Scripture by the chapter. Hence it is not strange that the name of the Danite Band . . . should derive its name from a scriptural quotation, Genesis XLIX, 17: 'Dan shall be a serpent by the way, an adder in the path, that biteth the horses heels so his rider shall fall backward.'" J. M. Reid, *Sketches and Anecdotes of The Old Settlers and New Comers, The Mormon Bandits and Danite Band*, 34.

38. Jessee and Whittaker, "The Last Months of Mormonism in Missouri," 23.

ment of Zion to the prophecy in Daniel in his 1837 *A Voice of Warning*. The eschatological kingdom of Daniel, Pratt explained, would never cease to roll until Jesus appeared in the clouds with power and great glory "as the King of kings, and Lord of lords, and destroy all these kingdoms, and give the kingdom and the greatness of the kingdom, under the whole heaven, to the saints." Pratt insisted this kingdom was the organized government of God on the earth.[39] Noting the violent implication of this passage, historians Matthew Grow and Terryl Givens write in their biography of Pratt,

> By 1838, the Saints' public invocation of Daniel 2:44–45, with its reference to a kingdom that should "break in pieces and consume" all other kingdoms, was common enough—and threatening enough—to be invoked at a court of inquiry as evidence of nefarious Mormon designs.[40]

The Daughter of Zion

A final name by which the Danites were known carries the imagery of all three purposes: fanning and separating the wheat from the chaff of apostasy, rising and threshing enemies from without the Church, and establishing the kingdom of God. In the book of Isaiah, the people of Israel are told to "Awake, awake; put on thy strength, O Zion; put on thy beautiful garments, O Jerusalem, the holy city." They are to be cleansed from "the uncircumcised and the unclean" among them. Sidney Rigdon's exhortation to the Saints to oust dissenters from their midst found justification in the ancient prophet's words: "Shake thyself from the dust; arise, and sit down, O Jerusalem: loose thyself from the bands of thy neck, O captive daughter of Zion" (Isa. 52:1–2).

The appellation "Daughter of Zion" is used symbolically by Old Testament prophets. Far from referring solely to females as the name might suggest, it represented the covenant people. Likewise, the term "Babylon" represented the worldly enemies of God. To the Saints, it was these enemies of God who were working to hamper their settlement of Missouri. "Behold, I will raise up against Babylon," was the powerful message of the Lord through the prophet Jeremiah,

> and against them that dwell in the midst of them that rise up against me, a destroying wind; And will send unto Babylon fanners, that shall fan her, and shall empty her land: for in the day of trouble they shall be against her round about. . . .
>
> [B]ecause it is the vengence of the Lord, the vengeance of his temple. . . .
>
> For thus saith the Lord of hosts, the God of Israel; The daughter of Babylon is like a threshingfloor, it is time to thresh her: yet a little while, and the time of her harvest shall come. (Jer. 51:1–2, 11, 33)

---

39. Parley P. Pratt, *A Voice of Warning and Instruction to All People, or, An Introduction to the Faith and Doctrine of the Church of Jesus Christ of Latter-day Saints*, 37, 99.

40. Terryl L. Givens and Matthew J. Grow, *Parley P. Pratt: The Apostle Paul of Mormonism*, 131.

In Micah 4, the "daughter of Zion" is redeemed from the hands of her enemies. She is told to "Arise and thresh . . . and thou shalt beat in pieces many
people" (vv. 8–13). Though nations are gathered against her, the daughter of
Zion is strengthened by the Lord and given the ability to rise as combatant
against her foes. In Micah, the daughter of Zion is a woman in travail; she will
bring forth and establish the political kingdom of God, which was the hope of
the beleaguered Mormons.

> Arise and thresh, O daughter of Zion: for I will make thine horn iron, and I will
> make thy hoofs brass: and thou shalt beat in pieces many people: and I will conse-
> crate their gain unto the Lord, and their substance unto the Lord of the whole earth.
> (Micah 4:13)

Here is found justification for appropriating the Missourians' assets and be-
longings and consecrating them to the Bishop's storehouse. The Mormons were
instructed to do these things both by scripture and prophetic authority. While
Danite morals and ethics seem repugnant today, Joseph Smith later explained the
underlying principle, which he observed applying "to all of God's dealings with
his children." In his letter to Nancy Rigdon, Smith stated:

> That which is wrong under one circumstance, may be, and often is, right under
> another. God said, "Thou shalt not kill"; at another time he said, "Thou shalt utterly
> destroy." This is the principle on which the government of heaven is conducted, by
> revelation adapted to the circumstances in which the children of the Kingdom are
> placed. Whatever God requires is right, no matter what it is, although we may not
> see the reason thereof till long after the events transpire. . . . Everything that God
> gives us is lawful and right.[41]

Applying this principle to the Saints' attempts to establish a theocratic kingdom
in Missouri is startling in its implications.

The three-fold philosophy of "Daniteism" was a response to Mormon prophecy and scripture in the context of the troubles the Saints experienced internally
in Ohio and externally in Missouri. Each Danite name-title had a specific function related to this concept, and Danite actions were consistent with these objectives throughout the Mormon-Missouri conflicts in 1838. The variant names of
the secret society were neither abandoned nor replaced; rather, they suggested in
the aggregate the full scope of Danite responsibilities in establishing a theocratic
empire. By use of each of these titles, the brothers signaled their overriding purpose: the restoration of Israel and the threshing of the nations.

Danite Structure, Signs, and Oaths

In every obligation a Freemason makes, he promises to be subject to the
Constitution of the Grand Lodge in his jurisdiction. Every constituent local lodge

---

41. "History, 1838–1856, volume D-1 [1 August 1842–1 July 1843]," The Joseph Smith
Papers, 3–4 [addenda].

also has a constitution, by-laws, rules, and regulations to which the initiate promises to conform.[42] Accordingly, a Danite constitution was drawn up, likely by Sampson Avard, a British-born physician who joined the Church in Pennsylvania with the Campbellites and eventually became a Danite general.[43] Avard told of taking his penned constitution to Sidney Rigdon's house where he read it to the Prophet and his counsellors. They subsequently approved the document, which vested executive power in these three men. In Freemasonry, a written constitution is a legitimizing document intended to express formality and durability. Similarly, the existence of a Danite constitution tends to demonstrate that, while the group may have largely operated *sub rosa*, they were considered a formal and legitimate Mormon institution and not merely an ad-hoc self-defense force. The language of the Danite Constitution contains complex theocratic aspirations that blossomed both in Nauvoo and in the Great Basin Kingdom that followed it. A melding of republican, secessionist, and Mormon millenarian thought, the preamble of the Danite Constitution calls to mind both the Book of Mormon account of the "Title of Liberty" as well as the United States Declaration of Independence:

> [W]e the members of the society of the Daughters of Zion do agree to regulate ourselves under such laws as, in righteousness shall be deemed necessary for the preservation of our holy religion and of our most sacred rights, and the rights of our wives and children. But to be explicit on the subject, it is especially our object, to support and defend the rights conferred on us by our venerable sires, who purchased them with the pledges of their lives, their fortunes, and their sacred honors. . . . Our rights we must have, and our rights we shall have, in the name of Israels God.[44]

Nineteenth-century Masons referred to the Bible in connection with their obligations, indicating the Christian character of the pledge:

> On yonder book that oath I took,
> And break it will I never,
> But swear by this, and this, and this,
> Forever and forever.[45]

In a similar vein, Luman Andros Shurtliff wrote of the Mormon Danite group with fond remembrance, describing its Masonic character and its Christian fraternal goals:

---

42. William Morgan, *Illustrations of Masonry by One of the Fraternity Who has Devoted Thirty Years to the Subject*, 68. This contemporaneous source shows that constitutions were in general use in Masonic lodges of the day.

43. Gentry, "The Danite Band of 1838," 425. Gentry, in particular, has suggested that Avard drew up the Constitution, basing this on both an accusation by Joseph Smith and John Corrill's testimony that he hadn't seen the document before. Yet, it seems unlikely that this document was simply thrown together on the fly after the fall of Far West in order to incriminate Joseph Smith (pp. 438–40).

44. "Appendix 2: Constitution of the Society of the Daughter of Zion, circa Late June 1838," The Joseph Smith Papers, 10–11.

45. Rob Morris, "The Mason's Vows," 57.

I received an invitation to unite with a Society called the Danite society and to meet with them at their next meeting which I did And found it was got up for our personal defence also of Our Families Property and our Religion Sighns and passwords given by which each member could know the other wherever they met night or day Each person to settle all difficulty if he had any with a member of the Society before he could be received I considered this a good institution for the benefit of society and a blessing for this people.[46]

Shurtliff's phrasing, "for our personal defense, also of our families, property, and our religion," likewise comes from the Book of Mormon story of Moroni's "Title of Liberty" (Alma 46:7–32). This account depicts a Nephite military captain who becomes angered by dissenters from among the Nephites. The internal rebellion jeopardizes the Nephites' repossession of land they believe the Lord has given them. Swearing God will not suffer them to be trodden underfoot and destroyed, Moroni rips a large piece of his clothing and writes upon it: "In memory of our God, our religion, and freedom, and our peace, our wives, and our children," and he fastens it upon a pole to wave as a banner (vv. 12–13). Those faithful to the cause swiftly assemble "with their armor girded about their loins" and make an oath of faithfulness complete with a token: pieces of their own rent garments, which they cast down at Moroni's feet (vv. 21–22). As an army, they then march forward against their enemies. This is just one example of how, within the first decade of the publication of the Book of Mormon, its stories were being applied directly to the Saints' situations as typological and prophetic.[47] The story of Captain Moroni was recognized as a portent of the challenges early Saints faced in their own day as they sought to establish the millennial kingdom.

The signs and passwords used by the Danites connect them directly with Freemasonry. Danites took oaths of secrecy, promised to defend each other, right or wrong, and swore to follow the leadership of the Church without question. Betrayal was punishable by death. Several available reports describe Danite oaths, showing how their phrasing closely followed the words of contemporaneous anti-Masonic exposures. For example, Sampson Avard testified that a covenant of secrecy was taken by all the Danite band who held up their right hands and swore

---

46. Luman Andros Shurtliff diary, in Leland H. Gentry and Todd M. Compton, *Fire and Sword: A History of the Latter-day Saints in Northern Missouri, 1836–39*, 223–24.

47. Another instance of such a usage is found in Parley P. Pratt's autobiography, where he tells of a time when he and his brother Orson were reading the Book of Mormon. They read the words of Ammon to King Lamoni: "Behold, my brother and brethren are in prison at Middoni, and I go that I may deliver them" (Alma 20:3). Said Pratt, "This was indeed a similar instance to ours. Ammon, on that occasion, had an own brother in prison, and also brethren in the ministry, and did deliver them. Our case was exactly similar, not in Middoni, but in Missouri." Parley P. Pratt Jr., ed., *The Autobiography of Parley Parker Pratt, One of the Twelve Apostles of the Church of Jesus Christ of Latter-day Saints*, 267. The Latter-day Saints were encouraged to "liken the scriptures" to themselves in this way (1 Ne. 19:23–24).

in the name of Christ "ever to conceal, and never to reveal, the secret purposes of this society called the Daughters of Zion," holding their lives as forfeit should they do so.[48] This wording is comparable to that of the obligation for the Entered Apprentice degree exposed by David Bernard in 1829: "I . . . do hereby and hereon most solemnly and sincerely promise and swear, that I will always hail, ever conceal, and never reveal any part . . . of the secrets, arts, and mysteries of ancient Free Masonry."[49] Avard explained that the Danites were given instructions that "if any of them should get into a difficulty, the rest should help him out; and that they should stand by each other, right or wrong."[50] Publicly exposed Masonic rituals used similar language, promising to extricate a companion from "any difficulty . . . whether he be right or wrong."[51] Added to these Masonically based oaths, Avard said, was an admonition that Smith and his counselors were the head of the Church, and the Danite band should feel themselves "as much bound to obey them as to obey the Supreme God."[52]

Danite John Corrill's description accords with Avard's, mirroring Bernard's version of the Royal Arch obligation mentioned above. It also contains principles contained in early Masonic Constitutions directing that a brother "must never go to Law about what concerneth Masonry," but to instead bring complaints before the Lodge.[53] Corrill testified,

> They secretly entered into solemn covenants, before God, and bound themselves under oath to keep the secrets of the society, and covenanted to stand by one another in difficulty, whether right or wrong, but said they would correct each others wrongs among themselves. As the presidency stood next to God, or between God and the church, and was the oracle through which the word and will of God was communicated to the church, they esteemed it very essential to have their word, or the word of God through them, strictly adhered to. They therefore entered into a covenant, that the word of the presidency should be obeyed, and none should be suffered to raise his hand or voice against it.[54]

Reed Peck's account corroborates with Avard and Corrill, detailing the duty to obey the prophet in all things: "It is not our business or place to know what is required by God, but he will inform us by means of the prophet and we must perform."[55] Peck also recalled:

> If any one of you see a member of the band in difficulty in the surrounding country contending for instance with an enemy, you shall extricate him even if in the wrong if

---

48. Sampson Avard, in *Document Containing the Correspondence*, 97–98.

49. Bernard, *Light on Masonry*, 20.

50. Sampson Avard, in *Document Containing the Correspondence*, 98.

51. Bernard, *Light on Masonry*, 130.

52. Sampson Avard, in *Document Containing the Correspondence*, 97–98.

53. James Anderson, *The Constitutions of the Free-Masons, Containing the History, Charges, Regulations, &c. of that Most Ancient and Right Worshipful Fraternity*, 54.

54. Corrill, *A Brief History*, 30–31.

55. Reed Peck, *The Reed Peck Manuscript*, 40.

you have to do with his adversary as Moses did with the Egyptian put him under the sand and both pack off to Far West and we will take care of the matter ourselves. . . . The secret signs and purposes of this Society are not to be revealed on pain of death.[56]

Masonic obligations often specified an explicit form of death as a symbolic penalty in the event of the breaking of the oath.[57] David Whitmer told Zenas Gurley that when he was "appointed in charge of church affairs in Zion Missouri," Joseph Smith and Sidney Rigdon paid a visit to the various branches of the Church. At this time, "they organized the Danites by which each member was sworn to sustain the Heads of the Church whether right or wrong—the penalty of refusing to do so being death, 'the throat cut.'"[58]

With so many Mormons flooding into the Missouri countryside in 1838, members were sometimes hard-pressed to know friends from foes. William Swartzell, who took Danite oaths in June of that year, detailed his observations about secret passwords and signs of recognition similar to those used among the Masonic fraternity. Swartzell revealed the Danite password "which was to be spoken at the moment of giving the hand of fellowship—'Who be you?' Answer— 'Anama.'" The meaning of this word was "by interpretation, a friend," and it was a sign to distinguish the Mormons "from all other people under heaven."[59] Luman Shurtliff wrote about the importance of Danite passwords, signs, and countersigns during the Missouri War, describing his part in a Danite expedition in October of 1838:

Under this tree I was stationed one night with orders to let no person pass except he gave the countersign about nine oclock I he[a]rd two men comeing from toward camp I knew by their voices it was our Prophet and his Br Hyrum when they came in hailing distance I hailed them enquired who they ware the answer was friends I bade them advance and give the Countersign which they did over the muzzle of my Rifle in true Military stile.[60]

Shurtliff used accepted military practices of the day to elicit signs of recognition from Joseph and Hyrum Smith, suggesting that all three men knew and used

56. Peck, 40–41. See also Lee, *Mormonism Unveiled*, 57: "The members of this order were placed under the most sacred obligations that language could invent. They were sworn to stand by and sustain each other. *Sustain, protect, defend*, and *obey* the leaders of the Church, under any and *all circumstances unto death*; and to disobey the orders the leaders of the Church, or divulge the name of a Danite to an outsider, or to make public any of the secrets of the order of Danites, was to be punished with death" (emphasis in original). After this telling, Lee digresses, agonizing over whether his revealing of the secrets of the Danites is justified.

57. For examples, see Bernard, *Light on Masonry*, 20, 45, 63.

58. David Whitmer, Interview by Zenas Gurley, Jan 14, 1885, in Romig, *Eighth Witness*, 329.

59. William Swartzell, *Mormonism Exposed, Being a Journal of a Residence in Missouri From the 28th of May to the 20th of August, 1838*, 22–23.

60. Shurtliff diary, in Gentry and Compton, *Fire and Sword*, 247.

Danite signs and countersigns. Shurtliff humorously related that later that same night he heard footsteps coming down the road and called out, but there was no answer. He pointed his rifle up and shouted "Halt!" To his relief, he saw that the source of the sound was a cow. "I stepped out of the road and let her pass without giving the countersign, thus giving the cow more leniency than I did the Prophet of God."[61]

During another expedition, Shurtliff and Apostle John Taylor were placed on guard to receive teams of horses from the brethren when they came into Adam-ondi-Ahman, a Mormon settlement in Daviess County, Missouri. Unable to recognize his fellow Mormons in the dark, Shurtliff relied upon signs and countersigns to accurately identify those who would pass into the settlement for safety. By this time in late October 1838, those who knew the Danite signs pervaded the community of Saints. Shurtliff wrote of his discovery that John Taylor was not a Danite, and he therefore felt uncomfortable using the signs and countersigns in Taylor's presence.[62] This passage demonstrates the signs and countersigns being used were distinctively Danite, not simply company or military codes.

The Danites, like the Masons, created a sign of distress under which they were obliged to respond, even at risk of death. Swartzell described it as follows:

When the High Priest had delivered himself of these charges, agreeably to the order of things, he next informed us that he would give us a *sign* "whereby ye may know each other anywhere, (either by day or by night,) and if a brother be in distress. It is thus: to clap the right hand to the right thigh, and then raise it quick to the right temple, the thumb extending behind the ear."[63]

John D. Lee explained that when the sign was given,

it must be responded to and obeyed, even at the risk or certainty of death. . . . The sign or token of distress is made by placing the right hand on the right side of the face, with the points of the fingers upwards, shoving the hand upwards until the ear is snug up between the thumb and fore-finger.[64]

---

61. Luman Andros Shurtliff, "Autobiography (1807-1847)."

62. In an 1870 narrative, John Taylor disavowed any knowledge of Danite activity in 1838. Leland Gentry acknowledges that Taylor's unfamiliarity with Danite oaths is not significant in assessing the Danite presence in Missouri: "John Taylor arrived in Missouri 'late in the summer of 1838' but, like many Canadian immigrants, stayed first in DeWitt, which had no Danite meetings. He was in DeWitt apparently until the exodus, on October 11. Many DeWitt Mormons never did become Danites." See Gentry and Compton, *Fire and Sword*, 260–61.

63. Swartzell, *Mormonism Exposed*, 22; emphasis in original.

64. Lee, *Mormonism Unveiled*, 59. These are John D. Lee's confessions at the time of his death, and some have suggested that his editor had a free hand with them. However, there is consistency in the account not expected from an editor. Many of the details fit together Masonically. The sign of protection is similar to a Masonic one, and the context seems to provide a level of description that only someone who was there could have known. The particulars agree with other tellings of the incident, making these confessions convincing.

Lee gave an instance of the Danite sign of distress being used at an election held at the new town of Gallatin, where pent-up bitterness of Missourians against Mormons exploded into violence. Nervous that the arrival of Mormons at the polls would signal their political domination of the county, locals sought to hinder them from voting. A drunken aggressor named Dick Weldon knocked one of the Mormons to the ground and another came flying to the victim's aid. After a half dozen other settlers also jumped into the fray, the Danite sign of distress was given by John L. Butler, one of the captains of "the Host of Israel":

> Seeing the *sign*, I sprang to my feet and armed myself with one of the oak sticks. I did this because I was a Danite, and my oaths that I had taken required immediate action on my part, in support of the one giving the sign. I ran into the crowd. . . . I was an entire stranger to all who were engaged in the affray, except Stewart, but I had seen the *sign*, and, like Samson, when leaning against the pillar, I felt the power of God nerve my arm for the fray. It helps a man a great deal in a fight to know that God is on his side.[65]

The story indicates the kinds of things one would expect from a "penny dreadful," or sensationalist dime novel, version of the Freemasons. The Danites' activities were an overblown caricature of Masonry, but like Lee, the men were fanatically serious about it. After their rout of the Missouri settlers at the polls, Mormons intentionally cultivated an atmosphere of terror surrounding the Danites as well as the perception that they were a Masonic-like body. Danite Albert Rockwood wrote: "the Missourians have nearly al[l] left Davies[s] Co[.] fear rest[s] down upon them and they flee when no man pursueth. . . . [N]ot a drop of blood has been spilt nor a gun fired as I have heard of, the Mob dispersed by 100ds on the approach of the Danites."[66]

Following the surrender, Daviess County Mormons deflected accusations for their various crimes onto Danites who had fled to Iowa. For example, Oliver Huntington wrote:

> [T]here was a great hu[e]-and-cry about the Danites, all over the county and among the Army. . . . [M]any stories were in circulation the most horrid and awfully distorted opinions their minds could immagine, and they all thought that every depridation was committed by the Danites. . . . [S]uch being their opinion and belief of Danites; and we knowing it, concluded to make the best of it. So every misterious trick and bold adventure which had been transacted, was palmed upon them and every body knew there had a company of Mormons fled to the Indian territories, (for they were pursued by their trail) and they, it was stated, were the Danites, a most daring band of braves, who were bound together like the Masons.[67]

It was to the advantage of the Mormons to foster stories about the fearsomeness of the Danites in order to deter citizens of Illinois and Missouri from

---

65. Lee, 59–60; emphasis in original.
66. Jessee and Whittaker, "The Last Months of Mormonism in Missouri," 23.
67. Oliver Huntington, Journal, Volume 2, 1845–1846, 40–41.

harming their people and property. This had the effect of placing many of the conceptions circulated about the Danites into the category of folklore, polemics, and propaganda. Nonetheless, Danite influence, with its decidedly Masonic character, was pervasive among the Latter-day Saints.

The "Knights Templar" of Mormonism, Danite members pledged their lives to each other's defense as literal Christian soldiers. Organized in a company with an elected leader, they became a band of obligated brothers in the military sense, committed to a single grand purpose and dedicated to principles of liberty and true religion. Some from high station and some low, they would all sacrifice their lives to defend a brother's honor. Men who spoke of their initiation into the Danite order expressed strong feelings and impressions, both positive and negative, in relation to their experience. For good or for ill, the Danite oath they had sworn linked them together in a durable brotherly union where their futures and fortunes were committed to the establishment of a literal Zion on the earth.

The nature of Joseph Smith's involvement in Danite activity is an issue that must periodically be revisited. The notion that Sampson Avard was the sole actor in the creation and execution of the Danite movement, and that he was a rogue member acting outside of Church authority, is a common way to exonerate Joseph of any responsibility for the Danites' behavior. Some of the first modern scholarly treatments of the Danite organization have promoted this view.[68] But other historians such as Steven LeSueur have established that Joseph Smith knew of and approved of the Danites.[69] Danite groups met in several locations under the direction of influential leaders including Jared Carter, Elias Higbee, David W. Patton, Lyman Wight, and John Smith, the prophet's uncle. Court records from Missouri and statements from a range of perspectives implicate church leaders in general, and Joseph Smith in particular, as the principal force in Danite activity in Missouri.

While imprisoned in Clay County in 1839, Smith denied his involvement in Danite misdeeds, expressly mentioning their Masonic context. With his life in peril, he wrote a letter cautioning the brethren against the organization of oath-bound bands or companies and announced his intention to reject such enterprises:

---

68. In his 1965 work on the Missouri War, Leland Gentry insisted that Sampson Avard "capitalized upon familiar and sacred LDS principles to further his work, using the concepts of consecration and of the kingdom of God to convince his followers of his fidelity." He "took advantage of the human desire to belong to exclusive, secret orders." He "skillfully convinced his followers that Church leaders approved of his operations." In Gentry's opinion, "Not until the Richmond hearing in November 1838 did Joseph Smith and his closest associates become aware of Avard's activities." See Gentry and Compton, *Fire and Sword*, 241–43.

69. Stephen C. LeSueur, "The Danites Reconsidered: Were They Vigilantes or Just the Mormons' Version of the Elks Club?" 35–51. See also Quinn, "The Culture of Violence in Joseph Smith's Mormonism," 24: "The Danites' military actions of 1838 were carried out under the general oversight and command of Joseph Smith, and their violent acts resulted in multiple disasters."

[L]et the time past of our experience and sufferings by the wickedness of Doctor Avard suffice, and let our covenants be that of the everlasting covenant, as it is contained in the Holy Writ, and the things which God has revealed unto us; pure friendship always becomes weakened the very moment you undertake to make it stronger by penal oaths and secrecy. Your humble servants intend from henceforth, to disapprobate every thing that is not in accordance with the fullness of the gospel of Jesus Christ, and which is not of a bold, frank, and upright nature.[70]

Here, Smith scapegoated Sampson Avard as instigator of the crimes of the group.[71] A defensive passage in Willard Richards' *Manuscript History of the Church* attempts to distance the Prophet from the Danite band and placed the blame for its formation on Avard. It asserts that his teachings were "manfully rejected by all." However, enthusiastic paramilitary activity under Avard's command is described in Mormon and non-Mormon primary sources. Still, the official history does contain insight into Danite origins and philosophy. Avard is quoted as saying: "This being a different dispensation, a dispensation of the fullness of times; in this dispensation I learn from the Scriptures that the kingdom of God was to put down all other Kingdoms, and He [Christ] himself was to reign, and his laws alone was the only laws that would exist."[72] Further, the Masonic connection of the group was recognized by the author of the passage.[73] Distinctive wording states that Avard's "craft was no longer in the dark" and that "little confidence was placed in him even by the warmest of the Members of his Danite Lodge." The word "Lodge" was later crossed out and replaced with "scheme."[74]

This account grants that Avard claimed to have been acting under orders of the first presidency, that he considered Daniteism an order of the Church, and that he justified the behavior of the Danites with an appeal to the scriptures.[75] Additional sources corroborate Joseph Smith's endorsement of the Danite band in its original inception. According to a testimony by John Corrill, Joseph Smith, his brother Hyrum, and Sidney Rigdon (the First Presidency) visited a meeting of Danites and approved the actions of Avard. They exhorted the men to be faithful and "pronounced a blessing on each" of them. Corrill wrote, "It was my understanding that Dr. Avard's teaching in the Danite society proceeded from

70. Joseph Smith Jr., "Extract of a Letter to Bishop Partridge," 72.
71. Stephen C. LeSueur maintains that, other than denouncing the "false and pernicious teachings" of Sampson Avard and recommending against reorganization of the band in Illinois, Joseph Smith's own statements were not critical of the Danites and do not contradict the evidence linking him with the group. See Stephen C. LeSueur, *The 1838 Mormon War in Missouri*, 43–44.
72. "History, 1838–1856, volume B-1 [1 September 1834–2 November 1838]," The Joseph Smith Papers, 844.
73. LeSueur attributes this passage in *History of the Church* to Morris Phelps, a Mormon resident of Missouri. See LeSueur, *The 1838 Mormon War in Missouri*, 44.
74. "History, 1838–1856, volume B-1 [1 September 1834–2 November 1838]," 844.
75. "History, 1838–1856, volume B-1 [1 September 1834–2 November 1838]," 843; see also Gentry, "The Danite Band of 1838," 433–50.

the presidency."[76] Simply stated, Sampson Avard did not have the authority or religious influence to take such actions without instruction from his superiors.

When defending himself, Joseph Smith went so far as to claim that Avard was the one who had given the group its name. However, Smith later contradicted this statement at a Nauvoo City Council session, saying the moniker grew out of an expression he had used. He clarified its meaning as follows: "If the enemiy comes, the Danites will be after them, meaning the brethren in self defince."[77] In his journal, the Prophet wrote of the plan for handling such opposition:

> Thus far, according to the ord[e]r of the Dan-Ites, we have a company of Danites in these times, to put to rights physically that which is not righ[t], and to cle[a]nse the Church of verry great evils which hath hitherto existed among us, inasmuch as they cannot be put to rights by teachings & persuaysons.[78]

Historian Dale Morgan asserted that Smith was "disingenuous in his entire explanation of the Danites; it is clear that he knew more of the Danites, over a longer period of time, than he cared subsequently to acknowledge."[79] John Cleminson, who was part of the Danite expedition to Daviess in which Gallatin was burned, testified that Joseph and Hyrum Smith personally participated. In fact, "it was generally understood that every movement made in Daviess was under the direction and supervision of the first presidency."[80] It is difficult to find any Danite action that did not have precedent in the public words of the First Presidency. Often, Sidney Rigdon was the spokesman, but Smith would follow closely after, giving prophetic endorsement to Rigdon's words.

In his public interactions with Danite participants, Smith rarely supported illegal actions overtly, but he preached homilies that made clear his objectives. For example, after Rigdon delivered the "Salt Sermon" and urged the Danites to

---

76. John Corrill, in *Document Containing the Correspondence*, 113. Corril further states, "President Smith got up. . . . [H]e observed to the people that they should obey the presidency, and, if the presidency led them astray they might destroy them" (p. 111). See also John Cleminson, in *Document Containing the Correspondence*, 114: "The three composing the presidency was at one of those meetings; and to satisfy the people, Dr. Avard called on Joseph Smith, jr., who gave them a pledge, that if they led them into difficulty he would give them his head for a foot-ball, and that it was the will of God these things should be so. The teacher and active agent of the society was Dr. Avard, and his teachings were approved of by the presidency."

77. "Nauvoo City Council Rough Minute Book, November 1842–January 1844," The Joseph Smith Papers, 36: "The Danite system never had any existence, the term grew out of a term I made an off when the brethren prepared to defend themselves from the mob in Far West,— the in reference to the stealing of Macaiahs images— [Judg. 18]."

78. "Journal, March–September 1838," 61; see also Quinn, "The Culture of Violence," 22.

79. Richard L. Saunders, *Dale Morgan on the Mormons: Collected Works, Part I, 1939–1951*, 228.

80. John Cleminson, in *Document Containing the Correspondence*, 115.

tread dissenters under foot, Smith addressed the men. Reed Peck describes him as stopping short of Rigdon's violent rhetoric:

> Joseph Smith in a short speech, sanctioned what had been said by Rigdon, though said he, I don't want the brethren to act unlawfully, but will tell them one thing, Judas was a traitor and instead of hanging himself was hung by Peter, and with this hint the subject was dropped for the day having created a great excitement and prepared the people to execute anything that should be proposed.[81]

Smith's retelling of the story of the biblical traitor Judas by having Peter hang him could thus be taken by his audience as an instruction to execute dissenters while he maintained plausible deniability. Indeed, his Missouri speeches frequently utilized this strategy. In one discourse, he "spoke of persons taking, at some times, what, at other times, it would be wrong to take; and gave as an example the case of David eating the shewbread, and also of the Saviour and his Apostles plucking the ears of corn and eating, as they passed through the cornfield."[82]

At a later meeting, Smith took the pulpit and described the Latter-day Saints as "an injured people, driven violently from Jackson county"; that they had "appealed to the Governor, magistrates, judges, and even to the President of the United States, and there had been no redress"; and that it was high time they take measures to defend their own rights. He told the crowd that he could not recommend they take property that did not belong to them in their upcoming expedition to Daviess County, but then related an anecdote about a captain who appealed to a Dutchman to purchase potatoes for his troops. The Dutchman refused to sell. The captain then charged his company several times not to touch the Dutchman's potatoes, but in the morning, there was not a potato left in the patch.[83]

By telling this story, Smith surreptitiously advised his followers to avoid the expenses of war by confiscating the enemies' property, all the while claiming adherence to the letter of the law. He used this technique often enough that these examples are not anomalies. They demonstrate Smith's intention and skill in directing military action in such a way as not to appear the originator.

The Danite band contained members of the leading bodies of the Church in Missouri and those who later were given positions of the highest responsibility.[84] From the several available journals, it is clear its members believed they were building that kingdom of God that Daniel prophesied would fill the earth and break to pieces all other nations. They felt justified in their actions to cleanse the Church, defend their occupation of the land, and retaliate against Missouri settlers.

---

81. Peck, *Reed Peck Manuscript*, 8.
82. John Corrill, in *Document Containing the Correspondence*, 112.
83. Sampson Avard, in *Document Containing the Correspondence*, 98–99.
84. LeSueur, "The Danites Reconsidered," 39–41.

Ecclesiastic and Military Entanglement

By 1838, Missouri Mormons had established a deeply clandestine militaristic "combination" from which Joseph Smith later distanced himself. Because of this, Mormon historians have found it difficult to disentangle the configuration, composition, and conduct of the Danites from other organized Church or civil endeavors.[85] Though the Danites were inseparably connected with ecclesiastic and military activity, some observers have attempted to dissociate them, absolving the Church from Masonic-like Danite activity. For example, though it is clear that the Danites utilized companies of tens, fifties, and hundreds, Willard Richards's *Manuscript History* claimed that these Danite companies were "altogether separate and distinct from those companies of tens and fifties, organized by the brethren for self defence, in case of an attack from the mob." The Church companies, it was claimed, were organized to perform such "righteous purposes" as cutting wood, gathering corn, butchering and distributing meat, and so forth.[86]

A letter written by Albert Perry Rockwood on October 22, 1838, counters this idea, demonstrating how contemporary Mormons viewed the companies as martial, spiritual, practical—and fundamentally Danite:

> Beloved parent Far West is the head quarters of the Mormon war. The armies of Isreal that were established by revelation from God are seen from my door ev[e]ry day with their captains of 10.s 50.s & 100. A portion of each Day is set apart for drill. after which they go to their several stations (VIZ.)
>
> 2 Companies of 10.s are to provide the familaes with meal[,] 2 provide wood[,] 2 or 3 Build cabbins[,] 1 Company of 10.s collect & prepare armes, 1 company provide me[a]t, 1 Company are spies, one Company are for express, 1 for guard[,] 2 Companies are to gather in the familaes that are scattered over the counties in the vicinity[,] 1 company is to see to & provide for the sick, and the familaes of those that are off on duty[,] Others are employed in gathering provisions into the city &c &c. Those companies are called Danites because the prophet Daniel has said they shall take the kingdom and possess it for-ever.[87]

Joseph Smith's journal, kept by George Robinson, connected the several elements of Danites, the principle of consecration, and companies of tens at an exhibition of the Danite company: "they [the Danite company] come up

---

85. D. Michael Quinn has concluded that nearly the entire fighting force of about 900 Mormon men in Caldwell and Daviess counties had become Danites, relying upon the September 4, 1838, affidavit of John N. Sapp who stated that the number of Danites was "betwixt eight and ten hundred men, well armed and equipped." Quinn further postulates that by the end of summer 1838, to be a member in full standing a Mormon must also have been a Danite. See Quinn, *The Mormon Hierarchy: Origins of Power*, 102–3. Alexander Baugh believes that the Danites were always "a select group," citing the testimony of John Corrill who gave the total number of Danites at 300. See Alexander L. Baugh, *A Call to Arms: The 1838 Mormon Defense of Northern Missouri*, 41.

86. "History, 1838–1856, volume B-1 [1 September 1834–2 November 1838]," 844.

87. Jessee and Whittaker, "The Last Months of Mormonism in Missouri," 23.

to consecrate, by companies of tens, commanded by their Captain over ten."[88] The Prophet's language surrounding consecration often reflected Masonic ideals; in the context of a lodge, all men were equal under the "leveling principle."[89] Furthermore, in Smith's revolutionary socio-economic order, members were expected to take vows to consecrate all of their substance to the Church. That this principle of consecration was a topic of discussion at Danite meetings is attested to by John Smith, who noted in his journal on September 1, 1838: "The Daughters of Zion meet today. Had a lecture on consecration by President [Lyman] Wight."[90]

The county militia under the command of Colonel George M. Hinkle in predominantly Latter-day Saint Caldwell County, Missouri, has contributed to confusion surrounding military activities conducted by the Danites. Not all Mormon military action was conducted by this sanctioned militia. A council composed of Colonel Hinkle, first presidency members Joseph Smith and Sidney Rigdon, and Danite leaders David W. Patten and Lyman Wight determined who would be the chiefs of the five hundred to eight hundred men constituting the Mormon troops, and they decided that Smith would carry out military action as commander-in-chief under the cover of this sanctioned militia.[91] According to Sampson Avard,

> [The Prophet] assembled the troops together at Far West, into a hollow square, and addressed them, and stated to them that the kingdom of God should be set up, and should never fall; and for every one we lacked in number of those who came against us, the Lord would send angels, who would fight for us; and that we should be victorious.[92]

Avard also reports that in another address at Far West, Smith said that "those troops were militia, and that we were militia too, and both sides clever fellows; and he advised them to know nothing of what had happened; to say nothing."[93] Anson Call went so far as to claim "the whole of the Military Force" at Far West

---

88. "Journal, March–September 1838," 61.

89. "Equality . . . stands foremost in the claims of Masonry. . . . [T]he levelling principle . . . that all Masons being bound to each other . . . to do good not only to each other, but to mankind at large." Thomas Cartwright Smyth, *Free Masonry; in It's Claims to the Regard of Men of Intelligence, Honor, and Christian Principle*, 62. Compare with Doctrine and Covenants 49:20: "It is not given that one man should possess that which is above another."

90. John Smith, journal, September 1, 1838.

91. Sampson Avard, in *Document Containing the Correspondence*, 100: "It was determined that Colonel Wight should be commander-in-chief at Adam on diahmon; Brunson, captain of the flying-horse of Daviess; Colonel Hinkle should be commander-in-chief of the Far West troops; Captain Patten, captain of the flying-horse, or cavalry; and that the prophet, Joseph Smith, jr., should be commander-in-chief of the whole kingdom."

92. Sampson Avard, in *Document Containing the Correspondence*, 100.

93. Sampson Avard, in *Document Containing the Correspondence*, 100.

belonged to the Danite organization.[94] On the strength of his religious authority alone, it is apparent that Smith intentionally melded Danites and county militia, giving the vigilantes pseudo-legitimacy.

The manner in which the Mormons fought exhibited the religious and ritual nature of Danite militarism. This was exhibited at the October 25, 1838, Battle of Crooked River, where an eyewitness placed Parley P. Pratt in the battle commanding part of the Mormon forces. Wrote one observer:

> [O]n that occasion—the officer who gave the command to the Mormons, after some kind of religious ceremony, [expressed himself] to about this amount: "In the name of Lazarus, God, and the Lamb, fire, Danites;" and after firing twice, they charged.[95]

The Mystic Tie

Oliver Huntington was made a Danite a few weeks before the Mormon surrender at Far West. Using Masonic language, he described his initiation into the group as taking "the first mistic step in the new and unknown bonds of the brothers and ites of Dan," and entering as "an apprentice in the divine brotherly union."[96] As part of Huntington's discussion on the Danites, he mentioned that on June 3, 1844, he was raised a Master Mason. Historian Michael Quinn notes, "the Masonic phrasing was no accident, and [Huntington] seemed enthusiastic about the similarity between his Danite . . . and . . . later Masonic initiation[s]."[97]

Huntington's language of taking a first mystic or apprentice step suggests the Danite ritual, like the Masons', was administered by degrees. An account by W. W. Phelps suggests three degrees may have been involved in Danite ritual.[98]

---

94. Quoted in Quinn, *The Mormon Hierarchy: Origins of Power*, 103. In this vein, Mormon writer Jeff Lindsay has built upon the work of Richard L. Anderson, Dean C. Jessee, and David J. Whittaker in postulating that the entire "Armies of Israel" were Danites, that most of these were "good Danites," and that a very small group of them, acting under the direction of Sampson Avard, were "bad Danites." He gives credit to a "legitimate public Danite organization," and blames questionable activities on "a smaller, secretive group lead [sic] by Avard who would have turned the loyalists into a renegade and bloodthirsty band." See Jeff Lindsay, "An Overview of the Danites and the Church in Missouri." The authors disagree with Lindsay's assessment, but it could be interesting to compare with Smith's possible understanding of true Masons and spurious Masons.

95. Nehemiah Odle [Odell] Testimony, in *Document Containing the Correspondence*, 108. What was reported as "Lazarus" may have been a version of "Eliazar," meaning "God is my help." Lazarus symbolically represented God's power over death.

96. Huntington, Journal, Volume 2, 1845–1846, 37.

97. Quinn, *The Mormon Hierarchy: Origins of Power*, 102.

98. "Mr. Rigdon then commenced making covenants, with uplifted hands. The first was, that, if any man attempted to move out of the county . . . that any man then in the house . . . should kill him. . . . The measure was carried in form of a covenant with uplifted hands. The next covenant, that, if any persons from the surrounding country came into their town, walking about—no odds who he might be—any one of that meeting should

Described in contemporaneous Masonic exposures, initiates of the Entered Apprentice Degree receive signs, grips, and words following their obligation. The Master of the Lodge then presents them with an apron, the working tools of an operative Mason, and a "new name."[99] Masonic name-titles could indicate a person's office within a specific degree. Sometimes these were relatively generic, such as "Father Adam" or "Brother Truth." Other such name-titles could be mystical or angelic, such as "Zaphriel," or "Uriel," or "Camiel."[100] This custom was revealed in Bernard's 1829 *Light on Masonry.*

The practice of giving code names to brethren who were entering into a covenant seems to have been adopted among the Mormons from at least the Kirtland period.[101] For example, Joseph Smith commanded the Church's armed forces in Kirtland as "Barak Ale," a code name meaning "Lightning of God," and he confirmed Lyman Wight a senior leader of the holy army and conferred upon him the name "Baneemy."[102] Further, contemporary accounts preserve appellations given to some of the Danite officers, demonstrating Masonic bestowal of a new name as well as the particular Mormon usage of new names as aliases. Apostle David W. Patten was widely known as "Captain Fear-Naught." Jared Carter, chief officer of the Danites was "the Brother of Gideon," a play on both his command of the Gideonites and his brother who was also named Gideon.[103] Jonathan Dunham was known as "Captain Black Hawk."[104] A lesser officer in the organization, King Follett, was named "Captain Bull."[105] Lyman Wight was "the Intrepid," and George Hinkle, though not generally recognized as a Danite, was "the Thunderbolt."[106]

---

kill him, and throw him aside into the brush. . . . The third covenant was, 'conceal all these things.'" W. W. Phelps, in *Document Containing the Correspondence,* 124.

99. Morgan, *Illustrations of Masonry,* 24–25. This follows the pattern found in Mark 3:17, where Simon is given the name of "Peter" and the others are given the appellation of "sons of Thunder."

100. Bernard, *Light on Masonry,* 259.

101. See, for examples, pre-1981 editions of Doctrine and Covenants 78:9 and 103:21–22, before the code names were removed.

102. Melvin C. Johnson, *Polygamy on the Pedernales: Lyman Wight's Mormon Villages in Antebellum Texas, 1845 to 1858,* 15. Baneemy may have been Smith's approximation of the Hebrew word "banai," which can be translated as "building master" or "restorer."

103. Apparently, Gideon Carter was in turn "the brother of Jared," a play on a Book of Mormon character. Jared Carter was introduced to the Book of Mormon by the Peck brothers of Friendship Lodge #129, S. Bainbridge, NY.

104. W. W. Phelps, in *Document Containing the Correspondence,* 125; Reed Peck, in *Document Containing the Correspondence,* 119; Harold Schindler, *Orrin Porter Rockwell: Man of God, Son of Thunder,* 44n51.

105. Reed Peck, in *Document Containing the Correspondence,* 119.

106. As a state militia man, Hinkle would naturally have wanted to keep any Danite affiliation secret. If he was not a Danite, he would have been the only non-Danite so honored at the Fourth of July ceremony.

Upon taking the Danite oath, William Swartzell alludes to a rite of illumination as well as a naming ceremony: "The promised revelations, said to have been received from heaven by Joseph Smith, Jr., then was, or should have been, possessed by me," preparatory to becoming "a man of God and a son of Thunder." He elaborated that others received this name as well, when "the High Priest stood up in the centre of a circle formed by eleven men, (that being the number initiated at a time,) and administered to them the oath word by word, each one of the circle at the same time repeating the word after him, with uplifted holy . . . hands."[107] The title seems to have been used in the Masonic fashion, given to each initiate as a reminder of his obligation and is derived from the name "Boanerges" that was bestowed by Jesus upon his followers James and John in the New Testament (Mark 3:17).

It is apparent that many of the companies also had code names. Dunham's company of fifty men went by the name of "the Fur Company."[108] Follett was captain of a small group of men called "the Regulators."[109] Orrin Porter Rockwell's company was called "the Destroying Angel," and there was another company labeled "the Destructives."[110]

Joseph Smith, likely the originator of these sobriquets, put them to use in directing action. At one Sunday meeting in Far West, a man entered the meetinghouse with a hat on his head. "The prophet ordered the *Brother of Gideon* to put that man out, for his presumption in daring to enter and stand in the house of God without uncovering his head."[111] According to later dissenter John C. Bennett, Smith directed the assassination of Missouri Governor Lilburn Boggs, who in 1838 ordered the extermination of all Mormons in Missouri, the same way, commanding: "The *exterminator* should be *exterminated* and the DESTROYING ANGEL should do it *by the right hand of his power*. I say it . . . in the name of the Lord God!"[112] Bennett further demonstrated his understanding of this naming practice when he wrote: "I feel . . . certain . . . that Rockwell, as a member of

---

107. Swartzell, *Mormonism Exposed*, 21. See also "Minutes and Blessings, 28 February–1 March 1835," The Joseph Smith Papers, 164–71, which reports that on February 28 and March 1, 1835, several men who had been members of Zion's Camp were given blessings and "endowments" and ordained members of the Seventy. As part of their blessings, several of these men were given names such as "son of consolation," "son of thunder," and "son of the waters."

108. Reed Peck, in *Document Containing the Correspondence*, 118–19.

109. Reed Peck, in *Document Containing the Correspondence*, 119.

110. Bennett, *History of the Saints*, 270–71.

111. Lee, *Mormonism Unveiled*, 56; emphasis added.

112. Bennett added that the prophet had declared in a First Presidency meeting, "The Destroying Angel will do the work; when God speaks, His voice must be obeyed." Bennett, *History of the Saints*, 281; emphasis in original.

the Daughter of Zion, acted as the *conductor* or *guide*; and that one of the twelve composing the Destroying Angel, assisted by Rockwell, *did the deed*."[113]

In the latter part of October 1838, Latter-day Saint troops were engaged in offensive military actions such as spying, seizing weapons, capturing and taking prisoners, firing cannons and other weapons as a show of force, burning buildings, appropriating property and supplies, and commandeering food from the farms and livestock of the Missouri settlers. From this point, some of the brethren, disturbed by the wartime mentality, began to betray the secrets of the Danite brotherhood. Thomas B. Marsh, one of the original members of the Quorum of the Twelve Apostles, was the most eminent among these defectors. Somewhat of a pacifist, Marsh was disturbed by Rigdon's speech condemning any of the male inhabitants who would not join with the Mormon military forces in the "Daviess county relief effort." After these Danite companies attacked the small non-Mormon settlements of Gallatin and Millport, Marsh and Orson Hyde left Far West with their families. Both testified before a justice of the peace in Richmond to improprieties committed by the Danites under the direction of Joseph Smith and David W. Patten.[114]

Danites in Nauvoo

The Danites were never disbanded at the exodus from Missouri in 1838. Rather, many were incarcerated or moved out of the state. In an affidavit made by the city council of Nauvoo, Illinois, on May 19, 1842, Church leaders testified there was no such thing as a Danite society in that city and that they had no knowledge of any combination other than the Masonic lodge.[115] However, the historical record shows that former Missouri-period Danites later became Joseph Smith's bodyguards and acted as part of Nauvoo's police force,[116] where they were often referred to as "life-savers." The Nauvoo Legion, with at least one-fourth of its officers being known Danites, were similarly called "lifeguards."[117] The diary of police chief and former Missouri Danite Hosea Stout makes it clear that Danites

113. Bennett, 286; emphasis in original.

114. William Shepard and H. Michael Marquardt, *Lost Apostles: Forgotten Members of Mormonism's Original Quorum of Twelve*, 187–89.

115. Affidavit of the City Council of Nauvoo, Ill., May 19, 1842, in "History, 1838–1856, volume C-1 [2 November 1838–31 July 1842]," The Joseph Smith Papers, 1357.

116. John Lee Allaman, "Policing in Mormon Nauvoo," 88–90. According to Quinn, "In May 1842, Joseph Smith reassembled a cadre of bodyguards, selecting primarily those with experience as Danites in Missouri. Former Danites such as Dimick B. Huntington, Daniel Carn, and Albert P. Rockwood began serving as Nauvoo's 'Night Watch.' Previously a Danite captain, Rockwood had already been serving as 'commander of my [Smith's] life guards.' The Prophet's bodyguards included such well-known Danites as John L. Butler, Reynolds Cahoon, Elias Higbee, Vinson Knight, Orrin Porter Rockwell, and Samuel H. Smith." Quinn, "The Culture of Violence in Joseph Smith's Mormonism," 25.

117. Quinn, *The Mormon Hierarchy: Origins of Power*, 479–90.

formed the "old police" or "high police" of Nauvoo, secret reinforcements to the "new police," and describes these men swearing "additional oaths" on top of their public oaths of office.[118] Far from being censured outcasts, they were among Smith's most trusted and loyal followers. Their vows were never renounced but were considered to be in effect for the rest of their lives; the hundreds of men who took the oaths continued to live those principles and were bound by them regardless of the different faces the organization took.

A telling meeting of the Nauvoo City Council demonstrates that men who had been Danites in Missouri integrated their previous oaths with Masonic principles from their newly formed lodges. On January 3, 1844, William Law came before the council with a complaint that he was in danger from the Nauvoo police. A lodge brother, Eli Norton, had warned him under "Masonic degradation" that he was suspected of being a traitor, largely because of his opposition to polygamy.[119] In true Danite style, it appears some of the policemen had taken secret oaths to terrorize the dissenter. When Norton was brought before the Council for an explanation, he equivocated, first denying that he knew anything about a private oath, and then blaming it on Daniel Carn, a Missouri Danite. Norton answered, "Cairns told me several times Daniteism was not down." Carn also "said it was a good system."[120]

Two Mormon exposés from 1842 and 1843 are significant regarding the existence of Danites in Illinois and their relationship to Freemasonry. The first is from Oliver Olney, a member of the Church who was coincidentally excommunicated on the very day the Mormon Masonic Lodge in Nauvoo was incorporated. Olney was familiar with the Danite band in Missouri, and in his idiosyncratic style, he wrote about the oaths in which they were bound "and a penalty annex'd." Their duty, he said, was "to take life" and "to defend each other at law." They were known by different names, "but mostly as the daughter of Zion."[121] With evident knowledge of their inner workings, Olney wrote about the Danites' later connection with the recently established Nauvoo Lodge U.D.:[122]

---

118. John S. Dinger, *Nauvoo City and High Council Minutes*, 200, 202. Officers of these special forces received "another oath" that was different than the regular oath of a police officer as a civil servant, which forty such men received on December 29, 1843. The secret oath was given along with "private" and "secret" instruction.

119. This phrase alludes to the promise of a punishment for revealing Masonic secrets. See "Dismissal of Dr. Oliver," 120. William Law told the City Council that he was under obligation not to tell who had warned him, but he soon revealed Norton's name under pressure from Joseph Smith. See Dinger, *Nauvoo City and High Council Minutes*, 200–201.

120. Dinger, 202.

121. Oliver H. Olney, *The Absurdities of Mormonism Portrayed: A Brief Sketch*, 8.

122. "U.D." means "under dispensation" and indicates that the lodge obtained an official dispensation from the Grand Lodge to begin work while preparing to receive a charter. After lodges were chartered, they received a consecutive number in the order they

Much has been said of this company in Missouri and in Illinois. But they have within the past year joined the Freemasons. Their name is changed. They unite with the Lodge free of expense. They now claim the name of Masons; but are a band bound to the Danite principles as before. In connection with the addition of Free Masonry, their oaths are to be true to one another; also to the Authorities of the church; suffer no one to speak reproachfully of them; to be as minute men to fulfil their word; not to let their left hand know what their right hand does. . . . [A] part of this band stands as a life-guard to the leaders of the church of L[atter] D[ay] Saints. . . . They[,] to strengthen themselves in faith and doings, quote the prophecies of the prophet Daniel 2:44, that speaks of the stone cut from the mountain without hand, that was to move until it filled the whole earth. They say to be this branch a'raising, as is spoken of in Isaiah 11:1.[123]

The second exposé, John C. Bennett's *History of the Saints,* was a publication intended to stir up fear of and opposition to the Mormons. The information contained in its pages is often exaggerated; however, Bennett's description of Joseph Smith's "Order Lodge," also known as the Quorum of the Anointed, is relevant:

This is a secret lodge or society, established by Joe Smith, in consequence of a special revelation from Heaven, which he pretended to have received respecting it. It was intended to enable him more effectually to execute his clandestine purposes. None but the very *elite* of the Mormons are admitted into this lodge, as the mysteries of the Holy Priesthood are there, more fully than elsewhere, explained to the members, who are initiated only after they have bound themselves, by a most solemn oath, to profound and inviolate secrecy.

"Order is *Heaven's* first law; and, that confessed,
Some are, and must be, greater than the rest."[124]

It is significant that when Bennett used fear of secrecy, elitism, and oath-taking to denounce the Quorum of the Anointed and Smith's proto-temple ceremonies, he linked these so closely with Masonic concepts.

The similarity of covenants taken in the Mormon endowment ritual to Freemasons' oaths has been covered at length by many authors. But one early Mormon temple vow called "Oath of Vengeance" has particular relevance to Danite and Masonic connections. This oath has passed from general knowledge among most Latter-day Saints, as it was removed from the temple ceremony by 1927.[125] As discussed, Danites obligated themselves to support and defend their

---

were chartered under the Grand Lodge of their state. For more on lodges being chartered, see Chapter 13.

123. Olney, *Absurdities of Mormonism,* 7–8. For additional references to Danites connected with Freemasonry in Oliver Olney's writings, see Richard G. Moore, ed., *The Writings of Oliver H. Olney: April 1842 to February 1843—Nauvoo, Illinois,* 25n2, 37, 39, 146, 148, 246, 253, 264–65.

124. Bennett, *History of the Saints,* 272–75.

125. A letter written by George F. Richards to the President of the St. George Temple shows that all vestiges of the oath were removed by 1927: "At request of President Grant we have already adopted some of the changes decided upon, and it will be in order for you

brothers even to the shedding of blood. After the death of one of their key leaders, David W. Patten, at the Battle of Crooked River, and the slaughter of other
members of the Church at Haun's Mill, both in the fall of 1838, the survivors
began to pledge themselves to avenge those who had been so cruelly slain. On
April 10, 1839, Danite Alanson Ripley wrote a letter to Joseph Smith and other
Church leaders in jail in Missouri. Passionately proclaiming his Danite legacy in
biblical language, he wrote he was ready to act: "I will be an Adder in the path."[126]
With a spirit like "fire in [his] bones," he declared that he could never be satisfied while one of the enemy remained "to piss against a wall, or draw a sword or
spring a trigger." Ripley vowed: "I from this day declare myself the Avenger of the
blood of those innocent men, and the innocent cause of Zion."[127]

According to Wilford Woodruff, this Danite-inspired sentiment became the
basis for the Oath of Vengeance in the endowment ceremony "long before the
death of Joseph and Hyrum."[128] Woodruff's early attribution links the oath with
murders that had taken place in Missouri, which remained very much upon the
minds of the Nauvoo Saints.[129]

Heber C. Kimball's journal reveals that by the end of 1845 the Oath of
Vengeance was considered a vow to avenge the deaths of Joseph and Hyrum
Smith. Kimball said the Twelve had placed temple patrons under oath "to avenge
the blood of the anointed ones. . . . I have covenanted, and never will rest nor
my posterity after me until those men who killed Joseph and Hyrum have been
wiped out of the earth."[130] In 1912, David H. Cannon detailed how the oath,
which he named "the law of retribution," migrated from an obligation given in
the Endowment House into the script of the endowment:

> The law of retribution is: To pray the Father to avenge the blood of the prophets and
> righteous men that has been shed, etc. In the endowment house this was given [as a
> personal responsibility] but as persons went there only once, it was not so strongly
> impressed upon their minds; but in setting in order the [script for] endowments for
> the dead it was given as it is written in [the] 9th Chapter of Revelations[,] and in

---

to do the same. . . . Omit from the prayer in the circles all reference to avenging the blood
of the Prophets. Omit from the ordinance and lecture all reference to retribution. This
last change can be made with a day's notice to those taking the parts that contain such
reference. This letter is written with the approval of the Presidency." George F. Richards,
letter to the President of the St. George Temple, February 15, 1927, quoted in Rocky
Hulse, *When Salt Lake City Calls: Is There a Conflict Between Mormonism and the Public
Trust?*, 354.

126. This passage in Genesis recounts Jacob's patriarchal blessings to his sons. Of Dan
he prophesies: "Dan shall be a serpent by the way, an adder in the path, that biteth the
horse heels, so that his rider shall fall backward" (Gen. 49:17).

127. "Letter from Alanson Ripley, 10 April 1839," The Joseph Smith Papers, 17.

128. "President Woodruff Speaks," 1.

129. See, for example, "We Were Not the Aggressors," 22.

130. George D. Smith, ed., *An Intimate Chronicle, The Journals of William Clayton*, 223–24.

that language we importune our Father, not that we may, but that He, our Father, will avenge the blood of martyrs shed for the testimony of Jesus.[131]

At Senate hearings held from 1904 to 1907 regarding the controversial seating of Apostle Reed Smoot, a witness disclosed the Oath of Vengeance as follows:

You and each of you do covenant and promise that you will pray, and never cease to pray, Almighty God to avenge the blood of the prophets upon this nation, and that you will teach the same to your children and your children's children unto the third and fourth generations.[132]

A preponderance of evidence from contemporaneous journal entries and exposés corroborates the content of this vow, though the placing within the ceremony varies.

With LDS temple patrons covenanting that they would petition God to avenge the blood of Joseph Smith, it is possible that this oath contributed to instances of violence perpetrated by Mormons in the Utah territory, not the least of which is the 1857 episode at Mountain Meadows where Mormons slaughtered close to 140 men, women, and children in the Baker-Fancher party, some of whom were accused of violence against Mormons. This horrific event provided further evidence to the greater community that their fears regarding Mormonism, oath-taking, and vengeance were reasonable concerns. Of the tragedy, Brigham Young is alleged to have said, "Vengeance is mine, saith the Lord, and I have taken a little."[133] Such reports did little to allay public fears.

Danites, Freemasonry, and Joseph's Theocratic Design

Historian Michael Quinn has observed that the Danite band "forecast a path the LDS church would increasingly take in Illinois and later Utah: creating its own alternative civil and political institutions as the basis of theocracy."[134] Recent scholarship on the 1838 Missouri War demonstrates that the Danites—far from being a rogue group distant from the aims and objectives of Mormon leadership—were an accepted and important part of mainstream Mormonism in Missouri. Historians of this period have demonstrated that Joseph Smith and his presidency approved of Danite activities, and that its undergirding "theocratic ethics" were widely accepted by increasing numbers of Saints in Ohio, Missouri, Illinois, and Utah.

---

131. *Minute Book*, St. George, February 22, 1912, in Devery S. Anderson, *The Development of LDS Temple Worship, 1846-2000: A Documentary History*, 163–64.

132. David John Buerger, *The Mysteries of Godliness: A History of Mormon Temple Worship*, 133, quoting Walter M. Wolfe's testimony at the Smoot hearings. Compare this oath with the obligation of the Masonic Elected Knights of Nine, who swear to avenge the murder of Hiram Abiff. See Bernard, *Light on Masonry*, 198.

133. John G. Turner, *Brigham Young: Pioneer Prophet*, 309.

134. Quinn, *The Mormon Hierarchy: Origins of Power*, 103.

Moreover, the Danite organization is one example of Masonic ritual ideology being actualized in early Mormonism. A close examination of the group's teachings, oaths, and rituals, together with its known practices and activities, displays more than coincidental similarities to Freemasonry. Details such as the specific formulation of the language of Danite oaths, and the public promotion of the group as fearsome and vengeful, point to the image of the Avenging Mason—common in the popular press—as an influential model in its conception. This has far-reaching implications both for our understanding of the nature of Daniteism and our appreciation of the extent of Masonic influence on the formation of early Latter-day Saint organizations. Furthermore, the connection between Daniteism and Freemasonry demonstrates that the relationship between Mormonism and Freemasonry was embedded at a much earlier time in Smith's teachings than has been heretofore recognized.

Smith laid the foundations for the Danites with religious teachings in Kirtland, such as the importance of consecration and how to deal with covenant-breakers. He organized military operations beginning with Zion's Camp and extending through the Armies of Israel in Missouri. Along with Sidney Rigdon, he spoke at public gatherings, inciting action from the "Big Fan." The prophet blessed and prophesied over the Danites, declaring they should be the means of bringing forth Christ's millennial kingdom.

The Masonic ideal of divine brotherly union formed a vehicle to bring about a theocratic kingdom and establish a utopian society. Like their Mormon counterparts, Freemasons were millennially minded: longing for peace but convinced that war and destruction would come first. Through both vigilante action and kingdom-building exercises, the Mormon Danites hoped to launch Joseph Smith's vision of a religiously grounded radical new social order. Oaths, signs of recognition, and private meetings gave men who were religious revolutionaries a means to stand together in defense of their rights. Holding sacred secrets inviolate within their hearts, they cultivated an image of energetic righteousness. Like the Freemasons, Danites promoted a connection with the ancient past and with scriptural figures in stirring allegorical tellings. To them, these stories served as justification for their acts defending their beliefs and standing against oppression. By their symbolical "fanning," "treading," "threshing," and "grinding," these latter-day brothers of the biblical Gideon cleansed their ranks and laid waste to the nations—that the stone "cut from the mountain without hands" would roll forth and the political kingdom of God would be established in its fullness.

When the Danite movement was exposed and publicly renounced at the close of 1838, the principles underlying this revolutionary impulse were not abandoned. The Masonic trappings in which it had been clothed would soon find other, increasingly sophisticated uses. Tellingly, the language associated with Danite oaths would find its way into Nauvoo Temple covenants. In this and other ways, Daniteism served as a vehicle for Masonic ritual forms within Mormonism.

CHAPTER 10

THE GRAND DESIGN: JOSEPH'S MASONIC KINGDOM ON THE MISSISSIPPI

Z. Most excellent Haggai, from whence came you?
H. From Babylon.
Z. Most excellent Jeshua, where are you going?
J. To Jerusalem.
Z. Most excellent chiefs, why leave you Babylon to go to Jerusalem?
H. To assist in rebuilding the second temple, and to endeavor to obtain the sacred word.
Z. Let us celebrate this grand design.
                    —Richard Carlile, *Manual of Freemasonry*

In the inspiring ritual of Royal Arch Masonry, Freemasons enact the biblical story of the rebuilding of the city of God and the House of the Lord in Jerusalem after returning from Babylonian exile. The establishment of the city of Nauvoo is equally magnificent and corresponds with the degree to a remarkable extent. On October 27, 1838, Governor Lilburn Boggs issued an order to exile the Latter-day Saints from the state of Missouri. Soon after, Joseph Smith and several church leaders were incarcerated in Liberty Jail from December 1, 1838, to April 16, 1839, as the Mormons scattered into Illinois. During this time, Sidney Rigdon learned of a large parcel of swampland for sale on both sides of the Mississippi River in western Illinois and Iowa surrounding the city of Commerce. Smith authorized the purchase of the land and, after his escape from prison, began to encourage the Saints to gather there. Informed by his years of both successes and failures in social experiments in New York, Ohio, and Missouri, Smith deftly stitched together various elements of contemporary society to compose his own vision for rebuilding and restoration. He would now begin what Masons might call his "master's piece" in a spot beautifully situated for such a vision of revolutionary theocratic social order. Smith renamed the city *Nauvoo*, a Hebrew word suggesting "that which is beautiful." During the years to follow, he would bend his efforts to the realization of a Christian utopian society that was, in fact, beautiful—socially, spiritually, economically, and politically. It would be a society in which each person would be of one heart and of one mind; in which they would be made one temporally so that they could be made one spiritually. In this way, they would be prepared by degrees to enter the presence

Hermann J. Meyer engraving, "Bird's-eye view from hill, across water to Nauvoo,"
ca. 1855.

of the Divine; perhaps they would even be translated to meet their coming Lord
in the air—like Enoch's fabled city in their new scriptural tradition.

The construction of the city itself was an exciting enterprise for those familiar with the Royal Arch degree who felt they were returning to a "New Jerusalem"
and building on the foundations of ancient religion. Nehemiah's call, "Come and
let us build up the wall of Jerusalem, that we be no more a reproach" (Neh. 2:17),
was echoed by nineteenth-century Freemasons who lamented, "Oh, the world
in ruins! Oh, the wrecks of humanity, lying about us on every hand, and crying
aloud for the Master Builder, who alone can reconstruct the edifices so fearfully
cast down."[1] Modeling the behavior of Jesus—the *tekton*,[2] or architect—Smith,
too, called upon this new Zion to "put on her beautiful garments" (D&C 82:14).
She was to become the proof of his prophetic calling and showcase his political
and theocratic vision.

The Royal Arch tradition specifies that the only ones who can participate in
the rebuilding of the Temple are those of the proper pedigree, the descendants
of the original builders. In Smith's theology, those who carried the royal blood of
Ephraim or Manasseh were called to gather the people and initiate this work of
restoration. In Kirtland, they had been told,

---

1. Rob Morris, "Building the Fane," in Rob Morris, *Masonic Odes and Poems*, 33.

2. *Tekton* is the ancient Greek term for architect, craftsman, builder, or carpenter. It is
used in the New Testament to describe the profession of Joseph (Matt. 13:55) and Jesus
(Mark 6:3).

Therefore, thus saith the Lord unto you, with whom the priesthood hath continued through the lineage of your fathers—

For ye are lawful heirs, according to the flesh, and have been hid from the world with Christ in God—

Therefore your life and the priesthood have remained, and must needs remain through you and your lineage until the restoration of all things spoken by the mouths of all the holy prophets since the world began.

Therefore, blessed are ye if ye continue in my goodness, a light unto the Gentiles, and through this priesthood, a savior unto my people Israel. (D&C 86:8–11)

Mormons who left their homes and possessions to move to Nauvoo believed that they were literal descendants of the ancient Israelites, enacting the restoration of the Holy City of God and its sacred temple. Further, they were taught that Joseph Smith and others who had been gathered as members of the Church were direct descendants of Jesus Christ. Through *translatio imperi*,[3] the kingdom of God was extended from Christ through his literal blood line to Smith and his followers, giving them the divine right to rule.[4]

Early Mormons believed it was no mistake that the kingdom of God was to be planted on American soil. Smith wrote that the land of America was a promised land to "all the tribes of Israel . . . with as many of the gentiles as shall comply with the requisitions [sic] of the new co[v]enant." The city of Zion, he pronounced, would be "built upon the Land of America."[5] When the Saints were expelled from Missouri, this dream did not fade.

Social experimentation was possible on a larger scale in North America than could be found elsewhere. Political, municipal, and religious freedom such as that found in the United States made possible the unique amalgamation of these elements characterizing the city of Nauvoo. Draftsmen of this kingdom on the Mississippi were new convert John C. Bennett, who became the primary architect of political and community workings in Nauvoo, and Joseph Smith, whose expertise lay in the theological and social development of the new religion. Both devised Masonic-like institutions to achieve civic and religious purposes. Experienced Freemasons, many of whom belonged to the Prophet's inner circle, understood what Smith and Bennett hoped to accomplish and participated in making their vision a reality.

---

3. The transfer of rule from one supreme governor to another.

4. Early Latter-day Saints believed that Jesus was married and that the Smith family, as well as other elect members of the church, had "Royal Blood"—that is, they were directly descended from Jesus Christ. Converts who came into the church who were not of the blood of Christ or of Abraham were "purged" by the Holy Ghost upon baptism and made "actually of the seed of Abraham." See "Discourse, between circa 26 June and circa 2 July 1839, as Reported by Willard Richards," The Joseph Smith Papers, 18; and Brigham Young, March 8, 1857, *Journal of Discourses*, 4:260.

5. "Letterbook 1," The Joseph Smith Papers, 17.

Four areas of interest apparent in the founding of the city of Nauvoo are: politics, economics, education, and sociality. Each of these vibrates with Masonic resonance.

Politics

Ever since Benjamin Franklin submitted a plan for a grand council of the American colonies based upon an identical plan of organization of American Provincial Masonic Grand Lodges, Freemasonry has been involved in politics in the United States.[6] During the founding of the nation, many of the leaders in the development of a federal union were Masons, which resulted in numerous Masonic concepts being introduced into American government. According to Masonic author James D. Carter, "the basic principles of government employed in Anderson's Constitutions are: popular sovereignty by majority rule; government limited by constitution; local lodges self-governing; Grand Lodge supreme in federal system; a type of judicial review by the Grand Lodge; [and] implied powers exist in constitutional provisions." These principles, he believes, "had been discovered and were being practiced, after 1734, in the area that became the United States." Carter concedes that "any serious student of American history and government can identify other institutions practicing some of these same concepts," but "no other institution was so widely distributed in the colonies as Freemasonry." He continues,

> Differences in religion, government, and economy, difficulties in transportation and communication, and a spirit of localism and individualism existed from north to south from east to west in varying degrees, but the basic principles of Freemasonry were identical in the approximately one hundred colonial lodges established by 1775. . . . This general acceptance by a large segment of the leaders of the people of fundamental concepts is significant in the formation of a federal union type of government and becomes doubly so when those leaders are bound to one another by fraternal ties which engender trust and confidence.[7]

Political involvement by Freemasons was common in the United States until the advent of the anti-Masonic movement when many Americans began to fear the power and influence exerted by the Fraternity. Midwesterners recognized a similar threat from the gathering of Mormons into their communities, yet political figures coveted the benefits such a large bloc of voters might provide.

In his introduction to Volume 4 of the *History of the Church*, B. H. Roberts noted that as the Saints began to stream into Illinois upon their exile from Missouri, their hearty welcome was due in part to the desire of the competing Democrats and Whigs for political advantage. It was this "rivalry for their sup-

---

6. "The plan was not adopted; Franklin explained in his Autobiography that the plan had too much prerogative in it to suit the colonial assemblies and too much democracy to suit the royal government." James Davis Carter, *Masonry in US History—through 1846*, 120.

7. Carter, 121.

port that doubtless made it possible for the Saints to obtain larger grants of power for their city government, and greater political privileges and influence in the State than otherwise could have been obtained." Roberts believed that the political parties' competitiveness made the Mormons "alternately fulsomely flattered and heartily disliked; fawningly courted, and viciously betrayed."[8]

John C. Bennett, Freemason and Quarter Master General of the Illinois State Militia before joining the Church, took advantage of this atmosphere as he developed a city charter for Nauvoo under the direction of Joseph Smith.[9] Bennett's "detailed knowledge of other [Illinois] charters" facilitated the formulation of a charter for Nauvoo drawing upon the most liberal policies then in existence.[10] The policies adopted in the document also gave the city a number of unique powers, including the absence of requirements for political office and the ability of city council members to remove city officers at will. Other distinctive functions dealt with city government, municipal justice, education, and an extraordinarily independent militia unit. Nauvoo's City Charter gave the Mormons the political independence necessary to establish an autonomous political kingdom within the bounds of the United States. The political agenda of the Mormons aligned with their religious aspirations:

> The government of the Almighty, has always been very dissimilar to the government of men; whether we refer to his religious government, or to the government of nations. The government of God has always tended to promote peace, unity, harmony, strength and happiness; while that of man has been productive of confusion, disorder, weakness and misery. . . .
>
> It has been the design of Jehovah, from the commencement of the world, and is his purpose now, to regulate the affairs of the world in his own time; to stand as head of the universe, and take the reigns [sic] of government into his own hand. When that is done judgment will be administered in righteousness; anarchy and confusion will be destroyed, and "nations will learn war no more."[11]

---

8. B. H. Roberts, ed., *History of the Church of Jesus Christ of Latter-day Saints*, 4:xxi.

9. James Kimball notes that both Bennett and Smith claimed credit for the Nauvoo Charter: "Bennett stated, 'I wrote and procured the passage of the . . . charters.' Joseph Smith asserted, 'The city charter of Nauvoo is of my own plan and device. I concocted it for the salvation of the Church.'" James L. Kimball Jr., "The Nauvoo Charter: A Reinterpretation," 45.

10. Kimball, 39–45. Nauvoo's charter included thirty-nine sections from article five of the Springfield charter. Its suffrage qualifications were identical to those in the Alton charter. The right to pass any ordinance not specifically conflicting with powers granted to the federal and state governments was drawn from provisions also seen in the charters of Galena, Quincy, and Springfield. In both Alton and Nauvoo, city courts possessed the authority to issue writs of habeas corpus. Lastly, there was a remarkable resemblance between the Nauvoo Legion and the Fairfield "Invincible Dragoons," an independent militia company that Bennett was instrumental in incorporating in 1837. Kimball suggests that the bulk of the Nauvoo City Charter was "based solidly on precedents" that were "not unheard-of."

11. Joseph Smith Jr., "The Government of God," 855–56.

In Nauvoo, the Latter-day Saints increasingly moved to consolidate political power in order to establish "the government of the Almighty." This would be administered by his mouthpiece, Joseph Smith, and the Council of Fifty, "the ultimate governing body for all mankind."[12]

Education

An early emphasis on education and universities came into Mormonism by way of John C. Bennett. Before coming to Nauvoo, Bennett had established a university and medical college in Virginia and a Christian college in Indiana, the latter from which he sold bogus degrees.[13] Despite indiscretions for which he was censured at both places, his interest in higher education continued. Building on the foundation laid in the School of the Prophets and the School of the Apostles initiated in Kirtland, he established the University of Nauvoo and a form of the popular Lyceum movement.[14] These were frequented with great enthusiasm by the Mormon population. Education may have been a principal concern throughout the less-than-a-century-old United States, but for Freemasons all forms of learning merged with spiritual matters. The figurative chariot of ascent that bears the Mason to heaven is constructed of the "seven liberal arts and sciences."[15] The lesson taken from this figure is that a person who gains knowledge is better able to ascend to higher glory. Education in Nauvoo was a literalization of this allegorical Masonic principle. The Doctrine and Covenants proclaims: "the glory of God is intelligence, or, in other words, light and truth" (D&C 93:36), and

---

12. J. D. Williams, "The Separation of Church and State in Mormon Theory and Practice," 46–47.

13. These degrees may be seen as bogus from a modern perspective. However, Bennett can also be viewed as highly innovative in developing the first independent study or long-distance degrees.

14. See Robert McNamara, "American Lyceum Movement." Josiah Holbrook originated the American Lyceum movement in Millbury, Massachusetts, in 1826. His 1829 book, *American Lyceum*, described a town lyceum as "a voluntary association of individuals disposed to improve *each other* in useful knowledge, and to advance the interests of their schools. To gain the first object, they hold weekly or other stated meetings, for reading, conversation, discussion, illustrating the sciences, or other exercises designed for their mutual benefit; and, as it is found convenient, they collect a cabinet, consisting of apparatus for illustrating the sciences, books, minerals, plants, or other natural or artificial productions." Josiah Holbrook, *American Lyceum, or Society for the Improvement of Schools and Diffusion of Useful Knowledge*, 3; emphasis in original. Though most nineteenth-century lyceums hosted educational lectures or programs by renowned speakers, Nauvoo lyceums seemed to emphasize training in public speaking and discussion of gospel subjects.

15. "In the seventh century, all learning was limited to the seven liberal arts and sciences; their introduction into Freemasonry, referring to this theory, is a symbol of the completion of human learning." Albert Gallatin Mackey, *The Symbolism of Freemasonry: Illustrating and Explaining its Science and Philosophy, its Legends, Myths, and Symbols*, 344.

"whatever principle of intelligence we attain unto in this life, it will rise with us in the resurrection" (D&C 130:18). Oliver Cowdery similarly preached,

> Intelligence is religion, and religion is intelligence. . . . The object of our religion, is to make us more intelligent, than we could be without it. . . . It is designed to evolve the faculties, to enlighten the understanding, and through this medium, purify the heart. It is calculated to make men better.[16]

In his autobiography, Master Mason Wandle Mace provided an interesting glimpse into how lyceums were organized in Nauvoo.[17] Mace had moved his family from Augusta, Iowa, across the river to Nauvoo in accordance with instructions from the First Presidency of the Church "to the Saints abroad." Members "who reside out of this [Hancock] county" were told "to make preparations to come in without delay."[18] Mace bought two lots of property during the summer of 1842, built a comfortable home, and started an iron foundry. During the winter, he spent the long, cold evenings improving his public speaking and religious knowledge at the lyceum, or "lecturing school."[19] He described it as follows:

> Our lyceum was composed of eighteen members, each presided over the meeting in turn, one of the principles of the gospel was chosen as a subject, and each member spoke an half hour upon it, three evenings was taken up with the one principle, before another was touched, six members occupied the first evening, the second evening six other members spoke upon the same subject, and the remaining six occupied the third evening; so that each one of the eighteen had equal time and opportunity to talk upon the subject.[20]

Mace remarked how curious it was that the same subject would be handled so differently by the members of the lyceum. Though their presentation was peculiar to themselves, they would all come "to the same conclusion, by the evidence adduced from the scriptures; there was no jarring, no contention nor discord, and all were entertained, instructed and edified." The prophet Joseph visited their lyceum whenever possible, encouraging the brethren by his presence, and giving them instructions and assistance. He charged them to "get into your lyceums, and investigate doctrine, and if you run against a snag, I am here, I will help you off." Mace recalled,

> There were days and nights of pleasure and profit,—to listen to a prophets voice and receive instruction from one who communed with angels and received his instruction

---

16. "Appendix 3: Discourse, circa 4 July 1838," The Joseph Smith Papers, 9.

17. Mace was raised a Master Mason in the Nauvoo Lodge on June 7, 1843.

18. "Letter to the Saints Abroad, 24 May 1841," The Joseph Smith Papers, 434.

19. Joseph Smith's history described lyceums in this way: "November 24: The young men have established a debating society in Nauvoo to discuss topics of various descriptions." See "History, 1838–1856, volume E-1 [1 July 1843–30 April 1844]," The Joseph Smith Papers, 1780. See also Gustavus Hills, "Nauvoo Lyceum," 2.

20. Wandle Mace, Autobiography of Wandle Mace.

from on high when or wherever I met him, whether in the lyceum, on the street, or at home, he spoke forth words of light and intelligence for the salvation of mankind.[21]

As in Freemasonry, education in the Nauvoo lyceums was markedly connected with religion. The McIntire Minute Book describes some of the first lyceum meetings in Nauvoo, commencing on January 5, 1841. Various gospel subjects were addressed, such as the creation of the earth, vice, resurrection and eternal judgment, true friendship, the Godhead, the law of consecration, the Second Comforter, and so forth. These were presented by speakers including Don Carlos Smith, Josiah Ells, Hosea Stout, Alexander Badlam Sr., Leonard Soby, Austin Cowles ("Father Cole"), Ebenezer Robinson, and others, with Joseph Smith often commenting and adding illumination upon the subject after the speaker concluded. In several of these 1841 lyceum meetings it appears that the Prophet was the only one to lecture.[22]

Economics

Masons believe in the development of the mind, intellect, and talents through education and learning—not only for individual benefit but for the benefit of society in general. All humankind enters the world helpless and dependent upon others. The retrospect of the third degree of Masonry reminds each new Master Mason that "your admission into Freemasonry in a state of helpless indigence, was an emblematical representation of the entrance of all men on this, their mortal existence." Because of this common mortality and dependence upon each other, Masonry teaches the need of "the active principles of universal beneficence and charity" and encourages each brother to extend "relief and consolation to your fellow-creatures in the hour of their affliction."[23] In the eighteenth century, the lodge room often served as a forum to discuss how Masonry could advance the temporal and spiritual well-being of its members. Economic experimentation was encouraged. As historian Mark Carnes observes,

> The [Masonic] rituals repeatedly contravened basic tenets of capitalism. The Improved Order of Red Men, for example, advised initiates to emulate the children of the forest, who held all wealth and property in common. Rather than reinforcing the forms and ideologies of capitalist social organization, the rituals often subverted them.[24]

During World War II, when Communism was being derided by members of the Craft as un-Masonic, it was nevertheless acknowledged that the "over 400 experiments in communal living" in the United States over the preceding two centuries had been beneficial:

---

21. Mace, *Autobiography*.
22. See William V. Smith, "The Parallel Joseph."
23. Richard Carlile, "To William Williams, Esq., M. P. Provincial Grand Master of the Association of Freemasons for the Country of Dorset. Letter IV," 112.
24. Mark C. Carnes, *Secret Ritual and Manhood in Victorian America*, 32.

Many of these have been Christian communal colonies. No doubt in their day of founding or organization they were referred to as socialistic or communistic enterprises. Many of these have developed to a satisfactory conclusion and are now absorbed within the boundaries of these United States. These groups known to you have definitely been an influence for good, and are in no way to be confused with the subject at hand.[25]

Joseph Smith's economic model was Christian communitarianism, a part of these utopian experiments mentioned above. After encountering the ideas through Campbellites Sidney Rigdon and Edward Partridge, Smith began to initiate some of these efforts in Ohio and Missouri. In the chill of February 1831, he established the office of bishop in his fledgling church and appointed Edward Partridge to the position (D&C 41:9; cf. 1 Tim. 3:1–7). Days later, Smith dictated a revelation that required the Saints to "consecrate" their property for the support of the poor. Each family would receive a portion of their holdings, over which they were to be "stewards" (D&C 42:29–32). The Saints viewed this "law of consecration" in Masonic terms: more than simply a temporal welfare program, it was designed to improve a man's character. According to Orson F. Whitney,

> [T]he redemption of Zion is more than the purchase or recovery of lands, the building of cities, or even the founding of nations. It is the conquest of the heart, the subjugation of the soul, the sanctifying of the flesh, the purifying and ennobling of the passions.[26]

In his new role, Partridge was made responsible for operating a storehouse to help the poor and for administering property transactions connected with the law of consecration (D&C 42:30–39; 58:17). In December 1831, Newel K. Whitney was also called as a bishop (72:1–8). The two served as regional or traveling bishops: Whitney for Ohio and the eastern states, and Partridge for Missouri.[27] Kirtland feasts, under the direction of Whitney, were a way for the Church to distribute items from the bishop's storehouse. Later they became associated with the giving of patriarchal blessings by Joseph Smith Sr.[28] As historian

---

25. Van Dyke Parker, "Freemasonry and Communism," 4. The "subject at hand" was defined as "Communism as promulgated by the doctrine of Karl Marx, as furthered by Lenin and Trotzky, and now practiced under the Dictatorship of Joseph Stalin in the Union of Soviet Socialistic Republic."

26. Orson Whitney, *Life of Heber C. Kimball, An Apostle; The Father and Founder of the British Mission*, 78–79.

27. Andrew Jenson, *Latter-day Saint Biographical Encyclopedia*, 1:219–20, 224.

28. These feasts became frequent by 1836 and were apparently the precursors to Fast Meetings. One such feast at the Whitney home lasted three days in January 1836: "Attended a sumptuous feast at Bishop Newel K. Whitney's. This feast was after the order of the Son of God—the lame, the halt, and the blind were invited, according to the instructions of the Savior. Our meeting was opened by singing and prayer offered up by father Smith, after which Bishop Whitneys father & mother were bless[ed] and a number of others, with a patriarchal blessing, we then recieved a bountiful refreshment, furnished

Mark Staker notes, these feasts were reminiscent of "the annual 'sumptuous dinners' that the Masons hosted for the widows, fatherless, and the poor in the area" that Whitney, as a Freemason, had likely participated in.[29]

In the same vicinity, on a large homestead near Kirtland, Ohio, Isaac Morley lived a communitarian lifestyle with Lyman Wight and several other families who had been influenced by the religious teachings of Alexander Campbell and Sidney Rigdon. After joining the Church in November 1831, Morley became devoted to Joseph Smith and meekly accepted his corrections on points of living the law of consecration. When called to sell his farm and move to Missouri, Morley promptly obeyed. He returned to Kirtland in time for the temple dedication and to receive initiatory ordinances there. The Morley family went back to Missouri in 1836, helped establish the town of Far West, and lived there until forced to leave in 1838. When the Saints began to settle in Nauvoo, the Morleys founded a nearby settlement in southern Hancock County that was cryptically named "Yelrome." Here and at the neighboring town of Lima, at least one hundred fifty-nine Latter-day Saint families lived in cooperation. About 76 percent of the over 880 individuals who lived in the area from 1839 to 1846 were linked by kinship relationships, prompting researcher Danny Jorgensen to identify them as a "tribe."[30] The Saints at the Morley Settlement "tithed, made special offerings for the poor and other specific projects, . . . contributed money, goods and labor for the construction of the Nauvoo temple," and "volunteered for service on periodic missions." Altogether, they "interacted with each other as a large extended family."[31]

Though the Morley settlement did not institute a common-stock economy, there was an instance of such an arrangement in the Nauvoo period. From 1841 to 1845, Latter-day Saints were sent to harvest lumber from the Wisconsin pineries for use in building the Nauvoo Temple and the Nauvoo House. Six logging camps were established on the Black River north of La Crosse. Workers in the pineries drew provisions, supplies, equipment, and occasionally cash from their accounts. When they finished their stint, they settled their accounts and were paid the balance in tithing credit, temple credit, and Nauvoo House stock certificates. Logging was a difficult chore and not profitable, but most of the workers participated as part of their service to build the city of God and the House of the Lord. The beauty of the country was spectacular, as Freemason George Miller expressed

---

by the liberality of the Bishop." See "Journal, 1835–1836," The Joseph Smith Papers, 101. Elizabeth Ann Whitney also reported: "According to our Savior's pattern and agreeably to the Prophet Joseph's and our own ideas of true charity and disinterested benevolence, we determined to make a Feast for the Poor, such as we knew could not return the same to us; the lame, the halt, the deaf, the blind, the aged and infirm." Elizabeth Ann Whitney, "A Leaf from an Autobiography: My husband traveled," 71.

29. Mark Lyman Staker, *Hearken, O Ye People: The Historical Setting of Joseph Smith's Ohio Revelations*, 245.

30. Danny L. Jorgensen, "The Morley Settlement in Illinois, 1839-1846," 153, 162.

31. Jorgensen, 160, 162–63.

in his journal on a wintry day in late November, describing it as possessing an "imposing grandeur so peculiarly calculated to captivate and lead the mind of the beholder to the author of our existence and Great Architect of the universe."[32]

The loggers, many of whom brought their families with them, worked together to build shelter, hunt and fish, plant crops, and gather fruits, nuts, berries, and maple syrup. Miller constructed a shoe factory to make sturdy shoes for the men who had not come prepared for the cold temperatures and heavy snow. Allen Stout, also a Freemason, built cabins for many of the company. He described the arrangement in a letter to his brother Hosea: "We hav[e] gon[e] in to the whole law of God on Black river." Every man, after giving an accounting of his property to the bishop, had "all things common according to the law in the book of covenants." Stout seemed pleased that all were "on an equality": every man "far[e]s alike labourse alike eats drinks wares alike" but also had his own small stewardship to do with what he pleased.[33] In another letter, Stout invited friends to join the company if they "thinks they can go the caper of concecration and equality." Said Stout, "[W]e wish you to come by all means and bring all the tools you can the law of black river is he that will not work shal[l] not eat."[34]

Sociality

In his 1775 classic, *The Spirit of Masonry*, author William Hutchinson articulated a commonly held vision of the coming ideal Masonic society in the late eighteenth century: "In the forming of this society, which is at once RELIGIOUS AND CIVIL, great regard has been given to the first knowledge of the GOD OF NATURE, and that acceptable service wherewith he is well pleased."[35] In this utopian vision, Hutchinson conceived of the future blending of the civil and the religious as necessary to a harmonious productive society. As Margaret Jacob has noted, this anticipated social harmony was intimately connected to notions of individual and social perfectibility:[36]

> The experience of this new fraternity occasionally set men to thinking about the larger society as they sought to perfect their own private sociability. They would wax, often eloquently, about the joys of order and harmony, about the sociable virtues prescribed now for all men. Much of eighteenth-century British masonic literature officially published by the lodges has a decidedly utopian cast about it.[37]

Joseph Smith went so far as to suggest that the order and harmony of such social utopianism reflects a heavenly verity:

---

32. George Miller diary, November 21, 1842, in H. W. Mills, "De Tal Palo Tal Astilla," 96.

33. Allen Stout, letter to Hosea Stout, September 13, 1843.

34. Allen Stout, letter to Hosea Stout, September 10, 1843.

35. William Hutchinson, *The Spirit of Masonry: In Moral and Elucidatory Lectures*, 9.

36. Margaret C. Jacob, *Living the Enlightenment: Freemasonry and Politics in Eighteenth-Century Europe*, 57.

37. Jacob, 50.

When the Savior shall appear we shall see him as he is. We shall see that he is a man like ourselves. And that same sociality which exists among us here will exist among us there, only it will be coupled with eternal glory, which glory we do not now enjoy. (D&C 130:1–2)

Here, God is depicted as a man, and as such is a social being living in a perfect and divine society in which mankind may share. To do so, a man must first demonstrate a willingness to live in that society by choosing to be subject to its various divine laws and sufficiently working to perfect his own personality. By attempting on the microcosmic level to approximate heavenly society, a human being may at length qualify for association with the Divine. In this way, he may as a grace subsequently be clothed upon with that "eternal glory" that Joseph Smith indicates is characteristic of the heavenly society to which the Saints aspired.

Jacob, however, notes how these utopian ideals may conflict with the rest of society:

> Continental reformers and visionaries could also find in their lodges a particular kind of social experience which, in certain circumstances, could create a dissonance between their personal experience in constitutionalism and the larger civil polity.[38]

Mormons likewise encountered dissonance in their own personal experience of "constitutionalism and the larger civil polity" as opposed to their own understanding of the nature of the coming decreed Mormon theocracy. Over time, this theocratic ideal was envisioned by Joseph Smith as a kind of heavenly compromise—it became a political body with a "Living Constitution" comprised of fifty men.[39] This theocratic body was an interesting twist on the notion of the philosopher kings that are described in eighteenth- and early nineteenth-century political philosophy and share similarities with the prophet kings of the Book of Mormon. The realization of a utopian society modeled upon the order of heaven and guided by the divinely appointed prophet-king was joined with a uniquely Mormon vision of divinely inspired constitutional monarchy.

Nauvoo Mormonism was a late but particularly vigorous flowering of American Masonic religious idealism, sharing a belief in the perfectibility of humanity and in its logical extension: the perfection of human society. This Masonic Millennialism had been part of the American fraternity in the early nineteenth century. David G. Hackett writes:

> Compared to colonial Freemasonry, in which men of good breeding and upright character attained the honor of membership as a means of entry into "polite" society, the early nineteenth-century version was a private world of warmth and intimacy, separated from an increasingly cold, competitive, and uncertain public sphere, with

---

38. Jacob, 50.

39. "Council of Fifty, Minutes, March 1844–January 1846; Volume 1, 10 March 1844–1 March 1845," The Joseph Smith Papers, 376.

rituals that spoke to the struggles and anxieties of young men living amid widespread social change.[40]

This thriving brotherhood had largely died with the William Morgan fiasco.

In the caricature of Freemasonry found in the anti-Masonic press, the fraternity seemed alienated from its own basic ideals and was presented as undemocratic, non-egalitarian, elitist, silly, pernicious, and morally dangerous. To some, Freemasonry appeared to have lost its way, becoming "drifted and diffused," having a "form" but lacking in any "power" (2 Tim. 3:5).[41] At best, in the estimation of many Americans—including many of its former members—Masonry had become irrelevant to the new order. Yet, in Nauvoo, Smith moved to export and transform Freemasonry and its powerful ideals.

In its heyday, Nauvoo was a thriving city of an estimated fifteen thousand. Thirty-two percent of the population were converts from England.[42] One of these, George D. Watt, was an example of the gentrification of these mostly lower-class converts.[43] Watt, a cobbler and weaver, and his wife Molly, a factory worker, were part of the urban poor of Preston, England. They emigrated to the United States and lived in Nauvoo from 1842 to 1846. Watt's enthusiasm for Mormonism and willingness to sacrifice for the cause provided him opportunities as a missionary preacher and a Church leader. He was self-educated and used his skills in shorthand to teach students and take notes of important speeches of the day. His services were highly appreciated and eventually lucrative. The ability of Watt and other working-class men like Brigham Young and Heber C. Kimball to undergo this type of transformation was part of the fundamentally egalitarian atmosphere of Nauvoo. They poured their creative energies into Mormonism, lifting themselves and others.

The Masonic ideal of equality puts men "upon the level," regardless of money or family connections. The Master of the lodge may be but a farmhand but is given an opportunity to participate in leadership directly. By participating in the lodge, he learns ritual manners, social niceties, and the shape of the gentlemanly life. In addition, he also draws close to God. Men were encouraged and moved by Masonic principle to rise to the level of their betters and to lift and exhibit charitable impulses toward the less fortunate. A popular poem by Masonic writer Rob Morris detailed the fundamental egalitarian nature of the Fraternity:

> We meet upon the Level, though from every station come —
> The King from out his palace and the poor man from his home;
> For the one must leave his diadem without the Mason's door,
> And the other finds his true respect upon the checkered floor. . . .

---

40. David G. Hackett, *That Religion in Which All Men Agree: Freemasonry in American Culture*, 5.

41. Samuel Morris Brown, *In Heaven as It Is on Earth: Joseph Smith and the Early Mormon Conquest of Death*, 172.

42. Dean May, "A Demographic Portrait of the Mormons, 1830–1980," 124.

43. Watt was raised a Master Mason in the Nauvoo Lodge on July 27, 1842.

There's a World where all are equal,—we are hurrying towards it fast,—
We shall meet upon the level there when the gates of death are past; . . .

O what words of precious meaning those words Masonic are,
We meet upon the level, and we part upon the Square.[44]

Such values were exported into the New World by the vast influx of British converts to Mormonism. They were then transformed by Joseph Smith and his contemporaries in a manner agreeable with the Mormon theocratic vision. Brought into alignment with their ideal of a new worldwide social order, this new Masonic culture and ideology was made agreeable to a pattern God had revealed to them. Co-opted and sanctified in the context of the Mormon kingdom-building enterprise, it was made congruent with the revolutionary concepts of liberty, equality, and fraternity.

Through the prophetic voice, Smith received his ability to populate a literal revolution. Mormons definitely had an upper echelon of leaders who were admitted to the School of the Prophets and the Quorum of the Anointed, but there was also an impulse toward bringing the gospel to the downtrodden. For example, Smith's political campaign advocated the emancipation of African slaves. Most Mormons espoused this idea, as well as the assimilation of Native Americans into society. From the earliest days of the Church, Native Americans were considered part of God's chosen people, and missionaries were sent to gather them, contrary to the then-current national policy of Indian removal.[45]

It was an irony that on one hand, people feared that Masonry was allowing too much influence by the upper classes while, on the other hand, they feared the working class uniting to cause social and economic change. For the brothers associated with the fraternity, Masonic affiliation crystallized what it was about the old social order that they didn't like and reflected their view of what American society ought to be.

True Religion and the New Society

There was a strong religious component in nineteenth-century Masonry. The divine attributes of God were imitated through ritual. No individual could be exalted on his own—restored Freemasonry was about the transformation of society. Attempts to construct a harmonious society "put the freemason on the side of virtue, as opponent of corruption."[46] In its New World incarnation, the coming Masonic utopia was at once Christian and benevolent, paradoxically both progressive and ancient, and socially stratified and egalitarian. It anticipated architectural feats like the design and construction of splendid monuments

44. Morris, *Masonic Odes and Poems*, 17–18.
45. Michael Scott Van Wagenen, *The Texas Republic and the Mormon Kingdom of God*, 15–16.
46. Jacob, *Living the Enlightenment*, 56.

as "harbingers of cultural revival," and it championed various social improvements.[47] Furthermore, Masonry emphasized the liberal arts and sciences and encouraged individual education and charitable action as important means to bringing about a specific social end: the establishment of True Religion. This in turn would lead to a revolution of the entire social order preparatory to the coming of the Son of Man and the establishment of his millennial kingdom. Masonic author David G. Hackett observes: "In its efforts to cross political and religious boundaries, Freemasonry rivaled Protestantism in influencing the creation of the new American society."[48]

The growing movement of American Evangelical Christianity was at odds with the type of religion embodied by Freemasonry. This rational Christian mysticism guided by human reason was at once too magical and too humanistic for mainstream Protestantism. But there were still folk steeped in Christian primitivism who yearned to restore the church's ancient foundations. These formed the foundation of the Masonic brotherhood. Masons believed that each individual had a responsibility to discover and live by the truth, whether scientific, moral, historical, or religious. Their social order encouraged each brother to be responsible to themselves and to God alone for the development of their innate divine qualities.

The manifesto of this social revolution was couched within the ritual and tradition of the Holy Royal Arch—the capstone and completion of Masonry as a Christian mystical tradition. "We have been liberated," Royal Arch Masons recited in their degree work, "and have come up to help, aid and assist in the noble and glorious work of rebuilding our city—and the House of the Lord—without hope of fee or reward."[49] This tendency towards radicalism and the yearning for primeval and even pre-Christian truth was part of the appeal of Freemasonry among Mormons. Nauvoo was a utopian experiment upon Masonic lines, wherein the Latter-day Saints, according to Mormon historian Marvin S. Hill, "did not separate society, economics, politics, and culture from religion."[50]

By bringing a Masonic temple and city of God from the figurative to the literal, Joseph Smith expanded ideas that he found first in Freemasonry, particularly the Royal Arch story—the compelling ritual portrayal of a group of God's people endeavoring to build an ideal community. The success of a utopian society requires that it be populated by ideal men and women. Like Freemasonry, nineteenth-century Mormonism sought to promote those ideals by recognizing that while mankind was fallible, they were also perfectible by virtue of being the

---

47. Jacob, 57.

48. Hackett, *That Religion in Which All Men Agree*, 4.

49. Malcolm C. Duncan, *Duncan's Masonic Ritual and Monitor or Guide to the Three Symbolic Degrees of the Ancient York Rite and to the Degrees of Mark Master, Past Master, Most Excellent Master, and the Royal Arch, Third Edition*, 259.

50. Summary of Marvin S. Hill, "Religion in Nauvoo: Some Reflections," 119–29, in the introduction to Roger D. Launius and John E. Hallwas, eds., *Kingdom on the Mississippi Revisited: Nauvoo in Mormon History*, 12.

offspring of a perfect deity. There is something divine and noble within each person, and given the proper opportunity, they could attain godhood.

Smith taught that one of the fundamental roles of his new social order was to help restore the individual to their own lost nature and to heavenly society. The teaching that heavenly directed social transformation and change would aid in the perfection of the individual, who was being prepared for the association of God and other perfected beings in God's own holy and heavenly society, was a powerful notion.

Borrowing a page from the Rosicrucian Enlightenment, the grand design of Freemasonry was to revolutionize the entire world. So, too, with Mormonism. By the early 1840s, Smith had a much clearer concept of what his utopian society would entail and had sufficiently developed the theological framework to begin implementing his plan. In Nauvoo, Smith began to move from a covert to a more overt Masonic model. Mormonism was a theocratic kingdom with a Davidic prophet-king at its head. It likewise was patriarchal, with its citizens joined by bonds of affection, kinship, and marriage. Through the temple and its theocratic laws, these bonds were made literal. This was Joseph Smith's "grand design" by which he aimed to revolutionize the world.

CHAPTER 11

THE ANCIENT ORDER OF THINGS: FREEMASONRY RESTORED

By the great Architect the grand fabric was form'd,
By wisdom contrived, and with beauty adorn'd;
Supported by strength, all its parts shall declare,
The order resulting from compass and square.
　　　　　—Joseph Thornton, "The Compass and Square"

Freemasonry possesses both a legendary and an authentic history, and the two have not always been carefully separated. This fact lies behind Albert Mackey's observation at the end of the nineteenth century that Freemasonry's traditional legends "have been invented by the makers of the rituals for symbolic purposes connected with the forms of initiation." Because these stories "are really to be considered as merely the expansion of a philosophic or speculative idea," Mackey concludes that "they can not properly be posited in the category of historical narratives."[1]

From the beginning of Freemasonry until his day, Mackey argued that "the legendary or traditional has too much been mingled with the historical element."[2] This was not seen as a problem by early framers of the Craft, as pre-modern historians often emphasized improving the reader, or demonstrating principles, rather than strict adherence to fact. This philosophy, which regularly included mythical elements, survived alongside the more scientific approach to history writing well into the nineteenth century.[3] It was not until the Progressive Era, beginning in the late 1800s, that histories more generally shifted toward confirmable, factual claims using source criticism.

---

1. Albert Gallatin Mackey, *The History of Freemasonry: Its Legendary Origins*, 1.

2. Mackey, 1. This is seen vividly in the works of George Oliver, a writer who pursued the legendary history of Masonry. Oliver was highly respected in his day, but a century later was disparaged by Masons who disapproved of his views. See "George Oliver, Early Masonic Writer," 245.

3. Ancient Greece and Rome can arguably be said to have valued the scientific philosophy of history. Herodotus and Thucydides both attempted to write objective accounts of history, though they were constrained to accept oral traditions and speculations for lack of written accounts. Mythic and sacred history largely took over during most of the Medieval and Renaissance periods. With the nineteenth century came Leopold von Ranke (1795–1886), who claimed that "historians should not interpret the past subjectively but re-present it *wie es eingentlich gewesen ist*, or 'as it really was.'" Anthony K. Jensen, "Philosophy of History."

Joseph Smith and his Mormon followers viewed Masonic history through the legendary lens. Thus, Mackey's caution applies to the student of Mormon-Masonic history who must be careful not to posit Smith's understanding of the Craft in the category of historical narrative. This standpoint, along with the folkloric paradigm in which early Mormons were steeped, allowed them to combine Christian symbolism, Masonic tradition, and early American myth to place Smith into the role of a prophetic restorer.

Restoring Ancient Freemasonry

Joseph Smith did not leave a detailed account of his reasons for establishing a Masonic lodge in Nauvoo, but his followers left several statements that illuminate their understanding of his intentions. According to this evidence, Smith not only embraced the Masonic worldview, but he believed his life to be the latter-day point and purpose for which that worldview existed.

In Masonic legend, priesthood had its beginning in the ancient past and ante-dated the Jewish priesthood. As Smith began to introduce the endowment, he connected his conception of priesthood with Masonry, closely following the Masonic legend of priesthood's ancient past and adding the idea that over the centuries it had become degenerated. Smith's colleague Heber C. Kimball seemed thrilled by these concepts and mentioned them in a letter to fellow apostle Parley P. Pratt:

> [W]e have recieved some pressious things through the Prophet on the preast hood that could caus[e] your Soul to rejoice[.] I can not give them to you on paper fore they are not to be [w]rit[t]en. So you must come and get them fore your Self . . . thare is a similarity of preast Hood in masonary. Bro Joseph Ses Masonary was taken from preasthood but has become degen[e]rated. but menny things are perfect.[4]

This letter, written in 1842, can be compared with Kimball's more dogmatic statement on November 13, 1858: "We have the true Masonry. The Masonry of today is received from apostasy, which took place in the days of Solomon and David. They have now and then a thing that is correct, but we have the real thing."[5]

According to Joseph Fielding, the Masonic degrees were "a Stepping Stone or Preparation for something else, the true Origin of Masonry," meaning the Nauvoo endowment.[6] "This I have also seen and rejoice in it," he exulted. "I have evidence enough that Joseph is not fallen. I have seen him after giving, as I before said, the origin of Masonry, organize the kingdom of God on the earth and am myself a member of it."[7]

Benjamin F. Johnson apparently had a similar understanding of Smith's teaching:

---

4. Heber C. Kimball, Letter to Parley P. Pratt, June 17, 1842.

5. Stanley B. Kimball, *Heber C. Kimball, Mormon Patriarch and Pioneer*, 85.

6. Andrew F. Ehat, ed., "'They Might Have Known That He Was Not a Fallen Prophet'—The Nauvoo Journal of Joseph Fielding," 145.

7. Ehat, 147.

[April of 1843] In lighting him [Joseph Smith] to bed one night he showed me his garments and explained that they were such as the Lord made for Adam from skins, and gave me such ideas pertaining to endowments as he thought proper. He told me Freemasonry, as at present, was the apostate endowments, as sectarian religion was the apostate religion.[8]

Johnson's statement reinforces Kimball's and Fielding's understandings, as it considers Freemasonry apostate and in need of restoration. Johnson also implies that the endowments Smith developed were the ancient, pristine, restored Freemasonry. Smith was taking a legendary tradition and making it literal, bringing the allegorical Masonic priesthood into reality.

Edward Tullidge further explained:

[Smith] understood that the chain of Masonry is the endless chain of brotherhood and priesthood, linking all the worlds,—the heavens and the earths,—but he believed that this earth had lost much of its purpose, its light, its keys, and its spirit,—its chief loss being the key of revelation. For instance, his conception might be expressed in the statement that the Masonic Church on earth ought to be in constant communion with the Masonic Church in the heavens, thus constituting a universal brotherhood indeed.[9]

This description clarifies Smith's views of a Masonic apostasy. The Craft had lost the keys of revelation; its communion with heaven had been broken. With this idea, part of the reasoning behind the Mormons joining the Masonic institution becomes evident. In order to revive the connection with the "Masonic Church" in the heavens and restore the "universal brotherhood," Mormons needed to become part of Masonry on earth.

The legendary view of ancient Freemasonry holds that it once had the power to impart the Lost Word: the name of Deity, representing a true knowledge of God's character and communion with the Divine. Nauvoo Freemasons recognized this as one of Smith's main objectives. According to Jesse C. Little,

The angel of the Lord brought to Mr. Joseph Smith the lost key-words of several degrees, which caused him, when he appeared among the brotherhood of Illinois, to "work right ahead" of the highest, and to show them their ignorance of the greatest truth and benefits of masonry.[10]

Likewise, Charles Charvatt is reported to have said that "there were some signs and tokens with their meanings and significance which we [Freemasons] did not have. Joseph restored them and explained them to us."[11]

---

8. Benjamin F. Johnson, *My Life's Review: The Autobiography of Benjamin F. Johnson*, 96.

9. Edward W. Tullidge, *The Life of Joseph Smith the Prophet*, 391–92.

10. Jesse C. Little, reported in Richard F. Burton, *The City of the Saints, and Across the Rocky Mountains to California*, 350.

11. Manuscripts of Samuel C. Young, as cited by Matthew B. Brown, "Of Your Own Selves Shall Men Arise," 130.

The belief that Masonry was of ancient vintage continued in the Church for some time. On January 1, 1877, in a talk given at the nearly completed St. George Temple, Brigham Young created sacred history by blending Masonic myth with biblical tradition, suggesting that Masonry is a remnant of the priesthood:

> It is true that Solomon built a Temple for the purpose of giving endowments, but from what we can learn of the history of that time they gave very few if any endowments, and one of the high priests was murdered by wicked and corrupt men, who had already begun to apostatize, because he would not reveal those things appertaining to the Priesthood that were forbidden him to reveal until he came to the proper place. I will not say but what Enoch had Temples and officiated therein, but we have no account of it.[12]

This view continued into the early twentieth century. Speaking at a conference on January 8, 1902, Apostle Matthias F. Cowley "spoke of Freemasonry as being a counterfeit of the true masonry of the Latter-day Saints."[13] In 1919, Apostle Melvin J. Ballard asserted that "modern Masonry is a fragmentary presentation of the ancient order established by King Solomon. From whom it is said to have been handed down through the centuries." Ballard claimed he was "not sorry there was such a similarity, because of the fact that the ordinances and rites revealed to Joseph Smith constituted a reintroduction upon the earth of the divine plan inaugurated in the Temple of Solomon in ancient days."[14]

Smith gave tangible, material shape to legendary concepts that were encountered in the Craft—the restoration of Christianity built on Biblical history as understood by the Masons. Masonry contributed the model that something vital had been lost, and he stepped in to restore the missing knowledge.

The Reorganization of the Grand Lodge of Illinois

The establishment of Freemasonry in Nauvoo relied first on the re-establishment of a grand lodge in the state. While a Grand Lodge of Illinois had operated from 1822 to 1827, it ceased to function after the Morgan affair. When the Saints arrived in Nauvoo in 1839, those Mormons who were already Freemasons had no serious opportunity to form a lodge. Only a handful of lodges existed in the state, and most were in the west-central part of Illinois, all operating under dispensations or charters from the grand lodges of other states. Of those states with organized grand lodges, only Kentucky and Missouri were nearby, the latter having begun to warrant Illinois-situated lodges only one year earlier. With the disastrous experience of the Mormons in Missouri, however, a petition to that grand lodge would have been fruitless. Grand Master Stephen W. B. Carnegy of

---

12. Brigham Young, January 1, 1877, *Journal of Discourses*, 18:303.

13. Stan Larson, ed., *A Ministry of Meetings: The Apostolic Diaries of Rudger Clawson*, 380.

14. *The Salt Lake Herald*, December 29, 1919, as cited in Samuel H. Goodwin, *Mormonism and Masonry: Origins, Connections and Coincidences Between Mason and Mormon Temple/Templar Ritual*, 61–62.

nearby Missouri had gladly given dispensations to Illinois-based lodges, but his close associate and newly elected successor, Grand Master Priestly H. McBride, was no friend to the Mormons. Destined to become the longest-serving Grand Master in Missouri history, McBride was appointed a circuit court judge by Governor Lilburn W. Boggs in 1836.[15]

The reorganization of the Grand Lodge of Illinois owed a great debt to James Adams, Master Mason raised on June 1, 1813, in Washington Lodge No. 220 at Blooming Grove, New York.[16] Later that year, Adams moved his family to Lysander, in Onondaga County, New York, where he served as a justice of the peace without the benefit of a law license.[17] Adams's career in New York came to a halt after he was indicted in 1818 for forgery of a deed record.[18] Making plans to meet up with his family at some future time, Adams fled the state before trial. By 1820, he appeared in Springfield, Illinois, where he became one of the first land-owners and the town's first lawyer. His reunited family thrived in Springfield, and Adams became a prosperous member of Springfield society, serving as a judge and running for a variety of public offices, including governor of Illinois.

In Springfield, Adams soon resumed his interest in Freemasonry. In December 1824, he attended the annual communication of the first Grand Lodge of Illinois as a visitor hailing from Skaneateles Lodge of New York. This gave Adams the distinction of being the only Mason attending meetings of the original Illinois Grand Lodge who would also be associated with the succeeding Grand Lodge. In 1839, he became the first Worshipful Master of Springfield Lodge No. 26 under the authority of the Grand Lodge of Missouri.[19]

Despite rumors that he had earlier secretly been a Mormon, it is generally believed that Adams converted to Mormonism in 1839 or 1840. A December 27,

---

15. *History of Audrain County, Missouri*, 231–32.

16. Records of the Grand Lodge of New York, as reflected in Tom Savini [Director, The Chancellor Robert R. Livingston Masonic Library, New York City], correspondence to Nicholas S. Literski, May 30, 2003.

17. Miscellaneous legal documents in James Adams Collection, Illinois State Historical Library Archives. Adams obtained his law license later, in 1817.

18. Certified copy of court record, published in "To the Public," 2. See also Wayne C. Temple, "An Aftermath of 'Sampson's Ghost:' A New Lincoln Document," 2.

19. Temple, "An Aftermath of 'Sampson's Ghost," 4. Adams reported that he hailed (originated) from "the Lodge at Skaneateles, New York, number not recollected." No record exists of a Masonic lodge at Skaneateles until 1826, well after Adams left New York. Further, that lodge appears to have disbanded the same year in the wake of the Morgan affair. As a result, at least one writer has suggested Adams falsified his Masonic history, insisting it was "almost unthinkable that a mason would ever forget his lodge number." Records of the Grand Lodge of New York, as reflected in Savini, correspondence to Literski, May 30, 2003. Another possibility is that Adams had been part of an earlier attempted lodge at Skaneateles that was never chartered, thus having no number. Many such lodges never appeared in the proceedings of their respective grand lodges and have been entirely forgotten as a result.

1840, letter from Ebenezer Robinson to Brigham Young mentions the baptism of Adams as news. Since Young had been absent on a mission to Great Britain since September 14, 1839, Adams's baptism must have occurred after that date.[20] In October 1839, Heber C. Kimball lodged with Adams and opined that Adams would "come into the Church soon."[21] In addition, between November 4 and November 8, 1839, Joseph Smith records that he became the guest of Adams, who "sought me out, and took me home with him, and treated me like a Father."[22] While not conclusive, these events seem to date Adams's baptism between October and November of 1839.

The timing of this baptism coincides with Adams's Masonic activities. He and his Masonic brethren signed a petition to the Grand Lodge of Missouri seeking a dispensation to form a lodge at Springfield on January 27, 1839.[23] Shortly after Smith's arrival at Adams's home on December 27, 1839, Adams met with representatives of the various Masonic lodges in Illinois at Jacksonville to consider the formation of a grand lodge. The delegates chose April 6, 1840—the tenth anniversary of the founding of The Church of Jesus Christ of Latter-day Saints—as the date upon which the grand lodge would be established.[24] The fact that the proposed reestablishment of Illinois Masonry was to take place on the same date as the Mormons' restoration of "true Christianity" suggests a connection of the two events in Adams's mind.

On the day appointed, officers were elected, with Past Grand Master of the Grand Lodge of Kentucky Abraham Jonas chosen in his absence as Grand Master.[25] Adams was elected Deputy Grand Master.[26] Another meeting was held on April 28, 1840, with Jonas still not in attendance. Not to be discouraged, the assembled delegates installed Jonas as Grand Master by proxy.[27]

On October 20, 1840, Grand Master Jonas finally attended, presiding over the annual convocation of the Grand Lodge of Illinois. Both Jonas and Deputy Grand Master Adams were reelected for the coming year.[28] At some time prior to

---

20. Kent Walgren, "James Adams, Early Springfield Mormon and Freemason," 127.

21. Helen Mar Kimball Whitney, "Life Incidents: No. II.," 26.

22. "History, 1838–1856, volume C-1 [2 November 1838–31 July 1842]," The Joseph Smith Papers, 972.

23. Everett R. Turnbull, *The Rise and Progress of Freemasonry in Illinois 1783–1952*, 97; Calvin A. Nevins, "Centennial History of Springfield Lodge No. 4 A.F. & A.M," 3.

24. Turnbull, *Rise and Progress*, 111.

25. Charles Snow Guthrie, *Kentucky Freemasonry, 1788–1978: The Grand Lodge and the Men Who Made It*, 241.

26. *Reprint of the Proceedings of the Grand Lodge of Illinois, From its Organization in 1840 to 1880 Inclusive*, 5.

27. Turnbull, *Rise and Progress*, 113–14. Turnbull notes that according to Article 36 of the General Regulations of 1722, a Grand Master cannot be elected in absentia unless "the old Grand Master, or some of the Masters and Wardens of Lodges, can vouch upon the honor of a Brother, that the said person so nominated or chosen, will readily accept the office."

28. *Reprint of the Proceedings of the Grand Lodge of Illinois*, 8.

1842, Adams loaned the Grand Lodge $109, facilitating its success.[29] There is no record of Adams having attended Grand Lodge again.[30]

A Masonic Lodge in Nauvoo

With the Grand Lodge of Illinois in place, the time was ripe for Freemasons in Nauvoo to organize. As the city took shape, an abundance of resources existed from which to draw in this endeavor. Heber C. Kimball owned a copy of William Morgan's exposure, *Illustrations of Masonry*;[31] Newel K. Whitney owned Webb's *Monitor*;[32] Oliver B. Huntington had access to Bernard's *Light on Masonry*; Lucinda Morgan Harris also owned Bernard's *Light on Masonry*;[33] and Brigham Young owned Bradley's *Some of the Beauties of Free-masonry*.[34] The large group of experienced Freemasons who became residents of the city made it possible to petition for a Nauvoo Lodge.

As a first step in this process, John C. Bennett and "others of the City of Nauvoo" wrote to nearby Bodley Lodge No. 1, located in Quincy, Illinois, asking them for a recommendation to the Grand Lodge.[35] This communication was discussed at Bodley Lodge's regular monthly meeting on June 23, 1841. The brothers of Bodley Lodge decided that "as those persons were unknown to this Lodge as masons it was thought prudent not to do so."[36] A careful examination

---

29. John C. Reynolds, *History of the Most Worshipful Grand Lodge of Illinois, Ancient, Free, and Accepted Masons, From the Organization of the first Lodge within the present limits of the State, up to and including 1850*, 170; *Proceedings of the Grand Lodge of Illinois*, 28.

30. See Michael W. Homer, *Joseph's Temples: The Dynamic Relationship Between Freemasonry and Mormonism*, 145. Homer notes, "In October [1841], when the Illinois Grand Lodge held its annual communication, Jonas was reelected Grand Master but Adams was replaced by Meredith Helm who, like Adams, was past master of Springfield Lodge. In fact, Adams did not attend Grand Lodge because he was in Nauvoo attending Church General Conference." Adams also received his patriarchal blessing during this visit to Nauvoo.

31. "I remember once when but a young girl, of getting a glimpse of the outside of the Morgan's book, Exposing Masonry, but which my father (Heber C. Kimball) always kept locked up." Helen Mar Whitney, "Scenes and Incidents in Nauvoo. The Next Important Event," 26.

32. Signed copy now owned by John Hajicek.

33. B. W. Richmond, "The Prophet's Death," 51–52. See discussion in Chapter 17 of this book.

34. Copy in possession of the Daughters of the Utah Pioneers museum in Salt Lake City.

35. As with most Masonic jurisdictions, the 1841 bylaws of the Grand Lodge of Illinois stated that in order for a dispensation to be granted for the formation of a new lodge, at least seven "known and approved Master Masons" must send a petition to the grand lodge nominating their first Master and Wardens. This petition must be "accompanied by a recommendation from the lodge nearest to the place in which the new lodge is to be holden." *Reprint of the Proceedings of the Grand Lodge of Illinois*, 35.

36. *Minutes of Bodley Lodge No. 1, A.F. & A.M. of Illinois*, June 23, 1841. These minutes remain in the care and custody of Bodley Lodge up until the present time, thus sparing

of the minute books of Bodley Lodge indicates that none of the Masons living in Nauvoo had ever visited there. Therefore, the brethren of Bodley Lodge were quite correct in stating that the petitioners were unknown to be Masons. Short of the Nauvoo Masons visiting Bodley Lodge and being duly examined before admission, the brethren at Quincy were unable to legitimately grant the requested recommendation.[37] In all probability, the brethren of Bodley Lodge expected the Nauvoo Masons to begin to visit Quincy and take the opportunity to form associations and demonstrate their good standing. Instead, the Mormons bypassed Bodley Lodge and turned to another for their recommendation. Columbus, Illinois, located a short distance east of Quincy, was home to Columbus Lodge No. 6, of which the founding master was Grand Master Abraham Jonas. Before the 1841 Grand Lodge communication ended on October 5, one of Jonas's last actions as master of Columbus Lodge was to issue the requested endorsement. Then, based upon his own recommendation, Jonas acted as Grand Master to issue a dispensation to Nauvoo Lodge while Grand Lodge was out of session.[38]

In the October 15, 1841, dispensation, Jonas made it appear that the Nauvoo Masons had been recommended "by the Master[,] Warden[,] and Brethren of Columbus Lodge, No. 6." However, the minutes of Columbus Lodge contain no discussion of such an approval. Masonic historian Robin L. Carr concludes that "Jonas must have issued the recommendation from himself to himself."[39] Having the recommendation from Columbus Lodge in hand, Jonas did not provide the dispensation until ten days after the annual meeting of the Grand Lodge of Illinois had concluded and the Grand Lodge was in recess. Brady Winslow has called this a "strategic maneuver" brought on, perhaps, by fear "that a proposal to grant a dispensation to Mormon Masons would have been rejected by the attendees at the meetings of the grand lodge."[40]

---

them from the general destruction of Illinois Masonic records in 1850.

37. While the Nauvoo Masons' letter no longer survives, its wording as recorded by the secretary of Bodley Lodge raises the likelihood that John C. Bennett was proposed as the first worshipful master of the new lodge. In Masonic records, the receipt of a petition for dispensation was generally referred to either by the names of the nominated master, senior warden, and junior warden, or just by the proposed master. The wording "John C. Bennett and others" suggests strongly that Bennett's name was at the head of this original petition, rather than listed as secretary as it would be later.

38. Dispensation Issued by Grand Master Abraham Jonas, Grand Master of Ancient Free and Accepted Masons of Illinois, as copied in "Nauvoo Masonic Lodge, Minute Book 1, 1841–1842."

39. Robin L. Carr, *Freemasonry and Nauvoo 1839–1846*, 9.

40. Brady Winslow, "Irregularities in the Work of Nauvoo Lodge: Mormonism, Freemasonry, and Conflicting Interests on the Illinois Frontier," 63–64. Historian Robin Carr writes, "On October 5, 1841 Jonas issued a dispensation to Nauvoo Lodge. Bodley Lodge immediately objected and the dispensation was rejected. Yet, ten days later, on October 15, 1841, Jonas defied the Grand Lodge, which was no longer in session, and again issued a dispensation for the new lodge." See Carr, *Freemasonry and Nauvoo*, 9. Some

A number of writers have speculated on the motives of Grand Master Abraham Jonas in issuing the above dispensation. In most cases, authors have pointed to Jonas's political ambitions as a reason to court Mormon favor.[41] This explanation is weak, however, as Jonas was running for the state legislature from Adams County, not Hancock County (which elected William Smith, the Prophet's brother).[42] Further investigation reveals a more likely explanation: Jonas sought a prominent national role in the Masonic institution. He already had favorable connections with Mormonism and had a vision of how this untapped resource could strengthen Freemasonry both in Illinois and nationally.

Jonas's association with Latter-day Saints began in January 1836, when certain elders in Kirtland sought an education in biblical Hebrew. Joshua Seixas, son of the first American-born rabbi, was hired as instructor. The Jewish population in the United States at the time was small, and the Seixas family was prominent in Masonic as well as religious circles.[43] Abraham Jonas and his brother Joseph, who helped form the first Jewish congregation west of the Allegheny Mountains, had married Sexias's sisters, Lucy and Rachel, in 1823.

While living in Cincinnati, Ohio, Abraham Jonas encountered anti-Semitism. However, among the group of men "whose bond was Freemasonry," he was welcomed as a friend and quickly showed an intense involvement in the Fraternity.[44] Jonas joined Miami Lodge No. 46 in Cincinnati, where he was initiated on August 12, passed on September 2, and raised on October 7, 1823.[45] A couple years later, tragedy struck when Jonas's wife, Lucy, and their newborn son died unexpectedly. Jonas moved forty miles south to Williamstown, Kentucky, where he maintained his ties with Masonry, opened a store, and began a new family. There, he united with a group of fellow Freemasons in opening Grant Lodge No. 85, where he served as the first master in 1827. For years Jonas led Freemasonry in Kentucky, serving in various positions in the Grand Lodge of Kentucky from

authors have followed Carr's lead and stated that Jonas first attempted to issue Nauvoo Lodge's dispensation at the Grand Lodge proceedings in 1841 and was rebuffed by Bodley Lodge. However, the authors have found no evidence that this was the case. Specifically, the official proceedings of the Illinois Grand Lodge do not contain such an occurrence.

41. For examples, see Michael W. Homer, "'Similarity of Priesthood in Masonry': The Relationship Between Freemasonry and Mormonism," 27–28; and Robert S. Wicks and Fred R. Foister, *Junius and Joseph: Presidential Politics and the Assassination of the First Mormon Prophet*, 6. Wicks and Foister claim that "Jonas's political campaign succeeded through Mormon support at the polls."

42. Theodore Calvin Pease, ed., *Illinois Election Returns 1818–1848*, 362–63.

43. See Alisa M. Flatow and Adina Anflick, eds., "Guide to the Papers of the Seixas Family, undated, 1746–1911, 1926, 1939."

44. Reg Ankrom, "Once Upon a Time in Quincy: Jonas Was Father of Freemasonry in Illinois."

45. Gayle Kozak [Assistant to the Grand Secretary at the Grand Lodge of F. & A.M. of Ohio], email to Joe Swick III, December 18, 2017.

Nauvoo Lodge Founding Members[1]

Name	Lodge Membership	Dispens.	Charter	12/29/41	12/30/41	1/3/42	1/6/42	1/20/42	2/3/42	2/17/42	3/15/42	3/16/42	3/17/42
Charles Allen	Nova Cesaraea Harmony 2, Cincinnati, OH		X	X	X	X	X	X	X	X	X	X	X
Josiah Arnold			X	X				X	X	X	X	X	X
John C. Bennett	Friendship Lodge 89, Barnesville, OH		X	X	X	X	X	X	X	X	X	X	X
Benjamin Brown	Forest Lodge 263, Pomfret, NY		X				X	X	X	X	X	X	
Ormond Butler												X	
Stephen Chase			X	X	X	X	X				X	X	X
Hiram Clark	Queen of Sheba Lodge, Antwerp, NY		X	X	X	X	X		X	X	X	X	X
Austin Cowles	Friendship Lodge 272, NY			X						X	X		X
William Felshaw	Hoosick, NY (prob. Federal Lodge 33)		X	X	X	X	X	X	X	X	X	X	X
Elijah Fordham	Hiram Lodge 10, New York City, NY		X			X	X	X	X	X	X	X	X
Samuel Henderson	Tyro Lodge 12, Caledonia, MO		X	X	X	X	X	X	X	X	X	X	X
Heber C. Kimball	Milnor Lodge 303, Victor, NY		X	X	X	X	X	X	X		X	X	X
Lyman Leonard	Tioga Lodge 79, Binghamton, NY[2]		X	X	X	X	X		X	X	X	X	X
John E. Mikesell	Blazing Star Lodge 3, VA						X	X		X			
Daniel S. Miles	Morning Dawn Lodge 48, Waterford, VT		X			X					X		
George Miller	Widow's Son Lodge 60, Charlottesville, VA	WM	X	X	X	X							
George Montague	Olive Branch 221 (later 40), Frankfort, NY		X							X	X	X	X
John D. Parker		SW		X									
John Patten	Friendship Lodge 129, S. Bainbridge, NY[3]		X	X	X	X	X			X	X	X
Hezekiah Peck	Friendship Lodge 129, S. Bainbridge, NY		X			X	X	X	X	X	X	X	
Ashael Perry	Augusta Lodge 233, Augusta, NY		X		X	X	X	X	X		X		

Name	Lodge / Affiliation										
David Pettigrew	Nova Cesaraea Harmony 2, Cincinnati, OH				X	X		X		X	X	
Noah Rogers	Morning Star Lodge 83, Mantua, OH	X		X	X	X	X	X	X	X	X	X
Noble Rogers	Morning Star Lodge 83, Mantua, OH	X		X						X	X	X
Samuel Rolfe	Blazing Star Lodge 30, Rumford, ME	X	X	X	X	X	X	X	X	X	X	X
Lucius Scovil	Morning Star Lodge 83, Mantua, OH	JW	X	X	X	X	X	X	X	X	X	X
Hyrum Smith	Mount Moriah Lodge 112, Palmyra, NY	X	X	X	X	X	X	X	X	X	X	X
John Smith	Harmony Lodge 187, NY			X	X				X			
Joshua Smith	Center Star Lodge 11, Granville, OH	X	X	X	X	X	X	X	X	X	X	X
William Vanansdale	Morning Dawn Lodge 7, Gallipolis, OH		X	X	X							
Newel K. Whitney	Meridian Orb Lodge 10, Painesville, OH	X	X		X	X		X		X	X	X
Christopher Williams	Fort George Lodge, Upper Canada	X	X		X	X		X	X	X	X	X
Members present of 32		26	18	19	21	17	15	20	18	26	21	18
[James Cummings]4	Maine Lodge 20, Farmington, ME	X								V5	V	P6
[Alvin C. Graves]7	Harmony Lodge 11, Virginia									V	V	
[Davison Hibbard]8	New England 48, Worthington, OH	X								V	V	P
[Lewis Hyde]	Allegheny Lodge 277, Pembroke, NY											
[Orson Hyde]	Meridian Orb Lodge 10, Painesville, OH											
[Samuel Miles]9	Rainbow, VT (Rainbow 26, Middletown?)									V	V	P
[O. Joseph Rose]10	St. Johns 21, N.Y.	X								V	V	P
[Henry Sherwood]11		X										
[William A. Weston]	Washington Lodge 256, NY											

1. Loosely based on Table 1 in Mervin B. Hogan, "Nauvoo Lodge at Work." Founding members are here identified as those whose names appear in Minute Book 1 as a clearly admitted member of the Lodge by the date of the installation of the Lodge. These members were made Masons in lodges other than Nauvoo. Also included with names in brackets are Nauvoo Mormons who were Masons before October 15, 1841, who may or may not have been admitted as members or attended Nauvoo Lodge meetings before installation. Lodge names and numbers have been revised and updated. 2. Or Binghamton Lodge No. 77 (once No. 79) of New York. 3. Lodge forfeited 3 June 1835, revived as Susquehanna No. 167, 11 Jun 1850. 4. Balloted for and received as member on April 7, 1842. 5. V=Marked as "visitor" in lodge minutes. 6. P=Petition submitted on March 17, 1842. 7. Later belonged to Hiram Lodge No. 7. 8. Balloted for and received as member on April 7, 1842. 9. Balloted for and received as member on April 7, 1842. 10. Balloted for, received as member, and signed the bylaws on April 7, 1842. 11. Balloted for and received as member on April 7, 1842.

1830 to 1834.[46] He then moved to Columbus, Illinois, in 1836—the year Joshua Seixas taught the Mormon schools. When Joseph Smith and his followers came to Illinois in 1839, Jonas may already have known a great deal about them through their association with his brother-in-law.

Jonas was instrumental in reviving Freemasonry following the Morgan affair. In 1841, he was in his eighth term as Grand Master in a second state Grand Lodge and was invested in increasing the membership of the Illinois lodges and expanding their work. The Latter-day Saints provided a likely means for accomplishing this task. With their dispensation firmly in hand from a sympathetic Grand Master, the Nauvoo Masons set about forming their new lodge.

On December 29, 1841, eighteen men met at Hyrum Smith's recently built brick office along the bank of the Mississippi River. Located across from Hyrum's residence on Water Street, it was built as an office wherein he could perform patriarchal blessings as Patriarch of the Church.[47] It subsequently served as a short-term Masonic hall, a high council room, and chambers for the Nauvoo City Council.

The dispensation from Grand Master Jonas was accepted,[48] and although the lodge "was not opened in due form," a slate of officers was nonetheless assembled. George Miller took his place as Worshipful Master, and Lucius Scovil as Junior Warden. Hyrum Smith was elected Senior Warden *pro tem*.[49] Additional officers were John C. Bennett, Secretary; Newel K. Whitney, Treasurer; Charles Allen, Senior Deacon; Heber C. Kimball, Junior Deacon; Hiram Clark and William Felshaw, Stewards; and Samuel Rolfe, Tyler. Eight other men also participated. The following day, the brethren adopted bylaws and scheduled regular meetings for the first and third Thursdays of each month. Before ending their meeting, the Lodge voted to request Grand Master Jonas to attend the official installation of Nauvoo Lodge on March 15, 1842.[50]

During the next few meetings, administrative details were tended to, including determining where each of the new lodge members hailed from. Prior to installation, the members of Nauvoo Lodge included the men listed in the ac-

---

46. Rob Morris, *History of Freemasonry in Kentucky: In Its Relations to the Symbolic Degrees: To Which Are Added, in the Form of Notes and Brief Historical Abstracts, an American Masonic Bibliography*, 447–48. Jonas served as Junior Grand Warden of the Grand Lodge of Kentucky in 1830–31, Senior Grand Warden in 1831–32, Deputy Grand Master in 1832–33, and Grand Master of the Grand Lodge of Kentucky in 1833–34.

47. "The Brethren Are Hereby Notified," 585.

48. "Nauvoo Masonic Lodge, Minute Book 1, 1841–1842," December 29, 1841.

49. Miller and Scovil had been appointed to their positions by Abraham Jonas in the Dispensation. Hyrum Smith was standing in for the absent Senior Warden John D. Parker, who was serving a mission in New Orleans (called October 7, 1841). The minutes state that Hyrum was elected "Junior Warden pro tem," but this is likely an error, since he served as Senior Warden pro tempore, and Scovil served as Junior Warden thereafter.

50. "Nauvoo Masonic Lodge, Minute Book 1, 1841–1842," December 30, 1841.

(Left) The Old Masonic Hall at Springfield, IL. The building was made of brick. The Masonic Hall occupied the upper story, and the only entrance was through the storeroom on the first floor. (Right) Joseph Smith's Red Brick Store. Meetings of the Nauvoo Lodge were held on the upper story.

companying table. By the first regular meeting, Nauvoo Lodge already had more members than any of the other five lodges under the jurisdiction of the Grand Lodge of Illinois.[51]

About the time the petition for a Lodge had been made, Joseph Smith's "Red Brick Store" was under construction with a structure and function very similar to that of the nearby Springfield Masonic Hall where James Adams had been Master. It opened on January 5, 1842, and served as the first regular meeting place for the newly constituted Lodge.

Irregularities in Nauvoo Lodge

In their great enthusiasm to establish the Nauvoo Masonic Lodge and restore apostate Freemasonry, the Mormons skated close to the established "landmarks" of the Craft, a code of ethics held to be ancient and sacrosanct. Violation of these landmarks made a lodge "irregular" and subject to sanction by the Grand Lodge. Grand Master Abraham Jonas gave the Latter-day Saints great leeway, even bypassing some of the accepted standards himself. However, to his dismay, Joseph Smith and the Mormons soon began to break through ice that caused even Jonas to shiver.

---

51. Bodley Lodge No. 1 had 31 members; Harmony Lodge No. 3 had 23; Springfield Lodge No. 4 had 38; Columbus Lodge No. 6 had 17; and Macon Lodge U.D. had 10. See *Reprint of the Proceedings of the Grand Lodge of Illinois*, 29–31. Heber C. Kimball later recalled that the "Lodge was organized on the 15 day of March 1842 with forty members." Heber C. Kimball, *Journals*, April 10, 1845. By October 1842, there were 256 members of Nauvoo Lodge.

While Smith never held an office in Nauvoo Lodge, his directing hand was evident from the very start when he officiated as Grand Chaplain at its installation without having first been initiated as a Mason. *The Masonic Trestleboard*, a guidebook coauthored by Stephen W. B. Carnegy and published the following year to regulate Masonic ritual throughout the United States, indicated that the Grand Chaplain was to precede the formal ceremony of installation with an "oration, or sermon, upon the design and principles of the [Masonic] Institution,"[52] to recite prayers of blessing, and to formally dedicate the lodge.[53] At the installation ceremony on March 15, 1842, Grand Master Jonas opened a Grand Lodge and constituted the new Nauvoo Lodge and installed its officers, with Joseph giving the Grand Chaplain's customary benediction. As the Grand Chaplain is an elected officer of the Grand Lodge, this apparent temporary appointment of a non-Mason was unusual.

Another odd feature of the installation was that the Master of the Lodge, George Miller, was not present; he was instead represented by Asahel Perry, who was acting as Master "pro tempore." The Nauvoo Lodge minutes are silent as to whether Perry was invested with the jewel of the Master's office and given a vicarious charge in behalf of Miller, as was the customary practice when installing the Master of a lodge.

Jonas continued to privilege Smith and his first counselor Sidney Rigdon by authorizing their immediate reception of the three degrees of Masonry.[54] Smith and Rigdon were initiated as Entered Apprentices that evening, March 15, 1842. The next day, they were passed as Fellowcrafts in the morning and raised as Master Masons separately in the afternoon and evening with no Master or acting Master of the Lodge present.[55] Miller was absent as before, and so was

---

52. Charles W. Moore and S. W. B. Carnegy, *The Masonic Trestleboard, Adapted to the National System of Work and Lectures, as Revised and Perfected by the United States Masonic Convention at Baltimore, MD, A.L. 5843*, 51.

53. Moore and Carnegy, 53.

54. "Know all ye brethren to whom come these presents, that I, Abraham Jonas, Grand Master of the Grand Lodge of the State of Illinois, in virtue of the power and authority in me vested as Grand Master aforesaid do hereby by these letters of Dispensation, authorize the Brethren of Nauvoo Lodge under dispensation, to receive the petitions of Joseph Smith and Sidney Rigdon, and act on the same instanter—and should the ballot be unanimous, in favor of said Smith and Rigdon, at a full meeting of said Nauvoo Lodge—then, in that case, the said Lodge is authorized to confer the three several degrees of Ancient York Masonry on the said Joseph Smith and Sidney Rigdon, as speedily as the nature of the case will admit—Provided, however, that nothing herein contained shall be deemed as authority by the said Nauvoo Lodge for violating any of the Ancient land marks of the order, or of acting contrary to the provisions of their by-laws except in the case herein authorized. Given under my hand as Grand Master, the day and date above named—A. Jonas G.M.G.L. Ill." See "Nauvoo Masonic Lodge, Minute Book 1, 1841-1842," March 15, 1842.

55. William Law, the second counselor in the First Presidency, was initiated, passed and raised six weeks later, on April 25–27, 1842.

Perry. The minutes do not show that anyone was chosen to act as Master pro tempore. Jonas may have felt that his presence precluded the need for a Worshipful Master, but since this was a lodge meeting and a Grand Lodge had not been opened on this day, there should have been an acting Master at hand.[56]

Smith and Rigdon were forwarded through the three degrees of Masonry in the space of two days without passing the usual time of about a month between degrees to develop the necessary proficiency. Many writers have considered this the first example of making Masons "at sight" in the state of Illinois.[57] However, the Masonic protocol for making a Mason at sight does not technically accord with the actions taken by Jonas in the initiation, passing, and raising of Smith and Rigdon.[58] Although in both cases the degrees are awarded by the authority of the Grand Master and the normal space between degrees is forgone, there are specific differences between the two. Both Smith and Rigdon submitted petitions and were balloted for, which is not necessary when being made a Mason at sight. Additionally, Jonas did not convene an "occasional lodge," another requirement when making Masons at sight.[59] Jonas's actions caused Bodley Lodge to call for an investigation. During a special meeting held on July 15, 1842, to consider charges against Nauvoo Lodge, they resolved:

That Bodley Lodge No. 1, of Quincy, request of the Grand Lodge of the State of Illinois, that a committee be appointed at the next meeting of said Lodge, to make inquiry into the manner the officers of Nauvoo Lodge U.D., were installed by the Grand Master of this State, and by what authority the Grand Master initiated, passed

---

56. In the Master Mason degree, the Master of the Lodge represents King Solomon. Jonas would have had to play this part, or at least assign someone else to do it if no one was acting as Worshipful Master.

57. Mervin B. Hogan, *The Founding Minutes of Nauvoo Lodge U.D.*, 1; Wicks and Foister, *Junius and Joseph*, 6; Carr, *Freemasonry and Nauvoo*, 13.

58. The expression is found at least as early as 1757, but it describes an action taken much earlier and found in the Ancient Constitutions where it is termed "making masons in an occasional lodge." The practice has been recorded in some form as early as 1731. It was officially authorized in Pennsylvania in 1825 but continued to be controversial throughout the United States. See Albert Gallatin Mackey, William James Hughan, and Edward L. Hawkins, *An Encyclopaedia of Freemasonry and its Kindred Sciences, Comprising the Whole Range of Arts, Sciences and Literature as Connected with the Institution*, 2:688–90.

59. In 1858 Albert Mackey defined twenty-five landmarks of Freemasonry, number 8 of which delineated making a Mason at sight: "The real mode and the only mode of exercising the prerogative is this: The Grand Master summons to his assistance not less than six other Freemasons, convenes a Lodge, and without any previous probation, but on sight of the candidate, confers the degrees upon him, after which he dissolves the Lodge, and dismisses the brethren. Lodges that thus convened for special purposes are called 'Occasional Lodges.' This is the only way in which any Grand Master within the records of the Institution has ever been known to 'make a Mason at sight.' The prerogative is dependent upon that of granting Dispensations to open and hold Lodges." Albert Gallatin Mackey, *A Text Book of Masonic Jurisprudence; Illustrating the Written and Unwritten Laws of Freemasonry*, 24.

and raised Messers Smith and Rigdon to the degree of Entered Apprentice, Fellow Craft and Master Mason, at one and the same time.[60]

Despite receiving the degrees so quickly, the Nauvoo Lodge minutes indicate that after their initiation, Smith's and Rigdon's "proficiency in the preceding degree was vouched for after which they were balloted for, the ballot found clear, and they duly received and passed to the degree of a Fellow Craft Mason."[61] Horace Cummings, the grandson of one of the founding members of Nauvoo Lodge, James Cummings, verified this while recounting his grandfather's personal stories of the Prophet. He writes that the elder Cummings was "quite intimate with the Prophet Joseph" and "being a Master Mason, officiated in conducting the Prophet thru all the degrees of Masonry," and that "the Prophet explained many things about the rites that even Masons do not pretend to understand but which he made most clear and beautiful."[62] In another account, he writes that Smith seemed "to under stand some of the features of the ceremonies better than any Mason and that he made explanations that rendered the rites more beautiful and full of meaning."[63]

After becoming a Master Mason, Smith quickly became involved in the lodge rituals. On April 13, 1842, less than one month after his formal initiation, his daily history indicates that he "introduced Mssrs. [Jacob] Backenstos, [George M.] Stiles, and [Chauncey] Robinson into the Lodge Room in the morning, and Samuel H. Smith, William Smith, and Vinson Knight in the evening."[64]

Comparison of this information with the Nauvoo Lodge record demonstrates that Smith was present that same day for conferral of all three degrees of Ancient York Masonry, the first three men being initiated Entered Apprentices and the last three being raised as Master Masons.[65] For Smith to say he "introduced" these men into the lodge room was Masonic parlance indicating he performed the ritually intensive role of Senior Deacon.[66] Playing a significant part in the new lodge, Smith was present at seventeen meetings of Nauvoo Lodge U.D. during its first three months of existence and a total of twenty-two meetings in 1842.

Acting as secretary of Bodley Lodge No. 1 in Quincy, Horace Cooley read an interesting letter to the nine brethren present at their May 2, 1842, meeting. The Masons at the recently constituted Lodge in Nauvoo had invited Bodley Lodge to join them in celebrating St. John's Day on June 24. Their letter, however, also contained distressing irregularities. The invitation was under the auspices of the LDS

60. Turnbull, *Rise and Progress of Freemasonry*, 130.

61. "Nauvoo Masonic Lodge, Minute Book 1, 1841–1842," March 16, 1842.

62. Horace H. Cummings, "True Stories from My Journal," 441.

63. Horace H. Cummings, "History of Horace Cummings," quoted in Kenneth W. Godfrey, "Causes of Mormon Non-Mormon Conflict in Hancock County, Illinois, 1839–1846," 86.

64. "History, 1838–1856, volume C-1 [2 November 1838–31 July 1842]," 1320.

65. "Nauvoo Masonic Lodge, Minute Book 1, 1841–1842," April 13, 1842.

66. David Bernard, *Light on Masonry: A Collection of All the Most Important Documents on the Subject of Speculative Free Masonry*, 17–26.

First Presidency, a religious organization not affiliated with Freemasonry. Attached to the letter were "sundry hieroglyphics," words that in Masonry signified material in a Royal Arch cipher. To the Bodley Lodge brethren, it must have seemed presumptuous for a Blue Lodge Mason to use a such a code when neither he nor the group of brethren he was addressing had attained the Royal Arch degree.

The brother secretary was instructed to respond coolly to the Nauvoo Lodge while "declining to accept of the invitation, on account of the great distance, and of our present pecuniary exigencies." Nauvoo Lodge was primly reprimanded and warned that the prestigious Bodley Lodge No. 1 "regrets that anything extraneous from pure masonry should be coupled with this communication, it having been, throughout all ages, the peculiar characteristic of Masonry, that she has sent forth her pure flame of living light, before the world, uncontaminated by Political dogmas, and untinged by Religious distinctions."[67] Bodley Lodge brothers bristled that this exchange from one lodge to another was tainted by Mormon as well as Royal Arch embellishments.

In addition to this communication to Bodley Lodge, Nauvoo Lodge committed several other indiscretions during its first few months of operation. When Abraham Jonas attended the installation of Nauvoo Lodge, he noticed several glaring irregularities in the record book, kept in the legible hand of John C. Bennett. On December 30, 1841, and February 3 and 17, 1842—all dates that occurred before the official installation—Nauvoo Lodge had accepted petitions for membership into the Masonic order. The petition was, and remains, a specific process that Freemasons undertake to become members. Petitioners submit a written application to the Lodge along with recommendations of current members of the Lodge in good standing. Next, an investigative committee conducts a background check and issues a report. Finally, Lodge members vote for each individual by secret ballot.[68] Not only had Nauvoo Lodge accepted a total of fifty-seven petitions, they had also accepted members who were already Masons and collected dues. They also balloted for forty-one men, likely en masse rather than on individual ballots, on February 3 and one additional applicant on February 17, 1841. Not only should these actions have taken place after the Lodge was officially constituted and bylaws accepted, but United States Freemasonry required balloting to be unanimous—one vote against a petitioner would disqualify him for membership.[69] By balloting en masse, the Nauvoo Lodge circumvented this requirement but was later censured by the Grand Lodge of Illinois for balloting on more than one applicant at a time. Additionally, the Lodge had received an individual of doubtful character on a promise of reformation and restitution,

---

67. Minutes of Bodley Lodge No. 1, May 2, A.L. 5842.

68. "[A candidate] must undergo a ballot, and he must be unanimously elected." Mackey, *A Text Book of Masonic Jurisprudence*, 317.

69. Henry Wilson Coil, *Coil's Masonic Encyclopedia*, 87a.

"with the view of holding his future conduct in check and making him a worthier and better man."[70]

Mervin Hogan has conjectured that at the time of dispensation, Jonas encouraged prospective officers of the lodge "to set to work directly and receive petitions for the degrees of Masonry from all the men in the vicinity who had an interest in becoming Masons."[71] Then, realizing the founding minute book could become a source of trouble for the new lodge, Jonas "directed Nauvoo Lodge to immediately secure a new minute book and rewrite the Minutes to show that no petition was received by the Lodge prior to the March 17 meeting."[72]

John C. Bennett's minutes have been designated by Hogan as the "Founding Minutes" and by other historians as "Minute Book 1." The forty-four pages consist of a copy of the dispensation given by Jonas, the Nauvoo Lodge bylaws, and minutes of meetings held from December 29, 1841, to May 6, 1842, all written in Bennett's hand.[73] One double-sided page of signatures to the bylaws is also included. The signers were Masons who were joining the new lodge as well as those who were made Masons there.

A second minute book was begun sometime before May 6, 1842, possibly at the suggestion of Jonas. These minutes, called the "Official Minutes" or "Minute Book 2," were written mostly by William Clayton, one of Joseph Smith's clerks.[74] They contain a copy of the dispensation, bylaws, and Bennett's minutes to May 6, 1842. The minutes are then continued in more than five hundred additional pages covering the dates of December 29, 1841, to September 15, 1845. This record includes sixteen pages of signatures of members of the Lodge.

After Bennett was expelled from the Lodge for egregious behavior, Minute Book 1 was retained by Nauvoo Lodge. Its pages were removed from their binding, along with the double-sided page of signatures. The signature page, which appears to come from the same book as the minutes, is currently placed after the entry for April 16, 1842. However, the tear does not match with its neighboring pages, indicating that the signatures were originally in a different place in the book. This signature page seems to have been replicated from an earlier one. One hundred twenty-three of the signatures are original holographs, but the remaining thirty-two signatures were written in the hand of one scribe, ending with Parley P. Pratt's name placed vertically between the two columns with the notation "and about 250 others not written down on this list."[75] It is assumed that

---

70. *Reprint of the Proceedings of the Grand Lodge of Illinois*, 71.

71. Mervin B. Hogan, *The Official Minutes of Nauvoo Lodge, U.D.*, 3.

72. Hogan, 4.

73. Although Bennett attended meetings until June 16, 1842, when he was expelled from the Lodge, the last time he took minutes was May 6 of that year. After that date, he was being investigated for numerous improprieties.

74. John A. Forgeus, Thomas Bullock, and Hosea Stout also made minute entries in Minute Book 2.

75. "Nauvoo Masonic Lodge minutes, 1841–1846."

Front and back of loose signature page in Nauvoo Lodge Minute Book 1. Courtesy of the Church History Library, The Church of Jesus Christ of Latter-day Saints.

the two hundred and fifty remaining signatures appeared on the original register. The pages of Minute Book 1 were folded in half and placed in the cornerstone of the Nauvoo Masonic Hall during the cornerstone ceremony of June 24, 1843. The contents of the cornerstone were unpublished and became lost to common knowledge. In 1954, Wilford Wood obtained the title to the old Masonic hall and the cornerstone was excavated. The minutes were found within, along with an extract from Joseph Smith's history, proceedings of the 1842 communication of the Grand Lodge of Illinois, and facsimiles from the Book of Abraham and the Kinderhook Plates. The pages from Minute Book 1 are now located in the LDS Church Archives with a copy held by the Grand Lodge of Illinois.

Not two months after the installation of the Lodge, persistent rumors and suspicion toward Bennett necessitated immediate action. Allegations of his misbehaviors before arriving in Nauvoo, and his indiscretions while in the city, were numerous. The Lodge met before dawn on Saturday, May 7, 1842, by special notice from the Worshipful Master, George Miller. Every officer was present, and Willard Richards served as secretary *pro tempore*. It was the first time since December 29, 1841, that Bennett did not keep the minutes, having reliably attended each and every one of the sixty-two meetings that heretofore had been held. A communication dated May 4 from Grand Master Jonas was read with a report that complaints had been made that Bennett had been expelled from a former lodge.[76]

---

76. Abraham Jonas, letter to George Miller, May 4, 1842.

Bennett, known in Nauvoo as a bachelor, was also alleged to have deserted a wife in Ohio. These accusations set off a furor in Nauvoo that resulted in Bennett's appearance before the High Council and being disfellowshipped from the Church.[77] Formal charges were filed in Nauvoo Lodge by Thomas Grover on May 19, which the brothers set about to investigate. [78] Because Bennett presented glowing letters of recommendation from his previous lodge, Nauvoo Lodge waited for a response from Pickaway Lodge, from which Bennett was said to have been expelled. Though Bennett was a rogue in many ways, he had indeed been honorably demitted from Pickaway Lodge.[79] Before word could be received, however, the uproar proved too much. Bennett was excommunicated from the Church on June 18 and publicly denounced by Joseph Smith for his miscreant behavior. Soon after, on July 7, 1842, Nauvoo Lodge resolved to strike Bennett's name from its rolls, the purported expulsion from Pickaway serving as justification.[80]

Doubtless the men of Nauvoo Lodge felt that they had given Bennett every chance to prove his innocence. Concerning such difficult matters among Freemasons, Masonic scholar William Preston wrote in his textbook *Illustrations of Masonry*:

> But if some do transgress, no wise man will thence argue against the institution, or condemn the whole fraternity for the errors of a few individuals. . . . Those who violate the laws, or infringe on good order, are kindly admonished by secret monitors; and when these have not the intended effect, public reprehension becomes necessary; at last, when every mild endeavour to effect a reformation is of no avail, they are expelled the Lodge, as unfit members of the society.[81]

---

77. For a detailed account of this process, see Homer, *Joseph's Temples*, 151–58.

78. "The W. M. then read the following charges preferred against Dr. John C. Bennett by Thomas Grover, to wit: 'that Dr. John C. Bennett has palmed himself upon the Masonic Brethren in the organization of Nauvoo Lodge U.D. as a regular mason in good standing, when I have reason to believe that he is an expelled mason from a lodge in Fairfield Ohio, or from Fairfield lodge Ohio.' signed 'Thomas Grover.' On motion, it was resolved that Dr. John C. Bennett be cited to appear before Nauvoo Lodge U.D. on the first Thursday in June next at 6 o clock P.M. to answer to the above charges." See "Nauvoo Masonic Lodge minutes, 1841–1846," May 19, 1842.

79. See the minutes of Pickaway Lodge, which confirm Bennett's membership from October 22, 1828, to August 12, 1829, and his service as Senior Deacon. He left in good standing and with a diploma recommending him to his new lodge (Friendship No. 89 in Barnesville, Ohio). Years later, George A. Patterson, a Protestant minister and past Grand Chaplain for the Grand Lodge of Ohio, filed charges against Bennett in Pickaway Lodge. They included "lying, selling diplomas, submitting petitions to the legislature with forged signatures, 'gambling and preaching,' submitting false plats, and falsely professing to be an officer of the U.S. army." The charges were never investigated, "presumably because Bennett was no longer a member." *History of Pickaway Lodge No. 23 Free and Accepted Masons*, 60. See also Mervin B. Hogan, "John Cook Bennett and Pickaway Lodge No. 23," 7–12.

80. "Nauvoo Masonic Lodge minutes, 1841–1846," July 7, 1842.

81. William Preston, *Illustrations of Masonry*, 18–19.

It seemed that such a procedure was followed, but Jonas was not satisfied. He instructed the Lodge that whether or not Bennett had previously been expelled it was their "duty to expel him for his conduct here [in Illinois]."[82] On August 8, another resolution was passed to expel Bennett from the Lodge for the charges of seduction, adultery, lying, perjury, embezzlement, and illicit intercourse with a Master Mason's wife.[83]

Throughout this process, Bennett was inflamed with fury over what he saw as unfair treatment by the Church, the city government, and the Lodge. Determined to settle the score, he penned a series of letters to the *Sangamo Journal*, several of which included accusations against the Masonic fraternity at Nauvoo. These attacks were specifically intended to "expose [Joseph Smith's] actings and doings in Nauvoo Lodge, U. D.," since Bennett claimed that the actions taken in Nauvoo Lodge were done "under the Supervision of Joe and his servile priest, George Miller—the little creature that does Joe's dirty work."[84] Bennett reported that in Nauvoo Lodge:

- Smith and five others were initiated, passed, and raised through the three Masonic degrees prior to its official installation by Abraham Jonas on March 15, 1842. After the Lodge was installed, Smith and four of those five were again advanced through the various degrees.[85]
- The Lodge's original minute book had been "sealed up, and a new one commenced,—the second was sealed up, and a third commenced,—and then a new record book procured" into which only the parts that they were willing to report to the Grand Lodge were copied.[86]

---

82. "Nauvoo Masonic Lodge minutes, 1841-1846," August 4, 1842.

83. At the request of Grand Master Jonas, Bennett was tried in the Nauvoo Lodge for the following grave charges: "1st Seduction. For seducing certain previously respectable females of our city by using Joseph Smith's name as one who sanctioned such conduct. 2nd Adultery. For illicit intercourse with various females frequently. 3rd Lying. In using Joseph Smith's name as before stated, saying that said Smith taught and practiced illicit intercourse with women, he knowing it to be false. 4th Perjury. In swearing that he was under duress when he made a certain affidavit before Esq. Wells when it is well known he never was under restraint or confinement at all while in this city. 5th Embezzlement. For making use of money belonging to the lodge without either knowledge or consent of said lodge. 6th For illicit intercourse with a Master Mason's wife." It was consequently "Resolved, That John C. Bennett be expelled from this [Nauvoo] Lodge and from all the privileges of Masonry." See "Nauvoo Masonic Lodge minutes, 1841–1846," August 8, 1842.

84. John C. Bennett, "General Bennett's Third Letter, July 4, 1842," 2.

85. John C. Bennett, "Astounding Disclosures! Letters from Gen. Bennett: For the Sangamo Journal, June 27, 1842," 2. These five were identified in Bennett's third letter as Job Snyder [John Snider], Brigham Young, Peter Haws, Willard Richards, and Adara [Amasa] Lyman. Bennett, "General Bennett's Third Letter," 2.

86. Bennett, "General Bennett's Third Letter," 2. Two minute books have been located with considerable changes made to Minute Book 2. Additional minute books have not been discovered.

- The suspension of a Mr. Stoddard "for blackballing Mr. Sessions" never appeared upon record.[87]
- A complaint from Henry G. Sherwood and Samuel H. Smith against Robert D. Foster never appeared upon record.[88]
- The Old Record was ante-dated and interlined to conceal irregularities.[89]
- Sixty-three men were balloted for in one ballot.[90]
- Three candidates were entered, three passed, and four raised, in one day, and the records made to appear as though only three were raised by antedating one.[91]
- A Mr. Hollister of Hannibal presented a petition and was entered, passed, and raised at Nauvoo, after visiting there only six or seven days.[92]
- Joseph Smith was making his own degrees.[93]

---

87. Bennett, 2. This incident does not appear in either Minute Book 1 or Minute Book 2. Further details are unknown.

88. Bennett, 2. Willard Richards reported in Joseph Smith's journal that Samuel H. Smith preferred charges against Foster for speaking "abusive language" toward him and for "abusing" Henry G. Sherwood. According to Richards, "The Masonic Breth[r]en met at 1 o clock P.M.," on May 20, 1842, "when the charges were substantatd[.] confession made by Foster. forgiveness granted. Joseph speaking at considerable length. to accomplish the decision." This incident was not reported in the Lodge minute book. See "Journal, December 1841–December 1842," The Joseph Smith Papers, 123; and Winslow, "Irregularities in the Work of Nauvoo Lodge," 71n74.

89. John C. Bennett, "Gen. Bennett's 4th Letter, July 15, 1842," 2. This charge has been substantiated. See examples of changes in Winslow, "Irregularities in the Work of Nauvoo Lodge," 72–76.

90. Bennett, "Gen. Bennett's 4th Letter," 2. Balloting for numerous applicants at a time occurred on February 3, 1842. The entire entry was omitted when Minute Book 1 was copied into Minute Book 2. However, Bennett's charge that the membership of the lodge voted on the petitions of sixty men that day is exaggerated. Minute Book 1 shows that the lodge membership voted on forty-one petitions on February 3. See Winslow, "Irregularities in the Work of Nauvoo Lodge," 70. Interestingly, there were fifty-eight men who petitioned the Lodge for membership prior to its official installation, another breach of Masonic protocol.

91. Bennett "Gen. Bennett's 4th Letter," 2. During Nauvoo Lodge's three gatherings on April 13, 1842, Minute Book 1 and Minute Book 2 show that the lodge brethren initiated three, passed three, and raised four. Neither record, however, shows any indication that one of the four raisings was antedated.

92. Bennett, 2. The record supports Bennett's claim as to David S. Hollister, who, along with Willard Richards and Brigham Young, was balloted for and made an Entered Apprentice on April 7th, passed to the degree of Fellowcraft on April 8th, and was raised a Master Mason on April 9th. Joseph Smith was present for the first and third degrees, while Worshipful Master George Miller was absent throughout. See "Nauvoo Masonic Lodge minutes, 1841–1846," April 7–9, 1842.

93. Bennett, "Astounding Disclosures!" 2; Bennett, "General Bennett's Third Letter," 2. Presumably Bennett was referring here to Smith's creation of the endowment ceremonies.

- Nauvoo Lodge did not deliver their minutes as required in the bylaws of the Grand Lodge.[94]

Bennett's claims in the *Sangamo Journal* have been thoroughly examined by researcher Brady Winslow, building on the work done by Andrew Smith in his biography of Bennett.[95] The available minute books demonstrate many of Bennett's accusations concerning Freemasonry were either completely justified or true but mildly exaggerated. Two exceptions are notable: his accusation that Joseph Smith and others were made Masons before the installation of the Lodge and his description of four separate copies of the Nauvoo Lodge minutes.

Because many of Bennett's other allegations in the *Sangamo Journal* (and his later book-length treatment of Mormonism, *History of the Saints, or, An Expose of Joe Smith and Mormonism*) were dramatic and overblown, those pertaining to Freemasonry have tended to be dismissed as well. But there is some evidence to show that they may indeed be accurate. Bennett's letter suggests that three copies of the minutes had been made in the original book, each containing his handwriting. A "new" book was procured in which William Clayton and others wrote the official, altered version. Bennett boldly insisted that "the original book be produced" to support his claims. The new book, he explained, had only his signature in it, but if a record could be produced that "has any of my hand writing in it," he could "show all the facts, unless the leaves have been torn out."[96] The leaves were in fact torn or cut out of the book.[97]

---

94. "Your Committee regret that the original records of said Lodge have not been sent up as was required by the M.W.G. Master in his order suspending the labor of said Lodge." *Reprint of the Proceedings of the Grand Lodge of Illinois*, 35, 58.

95. See Winslow, "Irregularities in the Work of Nauvoo Lodge," 69–79; and Andrew F. Smith, *The Saintly Scoundrel: The Life and Times of Dr. John Cook Bennett*, 98–103.

96. Bennett, "General Bennett's Third Letter," 2. Bennett had the Mormon Masons over a barrel. They could not produce the minute book in Bennett's handwriting with the irregularities, nor the one in Clayton's handwriting with the changes. See Winslow, "Irregularities in the Work of Nauvoo Lodge," 69. There was enough inconsistency with what the Mormons were doing in Nauvoo that Bennett's claims had legitimacy.

97. What is known today as "Minute Book 1" could possibly be a second draft of the minutes. One reason for believing they were copied is that under the entry for Wednesday, March 16, 1842, at 9 a.m., the word "meeting" is found once at the end of a line and again at the beginning of the next line. This dittography is described in textual criticism as a copyist's accidental mistake of repeating a letter, word, or phrase in a document they are duplicating. It does not tend to happen when a scribe is making an original record. Another anomaly found in this record was that the bylaws end with an "orphan" line carried over onto the next page which reads "by giving one month's previous notice, at a stated meeting." Normally, space would be left here after the bylaws for the members to sign. But in this version, the record continues with a list of people who petitioned the lodge for membership that day. The list of members signing the bylaws that is included later contains the same orphan line at the top, only using a different ink. This indicates that the signature page may have been torn from another copy of the minutes.

As most nineteenth-century Masons considered Freemasonry an ancient institution, they held their landmarks sacred and worthy of preservation.[98] Their
leaders attempted to keep these landmarks inviolate and regarded the slightest
change with suspicion. Writer Cecil McGavin captured the dynamics of Latter-
day Saint Masonry in Illinois:

> The Mormons were careless in some respects, failing to realize the sanctity of the "an-
> cient landmarks" and feeling free to make small innovations without consulting the
> Grand Lodge. Such a step, though not intended to trample underfoot the honored
> customs of the past, was perfectly natural for them. Their religion was a revolution-
> ary one. They never attempted to follow the religious pattern of the world, being free
> to introduce many teachings and institutions that were not practiced in any other
> church. This spirit of freedom and newness of growth with no attempt to follow the
> theological path of the past, may have influenced them to deviate from the ancient
> landmarks of Masonry.[99]

McGavin's remarks throw a charitable cloak over his nineteenth-century
religious forebears. It could equally be said of Latter-day Saints that they were in-
sensitive to the feelings of their "Gentile" neighbors, emboldened by their belief
that their religion was led by a prophetic voice. In doing so, they made radical
departures in both ritual and practice of the Craft that were important to their
Masonic brethren.

A Restored Lodge in the Ancient Order

Masonry has long been recognized as part of the secular social transformation in America. Joseph Smith, however, employed its tradition for the purpose
of religious transformation. The dissident John Bennett on the one hand and
the austere members of Bodley Lodge on the other saw Smith as irresponsibly
creating his own ritual, while he and his followers rejoiced in the restoration of a
priesthood that had gone astray. As seen from a Masonic legendary standpoint,
Smith was bringing back the perfect vision of an ancient order of things for the
first time in modern days. To his followers, the heavenly order was being reflected on earth through the institutions he was restoring. Even Bennett recognized
Smith's intent to bring together celestial and terrestrial power into a utopian
society when he accused the Mormon Prophet of founding an "Order Lodge."[100]

---

98. Landmarks are a set of universal principles, language, and laws governing Freemasonry.
99. E. Cecil McGavin, *Mormonism and Masonry*, 104–5.
100. John C. Bennett, *History of the Saints, or, An Expose of Joe Smith and Mormonism*, 272–78.

CHAPTER 12

KEEPING A SECRET:
THE ORGANIZATION OF
THE FEMALE RELIEF SOCIETY

*Let them therefore revive the lodges for women which undoubtedly existed in
the most ancient times with their appropriate ritual and ceremonial, which
women themselves must re-discover or devise. Such appropriate ritual and
ceremonial, if these are to be parallel and complementary to Freemasonry,
must be based upon the highest principles, the noblest moral teachings and
be applicable to woman's true development as those of Freemasonry are to
man's. Let them prove their organization, as Freemasonry has been proved,
to be a beneficent power in the life of the world.*
—Bro. Joseph H. Fussel, in *The Builder*, August 1921

Beyond fostering a Masonic renaissance in Nauvoo, Joseph Smith also designed Mormon counterparts of Masonic institutions. At the same time
that Freemasonry was coalescing in Nauvoo, plans were being made for
a Ladies' Society.[1] Sarah M. Kimball, Margaret Cook, and some neighbors first
devised a plan to form a Ladies' Society in 1842. They enlisted the talented writer
Eliza R. Snow to write a constitution and bylaws for a society of women desiring to
combine means and labor to assist in the building of the temple and other charitable works. After completing the document, Snow reportedly read it to Smith, who
praised her efforts but had a different order in mind for the women of the Church.
He directed Snow to invite the sisters to "meet me and a few of the brethren in
the Masonic Hall over my store next Thursday afternoon, and I will organize the
sisters under the priesthood after the pattern of the priesthood."[2] He thus adopted
the impulse of the sisters to assist with the building of the temple and gave them
"something better,"[3] expanding it to include the concerns of Freemasonry.

Masonic Origins and Forms in the New Society

On Thursday, March 17, 1842, twenty women and three men convened
in the same makeshift "Masonic Hall" where Joseph had been raised a Master

---

1. This chapter is adapted from Cheryl L. Bruno, "Keeping a Secret: Freemasonry,
Polygamy, and the Nauvoo Relief Society, 1842–44," 158–81.

2. Augusta Joyce Crocheron, *Representative Women of Deseret: A Book of Biographical
Sketches to Accompany the Picture Bearing the Same Title*, 27.

3. Relief Society Record, 1880–1892, 29.

Mason the previous day.[4] Evidence of the proceedings of that Masonic meeting lay in plain sight—an opened Bible with a scrap of paper upon which was penned a Masonic prayer.[5] No explanation has been given as to why the Bible lay open at the start of the sisters' meeting; however, such a thing would be expected in a Masonic event. Part of the "furniture" of a Masonic Lodge,[6] a copy of the Bible sits in an opened position upon the altar at each meeting and is called the Great Light of Masonry or the Volume of Sacred Law. No lodge in any regular Masonic jurisdiction may perform work or labor unless the Bible is open and the Square and Compasses are resting upon it. Likewise, the Bible is always closed when the Lodge is closed.

The Masonic prayer on that scrap of paper was deemed relevant to the aims of the proposed women's society. It was copied as a frontispiece in a blank book that Willard Richards presented to the ladies to use for the purpose of keeping minutes:

> O, Lord! help our widows, and fatherless
> children! So mote it be. Amen. With
> the sword, and the word of truth, defend
> thou them. So mote it be. Amen.[7]

As noted in Chapter 7, "So mote it be" was a signal Masonic phrase derived from the Masonic gothic constitutions.[8] No other organization at the time of Joseph Smith is known to have used the words. Similarly, "the widows and the fatherless" refers to a specific responsibility of Freemasons.[9] The sword and the word of truth were also common in Masonic usage.

As with many of the other early auxiliaries of the Church, Joseph Smith experimented with Masonic forms in several aspects of this new Society. The March 17 women's meeting was an installation with three men in charge: Smith

---

4. This upper room in Joseph's Red Brick Store was used as a Lodge room before the Masonic Temple (later "Cultural Hall") was built.

5. "Nauvoo Relief Society Minute Book," The Joseph Smith Papers, 4.

6. "Furniture" in this case meaning "physical items necessary for a Lodge to open and work."

7. "Nauvoo Relief Society Minute Book," 4. An example of a contemporary Masonic prayer is found in the Closing Lecture of the Entered Apprentice degree: "May the blessing of Heaven rest upon us, and all regular Masons, may brotherly love prevail, and every moral and social virtue cement us. So mote it be. Amen." Jabez Richardson, *Richardson's Monitor of Free-Masonry*, 18.

8. "A Poem of Moral Duties," or the Regius poem, was written for stonemasons in 1390 and is the oldest identifiable speculative Masonic document. The closing words of the poem are: "Amen! amen! so mote it be, Say we so all per charity." Quoted in James Orchard Halliwell, *The Early History of Freemasonry in England*, 38; spelling updated.

9. "In the opening of the Lodge is mention of the widowed and the fatherless, that we may never forget a Mason's duty to those whose natural protector is no more." See "Masonry in the Great Light."

appointed John Taylor as chair and Willard Richards as secretary.[10] This organizational form echoed the Masonic type, followed since Lodge meetings in the 1700s, of being held under a presidency of three.[11] This three-fold leadership was employed throughout Mormonism's organizational structure and would be used in the Relief Society with the ordinations of Emma Smith as President, Sarah M. Cleveland as First Counselor, and Elizabeth Ann Whitney as Second Counselor.[12]

After an opening song, the first order of business was to take a vote "to know if all are satisfied with each female present: and are willing to acknowledge them in full fellowship, and admit them to the privileges of the Institution about to be formed."[13] Throughout 1842 and 1843, Mormon women of the community were recommended for membership and then investigated to see if they were of good moral character.[14] Next, a vote was taken to assure that all were in agreement that the proposed members of the Society were respectable, virtuous, and trustworthy. In essence, the Relief Society was petitioning and balloting for membership.

In order to distinguish the new group from other women's organizations of the day, Emma rejected the proposed name "Female Benevolent Society" and instead chose "Relief" Society, which connected it further with Freemasonry. The three principal tenets of Masonry are Brotherly Love, Relief, and Truth. Here she used "Relief" in the title to show the emphasis of the Society.

In the early meetings of the Relief Society, Joseph Smith taught the sisters how to build up their organization in an acceptable manner and observe its rules. Each candidate should be closely examined, and they should not go too fast in adding members. The Society should "grow up by degrees,"[15] he said, echoing the language used to instruct a Fellowcraft that Masonry is a progressive system of morality taught by degrees.[16] Likewise, Smith used Masonic language when he directed that

10. In Masonic adoptive rites, it is required that men be present at any meeting. This was the case for the Relief Society at its organization and the first year of its existence. The men Joseph Smith brought with him to assist did not become Freemasons until several weeks following the meeting, but both men held the Priesthood. Willard Richards was Smith's personal secretary, and John Taylor's wife was present at the Society's organization.

11. James Burton Robertson, *Lectures on Some Subjects of Modern History and Biography*, 425.

12. "[Joseph Smith] propos'd that the Sisters elect a presiding officer to preside over them, and let that presiding officer choose two Counsellors to assist in the duties of her Office— that he would ordain them to preside over the Society— and let them preside just as the Presidency preside over the church." See "Nauvoo Relief Society Minute Book," 7–8 (March 17, 1842).

13. "Nauvoo Relief Society Minute Book," 6 (March 17, 1842).

14. Eliza R. Snow, "The Female Relief Society: A Brief Sketch of Its Organization and Workings in the City of Nauvoo, Hancock, CO., Ill.," 10.

15. "Nauvoo Relief Society Minute Book," 22 (March 30, 1842).

16. See, for example, Daniel Sickels, *The General Ahiman Rezon and Freemason's Guide*, 116.

the Society should "move according to the ancient Priesthood" and explained that he was going to "make of this Society a kingdom of priests, as in Enoch's day."[17]

By the eleventh meeting of the Relief Society, three months after its founding, Joseph Smith was still instructing the women that no person should be admitted to their ranks without "presenting regular petitions signed by two or three members in good standing."[18] But since the Nauvoo Masonic Lodge was initiating, passing, and raising Masons at a prodigious rate, he was no longer concerned about how fast the Society increased, as long as they were virtuous and not using the Society as a shelter for their iniquity.[19] In the Relief Society as well as in the Nauvoo Lodge, balloting procedure was not always strictly observed, but the Prophet often came before the Society to intervene.[20]

Precedents for Women in Freemasonry

Contrary to claims otherwise, Joseph Smith's organization of a women's society founded upon principles of priesthood and Freemasonry was not completely original.[21] In the 1790s, Hannah Mather Crocker, daughter of the well-known ministerial Mather family of Massachusetts, formed "a regular lodge" that claimed to be "founded on the original principles of true ancient masonry, so far as was consistent for the female character." Developed from a nucleus of several women studying ancient languages, the women's lodge received encouragement by a few Masons in good standing but "gave umbrage" to many others. Crocker's pamphlets on Freemasonry and women's intellectual capacity were published in

---

17. "Nauvoo Relief Society Minute Book," 22 (March 30, 1842). See also Reed C. Durham, "Is There no Help for the Widow's Son?," 9, who writes, "[E]vidence from a different bias came from Sister Eliza R. Snow, present at the organization as its first secretary, who strongly emphasized that the Society was Priesthood. Another charter member, Sister Mary Elizabeth Rollins Lightner, added that the Relief Society was an order of the Priesthood."

18. "Nauvoo Relief Society Minute Book," 61 (June 9, 1842).

19. "Nauvoo Relief Society Minute Book," 61 (June 9, 1842).

20. For example, Mahala Overton was blackballed in the ballot, but on June 9, 1842, Joseph Smith came before the Society to intervene. The objections to her membership were not recorded, but after he spoke to the Sisters, they were removed. The Prophet urged the Society to be merciful. "Respecting the reception of Sis. Overton," the minutes state, "Prest. Smith [said] It grieves me that there is no fuller fellowship— if one member suffer all feel it— by union of feeling we obtain pow'r with God. Christ said he came to call sinners to repentance and save them." "Nauvoo Relief Society Minute Book," 61–62 (June 9, 1842).

21. Samuel Morris Brown, *In Heaven as It Is on Earth: Joseph Smith and the Early Mormon Conquest of Death*, 188. Brown incorrectly states that the inclusion of women was a "rank heresy for American Masons." Similarly, Clyde Forsberg wrongly asserts that Mormonism was the first adoptive ritual of its kind in the United States. Clyde R. Forsberg, *Equal Rites: The Book of Mormon, Masonry, Gender, and American Culture*, 96.

the 1810s.[22] Shortly thereafter, "adoptive rites" of Masonry, sponsored by regular Masonic bodies, became well established in the United States.[23] By 1826, adoptive orders associated with the Royal Arch Degree had been inaugurated in Batavia, New York.[24] Royal Arch Masonry also came to embrace an appendant body, the Heroines of Jericho, which involved women.[25] Candidates in both groups participated in prayer circles, ritually experienced a "heavenly ascent" into the presence of a Grand Court or Council, and symbolically achieved exaltation.[26] Because of the importance of maintaining familial links, which Freemasons believed would last beyond death, there was an impulse to recognize and involve women in legitimate Masonic activities. This might explain why, in all their objections to the proceedings of the Nauvoo Masonic Lodge, the other Illinois Masons never mentioned bringing women into the Lodge as a point of contention.

Involving women in Masonry was however frowned upon by the greater society. Many felt secret societies would lead to the corruption of women.[27] Especially feared was the possibility that Masons might covertly accept women into their nighttime meetings.[28] Spurious Masonic lodges that indulged libertine sexual practices were rumored to exist, inducting women into Masonic degrees

---

22. Steven C. Bullock, *Revolutionary Brotherhood: Freemasonry and the Transformation of the American Social Order, 1730-1840*, 160–61.

23. Robert Macoy, *Adoptive Rite Ritual: Instruction, Organization, Government and Ceremonies of Order of the Eastern Star, Queen of the South, Administrative Degree, Installation, Dedication of Hall, Chapter of Sorrow, Burial Service*, 10. An adoptive rite is one that is sponsored by a regular Masonic body. Women who are related by blood or marriage to Master Masons in good standing are entitled to Masonic relief, respect, and attention of the entire fraternity. Adoptive rites grew up around the need for such women to make themselves known.

24. Henry Wilson Coil, *Coil's Masonic Encyclopedia*, 13b.

25. The first printed exposure of the Heroine of Jericho degree was published in 1831. Avery Allyn, *A Ritual of Freemasonry*, 172–77.

26. *Book of the Scarlet Line: Heroines of Jericho*, 84 (exaltation of sister); 124–25 (prayer circle/ascent from earthly to heavenly court).

27. In Olney's exposé of Mormonism, he said "there was some few degrees of Masonry for the fair sex of the land. That such encouraged the Mormon sisters. They soon came together and formed a lodge . . . received many instructions, in their daily moves, by the authorities of the Church, got their society organized. . . . They continued their meetings from time to time, until it was made known to them, that had been regular members, that there was certain degrees of Masonry for them to receive. . . . As the cords were tightened from time to time, That they were brought into subjection, And a rush was made for a plurality of wives. I saw difficulty that soon arose." Oliver Olney, *The Absurdities of Mormonism Portrayed: A Brief Sketch*, 11–12.

28. "'Were women to be admitted to our Lodges,' the Reverend brother Ezra Ripley of Concord, Massachusetts, pointed out in 1802, 'though they should be pure, as angels are, they could not avoid infamous charges from the envious and uncharitable world abroad.'" Bullock, *Revolutionary Brotherhood*, 181.

based on sexual favors. For example, Cagliostro's Egyptian rite was androgynous and was said to include female Masonic consorts known as "doves."[29]

The Relief Society and Polygamy

In his exposés, John C. Bennett claimed that the women of Nauvoo were involved in the kinds of ritual orders mentioned above.[30] While Joseph Smith was secretly practicing plural marriage, and members of the Relief Society were sealed to Smith, Bennett's claims were exaggerated, and Emma Smith did all she could to combat this perception. One of the stated goals of the Relief Society was "correcting the morals and strengthening the virtues of the female community," though Emma and Joseph differed on how this was to be done.[31] For instance, tensions surrounding the investigation and balloting process in the Relief Society can best be seen in light of disagreement between the two concerning Joseph's practice of plural marriage, with each seeming determined to promulgate their views using Nauvoo's fledgling women's organization. From the beginning, Emma seems to have had a desire to use the organization to promote opposition to her husband's teachings about plural marriage.[32] But in the two years between June 1842 and July 1844, the key officers and founding members of the group were taught and began to practice "celestial marriage," many becoming Joseph's plural wives. These women were informed as to Joseph's quite different aims for the Relief Society, and they kept the secret from Emma. Meanwhile, reports in local newspapers cited Bennett's accusation of the Mormon prophet "introducing a new order or degree of masonry." Bennett claimed that in Smith's "Order Lodge," Smith revised a Masonic oath of chastity to read: "I furthermore promise and swear, that I will never touch a daughter of Adam *unless she is given me of the Lord.*"[33]

One of the many plural wives and members of the Relief Society who "was given . . . by the Lord" was Agnes Coolbrith Smith, the widow of his late brother, Don Carlos. The marriage took place several months before the founding of the Relief Society. Brigham Young wrote about this event in his journal in Masonic code. Deciphered, it read: "I was taken in to the lodge J Smith *was* Agness."[34] The

---

29. Timothy O'Neill, "The Grand Copt," 28; Massimo Introvigne, "Arcana Arcanorum: Cagliostro's Legacy in Contemporary Magical Movements," 122–23; Henry R. Evans, *Cagliostro and his Egyptian Rite of Freemasonry*, 23–24.

30. John C. Bennett, *History of the Saints, or, An Expose of Joe Smith and Mormonism*, 220.

31. "Nauvoo Relief Society Minute Book," 7 (March 17, 1842).

32. See Minutes of General [Women's] Meeting, July 17, 1880, in "R.S. Reports," 53–54; and Valeen Tippetts Avery, "Emma, Joseph, and the Female Relief Society of Nauvoo: Unsuspected Arena for a Power Struggle."

33. See "The Difficulties at Nauvoo—the other side of the story—John C. Bennett—'Spiritual Wives,' &c. &c."; emphasis added.

34. Brigham Young Diary, January 6, 1842, cited in Todd M. Compton, *In Sacred Loneliness: The Plural Wives of Joseph Smith*, 153–54; emphasis added.

abbreviation "*was*" has been interpreted to mean "wedded and sealed."[35] Though Emma might have known about Joseph's predilections, she probably did not realize just how far things had gone. As she investigated the rumors surrounding her husband and Agnes Coolbrith, a power struggle developed between Emma and Joseph.

According to Masonic writer Joshua Bradley, "Whoever would be a Mason, should know how to practice all the private virtues. . . . [T]he virtue indispensably requisite in a Mason, is *secrecy*. This is the guard of their confidence, and the security of their trust."[36] Likewise, Joseph understood and taught that "the secret of Masonry is to keep a secret,"[37] and he exhorted the sisters of the Relief Society to uphold this principle.

In an epistle signed by Joseph as President of the Church, Brigham Young as President of the Twelve, and four other men, which Emma was asked to read to the sisters,[38] the Prophet ostensibly warned those in the Relief Society to beware of "unprincipled men" who were teaching precepts "contrary to the old established morals and virtues" without his sanction. The names of these "iniquitous characters" were not mentioned, "not knowing but what there may be some among you who are not sufficiently skill'd in Masonry as to keep a secret."[39] This phrase reveals some of Joseph's chief designs for the women's Relief Society: to instruct the sisters in his version of Masonry, to maintain a semi-autonomous female lodge, and to retain a loyal following supportive of his teachings. Not mentioning the names of the accused allowed him to appease Emma's concerns about church leaders who were teaching a sanctioned form of plural marriage while plausibly condemning John C. Bennett's more profligate "spiritual wifery."[40] "Let this Epistle be had as a private matter in your Society," Joseph concluded, "and we shall learn whether you are good Masons."[41]

With this epistle, Joseph Smith employed a method of communicating that allowed him to denounce adultery and other moral transgressions while at the same time promulgating the principle of plural marriage to those who were part of the inner circle. He did this by using signal phrases such as "the commandments of God in all things," "every word that proceedeth out of the mouth of the Lord,"

---

35. Passages in Brigham Young's journal written in a variation of the Royal Arch cipher were first decoded by Arturo de Hoyos in 1991.

36. Joshua Bradley, *Some of the Beauties of Free-masonry*, 149, 151.

37. "History, 1838–1856, volume E-1 [1 July 1843–30 April 1844]," The Joseph Smith Papers, 1756. This was later echoed by Brigham Young who averred "the mane [main] part of Masonry is to keep a secret." Wilford Woodruff journal, January 22, 1860.

38. Kent Walgren, "James Adams, Early Springfield Mormon and Freemason," 131.

39. "Nauvoo Relief Society Minute Book," 87.

40. The term "spiritual wifery" was sometimes used contemporaneously to refer to Joseph Smith's brand of sanctioned plural marriage, but more recently it is used to distinguish unsanctioned relations in Nauvoo polygamy.

41. "Nauvoo Relief Society Minute Book," 88.

and "the responsibilities that we conferred upon you."[42] Later, he would employ such code words as "true and divine order," "new and everlasting covenant," or even simply "blessings" which those in the know understood to mean plural marriage.[43]

Without an awareness of the secret practice of polygamy that underlay many of Smith's discourses to the Relief Society sisters and a conception of the Masonic structure used to protect this secret, it is difficult to arrive at a correct understanding of his teachings. For example, on April 28, 1842, Smith spoke of delivering "keys" both to the Society and to the elders. The Relief Society Minute Book reports, "[T]he keys of the kingdom are about to be given to them, that they may be able to detect every thing false."[44] A few days later, on May 1, 1842, he said to the Nauvoo populace that the keys were "certain signs and words by which false spirits and personages may be detected from true, which cannot be revealed to the Elders till the Temple is completed. . . . There are signs . . . Elders must know . . . to be endowed with power, to finish their work, and prevent imposition."[45] In Freemasonry, keys alluded to the secrets of the Craft, and keys of detection were grips of the hand by which one could "tell another in the dark as well as in the light."[46] Willard Richards reported further instruction from Smith expanding on this Masonic practice: "A [drawing of a key] Key to detect Satan. As there are many Keys to the Kingdom of God the following one will detect Satan when he transforms himself nigh unto an Angel of Light. When Satan appears in the form of a personage unto man &—reaches out his hand unto him & the man takes hold of his hand & feels no substance he may know it is satan."[47]

"I now turn the key to you in the name of God," Smith told the sisters, "and this Society shall rejoice and knowledge and intelligence shall flow down

---

42. "Nauvoo Relief Society Minute Book," 88.

43. "An 1886 article in the *Deseret News* detailed specific code words and the rationale for their use. 'When assailed by their enemies and accused of practicing things which were really not countenanced in the Church, they were justified in denying these imputations and at the same time avoiding the avowal of such doctrine as were not yet intended for the world. . . . *Polygamy*, in the ordinary and Asiatic sense of the term never was and is not now a tenet of the Latter-day Saints. That which Joseph and Hyrum denounced . . . was altogether different to the order of *celestial marriage*, including a *plurality of wives*. . . . Joseph and Hyrum were consistent in their action against the *false doctrines* of *polygamy* and *spiritual wifeism*, instigated by the devil and advocated by men who did not comprehend sound doctrine nor the purity of the *celestial marriage* which God revealed for the holiest of purposes.'" Linda King Newell and Valeen Tippets Avery, *Mormon Enigma: Emma Hale Smith*, 113, citing a May 20, 1866, *Deseret News* article; emphasis in original. See also "Revelation, 12 July 1843 [D&C 132]," The Joseph Smith Papers, 1, 4.

44. "Nauvoo Relief Society Minute Book," 37–38 (April 28, 1842).

45. "History, 1838–1856, volume C-1 [2 November 1838–31 July 1842]," The Joseph Smith Papers, 1326.

46. Richardson, *Richardson's Monitor of Free-Masonry*, 13b.

47. "Discourse, 27 June 1839, as Reported by Willard Richards," The Joseph Smith Papers, 9–10.

from this time."[48] According to previous revelation, he had described keys as being connected with the mysteries of the kingdom, the knowledge of God, and the ordinances of the priesthood (D&C 84:19–21). The keys to the spiritual blessings of the Church, he wrote, gave the bearers "the privilege of receiving the mysteries of the kingdom of heaven, to have the heavens opened unto them, to commune with the general assembly and church of the Firstborn, and to enjoy the communion and presence of God" (D&C 107:19). Masonic secrets that were hidden in the heart both concealed and revealed; they were keys of power that could bring a candidate into the presence of God. Turning the key to the Relief Society was equivalent to giving the women independent power to open the heavens and associate with the Divine.

From indications in Joseph's diary, Emma became aware of the extent of her husband's involvement in plural marriage on April 29, 1842.[49] It has been speculated that this may be the reason why no Relief Society meeting was held the following week and why Emma was absent at the next.[50] But the wrestle for control continued as Joseph continued cautioning the sisters against intolerance while Emma continued denouncing plural marriage. "There is another error which opens a door for the adversary to enter," Joseph chided. "As females possess refin'd feelings and sensitivenes[s], they are also subject to an overmuch zeal which must ever prove dangerous, and cause them to be rigid in a religious capacity—[they] should be arm'd with mercy notwithstanding the iniquity among us." Then, addressing Emma directly, he requested that the president should hold her tongue.[51] In Masonic tradition, keys of silence are associated with the tongue. They are kept "in a box of coral which opens and shuts only with ivory keys." The tongue is to be obedient to reason and to speak well of others in their absence as well as in their presence.[52] Joseph was not just telling Emma to silence herself, but in the Masonic sense to be circumspect about things that she might know. "At this time the truth on the guilty should not be told openly—Strange as this may seem, yet this is policy." Emma responded by observing that sin should not be covered, the guilty should reform, and that no one should be in the Society who had violated the law of virtue.[53]

48. "Nauvoo Relief Society Minute Book," 40 (April 28, 1842).

49. On this day, Joseph recorded: "A conspiracy against the peace of my household was made manifest, and it gave me some trouble to counteract the design of certain base individuals, and restore peace. The Lord makes manifest to me many things, which <it> is <not> wisdom for me to make public until others can witness the proof of them." See "History, 1838–1856, volume C-1 [2 November 1838–31 July 1842," 1326.

50. Avery, "Emma, Joseph, and the Female Relief Society of Nauvoo."

51. "Nauvoo Relief Society Minute Book," 52 (May 26, 1842).

52. Albert Gallatin Mackey, William James Hughan, and Edward L. Hawkins, *An Encyclopaedia of Freemasonry and its Kindred Sciences, Comprising the Whole Range of Arts, Sciences and Literature as Connected with the Institution*, 1:380.

53. "Nauvoo Relief Society Minute Book," 51–53 (May 26, 1842).

Through public exchanges such as this, it is apparent that Emma rejected the doctrine of celestial plural marriage. So much wrangling was occurring over the "immoral character" of some of the sisters who were being considered for membership that the Relief Society began to founder. Joseph attempted to buoy their spirits with a speech prophesying the blessings of the endowment. When they saw this work rolling on, he promised, "The kingdom increasing and spreading from sea to sea; we will rejoice that we were not overcome by these foolish things."[54] Such a prophecy indicates that he may have initially intended the Relief Society to be the vehicle through which they would receive or be prepared to receive the temple rites. According to Elder Reynolds Cahoon, there was no doubt "but this Society is raisd [sic] by the Lord to prepare us for the great blessings which are for us in the House of the Lord in the Temple."[55]

The Relief Society minutes for September 28, 1842, showed that the meeting was adjourned "sine die" (for an indefinite period of time).[56] The women would not meet again in this capacity until nine months later. When they resumed in 1843, Emma was no longer attending and was not present at any of the meetings held that year, although she remained its "presidentess" in name.

The Relief Society went from a vibrant, growing organization to one that quickly diminished in membership. At the end of July 1843, Elizabeth Ann Whitney said that so few attended that she hoped the meetings would not be discontinued.[57] Following the twelfth 1843 meeting, which concluded with a proposal that they meet the next Thursday, all future meetings were indeed suspended. By that time, Emma had become the first woman Latter-day Saint to receive her own endowments and be admitted into the Quorum of the Anointed.[58]

Though she never attended Relief Society that year, Emma became active in administering the washing, anointing, and sealing ordinances to her fellow sisters through the rest of 1843 and the beginning of 1844. It appears Joseph transferred his hopes for an androgynous ritual to the Quorum of the Anointed. Susa Young Gates, a daughter of Brigham Young, later wrote: "The privileges and powers outlined by the Prophet in those first meetings [of the Relief Society] have never been granted to women in full even yet."[59]

In 1844, on two successive Saturdays in March, Emma staged a dramatic repossession of the Relief Society. Rumors of John C. Bennett's "spiritual wife system"[60] and accusations of adultery against Hyrum Smith by a Mr. Bostwick excited the indignation of the majority of the Saints who were unaware that

---

54. "Nauvoo Relief Society Minute Book," 82 (August 31, 1842).
55. "Nauvoo Relief Society Minute Book," 110 (August 13, 1843).
56. "Nauvoo Relief Society Minute Book," 85, 90 (September 28, 1842).
57. "Nauvoo Relief Society Minute Book," 100 (July 28, 1843).
58. Devery S. Anderson and Gary James Bergera, eds., *Joseph Smith's Quorum of the Anointed, 1842–1845: A Documentary History*, xxviii.
59. Susa Young Gates, "The Open Door for Woman," 117.
60. "Nauvoo Relief Society Minute Book," 125 (March 16, 1844).

polygamy was being practiced and promoted by the prophet.[61] In response, W. W. Phelps composed a twelve-hundred-word statement titled "The Voice of Innocence," which was read and approved on March 7 at a general meeting of priesthood leaders and "about eight thousand" members of the Church. Emma appropriated this statement and called for the female Relief Society to "resume its meetings."[62] On the morning and afternoon of March 9, and again on the morning and afternoon of March 16, Emma read the document and called for a vote of those "willing to receive the principles of virtue, keep the commandments of God, and uphold the Presidentess in putting [down] iniquity."[63] It was ratified by unanimous vote.[64]

Though Emma was making a strong public stand against polygamy, she did it in a way that she may have believed was supportive of her husband. Her exhortation to the sisters was that they follow the teachings of Joseph as he spoke against vice *from the stand*. At the final Saturday session, Emma announced her intention to examine the conduct of the leaders of the Relief Society and present officers when a place could be found that was large enough for all the sisters to gather together; for, she said, "if their [sic] ever was any authourity on the Earth she had it—and had [it] yet."[65]

The Relief Society never met again in Nauvoo. John Taylor later explained, "The reason why the Relief Society did not continue . . . was that Emma Smith . . . taught the Sisters that the principles of Celestial Marriage as taught and practiced was not of God."[66]

Mormon Women and Masonic Orders

The Mormons' secrets were becoming widely known in the community and throughout the world. Four months later, Joseph Smith and his brother Hyrum were killed at Carthage, Illinois. Small groups of women continued to meet in private homes where they encouraged and blessed each other, often exercising spiritual gifts such as speaking in tongues. An excerpt from Zina Diantha

---

61. "Nauvoo Relief Society Minute Book," 124 (March 16, 1844).

62. "Nauvoo Relief Society Minute Book," 123 (March 9, 1844); Emma Smith, "Virtue Will Triumph," 187.

63. "Nauvoo Relief Society Minute Book," 123 (March 9, 1844).

64. Smith, "Virtue Will Triumph," 187.

65. "Nauvoo Relief Society Minute Book," 126 (March 16, 1844).

66. John Taylor, Statement, June 29, 1881, quoted in Avery, "Emma, Joseph, and the Female Relief Society of Nauvoo." At another meeting Taylor elaborated, "I . . . think that some of those circumstances should be known. Sister Emma got severely tried in her mind about the doctrine of Plural Marriage and she made use of the position she held to try to pervert the minds of the sisters in relation to that doctrine. She tried to influence my first wife and to make her believe the revelation was not correct." John Taylor, July 17, 1880, in "R.S. Reports," 53–54.

Huntington Jacobs's journal less than three months after the final approved Relief Society meeting provides a glimpse into a possible direction the sisterly impulse for communion took:

> June 1844
>
> 5, 6, 7, 8 , 9. Went with Henres [Henry's] uncles family uppon the hill. From this day I understand the Kinsmans degree of freemasonry. (3) My husband, being a Master Mason, attended meeting. Hiram Smith spoke exceeding well also re[a]d a revelation. . . .
>
> 18. I went to the Masonic hall with the sisters. [67]

As previously discussed, the Heroines of Jericho was a Masonic women's rite associated with the Royal Arch Degree.[68] This order had three rites or degrees: The Master Mason's Daughter, the True Kinsman's Degree, and The Heroine of Jericho Degree.[69] The statement "from this day I understand the Kinsmans degree" indicates Zina had received this Masonic degree offered to the close female relatives of Master Masons—that adoptive rites for women were operating in Nauvoo. Zina's husband Henry Jacobs was a Master Mason,[70] and she had been sealed to Joseph Smith, another Master Mason. Her father and brothers had also been raised Master Masons in the Nauvoo Lodge.[71] Years later, in 1878, Zina spoke in protest of anti-polygamy campaigns at a mass meeting where she declared her personal connection with Masonry:

> I am the daughter of a Master Mason! I am the widow of a Master Mason, who, when leaping from the windows of Carthage jail, pierced with bullets, made the Masonic sign of distress. . . . I wish my voice could be heard by the whole brotherhood of Masons throughout our proud land. That institution I honor. If its principles were practiced and strictly adhered to, would there be a trespass upon virtue? No indeed. Would the honorable wife or daughter be intruded on with impunity? Nay verily.[72]

When Zina proudly announced that she was the daughter of a Master Mason she could have been hinting at her participation in the first degree of adoptive Masonry: "The Master Mason's Daughter." As such, she would have been entitled to respect and relief from "the whole brotherhood of Masons throughout [the] land."

Another possible member of an adoptive rite in Nauvoo was Sarah Rich, wife of Charles C. Rich. A cryptic handwritten note in the CC Rich manuscript

---

67. Maurine Ursenbach Beecher, ed., "All Things Move in Order in the City: the Nauvoo Diary of Zina Diantha Huntington Jacobs," 291.

68. *Book of the Scarlet Line: Heroines of Jericho*, v; Moses Dickson, *Landmarks and Ceremonies of Courts of Heroines of Jericho.*

69. *Coil's Masonic Encyclopedia*, 13b.

70. Henry Jacobs received Masonic degrees on August 8, 9, and 10, 1842.

71. The three Huntington men were initiated in the Nauvoo Lodge in 1842. Her third brother, Oliver, recounts his rising to Master Mason in June 1844. See Oliver Huntington, "History of the life of Oliver B. Huntington, also his travels & troubles / writen by himself, 1843-1844," 48.

72. Zina D. H. Young, "Woman's Mass Meeting. Salt Lake Theater, Nov. 16, 1878," 98.

collection with a date of April 24, 1906, states: "The Masonic Temple in the City of Nauvoo was Dedicated April 6th 1844.[73] CC Rich was a member of the Lodge. his wife took Degree allowed to Women."[74]

Unlike his Masonic predecessors, Joseph Smith's revolutionary perspective did not discriminate based on gender. If one operates from the assumption that Smith was encouraging Freemasonry for men as a "stepping stone to something greater," then it is not insignificant that Mormon women were involved in the female equivalent of Masonic bodies.

As the Saints moved west, connections with Freemasonry were severed. Typically, the brothers remained loyal to their fraternal ties, but Mormon Masons felt betrayed by the involvement of Illinois Freemasons in the deaths of Joseph and Hyrum Smith. Likewise, sisters felt conflicted about their Relief Society connections. They would continue to meet in relief groups, but the organization was not officially recognized again until 1866.

---

73. The Masonic Lodge in Nauvoo was actually dedicated on April 5, 1844.

74. "Charles C. Rich biographical information, circa 1906," 6.

CHAPTER 13

GREATER THAN SOLOMON: JOSEPH SMITH'S "GRAND" ASPIRATIONS

The straight path of Masonic rectitude positively requires that every rough corner of every stone should be beaten off so completely that the square of virtue will set easy.
   —James E. Seaver, letter to Mr. William Seaver

In ancient times, operative masons removed coarse stones from a quarry in the shape of a rectangular solid. These rough "ashlars" were intended for use in the construction of a building. But before any such stone could be placed in a building, it required smoothing and shaping by tools in the hands of a stonemason.

Every lodge room holds both a rough ashlar and a smooth ashlar. The rough ashlar is placed in the northeast corner of the lodge to signify the rough human personality in its natural state. The smooth ashlar is in the southwest corner and represents the refinement of character to which Freemasons aspire. Together, these stones symbolize their journey from natural crudeness to spiritual sophistication and excellence. Initiates are charged to engage continually in self-improvement, to allow life to smooth their rough edges, and to become better men and Freemasons. This allegory was applied by Joseph Smith to himself on May 21, 1843, when he stated:

> I am like a huge rough stone rolling down from a high mountain, and the only polishing I get, is when some corner gets rubbed off by coming in contact with something else . . . all hell knocking off a corner here and a corner there; thus, I will become a smooth and polished shaft in the quiver of the Almighty . . . while these smooth polished stones with which I come in contact, become marred.[1]

Heber C. Kimball, by then a Freemason for about fifteen years, repeated this metaphor at a church conference in Boston a few months later:

> Joseph Smith never professed to be a dressed, smooth, polished stone, but to have kicked himself rough out of the mountain; and he has been rolling among the rocks and trees, yet it has not hurt him at all; but he will be as smooth and polished in the end as any other stone, while many who were so very polished and smooth in the beginning get badly defaced and spoiled while they are rolling about.[2]

---

1. "History, 1838–1856, volume D-1 [1 August 1842–1 July 1843]," The Joseph Smith Papers, 1556.

2. "History, 1838–1856, volume E-1 [1 July 1843–30 April 1844]," The Joseph Smith Papers, 1725.

"King Solomon and the Iron Worker," steel mezzotint engraving by John Sartain of the 1863 painting by Christian Schussele.

The Mormon prophet easily fit himself into the legendary Masonic worldview. Not only did he apply Masonic parables to himself, he seemed to stride into the mythical history of the Craft. His keen perception of the ancient myths allowed him to penetrate their mysteries, gather them about him, and cloak himself in the legend.

Freemasons familiar with these stories will notice that Smith was playing the part of King Solomon, stepping into the monarch's Masonic shoes. In the narrative told by George Oliver, Solomon erected the Temple at Jerusalem assisted by two groups of builders. He began by calling together skillful architects from the city of Tyre who were disciples of spurious Masonry. When they arrived, they united with "Jewish workmen who practiced the pure system," and Solomon was said to have "reorganized the system of Masonry," providing the ritual and structure that would guide Masons through future generations.[3] Masonic author Albert Mackey explained: "Temple Masonry . . . was formed by a union of the Primitive, or Pure, and the Spurious systems."[4]

---

3. Albert Gallatin Mackey, *The History of Freemasonry: Its Legendary Origins*, 148.

4. Albert Gallatin Mackey, *The Symbolism of Freemasonry: Illustrating and Explaining its Science and Philosophy, its Legends, Myths, and Symbols*, 302. "This spiritualizing of the temple of Solomon is the first, the most prominent and most pervading of all the symbolic instructions of Freemasonry. . . Take from Freemasonry its dependence on the temple, leave out of its ritual all reference to that sacred edifice, and to the legends connected with it, and the system itself must at once decay and die, or at best remain only as some fossilized bone, imperfectly to show the nature of the living body to which it once belonged" (p. 86).

Similarly, Smith associated with what he saw as spurious Freemasonry as he prepared to restore the Temple of God, hoping to unite the apostate Illinois Masons with the Mormon workmen who "practiced the pure system." He did this by placing himself into the Royal Arch Masonic archetype of Millennialism, an eschatological restoration of "that which had been lost." Additionally, he re-organized Masonry into a new form and provided the endowment as a puri-fied ritual to govern revivified Freemasonry in preparation for the coming of the Son of God. Freemasonry was thus not merely incidental in the emergence of Mormonism; it was centrally important to the Restoration.

From 1842 to 1844, Nauvoo Lodge and several other Mormon Masonic lodges in the immediate vicinity enabled the two systems of Mormonism and Freemasonry to converge in a major way. Wilford Woodruff demonstrated his understanding that the Mormon lodges were restoring existing Freemasonry in his diary. Often, he would illustrate his entries with miniature symbolic figures. According to historian Laurel Thatcher Ulrich, "To mark a day spent performing baptisms for the dead, he drew a crowned figure. . . . Above an entry reporting his own work in performing baptisms, he inserted a tiny key." In like manner, "above a reference to the Masonic lodge, he sketched a tiny bird emerging from fire like a phoenix."[5]

Irregularities in Illinois

Joseph Smith and other Mormon Masons perceived contemporary Freemasonry as spurious, but brothers in the Illinois lodges were in turn quick to point out the irregularities they noticed coming from Nauvoo. In 1842 and 1843, the lodge at Nauvoo and other Mormon lodges were found to be in vio-lation of Masonic procedure. They were not the only lodges in violation, but Illinois Freemasons were not as amenable to granting the Mormons the generos-ity and flexibility allowed to other local lodges.

As irregularities in new lodges became evident, Masonic Grand Officers en-deavored to correct the mistakes and formulate policies to regulate the lodges under their jurisdiction. For example, at the annual Grand Communication on October 5, 1841, both Springfield Lodge and Macon Lodge were found to have "in several instances, received the petition and initiated the candidate on the same evening; and also have passed and raised candidates at the same sitting of the lodge."[6] These practices did not allow enough time to thoroughly investigate a brother or allow him to become fully proficient in one degree before proceeding to the next. The committee recommended that the subordinate lodges "not act on any petition unless the same has laid over at least one month, or from one

---

5. Laurel Thatcher Ulrich, *A House Full of Females: Plural Marriage and Women's Rights in Early Mormonism, 1835–1870,* 59–60.

6. *Reprint of the Proceedings of the Grand Lodge of Illinois: From its Organization in 1840 to 1850 Inclusive,* 22.

stated meeting until the next regular stated meeting of the lodge."[7] Irregularities notwithstanding, Springfield Lodge retained its standing and Macon Lodge was granted a charter. The same practices were evident as the Mormon lodges grew. However, the procedure for dealing with these were harsh, perhaps because irregularities were introduced in innovative ways and on a grander scale in the Mormon lodges than in any other.

On August 5, 1842, five months after Nauvoo Lodge was constituted and its officers installed, the Rising Sun Lodge in Iowa was constituted under the Grand Lodge of Illinois, with its officers installed by James Adams.[8] These officers included Stephen H. Burtis, Worshipful Master;[9] D.C. Davis, Senior Warden;[10] Christopher Williams, Junior Warden;[11] William Vanansdall, Senior Deacon; and David A. Pettigrew, Junior Deacon. Three days later, Nauvoo Lodge held two meetings, the first at eight in the morning and the other at four in the afternoon. Startlingly, at the afternoon meeting, twelve brethren from Rising Sun Lodge, Iowa, petitioned and were granted a demission from Nauvoo Lodge.[12] Included in this list were the five principal officers named above, none of whom had demitted from the Nauvoo Lodge. Joining a lodge while still belonging to another in that same jurisdiction was a Masonic *faux pas*,[13] and the Grand Lodge of Illinois would soon officially prohibit dual memberships.[14]

---

7. *Reprint of the Proceedings of the Grand Lodge of Illinois*, 23.

8. Wilford Woodruff journal, August 6, 1842: "I left the Boat. Took stage. Arived at Montrose in the midst of a Masonic possession (sic). A lodge was instituted in Montrose."

9. Stephen H. Burtis was raised a Master Mason in Nauvoo Lodge on May 24, 1842.

10. Daniel C. Davis was raised a Master Mason in Nauvoo Lodge on April 25, 1842.

11. Christopher Williams was a founding member of Nauvoo Lodge.

12. Demits to form Rising Sun Lodge were Stephen H. Burtis, Daniel C. Davis, Christopher Williams, David Pettigrew, William Vanansdall, James Anderson, Asahel A. Lathrop, Joseph A. Swasey, Henry Hoagland, David A. Pettigrew, John Smith, & John Patten. On the same day, Hosea Stout, Allen J. Stout, George Morey, Anson Call, George Watt, and Benjamin S. Wilber demitted from Nauvoo Lodge. See "Nauvoo Masonic Lodge minutes, 1841–1846," August 8, 1842.

13. "The provision [is] contained in the earlier, and, very generally, in the modern Masonic constitutions, that 'no brother shall be a member of more than one Lodge at the same time.'" John C. Reynolds, *History of the Most Worshipful Grand Lodge of Illinois, Ancient, Free, and Accepted Masons, From the Organization of the first Lodge within the Present Limits of the State, Up to and Including 1850*, 301.

14. The following resolution was adopted at the Grand Lodge meeting of 1845: "*Resolved*, That it is the duty of every Mason to belong to some Lodge, but that no Mason may belong to two Lodges at one and the same time, but that it is his duty regularly to withdraw from the Lodge to which he belongs before he makes application for membership in another." Reynolds, 305.

A few weeks earlier on July 21, 1842, thirty men demitted from Nauvoo Lodge in a similar manner to the brethren of Rising Sun Lodge.[15] The reason for the demission is undetermined. It seems possible that these brothers also planned to "hive off," though no known lodge was proposed at that time.[16] Many of the men continued to attend Nauvoo Lodge. Some, like Albern Allen and John Hatfield, were counted as members, and others, like Eliphas Marsh and Duncan McArthur, were included in subsequent minutes as "visiting brethren."[17] On January 5, 1843, four of the thirty men made application for membership in Nauvoo Lodge, the same lodge they had demitted from five months earlier.[18] They were readmitted on January 19.[19] It appears that all the brethren who demitted either reapplied for membership or were eventually reincluded in the minute book as members of Nauvoo Lodge.

Between August 8 and 11, 1842, in the heat of the Midwest summer, the Nauvoo Lodge met as usual to perform Masonic work. During the week, thirty-four brothers received degrees. At the close of the August 11 meeting, the minute book shows a copy of an injunction to suspend work in Nauvoo Lodge pending further investigation. The injunction, dated July 30, 1842, was signed by Abraham Jonas in response to accusations put forth by Bodley Lodge. The message had taken almost two weeks to arrive in Nauvoo.[20]

Worshipful Master George Miller was incensed that the work of Nauvoo Lodge had been suspended. He believed that the Lodge had been unfairly judged

---

15. These were "John D. Parker, Hamilton Jett, Alvin Horr, Alexander Badlam, Albern Allen, Levi Stewart, Josiah Arnold, Erastus H. Derby, Philander Colton, David Brinton, John Hatfield, David Grant, James Brown, Alfred Brown, Eliphaz Marsh, Wm Summerville, Duncan McArthur, Samuel H. Rogers, Elisha H. Groves, Joseph W. Johnson, David Lewis, Alexander McRae, Jacob F. Abbott, Horace M. Alexander, Josiah Fleming, Wm Davis, Harvey Green, Wm Huntington Senr., Wilber J. Earl, & Charles C. Rich. Their names were accordingly stricken from the list of members." See "Nauvoo Masonic Lodge minutes, 1841–1846," July 21, 1842.

16. Lodges of Freemasons were once known as hives, corresponding to the symbolic importance of the bee. When a portion of a lodge's members separated to form a new lodge, the process was called "swarming" or "hiving off."

17. "Nauvoo Masonic Lodge minutes, 1841–1846," November 10, 1842, December 7, 1842.

18. Namely, Alvin Horr, William Huntington, Charles C. Rich, and David Grant.

19. "Nauvoo Masonic Lodge minutes, 1841–1846." On January 19, 1843, Levi Stewart applied for membership and was readmitted on February 16. On January 24, 1843, Josiah W. Fleming, David Brenton, and Harvey Green made applications for membership. On February 1, 1843, Alexander McRae and David Lewis applied for membership. On February 16, Philander Colton was readmitted to the Lodge. On April 1, 1843, Josiah Arnold and Samuel H. Rogers made application for membership. On April 6, 1843, Erastus H. Derby applied for membership.

20. On August 11, 1842, Nauvoo Lodge attached the injunction to its minutes and did not meet again until November when the injunction was removed.

by those who were prejudiced against Mormons. Miller had been a Freemason since 1819, and after twenty-five years of what he described as "respectable standing as a member of the fraternity," he had never seen a Masonic lodge disqualified on religious grounds.[21] The suspension, however, may have been provoked by issues more complex than Bodley Lodge's complaints.

Looking back in the Nauvoo Lodge Minute Book to the date of July 30 reveals a significant occurrence. At seven o'clock that Saturday morning, the Lodge was visited by Priestly H. McBride, Grand Master of the Grand Lodge of Missouri and political appointee of Lilburn W. Boggs. The lodge at Nauvoo was no stranger to visitors, often admitting two to five visiting brethren from lodges all over the States, Canada, and even France and Scotland as a matter of course. Under normal conditions, a visit from the Grand Master of a nearby jurisdiction would have elicited treatment as a guest of honor. But in McBride's case, he was left to cool his heels outside the lodge while the meeting was opened and the minutes read. A committee was then selected to "examine" McBride and another brother who accompanied him. A Masonic examination is a test of knowledge given to someone who is visiting a lodge to make sure they are worthy to participate. It was rarely done at Nauvoo. To investigate Missouri's Grand Master in this way was an intentional slight. Perhaps it was not coincidental that later that day, Nauvoo Lodge's dispensation was suspended.[22]

Rising Sun Lodge No. 12, Montrose, IA

In accordance with Jonas's injunction, Nauvoo Freemasons ceased their work throughout the Fall. Meanwhile, directly across the Mississippi River at Montrose, Iowa, Rising Sun Lodge became the focus of Masonic activity for the Mormons. Montrose was an ideal location to launch the second Mormon Masonic Lodge. As the Church was being established on the Illinois side of the Mississippi River, many members settled on the Iowa side as well. Referred to as the "Greater Nauvoo" by historian Stanley Kimball, the eastern part of Lee County had abandoned military barracks that provided temporary shelter for destitute Mormons arriving from Missouri. These included the families of Brigham Young, John Taylor, Wilford Woodruff, Orson Pratt, and others.[23] In October 1839 the Iowa Stake of the Church was formed with its center in Montrose. The west part of Montrose, where the Saints lived, was named Zarahemla after a land in the Book of Mormon. At the stake conference of 1841, there were 326

---

21. George Miller, Letter to Abraham Jonas, September 29, 1842.

22. "Copy of Injunction," in "Nauvoo Masonic Lodge minutes, 1841–1846," July 30, 1842. Days later, Joseph Smith would be arrested on a Missouri writ, as an accessory to the Boggs shooting, only to be released after the exercise of a writ of habeas corpus. See "Persecution," 887–88.

23. Stanley B. Kimball, "Nauvoo West: The Mormons of the Iowa Shore," 136.

members in the Zarahemla Branch, and in August that year the name of the Iowa Stake was changed to the Zarahemla Stake.[24]

In January 1842, the Zarahemla Stake was discontinued, and members were encouraged to move across the river to strengthen Nauvoo. However, many prominent Latter-day Saints remained in Montrose, including the Prophet's uncle, John Smith, who had been president of the stake. John was one of the men who demitted from Nauvoo Lodge on August 8, 1842, to form Rising Sun Lodge in Montrose two days earlier.

Joseph Smith crossed the river to participate in the installation of Rising Sun Lodge on August 6, 1842. Following the installation, Deputy Grand Master James Adams took Stephen Burtis aside to instruct him in his responsibilities as Master of the new lodge, while Joseph Smith and a few of the other brothers stood in the shade of a building to cool themselves from the hot summer sun. An addition to Smith's history depicts the Prophet at the same time foretelling that "the Saints would continue to suffer much affliction and would be driven to the Rocky Mountains." He prophesied to some of the Masonic brothers that they would "live to go, and assist in making settlements and build cities and see the Saints become a mighty people in the midst of the Rocky Mountains."[25]

Lodge members at Rising Sun were prodigious in establishing Freemasonry in the Montrose and Zarahemla area. Without delay, they "built a new hall . . . had completely furnished the same and had procured suitable jewels and Masonic clothing."[26] At the 1842 Grand Lodge Communication in October, a scant two months after their installation, the delegate from Rising Sun Lodge presented a complete and thorough report of their work and paid their dues.[27] The Grand Lodge Committee on Returns and Work of Lodges was impressed enough to recommend they receive their charter, a process that usually took at least a year under dispensation. Rising Sun Lodge became "No. 12," indicating that they were the twelfth lodge to be chartered under the new Grand Lodge of Illinois.

Nauvoo Lodge Returns to Work, Proposes New Lodges

On the other hand, Nauvoo Lodge, represented at the Grand Communication by Henry Sherwood and Lucius Scovil, was reprimanded by the Grand Lodge Committee on Returns and Work of Lodges. Their return had been submitted, and the work "appear[ed] to conform to the requirements of the Grand Lodge." However, Nauvoo Lodge had not sent up "the original records" of the work of

---

24. Kimball, 139.

25. "History, 1838–1856, volume D-1 [1 August 1842–1 July 1843]," *The Joseph Smith Papers*, 1362.

26. Joseph E. Morcombe, *History of Grand Lodge of Iowa, A.F. and A.M.*, 1:156.

27. *Reprint of the Proceedings of the Grand Lodge of Illinois*, 56. Upon examination, Rising Sun Lodge's returns were reported correct. However, the actual return is not included with the proceedings, as is the case for all of the other lodges who submitted returns.

their lodge, as requested by the Grand Master in his suspension order.[28] These
records would have included the minutes and proceedings of the Lodge as well as
the return.[29] The wording of this report is interesting, as it may reflect the Grand
Lodge's knowledge of John C. Bennett's accusation that the original minute book
had been altered.

Sherwood wrote a passionate account of the Grand Lodge proceedings,
defending Nauvoo Lodge. In the report, he shows himself as a bit of a hot-
head, refusing a request to pay the lodge dues before being granted a seat at the
proceedings. The more refined Lucius Scovil urged him to consent. Sherwood,
like George Miller, felt the sting of religious persecution from the time Bodley
Lodge refused to recommend Nauvoo Lodge's charter to the present suspension.
Nauvoo's lodge reports, which had been kept by Sherwood as acting secretary
since June, were examined. He proudly recounted:

> Then G[rand] M[aster] Jonas made a flaming speech in behalf of the N[auvoo] Lodge
> saying they were the fairest books and papers that had been brought from any Lodge
> to the Grand Lodge, and . . . he verily believed that if they were not Mormons, the
> Lodge would stand the highest of any Lodge, that had come to that Grand Lodge.[30]

Although no great discrepancy had been discovered in Nauvoo Lodge's return, the committee had a niggling concern that there might be "some reason
to fear that the intention and ancient landmarks of our institution have been
departed from."[31] The Mormon lodge had initiated 256 candidates, almost all
going on to become Master Masons. Such a large number of new members was
unheard of in any other Masonic lodge in any country or time period, and it was
not understood exactly how it had been accomplished. In fact, Nauvoo Lodge
had been holding daily meetings, often two or three times a day. As allowed
by the Grand Lodge of Illinois, up to three men were receiving degrees at each
meeting.[32] This effort required such a large time commitment from the officers
of Nauvoo Lodge that Hyrum Smith, acting as Master of the Lodge on April

---

28. *Reprint of the Proceedings of the Grand Lodge of Illinois*, 58–59.

29. A Lodge return is a yearly summation of the work, which in the case of the Illinois
Grand Lodge included: name and place of Lodge; when meetings were held; names of
officers with dates and places of their Masonic initiations; names of past Masters, Master
Masons, and Fellowcrafts Entered Apprentices; names and dates of those who were initiated,
passed, and raised during the year; names and descriptions of those who were rejected;
names and dates of those suspended, expelled, and reinstated; names of those who died
during the year; and the amount of financial contributions to the Grand Lodge.

30. "Henry G. Sherwood Statements, circa 1854," 4. See also "Lucius N. Scovil statement,
circa 1854–1856."

31. *Reprint of the Proceedings of the Grand Lodge of Illinois*, 58.

32. John C. Bennett accused Nauvoo Lodge of exceeding this maximum number, and
indeed on at least one occasion on April 13, 1842, Minute Books 1 and 2 demonstrate
that during the three meetings held that day the lodge brethren initiated three, passed
three, and raised four. See John C. Bennett, "Gen. Bennett's 4th Letter, July 15, 1842," 2.

8, 1842, had ordered that "officers be entitled to a reasonable compensation for their services."[33] Paying members of the Lodge for their work in this way was highly unusual, even dodgy. Remuneration to the officers of the Lodge likely continued until at least September 1845. The final pages of the minute book contain an attendance roster of the officers and acting officers that was almost certainly used for that purpose.

Allen Stout was one of those who benefitted from this practice. As a member of the "Old Police" in Nauvoo, he "drew one dollar per day for services in city scrip" until after the assassinations of Joseph and Hyrum Smith. Thereafter, Brigham Young asked the Old Police to continue to guard the city though there was no available means of pay. Young told them "the Lord would open some way for there [sic] support," and Stout kept on guard, though many others quit their service. "Soon after I got a birth [sic] in the Nauvoo Lodge," Stout wrote, "where I got $1.50 per day and only had to act [in the rituals] about 3 hours each day."[34]

Non-Mormon Freemasons of the day were leery of too-rapid growth in their lodges. In 1839, when Abraham Jonas and several compatriots had petitioned the Grand Lodge of Missouri for a new lodge in Columbus, Illinois, Grand Master Stephen W. B. Carnegy had cautioned them:

> [S]o long as we are but few in number, and consist of the true, the moral, and temperate, we are safe, and may be happy. The best evidence of speedy ruin to any Lodge, is that they increase very fast that they are very numerous.[35]

Having been thus cautioned, it is surprising that Jonas accepted and actually seemed to facilitate such rapid growth at Nauvoo. His successors were less accommodating. Accordingly, members of the Grand Lodge of Illinois decided that a special committee should be appointed to travel to Nauvoo, observe their work and examine their minutes, and then make a recommendation whether their dispensation should be continued.[36] Additionally, as a safeguard, the Grand Lodge decided:

> 1st. *Resolved,* That no lodge under the jurisdiction of this Grand Lodge shall be allowed to ballot for a candidate for initiation except at a stated meeting, nor in a shorter time than one lunar month from the reception of the petition, except by dispensation from the M. W. G. Master.[37]

---

33. "Nauvoo Masonic Lodge minutes, 1841–1846," April 8, 1842.

34. Allen J. Stout, Reminiscence and Journal, 1845–1850, 1865–1889, 22.

35. Everett R. Turnbull, *The Rise and Progress of Freemasonry in Illinois, 1783–1952,* 101.

36. *Reprint of the Proceedings of the Grand Lodge of Illinois,* 59–60.

37. Nauvoo Lodge was skirting this regulation by having regular meetings every two weeks. For just one example among many, the petitions of William Weeks, King Follett, Isaac Morley, and forty-two others were received at the regular communication of May 5, 1842. The petitions were reported on and balloted for at the next regular communication of May 19, 1842. See "Nauvoo Masonic Lodge minutes, 1841–1846," May 5, 1842; May 19, 1842.

2nd. *Resolved,* That a lodge ought not to confer more than one degree on a candidate in a shorter time than from one regular [monthly] meeting to another, except in cases of emergency.[38]

By his authority as Grand Master, Meredith Helm appointed Brothers Jonathan Nye, Grand Secretary W. B. Warren, and Hiram Rogers of Quincy to form the committee of investigation.[39] Nye had been Master of the Grand Lodge of Vermont from 1815 to 1817, where he may have been acquainted with Joseph Smith Sr., was involved in Royal Arch Masonry at the national level as Grand King, and served as second Grand Master of the Grand Encampment of the Knights Templar. He was also the first Grand Master of the Grand Council, Royal and Select Masters of New Hampshire.[40] After he moved to Illinois, he was a highly respected organizing lecturer, helping the newly formed lodges learn ritual work. On November 1, 1842, a month after the assignment was made, Nye reported to Illinois's Grand Master Meredith Helm that the charges against Nauvoo Lodge appeared to be without substance, while acknowledging that some irregularities were present.[41] The committee issued a resolution that the dispensation of Nauvoo Lodge be continued until the following annual meeting and suggested that a brother be appointed to attend Nauvoo Lodge meetings to admonish the Mormon Masons "in the most friendly manner" not to continue their breaking of the bylaws. Helm then lifted the injunction and authorized Nauvoo Lodge to continue their work. This order was signed by Grand Master Helm on November 2 and was attached to the October 1842 Grand Lodge minutes and to the Nauvoo Lodge minutes on the date of November 10, 1842. On that day, they returned to work after a three-month hiatus.[42]

One week later, on November 17, Jonathan Nye arrived in Nauvoo. For three months he attended numerous meetings of the Lodge, allowing him to keep his finger upon the pulse of the daily work of Freemasonry in the city until he left on February 10, 1843.

At the 1842 Grand Lodge meeting, Lucius Scovil had spoken to Grand Master Helm about the difficulties that Nauvoo Lodge was having because of the

---

38. *Reprint of the Proceedings of the Grand Lodge of Illinois,* 61.

39. *Reprint of the Proceedings of the Grand Lodge of Illinois,* 62. W. B. Warren is not mentioned by name here, only by his office of "G. Secretary."

40. George L. Marshall Jr., "Reverend Jonathan Nye, 2nd Grand Master of the Grand Encampment 1829–1835."

41. In particular, the Committee of Investigation felt that Nauvoo had committed irregularities in "balloting for more than one applicant at one and the same time," and that "an applicant of at least doubtful character was received on a promise of reformation and restitution." This committee consisted of Jonathan Nye and Grand Secretary W. B. Warren and did not include original appointee and member of Bodley Lodge Hiram Rogers. *Reprint of the Proceedings of the Grand Lodge of Illinois,* 70.

42. "Copy of Removal of Injunction," signed November 2, 1842, in "Nauvoo Masonic Lodge minutes, 1841–1846."

"unavoidable but protracted absence of its first two officers." George Miller, the Master of Nauvoo Lodge, served a mission to Kentucky in 1842 and thereafter was sent to the Wisconsin pineries to obtain lumber for the Nauvoo Temple and other building projects, and John D. Parker, who had been appointed Senior Warden on Nauvoo Lodge's dispensation, had never acted in the position, having been on a mission in Louisiana. Beginning in January 1842, Hyrum Smith generally acted from day to day as Worshipful Master *pro tempore* in Miller's stead. Whenever Miller was in town, he would either "assist" Hyrum,[43] or he would simply attend as a member of the Lodge,[44] deferring to Hyrum who outranked him in the Church hierarchy. Notable exceptions were at three of the twice-monthly regular communications, which included the trial and expulsion of John C. Bennett[45] and the celebration of St. John's Day,[46] at which occasions George Miller took his place as Master of the Lodge. Additionally, Nauvoo Lodge was in need of a permanent secretary, having expelled John C. Bennett. Several men had acted as Secretary *pro tem*, most often William Clayton and Henry G. Sherwood.

In response to Scovil's concerns, Meredith Helm authorized the Lodge to "proceed to fill the offices of said Lodge anew by election," empowering Jonathan Nye and Stephen Burtis, the master of Rising Sun Lodge, to install the new officers. Accordingly, in the presence of Joseph Smith, an election was held on November 10, 1842. The installation took place the following week by Nye, assisted by Newel K. Whitney. The new slate of officers, reported in the minute book in a decorative motif, was as follows:

Hyrum Smith, Worshipful Master
Lucius Scovil, Senior Warden
Noah Rogers, Junior Warden
James Sloan, Treasurer
William Clayton, Secretary[47]
Joshua Smith, Senior Deacon
Shadrach Roundy, Junior Deacon
Albert P. Rockwood and Joseph K. Allen, Stewards
Asahel Perry, Tyler[48]

Samuel Rolfe had actually been elected Junior Warden by a majority of sixty-nine votes, and William Felshaw captured the vote for Treasurer with fifty-two of the total votes. But at the installation on November 17, Hyrum Smith announced

---

43. "Nauvoo Masonic Lodge minutes, 1841–1846," April 22, 1842.
44. "Nauvoo Masonic Lodge minutes, 1841–1846," April 24, 28, May 5, 30, June 1, 16, 20, July 5, 11, 1842.
45. "Nauvoo Masonic Lodge minutes, 1841–1846," May 7, June 16, July 7, 1842.
46. "Nauvoo Masonic Lodge minutes, 1841–1846," June 24, 1842.
47. Clayton was not present, and George W. Thatcher acted as his proxy at the installation.
48. Perry was not present, and Samuel Rolfe acted as his proxy at the installation.

that these two brothers "declined serving in the offices they were elected to fill."[49] This seemed surprising, since Rolfe and Felshaw were founding officers of the Lodge, appointed as Steward and Tyler respectively. Furthermore, they both had attended the great majority of near-daily meetings, each serving in many *pro tem* capacities. It would, however, soon become clear why the two had demurred.

The evening after the election, Saturday, November 11, Jonathan Nye presided over sixty-two Nauvoo Lodge brothers, assisted by Hyrum Smith. Nye gave an eloquent address mentioned in the minutes, followed by Hyrum stating that "there had been some conversation upon the subject of dividing the Lodge."[50] Three hundred and eight members had now signed the bylaws, and the Lodge was growing so large that it was impossible to involve all the members in the work. Hyrum suggested appointing a committee to consider "the expediency of dividing this Lodge," and the following men were nominated: Hyrum Smith himself, Lucius Scovil, Noah Rogers, Henry G. Sherwood, and Samuel Rolfe.

The committee's report was given at the regular bi-monthly meeting on November 23, with Past Grand Master Nye in attendance. Their opinion voiced the necessity that Nauvoo Lodge be divided into three bodies as soon as possible "for the better accommodation of the Brethren and to enable them more correctly and promptly to discharge various duties incumbent on them as true and faithful Masons, and to enable them also to become more correctly acquainted with the labour, work, discipline and Lectures of the several degrees."[51] They resolved to obtain the consent of the Grand Master of Illinois, Meredith Helm, and apply for a dispensation for two new lodges, to be named "Nye Lodge," a nod to the venerable Jonathan Nye who was sitting in their midst, and "Hiram Lodge," a common enough Masonic name for a lodge but also a possible reference to their own Worshipful Master, Hyrum Smith. Names for officers were also drawn up with committee members Henry Sherwood and Samuel Rolfe as the respective Masters. William Felshaw was proposed as Senior Warden for Hiram Lodge.[52] The committee ended their report with an unusual and heartfelt pledge that if this division of the Lodge was granted, they would remain unified:

> Resolved that if our request should be granted we do most Solemnly and Sincerely pledge ourselves to the M. W. Grand Master and through him to the Grand Lodge as

---

49. "Nauvoo Masonic Lodge minutes, 1841–1846," November 18, 1842.

50. "Nauvoo Masonic Lodge minutes, 1841–1846," November 11, 1842.

51. "Nauvoo Masonic Lodge minutes, 1841–1846," November 23, 1842.

52. The slate of officers for the proposed Nye Lodge was as follows: Henry G. Sherwood, Master; John D. Parker, Senior Warden; Charles Allen, Junior Warden; John A. Forgeus, Treasurer; George W. Thatcher, Secretary; Dimick B. Huntington, Senior Deacon; Hosea Stout, Junior Deacon; Theodore Turley and George Watts, Stewards; William D. Huntington, Tyler. Officers for the proposed Hiram Lodge were: Samuel Rolfe, Master; William Felshaw, Senior Warden; Ebenezer Robinson, Junior Warden; Aaron Johnson, Treasurer; Ephraim Potter Jun., Secretary; George A. Smith, Senior Deacon; Arthur Millikin, Junior Deacon; James H. Rollins and David Grant, Stewards; and Gilbert Rolfe, Tyler.

in the presence of the great Ruler of the universe, that we will indulge no jealousies, or unkind feelings toward these respective bodies or any individual thereof in consequence of this seperation, but will exert ourselves in every consistent and rational manner to promote and advance peace & harmony throughout the whole.—and by a prudent discreet and truly masonic conduct ~~towards~~ ^render^ these Lodges useful faithful and honorable Branches of the W. Grand Lodge of this State.[53]

The members present at this meeting of November 23 decided to wait for "some future expedient time" to make their request to the Grand Master. Little information is available about when the application for these two lodges was received or when the dispensations were given. In a speech at the proceedings of the next Grand Lodge meeting on October 2, 1843, Grand Master Meredith Helm commented that "since your last annual meeting" (in October 1842) he had granted dispensations for the formation of new lodges at Nauvoo.[54] These were Nye Lodge U.D. and Helm Lodge U.D., both of which were represented by J. S. Myers. Presumably, the dispensations had been granted in early 1843. However, these two new lodges at Nauvoo were not the lodges envisioned by Nauvoo Lodge in their November meetings.

Nauvoo Masons Install Warsaw Lodge Officers

The early days of January 1843 found Meredith Helm and Jonathan Nye up to their elbows in intrigue. In fellowship with Mormon Freemasons, they began to work outside procedures accepted and normative throughout the Masonic system. A lodge located in Warsaw, Illinois, was given a dispensation by Meredith Helm acting as the installing officer. On January 9, Helm gathered a group consisting largely of Nauvoo Masons who traveled together to Warsaw to assist in organizing the lodge. Each man was given a *pro tempore* Grand Lodge office, and under these they installed the new officers of the Warsaw Lodge under dispensation.[55] Mormon Masons may have been quite earnest in their support, but given the political environment, such a large group of Mormon Masons may have been threatening to the new lodge members. Some of the men in the Warsaw Lodge, such as Mark Aldrich and the Chittenden brothers, became staunchly anti-Mor-

---

53. "Nauvoo Masonic Lodge minutes, 1841–1846," November 23, 1842.

54. Reynolds, *History of the Most Worshipful Grand Lodge of Illinois*, 193.

55. Reynolds, 218–19. Reynolds names the following brethren who officiated as grand officers: "Louis Ervin, D.G.M., *p.t.*; L.N. Scovil, S.G.W., *p.t.*; D.S. Hollister, J.G.W., *p.t.*; S. Comer, G. Treas., *p.t.*; C. Robinson, G. Sec., *p.t.*; B.L. Gallup, S.G.D., *p.t.*; W. Folshaw [Felshaw], J.G.D., *p.t.*; E.H. Spinning, G.S.B., *p.t.*; J.A. Forgis [Forgeus], G.M., *p.t.*; E.B. Baldwin, G.T., *p.t.* The following additional brethren were present: L.B. Stoddard, J.W. Collidge, J.B. Nobles, and Benjamin Avise. Of these, all except Ervin and Avise were members of the Mormon Lodges at Nauvoo." Actually, Benjamin Gallop, Samuel Comer, and E. B. Baldwin were from Hancock Lodge of Carthage and had never been members of the Mormon Lodges. Nine of the above-named brothers were from Mormon lodges.

mon and participated in the mob action culminating in the murders of Joseph and Hyrum Smith in 1844 (see Chapter 17).

The day after the Warsaw Lodge installation on January 10, 1843, Nye presided as two new candidates for Warsaw Lodge were initiated, passed, and raised to Master Mason all in the same day. Joseph Smith and Sidney Rigdon had been made Masons in a similar procedure, which had drawn great criticism from other Illinois lodges. Not two weeks later, one of these new Warsaw Masons made a motion that Nye be sent as delegate to the National Masonic Convention in Baltimore, Maryland, to be held May 8–17, 1843.[56]

The Baltimore Convention

The Baltimore Convention's professed purpose was "to produce uniformity of Masonic work and to recommend such measures as should tend to the elevation of the Order."[57] For nine days, delegates from Masonic Grand Lodges in fourteen states attempted to perfect the ritual and eliminate discrepancies among lodges in the United States.[58] Additionally, they adopted a report endorsing "the establishment of a Grand National Convention possessing limited powers . . . and to act as referee between Grand Lodges at variance."[59]

The possibility of a National Grand Lodge generated great excitement and speculation among the lodges located across the United States. Jonathan Nye had been actively campaigning for a General Grand Lodge since 1822.[60] The Mormons were

---

56. At this occasion, the Committee on Masonic Jurisprudence met to facilitate purity and unity of work and correct the evils that prevailed because of the individual action of the numerous Grand Lodges in the United States. The committee considered two plans: "1st. A General Grand Lodge of the United States. 2nd. A triennial convention of representatives of the several Grand Lodges of the United States." The latter course was recommended, and a date suggested for another meeting to be held in Winchester, Virginia, on May 11, 1846. On that date there was a lack of a quorum, so the meeting adjourned without action.

57. Albert G. Mackey, William J. Hughan, and Edward L. Hawkins, *An Encyclopaedia of Freemasonry and its Kindred Sciences, Comprising the Whole Range of Arts, Sciences and Literature as Connected with the Institution*, 1:96.

58. These were New Hampshire, Rhode Island, New York, Maryland, District of Columbia, North Carolina, South Carolina, Georgia, Alabama, Florida, Tennessee, Ohio, Missouri, and Louisiana. R. W. E. Cruben of Louisiana was numbered as a visitor at the Convention. See Gustav A. Eitel, "The Baltimore Convention."

59. Stephen Dafoe, ed., The Masonic Dictionary Project, s.v., "The Baltimore Convention."

60. In a letter to Past Grand Master of Ohio John Snow, written March 5, 1822, Nye wrote: "I wish to call your attention to a subject, in my view, important and desirable. It is the establishment of a General Grand Lodge for the United States. Such an establishment would strengthen the cord which now feebly unites the brethren of the different states and induce them to feel and take a deeper interest in disseminating the true principles of the institution. . . . Let us form a solid column and present to the world our harmonious

well aware of the power and opportunities such an organization could present—it was mentioned in the Nauvoo Lodge minutes twice—in both 1843 and 1844.[61] The Illinois Grand Lodge came out strongly in favor of a National Grand Lodge in 1845,[62] with Abraham Jonas, Jonathan Nye, and even Meredith Helm all being well placed to play a role in the anticipated body. It is even likely that Joseph Smith with his brother Hyrum, then Worshipful Master of Nauvoo Lodge, entertained the same ambition. The growth of the Illinois lodges had been astonishing due to Smith's encouragement of the Fraternity among church members and the zeal of Jonas, Nye, and Helm in supporting the growth of Freemasonry under the reestablished Grand Lodge of Illinois. In 1842, Nauvoo Lodge membership topped 256, and there were forty-five known members of Rising Sun Lodge at Montrose, Iowa Territory. (Unfortunately, records for the other Mormon lodges are unavailable.) Comparatively, Masonic membership in the rest of the state totaled 230.[63] Explosive growth of Mormon Freemasonry in Nauvoo continued until early 1846, culminating in about 1,300 members of the Nauvoo Lodge alone and hundreds more in the other lodges. Masonic historian John C. Reynolds expressed the fear of many of the Illinois Masons when he speculated, "[I]f the Lodge had been suffered to work two years longer, every Mormon in Hancock County would have been initiated."[64]

The first two Grand Masters of the Grand Lodge of Illinois were initially pleased to see so many new Masons. They were flexible and forgiving, wishing to build the Fraternity after the decline following William Morgan's disappearance. However, Bodley Lodge vehemently opposed granting a charter to Nauvoo Lodge. Other lodges expressed the same misgivings because a preponderance of Mormon Masons threatened the power dynamics in the Illinois Grand Lodge and potentially at the national level. If Helm, Jonas, or Nye planned to play a role in the projected National Grand Lodge, huge numbers of Mormon Masons under the control of a powerful leader now seemed incompatible with these designs.

The vision of a National Grand Lodge in the United States was never achieved. Following a recommendation of the 1843 Convention to meet in three years' time, representatives from eight Grand Lodges met at Winchester,

---

efforts. . . . If you feel engaged in this pursuit, I wish you to converse with some of your influential brethren and ascertain their views and feelings, and communicate to me without delay the result as well as your opinion." See Jonathan Nye, "For a General Grand Lodge!"

61. "Nauvoo Masonic Lodge minutes, 1841–1846," November 2, 1843; January 4, 1844.

62. *Reprint of the Proceedings of the Grand Lodge of Illinois*, 196–97, 223.

63. According to Grand Lodge returns, 1842 Illinois Lodge Membership was: Bodley Lodge No. 1, 23; Harmony No. 3, 21; Springfield No. 4, 43; Columbus No. 6, 23; Macon No. 8, 22; Juliet No. 10, 25; Rushville UD, 20; Western Star UD, 23; Cass UD, 12; St. John's UD, 10; Warren UD, 8; for a total of 230 non-Mormon Masons in the entire state. Comparatively, Nauvoo Lodge reported 256; and Rising Sun Lodge at Montrose, Iowa Territory, 45; totaling 301. See *Reprint of the Proceedings of the Grand Lodge of Illinois*, 73–78.

64. Reynolds, *History of the Most Worshipful Grand Lodge of Illinois*, 184.

Virginia, on May 11, 1846. Due to the minority attendance, the Convention adjourned without doing any business. Another Masonic Convention was held at Baltimore on September 23, 1847, to consider the propriety of forming a national General Grand Lodge. This time only seven accredited delegates were in attendance. Nonetheless, they drafted a Constitution that was sent to all the US Grand Lodges. It was resolved that if sixteen of them approved the measure before January 1, 1849, it would go into effect. The Constitution, however, failed to receive approval from any of the Grand Lodges. Other attempts to form a National Grand Lodge in 1853, 1855, and 1859 were similarly fruitless.[65]

Regardless of the National Grand Lodge's eventual fate, Mormon lodges continued to flourish on the Illinois frontier.

Keokuk Lodge U.D., Keokuk Iowa

Across the Mississippi River and twelve miles southwest of Nauvoo lay the township of Keokuk, Iowa. It was named in honor of Chief Keokuk, a Sac and Fox Indian who visited Joseph Smith in August of 1841 with approximately one hundred other Native Americans. Smith addressed the group upon the topic of the promises contained in the Book of Mormon respecting "themselves, the despised remnants of a once splendid race."[66] At that time, the population of Keokuk was estimated at 150. Smith owned land in Keokuk, which he obtained from Isaac Galland when he bought the Commerce town site that became Nauvoo. Displaced Mormons from Missouri and elsewhere trickled into town in the first years of the 1840s, adding to the sparsely scattered inhabitants. The Zarahemla Stake Conference of August 8, 1841, reported thirteen members attending from Keokuk.[67] By December 28, 1842, several of the Mormon settlers had obtained a dispensation from the Grand Lodge of Illinois to start a Masonic Lodge in their Iowa township.

The year of 1843 began with an installation ceremony at Keokuk, presided over by Jonathan Nye. This experienced Freemason constituted the Lodge and installed the officers on January 17, 1843, with Henry King as the founding Master. King had been made a Mason at Sylvan Lodge No. 229 in New York and had been present at the installation of Nauvoo Lodge on March 15, 1842, and at several other occasions. Keokuk Branch President Abraham O. Smoot was initiated and passed in Keokuk Lodge.[68]

---

65. Mackey, Hughan, and Hawkins, *Encyclopedia of Freemasonry*, 1:292–94; Henry Wilson Coil, *Coil's Masonic Encyclopedia*, 277b–280a.

66. B. H. Roberts, *The Rise and Fall of Nauvoo*, 106–7.

67. Lyman D. Platt, "Early Branches of the Church of Jesus Christ of Latter-day Saints, 1830–1850," 20–21.

68. Smoot attended Nauvoo Lodge on December 7, 1843, hailing "from Keokuk Lodge U.D., a F.C. petitioning for 3rd degree." See "Nauvoo Masonic Lodge minutes, 1841–1846," December 7, 1843.

At the end of the year, the Grand Lodge deemed the work of Keokuk Lodge "very irregular and highly censurable" because there had been several instances when the ballot was taken in less than one full lunar month after the petition. "In every other respect," however, the committee admitted that "the work appears to have been correct."[69] Nonetheless, at this Grand Lodge Communication of October 1843 the dispensation of Keokuk Lodge was revoked, as were the dispensations of Nauvoo, Nye, and Helm Lodges, while the charter of Rising Sun Lodge was suspended. In his history of the Grand Lodge of Iowa, Joseph Morcombe gave as his opinion:

> The matters criticized are not in themselves sufficient to justify the action recommended and taken—they were used only to veil or hide the social, political and religious difficulties, which were rightfully regarded as dangerous subjects to bring before the Grand Lodge.[70]

During the period of time that Rising Sun and Keokuk Lodges were in operation, they became part of a movement to form a Grand Lodge in the state of Iowa. In October 1842 Jonathan Nye visited Burlington Lodge U.D. The minutes record that, when asked to give his opinion as to forming a Grand Lodge of Iowa, Nye was found in favor and a committee was appointed for that purpose. Finally, on January 2, 1844, four Iowa Lodges met to organize a Grand Lodge in their state. Although Rising Sun and Keokuk Lodges had not been invited to the meeting, representatives from both of these lodges appeared and insisted they be recognized. Ansel Humphreys, the prime contender for Grand Master of the new Grand Lodge, asserted that the Mormon representatives were "without a Masonic home by virtue of the withdrawal of charter and dispensation of these lodges by the Grand Lodge of Illinois." Though Des Moines Lodge was in favor of seating the Mormon delegates, the other three lodges "upheld its chairman in his ruling. . . . This decision provoked a breach among the delegates which ultimately prevented election of Ansel Humphreys as the first Grand Master of Masons in Iowa."[71] The difficulties with Mormon lodges clearly extended beyond Illinois.

Nye Lodge U.D., Nauvoo, Illinois

Jonathan Nye's involvement in the formation of Nye Lodge was unconventional and intriguing. Nye was present at the November 23, 1842, Nauvoo Lodge meeting where the brothers decided upon a slate of officers for a lodge to be called Nye Lodge. In order to avoid confusion, we will refer to this proposed lodge as "Nye Lodge (1)." By February 1843, Jonathan Nye organized a lodge in Nauvoo in opposition to the one proposed in November with a different slate of officers. This was also named "Nye Lodge." We will refer to this lodge as "Nye

69. *Reprint of the Proceedings of the Grand Lodge of Illinois*, 89.
70. Morcombe, *History of Grand Lodge of Iowa*, 160.
71. Tom B. Throckmorton, "Morgan, Mormons, and Masonry, a New Approach," 38.

Lodge (2)." Of this rival lodge, Joseph Smith opined, "they will do us all the injury they can, but let them go ahead, altho' it will result in a division of the [Nauvoo] lodge."[72]

The little evidence available presents a possible reason for Nye's opposition. An insertion in Smith's journal for February 9, 1843, reads: "conversation with Master Nye & W.W. Phelps[.] went to Keokuk." Notes for the same day discuss Smith's explanation to "Parley Pratt and othe[r]s" about classes of angels and devils. Freemasonry contains the idea that a certain grip might provide information about the one giving the handshake, and Smith had spiritualized the concept and retooled it for Mormonism.[73] He thus gave three keys by which one could identify angelic messengers by asking them to shake hands: the "spirit of a just man made perfect" (a resurrected being) would have tangible flesh and bones, one could not feel the handshake of a devil, and a "true spirit" would not offer his hand to be tested at all.[74]

It is not clear whether Nye was present for Smith's remarks on the classes of spirits, but if Nye, a notable ritualist himself, was in attendance, he may well have been stunned to see a Masonic tradition expressed in Mormonism, likely viewing Smith's borrowing as an arrogant overreach. He might have even viewed it as a corruption of Freemasonry or a betrayal of Smith's oath not to share Freemasonry's esoteric wisdom with the uninitiated. Innovation and exploration have always been crucial to the spiritual and intellectual vitality of Freemasonry, but there are limits on what sort of innovation is acceptable; it is certainly not permissible to mine Freemasonry's secret knowledge for wisdom to enrich other organizations. As a man more than twenty years Smith's senior, and as a far more experienced Mason, Nye may well have felt entitled to chastise Smith for his misappropriation of Masonry's hermetic lore.

On the other end, Smith seemed to see as spurious any form of Masonry that did not let him adapt it as he pleased. He certainly felt that Nye was "trying to pull me by the nose and trample on me" and "enquired of the Lord if I was to be led by the nose and cuffed about by such a man." The answer he received

---

72. "History, 1838–1856, volume D-1 [1 August 1842–1 July 1843]," The Joseph Smith Papers, 1541.

73. At the funeral of Freemason James Adams, Joseph Smith preached on this concept in connection with priesthood keys. The prophet explained that the keys of power and knowledge were given to men through communication with the spirits of just men made perfect— "hence the importance of understanding the distinction between the spirits of the just, and angels. Spirits can only be revealed in flaming fire, or glory. Angels have advanced farther—their light and glory being tabernacled, and hence appear in bodily shape." Adams had been a close friend, and Smith "had annointed him to the Patriarchal power—to receive the keys of knowledge, and power, by revelation." See Gustavus Hills, "Minutes of a Special Conference," 331.

74. "Journal, December 1842–June 1844; Book 1, 21 December 1842–10 March 1843," The Joseph Smith Papers, 172–74.

from the Lord was "Wait a minute."[75] Smith accused Nye of violating his oath as a Master Mason by committing adultery, and Nye "speedily fled from Nauvoo," fearing the penalty of the city ordinances. On April 1, 1843, he traveled to Fort Madison, Iowa, to make a Masonic speech. While there, Nye died suddenly under suspicious circumstances. Smith learned the news on April 25 from Lucius Scovil and other Masons who had come to speak with him "concerning H[enry] G. Sherwood," who had originally been proposed as Master of Nye Lodge (1). Smith told the brethren: "Nye is dead, and any man or mason who attempts to ride me down, and oppress me, will run against the boss of Jehovah's buckler, and will be quickly moved out of the way."[76] Such language is reminiscent of similar biblically based code utilized by the Danites. Adding to the mystery, despite an exhaustive search through cemeteries, burial records, and newspapers on both sides of the Mississippi River, no evidence has been found regarding the location of Nye's final resting place.

Two days later, on Thursday, April 27, 1843, Nye Lodge (2) "was installed on the hill."[77] Henry G. Sherwood never served as the Master of Nye's rival lodge. Instead, he and the rest of the slate of officers for the earlier proposed Nye Lodge (1) continued to attend Nauvoo Lodge, some reapplying for membership or filling in as *pro tem* officers.[78] Nye Lodge (2) is discussed in the minutes of the Grand Lodge of Illinois. It was granted a dispensation to begin Masonic work, but the Lodge never submitted a yearly return.[79] Therefore, it is difficult to discover who the officers or members were.[80]

The argument that Nye Lodge (2) was an opposition lodge distinct from the Nye Lodge (1) proposed in 1842 is strengthened by events recorded in the Nauvoo Lodge minutes for August 10, 1843. In that meeting it was decided that "the time had arrived for dividing the Lodge." Sidney Rigdon, who was not an officer and had only attended the Lodge a mere six times since being raised—but still had great influence because of his position in the Church—motioned "that Nauvoo Lodge be divided into 3 branches" and that Nye and "Hyram" Lodges should "have their proportion of the funds of Nauvoo Lodge" and share the use of the new Masonic Hall. A slate of officers was chosen for the "New Lodge"—

---

75. "History, 1838–1856, volume D-1 [1 August 1842–1 July 1843]," 1541.

76. "History, 1838–1856, volume D-1 [1 August 1842–1 July 1843]," 1541.

77. "History, 1838–1856, volume D-1 [1 August 1842–1 July 1843]," 1541.

78. See, for example, "Nauvoo Masonic Lodge minutes, 1841–1846," June 19, 1843, when John D. Parker filled in as Junior Deacon *pro tem.*; and September 14, 1843, when he acted as Junior Deacon *pro tem.* and reapplied for membership the same day.

79. Nye Lodge (2) is thus known in Masonic terms as "Nye Lodge U.D." It was authorized by the Grand Lodge of Illinois, while Nye Lodge (1) was not.

80. Nathaniel Case was named on the Nauvoo Lodge minutes of July 3, 1843, as a visitor from Nye Lodge. John Olney and George W. Robinson each have a notation following their signature to the Nauvoo Lodge Bylaws reading "Nye Lodge." See "Nauvoo Masonic Lodge minutes, 1841–1846."

Nye Lodge (1). The officers were enjoined to rename their lodge "in consequence of another Lodge in this County be[ing] called Nye Lodge."[81] It was resolved that "the Brethren nominated for officers be recommended to the M. W. G. Master of the M. W. G. Lodge of Illinois." It is not known if this ever took place since all the Mormon Lodges' charters and dispensations were revoked by the Grand Lodge communication in October.

La Harpe Lodge, La Harpe, Illinois

La Harpe, Illinois, is located about twenty-five miles east of Nauvoo. First settled in 1830, it was renamed, platted, and developed by 1836. Latter-day Saint Erastus Bingham arrived in the town around 1839 as a missionary, and his work was successful enough that before long a branch of the Church was established. According to historian Donald Q. Cannon, on March 15, 1841, Elder Zenas Gurley "reported that he had labored for a few weeks at La Harpe, where, in six days he had baptized 52 persons." Some of the leading citizens of La Harpe were eventually converted, including Dr. George Coulson and merchant and postmaster Lewis R. Chaffin.[82] By 1845, there were 250 members of the Church in La Harpe.[83]

On February 1, 1843, several Mormon brethren in La Harpe brought a petition before the Nauvoo Lodge. It was directed to the Most Worshipful Grand Master of the Grand Lodge of Illinois asking "for a Letter of dispensation empowering them to open a Lodge in said Town of Laharpe." In order to send such a petition to the Grand Lodge, they needed the endorsement of a regularly constituted lodge. According to their minutes, the brothers of Nauvoo Lodge duly approved the petition and recommended the new lodge.[84]

It appears that La Harpe did form a lodge, although no record of dispensation from the Grand Lodge is available. On June 15, 1843, Nauvoo Lodge members resolved to invite local lodges to participate with them in their annual celebration of the Feast of St. John the Baptist and cornerstone laying of the new Masonic Hall. Six lodges were mentioned: Warsaw, Carthage, Keokuk, Rising Sun, Helm,

---

81. "Nauvoo Masonic Lodge minutes, 1841–1846," August 10, 1843. The new officers were D. S. Hollister, WM; Aaron Johnson, SW; and Joseph W. Coolidge, JW.

82. Donald Q. Cannon, "Spokes on the Wheel: Early Latter-day Saint Settlements in Hancock County," 62–68.

83. Platt, "Early Branches of the Church," 22. According to FamilySearch.org, in 1855, there were 1201 residents of La Harpe.

84. "Nauvoo Masonic Lodge minutes, 1841–1846," February 1, 1843. Some of the brothers who were living in La Harpe and had petitioned for or received degrees in Nauvoo Lodge before that date were John F. Olney (raised May 31, 1842), John Jackson (raised June 13, 1842), Louis R. Chaffin (petitioned June 2, 1842), and Thomas Walinsley (petitioned July 7, 1842, but died of bilious fever on November 16, 1842).

and La Harpe.[85] At least one of the members of La Harpe Lodge, Rufus Beech, joined the celebration on June 24 and appears in the roster of attendees.[86]

If La Harpe had received a dispensation during 1843, it should have been mentioned in the Grand Lodge proceedings in October of that year. It was not. In his opening speech, Grand Master Meredith Helm stated that he had granted dispensations "for the formation of new Lodges at Warsaw, Carthage, Macomb, Chicago, Nauvoo, and Pekin . . . at Keokuk, Iowa; and at Milwaukee, Wisconsin Territory."[87] It is possible that La Harpe Lodge did not send a representative to Grand Lodge, so Helm—who was already under censure for granting dispensations to so many Mormon lodges—did not mention it. It is also possible that La Harpe was already meeting despite not having yet received a dispensation.

Helm Lodge and the Proposed Hiram Lodge, Nauvoo, Illinois

Like the proposed Nye Lodge, Hiram Lodge was planned with a complete slate of officers as one of the divisions of Nauvoo Lodge on November 23, 1842.[88] As mentioned above, it was again discussed on August 10, 1843, but no petition has been found, and it was never constituted. Instead, its proposed officers remained active members of Nauvoo Lodge. While it is commonly assumed that this proposed Hiram Lodge later became Helm Lodge,[89] the evidence shows that these were two separate groups.

On March 27, 1843, a petition was brought before Nauvoo Lodge by several brethren seeking a recommendation for a dispensation from the Grand Master to open a new lodge in the city of Nauvoo. These brothers were not the ones mentioned as officers for the proposed Hiram or Nye Lodges the previous November. The petition was discussed with several men remarking "on the impropriety of granting the request."[90] The matter was deferred until the next regular meeting on April 6, 1843. That meeting was attended by fifty-seven men, including Joseph Smith, Worshipful Master Hyrum Smith, Senior Warden Lucius Scovil, and Master of the proposed Nye Lodge Henry G. Sherwood, all of whom spoke in

---

85. "Nauvoo Masonic Lodge minutes, 1841–1846," June 15, 1843. The minutes for that day refer to the Masonic Hall as the "Masonic Temple."

86. "Nauvoo Masonic Lodge minutes, 1841–1846," June 24, 1843.

87. *Reprint of the Proceedings of the Grand Lodge of Illinois*, 85.

88. This resolution was read at a meeting of Nauvoo Lodge in the presence of Jonathan Nye. The proposed officers were Samuel Rolfe, WM; William Felshaw, SW; Ebenezer Robinson, JW; Aaron Johnson, Treas.; Ephraim Potter, Jun., Sec.; George A. Smith, SD; Arthur Millikin, JD; James H. Rollins and David Grant, Stewards; and Gilbert Rolfe, Tyler. "Nauvoo Masonic Lodge minutes, 1841-1846," November 23, 1842.

89. Michael W. Homer, *Joseph's Temples: The Dynamic Relationship between Freemasonry and Mormonism*, 165.

90. "Nauvoo Masonic Lodge minutes, 1841-1846," March 27, 1843. The petitioners were Jack S. Miles, Reuben Hadlock [Hedlock], Ira S. Miles, Asahel A. Lathrop, Henry Hoglan, Gustavus Hills, and Jacob Shoemaker.

opposition to the recommendation. A motion was made "not deeming it wisdom to divide" and resolving to "write a letter to the G[rand] Master informing of our reasons for not recommending those Brethren."[91] Nauvoo Lodge seemingly had their own plans for the division of the Lodge and were not amenable to other proposals. However, this group of brothers must have speedily gone ahead with their plans to form a lodge, obtain a dispensation, and seek installation, as Helm Lodge was mentioned for the first time in the Nauvoo Lodge minutes at the end of the month.[92] Later, at the Nauvoo Lodge cornerstone ceremony on June 24, 1843, several of these brothers were included on a list of visitors from Helm Lodge.

Influence of Joseph Smith on Nauvoo Lodge

In nineteenth-century Illinois lodges, it was common that the Fraternity meet once monthly to conduct business as well as to receive petitions and perform ritual work. Officers of a lodge who were present at every meeting would have a yearly attendance at twelve meetings plus a couple of extra for funerals or Masonic events. At Nauvoo, regular (or "stated") meetings were held twice a month while ritual work was at times carried out almost daily—two and sometimes three times a day. Although Joseph Smith was not present at each day-to-day meeting of the Nauvoo Lodge, at which ever-increasing numbers of men were being made Masons, he held a governing influence upon its major operations. Smith attended many of the stated meetings of the Lodge. He was also actively involved when important business was conducted. In 1842 Smith's total recorded attendance at lodge meetings was twenty-seven meetings on nineteen different days.[93] He attended more than twice as many Masonic meetings than any other member or officer of a non-Mormon Illinois lodge in that year, and he continued to attend, though less often, in the years 1843 and 1844.[94]

Even though the Mormon lodges were raising members very quickly, there is evidence that the new Freemasons took the work seriously. Allen Stout, third lieutenant in a company of the Nauvoo Legion, was initiated, passed, and raised in Nauvoo Lodge in June 1842. Stout says that he "took great delight in this order of things insomuch that [he] improved every opportunity to learn the lec-

---

91. "Nauvoo Masonic Lodge minutes, 1841–1846," April 6, 1843.

92. At the death of Joseph Allen, Nauvoo Lodge planned a funeral with a Masonic procession. They resolved to invite the brethren of Rising Sun Lodge "and also Helm Lodge in this city to unite with us in procession." The "opposition" Nye Lodge, also in the city, was not invited. "Nauvoo Masonic Lodge minutes, 1841–1846," April 28, 1843.

93. "Nauvoo Masonic Lodge minutes, 1841–1846," March 15 (2), March 16 (3), April 7, April 9 (2), April 13 (3), April 14 (2), May 19, May 20, May 25, May 26, June 2, June 16, June 24 (2), July 6, November 10, December 5, December 7, December 20, December 23, 1842.

94. "Nauvoo Masonic Lodge minutes, 1841–1846," January 18, January 31, February 1, April 6, August 3, 1843, and April 5, 12, and 23, 1844.

tures and all the principles pertaining to that ancient and honorable order."[95] He immersed himself in Freemasonry so much that in the winter of 1844 through the spring of 1845, he taught an evening class on Masonry, tutoring those who had been through the degrees to learn the lectures.[96]

No doubt Jonathan Nye, who spent a great deal of time in Nauvoo Lodge from November 1842 to February 1843, also assisted the Lodge members in learning the degrees. Nye's appointment from the Grand Lodge of Kentucky had been "Grand Visitor," with the assignment of visiting all the area lodges and during several days' time "teach[ing] the Lectures, and inculcat[ing] the moral precepts of the Institution."[97] He held the same role as "Organizing Lecturer" in Illinois. Nye was well suited to this responsibility as he was well acquainted with Thomas Smith Webb and Jeremy Ladd Cross, both of whom had been instrumental in the development of Craft Masonry and York Rite Masonry in the United States.

Joseph Smith's particular talent lay in ritual-making, and he had an interest in making the Mormon degrees unique: pure, restored, and hearkening back to antiquity. This interest was likely shared by many Nauvoo Freemasons. In August and September 1843, Nauvoo Lodge hosted an entertaining visitor: Royal Arch Mason Edwin Cruben, who was known for "travelling from place to place, assuming a right to confer [the Royal and Select Master Mason] degrees upon individuals when and where it may best suit his pleasure or convenience."[98] While at Nauvoo, Cruben demonstrated "the mode of lectures as given in the French Lodges in New Orleans" to the Mormon Masons.[99] It seems possible that the Mormons may have been interested in receiving the degrees that Cruben was peddling. In any event, Nauvoo Lodge adopted a resolution that a letter of thanks be written to Brother Cruben "for services rendered during his late visit at Nauvoo," and the secretary was instructed to write a letter telling him what a privilege it was for Nauvoo Lodge to receive his visits.[100]

Charters Revoked

By late June 1843, 382 men had been raised in Nauvoo Lodge. The cornerstone had been laid for the Masonic Hall, and Freemasonry was a respected institution in the city. The day after the cornerstone ceremony, on June 25, 1843,

---

95. Allen Stout, *Allen Stout Journal*, 19.

96. Stout, 22–23.

97. Rob Morris, *History of Freemasonry in Kentucky: In Its Relations to the Symbolic Degrees*, 122.

98. *Proceedings of the Grand Chapter of Royal Arch Masons of the State of New York, at its Eighty-Fifth Annual Convention, Held at the City of Albany*, 134. This source is quoting a communication received by Alexander T. Douglas under the date of March 18, 1844.

99. "Nauvoo Masonic Lodge minutes, 1841–1846," September 7, 1843.

100. "Nauvoo Masonic Lodge minutes, 1841–1846," September 21, 1843.

Wilford Woodruff was attending a Sunday afternoon meeting. In the middle of one of the talks, Hyrum Smith "came onto the Stand & requested the Masonic fraternity to meet him at the Lodge Room in 30 minutes." Immediately, the men followed his directions, but a quarter of the men could not get into the room. They went outside onto the green and "formed a hollow square." Hyrum Smith then informed the men that his brother Joseph had been captured and taken to Missouri. About two hundred men volunteered to form a company to bring him back.[101] This incident illustrates the close relationship between Masonic, military, and ecclesiastical affairs in Nauvoo.

The Grand Lodge of Illinois finally revoked all charters and suspended all dispensations for the so-called "Mormon Lodges" in October of 1843.[102] Within days, the Grand Lodge of Missouri applauded this action, declaring that the Grand Lodge of Illinois had "resolved, in the strength of her truly Masonic principles, to separate from herself the unskillful and unworthy who have for a short time taken shelter under her good name."[103] Nauvoo Lodge, however, paid little attention to the action of the Grand Lodge of Illinois. In a business meeting on November 2, 1843, Worshipful Master Hyrum Smith urged the members to entirely ignore the withdrawal of their dispensation and continue work upon their own authority. The vote in favor of his proposal was unanimous: Nauvoo Lodge continued its labors, including its construction of the three-story Masonic Hall begun in June 1843 and dedicated on April 5, 1844.[104]

The Nauvoo Masonic Hall, said to have been the largest building in Nauvoo at the time of Joseph Smith's death in 1844, was a physical testament of the importance of Freemasonry in establishing the kingdom of God. The building committee consisted of Samuel Rolfe, Aaron Johnson, and chairman Lucius Scovil, whose home and bakery were located on the lot next door. William Weeks, designer of the Nauvoo Temple and many other public buildings in Nauvoo, was the principal architect. The Hall was built of fine red brick, set on a full basement with walls three feet thick. The front face of the building was overlaid with stucco crafted to give the appearance of marble from a short distance.[105] A large foundation stone, about three feet wide and tall, was engraved with the date 1843 and the name of the Grand Master of Illinois, A. Helm. The gable end of the building was set to the east. On this end was painted a representation of the All-Seeing Eye.[106] Three symmetrical front doorways offered access to the build-

---

101. Wilford Woodruff journal, June 25, 1843.

102. *Reprint of the Proceedings of the Grand Lodge of Illinois*, 96.

103. *Proceedings of the Grand Lodge of the State of Missouri, at their Grand Annual Convocation, Held at the City of Saint Louis, on Monday, the 9th of October, A.D. 1843, A.L. 5843*, 25.

104. "Nauvoo Masonic Lodge minutes, 1841–1846," November 2, 1843.

105. James B. Allen, "Nauvoo's Masonic Hall," 39.

106. May 22, 1896, description by B. Mendenhall, 1882 District Deputy Grand Master of the Grand Lodge of Illinois, in Albert Clark Stevens, comp., *The Cyclopaedia of Fraternities,*

Preliminary plans for the Nauvoo Masonic Hall from William Weeks's Nauvoo Architectural Drawings collection. Shows dome and all-seeing eye, both of which were not part of the 1967 reconstruction.

ing. The second-story windows, with six-inch blocks of limestone on the top and bottom, were placed above the doors. Graceful, arched third-story windows completed the picture. Their limestone arches were held in place by keystones in true Masonic fashion.

The basement rooms, well-lit by three large chandeliers, had several functions. At times they served as schoolrooms, and later they were used to store ammunition or build wagons for the trek West. A large main floor was suitable for plays, dances, and community activities. It likely included a stage similar to the one constructed in the building's restoration.

The Masonic Hall was sold when the Latter-day Saints left Nauvoo in 1846 and became a private residence. The third floor, where lodge meetings were held, was removed in 1884 but reconstructed after the LDS Church acquired the building in 1967. Both the original lodge room and the reconstruction were painted sky blue, and a white ornamental molding extended eight inches from the walls to separate them from the elevated arched ceiling. The west end of the room contained a two-story set of preparation rooms—an unusual feature that was called for by the volume of Masonic work being carried out daily.[107] The original yellow pine floor, which was left intact when the third story was removed, shows wear marks from the impact of hundreds of Mormon Masons circumambulating the central altar.

The focal point of the majestic lodge room was without doubt the dais in the East, where the Master's chair was strategically placed in front of the arched windows. Two twelve-foot pillars flanked three steps leading to the platform that was placed under an impressive dome. The white pillars were marbled with blue paint that matched the walls. An elegant bronze "G," the Masonic symbol for Deity, was suspended above the chair. Given the investments of time, money, energy, and devotion the men of the Nauvoo Lodge made in their Temple, it's easy to understand why they were unwilling to give up using it in ways that seemed right to them.[108]

Learning of Nauvoo Lodge's refusal to cease work, a new Grand Master of Illinois deputized the Master of Bodley Lodge to demand Nauvoo's officers' jew-

---

A Compilation of Existing Authentic Information and the Results of Original Investigation as to the Origin, Derivation, Founders, Development, Aims, Emblems, Character, and Personnel of More than Six Hundred Secret Societies in the United States, Second Edition, 71.

107. In the restoration following the LDS Church's purchase of the building in 1967, a "musician's balcony" was added that was not present in the original room. The western wall of the lodge room came fully down to the floor, where the floor planks under the balcony are not original. On the remaining original planks, it is evident that the Senior Warden's dais extended from the wall. Wear marks indicate the location where the candidates stood before him.

108. Description of the lodge room is taken from James B. Allen, "Nauvoo's Masonic Hall," 39–41. Allen drew heavily from Charles Mulch's 1937 depiction of the building. Mulch had remodeled the building in 1884 but provided a description of what it looked like before the changes.

els and records. Rather than comply, the officers of Nauvoo Lodge gave notice that they intended to appeal the Grand Lodge's decision to the next "Triennial Convention" of American Masons—a meeting not scheduled until late March of 1846.[109] The Nauvoo Masons had placed themselves irrevocably in opposition to the Grand Lodge of Illinois.

The members of Bodley Lodge, meanwhile, were obsessed with the actions of the Mormon lodges. In an April 1, 1844, meeting of Bodley Lodge, Worshipful Master J. B. Conyers took up the subject:

> The W. Master remarked that the Nauvoo Lodges still were working & finishing their Hall, notwithstanding their dispensation had been withdrawn by the Grand Lodge.
>
> Bro. Truman was called upon, & stated that he had learned that the Nauvoo Lodges were still at work, receiving passing & raising masons, and that the Brethren of Warsaw Lodge had notified the Grand officer on the Subject.
>
> On motion of Bro. Stehls, Resolved, that the Secy be instructed to inform the G. Master of this State that the Nauvoo & Keokuk, the Lodges in & about Nauvoo continue to work, & that they have given notice in a public paper of their intention, to consecrate their Masonic Hall on the 5th inst. & that the said Masons pretend not to be in possession of official notice, that they were deprived of their Charter & dispensation.[110]

While the minutes of Bodley Lodge No. 1 are not explicit, the chief concerns may have been the status of Illinois Masonry among the other US Grand Lodges if they did not respond to the Mormon lodges' violations.

Hiram Lodge No. 7, Augusta, Iowa

The community of Augusta was located a few miles upriver from Nauvoo on the Western bank of the Mississippi in Iowa Territory. It had been established in 1835, when Frederick Kesler surveyed the town site and Levi Moffitt built a water-powered flour mill, bringing customers from a distance of up to one hundred miles. Both men soon converted to Mormonism, joining several Mormon families who fled Missouri in 1838–39. A few years later, on April 1, 1843, James Brown was made president of the Augusta branch, consisting of eighty-four members.[111]

On April 1, 1844 (the same day that Bodley Lodge discussed the renegade behavior of the lodges), six men "all of Nauvoo Lodge" appeared in Des Moines, Iowa, Lodge No. 1 and presented a proposal for a lodge to be established in

---

109. *Proceedings of the National Masonic Convention, Held at Baltimore, Maryland, May, A.L. 5843, A.D. 1843*, 91.

110. Minutes of Bodley Lodge No. 1, A.F. & A.M. of Illinois, April 1, 1844.

111. William G. Hartley, "Mormons and Early Iowa History (1838 to 1858): Eight Distinct Connections," 228.

Augusta.[112] A recommendation was granted, and a petition was made that day to the Grand Lodge of Iowa by William A. Weston,[113] Jacob F. Hutchinson,[114] Clark L. Whitney,[115] David Kneeland, Jacob F. Abbott,[116] and Alvin C. Graves.[117] Grand Master Oliver Cock granted a dispensation for this lodge by April 16, 1844. Thus, although five Mormon lodges had been declared clandestine by the Grand Lodge of Illinois, another was constituted before the death of Joseph Smith in 1844. This lodge, Hiram Lodge No. 7, would receive its charter on January 7, 1845, from the Grand Lodge of Iowa.

Hiram Lodge No. 7 was constituted predominantly of Mormons for some years. As in Nauvoo Lodge, petitions were received in large numbers, candidates were rushed through in blocs, and the lodge was consistently short of funds, indicating a system of rebates or remission of fees.[118]

A Mormon Grand Lodge

In April 1844, the six Mormon lodges included Nauvoo, Rising Sun No. 12, Keokuk, Helm, Nye, and Hiram No. 7. There were possibly three other unofficial lodges at La Harpe and in Nauvoo (the original proposed Nye and Hiram Lodges). Because the other Mormon lodges were accused of some of the same irregularities as Nauvoo Lodge, including rushing candidates through the degrees, it can be assumed that they had many more than an average amount of members for a lodge.[119] Even though the records of these lodges are not extant, we are able to discover the identities of fifty-eight members of Rising Sun Lodge No. 12, nine at Keokuk, seven at Nye Lodge, twenty at Helm Lodge, and thirteen at Hiram Lodge No. 7.

---

112. Morcombe, *History of Grand Lodge of Iowa*, 1:171. These were Brothers McCormack, Stewart, G. P. Adams, A. F. Hutchison, C. L. Whitney, and Jacob Abbott.

113. "William A. Weston, et. al., to The Most Worshipful Grand Lodge of the Territory of Iowa," April 1, 1844. Weston, a High Priest in the Springville, IA branch, died on July 13, 1853, en route from Iowa to Utah. He married Cynthia Shurtliff on May 9, 1850, in Pottawattamie, Iowa.

114. Hutchinson and his wife Constantia received their endowments in the Nauvoo Temple December 22, 1845. He played clarinet in the Nauvoo Band and later died in Springville, Utah.

115. Whitney was a carpenter on the Nauvoo Temple and a Nauvoo Freemason raised March 2, 1843.

116. Abbott was a Nauvoo Freemason raised June 27, 1842, and member of the Nauvoo Legion. He died in Paradise, Utah.

117. Graves stayed in Iowa and was Treasurer of Hiram Lodge No. 7 in 1852.

118. Morcombe, *History of Grand Lodge of Iowa*, 1:170–72.

119. In an 1845 estimation of the total number of Freemasons in the United States, the Grand Lodge of Illinois supposed that the "average number of Masons in each Lodge" was twenty. Reynolds, *History of the Most Worshipful Grand Lodge of Illinois*, 308.

Mormon Lodges 1842–1844				
Name	(Proposed)/ Petition	Dispensation	Installation	Charter
Nauvoo Lodge U.D.	abt 7/28/41	10/15/41	3/15/42	none
Rising Sun No. 12	10/5/41	1841	8/6/42	10/3/42
Nye/New Lodge	(11/23/42) (8/10/43)			none
Hiram Lodge	(11/23/42) (8/10/42)			none
Keokuk Lodge U.D.		12/28/42	1/17/43	none
Nye Lodge U.D.		early 1843	4/27/43	none
Helm Lodge U.D.	(3/27/43)	by 4/28/43		none
LaHarpe Lodge	2/1/43			none
Hiram Lodge No. 7 (Iowa)	4/1/44	4/16/44	4/25/44	1/7/45

According to the Illinois Grand Lodge proceedings, the reason for making new lodges at Nauvoo was that the number of members was "too large for convenience in working."[120] But it is also likely that the Mormons were establishing numerous lodges so they would have enough for their own independent Grand Lodge. With at least six and perhaps as many as nine lodges functioning outside the control of the Grand Lodge of Illinois, sufficient bodies existed to form a Mormon Grand Lodge—as five lodges had formed the Illinois Grand Lodge in 1840, and four lodges were enough to form the Iowa Grand Lodge in 1844.

It would have been as easy as mortaring a brick for the Mormon lodges to come together and form a Grand Lodge. They simply needed one Grand Lodge to sponsor them. The problem they would have faced was that other United States Grand Lodges may not have wished to recognize them as legitimate (or "regular"). This was the case when, in 1808, Freemasons of color had formed the African Grand Lodge (later renamed "Prince Hall") under the sponsorship of the United Grand Lodge of England. It was many years before Grand Lodges in the United States would officially recognize these lodges.

While the formation of a Mormon Grand Lodge never occurred in Joseph Smith's lifetime, the idea persisted. On December 19, 1844, the Nauvoo Lodge record indicates that:

> The subject of the Grand Lodge [of Illinois] towards us was then taken up, when it was strongly urged by some, that the oppressive and tyrannical treatment which not only this Lodge, but also four other Lodges in this vicinity have received from the Grand Lodge of the State of Illinois in withholding from us our masonic rights and privileges, and that is they continually sought to tyrannize over and oppress us, it was

120. *Reprint of the Proceedings of the Grand Lodge of Illinois*, 85.

not only our right and privilege but also our duty to fall back on our reserved rights, and *call a convention of the several Lodges thus oppressed and form a Grand Lodge.*[121]

The proposition failed when, after consideration, the Worshipful Master Lucius N. Scovil "said that he thought it was bad policy under existing circumstances to form a grand lodge at this time."[122] Not until 1860, when the Mormons were confronted with the formation of a non-Mormon or "gentile" lodge at Camp Floyd, Utah, would George A. Smith and Lucius N. Scovil propose a similar plan. Brigham Young, acting in the role he inherited from Joseph Smith, vetoed the idea, predicting that such an action would "bring down all hell upon us as far as they (gentile Masons) had the power."[123]

What King Solomon Could Not Do

Having learned through Masonic lore that ancient prophets functioned as Grand Masters of Freemasons, Joseph Smith appears to have appropriated that role. Even without a Grand Lodge to preside over, Smith looked to the past to provide his blueprint. Grand Masters King Solomon and the two Hirams each represented an aspect of human potential and were often on the Mormon Prophet's mind.

On Thursday, February 8, 1844, Smith spoke at a political meeting with Elders Orson Hyde and John Taylor.[124] William W. Phelps publicly announced for the first time Smith's intention to run for president and read aloud the candidate's "Views on the Powers and Policy of the Government of the United States."[125] The *Nauvoo Neighbor* called the essay "an able document, big with meaning and interest, clearly pointing out the way for the temporal salvation of this union."[126] It must have been a stirring occasion for the former farm boy.

Later that evening, several of the Masonic brethren were gathered together in the upper room of Smith's Red Brick Store following their 6 p.m. meeting. Smith arrived and gave the proper entrance signal to Asahel Perry who was acting as Tyler at the door. "Let him enter," responded George A. Smith, who had taken the place of Worshipful Master that day. The Prophet burst in the room, "strode up and down the lodge," and, according to the report of Dimick B. Huntington, exclaimed, "Hallelujah, hallelujah, hallelujah!" Joseph Smith continued, "I have done what king Solomun[,] King Hiram[,] & Hiram Abif could not do[:] I have

---

121. "Nauvoo Masonic Lodge minutes, 1841–1846," December 19, 1844; emphasis added.

122. "Nauvoo Masonic Lodge minutes, 1841–1846," January 2, 1845.

123. Wilford Woodruff journal, August 19, 1860.

124. "Journal, December 1842–June 1844; Book 3, 15 July 1843–29 February 1844," The Joseph Smith Papers, 259.

125. Wilford Woodruff journal, February 8, 1844.

126. "History, 1838–1856, volume E-1 [1 July 1843–30 April 1844]," 1887.

set up the kingdom no more to be thrown down forever nor never to be given to another people."[127]

Such a bold statement implicitly placed Smith in the company of the men Freemasons called their "Ancient Grand Masters," even portraying him in a superior role. Smith had found the Word that they had lost. It was the culmination of all his literal and figurative treasure seeking and the playing out of the Royal Arch degree. The event demonstrates that Freemasonry was integral to Smith's restoration project and his efforts to establish the theocratic kingdom of God. On June 15, 1844, William Clayton wrote in his journal,

> [Joseph Smith] spoke concerning key words. The g[rand] key word was the first word Adam spoke and is a word of supplication. He found the word by the Urim and Thummim. It is that key word to which the heavens is opened.[128]

Masonic author Manly Hall's description of the coveted attainment of a Freemason entirely captures Smith's accomplishment:

> The true Word of the three Grand Masters has never been concealed from those who have the right to know it nor has it ever been revealed to those who have not prepared a worthy shrine to contain it. The Master knows, for he is a Temple Builder. . . . The Word is found when the Master himself is ordained by the living hand of God, cleansed by living water, baptized by living fire, a Priest-King after the Order of Melchizedek, who is above the law.[129]

On April 5, 1844, the Mormons carried out plans to dedicate their new Masonic Hall. Attending the dedication were over five hundred Masons, including twenty-two members of Helm Lodge, twelve members of Rising Sun Lodge, five members of Nye Lodge, one member of LaHarpe, and two members of what would soon become Hiram Lodge of Augusta, Iowa.[130] Once again, the ceremonies followed the outline of *The Masonic Trestleboard*, but with Worshipful Master Hyrum Smith performing the duties ordinarily assigned to a Grand Master.[131] It

---

127. Dimick B. Huntington, "Statement of Dimick B. Huntington, December 12, 1878, Salt Lake City." Huntington's statement places the date of the event as February 8, 1844, the date of the only Masonic meeting of Nauvoo Lodge where both George A. Smith presided as Worshipful Master and Ashael Perry acted as Tyler. See "Nauvoo Masonic Lodge minutes, 1841–1846," February 8, 1844.

128. George D. Smith, ed., *An Intimate Chronicle, The Journals of William Clayton*, 133–34. George Smith explains that "Clayton's entries from June 14 to June 22, 1844, comprise a small separate journal," which the compiler "included chronologically within the second Nauvoo journal, 1843–44." The final sentence was found in the concurrent (June 15, 1844) entry in Clayton's second Nauvoo journal notebook.

129. Manly P. Hall, *The Lost Keys of Freemasonry, or The Secret of Hiram Abiff*, 88.

130. "Nauvoo Masonic Lodge minutes, 1841–1846," April 5, 1844.

131. Charles W. Moore and S. W. B. Carnegy, *The Masonic Trestleboard, Adapted to the National System of Work and Lectures, as Revised and Perfected by the United States Masonic Convention at Baltimore, MD, A.L. 5843*, 64–68; "Nauvoo Masonic Lodge minutes, 1841–1846," April 5, 1844.

is notable that Joseph Smith was ill, preventing him from delivering the lengthy King Follett funeral discourse—a sermon filled with familiar Masonic images and themes (see Chapter 16).[132] Joseph's participation was limited to a closing oration, whereas he had originally planned to take a greater role.

With the Masonic Hall completed, work continued apace on the Church's own temple six city blocks away. On a visit to Nauvoo, United States political figure Josiah Quincy wrote his impressions of the "odd and striking" Mormon temple. He considered it a "grotesque structure on the hill, with all its queer carvings of moons and suns," and quoted Joseph Smith's opinion of the edifice as follows:

> In a tone half-way between jest and earnest, and which might have been taken for either at the option of the hearer, the prophet put this inquiry: "Is not here one greater than Solomon, who built a Temple with the treasures of his father David and with the assistance of Huram, King of Tyre? Joseph Smith has built his temple with no one to aid him in the work."[133]

Joseph Smith's prophetic charisma and magnetic personality allowed him to use many different avenues to animate Mormonism. Freemasonry was not the only ingredient that went into the mix, but it was a vital one. His interpretation of Masonic ritual deepened its value for Latter-day Saint participants, and once he had given his followers an idea of the possibilities inherent in Masonry, they united to draw friends and associates to their prophet's vision of Freemasonry restored. Smith was not a daily participant in the Lodge, but he was a regular and an influential one. The Mormon lodges came close to dominating Freemasonry in Illinois and were well on their way to becoming a presence on the national Masonic stage. With a few minor tweaks in the historical record, the Mormons, with Smith as their leader, could have played a leading role in a national governing body. There, the Prophet's ritual proclivities might well have re-envisioned the Craft. As it was, these natural talents, strengthened by a divine calling and powerful Masonic patterns, found their way into a uniquely Mormon ritual that would inspire millions.

---

132. Wilford Woodruff journal, April 5, 1844.

133. Josiah Quincy, *Figures of the Past from the Leaves of Old Journals*, 390.

CHAPTER 14

THE GLORY OF THIS LATTER HOUSE

And since sin has destroyed within us the first temple of purity and innocence, may thy heavenly grace guide and assist us in rebuilding a second temple of reformation, and may the glory of this latter house be greater than the glory of the former! Amen, so mote it be.
— Malcolm C. Duncan, *Duncan's Masonic Ritual and Monitor*

Through the poetic and vibrant enactment of the Royal Arch Degree, nineteenth-century American Freemasons sought to preserve a spiritual connection to King Solomon and his temple, and Mormon understanding of the literal and allegorical significance of temples appears to derive from this Holy Royal Arch tradition. After their relocation out of Kirtland, site of their first temple, and exile from their garden spot in Missouri, Latter-day Saints began building a second temple to God in Nauvoo. In doing so, Joseph Smith worked to recover the mystery and ritual of ancient temple work and to teach his followers the true path to God.

The Latter-day Saint temple in Nauvoo had numerous parallels with the Masonic conception of Solomon's Temple, and the rites revealed by Smith for that edifice shared common perspectives and symbolism with contemporaneous Masonic ritual. Similarities extended from the outer and inner architecture and appointments of the temple to the use of ritual space, clothing, signs, tokens, obligations, and penalties. Furthermore, the two traditions shared biblical references and even ritual framing and precise ritual phrasing. Because of this, the many Latter-day Saints who had previously become Freemasons by 1844 would have been keenly aware of these resemblances, and they understood them to be part of the continual efforts of the Prophet to restore ancient authority, knowledge, and sacraments. They envisioned the Mormon temple with its prophetically revealed ordinances as something that had been lost both to ancient Israel and to Masonry through apostasy but restored to its original pristine form by Smith for the salvation of the Saints in the Dispensation of the Fullness of Times.[1] Continuing to the present day, many modern Latter-day Saints believe that both

---

1. David John Buerger observed that "some scholars feel that anti-Masonry may be seen in the Book of Mormon and interpret some passages . . . as anti-Masonic," as "these passages condemn secret combinations, secret signs, and secret words in a manner . . . reminiscent of anti-Masonic rhetoric prevalent during this period." David John Buerger, *The Mysteries of Godliness: A History of Mormon Temple Worship*, 47. However, as the Book of Mormon also contains genial Masonic elements, it can be argued that such passages suggest apostate or spurious Masonry rather than anti-Masonry (see Chapter 6).

Mormonism and Freemasonry draw from common ancient sources and that this explains ritual similarities. This view is, however, untenable for several reasons, the foremost being that the further one goes back in time, the more dissimilar Mormon and Masonic rituals become. Moreover, the Masonic ritual source (i.e., the Entered Apprentice, Fellowcraft, and Master Mason degrees, including the Royal Arch) cannot reliably be traced beyond the early eighteenth century.

Whether or not one believes in divine inspiration for Mormon temple ritual, nineteenth-century Freemasonry was certainly one of its shaping factors. Freemasonry's influence on the shape and content of the Mormon restoration movement has been demonstrated throughout the Church's history. It was especially evident in the temple-building impulse that began in Ohio and Missouri and reached its culmination in Nauvoo. The idea that ancient knowledge and authority was to be recovered in the Mormon temple was foreshadowed in the Book of Moses and expressly claimed in the Book of Abraham (see Chapters 6 and 7). By the Nauvoo period, the temple was envisioned as a way to ritualize LDS textual traditions, making use of a Mormon midrash with significant Masonic elements.

At the crest of Nauvoo Mormonism in the 1840s, Masonic ritual was rich with symbolism and allegory. Masons were taught how to interpret symbolism and were given lectures along with the ritual that explained some of these symbols while encouraging participants to uncover further meanings of their own. Because many of the men receiving LDS ordinances were familiar with this system, they were able to understand the meanings behind the Masonic allegories employed in the Mormon endowment and appreciate the innovative use to which they were put.

Freemasons both early and late have described their own institution as divine, its ritual as sacred, and its doctrine as holy.[2] Freemasonry's early connection with the Christian mystical tradition means that for Masons in the early nineteenth century, the innermost confidential instruction provided by the Fraternity was considered a divine secret, and the Lodge in which such divine secrets were imparted was the adytum of God—the symbolic *sanctum sanctorum* of God's holy temple. Such divine secrets included the Sacred Word—for example, the Name of God so holy that no single individual could speak it and thus required a covering word to veil it. They also included mysteries and legends meant only for the initiated, intended to lead the receptive mind of the properly prepared to authentic spiritual illumination. Masonry was never intended to be mere mummery or a humbug for the credulous. To receive its symbolic instruction, candidates for Masonic degrees have always been advised to prepare carefully, and Masons have been cautioned not to allow the unworthy or improperly prepared to enter the Lodge.

---

2. For instance, modern Masonic interpreter Rex Hutchens declares that the purpose of Freemasonry is to make a man "both priest and king, like all those who before have been entrusted with the Holy Doctrine and the Royal Secret." Rex R. Hutchens, A *Bridge to Light*, 320.

In the early nineteenth century, there was little doubt among Freemasons that God's glory would rest upon their Lodge and that God himself would direct their proceedings. Latter-day Saints today often fail to appreciate the spiritual nature of Freemasonry's temples and the Mason's sacred obligations to God. Seeking to segregate themselves from Masonic temple tradition, Mormons will sometimes characterize differences between the two ritual systems in language that reveals this misunderstanding and prejudice. For example, Latter-day Saint author Matthew B. Brown claimed:

> It is apparent that the temples of The Church of Jesus Christ of Latter-day Saints are genuine houses of the Lord, while the Masonic lodges do not attempt to take upon themselves such a lofty and holy status. The "temple" of the Freemasons is just an allegorical instructional device, whereas the Mormon temple is a replica of the hallowed sanctuaries of biblical times.[3]

Given this is a commonly held view among contemporary Mormons, it seems worthwhile to emphasize that every Masonic temple "is a replica of the hallowed sanctuaries of biblical times." Masonry's main allegory is unarguably centered upon King Solomon's Temple, and every lodge of Ancient Craft Masonry is modeled thereon.[4] It is certainly true that Masonic lodges or temples serve as allegorical and instructional devices intended to convey instruction devised by their Christian originators;[5] however, this can likewise describe every LDS temple, including the instructional rooms used in Newel K. Whitney's store in Kirtland and Joseph Smith's Red Brick Store in Nauvoo. These structures were similar to contemporary nineteenth-century lodges, which frequently occupied an upper room in an existing building, and in which both important civil events and holy rituals took place.

In a related line of reasoning, Latter-day Saints often stress that Masonic ritual is "horizontally oriented" and primarily intended to connect men fraternally "for their personal advancement within the Masonic organization," while LDS ritual is "vertically oriented" and intended to point us toward and connect us with God.[6] At first glance this might seem to be a reasonable distinction; after all, Freemasonry is a fraternal organization and not a religion. Yet, such explanations overlook the context in which speculative Masonry arose. As early as 1775, Freemasons associated themselves with revolutionary notions regarding religion and proudly published in their own works references to what others of more staid

---

3. Matthew B. Brown, *Exploring the Connection between Mormons and Masons*, 15.

4. Note the influence of Sam Lee's *Orbis Miraculum* (1659) and John Bunyan's *Solomon's Temple Spiritualized* (1688) upon the symbolism of Masonic Temples.

5. As Masonic scholar Bernard Jones notes, "[Masonic Craft and Royal Arch rituals in the] early nineteenth century were definitely of a Christian character." Bernard E. Jones, *Freemasons' Book of the Royal Arch*, 27–30.

6. Brown, *Exploring the Connection between Mormons and Masons*, 16.

religious views would find problematic. The point and purpose of Masonic ritual as it existed in its earliest years was to connect men with God.

It should be readily apparent why Freemasonry held great appeal for Joseph Smith. Its central allegory of the search for a connection with the Divine spoke to the inner desires he had felt since his youth. Its esoteric qualities captivated his proclivities for secrets and mysteries. Its ritual helped him bring his thoughts and longings into physical form. Smith's passion for learning, his interest in lost scripture and ancient mysteries, and his yearning for a deep bond with his friends and family were all fed by the legend and structure of the Fraternity. The Mormon prophet began introducing secret, oath-bound associations from the Kirtland period, throughout Missouri, and into Illinois. With the Nauvoo temple endowment, he would finally use his considerable talents as a ritualist to put together a restored ritual, Masonic in character, but imbued with his prophetic authority.

The Nauvoo Temple and its Ritual

Joseph Smith was not alone in creating new Masonic ritual in the nineteenth-century United States. Two American exposés from the post-Morgan period, David Bernard's 1829 *Light on Masonry* and Avery Allyn's 1853 *A Ritual of Freemasonry*, contain several examples of such "side degrees." These were Masonically inspired rituals based on scriptural or legendary themes. Out of this tradition sprang up degrees such as the "Knight of the Holy Sepulchre," the "Secret Monitor," "Aaron's Band," and others.[7] They were written by Masonic ritualists with little formal authority and often conferred by itinerant lecturers. As mentioned in Chapter 13, Nauvoo Lodge engaged one such traveler, Edwin Cruben, who was known for giving degrees "irregularly."[8]

The same impulse to create a ritual that would be uniquely suited to his people can be seen in Smith's development of LDS temple ritual. Nonetheless, the magnificent accomplishment the Nauvoo temple ceremony represented for the Latter-day Saint community cannot be overstated. It seems clear that Smith felt divinely led to restore an ordinance that would be salvific and represent pure truth.

Sixty-five people received at least a portion of the anointing, endowment, and sealing ordinances before the death of their Prophet on June 27, 1844. In 1845 and 1846, over five thousand men and women experienced temple rites in the newly completed Nauvoo Temple. It remains difficult to discover exactly which details of the temple ceremony were initiated by Smith himself and which were added or adjusted by Brigham Young, Heber C. Kimball, and others who worked on refining the ritual following the Prophet's death. According to Young, the Prophet apologized for the arrangement of the improvised quarters where he

---

7. S. Brent Morris, "The High Degrees in the United States: 1730–1830."

8. Irregular in the Masonic sense means not following accepted Masonic practices or not being formally recognized by an authoritative body.

first offered the endowment, and Young noted his own effort to stay true to what Smith had shown them:

> "[W]e have done the best we could under the circumstances in which we are placed, and I wish you all to take this matter in hand . . . organize and systematize all these ceremonies with the signs, tokens, penalties and key words." I [Young] did so and each time I got something more; so that when we went through the Temple at Nauvoo, I understood and knew how to place them there. We had our ceremonies pretty correct.[9]

It is apparent that some modification to the ceremony did take place before it was presented to the majority of the Saints in the Nauvoo Temple; however, the closer the evidence places these elements to June 1844, the more certain we can be that Smith himself had a hand in their construction. The conception of the ritual was his, and it had already been presented to dozens of the most influential people in Nauvoo. Young, whose succession was in question for some years, would not likely have been able to make too many unchallenged alterations.

There are few contemporary exposures authored by eyewitnesses of the Nauvoo temple ritual. Brief details were noted by William Clayton, Brigham Young, Heber C. Kimball, George A. Smith, Amasa Lyman, Newel K. Whitney, Wilford Woodruff, and in Joseph Smith's diary kept by Willard Richards. The earliest complete exposé of the endowment is the article "Mormon Endowments" by a woman calling herself "Emeline." This was published in the *Warsaw Signal* on April 15, 1846.[10] In 1847, Increase McGee Van Dusen published his and his wife's experience of the Nauvoo endowment.[11] Nauvoo temple records, including the "Book of Anointings," contain short descriptions and are available in the Nauvoo Temple Records Collection in LDS Church History Archives in Salt Lake City. Later recollections important in reconstructing Smith's incipient ritual ceremonies come from Lucius Scovil,[12] Dimick B. Huntington,[13] Heber C. Kimball, Brigham Young,[14] and Bathsheba W. Smith.[15] These sources can be compared with Masonic exposures of that period such as David Bernard's *Light on Masonry* and William Morgan's *Illustrations of Masonry.*

Features identical in Masonry and the endowment have become less obvious as a result of drastic revisions to the endowment in the 1920s, 1990s, 2019, and 2020. Alterations to Masonic ritual have been made as well over the years.

---

9. L. John Nuttall diary, February 7, 1877, in Ogden Kraut, ed., *L. John Nuttall: Diary Excerpts*, 13–14.

10. Emeline, "Mormon Endowments," 2.

11. Increase McGee Van Dusen, *Positively True: A Dialogue between Adam and Eve, the Lord and the Devil, Called the Endowment.*

12. Lucius N. Scovil, letter to editor, *Deseret News*, February 20, 1884.

13. Dimick B. Huntington, "Statement of Dimick B. Huntington, December 12, 1878, Salt Lake City."

14. Nuttall diary, February 7, 1877, in Kraut, *L. John Nuttall*, 13–14.

15. Bathsheba Smith, "Recollections of Joseph Smith," 345.

Nonetheless, the philosophical context of the temple as well as the ritual similarities between Mormonism and Freemasonry in the 1840s remain striking.

Many authors have written about the relationship between the Mormon endowment and Masonic ritual. However, without understanding the historical and philosophical context of Masonic ceremony, it is difficult to fully grasp the relationship between these two systems—that is, precisely where they converge and diverge. For Latter-day Saints investigating this subject, no meaningful discussion can occur unless one is first willing to examine Masonic ritual without the natural tendency to distort,[16] trivialize,[17] or censure.[18]

Parallels between Masonry and the endowment become problematic when contemporary Saints see them as opposing a belief that Joseph Smith received the temple ceremony by revelation from God. Likewise, accusations that Smith cobbled together ritual from items found in his environment miss his intentions as well as his genius in developing a meaningful religious ceremony for nineteenth-century seekers. The Mormon Prophet's usage of Masonic ritual was informed and brilliant, and his positioning and development of elements of the different degrees can certainly be viewed as inspired.

As noted by Paul Toscano, Latter-day Saints need not assume that their temple endowment's construction "from elements of Masonry disqualify it as either a revelation or as a . . . sacrament":

> Transformation of the profane into the sacred is the heart of Christ's teachings. Jesus' first miracle was the turning of water into wine. It should not be an impediment to faith that a Masonic ceremony was transformed to serve a Messianic purpose or that a rite that served such a purpose for Masons was borrowed and restructured as a sacrament of the Mormon Restoration.[19]

Three chief concepts found in early Masonic ritual relate more closely to Mormon temple ordinances than has been previously understood. These are the ideas of endowment, the mysteries of godliness, and celestial ascent.

---

16. In many exposés, Masonry is distorted and taken out of its natural context. Distortion also involves mischaracterizing Masonic ritual and its meaning primarily for polemical purposes.

17. Specifically, to trivialize means to treat Masonic ritual as fundamentally inferior to its Mormon counterpart—as cobbled together, as a jumble or mishmash, as philosophically inconsistent, as uninspired, or as essentially valuable only because Joseph Smith used it in some way in shaping his own ritual system. Wellins Calcott responds to those who object to Masonry as "a trifling institution" which contains "nothing valuable" by remarking that "it is easier to decry a science than to understand it." See Wellins Calcott, *A Candid Disquisition of the Principles and Practices of the Most Ancient and Honorable Society of Free and Accepted Masons*, 55.

18. In this case, to censure is to condemn Freemasonry as unspiritual, evil, immoral, literally apostate, or even a satanic counterfeit of "the real thing" (i.e., Masonic ritual is manmade and satanic, but LDS ritual is God-given and celestial).

19. Paul Toscano, *The Serpent and the Dove: Messianic Mysteries of the Mormon Temple*, 41.

Masonic "Enduement"

Beginning in Kirtland, early Latter-day Saints referred to blessings received in LDS temples as an "enduement" and its candidates as being "endued." As in Freemasonry, the word was similar in meaning and often used interchangeably with "endow." In Nauvoo, the idea was further developed and came to be associated with the ritual ceremony itself.[20] The sense of endue, meaning "to put on" or "to be clothed," was evident in several aspects of the temple endowment, from the putting on of special clothing to participate in the ritual to the bestowal of divine blessings. A deeper look into the Masonic use of "endue" or "endow" can illuminate how some of the practices early Mormons adopted related to the concept of endowment.

As early as 1769, a Masonic candidate was "duly and truly prepared" for his first entrance into the lodge by being ritually "clothed." In William Morgan's exposure of the Entered Apprentice degree, the candidate "is divested of all his apparel (shirt excepted) and furnished with a pair of drawers kept in the lodge for the use of Candidates. The Candidate is then blindfolded, his left foot bare, his right in a slipper, his left breast and arm naked, and a rope called a Cable-Tow round his neck and left arm."[21] In the Entered Apprentice degree, the candidate is taught that the "wearing of special garments furnished by the Lodge" emphasizes the Mason's "concern with man's internal qualifications, rather than his worldly wealth and honors. By wearing these garments, the candidate signifies the sincerity of his intentions."[22] Further, this ritual of being "clothed upon" symbolizes that the candidate is being furnished with esoteric knowledge and heavenly power. Finally, it suggests the future state of the new initiate:

> Even the ceremonies of gaining admission within these walls are emblematical of events which all mankind must sooner or later experience. They are emblematical at least in some small degree to your great and last change; of your exit from this world to the world to come. You are undoubtedly aware that whatever man may acquire on earth, whether wealth, honor, titles or even his own merits, can never serve him as a passport to the Grand Lodge above, but previous to his gaining admission there he must find himself poor and penniless, blind and naked, dependent upon the will and pleasure of the Supreme Grand Master. He must be divested of the rags of his own righteousness, and clothed in a garment from on high.[23]

---

20. "You shall be blesst [sic] with your portion of the Priesthood which belongeth to you, that you may be set apart for your Anointing and your endument." Hyrum Smith, Patriarchal Blessing to Leonora Cannon Taylor, July 28, 1843.

21. William Morgan, *Illustrations of Masonry by One of the Fraternity Who has Devoted Thirty Years to the Subject*, 18.

22. "The Three Degrees of Freemasonry," North Raleigh Masonic Lodge.

23. "In the Ante-Room," 452–53. See also Julius Reynolds Kline, "Some Things an Entered Apprentice Should Know," 73.

The endowment of a candidate with ceremonial clothing has several alle-gorical meanings: humility, purity of intention, interior qualification, equality or "meeting on the level," man's transition to his immortal future life with God, and God's grace in his redemptive and purifying work in man. Esoteric Freemason Arthur Edward Waite illustrated this symbolism in his poem, "Misfits":

> 'Tis scarcely true that souls come naked down
> To take abode up in this earthly town,
> Or naked pass, of all they wear denied.
> We enter slipshod and with clothes awry,
> And we take with us much that by-and-by
> May prove no easy task to put aside.
> Cleanse, therefore, that which round about us clings,
> We pray Thee, Master, ere Thy sacred halls
> We enter. Strip us of redundant things,
> And meetly clothe us in pontificals.[24]

In the washing and anointing ceremony that Joseph Smith introduced, initi-ates were also divested of their street apparel and clothed with a garment, an item of attire to be worn routinely underneath one's regular clothing. To the significa-tion described above, which would have been understood by those who had al-ready been made Masons, was added the concept of protection imparted to those who wore the garment faithfully. Smith designed the garment to include Masonic markings corresponding to certain actions in the ritual, bringing the symbolic into the literal. Immediately prior to the prayer of enduement in the Entered Apprentice degree, a petitioner is given permission to come into the lodge and, according to William Morgan,

> The Candidate then enters, the Junior Deacon at the same time pressing his naked left breast with the point of the compass, and asks the candidate, "Did you feel any-thing?" *Ans.* "I Did." Junior Deacon to Candidate, "what was it?" *Ans.* "A torture."
>
> The Junior Deacon then says, "as this is a torture to your flesh, so may it ever be to your mind and conscience if ever you should attempt to reveal the secrets of masonry unlawfully.["][25]

Later, in the Fellowcraft degree, the initiate is again brought to the door of the lodge. This time, "the angle of the square is pressed hard against his naked right breast," and the Junior Deacon says,

> Brother, when you entered this Lodge the first time, you entered on the point of the compass pressing your naked left breast, which was then explained to you. You now enter it on the angle of the square pressing your naked right breast, which is to teach you to act upon the square with all mankind, but more especially with the brethren.[26]

---

24. Arthur Edward Waite, *Strange Houses of Sleep*, 231.
25. Morgan, *Illustrations of Masonry*, 19.
26. Morgan, 47.

In the early Mormon initiatory ordinance, the left breast of the garment was cut in the shape of a compass and the right breast in the shape of the Mason's square while the garment was being worn by the individual.[27] Later in the endowment ceremony, Masonic penalties as well as further admonitions were associated with these marks. In an 1886 meeting, John Taylor remarked on "the correct understanding of the pattern and meaning of the [garment] marks":

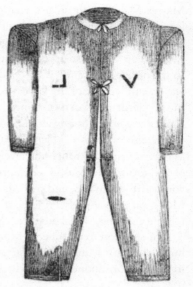

Mormon temple garment circa 1879, in *Salt Lake Tribune*, September 28, 1879.

The Collar: "My yoke is easy and my burden is light."

The strings: 3 strings on each side, had a double meaning. The strings being long enough to tie in a neat double bow-knots, representing the Godhead. The double bow-knots meaning the marriage tie, man and wives.

The compass: a guide to the wearer as the North Star is a guide in the night to those who do not know the way they should go.

The Square: Representing the justice and fairness of our Heavenly Father, that we will receive all the good that is coming to us or that we earn, on a square deal.

The Navel Mark: Meaning strength in the navel and marrow in the bones.

The Knee Mark: Representing that every knee shall bow and every tongue confess that Jesus is the Christ.

Adam and Eve, he told us, were without clothing and the garment was also given to cover their nakedness and for the protection from the enemy. The sleeves reaching to the wrist and the legs to the ankles; not fitting tight but flowing. This pattern was given to the prophet Joseph Smith by two heavenly beings.[28]

Masons are also clothed with an apron of white leather or lambskin that represents purity and innocence and calls to mind the sacrifice of Jesus Christ. The Master Mason's apron is fourteen by sixteen inches large and embroidered with Masonic symbols in blue thread. The apron is presented to the newly made

---

27. Nelson Winch Green, *Fifteen Years among the Mormons; Being the Narrative of Mrs. Mary Ettie V. Smith, Late of Great Salt Lake City*, 48–49. This practice may have continued in some places into the twentieth century. By March 1937, Elder George F. Richards and wife, Supervisors of Temples, instructed workers at the Manti Temple: "When marking the garments place the garment on the person unmarked, place pins in the marked space, take the garments off and proceed to cut the marks." See Manti Temple Historical Record, March 1937, in Devery S. Anderson, *The Development of LDS Temple Worship, 1846–2000: A Documentary History*, 243.

28. Daniel Bateman, statement, Midvale, Utah, June 20, 1932.

Master Mason with an explanation of its important emblematic character. In legend, the apron is associated with Melchizedek, "the Most High Priest and the first to wear the apron as the badge of religious authority."[29]

The apron is also an important part of the Mormon endowment ceremony. In the nineteenth century, Latter-day Saints wore white aprons embroidered with leaves, emblematic of the fig leaves with which Adam and Eve covered themselves in the Garden of Eden. During the ceremony, however, the apron is also recognized as a symbol of power and priesthood. As Masons fold their aprons down in a different way for each degree, early LDS temple patrons adjusted their clothing as they advanced through the levels of priesthood in the temple. On the occasion of the death of a Mason, the apron is "placed upon the coffin which contains your earthly remains, and with them laid beneath the silent clods of the valley."[30] Mormons are similarly buried with the apron, as well as being dressed in all their temple clothing, when they are laid in the coffin.

In addition to clothing, a Mason was endowed with virtues that would assist him in his earthly mission. Unsurprisingly, a Masonic "endowment" was threefold in nature, corresponding to each of the three degrees of Ancient Craft Masonry:

> May he be endowed with wisdom[31] to direct him in all his ways, strength, to support him in all his difficulties, and beauty, to adorn his moral conduct; and may we jointly and individually walk within compass, and square our actions by the dictates of virtue and conscience, and the example of the wise and the good. *Amen.*[32]

In Mormonism, endowment also carried a great weight of spiritual meaning. Early members were urged to study the implications of their ritual but were not always diligent in this effort. By 1853, Brigham Young admonished: "Be assured, brethren, there are but few, very few of the Elders of Israel, now on earth, who know the meaning of the word endowment."[33]

The Mysteries of Godliness

The Masonic phrase "mysteries of godliness" is drawn from 1 Timothy 3:16: "And without controversy great is the mystery of godliness: God was manifest

---

29. Simon Pierce, "Master Mason Apron."

30. Stephen Dafoe, ed., *The Masonic Dictionary Project*, s.v. "apron lecture."

31. While both Laurence Dermott's 1764 *Ahiman Rezon, Or a Help to All that are (or Would Be) Free and Accepted Masons* and William Preston's 1775 *Illustrations of Masonry* contain the phrase "endue him with a competency/competence of thy divine wisdom," respectively, other early versions omit this portion, preferring instead: "*endue him with divine wisdom,* that he may, with the secrets of masonry, be able to unfold the mysteries of godliness and Christianity." See, for example, Calcott, *A Candid Disquisition*, 199; emphasis added.

32. James Hardie, *The New Free-Mason's Monitor; or, Masonic Guide. For the Direction of Members of that Ancient and Honourable Fraternity, as well as for the Information of those, who may be Desirous of Becoming Acquainted with its Principles*, 219.

33. Brigham Young, April 6, 1853, *Journal of Discourses*, 2:31.

in the flesh, justified in the Spirit, seen of angels, preached unto the Gentiles, believed on in the world, received up into glory." The revealing of these mysteries is central to the fundamental purposes of Masonic initiation, as explained in the various iterations of its initiatory prayer. For example, "The Ancient Prayer at Making, or Opening a Lodge" asks:

> And we beseech thee, O Lord God, to . . . grant that this our new made brother, may prove true and faithful. [1] Endue him with a competency of thy divine wisdom, that [2] he may, with the secrets of free-masonry, be able to unfold the mysteries of godliness; and [3] may he and we walk in the light of they countenance, and [4] when all the trials of our probationary state shall be over, be admitted into the temple not made with hands, eternal in the heavens. *Amen.*[34]

This final hope was described in Wellin Calcott's 1769 *Candid Disquisition*:

> Let GOD's holy word be the guide of our faith; and, justice, charity, love and mercy, our characteristicks, then we may reasonably hope to attain the *celestial pass-word,* and gain admittance into the lodge of our *Supreme grand-master, where pleasures flow for evermore.*[35]

The Masonic endowment with a knowledge of the Divine Name seems similar to what Joseph Smith was claiming for the Latter-day Saints who received his revelation of the Mormon endowment. For decades, temple patrons were expressly taught that the LDS endowment represented "what are termed the mysteries of godliness—that which will enable you to understand the expression of the Savior, made just prior to his betrayal: 'This is life eternal, that they might know thee, the only true God, and Jesus Christ, whom thou has sent [John 17:3].'"[36] This language was removed from LDS ritual in 1990, although it continues to be popularly associated with the temple experience. In fact, the reception of the confidential Name of God is the ostensible purpose for the LDS temple-goer when "approaching the Lord" in the Ceremony at the Veil. This Name also serves as a password, the reception of which precedes the Mormon temple patron's passing into the room representing the Celestial Kingdom.

It is noteworthy that while the precise phrase "mysteries of godliness" (in the plural) is not found in the Bible nor LDS scripture, it is common to both the Masonic prayer at the initiation of a candidate and to the LDS Temple's "Lecture

---

34. Hardie, *The New Free-Mason's Monitor*, 18; bracketed numbers added. That "unfolding the mysteries of godliness" was understood as living a godly life is demonstrated by later versions of this prayer, which replaced the phrase with the words "better enabled to display the beauties of brotherly love, relief, and truth" (Malcolm C. Duncan, *Duncan's Masonic Ritual and Monitor or Guide to the Three Symbolic Degrees of the Ancient York Rite and to the Degrees of Mark Master, Past Master, Most Excellent Master, and the Royal Arch*, 30), or, in some exposures, "better enabled to display the beauties of holiness" (William Morgan, *Illustrations of Masonry*, 19).

35. Calcott, *A Candid Disquisition*, 175; emphasis in original. See also pages 155–56.

36. This instruction was found at the conclusion of the LDS Temple's pre-1990 "Lecture at the Veil."

at the Veil" (deleted *in toto* in 1990), as well as in public discussions of the respective rituals by both Mormons and Freemasons.

Let Us Go Up: Masonic Ascent to the Heavenly Temple

The prayers associated with the initiation of the candidate demonstrate the belief that a Mason's *enduement* is received in the context of a spiritual ascent in which he passes into the presence of God and those who have been sanctified. He then enters the sublime glory of a heavenly temple,[37] emblematically prefigured by the "all-perfect Lodge in Heaven."[38]

Historian Michael Quinn asserted that the "Mormon endowment or Holy Order had the specific purpose of preparing the initiate for 'an ascent into heaven,' whereas Freemasonry did not."[39] Modern Latter-day Saint scholars have generally accepted this as true,[40] and Quinn's initial assessment has come to be used by writers both friendly and unfriendly to Mormonism's claims.[41] While Quinn's original argument was that Freemasonry did not have this heavenly ascent as its primary *objective*, others have suggested that Freemasonry simply has no celestial ascent in it—that it neither contains the elements of heavenly ascent nor claims to be such. Yet, to make this argument is to ignore both the language and the symbolic instruction implicit in Masonic ritual. Ascent—social, moral, and spiritual—is a significant theme, expanded and developed in each successive degree, and culminating in the Royal Arch.

---

37. Samuel Cole, *The Freemasons' Library and General Ahiman Rezon: Containing a Delineation of the True Principles of Freemasonry, Speculative and Operative, Religious and Moral*, 134–35.

38. Cole, 134.

39. D. Michael Quinn, *The Mormon Hierarchy: Origins of Power*, 115.

40. The first chapter of the Book of Moses, published in the same month and year as the Book of Mormon, has been recognized by Latter-day Saints as containing themes of Celestial Ascent consistent with what can be found in the ancient world. See, for instance, Jeffrey M. Bradshaw and David J. Larsen, "The Vision of Moses as a Heavenly Ascent," 23–50. However, this principle is also consistent with what may be found in Royal Arch Masonry and—together with the content of the Book of Mormon itself—argues powerfully for Smith's early contact with the Masonic tradition. It is perhaps best to say that Mormonism shares with Masonry themes consistent with heavenly ascent in the ancient world.

41. See, for instance, Richard L. Bushman, *Joseph Smith—Rough Stone Rolling: A Cultural Biography of Mormonism's Founder*, 647n55: "Michael Quinn emphasizes the temple endowment's ascent into heaven as a distinguishing feature." See also Devery S. Anderson, "The Anointed Quorum 1842–1845," 140; and Devery S. Anderson and Gary James Bergera, *Joseph Smith's Quorum of the Anointed, 1842–1845: A Documentary History*, xxiii. For citations in sources critical to Mormonism, see Joel B. Groat, "Occultic and Masonic Influence in Early Mormonism."

The symbols of ascent appearing in Craft Masonry are Jacob's Theological Ladder in the First Degree,[42] the Winding Stair upon which one ascends to obtain a reward in the Second Degree,[43] and the "raising" of the candidate in mystical embrace in the Third Degree. From very early on, both Freemasons and their critics interpreted these symbols as references to a heavenly ascent. For example, as early as 1720, Masons understood the Lodge itself as symbolically "reach[ing] . . . to heaven."[44]

The culminating event of the celestial ascent is the "exaltation" of the recipient of the heavenly vision. In such accounts heaven is depicted as a temple; the seer—or Masonic candidate—enters into the Holy of Holies and experiences the *visio dei* or beatific vision of God. In so doing he is transformed, reflecting the image of the Divine; he is clothed in divine glory and crowned, and having received the secret knowledge of God and mysteries of the heavens, he is seated on a throne beside God.

The theme of heavenly ascent is even more express in the Royal Arch Degree. There is a "going up" to the Holy City from captivity in Babylon, an entering into the Sacred Tabernacle, a passing through of veils and challenges and tests of knowledge, a deliverance from a subterranean cavern by which one recovers "That Which Was Lost," and finally an entry into the Holy of Holies and into the presence of a Grand Council where the Mason is crowned for his labors and obtains secrets, including the Secret of the Divine Name. Significantly, this is known by Royal Arch Masons as "The Rite of Exaltation," and Royal Arch Companions are said to be "exalted."

---

42. As early as 1826 the exceedingly popular Masonic author George Oliver noted that "Jacob, in reference to the lower *stave* of his Ladder, exclaimed, 'this is the . . . gate of heaven.' Here we find the notion of ascending to heaven by means of the practice of moral virtue, depicted by the Hebrew Patriarchs . . . under the idea of a Ladder; which we hence may conclude was a Masonic symbol [from at least] the time of Jacob." Oliver further explained that the ascent of Jacob's Theological Ladder was a variation of the idea of "ascent to the summit of the paradisiacal mount of God, by means of a pyramid consisting of seven steps." George Oliver, *Signs and Symbols: Illustrated and Explained in a Course of Twelve Lectures on Freemasonry*, 146, 142.

43. The Second, or Fellow-crafts', degree, unambiguously illustrates the theme of heavenly ascent. Here, the degree involves the candidate's ascent of a flight of winding stairs of fifteen or more steps "into the Middle Chamber of the Temple" and "the objects that attract his attention there." See John Sherer, *The Masonic Ladder: Or the Nine Steps of Ancient Freemasonry*, 59. It is in this place that on the day of rest the workman symbolically receives his wages and encounters that particular Masonic symbol so emblematic of the Deity—the letter "G."

44. "(Q) how high is your Lodge (A) without foots yards or Inches *it reaches to heaven*." The Sloan MS. 3329, circa 1700, as quoted in Harry Carr, ed., *The Early Masonic Catechisms*, 48.

The Quorum of the Anointed

In May 1842 Joseph Smith created the Quorum of the Anointed, a select secret society, also Masonic in conception, to whom he taught the concept of heavenly ascent. Smith had been using the term "Quorum," a word also found in Masonic parlance, to indicate a group possessing a certain level of priesthood. Since the 1700s, Masonic ritual had determined the requisite number of men needed to open a lodge and proceed to work or business. This number, known as a quorum, was seven in an Entered Apprentice's Lodge, five in a Fellow Craft's, three in a Master Mason's, nine in a Chapter of Royal Arch Masons, and eleven in a Commandery of Knights Templar.[45]

Smith first introduced the full endowment ceremony on May 4, 1842, to a group of nine Mormon Freemasons (significantly, enough to make a quorum in a Royal Arch Chapter).[46] The morning before, a Tuesday, Smith called together Lucius Scovil and a small group of men to assist him in preparing the entire upper story of his brick store for a ritual enactment of the biblical story of the Creation. From then until just before noon on Wednesday, the men industriously arranged everything "representing the interior of a temple as much as the circumstances would permit, he [Smith] being with us dictating everything."[47] The furnishings resembled those found in a Masonic temple, including the mural of a pastoral scene,[48] a carefully constructed altar, and canvas fabric to section the room. Boxed and potted bushes and trees were set up to adorn the "garden room."[49]

---

45. Albert G. Mackey, William J. Hughan, and Edward L. Hawkins, *An Encyclopedia of Freemasonry and Its Kindred Sciences, Comprising the Whole Range of Arts, Sciences and Literature as Connected with the Institution,* 2:606.

46. "Wednesday 4 [May 1842] In council in the Presidents & General offices with Judge Adams Hyram Smith Newel K. Whitney. William Marks, Wm Law, George Miller, Brigham Young, Heber C. Kimball & Willard Richards. [blank space] & giving certain instructions concerning the priesthood. [blank space] &c on the Aronic Priesthood to the first [blank space] continueing through the day." Eight of the men continued in council the next day to endow both Joseph and Hyrum Smith, while James Adams returned to his home in Springfield. See "Journal, December 1841–December 1842," The Joseph Smith Papers, 94. Adams, Hyrum Smith, Whitney, Miller, and Kimball were Freemasons before Nauvoo. Marks, Law, Young, and Richards were made Masons in Nauvoo Lodge in April 1842.

47. Lucius N. Scovil, letter to editor, *Deseret News,* February 20, 1884.

48. See, for example, an 1867 description of a Masonic Hall in *The Lorain County News*: "The walls and ceilings are frescoed in the finest manner. Four large paintings decorate the walls. The one in the east represents the rising sun reflecting its rays upon the ruins of castles on the distant hills. The one in the south represents midday with the trees and plants of the tropics. The north represents icebergs with a frail ship dashing among them and overtopping all is the Aurora Borealis sending up its glare to the blue sky above. The west represents rocky hills and extension plains, with wild scenes almost to the setting sun. The ceiling overhead represents the blue sky interspersed with clouds with twinkling stars glistening beautifully in the light of the splendid chandelier." See "Masonic Hall," 3.

49. Huntington, "Statement."

Brigham Young remembered that the men were washed and anointed in "a little side room" and given a new name and a specially marked undergarment, as well as other ceremonial clothing. The next part of the ceremony took place in the larger room, where candidates were given instructions and tests "as we passed along from one department to another." During this portion of the ritual, they received "signs, tokens, [and] penalties with the Key words." These enabled them to gain their eternal exaltation as well as to participate in the "true order of prayer."[50]

From reminiscences and other documents, Thomas Bullock and Willard Richards wrote the following description of the event for the Manuscript History of the Church, compiled in 1845. In Masonic terminology they described Smith instructing the Council

> in the principles and order of the Priesthood, attending to washings, anointings, endowments and the communication of Keys pertaining to the Aaronic Priesthood, and so on to the highest order of Melchisedec Priesthood, setting forth the order pertaining to the ancient of Days, and all those plans and principles, by which any one is enabled to secure the fulness of those blessings, which have been prepared for the Church of the first born, and come up and abide in the presence of the Eloheim in the Eternal worlds. In this Council was instituted the Ancient order of things for the first time in these last days.[51]

Andrew F. Ehat wrote that by this time in his ministry, Smith had "developed and solidified his conceptions of the ordinances that were essential to the restoration of 'the ancient order of things.'" By introducing temple ordinances, he institutionalized the Mormon theology of God and man and "ceremonialized the process by which such powers, blessings, and authority could be conferred on the 'true and faithful.'"[52] Over the next two years, the endowment ceremonies would be refined and expanded and bestowed upon thirty-six men and twenty-nine women before the death of the Prophet.[53]

At the April 28, 1842, meeting of the Relief Society, Smith promised that women could eventually "come in possession of the privileges, blessings, and gifts of the Priesthood" and would be given "the keys of the kingdom" if they were virtuous and diligent.[54] However, females were not admitted into the Anointed Quorum until over a year later.

After a few gatherings that year for prayer and discussion of church affairs, the Anointed Quorum met again (minus William Marks and George Miller, who were absent) on May 26, 1843, to receive "inst[r]uction on the prie[s]thood,

---

50. L. John Nuttall, *Diary of L. John Nuttall*, February 7, 1877.

51. "History, 1838–1856, volume C-1 [2 November 1838–31 July 1842]," The Joseph Smith Papers, 1328.

52. Andrew F. Ehat, "Joseph Smith's Introduction of Temple Ordinances and the 1844 Succession Question," 17.

53. Ehat, 14. See also D. Michael Quinn, "Latter-day Saint Prayer Circles," 86–87.

54. See "Journal, December 1841–December 1842," 94; "Nauvoo Relief Society Minute Book," The Joseph Smith Papers, 38.

the new and everlasting covena[n]t, &c." A later insertion has them being given "their endowments" again at this time.⁵⁵ This was perhaps in preparation for several sealings in celestial marriage, which took place among some of the men and their wives days later on May 28 and 29. The sealings included Joseph and Emma Smith, James and Harriet Adams, Brigham and Mary Ann Angell Young, Hyrum and Mary Fielding Smith, and Willard and Jenetta Richards. Yet, later that summer on August 6, 1843, Brigham Young stated that the fullness of the Melchisedek Priesthood had not yet been given, "for any person to have the fulness of that pri[e]sthood must be a king & a priest."⁵⁶ This understanding follows the ritual in the Royal Arch Degree, when men receive priesthood and are crowned kings. That this teaching was initiated by Joseph Smith is evident by his remarks on August 27, 1843, that no man could be a joint heir with Christ "with out bein[g] administered to by one having the same power & Authority of Melchisede[c]." This authority came only from a "King or Priest to God."⁵⁷

On September 28, 1843, women began to receive their endowments and were admitted into the Quorum. In addition, Smith's history for that day reports: "by the common consent and unanimous voice of the Council, ~~Baurak Ale~~ ^I^ was chosen President of the Quorum, ~~and anointed and ordained to the highe[s]t and holiest order of the Priesthood. (with his companion [Emma])~~."⁵⁸ This "Second Anointing" ordinance was a realization of the promise given in the endowment that men would become kings and priests and women queens and priestesses. By the end of the year, Emma had washed and anointed several of the women in the Mansion House preparatory to their receiving the endowment in the Red Brick Store, and Brigham and Mary Ann Young had received the Second Anointing ordinance—the fullness of the priesthood. The Prophet then directed

---

55. "History, 1838–1856, volume D-1 [1 August 1842–1 July 1843]," The Joseph Smith Papers, 1561. The history reads as follows: "26 [May 1843] At 5 p.m. I met in Council in the upper room, with my brother Hyrum, B[righam] Young, H[eber] C Kimball, W[illard] Richards, Judge <James> Adams, Bishop N[ewel] K. Whitney, and William Law, and gave them <their endowments, and also> instructions in the Priesthood, on the New and everlasting covenant &c."

56. Wilford Woodruff journal, August 6, 1843. See also Ehat, "Joseph Smith's Introduction of Temple," 80: According to Brigham Young, "those who . . . come in here [the Nauvoo Temple] and have received their washing & anointing will [later, if faithful], be ordained Kings & Priests, and will then have received the fullness of the Priesthood, all that can be given on earth. For Brother Joseph said he had given us all that could be given to man on the earth."

57. "Discourse, 27 August 1843, as Reported by Franklin D. Richards," The Joseph Smith Papers, 31.

58. "History, 1838–1856, volume E-1 [1 July 1843–30 April 1844]," The Joseph Smith Papers, 1738. "Baurak Ale" is a code name that Smith had also used for himself for the 1844 publication of the Doctrine and Covenants 101:4–6 and 102:5, 8 (now 103:21–35 and 105:16, 27).

Brigham Young to anoint the Twelve "kings and priests to God."[59] By the end of January 1844, that goal had been accomplished.

Finally, in December 1845, members of the Anointed Quorum who had not died or apostatized were administered to in the Nauvoo Temple at the first endowment ceremony given there. This allowed them to receive the ordinance in a more complete fashion.

In describing her early endowment, Lucy M. Smith, married to Joseph Smith's cousin, George A. Smith, intermingled the Mormon ceremony with contemporary women's Freemasonry:

> The party who anointed me in Emma's bedroom . . . poured oil on my head and blessed me. . . . I had different clothing on from what I wore when I went to the house first. This anointing was for the purpose of initiating me in the . . . endowments. *The Order of Rebecca* is a side degree of Masonry, for I think I had one or two degrees of it in that lodge. . . . [T]here was no curtain separating the ladies from the gentlemen. . . . Afterwards we promised not to reveal our endowments, or tell what it was.[60]

Masonic similarities are apparent in several unique features of the Nauvoo Temple and its ritual. However, they seem to have been transformed under the Prophet's hand to adapt their symbolic meaning to a fresh and innovative purpose. In these adaptations, Joseph Smith's particular ritual genius can be appreciated.

Nauvoo Temple Architecture and Furnishings

Nineteenth-century American Freemasons did not generally use symbols to adorn their buildings. An exception to this rule might be the square and compasses with a letter "G" that could be seen on the front of some of the buildings. This custom was followed in the architecture of the Nauvoo Masonic Hall, which was, like others of its time, a boxy structure free of outer ornamentation. The Mormon temple in Nauvoo, however, was decorated with exterior symbolic embellishment. Virtually every symbol used in the temple's outer architecture could be found on a Masonic apron or tracing board. It was as if the temple was being used as a giant tracing board upon the hill.

Joseph Smith had a pronounced influence in the placing of these symbols. As in almost all aspects of Nauvoo's government, scarcely anything could be done without the influence and approval of the Prophet. A revelation concerning the temple given on January 19, 1841, has the Lord Jesus Christ stating: "I will show unto my servant Joseph all things pertaining to this house" (D&C 124:42).

---

59. Ehat, "Joseph Smith's Introduction of Temple Ordinances," 122.

60. Lucy M. Smith testimony, as quoted in Linda King Newell and Valeen Tippets Avery, *Mormon Enigma: Emma Hale Smith*, 105; emphasis added. It is not certain precisely why she combined her description of the Mormon anointings with the Order of Rebecca, which since 1851 has been a side degree of Odd Fellowship rather than Masonry. Perhaps she was mislabeling the degree. However, her memory does demonstrate the presence of fraternal organizations in Nauvoo as well as their admission of women.

To William Weeks, the temple's chief architect, Smith elaborated, "I have seen in vision the splendid appearance of that building." The Prophet directed the draftsmen and workers to assemble it in the "pattern" that he had been shown.[61] A personal experience told by Josiah Quincy, visitor to Nauvoo at the time the temple was being built, illustrates the direct control Smith held over every detail of its ornamentation:

> Near the entrance to the Temple we passed a workman who was laboring upon a huge sun, which he had chiselled from the solid rock. . . .
>
> "General Smith," said the man, looking up from his task, "is this like the face you saw in vision?"
>
> "Very near it," answered the prophet, . . . "except that the nose is just a thought too broad."[62]

In a late description of the "order of architecture" on the Nauvoo Temple, Wandle Mace, a foreman over its framework, gave the symbols a biblical interpretation. Mace stated that the temple was "a representation of the Church, the Bride, the Lamb's wife." He quoted the book of Revelation 12:1: "And there appeared a great wonder in heaven; a woman clothed with the sun, and the moon under her feet, and upon her head a crown of twelve stars." Mace said that this verse was "portrayed in the beautifully cut stone of this grand temple."[63] When taken together, however, the many Masonic elements occurring collectively on the temple demonstrate not merely a biblical presence but a Christian Masonic one.

As well as sun, moon, and star stones, the temple featured pillar and arch motifs and inverted five-pointed stars that were carved in stone and incorporated into stained glass windows. The edifice was crowned with a Masonic angel as a weathervane; it wore a Royal Arch style turban. In William Weeks' blueprint drawings, the angel was pictured with the Book of the Law, square, compasses, and flaming heart.

William Clayton, the Nauvoo Temple Recorder, described the attic story of the Nauvoo Temple in a journal entry for December 11, 1845. Its sectioning into parts is reminiscent of that done in the Royal Arch Degree:

> I will now give a description of the way the attic Story is finished. The main room is 88 feet 2 inches long and 28 feet 8 inches wide. It is arched over, and the arch is divided into six spaces by crop beams to support the roof. There are 6 Small rooms on each side [of] the main room about 14 feet square each. The last one on the West end on each side is a little smaller.[64]

---

61. "History, 1838–1856, volume E-1 [1 July 1843–30 April 1844]," 1876.

62. Josiah Quincy, *Figures of the Past from the Leaves of Old Journals*, 389.

63. Wandle Mace, *Autobiography of Wandle Mace*, 207. Mace became a Master Mason in the Nauvoo Lodge on June 7, 1843.

64. William Clayton journal, December 11, 1845, in George D. Smith, ed., *An Intimate Chronicle, The Journals of William Clayton*, 204.

Nauvoo Temple Sunstone.

Small rooms were assigned to Apostles, Seventies, Elders, High Priests, and the High Council, with two rooms reserved as "preparation rooms" for male and female members respectively. Here they were washed and anointed, and received a "new name." The main room was "divided into apartments for the ceremonies of the endowment."

> Beginning from the door at the West end is an all[e]y about 5 feet wide extending in about 3 feet beyond the first Beam of the arch. On each side of the alley is a small room partitioned of[f] where they saints receive the first part of the ceremony or where the man is created and a help mate given to him. From these rooms to the third partition in the arch is planted the garden, which is nicely decorated and set off with shrubs and Trees in pots & Boxes to represent the Garden of Eden. In this apartment is also an alter. Here the man and woman are placed & commandments given to them in addition to what is given in the creation. Here also after the man & women has eaten the forbidden fruit is given to them a charge at the alter. And the first and second tokens of the Aaronic Priesthood.[65]

Upon eating the forbidden fruit, initiates were thrust into a dark room under the arch representing the "telestial kingdom or the world." They progressed through this and the terrestrial kingdom, receiving further signs, tokens, and charges. After reaching the altar, they were given "the key word on the five points of fellowship." After every member of the company received the tokens, words, and signs of the

---

65. Smith, 205.

Melchizedek Priesthood, they were led to the veil, where "they give each to Eloheem [sic] through the vail and are then admitted into the Celestial Room."[66]

The Celestial room of the Nauvoo Temple was a main area located "in the space between the two divisions of the arch." Its appearance was comparable to many Masonic Lodge rooms and Celestial rooms in modern LDS temples, adorned with ornate mirrors, paintings, portraits, and maps. The room was comfortably carpeted and furnished with handsome chairs, tables, and four splendid sofas. Upon a small table opposite the large window on the East end of the room were placed "the Celestial and terrestrial globes," two paired globes usually found on tripod stands or pillars in Masonic lodges.[67]

Mormon and Masonic Ritual Similarities

The Tyler

Both Masonic and Mormon rituals were restricted and confidential. In order to hold their meetings inviolate, Freemasons employed an officer of the lodge to guard the entrance. The Tyler's responsibility was to prepare the room for meetings and to check the eligibility of those wishing to enter. He would inform latecomers upon what degree the lodge was opened so that they could give the proper sign of recognition. A Masonic Tyler carried a sword that represented the biblical flaming sword carried by the cherubim who guarded the way to the Tree of Life in the Garden of Eden. Often the sword was crafted with a wavy shape to represent the flame.

Joseph Smith seemed to place a great deal of importance upon the detecting of imposition such as was done by a Masonic Tyler. In a letter to the Church dated September 6, 1842, which later became part of the Doctrine and Covenants, Smith writes of "the voice of [the archangel] Michael on the banks of the Susquehanna, detecting the devil when he appeared as an angel of light!" (D&C 128:20).

Smith preached both publicly and privately on keys that would allow one to distinguish between angels of light and of darkness. As early as June 27, 1839, in a meeting with the Twelve, he presented to them one key "among the vast number of the Keys of the Kingdom of God." By means of sensing corporeality with a handshake, he told them, they could tell if a personage was an angel, a devil, or a deceased person who had not yet been resurrected. On May 1, 1842, in the Grove, Smith preached that the keys of the kingdom consisted of "certain signs & words by which false spirits & personages may be detected from true.— which cannot be revealed to the Elders till the Temple is completed." He further stated

---

66. Smith, 205.
67. Smith, 206.

that the elders must know all the signs in heaven, earth, and hell "to be endued with power to finish their work & prevent imposition."[68]

Two incidents suggest that a Masonic-style Tyler was utilized at the introduction of the endowment, one at Smith's Red Brick Store and the other in the Nauvoo Temple. The first comes from Ebenezer Robinson, former editor and publisher of the *Times and Seasons*, the Church's official newspaper. The journalist walked one day with the Prophet to his store. As they parted company, Smith climbed the back stairs to the upper floor to attend to the administration of the ordinances. Moments later, Robinson remembered that he had something else to say to the Prophet. When he ascended the stairs, he instead found John Taylor "in a long white garment, with a drawn sword in his hand, evidently representing the 'cheribims and flaming sword which was placed at the east of the garden of Eden, to guard the tree of life.'" Taylor informed Robinson that Smith was already inside and could not be summoned.[69]

A more explicit mention of a Tyler comes from John D. Lee's description of his duties as a worker in the Nauvoo Temple. The Masonic language he employs in this account, as well as terms which correspond with aspects of Solomon's Temple, are unmistakable:

> Tuesday Dec 16[th] 1845 about 4 oclock in the morning I entered the Poarch in lower court where I met the Porter who admitted me through the door which led to the foot or nea[r]ly so of a great flight of Stairs which by ascending led me to the door of outer court, which I found tyled within by an officer. I having the proper implements of that degree gained admittance through the outer and inner courts which opened and led to the sacred departments, the Titles of these apartments are not lawful for me to give at present. having entered I found myself alone with the Tyler that kept the inner courts or rather the door of the inner court, set about & soon got fires up in the different rooms and setting things in order—for the day—at about 9 oclock in the morning the washing and anointing commenced.[70]

Lee's deliberate use of Masonic terminology associated with the temple demonstrates his reverence for even the menial work he was performing. Lee firmly linked Smith's teachings about Freemasonry with the restored ordinances in which he was now dutifully engaged. Like the Tylers guarding the work of a lodge, Latter-day Saints involved in detecting imposition participated with Smith in protecting divine secrets and keeping them sacred.

The Creation Drama

Joseph Smith's endowment ritual drew upon Masonic motifs, biblical stories, and esoteric legends passed down from ancient pseudepigrapha. Of the thirty-

---

68. "Discourse, 1 May 1842, as Reported by Willard Richards," The Joseph Smith Papers, 94.

69. Ehat, "Joseph Smith's Introduction of Temple Ordinances," 112.

70. John D. Lee journal, December 16, 1845.

six men who received the endowment when Smith was alive, thirty-three were documented Freemasons. To these men, the new ritual was still familiar and often identified with Freemasonry. After washing and anointing in a small side room, the ritual drama began with a review of the creation of the earth—a theme that had been in use in eighteenth-century Masonic rituals. While the current American working is abbreviated, earlier versions of Masonic ritual traditionally included as its backdrop an unfolding of the periods of divine creation from unorganized matter to the present orderly state:

> [F]or before he was pleased to command this vast World into Perfection, the Elements and the Materials of the Creation lay blended without Form or Distinction. Darkness was upon the Face of the Deep, and the Spirit of God moved upon the Face of the Waters; when the Great Jehovah, as an example to Man, that things of Moment ought to be done with Deliberation, was pleased to be Six Days in periodically bringing it from *Chaos* to *Perfection*.[71]

Hearing the words "Let there be light" in the Mormon endowment Creation narrative, Nauvoo Freemasons would doubtless be reminded of the Rite of Illumination in which they had participated in the Entered Apprentice Degree. In this ritual context, Man is created and by degrees is brought to philosophical and spiritual light. In Masonry, this bringing to light is still associated with the potent allegory of God's work of creation.[72] Just as the Entered Apprentice's degree is calculated to bring a man to light when his hoodwink is removed, the endowment was Smith's "response to skepticism"[73] that utilized early Masonic themes to reveal the Divine hand in the creation of all things.

The Number Three

Number mysticism plays an important part in Freemasonry. One example of this is the frequent purposeful use of the number three. In the Craft Lodges there are three degrees, three perambulations around an altar, and three ruffians who assault Hiram Abiff. The Royal Arch sign is the "Triple Tau," consisting of three T's united. Also present in the Royal Arch are three stones of the arch, three

---

71. John Browne, *Browne's Masonic Master-Key through the Three Degrees by way of Polyglot. Under the Sanction of the Craft in General, Second Edition, with Many Additions,* 49; emphasis in original. See also "The Grand Architect's Six Periods," in Hardie, *New Free-Mason's Monitor*, 122–23.

72. In his recounting of "The Almighty's Six Periods of Creation," John Browne continues a discussion of the phrase "Let there Be Light" as follows: "he [the Almighty] gave it his sacred Approbation, and distinguished it by a new Name, calling Light, Day, and Darkness, he called Night; in order to keep new framed *Matter* within just Limits." To the careful reader, Browne is providing the creative illumination with the bestowal of the New Name in Masonic initiation ritual. See *Brown's Masonic Master-Key*, 49; emphasis in original.

73. Robert N. Hullinger used this phrase in the title of his book, *Joseph Smith's Response to Skepticism*.

Principals, three Sojourners, and three words that form the Grand Omnific Royal Arch Word, with three parts to each word.

The appearance of trios in Freemasonry calls to mind the Christian Trinity and has deep allegorical significance. The three officers who lead the ceremonies include the Worshipful Master, Senior Warden, and Junior Warden. In the Mormon endowment, the allegory is expressly revealed by the presence of Elohim, Jehovah, and Michael, with a later appearance of Peter, James, and John. As part of the pre-1990 LDS temple ceremony, patrons recited three syllables in a sacred language, said to be Adamic. The word is analogous to several tri-syllabic code words that are given to Masonic seekers in the Royal Arch Degree.

In another example of the use of three in Masonic ritual, the words of the Master of the Lodge are repeated verbatim by the Senior Warden and then the Junior Warden in a three-fold composition. This emphasizes the line of authority. The Master's words are communicated in a chain through his representatives. Again, the Mormon iteration of this practice highlights the Masonic inference. In the pre-2019 endowment, Elohim gives his instructions to Jehovah, who repeats them to Michael, who puts them into action. The sequence is then repeated in a series of reports back to Elohim. Through this ritual, Mormons are meant to understand that the chain of authority they observe in their ecclesiastical experience literally connects heaven and earth.

Freemasonry includes four obligations: one for each of the three Blue Lodge degrees, and one associated with the Royal Arch. Similarly, there are four covenants made in the nineteenth-century Mormon temple ceremony, each associated with a sacred sign, token (handclasp), and penalty. In his book *The Mysteries of Godliness*, David Buerger has made a side-by-side comparison of the signs, tokens, and penalties in William Morgan's 1826 exposé of his local Craft degrees and former Mormon Catherine Lewis's 1848 description of the LDS temple ceremony, which demonstrates that the two ceremonies are almost identical.[74] Additional near-contemporary Masonic exposures, such as Giddins's *Anti Masonic Almanac for the year 1831*, make these correspondences evident by means of simple line drawings.[75] This portion of the LDS temple ceremony is perhaps the most distinct evidence for direct assimilation of Masonry into Mormonism.

Signs, Tokens, and Penalties

Hearkening back to operative Masonry, signs, tokens, and penalties were observed as a means of recognizing a member's position in the craft. As Freemasonry gradually became more speculative, this system was expanded. Particularly in the Master Mason degree, the tokens acquired the allusion of divine power, the power by which mortals are raised into immortality. In *The Spirit of Masonry*,

---

74. Buerger, *Mysteries of Godliness*, 53–55.
75. Edward Giddins, *Anti Masonic Almanac for the year 1831*, 55–64.

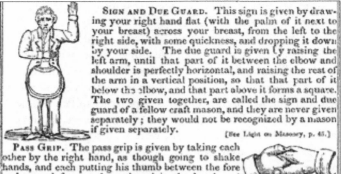

The sign and grip for a Fellow Craft degree, from Edward Giddins, *Anti Masonic Almanac*, no. IV (1831).

William Hutchinson explains that "the MASTER MASON represents a man under the christian doctrine, saved from the grave of iniquity, and raised to the faith of salvation."[76]

The Mormon ritual used the same or similar tokens, signs, and penalties, but they were given more overt religious significance. In the early Mormon endowment ceremony, not only the final token but all four alluded to some aspect of divine grace. Each one was itself a vehicle of God's mercy and also a point of entrance by which one could receive divine knowledge. Each was revelatory of the character or nature of God. Placing these together in the endowment ceremony emphasized their significance.

In a discourse given in the Nauvoo Temple, December 28, 1845, Brigham Young explained the peculiarly Mormon application of the signs in prayer:

> There are 4 Penal Signs & 4 Penal Tokens and should I want to address the Thorone (the Throne) to enquire after Ancient things which transpired on Plannets that rol[l] ed away befofore this Plannet came into existence—I should use my New Name which is Ancient & refers to Anci[e]nt things. Should I wish to enquire for [crossed out word] ^present^ things I should use my own Name which refers to presant things & should I want to enquire for [crossed out word] ^Future^ things= I would use the 3rd Name which refers to the first token of the Melchizadich Priesthood.[77]

Early Mormons thus associated the signs and tokens with keys of asking and receiving.

---

76. William Hutchinson, *The Spirit of Masonry: in Moral and Elucidatory Lectures*, 162.

77. "General Record of the Seventies Book B, Commencing Nauvoo 1844," December 28, 1845, quoted in Devery Scott Anderson and Gary James Bergera, eds., *The Nauvoo Endowment Companies, 1845–1846: A Documentary History*, 211–12.

Three Distinct Knocks

The earliest known Masonic legends of the death of the Master and loss of divine truth and power are associated with "three great knocks." In Pritchard's 1737 exposure of the Master Mason degree, the candidate is asked:

Ex. What was that which was lost and is now found?

R. The Master-Mason's Word.

Ex. How was it lost?

R. By Three Great Knocks, or the Death of our Master *Hiram*.[78]

This refers to the murder of Hiram Abiff, killed by three blows of his assassins. Echoing this point, "three distinct knocks" are given at the entrance door of the lodge. Going through the door of the lodge represents moving to a new phase of existence where the initiate's very being is about to be transformed. His former understanding must pass away before he can receive the further light that his initiation offers him. As Wilmshurst expresses it: "'*Mors janua vitae*'; death to self is the portal to true life. There is no other way."[79]

Mormonism utilizes this symbol as part of the temple endowment, significantly placing the three knocks towards the end of the ceremony in connection with a ritual embrace (originally "The Five Points of Fellowship") and passing through the veil. Taken together, these symbols are a vivid and powerful allusion to the patrons' death, transformation, and resurrection, and what Freemasons would know as the entrance into the "Celestial Lodge above."

Both rituals represent the sojourn of life. The initiates are tested based upon what they have learned. Smith's transposition of the knocks demonstrates his understanding of Masonic symbolism and his facility with ritual itself. He recognizes the purpose of the symbol at the door of the lodge but gives it a more prominent place at the climax of the Mormon ceremony.

Five Points of Fellowship

The ceremony at the veil, beginning with the three knocks of death and concluding with a sacred embrace with an officiator representing God, is the culmination of the temple endowment. Contact with the officiator upon "Five Points of Fellowship" was a part of Latter-day Saint temple liturgy until 1990. It was an important emblematic ritual that had its origins in Nauvoo-era Freemasonry.

The Masonic "Five Points of Fellowship" served several purposes. The brief ritual embrace instructed the Mason in fraternal duties, emphasizing the need for brotherly love, co-operation, and unity; it provided a mode of recognition; and, significantly, it stood as a symbol of the Mason's hope of a resurrection, in

---

78. Samuel Prichard, *Masonry Dissected: Being a Universal and Genuine Description of All Its Branches from the Original to this Present Time*, 26; emphasis in original.

79. Walter L. Wilmshurst, *The Meaning of Masonry*, 142.

which he would be raised "from a dead level . . . on the five points of fellowship, to a living perpendicular."[80] William Morgan's *Illustrations of Masonry* explains the Masonic significance of each of the points of fellowship. "Foot to foot" represents a Mason stepping out of his way to extend mercy and benevolence to his brother. "Knee to knee" describes the bent knee during intercessory prayer and in asking forgiveness for his own sins. "Breast to breast" cautions the Freemason to guard the secrets he learns within his breast. "Hand to back" recalls the Mason's duty to support and lift up his brother. This may also hold some symbolism of being "raised up" in other ways. Finally, "mouth to ear" instructs the Mason to whisper good counsel into his brother's ear and to warn him of coming danger.[81] The Mormon version of the Five Points of Fellowship was similarly described as: (1) inside of right foot by the side of right foot, (2) knee to knee, (3) breast to breast, (4) hand to back, and (5) mouth to ear.[82] Freemasons found additional meaning in this ritual—it came to symbolize human perfection. In the words of Paul to the Ephesians, the Church exists for the "perfecting of the Saints"—that perfect man coming "unto the measure of the stature of the fulness of Christ" (Eph. 4:12–13). In other words, the participant in this temple rite would stand foot to foot, knee to knee, breast to breast—matching the Divine, feature to feature and face to face.

In the now-obsolete Mormon ceremony, the petitioner was not allowed into the symbolic presence of the Lord until he or she had conversed with Him upon the Five Points of Fellowship "through the veil." Since one cannot enter into the Celestial sphere without first having died and then been raised, this typology is an important part of the ritual.

Freemasons associate each of the five points of fellowship with scriptures in the Bible, and Mormon apologists have claimed that these Bible verses are the point of origin for both traditions. However, a comparison demonstrates that the Masonic points and the Mormon points of fellowship are much more similar to each other than either is to the biblical passages. For example, one biblical source for the Five Points recounts the story of the prophet Elisha raising a child from death: "And he (Elisha) went up, and lay upon the child, and put his mouth upon his mouth, and his eyes upon his eyes, and his hands upon his hands, and he stretched himself upon the child; and the flesh of the child waxed warm" (2 Kgs. 4:34). Clearly, the

---

80. Avery Allyn, *A Ritual of Freemasonry: Illustrated by Numerous Engravings*, 81.

81. See Morgan, *Illustrations of Masonry*, 76.

82. This follows almost word-for-word the description by William Morgan: "[The Master Mason] proceeds to raise the candidate, alias the representative of the dead body of Hiram Abiff. He (the candidate) is raised on what is called the five points of fellowship, which are foot to foot, knee to knee, breast to breast, hand to back, and mouth to ear. This is done by putting the inside of your right foot to the inside of the right foot of the person to whom you are going to give the word, the inside of your knee to his, laying your right breast against his, your left hands on the back of each other, and your mouths to each other's ear (in which position alone you are permitted to give the word) and whisper the word *Mah-hah-bone*. . . . He is also told that *Mah-hah-bone* signifies marrow in the bone." Morgan, 76; italics in original.

Mormon ritual owes more of a debt to the Masonic rite than to the biblical passage.

Similarly, resemblances to other ancient traditions are less pronounced than those of the nineteenth-century Masonic ritual. Brent Metcalfe has remarked that Hugh Nibley's comparisons of Egyptian embraces "pale in comparison to the identical congruity between the Masonic and LDS embrace. Nibley's ritual verisimilitude also suffers from the lack of a coherent theory of ritual interdependence." Metcalfe concludes that "Smith's Points clearly owe their genealogy to 19th-century Masonry, not some antediluvian tradition."[83]

Gerald B. Gardner, a Freemason, was responsible for much of the modern revival of Wicca. He brought some of his personal idiosyncrasies as well as borrowings from Freemasonry into this occultist group. Thus, in Wicca we see the ritual of the "Fivefold Kiss," a form of the Five Points

The Five Points of Fellowship, in William Morgan, *Illustrations of Masonry*, 1827 ed.

of Fellowship. The Fivefold Kiss is a ceremony involving kissing five parts of the body. Each kiss given is accompanied by a blessing that is reminiscent of the early LDS initiatory work:

> Blessed be thy feet, that have brought thee in these ways
> Blessed be thy knees, that shall kneel at the sacred altar
> Blessed be thy womb, without which we would not be
> Blessed be thy breasts, formed in beauty and in strength
> Blessed be thy lips, that shall utter the sacred names.[84]

It is intriguing that the Wiccan ceremony preserves the symbolic nature of the elements, while the Mormon ritual did not. This is perhaps the reason the ritual did not survive in the LDS Church. As the significance, symbolism, and historical background of certain Mormon rituals were lost, they became less vital to temple worship.

---

83. Brent Lee Metcalfe, "Whence and Whither the Five Points of Fellowship? Being a Treatise on the Evolution of the Embrace from 1696 to 1990."

84. Gerald B. Gardner, "Drawing Down the Moon."

Recovery of the Lost Word

The loss and recovery of something magical or sacred has always been a powerful myth for humanity, as seen in ancient legends such as Shangri-La, Atlantis, the Fountain of Youth, the Ark of the Covenant, Excalibur, or the Holy Grail. This same idea can be observed throughout early Masonic ritual in Enoch's pillars of knowledge, the body of Hiram Abiff, and in a golden delta inscribed with a message to mankind.

In Freemasonry, the Lost Word represents the lost Name of God—something that Masons are tasked to search for and recover. As with many other Masonic concepts, Joseph Smith worked to bring the idea of the Lost Mason's Word into literal reality. The ability to use the Lost Word was the ability to use God's creative power. The idea of building a temple was to create a space where Latter-day Saints would have an opportunity to obtain and be taught to use the Word. William Clayton explained, "[the man and the woman] are admitted into the terrestrial kingdom, where at the alter [sic] they receive an additional charge and the second token of the Melchizedek Priesthood and also the key word on the five points of fellowship."[85]

Here, the Word is identified as a "key word," as it is in the Book of Abraham. One of the figures in this book of scripture represents "God . . . clothed with power and authority; with a crown of eternal light upon his head; representing also the grand Key-words of the Holy Priesthood, as revealed to Adam in the Garden of Eden, as also to Seth, Noah, Melchizedek, Abraham, and all to whom the Priesthood was revealed" (Abr., facsim. 2, fig. 3). Another figure "represents God . . . revealing through the heavens the grand Key-words of the Priesthood" (Abr., facsim. 2, fig. 7).

In the Mormon endowment, just as in Freemasonry, the restoration of the Divine Name occurs in a five-point embrace. According to William Morgan's *Illustrations of Masonry,* after being whispered a tri-syllabic code word in the embrace,

> [T]he candidate [is told] to repeat it, telling him at the same time that he must never give it in any manner other than that which he receives it.—He is also told that [the code word] signifies marrow in the bone.[86]

By virtue of having experienced the Masonic ritual, Mormon Freemasons were prepared to know that the name given at the ceremony at the veil is not the name of God, but only a substitute. The purpose of the endowment was to teach initiates how to part the veil and obtain knowledge. The quest for the true name of God was to continue throughout mortality.

---

85. William Clayton journal, December 11, 1845, in Smith, *An Intimate Chronicle,* 205.
86. Morgan, *Illustrations of Masonry,* 76.

Passing the Veils

In the United States, the dramatic ceremony of Passing the Veils appears in the Royal Arch Degree.[87] It is based on a description of King Solomon's Temple in Josephus's *Antiquities of the Jews*. The first-century historian wrote that Solomon "also had veils of blue, and purple, and scarlet, and the brightest and softest linen, with the most curious flowers wrought upon them, which were to be drawn before those doors."[88]

According to Masonic tradition, those who had been liberated from Babylonian captivity and desired to participate in rebuilding the holy city and its temple had to pass through these three sections of the tabernacle, ostensibly built by the exiles on their return from Babylon. Royal Arch ritual depicts the traversing of these sections, which are divided by colored veils. At each partition, there are readings of the Book of Exodus and passwords recalling Old Testament characters or phrases. [89] The ceremony of the Passing of the Veils signifies— among other things—the process of discovery and enlightenment that comes with Masonic progression. After a threefold test, the candidates pass through a fourth and final white veil and symbolically enter the presence of the Prophet, Priest, and Scribe in the Holy of Holies, also designated as the "Supreme Grand Master" or God.[90]

Royal Arch Freemasons have understood their ritual as an allegory of our future life after passing through the barrier of death. In both Mormon and Masonic ritual, the veil represents that which separates humans from divine knowledge (i.e., mortality). God is depicted as being on the other side of a veil, and the passing of mortals across that veil suggests their enlightenment. The LDS endowment ritual presents yet another example of Masonic allegory made literal. Brigham Young described the purpose of the ceremony in language that recalls the Masonic Rite of Exaltation, with the associated Passing of the Veils:

> Your endowment is, to receive all those ordinances in the House of the Lord, which are necessary for you, after you have departed this life, to enable you to walk back to the presence of the Father, passing the angels who stand as sentinels, being enabled to give them the key words, the signs and tokens, pertaining to the Holy Priesthood, and gain your eternal exaltation in spite of earth and hell.[91]

Like the Mormon endowment, the Royal Arch Degree includes a symbolic ascent, a knocking, a passing through veils with tests of knowledge, a recovery of "That Which Was Lost," and an entering into a Grand Council (which Masons are told represented a Grand Council in Heaven) in the presence of

---

87. Richard Carlile, *Manual of Freemasonry: In Three Parts. With an Explanatory Introduction to the Science, and a Free Translation of some of the Sacred Scripture Names*, 2:12–18.

88. Flavius Josephus, *Antiquities of the Jews*, Book VIII, Ch. 3:3. See also 2 Chronicles 3:14.

89. Allyn, *A Ritual of Freemasonry*, 120–141.

90. Calcott, *A Candid Disquisition*, 175.

91. Brigham Young, April 6, 1853, *Journal of Discourses*, 2:31.

which the person is crowned a Companion. According to Masonic symbolist W. L. Wilmshurst,

> The Royal Arch is the natural conclusion and fulfillment of the Third Degree. The latter inculcates the necessity of mystical death and dramatizes the process of such death and revival therefrom into newness of life. The Royal Arch carries the process a stage farther, by showing its fulfilment in the "exaltation" or apotheosis of him who has undergone it. The Master Mason's Degree might be said to be represented in the terms of Christian theology by the formula "He suffered and was buried and rose again", whilst the equivalent of the exaltation ceremony is "He ascended into heaven."[92]

At the end of each Masonic Degree and following the presentation of the pre-1990 temple endowment ceremony, the initiate was given a lecture that reviewed the elements of the ritual presented thus far. For example, a portion of the LDS Lecture at the Veil stated:

> You were first washed and anointed, a garment was placed upon you, and a new name was given you. This name you should always remember; but you must never reveal it to any person, except at the veil. . . .
>   You then entered [the Creation Room]. [There] you heard the voices of persons representing a council of the Gods.[93]

In the Royal Arch lecture, a similar review takes place:

> You have been conducted around the outer courts of the Temple-viewed its beautiful proportions. . . . You have been introduced into the Middle Chamber—and you learned—by the example of our ancient brethren—to reverence the sacred name of Deity. . . .
>   You have wrought in the quarries-and exhibited specimens of your skill—and have been taught how to receive—in a proper manner—your Masonic wages.[94]

Freemasons are then told that they can "only justly claim the noble name of free mason" if they have entered into the spirit of the ceremonies, tried to understand the full import of the symbols, and had the great and fundamental principles of the institution deeply impressed upon their minds.[95] Likewise, Latter-day Saints were told to "give prayerful and earnest thought to the holy endowment" in order to "obtain the understanding and spirit of the work done in the temples of the Lord." They were charged to "strive to comprehend the glorious things presented to you this day. . . . [T]hese are what are termed the mysteries of godliness," which enable patrons to understand the Savior's words in John 17:3: "This is life eternal, that they might know thee, the only true God, and Jesus Christ, whom thou hast sent."[96]

---

92. Wilmshurst, *The Meaning of Masonry*, 140. Note that Wilmshurst here equates "exaltation" with apotheosis or divinization.

93. "The Veil," The LDS Endowment.

94. Stichting Argus, "Ritual for the Royal Arch Degree, Indiana, 1952."

95. Stichting Argus, "Ritual for the Royal Arch Degree, Indiana, 1952."

96. "The Veil."

The Power of Ritual

One of the most sublime uses of scripture is to ritualize it, thereby making it experientially available. Masonic ritual serves this purpose. By the enactment of its myths, it brings candidates into sacred time and space so that participants share together in divine mystery and experience divine power. Masonry's mysteries forge men together into a brotherhood, bound by voluntary oaths, ethical standards, and common moral and spiritual values.[97] Using symbolism, allegory, and scriptural reenactment, Masons learn how to achieve union with the Divine: they not only read the sacred myths, but actually enter into them, thereby becoming "partakers of the divine nature" (1 Pet. 1:4).

The story of the collapse of Solomon's Temple and its rebuilding is a powerful and meaningful symbol to Freemasons. It is a metaphor for fallen human nature restored by God to something greater than it was. By their very nature, all humans fall, deteriorate, and crumble. It is a great comfort to be able to rely on a power that lifts, strengthens, and rebuilds. To Masons, the allegorical telling is as important as any literal rebuilding of the temple. They can relate the inspiring tale to themselves and their quest for improvement.

The context of Masonic ritual includes the unfolding of the periods of creation and a description of our mortal sojourn. By degrees, man is brought to light. Joseph Smith followed a similar pattern, using the same structure and formalities as Masonic rites. He ritualized the story of Adam and Eve and placed participants in mythic time, which patrons could experience as past, present, or future events. The Adam and Eve story simultaneously teaches truths about the creation of humankind, figurative events in their present state of being, or the future creation of worlds as a god. In this way, Smith was not slavishly borrowing from Masonry, nor harking back to an earlier tradition, but creatively adapting Masonic rites.

Hundreds of Nauvoo Freemasons, as well as countless more who had lived through the disclosure of Masonry resulting from the Morgan affair, would have noticed similarities between Mormon and Masonic ritual. These included oaths with the use of a Bible, vows not to reveal ceremonial secrets, and prayer offered while kneeling at an altar. Both ceremonies contained identical phrases, such as "Has it a name?" "three distinct knocks," and "Let him enter." Mormon and Masonic rituals used dialogues or catechisms to test initiates or to solicit passwords. They gave initiates a new name. Both ceremonies comprised acting out a ritual drama in which the initiate represents a biblical figure: Adam or Eve in the endowment, and Hiram Abiff in Masonry. As in the Royal Arch degree, initiates wore priestly robes of an Old Testament pattern and passed through a

---

97. Freemasonry seems to intentionally play with several definitions of "mystery": Masonry centers around a trade; it provides special knowledge known only to the skilled, those who are involved in a specific activity, or to a particular group; it presents dramas like those staged by medieval craft guilds, generally based upon a story from the Bible.

veil. Mormons were not ashamed to claim the connection between the two sys-
tems. Eliza Young wrote: "It is claimed that the mysterious rites were taken from
Masonry, and that the Endowments are a direct outgrowth of the secret society.
Brigham Young delights, I know, to speak of it as 'Celestial Masonry.'"[98]

Joseph Smith believed in an ancient, authentic Masonry. As he began the
work of literally building an Old Testament-style temple and restoring ancient
religion, he came up with something magnificent that inspired both him and
his followers. He was comfortable and skilled with the Masonic ritual style and
populated the temple with a ceremony supporting his views on priesthood. In
doing so, he tapped into the emotion of the legend and began to recover real
truths about the human soul. To understand this point is to see in some small
measure what it was about Masonry that captured the imaginations of men for
generations. It deepens one's understanding and appreciation of the Masonic degrees and unveils the profound ritual power in Masonry—something that cannot
be passed over as mere pageantry. The Mormon temple endowment oftentimes
makes explicit the concealed Masonic meaning in a shared ritual element. At
other times, portions of the LDS ritual yield increased meaning when understood in their original Masonic context.

Mormon temple ritual sacralized Masonic concepts such as the Five Points of
Fellowship. While retaining the fundamental symbolic significance of these ideas,
Smith made them explicit and literal. The Mormon prophet sought to transform
and elevate Masonic ritual into ordinances holding divine, salvific power reflecting his own vision of the heavenly pattern. Thus, the endowment recognizes the
concealed meaning in Masonry and makes it more overt. Mormon temple rites
claim to be a fulfillment, adding divine power to Masonic forms. These rituals respond to Freemasonry rather than imitate it. Masonic in style and structure, and
redolent with scriptural themes, the endowment brings the initiate into fellowship with Deity. For this reason, Smith was anxious to bestow this endowment
upon every member of the Church as part of his divine mission.

Nauvoo Saints were tutored to embrace the principles of Smith's radical social and spiritual vision by oath or covenant. Obedience to these vows overturned
contemporary economic, social, spiritual, and moral conventions in favor of a
society more closely aligned to the Prophet's revealed ideal. The pattern for a renewed society was revealed in the temple through its ordinances and instruction.
The Mormon temple endowment not only speaks to Latter-day Saints' relationship to God but also to their relationships with family and neighbors. Chains of
virtuous social action are forged in the temple. According to Smith, Zion—the
order of heaven—is the society of exalted beings. It is the grand leveling principle
of Masonry applied socially where there will be "no poor among them" (Moses
7:18) and where they will be one in spiritual blessing and temporal reward.

---

98. Ann Eliza Webb Young, *Wife No. 19: Or, The Story of a Life in Bondage*, 371.

CHAPTER 15

LOOK TO THE WEST:
THE POLITICAL KINGDOM OF GOD

Go, Brothers! Thus enjoined, farewell!
Spread o'er the darkened West;
Illume each clime
With ART sublime,
The noblest truths attest.
　　　　　　—Rob Morris, *Masonic Odes and Poems*

Following early Christian practice, Masonic lodges are symbolically oriented due east and west. The Master's station in a lodge is in the east, reminding Freemasons that "as the sun rises in the East to open and govern the day,"[1] the Master's duty is to open and govern his lodge. Similarly, the Senior Warden stands in the west to assist the Master in this work. While the Master represents wisdom, or the power to conceive, the Senior Warden symbolizes the strength needed to bring about the Master's plan; he is therefore charged to remember this duty with the words: "Look well to the West."[2]

For early American Freemasons, the phrase "Look well to the West" was a positive admonition from a fraternity that was fundamentally Christian in character, rational in perspective, tolerant to religion, enlightened in philosophy, and, in this sense, revolutionary. In the first fifty years of the history of the United States, Freemasonry had profound influence on society, with Masonic political influence in the states being apparent from its very beginnings. Freemasonry was imported from England to the large seaport cities of the colonies: Boston, Philadelphia, Savannah, Charleston, and Portsmouth were sites of the first official lodges. Their influence was seen during the Revolution—Benjamin Franklin served as Grand Master in Philadelphia, and George Washington and most of his generals were Freemasons. Nearly one in twenty-five eligible adult males were Masons in the 1820s, a number which does not include those women and children affiliated with adoptive rites and orders.[3] The Lodge was perceived as a social good, which spread liberty and encouraged public virtue. Many leading religious

---

1. Malcolm C. Duncan, *Duncan's Masonic Ritual and Monitor or Guide to the Three Symbolic Degrees of the Ancient York Rite and to the Degrees of Mark Master, Past Master, Most Excellent Master, and the Royal Arch*, 15.

2. Jeremy L. Cross, *The True Masonic Chart, or Hieroglyphic Monitor*, 67.

3. A rough estimate. In 1826 there were an estimated 50,000 Freemasons in the United States, and according to the 1820 US Census, there were just over 1,260,000 "free white

and political figures chose to join as part of the traditional course for entering public life, as a place to learn and practice genteel behavior, and as a way of encouraging the love that held society together.

Yet, by the early 1800s the tide of fraternal fortunes shifted on the waters of American social and political change. The William Morgan affair of 1826 was a watershed event. Manipulated and skillfully guided by the politically savvy, it stirred the passions of Americans, resulting in the establishment of the Anti-Masonic Movement that launched the first political third party in United States history.[4] What had once been seen as a social good was increasingly viewed as a social evil, and even positive aspects of the Lodge were cast in an unholy light.

As the nascent anti-Masonic political movement aspired to become a major party, it attracted men of real political acumen, such as Thurlow Weed and Thaddeus Stevens. Political anti-Masons argued that a free society could not thrive in the presence of secret organizations, that secret rituals concealed immoral practices, and that secret combinations colluded outside the boundaries of the political process. Most troubling to these thinkers, Freemasonry seemed to blur the line between the religious and the secular. In one of his speeches before the Legislature, Stevens laid out a concise summary of the position and platform of the Anti-Masonic Party. He charged that Masonry gave an unmerited advantage to Masons over honest American citizens in ordinary business as well as politics and that it prevented the just administration of the legal system.[5] He further contended that it contained oaths inconsistent with law, was anti-republican, promoted political and social favoritism, and violated the Constitution by encouraging aristocratic power. In 1834, Stevens asserted that Freemasonry had formed "a regularly organized kingdom within the limits of this [American] republic."[6]

In retrospect, many of these concerns seem to have been unfounded—largely an expression of much broader social and political tensions of the day. Yet, Stevens's fears reflected the negative perception of Freemasonry held by a growing segment of American society. While there is not and never was a Masonic conspiracy to gain control of the national political life of Americans, nor has there ever been a literal "Masonic Political Empire" with its seat in New York, American anti-Masonic suspicions seemed confirmed in the apparent abduction and murder of William Morgan by conspiring Masons.

---

males" twenty-six and older in the United States. See Martin L. Wagner, *Freemasonry: An Interpretation*, 10; *Census for 1820*, 18.

4. Charles McCarthy, *The Antimasonic Party: A Study of Political Antimasonry in the United States, 1827–1840*, 370. See also Steven C. Bullock, *Revolutionary Brotherhood: Freemasonry and the Transformation of the American Social Order, 1730–1840*, 281.

5. Thaddeus Stevens, *Free-masonry Unmasked, Or, Minutes of the Trial of a Suit in the Court of Common Pleas of Adams County*, as quoted in Thomas Frederick Woodley, *The Great Leveler: The Life of Thaddeus Stevens*, 52–54.

6. Bullock, *Revolutionary Brotherhood*, 296.

In 1842, John C. Bennett, former confidante of Joseph Smith and disaffected member of the Church's governing First Presidency, wrote a widely read exposé, *The History of the Saints, or, An Exposé of Joe Smith and Mormonism*. Here, he pointed to Jackson County, Missouri, as the prospective seat of Mormon power in Joseph Smith's aspirations to establish a vast religious empire. Bennett warned that while recent providence had scattered the Mormons and foiled their immediate plans for a world government, the nation should be vigilant regarding future Mormon plans:

> As the GREAT PLOT AND LEAGUE is now fully before the nation . . . the public weal requires the vigilant eye of the body politic to **LOOK WELL TO THE WEST!**[7]

Bennett may have hoped language so reminiscent of Masonic ritual discourse would rouse fears against the Latter-day Saints amongst Americans who had shuddered at the hobgoblin of Masonic political subversion and had successfully dismantled the entire Masonic order. Bennett's use of a Masonic phrase such as "look well to the West" when speaking of the political designs of the Church leadership and the Mormon theocratic kingdom was bound to raise troubling questions for his contemporaries.

Smith's Mormonism was one of the last great flowerings inspired by pre-Morgan style American Freemasonry. Key Latter-day Saint rituals were performed in what Bennett called "Order Lodge," and sermons, new scripture, and doctrine all bore the marks of Masonic influence. Largely incorporating the Masonic worldview, Mormonism was seen by some as a fulfillment of millenarian Masonic hopes. Yet for others, it may have seemed that the very literal Mormon political kingdom had grown to embody everything Stevens had feared about Masonry. From the School of the Prophets in Kirtland and the Danites in Missouri to the Nauvoo Legion, the Mormon Masonic lodges, the Anointed Quorum, and even the Relief Society, the Mormons participated in exclusivist, ritualized, covenant-bound associations. These, in addition to the cohesive, economically self-sufficient, and largely self-governing communities they had established, isolated them from their neighbors and set them up not simply as a group of worshippers but as a people apart. This emerging theocratic kingdom struck fear in the hearts of many, both inside and outside the Church. Concerns expressed regarding Smith and his Mormon kingdom sound remarkably like Thaddeus Stevens's fears of the Masonic Institution.

---

7. "Independence, in Jackson county . . . is considered their ZION, or haven of ultimate repose. . . . I cannot but admire the judgment with which the Mormon leaders selected this, the very heart of North America, as the chief seat of their vast empire. Could they have succeeded in erecting there an independent military organization, they would have been able to control, in time, almost the whole continent. . . . Illinois and Iowa, these extensive regions of country . . . were to form the remaining portion of the vast domain of the nucleus before which nations, kingdoms, and empires, were to fall." John C. Bennett, *History of the Saints, or, An Exposé of Joe Smith and Mormonism*, 300, 302; emphasis in original.

Anti-Masonic Fears and Their Manifestations in Masonry and Mormonism		
Anti-Masonic Fears	Masonic Manifestation	Mormon Manifestation
Exclusiveness	Ritualized, covenant-bound instruction	School of the Prophets Anointed Quorum
Oaths and avengement	Morgan Affair The "Avenging Mason"	Danites, Nauvoo Police, Oath of Vengeance, Nauvoo Legion
Circumvention of the legal process	Morgan Affair (aftermath) Members of the Fraternity above the law	Mormon disregard for Law Nauvoo Charter
Immoral practices covered by secrecy	Cagliostro's Egyptian rite	Polygamy
Secret combinations	Masonic Lodges	Secret combinations in Book of Mormon Nauvoo Lodge and other Mormon lodges
Political influence	Masonic political involvement Anti-Masonic Party	Mormon political involvement Anti-Mormon party
Political kingdom of God	Illuminati Andrew Jackson presidency	Council of Fifty Joseph Smith Presidency Plans for Occupation of Texas

When William Morgan disappeared, it was not the allegations that he was kidnapped to prevent him from revealing Masonic secrets that set off such bitter anti-Masonic sentiment throughout New York and the Northeast. It was not even the idea that Freemasons may have murdered him for threatening to reveal the innermost secrets of the Royal Arch. These claims alone could never have generated the first organized third-party movement in American political history. This occurred only when it began to seem that Freemasonry was fully removed and isolated from the superintending power of the law. Police cooperated with Masons from many different lodges. Fellow Freemasons were allowed to sit on the jury. Evidence was covered up, and the investigation was stalled over and over. Although "the event implicated Masons all the way from the Finger Lakes to the Niagara frontier,"[8] the only convictions were Eli Bruce, the deputy sheriff

---

8. Whitney R. Cross, *The Burned-Over District*, 115.

of Niagara County (sentenced to two years and four months), and carriage driver John Whitney (sentenced to one year and three months).[9] It was only then that people all over the nation responded with growing indignation. They "began to organize politically, to form new counter-associations, to publish newspapers and magazines, and to doubt whether Masonic morality and the rule of law could ever coexist in the American republic."[10] By the late 1820s there was widespread disapproval and fear of any political influence that could be gained by way of membership in a lodge. Even Masons themselves were largely horrified by the Morgan case, which led to a mass exodus from lodges throughout the United States.

In the heyday of the Anti-Masonic Party, Freemasonry was in a steep decline. In New York over four hundred lodges became defunct, and in Illinois the Grand Lodge itself went under. In round numbers, it is estimated that of the 50,000 Masons in America at the time, 45,000 withdrew their membership and renounced their oaths, forcing the closure of two thousand lodges.[11] There no longer remained a large enough body of Masonic brothers to wield much political influence, even were they so inclined. Gradually, as Masonic historian Stephen C. Bullock describes, anti-Masonic fervor began to cool. The few remaining brothers in shrunken lodges "could not provide the plausible demon that opponents required."[12]

A decade later, the Mormons were in the public eye, saying and doing things that raised the old fears about Masonry. In quotations, newspaper articles, exposés, and journals, the Latter-day Saints passionately identified with the kingdom of God prophesied by Daniel to come forth in the Last Times. In their zeal to build this kingdom, they began relinquishing an identity as United States citizens, freeing themselves from the country's laws and alienating their neighbors in the process. Danite leader George W. Robinson stated that "when God spoke he must be obeyed, whether his word came in contact with the laws of the land or not; and that, as the kingdom spoken of by Daniel has been set up, its laws must be obeyed."[13] Later in Nauvoo, while still in the First Presidency, Sidney Rigdon recalled that a principal reason for harassment in Missouri was because the Saints "would not have any thing to do with the laws[. W]e did not break any[;] we lived above them[,] so they sent a mob upon us."[14] In 1857, William Smith

---

9. Thurlow Weed, *Life of Thurlow Weed Including his Autobiography and a Memoir*, 1:270, 273.

10. Kevin Butterfield, "The Right to Be a Freemason: Secret Societies and the Power of the Law in the Early Republic."

11. William T. Still, *New World Order: The Ancient Plan of Secret Societies*, 107.

12. Bullock, *Revolutionary Brotherhood*, 315.

13. Testimony of James B. Turnur, in *Public Documents Printed by Order of the Senate of the United States, During the Second Session of the Twenty-Sixth Congress, Begun and Held at the City of Washington, December 7, 1840, and in the Sixty-Fifth Year of the Independence of the United States*, 4:33.

14. Wilford Woodruff journal, April 6, 1844.

looked back at groups of men under the control of Brigham Young in Nauvoo before moving west, labelling them "secret Danite banditti, or '*destroying angels*,' as they are called by the Mormons."[15] William exposed the "sixth degree" charge he said was given to this company as follows:

> Mormon, though you have eaten of the bread of life, you are still liable not only to the natural but to an eternal death. But such can only befall you through faithlessness to your oath of initiation, for otherwise you are superior to all mortal sin. BETRAY THAT OATH and you hang for all time and burn for all eternity. . . . Against a Mormon you must never fight; against a Mormon you must never swear. Your words must comfort them—your money must succor them. As judges you must deliver them—as jurors, acquit them—as brothers and sisters, live and die for them. You must exalt them into all offices which they covet; you must abandon clan, kin and country for their sake; and in fine, you must make Mormonism and everything that effects its interests the great aim and object of your life. And now go forth upon your mission and be this your motto:
>
>> An oath I have given
>> Let me honor it well;
>> For to keep it is heaven,
>> And to break it is hell.[16]

After 1840, Mormonism grew in size and influence and became a concern to local caucuses. Thomas C. Sharp, editor of the *Warsaw Signal* and a former lawyer, first expressed his apprehensions about Mormon political influence after being invited to the Nauvoo Temple cornerstone-laying ceremony on April 6, 1841. With growing alarm, he watched a parade of fourteen companies of the Nauvoo Legion, accompanied by two companies of volunteers from Ohio and a brass band. The ceremony began with hymns and prayers, and it continued with speeches by Joseph Smith and other Church leaders speaking "about the prospects for the growth of Nauvoo and the kingdom of God." That day, Sharp fathomed the potential Mormonism had acquired to become a powerful political influence in Illinois, and he viewed the religion as a dangerous threat to the balance of church and state. Galvanized by his fears, Sharp went back to his Warsaw newspaper and immediately fired up a spirited crusade to break the influence of the Church and their autonomous Nauvoo Charter.

Just months later, in June 1841, using the model of political anti-Masonry, Sharp helped form the Anti-Mormon Party in Hancock County that held conventions in Warsaw and Carthage, as well as public meetings in other smaller communities. Individuals from both national political parties united to oppose political Mormonism. In county elections in July, an anti-Mormon slate was elected, which thwarted the political influence of the Saints, even when they voted as a bloc. But as Latter-day Saints continued to stream into Hancock County,

---

15. William Smith, "Mormonism. A Letter from William Smith, Brother of Joseph, the Prophet," 5.

16. Smith, 5.

including many British converts who quickly became United States citizens, the political power of the Saints grew and further alienated their new enemies in Hancock County. For many who were socially and politically dispossessed, it was precisely the idea of a political kingdom of God that drew them to Mormonism.

Joseph Smith experimented with Mormon voting strength to promote their interests. The Saints had voted Democrat in Missouri, but in 1840 and 1841 they voted solidly Whig in Illinois. The first example of possible "vote trading" by Latter-day Saints was the legislative vote in favor of the Nauvoo charter in December 1840 promoted by Democrats but also voted for by the Whig Abraham Lincoln. The resulting Nauvoo Municipal Court, Nauvoo Legion, and Agricultural and Manufacturing Association formed the backbone of a self-governing theocracy—something that did not sit well with most non-Mormon Illinois citizens.

One telling incident shows the importance of the Mormon voting bloc. Cyrus H. Walker, a Whig congressional candidate in 1843, helped the Mormon prophet obtain release after Smith's arrest on June 23. In return, Smith promised Walker nine out of every ten Mormon votes in Illinois's Sixth District. Before a vast audience of Saints, Smith explained that Walker supported the Nauvoo Municipal Court's power to issue writs of *habeas corpus*, so they should vote for him. "Will you all help me? If so, make it manifest by raising the right hand," Smith asked. The response by the thousands there gathered was unanimous, "a perfect sea of hands being elevated." Then, on July 7, an article appeared in the Illinois State Register charging that Smith's arrest, which enabled Cyrus Walker to offer him assistance and solicit a quid pro quo, was a "Whig conspiracy" to get the Mormon vote. Latter-day Saints were disillusioned by this information. Just before the election of August 7, Hyrum Smith spoke at a political rally at the Grove, advising the people to now vote for Walker's opponent, Joseph Hoge. William Law objected, "Bro. Hyrum does not say he had a revelation." In response,

> Hyrum rose and took the stand a second time. He told the people he knew with a certainty how they were to vote the coming Monday, for "he had sought to know, and knew from knowledge that would not be doubted, from evidences that never fail, that Mr. Hoge was the man, and it was for the interest of this place and people to support him." He raised both arms and held up an election ticket ("printed on yellow post office wrapping paper"). "Thus saith the Lord," Hyrum proclaimed, giving his words the stamp of heavenly approval, "those that vote this ticket, this flesh colored ticket, this Democratic ticket, shall be blessed; those who do not, shall be accursed."[17]

---

17. Robert S. Wicks and Fred R. Foister, *Junius and Joseph: Presidential Politics and the Assassination of the First Mormon Prophet*, 40–45.

Joseph Smith kept his word and cast his personal vote for Walker, but he supported Hyrum's revelation. Thus, the bulk of the Mormon vote went to Hoge, and he won the election.[18]

The Political Kingdom of God

One of the greatest misgivings expressed by anti-Masons was that secret combinations would gain control of the United States, supplanting its constitutional government with its own privileged monarchy, led by a hand-picked Masonic king. When Freemason Andrew Jackson won the 1828 election after a particularly vicious campaign of mudslinging and name-calling, anti-Masons must have felt their darkest fears had been realized. Nonetheless, Jackson proved to be a popular president, easily winning reelection in 1832. In 1835, he paid off the entire national debt—the only time in U.S. history that this has ever happened. In 1837, Martin Van Buren—who had been Jackson's vice president—won the election and served a single term as president. Clearly, the anti-Masons were wrong about Masonic empire-building. Yet, in 1842, events in Nauvoo raised the specter of *imperium in imperio* again.

In January of 1842, Joseph Smith's journal depicts the Saints looking forward to the completion of the temple "of the Most High God" as a first step in the restoration of the theocratic kingdom. Smith wrote in his journal:

> Truly this is a day long to be remembered by the saints of the Last Days; A day in which the God of heaven has begun to restore the ancient ^order^ of his Kingdom . . . to prepare the earth for the return of his glory, even a celestial glory; and a kingdom of Priests & Kings to God & the Lamb forever.[19]

Just as Masons saw their temple as the vessel of the heavenly plan as it applies to both individuals and societies, so the Mormons pictured the Nauvoo Temple. Temple building was framed in Masonic terms, referring to an "ancient order" and "a kingdom of priests and kings." The temple and its rites were the spiritual vehicle for the recovery of That Which Was Lost—what Freemasons know as the Grand Omnific Word—by which the worlds subsist, and by which initiates are personally transformed.

In Masonic thought, the heavenly pattern recovered in the sacred context of the House of the Lord is implemented in the theocratic kingdom. This kingdom is also the Strength of God, the power to execute what the Master of All has conceived. It is also associated with the great leveling power of the West. Together

---

18. "President Joseph made some remarks on the election showing that he had taken no part in it. Stated that Hyrum had had a manifestation that it was for our interest to vote for Hoge." William Clayton journal, August 6, 1843, in George D. Smith, ed., *An Intimate Chronicle, The Journals of William Clayton*, 114.

19. "Journal, December 1841–December 1842," The Joseph Smith Papers, 57.

with the East, Masons see the Power of God to both build up true forms (symbolized by the rising sun) and to break down the false (symbolized by the setting sun).

Mormon Theodemocracy and the United States Presidency

With Joseph Smith's enthusiastic approval, and his brother Hyrum's quiet, competent leadership, Freemasonry grew rapidly in Nauvoo, surpassing pre-Morgan numbers. In his final year, Smith focused his energy on the political kingdom of God. On January 29, 1844, he met with Hyrum Smith, John P. Greene, and the Twelve to discuss which candidate they would support in that year's United States presidential election. Willard Richards moved that the Mormons form an independent electoral ticket and nominated Joseph Smith for president. A campaign strategy was discussed, and in the coming weeks W. W. Phelps would assist in writing up a platform statement: *General Smith's Views of the Powers and Policy of the Government of the United States.*[20] With undeniable hubris, Smith drew up a plan dated February 6, 1844, eight days after the nomination, listing his choices for members of the Cabinet, House of Representatives, and thirteen members of the Senate (sixteen spots being available for election in 1844). The list bore the title "Proposed plan for a Moot Organization & Congress" (*moot* defined in its sense of "open for discussion" or "not finalized"), and it demonstrates the dependence Smith placed upon these proposed officials being Freemasons. Of the proposed men, 91.6% of them are known to have been Masons, all were Mormons, and many had ties to the States to which he assigned them Representatives.[21]

In March 1844 the candidacy was publicly announced with Smith running on his coined term of "theodemocracy." He described this principle as a system "where God and the people hold the power to conduct the affairs of men in righteousness."[22]

Smith's unique form of theocracy provided for the rule of God over the population yet left room for Jacksonian democracy and individual freedom of choice. It addressed the sense of betrayal the Mormons felt by the failure of government to redress the loss of their homes and property in Missouri. Smith longed to set up a foundation for the coming millennial kingdom, which would "revolutionize the whole world" and put all nations "under the necessity of obeying the gospel."[23] As conceived by Smith, theodemocracy had several unique features. Like Freemasonry, it would be based on religious principles, yet it would not

---

20. Andrew F. Ehat, "Joseph Smith's Introduction of Temple Ordinances and the 1844 Mormon Succession Question," 150–51.

21. It is very likely that the four men who were not members of the Nauvoo Lodge—Benjamin Winchester, Edmund Ellsworth, Orson Spencer, and Phinehas Richards—were members of other Mormon Lodges.

22. Joseph Smith Jr., "The Globe," 510.

23. "History, 1838–1856, volume F-1 [1 May 1844–8 August 1844]," The Joseph Smith Papers, 18.

~~March~~ 6 Feby 1844
Proposed plan for a Moot ~~congress~~ Organization & Congress

Proposed role	Name	Master Mason	Member of 50
?Prest.	B[righam] Young	4/9/1842	Y
Vice President	John Taylor	4/30/1842	Y
Secretary of State	W[illard] Richards	4/9/1842	Y
Sec[r]etary ~~war~~ Treasury	O[rson] Pratt	4/11/1843	Y
War	Geo[rge] A Smith	5/21/1842	Y
Navy	~~W Woodruff~~ ^O Hyde^	1/18/1843	Y
Post master-Gen	W[ilford] Woodruff	4/29/1842	Y
Attorney General	WW Phelps	bef 1826, renounced	Y
Members of the House			
Maine	~~Johnathan Hales~~ & Sylvester B. Stod[d]ard	4/20/1842	N
N[ew] Hampsh[i]re	Jonathan H. Hale	8/10/1842	N
V[ermon]t	Erastus Snow	12/22/1843	Y
Mass[achusetts]	Franklin Richards	4/29/1843	a
Rhode isl[an]d	Truman Angel	3/9/1843	N
C[onnecticu]t.	Quartus S. Sparks	2/2/1844	N
N[ew] York	Phinehas Young	2/16/1844	a
N[ew] Jersey	B[enjamin] Winchester		N
Pennsylvania	D[avid] D. Yearsly	5/30/1842	Y
Delaware	E[dwin] D Wooly	4/20/1842	N
Maryland	Jesse P. Nichols	Helm Lodge	N
~~North~~ Virginia	Josiah Flemming	6/29/1842	N
N[orth] Carolina	A[braham] O. Smoot	1/5/1844	a
S[outh] Carolina	~~Benjamin Clapp~~ – Alexander Randolf	6/7/1842	N
Georgia	John D. Lee	8/9/1842	Y
Alabama	David Fulmer	7/11/1842	a
Mississippi	John Fulmer	6/22/1842	a

Proposed role	Name	Master Mason	Member of 50
Louisiana	Edmund El[l]sworth	3/14/1845	N
Tennesse[e]	Alphonso? Young		N
Kentucky	Charly C. Rich	4/28/1842	Y
Ohio	William Snow	12/22/1843	a
Indiana	Truman Gillet	2/28/1844	N
Michigan	Samuel C. Bent	5/20/1842	Y
Illinois	Demit		/
Missouri	Rule		/
Arkansas	Hosea Stout	6/15/1842	a
Florida	Wandall Mace	6/7/1843	N
Iowa	Elias Smith	3/22/1844	Y
Wisconsin	Lucius Scovil	[bef 1840]	N
	Geo. D. Watt. Reporter	7/27/1842	N
Senate [16 members requiring reelection in 1844]			
	S[idney] Rigdon	3/16/1842	Y
	O[rson] Spencer		Y
	J[ohn] P. Green[e]	5/10/1842	Y
	John Pack	5/2/1842	a
	Winslow Farr	11/15/1843	a
	A[a]ron Johnson	4/18/1842	N
	E[benezer] Robinson	5/12/1842	N
	Levi Richards	1/3/1844	Y
	Phinehas Richards		a
	R[obert] D. Foster	5/11/1842	N
	Morris Phelps	7/9/1842	N
	Alexander McRay	6/28/1842	N
	Theodore Turl[e]y	4/19/1842	a

be subject to any particular creed or denomination. God would be the ultimate power but would not impose His will on the unwilling, allowing all people complete moral agency to choose to be governed in this manner. The system pointed out what an expanded role of government might look like. Smith's presidential run had a somewhat naïve theocratic design, yet he was prepared to back it up with a framework to support such a system.

The Council of Fifty

Beginning on March 10, 1844, Joseph Smith instituted an organization that embodied his political objectives and named it "The Kingdom of God and His Laws with the Keys and Power thereof, and Judgment in the Hands of His Servants," also known as the Council of Fifty.[24] The conception of this body began by revelation in 1842, and in the interim two-year period, Smith prepared for its institution by introducing "Second Anointing" ordinances by which men became kings and priests. As described by historian Andrew Ehat, "the Prophet taught that only through such ordination would men have the ultimate, legitimate power of government." Between September 28, 1843, and February 26, 1844,

> Joseph Smith conferred such ordinations on the twenty men who received these blessings during his life. With only one exception all of these men became members of the "Kingdom" during the Prophet's lifetime. Moreover, of the nine other men in the Quorum who had thus far received the endowment ordinances, seven also became members of the "Kingdom."[25]

Smith's Masonically inspired associations were designed to foster loyalty to the Prophet and to the Mormon institution. At least twenty percent of the members of the Council of Fifty held a four-fold bond with Smith, each sealed by a blood oath of allegiance.[26] Virtually every member of the Council of Fifty was a Freemason and thus obligated to keep each other's secrets and to "obey all regular signs, summonses, or tokens given, handed, sent, or thrown to me from the hand

---

24. Reading this phrase in context, one can see that the final words which are usually added, "Ahman Christ," are a mode of signature by He who is bestowing the title.

25. Ehat, "Joseph Smith's Introduction of Temple Ordinances," 156.

26. Samuel Bent, Reynolds Cahoon, Joseph W. Coolidge, Cornelius P. Lott. Amasa M. Lyman, Parley P. Pratt, Sidney Rigdon, Hyrum Smith, John Smith, George A. Smith, and Lyman Wight were known members of the Missouri Danites, Nauvoo Masonic Lodge, Quorum of the Anointed, and Council of Fifty. This number is probably much larger—not all Danite participants or Mormon Freemasons are known. Complete lists of members of the Keokuk Lodge, Rising Sun Lodge, and Helm and Nye Lodges are unavailable. D. Michael Quinn estimates that "at least 15 percent of Smith's Fifty were bound by four different oaths of secrecy: Danite, Masonic, endowment, and Council of Fifty." D. Michael Quinn, *The Mormon Hierarchy: Origins of Power*, 131.

of a brother Master Mason."[27] Many members of the Fifty had been Danites in
Missouri, making a covenant "to sustain the Heads of the Church whether right
or wrong—the penalty of refusing to do so being death, 'the throat cut.'"[28] Smith
himself initiated members of the Anointed Quorum with key words, signs, and
tokens, along with penalties for revealing these secrets.[29] Finally, the Council of
Fifty took a similar oath with a penalty.[30]

The potency of these oaths and obligations is clear, as Smith's colleagues were
willing to protect him to the point of lying in a legal document. At a hearing
on January 4, 1843, a federal court investigated accusations that Smith was an
accessory in orchestrating an assassination attempt on former Missouri governor
Lilburn Boggs. Several affidavits were provided to support Smith's alibi that he
had been in Nauvoo during the assassination attempt.[31] One affidavit has depo-
nents Hyrum Smith, Willard Richards, Henry G. Sherwood, John Taylor, and
William Clayton stating they "were with the said Smith, at Nauvoo aforesaid
during the evening of the sixth day of May last & sat with said Joseph Smith in
Nauvoo Lodge from Six until nine oclock. of said evening."[32] Comparison with
the Nauvoo Lodge minutes for the evening of May 6, however, demonstrates that
neither Joseph Smith nor many of the above testators were present at the meeting
on that date.[33] Even assuming Smith was innocent of any role in the assassination
attempt, using an association with Freemasonry to provide an alibi is disturbing. Though this action calls into question the integrity of Nauvoo Masons, it

---

27. William Morgan, *Illustrations of Masonry by One of the Fraternity Who has Devoted
Thirty Years to the Subject*, 75.

28. David Whitmer, interview by Zenas Gurley, January 14, 1885, in Ronald E.
Romig, *Eighth Witness: The Biography of John Whitmer*, 329.

29. "[W]hen we got our washings and anointings under the hands of the Prophet Joseph
at Nauvoo . . . we were washed and anointed [and] had our garments placed upon us
and received our New Nam[e], and after he had performed these ceremonies, he gave the
Key Words[,] signs, togkens [*sic*] and penalties." Brigham Young, quoted *Diary of L. John
Nuttall, Dec. 1876–Mar. 1884*, February 7, 1877. William Law, Isaac Morley, and Joseph
Young were the only living members of the thirty-seven men who belonged to the Anointed
Quorum during Smith's lifetime who were not part of the original Council of Fifty.

30. George T. M. Davis, *An Authentic Account of the Massacre of Joseph Smith, the
Mormon Prophet, and Hyrum Smith, His Brother, Together with a Brief History of Rise and
Progress of Mormonism, and All the Circumstances Which Led to Their Death*, 7–8.

31. "Appendix 1: Missouri Extradition Attempt, 1842–1843, Selected Documents,
Introduction," The Joseph Smith Papers.

32. "Wilson Law and Others, Affidavit, 4 January 1843, Willard Richards Copy
[*Extradition of JS for Accessory to Assault*]," The Joseph Smith Papers, 29.

33. Present were Hyrum Smith, Samuel Rolfe, Lucius N. Scovil, Hiram Clark, John
C. Bennett, Charles Allen, William Felshaw, Dimick B. Huntington, J. B. Backenstos,
Jared Carter, George W. Robinson, Warren Smith, Elias Higbee, and Lorenzo D. Warson,
members. A. Thayer, Moses Wade, and J. King appeared as visiting brethren. Chancy
Robison, Erastus H. Derby, & Hamilton Jett were made Fellow Craft Masons.

also demonstrates that their loyalty to the Prophet superseded all other considerations.

Members of the Fifty were charged with establishing the political and theocratic kingdom of God. The group was to include token non-Mormons since doing so, as Klaus Hansen observed, "allowed Mormons to insist that at least theoretically they observed the American doctrine of separation of church and state."[34] Nonetheless, Thomas Sharp's apprehensions about the Church's political ambitions were prescient. Following a call in the April 1844 general conference, a group of about 340 political missionaries volunteered to electioneer throughout the country.[35] On May 17, 1844, Latter-day Saints organized their own "state political convention" held in the upper room of Smith's Red Brick Store to formally nominate the Prophet as candidate for United States president. Representatives of the Council were sent to different states to publicize his campaign, as well as to the nations of the world to gain recognition.

Handbill for Joseph Smith's presidential campaign.

Much of the media of the day did not take Smith's candidacy seriously—a representative headline in the *Niles National Register* read, "A New Candidate in the Field! Stand out of the way—all small fry."[36] Yet, others warned, "[L]et no man sneer at these people or deem them of little consequence, either for good or evil. They are becoming a potent influence to the people of the State of Illinois. It is a serious question: What will be the end of things?"[37] After nearly four hundred political missionaries made their views known throughout the states, concerns about the Mormons' potential influence became more prominent. Thousands of copies of *General Smith's Views* were printed and distributed and "took like wild fire."[38] Methodist frontier preacher Peter Cartwright wrote that when Smith was announced as a presidential candidate, "almost every infidel association in the Union declared in his favor." In his extensive travels through both eastern and western cities, Cartwright personally verified that "this was literally true, as far as

---

34. Klaus J. Hansen, "The Metamorphosis of the Kingdom of God: Toward a Reinterpretation of Mormon History," 222.

35. Willard Richards, "Special Conference," 504–6.

36. Wicks and Foister, *Junius and Joseph*, 90.

37. "W." [Nauvoo, Illinois], letter to the editors of the *Missouri Republican* (April 25, 1844), quoted in Wicks and Foister, *Junius and Joseph*, 109.

38. Stephen Markham, letter to Wilford Woodruff, June 20, 1856, cited in Wicks and Foister, *Junius and Joseph*, 165, 124–29.

I conversed with, or obtained reliable information of those infidel associations or individuals."[39]

Smith had matured in his leadership abilities since the days of Kirtland and Missouri. Though he fully committed his resources to the campaign, he worked through the Fifty to arrange two additional backup plans. Three members of the Council were sent to negotiate with Sam Houston, president of the Republic of Texas, where Smith had envisioned the establishment of a Mormon state located between the Nueces and Rio Grande rivers. There, the settlers would serve as a buffer between territory claimed by the United States and the hostile Mexican army. The location was sufficiently remote that a theocratic body could be established without interference from United States citizens. Members of the Fifty were also assigned exploring expeditions in the trans-Mississippi area while a committee drafted missives to petition the government for funds and authority to organize patrols of the West.[40]

With the Council of Fifty engaged in so many different efforts—managing Smith's presidential campaign and the political missionaries, negotiating in Texas, forming surveying parties in the West, appealing to the Federal government for redress of grievances and other concerns, and traveling throughout the United States and other countries—the body was more significant than has been apparent.

Structure and Characteristics of the Council of Fifty

Several aspects of the structure of the Council were apparently modeled upon Masonic practices. For example, the group used a revised form of parliamentary procedure to conduct its meetings. Modifications made by the Fifty are similar in form and purpose to those made by Freemasons in their meetings. One of these Masonic adaptations is described as follows:

> In a secular body, the presiding officer is subject to the dictates of the organization and may be removed by it. . . . The Master of a Lodge is not controlled by the Lodge and can only be removed by the Grand Master. In a secular body the presiding officer's decision can be overturned by the body itself. . . . The Master's Decision in a Masonic Lodge can only be appealed to the Grand Master or the Grand Lodge. The Presiding officer of a secular body is supposed to conduct its meetings according to the "Rules of Order." . . . The Master of a Masonic Lodge is totally responsible to the Grand Lodge, The Grand Master and the fraternity in general for all that his Lodge does and, as such, is clothed with all the authority needed to exercise full control.[41]

Similarly, Joseph Smith retained full control of Council of Fifty meetings. The council was to be "convened and organized by the president of the church"

---

39. Peter Cartwright, *Autobiography of Peter Cartwright: The Backwoods Preacher*, 346–47.

40. See Hansen, "The Metamorphosis of the Kingdom of God," 224–25; Ehat, "Joseph Smith's Introduction of Temple Ordinances," 159–60.

41. Masonic Code of Georgia, quoted in Earl D. Harris, "An Outline of Rules of Order (Parliamentary Procedure) for use in Georgia Masonic Lodges," 2.

who was "elected standing chairman upon convening of the council." The chairman voted first upon all motions. Although each member was obliged to make his objections known, his vote needed to be unanimous with the chairman or else his membership in the Fifty would have to be withdrawn.[42]

At each meeting of the Council of Fifty, members took a Masonic-like oath of secrecy under the penalty of death. Knowledge of this procedure first became publicly available from a diary entry made by Joseph F. Smith describing an October 12, 1880, meeting of the reconstituted Council of Fifty in Utah. At ten that morning, two new members—John Van Cott and Lorin Farr—were unanimously voted into what Smith artfully termed the "Council of L." After "affirming that they were in fellowship with every other person in the room," they were given a "Charge," a "Name," a "Key word," the "Constitution," and a "Penalty."[43]

At this point, Joseph Young objected to the "penalty," an oath that members of the council would not disclose its proceedings under penalty of death by certain means. Young believed it was "first suggested by the 'Pagan Prophet'" (Lucien Woodworth), and not sanctioned by Joseph Smith himself.[44] After a lively discussion by Young, Franklin D. Richards, C. C. Rich, and Wilford Woodruff, George Q. Cannon read aloud the original Nauvoo Council of Fifty minutes, and all agreed that the first organization had sanctioned a penalty.[45]

After publication of the Council of Fifty minutes in 2016 it was possible to verify Joseph Smith's involvement. At 4:30 p.m. on the day of the organization of the Council, March 10, 1844, Smith insisted upon perfect secrecy, asking, "Can this council keep what I say, not mak[ing] it Public[?]" The minutes record "all held up th[e]ir hands."[46] In a reconvening of the meeting at seven that evening in the assembly room above his store, the men met in council and Smith

---

42. Andrew F. Ehat, "'It Seems Like Heaven Began on Earth': Joseph Smith and the Constitution of the Kingdom of God," 260–61.

43. Joseph F. Smith journal, October 12, 1880, quoted in D. Michael Quinn, "The Council of Fifty and Its Members, 1844–1945," 178. Quinn also cites Franklin D. Richards's journal entry for April 8, 1881, concerning new members of the Council of Fifty and referring to "charge obligation & password."

44. On Tuesday, February 21, 1843, Joseph Smith so referred to Lucien Woodworth after he chastised some workmen who demanded to receive their pay and something to eat before continuing to labor on the Nauvoo House. Woodworth said that they should "go to hell & get it," for he had "set me down to a dry Johncake & cold water," and "when I have had a pou[n]d of meat or quart of meal I have divided with the workman." Smith remarked that was "pretty good Doctrin[e] for paganism," and that "the pagan prophet has preached us a pretty good sermon thiss morni[n]g— to break off the yoke of oppressesion. I dont know as I can better it much." See "Journal, December 1842–June 1844; Book 1, 21 December 1842–10 March 1843," The Joseph Smith Papers, 202.

45. Joseph F. Smith journal, October 12, 1880, quoted in Quinn, "The Council of Fifty and Its Members," 178.

46. "Journal, December 1842–June 1844; Book 4, 1 March–22 June 1844," The Joseph Smith Papers, 31.

"enjoined perfect secrecy of them."[47] The following day, Lucien Woodworth supported Smith's directive, calling for "every member of it [the Council] to be bound to eternal secrecy as to what passed here." The men were not even to tell their own wives, "and the man who broke the rule 'should lose his cursed head.'" Woodworth's resolution passed unanimously, including the vote of Smith, and "became a law of the council."[48]

Secrecy was necessary, since the public would easily view the concept of political power enforced by God through the medium of a human municipality as highly dangerous and even treasonous. For example, one of the reasons for Oliver Cowdery's early disaffection was his considered opinion on the combination of civil and religious authority. In 1834 he wrote:

[T]he moment any one religious sect . . . gains the ascendancy sufficient to hold the administration of our government, the human heart is so easily corrupted that a spirit of intolerance would immediately transcend that of justice and equality that we should be compelled to immediately bid an everlasting adieu to our hard bought liberty.[49]

By March 15, 1844, an anonymously written letter by "A Friend to the Mormons," first published in the *Quincy Herald* and reprinted in the *Times and Seasons*, criticized the very separation of church and state and concluded, "Church must not triumph over State, but actually swallow it up."[50] These sentiments were approved and expanded in Council meetings.

Notwithstanding the vow of secrecy, some members did make records of events relating to the Council, albeit at a later date, regarding an event that reportedly took place on March 23, 1844. In what came to be known as "the Last Charge," they claimed that Smith transferred "all the ordinances, keys, covenants, endowments, and sealing ordinances of the priesthood" onto the Twelve in connection with the Council of Fifty. Furthermore, Smith was said to have conferred upon Brigham Young the "keys of the sealing power, as conferred in the last days by the spirit and power of Elijah," or "this last key of the priesthood . . .

---

47. "Journal, December 1842–June 1844; Book 4, 1 March–22 June 1844," 33. The editors of the Joseph Smith Papers transcribe this word as "enquired," but it seems better read as "enjoined," as transcribed in Quinn, "The Council of Fifty and Its Members," 165. An account by George Davis elaborated: "And accordingly Joe swore them all [the Council of Fifty] to present secrecy, *under the penalty of death!*" Smith was murdered before he could stand trial at Carthage, but Davis stated "unhesitatingly, upon the best authority, that the above facts in regard to the crowning of Joe, the revelation he professed to have received, and his swearing those entrusted with taking part, to secrecy, *under penalty of death*, would all have been proved upon their trial for treason, by at least two witnesses." See Davis, *An Authentic Account of the Massacre of Joseph Smith*, 7–8; emphasis in original.

48. "Council of Fifty, Minutes, March 1844–January 1846; Volume 1, 10 March 1844–1 March 1845," The Joseph Smith Papers, 26.

49. Oliver Cowdery, letter to Lyman Cowdery, January 13, 1834.

50. Friend to the Mormons, "Mr. Editor," 477.

most sacred of all."[51] As part of this ceremonial bestowal of authority, Smith was recognized as the Council's grand key-holder. William Clayton, the scribe of the Council, recorded: "[April 11, 1844. Thursday] . . . Afterwards in the Council. We had a glorious interview. President Joseph was voted our P[rophet] P[riest] and K[ing] with loud Hosannas."[52]

With his leadership of the Church, his ordination to the Anointed Quorum, and his bid for the presidency of the United States, Smith was now in the position to be a prophet, priest and king and bring to pass the theocratic kingdom of God in true Masonic fashion.

The Grand Council and *Translatio Imperii*

The Royal Arch has a tradition of a Grand Council as the center of the earthly Government of God. Ruled by a prophet or scribe, a priest, and a king, this Grand Council is a reflection or earthly type of a Grand Council in the Heavens. This is expressly mentioned by one of the prayers that have been part of the Royal Arch since at least the early 1800s:

> O merciful Father, when we shall have passed through the outward veils of these earthly courts, when the earthly house of this tabernacle shall be dissolved, may we be admitted into the Holy of Holies above, into the presence of the Grand Council of Heaven, where the Supreme High Priest for ever presides, for ever reigns.[53]

The earthly high priest, represented by Joshua, presides with his two counselors, the king and the prophet, to govern the work of restoration as a type and shadow of the heavenly council: "[The High Priest] is stationed in the sanctum sanctorum. His duty, with the King and Scribe, [is] to sit in the Grand Council, to form plans and give directions to the workmen."[54]

The tradition of a Grand Council in heaven found its way into Mormonism by at least 1839. In an epistle to the Church while in Liberty Jail, Joseph Smith wrote that in the dispensation of the fulness of times, all would be revealed "according to that which was ordain[e]d in the midst of the councyl [*sic*] of the eternal God of all other Gods before this world was."[55] Four years later, in a discourse

---

51. Parley P. Pratt, "Proclamation to the Church of Jesus Christ of Latter-day Saints: Greeting," 151.

52. Smith, *An Intimate Chronicle*, 129.

53. Cross, *The True Masonic Chart*, 103. See also Henry Clinton Atwood, *The Master Workman; Or, True Masonic Guide: Containing Elucidations of the Fundamental Principles of Free-masonry, Operative and Speculative—Morally and Beneficially*, 148; and Cornelius Moore, *The Craftsman, and Freemason's Guide; Containing a Delineation of the Rituals of Freemasonry*, 139.

54. David Bernard, *Light on Masonry: A Collection of All the Most Important Documents on the Subject of Speculative Free Masonry*, 127.

55. "Letter to the Church and Edward Partridge, March 20, 1839," The Joseph Smith Papers, 14. See also Doctrine and Covenants 121:32.

reported by Franklin D. Richards on June 11, 1843, Smith pointed to this divine council again when he preached, "The Order & Ordinances of the Kingdom were instituted by the Priesthood in the council of Heaven before the world was."[56]

It is apparent that the Council of Fifty was an earthly representation of the heavenly council. While writing up the fair copy of the "records of the Kingdom" on March 10, 1845, William Clayton wrote that "[t]he Council of the Kingdom of God now organized upon this earth" was making laws that would govern the Saints after the resurrection. He added, "And is there not a similarity between this grand council and the council which sat previous to the organization of this world[?]"[57]

One form of the Mormon Grand Council is described by Parley P. Pratt in his work *The Angel of the Prairies; A Dream of the Future*, composed between 1843 and 1844 and read in the presence of the Prophet in the Council of Fifty. Pratt's story offers an insight into the expansionist hopes of the early Church. His dream begins with an angel showing him the United States, the "spot which is destined for the seat of empire," which, according to the angel, "began in the eastern Eden, but its progress has always been westward."[58] Ernest Lee Tuveson, author of *Redeemer Nation: The Idea of America's Millennial Role*, writes of the early Mormons' drive for Manifest Destiny exemplified by Pratt's tale. "The capital not alone of the United States but of the world," Tuveson notes, would be "in the middle of the North American continent. . . . Pratt's divine romance represents perhaps the most complete assimilation of the millenarian doctrine of the Latter-Day Saints with the American millennial dream."[59] In a second vision, Pratt's angel displayed "[t]he Grand Presiding Council organized in wisdom, and holding the keys of power to bear rule over all the earth in righteousness. And of the increase and glory of their kingdoms their [*sic*] shall be no end."[60]

In connection with Mormonism's theocratic kingdom and its concept of successive westward movements, Tuveson mentions the Latin phrase *translatio imperii*, meaning "transfer of rule." The concept was invented in the Middle Ages and describes history as a succession of transfers of *imperium* or supreme governing authority. The authority often began with a scriptural or mythical character and was passed down through carefully constructed genealogies to bolster a particular kingdom's right to reign. Latter-day Saints conceived of the right to rule originating East in Jerusalem and ever moving toward the West, finally to rest in Zion, located in the very center of the American continent.

Tuveson's description is fitting not only because of Pratt's description of Westward-moving *imperium*, but also because Latter-day Saint leaders believed

56. "Discourse, 11 June 1843–A, as Reported by Franklin D. Richards," The Joseph Smith Papers, 21.

57. Smith, *An Intimate Chronicle*, 159.

58. Parley P. Pratt, *The Angel of the Prairies; A Dream of the Future*, 10.

59. Ernest Lee Tuveson, *Redeemer Nation: The Idea of America's Millennial Role*, 182, 184.

60. Pratt, *Angel of the Prairies*, 14.

they had a right to the priesthood—the right to sacred rule—by lineage and birth. An 1832 revelation by Joseph Smith declared:

> Thus saith the Lord unto you, with whom the priesthood hath continued through the lineage of your fathers—For ye are lawful heirs, according to the flesh, and have been hid from the world with Christ in God—Therefore your life and the priesthood have remained, and must needs remain through you and your lineage until the restoration of all things spoken by the mouths of all the holy prophets since the world began. Therefore, blessed are ye if ye continue . . . a light unto the Gentiles, and through this priesthood, a savior unto my people. (D&C 86: 8–11)

The tradition of the gathering of the noble-born to restore the Holy City and its sacred temple is a significant element in the central legend in Royal Arch Masonry. In that tradition, three masters from the Babylonian captivity "heard that the Temple of the Lord God was about to be rebuilt at Jerusalem" and so came up to offer their services "to assist in the completion of that great and glorious undertaking." When questioned by the Grand Council as to their lineal descent, they replied that they were nobly born and that "they were descended from the Princes and Rulers of the House of Judah."[61] Because of their appropriate blood line, the masters were admitted into the city to work on the temple.

Possibly adapting this concept from Royal Arch Masonry, Latter-day Saint leaders believed they were noblemen in literal fact. Heber C. Kimball explained:

> Now, I will refer to brother Brigham, brother Heber, brother Joseph Smith, Oliver Cowdery, Bishop N. K. Whitney, and lots of other men. Brother Joseph actually saw those men in vision; he saw us in a day when we were all together. We have been separated by marriage and thrown apart; but he saw the day when we all came out of one stock, and that was out of the aristocracy. Yes, we came directly down through the Prophets, and not only us, but . . . the whole Smith race.[62]

Kimball further voiced the right of dominion that this lineage possessed:

> Did you actually know Joseph Smith? No. Do you know brother Brigham? No. Do you know brother Heber? No, you do not. Do you know the Twelve? You do not, if you did, you would begin to know God, and learn that those men who are chosen to direct and counsel you are near kindred to God and to Jesus Christ, for the keys, power, and authority of the kingdom of God are in that lineage.[63]

This suggests why the early Latter-day Saint belief that Jesus was married was not idle doctrinal speculation; rather, it was intimately connected with the idea that there were Latter-day Saints, the Prophet Joseph Smith in particular, who held by birth the prophetic, kingly, and priestly authority needed to restore the city of God and its holy temple as well as to establish the theocratic kingdom of God on earth.

---

61. Thomas Sargant, *The Royal Arch Companion, a Manual of Royal Arch Masonry*, 84–85.
62. Heber C. Kimball, September 6, 1857, *Journal of Discourses*, 5:215–16.
63. Heber C. Kimball, March 1, 1857, *Journal of Discourses*, 4:248.

As Michael Quinn has pointed out, those who had received Smith's "last charge" understood their role as rulers in the kingdom of God "in literal terms and did not perceive or accept the essentially symbolic nature of everything connected with the Council of Fifty." Men like "Alpheus Cutler, James Emmett, Peter Haws, George Miller, Lyman Wight, and Lucien Woodworth" all felt they had received "personal missions" from Smith. "They did not agree that the Council of Fifty derived its authority from the Church and was subject to Church leadership," and they later "dissented from the Church in order to preserve what they felt were their missions in the Kingdom of God."[64]

A Foundation to Revolutionize the World

In 1826, Freemasonry was broken upon the wheel of American social change. Local communities enlisted the government as their agent to destroy the Lodge. Later, these communities would similarly ask for this kind of assistance from the state to aid in the destruction of the Mormon empire.

Joseph Smith's fraternal and sororal organizations—including the School of the Prophets, the Danite band, the Relief Society, the Quorum of the Anointed, and the Council of Fifty—were all revolutionary experiments based upon Masonic form, ideals, and structure. To these he added expressions of his own personality as well as his authority as a prophet of God. It was his prophetic authority that lent these auxiliaries and their parent denomination religious authenticity in the eyes of his followers. "God will always protect me until my mission is fulfilled," declared Smith, and further said,

> I calculate to be one of the instruments of setting up the Kingdom of Daniel by the word of the Lord, and I intend to lay a foundation that will revolutionize the whole world. . . . The power of truth is such that all nations will be under the necessity of obeying the Gospel. . . . It may be that the Saints will have to beat their plows into swords, for it will not do for men to sit down patiently and see their children destroyed.[65]

The prophet's revolutionary and even treasonous plans were seen by the Latter-day Saints to be "the design of Jehovah, from the commencement of the world." God's purpose was "to regulate the affairs of the world in his own time; to stand as head of the universe, and take the reins of government into his own hand."[66]

Days before his final arrest, Joseph Smith crossed the Mississippi River into Iowa, intending to flee to the West. The writers of the *History of the Church* describe his brother Hyrum as saying, "A company of men are seeking to kill my brother Joseph, and the Lord has warned him to flee to the Rocky Mountains

---

64. Quinn, "The Council of Fifty and its Members," 182–83.
65. "History, 1838–1856, volume F-1 [1 May 1844–8 August 1844]," 18–19.
66. Joseph Smith Jr., "The Government of God," 856.

to save his life. Goodbye, Brother [Reynolds] Cahoon, we shall see you again."[67] Fearing destruction of life and property, a number of brethren urged the Prophet to return and give himself up. Emma Smith sent a message as well, saying "unless they returned and went to Carthage, Nauvoo would be burnt up and the people massacred."[68]

In later years, Brigham Young expressed his opinion that "if Bro. Joseph Smith had been led by the Spirit he had, he would never [have] given himself up and gone to Carthage but he would have gone right to these mountains and would have been alive today to lead this people."[69] However, at the time of the occurrence, Vilate Kimball wrote, "Joseph went over the river out of the United States, and there stop[p]ed and composed his mind, and got the will of the Lord concerning him, and that was, that he should return and give himself up for trial."[70] In 1844, Smith's gaze had turned to the West. Whether the Lord's will or not, turning back cost him his life.

---

67. According to Abraham C. Hodge, Joseph Smith met in the upper room of his store with several brethren and had Governor Boggs' letter read aloud. "After it was read through Joseph remarked 'there is no mercy— no mercy here.' Hyrum said 'No; just as sure as we fall into their hands we are dead men.' Joseph replied 'yes; what shall we do brother Hyrum?' He replied, 'I don't know.' All at once Joseph's countenance brightened up and he said, 'the way is open— it is clear to my mind what to do; all they want is Hyrum and myself—then tell every body to go about their business, and not to collect in groups but scatter about; there is no doubt they will come here and search for us— let them search; they will not harm you in person or property, & not even a hair of your head. We will cross the river tonight and go away <to the West>.'" See "History, 1838–1856, volume F-1 [1 May 1844–8 August 1844]," 147.

68. "History, 1838–1856, volume F-1 [1 May 1844–8 August 1844]," 148.

69. A. Karl Larson and Katharine Miles Larson, eds., *Diary of Charles Lowell Walker*, 1:25.

70. Ronald K. Esplin, "Life in Nauvoo, June 1844: Vilate Kimball's Martyrdom Letters," 235.

CHAPTER 16

TREASURES HIDDEN IN THE GRAVE

By the yearning to retrieve
treasures hidden in the grave…
hark unto the earnest cry,
notes celestial, make reply!
Christian, unto thee 'tis given:
Death's a passage unto heaven!
—Rob Morris, *The Poetry of Freemasonry*

Masonic legend addresses loss on a cosmological scale. It is a theme with universal relevance as all humanity feels the pain of physical loss. On the individual level, Masonic restoration involves a reversal of the powerful blow suffered through the discovery of one's very real mortality. This is symbolically represented by the Master's Word—lost at the death of Hiram Abiff. When Hiram was buried, he had a jewel on his body representing the lost key of revelation that all Masons are charged to search for throughout their mortal lives. The Royal Arch degree ends with the symbolic restoration of the lost Master's Word and the subsequent exaltation of the candidates. Recovery of this treasure makes possible a reversal of the three great knocks of death, which not only sets right the lives of individuals but also transforms, empowers, and revives human society.[1]

As Joseph Smith experienced premonitions of his own impending death, he began to declare that he had found this Masonic "Lost Word." That is, he had recovered what was needed to complete the temple endowment and make it available to the entire body of the Saints. In a revelation recorded in Doctrine and Covenants 124, these Saints had been commanded to build a temple, and concordantly they were promised keys that would allow them to pierce the veil, receive revelations, and achieve apotheosis. Through recontextualizing Masonry as a religious ordinance, Smith provided the Saints a way to approach God ritually and experience

---

1. "Eternity in the midst of time [is] a divine-human experience possible in the Here and Now. To reach such an existence is in the power of every man; nay, it is the birthright, the God-intended plan, of every child of the race. Herein, it seems to me, we have the reality of which the Lost Word is the mystic symbol; and he who has found that Word within himself is victorious always, whatever betide. If he is betrayed by the friends in whom he has trusted, waylaid by ruffians, put to death in the midst of his creative and benignant work, and thrown into an unmarked grave, he is not defeated or destroyed; the God-like spirit within him, dedicated to the Eternal Values, raises him up from the level of death to the perpendicular of the life that is endless." Harry L. Haywood, *Symbolical Masonry: An Interpretation of the Three Degrees*, 276.

divine power. The restoration of the temple was the restoration of a pure form of Masonry, and, for Joseph Smith as prophet, the end was now in sight.

On April 7, 1844, during the second session of the general conference of the Church, in front of an estimated fifteen thousand Latter-day Saints, Smith preached a powerful discourse in honor of a deceased Mormon elder and Masonic brother, King (his first name) Follett.[2] Five weeks earlier, on February 27, Follett was digging a well for the use of his family when a rope holding a large tub of rocks broke. The falling rocks and dirt crushed him, and he was carried to his house where he lived for eleven more days, in great pain, before finally expiring on Saturday, March 9, 1844. That evening, his death was announced during a meeting of the Nauvoo Lodge where he had been a Master Mason. There, William S. Hathaway reported that "Brother King" had indicated his desire to receive a Masonic burial.[3]

The next day, Sunday, March 10, one hundred and nineteen members of the Masonic lodge met at the newly built but still undedicated Masonic Hall in Nauvoo. The Lodge was "called from adjournment" to labor on the third degree, and Worshipful Master Hyrum Smith stated that the object of the meeting was "to carry to the grave a worthy brother, King Follet[t] who has for some time been a worthy member of our Lodge and continued in good standing while he lived on the earth."[4] Brief remarks were made by Hyrum Smith, during which he presumably opened a Lodge of Sorrow in memory of their deceased Brother. Then a procession was assembled in due Masonic form.[5] Accompanied by the Nauvoo Brass Band, Lodge members proceeded to the Follett home to dress and

---

2. Contemporary accounts estimate the audience at fifteen to twenty thousand, but the total population of Nauvoo at the time was closer to eleven thousand (11,057). Perhaps additional people coming from outlying areas for general conference could have swelled the number this much, but this would have pushed the upper limit of the capacity of the grove where the conference was held.

3. "Nauvoo Masonic Lodge minutes, 1841–1846," March 9, 1844.

4. The usual procedure for a Masonic funeral would have been to formally open the Lodge at this time. But the Nauvoo Lodge typically conducted procedures a bit differently. Often, they did not close the Lodge at the conclusion of their meetings but left them open and adjourned until the next day. This allowed them to save time and dispense with the ceremony of opening the Lodge each time they wished to confer degrees. Sometimes ten or more degrees were given during a meeting.

5. The earliest known record of a Masonic funeral was for the Rev. Dr. James Anderson, author of the first Book of Constitutions of the first Grand Lodge. According the William Denslow, "[h]e was buried in Bunhill Fields with Masonic services, and accounted for the earliest known account of a Masonic funeral which appeared in the London Daily Post of June 2, 1739: 'Last night (June 1) was interr'd the corpse of Dr. Anderson, a Dissenting Teacher, in a very remarkable deep Grave. His pall was supported by five Dissenting Teachers, and the Rev. Dr. Desaguliers; it was followed by a dozen of Freemasons who encircled the Grave; and after Dr. Earle had harangued on the Uncertainty of Life &c, without one word of the Deceased, the Brethren, in the most solomn dismal Posture, lifted up their Hands,

prepare his body for burial and place it in his coffin.[6] By all accounts, the procession from the Follett home to the grave site was a stunning spectacle. The band played somberly with their drums "muffled and trim[m]ed with black lace."[7] Led by Nauvoo Lodge Marshal John P. Green, the Masons were dressed in dark suits. Around their waists were tied aprons of white lambskin, that Masonic emblem of innocence that represented the Mason's lifelong commitment to purity of life and rectitude of conduct. Wearing white gloves, the lodge officers were decked in the glittering regalia of their respective offices; the deacons and stewards additionally carried staffs. It was likely that the procession accompanying Follett's coffin followed the Masonic tradition of the day, forming two columns roughly five feet apart, with the members of the Nauvoo Lodge in the front and those from visiting Lodges behind. Friends and family followed in carriages, on horseback, and on foot in a procession described as being a mile in length.[8] Follett's funeral service adhered to the Masonic convention that "a masonic Lodge should not take part in funeral services when conducted by any other organization."[9] Thus, the Nauvoo Lodge, not the Church, was in charge of the body of the deceased and all of the funerary ceremonies and procedures.

That evening, Joseph Smith preached at the regular Sunday evening meeting in the Grove. Although Follet's friends and family specifically requested Smith to

---

sigh'd, and struck their aprons three times in Honour to the Deceased.'" See William R. Denslow, *10,000 Famous Freemasons*, s.v. "James Anderson."

6. Joann Follett Mortensen, *The Man behind the Discourse: A Biography of King Follett*, 393–97; "Nauvoo Masonic Lodge Minutes," March 10, 1844. The Minute Book described Brother Follett as "a man universally respected by a large circle of friends, having the friendship and esteem of all around him, whether he was viewed as a father, a neighbor, a Mason or a Christian his character was equally honorable and virtuous. He has borne a large portion of sufferings with the Saints of God, having been amongst the number of those who were so cruelly and inhumanly ejected from the State of Missouri by executive authority at the point of the bayonet, his property destroyed and with his family and friends turned naked & destitute upon the world in a solitary wilderness; but he bore his sufferings with patience, fortitude and courage. He lived long enough to witness the unjust, and oppressive conduct of the Grand Lodge of this State towards Nauvoo Lodge in consequence of their religion, and had a disposition with his brethren to contend for his rights as a man and a Mason even though his life must be a forfeit for the attempt."

7. Aroet Lucius Hale, letter to Ebenezer Beesley, circa 1897, quoted in Mortensen, *Man Behind the Discourse*, 396.

8. "Brother Follet's funeral was attended with the highest honors and most marked respect. A procession a mile in length, followed his remains to the 'narrow house.' The emblems and paraphornalia of the 'fraternity,' that glittered along the lengthened line, showed that his 'fidelity' had entitled him to the benefits of Masonry, under the honors of which, in due Masonic form, he was consigned to the solitude of the grave." Lyman O. Littlefield, "Communicated," 2.

9. *Ceremonials Compiled for Use of Lodges Working Under Jurisdiction of the M. W. Grand Lodge of Free And Accepted Masons of the State of Illinois*, 76.

speak at the funeral, the Prophet did not take the opportunity to present a eulogy at that time. Instead, his address was a sermon on Elias and the priesthood, and it contained no reference to Follett or to death in general. However, some weeks later, apparently having been profoundly affected by Follett's death, the Prophet delivered a stirring address which has come to be known as the "King Follett Discourse."

On April 7, 1844, an audience gathered in a grove located on a bluff near the unfinished Nauvoo Temple. Notwithstanding a stiff wind, the spring weather accentuated the beauty of the Mississippi River, and trees could be seen blossoming on the Iowa side. "Inasmuch as there are a great many in this congregation who live in this city, as well as elsewhere, and who have lost friends," Smith explained, "I feel disposed to speak on the subject in general, and offer you my ideas so far as I have ability, and so far as I shall be inspired by the Holy Spirit to dwell on this subject."[10]

The speech is often referred to as a eulogy or funerary discourse[11] for the deceased, though it was given almost a month after Follet's funeral. It has also been seen as a conference address wherein the Prophet used the circumstances of the tragic death of a prominent member of the Church and Fraternity to speak on the eternities and the status of the dead. However, its Masonic connections should not be overlooked. It was originally intended that Smith speak a few days earlier on Friday, April 5, 1844, the day of the dedication of the Nauvoo Masonic Hall.[12] This speech would have taken place in front of an audience that included Mormon and non-Mormon Illinois Freemasons who had gathered for the ceremonies. Being somewhat ill that day, Smith opted to postpone his speech and presented it at Sunday's Conference, bringing Masonic elements to a sympathetic and specifically Latter-day Saint congregation. In this, one of the best attested of all of the Prophet's sermons, Smith engaged the central Masonic theme of human mortality and perfectibility in his own unique way, utilizing language that would have been familiar to the hundreds of Mormon Freemasons in his audience.

Official notes of the speech were taken by three men. Thomas Bullock was formally trained in England as a law clerk and filled many clerical positions in Nauvoo, beginning in October 1843 as Joseph's personal clerk. His journal indi-

---

10. John Taylor, "Conference Minutes," 613.

11. B. H. Roberts's description of the April 7 discourse in *History of the Church* states: "President Joseph Smith delivered a discourse before twenty thousand Saints, being the funeral sermon of Elder King Follett." Joseph Smith Jr. et al., *History of the Church of Jesus Christ of Latter-day Saints*, 6:301.

12. "In the fore part of the day President Joseph Smith was to have preached the fun[er]al sermon of King Follet but in consequence of Ill health He omitted it & called upon Elder A. Lyman to take the stand & he arose & gave an interesting address to the vast multitude who had assembled for the purpose of hearing a discourse from Presiden[t] Smith." Wilford Woodruff journal, April 5, 1844. However, the minutes from the Nauvoo Lodge for that date state that addresses were given at the afternoon dedication by Hyrum Smith, William Goforth, and Joseph Smith.

cates that he had been assigned to take minutes of the meeting.[13] Bullock would not become a Freemason until months later, and his account demonstrates that he missed some of the Masonic references the other scribes were able to pick up.[14] William Clayton had joined the Nauvoo Masonic Lodge in 1842 in the first month of its existence.[15] He served as secretary to Smith and has been described as "a clear writer" with "a love for order."[16] Willard Richards also joined the Lodge in April of 1842.[17] As Church historian, Richards was responsible for making an official account of the proceedings. He was also the Prophet's private secretary and historian, keeping Smith's daily journal from 1842 through 1844, and he recorded his summary of the discourse into Smith's journal.[18] An unofficial account of the discourse was taken by Wilford Woodruff, another early Nauvoo Freemason and one of the most prodigious journal keepers of the day.[19] While standing in the congregation, Woodruff removed his hat and used the crown as a surface upon which to place his paper while taking notes.[20] The following August, four months after the sermon was given, and nearly two months after the death of Smith, a version of the discourse was put together from an amalgamation of these four accounts and published in the *Times and Seasons*.[21]

Even had the speech been given at the dedication of the Masonic Hall as planned, it would have been a public address. Attending the dedication of the Hall were 334 Masons from Nauvoo Lodge, along with brethren from Mormon lodges Helm, Nye, Hiram (Augusta, IA), and Rising Sun (Montrose, IA). Other lodges in the area had been invited as well, though only eight non-Mormon Masons were marked in attendance. One of these was Brother William G. Goforth from St. Clair Lodge No. 24 in Belleville, who was daring enough not only to appear at the dedication of a lodge that had been declared clandestine

---

13. Donald Q. Cannon, "The King Follett Discourse: Joseph Smith's Greatest Sermon in Historical Perspective," 183. Bullock was secretary of the courts-martial for the Nauvoo Legion, clerk for the "Maid of Iowa," and clerk of conferences of the Church, and he was assigned to write brief synopses of sermons given by the Prophet.

14. Two persons named Thomas Bullock were raised in Nauvoo Lodge in 1844: one on May 3, 1844, and the other on August 31, 1844.

15. Clayton was raised April 23, 1842, and made a member of the Anointed Quorum February 3, 1844.

16. Cannon, "The King Follett Discourse," 183.

17. Richards was raised April 9, 1842, and made a member of the Anointed Quorum May 4, 1842.

18. Cannon, "The King Follett Discourse," 183. Of Richards's abilities as a scribe, Orson Spencer wrote that he "was eminently gifted. He chronicled events, dates, circumstances, and incidents with rare accuracy of judgment and rare tenacity of memory." See "Death of our Beloved Brother Willard Richards," 2.

19. Woodruff was raised April 29, 1842, and made a member of the Anointed Quorum December 2, 1843.

20. Cannon, "The King Follett Discourse," 184.

21. "Conference Minutes: Continuation of Last April's Conference," 612–17.

but also to give a speech. He was later reprimanded for this action by his lodge.[22] Numerous additional spectators from many miles around who were not Masons also gathered to witness the ceremonies. These lingered in town and joined the thousands of Latter-day Saints who made up the conference audience of April 7.

The public nature of the event presented Smith with a predicament. As part of his Masonic obligation, he had promised at the altar of the lodge that he would always "conceal, and never reveal any part, or parts, art, or arts, point, or points of the secret arts and mysteries of ancient freemasonry." Knowing that his address would likely be reproduced in the *Times and Seasons*, he also needed to keep in mind his obligation not to "write, print, stamp, stain, hugh [hew], cut, carve, indent, paint, or engrave" the secrets of Masonry "on any thing moveable or immoveable, under the whole canopy of Heaven, whereby, or whereon the least letter, figure, character, mark, stain, shadow, or resemblance of the same may become legible or intelligible . . . to any other person in the known world."[23]

In order to include Masonic elements, Smith would have to give his discourse in the manner that other Masons had utilized to give public addresses. These speakers alluded to Masonic themes in such a way that Freemasons would catch the references but common listeners would not. An example of this technique is seen in a speech by Salem Town:

> On the apostacy of our first common parent, not a gleam of light was left to irradiate and cheer his desponding mind. To his surprise and amazement, he found himself in total obscurity, as to those future and interesting scenes, on which he was entering. Soon, however, to his inexpressible joy, the first kind promise was made. This promise, though but a single ray, afforded much consolation. Although the true light now began to shine, yet how faint were its beams compared with that bright and meridian splendor, afterwards to illuminate the moral world.[24]

A non-Mason might catch the symbolism that "our first parent"—Adam—was in the darkness of ignorance and found himself brought to the light of knowledge concerning his future. However, a Mason listening to the talk would immediately see that Salem Town was suggesting that Adam was a Freemason. In the first degree, a Mason enters the darkened lodge in which "not a gleam of light" is seen. He is led to the altar where "the first kind promise" is made. To a Freemason, Town's wording brings to mind all of the details of the ceremony of the first, or Entered Apprentice, degree.

Wilford Woodruff would later report Brigham Young's understanding of this method of discourse: "I Could preach all about the Endowments in Public and the

---

22. Mervin B. Hogan, *The Dedication of the Nauvoo Masonic Temple and the Strange Question of Dr. Goforth*, 4–8.

23. William Morgan, *Illustrations of Masonry by One of the Fraternity Who has Devoted Thirty Years to the Subject*, 21.

24. Salem Town, *A System of Speculative Masonry in its Origin, Patronage, Dissemination, Principles, Duties, and Ultimate Designs, Laid Open for the Examination of the Serious and Candid*, 75–76.

world know Nothing about it. I Could preach all about Masonry & None but a mason know any thing about it."[25] Similarly, members of the congregation listening to the Smith's discourse who were not Freemasons might not have noticed his Masonic allusions. However, Smith was moving these ideas directly into Mormonism in a way that he had rarely done before outside of the temple endowment.

The Character of God

After introducing his topic, Joseph Smith set the scene with ideas that accorded well with Masonic interests. The Prophet first expounded upon the character of God, and he expressed the importance of understanding God's nature, asking the congregation, "What kind of being is God?" He asked if any had seen him, heard him, or communed with him. "Here [is] a subject that will peradventure occupy you[r] attenti[o]n while you live. . . . There can be eternal life on no other principle."[26] In *The Symbolism of Freemasonry*, Albert Mackey explains that Freemasonry is "a science which speculates on the character of God and man, and is engaged in philosophical investigations of the soul and a future existence, for which purpose it uses the terms of an operative art."[27] Reflecting upon the character of God is thus a principal pursuit of Masons.

In his presidential platform, Smith's principle of theocratic democracy included the provision that humans have a right to believe as they chose about God. This was the evolving wisdom of the age. Enlightenment thinking had taken hold of the developed world, with America being the ground of experimentation. Freemasonry's position on religious freedom developed in harmony with this thinking. In the eighteenth century, it was one of the first organizations to practice the concept of separation of church and state and acted accordingly as a powerful force for religious freedom. The Masonic Service Association of North America's "Statement on Religion" specifies that "Masons believe that there is one God and that people employ many different ways to seek, and to express what they know of God." Non-sectarian titles for Deity such as "Grand Architect of the Universe" are used so that "persons of different faiths may join together in prayer, concentrating on God, rather than differences among themselves. Masonry believes in religious freedom and that the relationship between the individual and God is personal, private, and sacred." Furthermore, although "Freemasonry lacks the basic elements of religion, . . . Freemasonry is far from indifferent toward religion. Without interfering in religious practice, it expects each member to follow his own faith and to place his Duty to God above all other duties."[28] Mirroring this sentiment, Smith emphasized the privilege of religious

---

25. Wilford Woodruff journal, January 22, 1860.

26. "Discourse, 7 April 1844, as Reported by William Clayton," The Joseph Smith Papers, 12.

27. Albert Gallatin Mackey, *The Symbolism of Freemasonry: Illustrating and Explaining its Science and Philosophy, its Legends, Myths, and Symbols,* 356.

28. Masonic Information Center, "Statement on Freemasonry and Religion."

freedom: "But meddle not with any man for his religion, ev[e]ry gover[n]ment ought to permit ev[e]ry man to enjoy his religion."²⁹

After establishing this principle, Smith revealed a "great secret"³⁰ about Deity in a statement that was to shock many in the audience:

> God himself who sits enthroned in yonder Heavens is a man like unto one of your-selves who holds this world in its orbit & upholds all things by his power[.] if you were to see him to day you wo[ul]d see him a man for Adam was an man like in fashion & image like unto him.³¹

Smith further taught that God had not been God for all eternity; rather, "he once was <a> man like us, and the Father was once on an earth like us."³² Using John 10:17 as a reference, the prophet taught that as the Father had power in himself, "so hath the son power in himself to do what the father did even to lay down my body and take it up again." He reasoned that the Father must have also once had a body of flesh and bones that was resurrected. Understanding this principle was necessary for his followers to be able to understand the character and being of God.

Having taught that God had once been mortal, Smith explained the corol-lary that men could become deities in their own right:

> You have got to learn how to be a god yourself in order to save you[r]self— to be priests & Kings as all Gods has done—by going from a small degree to another[,] from exaltation to ex[altation]—till they are able to sit in glory as doth those who sit enthroned . . . how consoling to the mourner when call[e]d to part with husband father wife [and] child to know that those being[s] shall rise in immortal glory to sor-row die nor suffer anymore. & not only that[,] to contemplate the saying they shall be heirs of God &c[.] What is it[?]—to inherit the same glory[,] power & exal[ta] tion with those who are gone before.³³

Three accounts of this portion of the discourse use the terminology of go-ing from a small to a great "capacity." William Clayton, however, instead used the Masonic term "degree," indicating that he likely recognized this teaching as a Masonic principle. Wilford Woodruff's account also uses the Masonic locution "arrive at the station of a God,"³⁴ an allusion to the progression of the officers of a Lodge, wherein Brothers move from station to station, each one taking the place of the Brother who has sat in that station previously, advancing by degrees, until arriving at the station of the Worshipful Master in the East and "ascending the

---

29. Wilford Woodruff journal, April 7, 1844.

30. "Discourse, 7 April 1844, as Reported by William Clayton," 13.

31. "Discourse, 7 April 1844, as Reported by Thomas Bullock," The Joseph Smith Papers, 16.

32. Woodruff journal, April 7, 1844. Clayton reports "a planet" instead of "an earth." See "Discourse, 7 April 1844, as Reported by William Clayton," 13.

33. "Discourse, 7 April 1844, as Reported by William Clayton," 14.

34. Woodruff journal, April 7, 1844.

[Master's] throne."[35] Such language appears in Thomas Bullock's account, which was incorporated into the official report of the discourse in the *Times and Seasons*: "What is [to be a joint heir with Christ]? to inherit the same glory, the same power and the same exaltation, until you ascend the throne of eternal power the same as those who are gone before."[36]

Two years later, Orson Hyde would use similar Masonic terminology in a discourse at the dedication of the Nauvoo Temple on May 3, 1846:

> [T]here are different stations in the next world and men will be de[a]lt with ~~here~~ according to the deeds done in the body. A man ought to be good Here as he grows older. A man that does his duty and obtains the Priesthood and honors it will have his reward, His exhaltation, thrones, & dominions according to his faithfulness. We like our Master have des[c]ended below all things so shall we arise above all things. I have seen this by vision. We shall be connected with the kingdom of Jesus Christ To the very place and station will a man arise in the resurrection to which He Has been sealed & anointed on earth.[37]

In Freemasonry, the Master of the Lodge symbolizes Deity. Smith's explanation that if his audience were to see God today, they would see him like a man in form, would have naturally brought to Freemasons' minds the image of the Worshipful Master of the Lodge standing in for God. His comments regarding the goal to "ascend the throne of eternal power" invoke an image of the Master of the Lodge, sitting upon his elaborate dais in the East. He represents God, just as the Lodge itself is symbolic of the created universe. Furthermore, his description of Saints inheriting the same glory, power, and exaltation with "those who are gone before" uses the same wording as a three-fold repetition in the Entered Apprentice degree where a candidate petitions to receive the rights and benefits of the lodge "as all true fellows and brothers have done, who have gone this way before him."[38]

This process of exaltation described by Smith points to it being a theological expansion of the concept of "progression up the line of officers" in a lodge. In this instance, Smith specifically applied the idea to God the Father and the Son. Additionally, he employed the use of figures such as that of a ladder, featured in the Entered Apprentice degree, to teach heavenly ascent and exaltation:

---

35. See also George Laub's summary of the discourse, which evokes this same Masonic progression: "For we are to goe from glory to glory & as one is raised the Next may be raised to his place or Sphere and so take their Exaltation through a regular channel. And when we get to where Jesus is he will be as far ahe[a]d of us in exaltation as when we started." See Eugene England, ed., "George Laub's Nauvoo Journal," 173.

36. "Conference Minutes: Continuation of Last April's Conference," 614. See also "Discourse, 7 April 1844, as Reported by Thomas Bullock," 17: "they shall be heirs of God & jt. hrs [joint heirs] of J. C. to inherit the same powers exalt[atio]n. until you asc[en]d. the throne of Etl. power same as those who are gone bef[ore]."

37. Orson Hyde, discourse at the dedication of the Nauvoo Temple, in Wilford Woodruff journal, May 3, 1846.

38. Morgan, *Illustrations of Masonry*, 18.

what J[esus] did I do the things I saw my Fa[the]r do before worlds came roll[e]d into existence I saw my Fa[the]r work out his K[ingdom] with fear & trembling & I must do the same when I shall give my K[ingdom] to the Fa[the]r so that he obt[ai]ns K[ingdom] roll[in]g upon K[ingdom] so that J[esus] treads in his tracks as he had gone before[.] it is plain beyond comprehens[io]n & you thus learn the first prin[ciple] of the Gospel when you climb a ladder you must begin at the bottom run[g] until you learn the last prin[ciple] of the Gospel for it is a great thing to learn Sal[vatio]n. beyond the grave & it is not all to be com[prehended] in this world.[39]

In Freemasonry, the symbol of a ladder is taken from Jacob's dream of a ladder ascending to heaven (Gen. 28). For Entered Apprentice Masons "[e]ither resting upon the floor-cloth or upon the Bible: the compasses and the square should lead the thoughts of the brethren to heaven."[40] The ritual describes the ascension of a brother up the "Theological Ladder" through the steps of Faith and Hope and then leading to the summit of Charity. He who attains this virtue "may justly be deemed to have attained the summit of his profession, figuratively speaking, an ethereal mansion veiled from mortal eye by the starry firmament."[41]

Perfection of Human Personality

The perfection of human personality is a doctrine that Joseph Smith had been developing since at least 1834. The fifth Lecture on Faith discusses becoming partakers of the divine nature, or "partaking of the fulness of the Father and Son, through the spirit."[42] The Masonic variation on this biblical doctrine is that not only can humans develop God-like qualities by perfecting themselves, but they have the innate potential to actually become gods. Masonic philosopher Manly Hall wrote that

> Man is a god in the making, and on the potter's wheel he is being molded, as in the mystic myths of Egypt. When his light shines out to lift and preserve all things, he accepts the triple crown of godhood, and joins that throng of Master Masons . . . in their garments of glory.[43]

F. V. Mataraly expounded upon this idea, speaking of a "hidden Master" inside each person who could be revealed through the purification of an individual:

> By the exercise of the three Working Tools, a straight-edge, a chisel (also represented by a line), and a gavel (represented by two lines at right angles), the rough material is wrought into due form and the perfection of the whole brought into manifestation.

---

39. "Discourse, 7 April 1844, as Reported by Thomas Bullock," 17.

40. George Oliver, *A Dictionary of Symbolical Masonry, Including the Royal Arch Degree; According to the System Prescribed by the Grand Lodge and Supreme Grand Chapter of England*, 194.

41. Richard Carlile, "To William Williams, Esq., M. P. Provincial Grand Master for the County of Dorset of the Association of Freemasons. Letter II," 49.

42. "Doctrine and Covenants, 1835," The Joseph Smith Papers, 54.

43. Manly P. Hall, *The Lost Keys of Freemasonry: The Legend of Hiram Abiff*, 123–24.

So in the individual, the material is rough, albeit sound, stone; else he would not have been accepted as a candidate, but by the exercise of the Working Tools of the personality, purified thought, action, and desire, the individual is wrought into due form and the hidden Master brought to light.[44]

Mormon teachings encompass this distinctive Masonic belief. As noted in the King Follett discourse, Smith taught that God had once been a man and that humans could learn to become gods themselves, and this idea of humans being gods in the making has continued in The Church of Jesus Christ of Latter-day Saints. After arriving in Utah, apostle and future president John Taylor taught, "[W]e look at him [man] as emanating from the Gods—as a God in embryo—as an eternal being who had an existence before he came here."[45] This teaching by Taylor was selected for the very first entry in the Church's 2001 *Teachings of Presidents of the Church: John Taylor* manual for adult weekly study.[46] Likewise, in his still-popular 1901 *Articles of Faith*, Elder James E. Talmage declared, "[I]n his mortal condition man is God in embryo. However . . . any individual now a mortal being may attain the rank and sanctity of godship."[47] And more recently, the Church clarified its teaching that

[A]ll people [are] children of God in a full and complete sense. . . . Each possesses seeds of divinity. . . . Just as a child can develop the attributes of his or her parents over time, the divine nature that humans inherit can be developed to become like their Heavenly Father's.[48]

Joseph Smith and Kabbalah

While preaching these principles, Joseph Smith exhibited a connection with what some authors have identified as Kabbalistic thought. This ought to be expected, since the earliest Masonic legends are based in Christian mysticism, which itself is rooted in Jewish mystical teaching (Kabbalah). In the nineteenth century, these interests came to most Americans through the cultural saturation of Freemasonry throughout society.

The concept of the perfection of human personality is a Masonic teaching that comes through Christian Kabbalah. In turn, this idea was the core confidential teaching in Jewish Kabbalah. Critic and scholar Harold Bloom recognized the use of Kabbalah in Smith's teachings. He postulated: "Either there was a more direct Kabbalistic influence upon Smith than we know, or, far more likely, his genius re-

---

44. F. V. Mataraly, "The Spiritual Significance of Some of Our Symbols."

45. John Taylor, February 19, 1850, *Journal of Discourses*, 8:1.

46. *Teachings of Presidents of the Church: John Taylor*, 2.

47. James E. Talmage, *Articles of Faith, A Series of Lectures on the Principal Doctrines of the Church of Jesus Christ of Latter-Day Saints*, 461.

48. "Becoming Like God," The Church of Jesus Christ of Latter-day Saints.

invented Kabbalah in the effort necessary to restore archaic Judaism."[49] Even more likely, the direct Kabbalistic influence upon Smith came through Freemasonry.

Author Lance Owens posits that Smith was influenced by Kabbalah in several distinct ways: "through contact with ceremonial magic in his youth"; through personal inclination during his Kabbalistic hermeneutic method while translating the Book of Mormon; through initiation into Masonry in 1842; through his friendship with Alexander Neibaur, a Jewish Kabbalist; and through the possible possession of a collection of Kabbalistic books and manuscripts.[50] Owens points out that in the King Follett discourse, Smith "quotes almost word for word from the first section of the *Zohar*,"[51] a fundamental text of the Jewish Kabbalah that begins with remarks on the first sentence in the Hebrew scriptures, *Bereshith bara Elohim*. In William Clayton's transcription of the discourse, Smith remarks, "Rosheit signifies to bring forth the Eloheim." This is comparable with the analysis in the *Zohar*:[52]

> This "beginning" [*Reshith*] then extended, and made for itself a palace for its honour and glory. . . . This palace is called Elohim, and this doctrine is contained in the words, "By means of a beginning [*Reshith*, it,] created Elohim."[53]

According to Owens, the objection that Smith exhibited "audacious independence" in interpreting *Bereshith* as *Rosh*, the "head" or "head God," is explained by the use of Kabbalah. He writes, "A basis for this reading is actually found in the next verse of the *Zohar*. . . . [T]he *Zohar* explains that the word *Reshith* 'is anagrammatically Rosh (head), the beginning which issues from Reshith."[54]

Owens additionally shows that Smith followed the *Zohar* in translating *Elohim* in the plural rather than the orthodox singular he was taught in his Kirtland Hebrew class. In the same passage quoted by Owens is found "both the concept of plurality and the hierarchy of Gods acting 'with the permission and direction of the one above it, while the one above did nothing without consulting its colleague.'" He concludes that these themes from the *Zohar* were echoed in the King Follett discourse and again two months later (June 16, 1844) in Smith's last public doctrinal address. Thus, Kabbalistic ideas "became a foundation for all subsequent Mormon theosophy."[55]

---

49. Harold Bloom, *The American Religion: The Emergence of the Post-Christian Nation*, 99, 105.

50. Lance S. Owens, "Joseph Smith and Kabbalah: The Occult Connection," 119.

51. Owens, 178.

52. "Discourse, 7 April 1844, as Reported by William Clayton," 15.

53. Harry Sperling, *The Zohar*, I:15a, as quoted in Owens, "Joseph Smith and Kabbalah," 181.

54. Owens, 182.

55. Owens, 182–83. According to Owens, "Two months after giving the King Follett Discourse, Joseph returned to these first Hebrew words of Genesis and the subject of plural Gods. Thomas Bullock transcribed his remarks on the rainy Sunday morning of 16 June 1844. . . . As he began his exegesis of the opening Hebrew phrase of Genesis in the King Follett Discourse, Joseph stated that he would go to the 'old Bible.' In Kabbalistic lore, the commentary of the *Zohar* represented the oldest biblical interpretation, the secret

The Jewish mystical tradition held that Kabbalah consisted of the original knowledge Adam received from God. Not only was Kabbalah considered to be the guardian of this original knowledge, but "its function was to hand down to its disciples the secret of God's revelation to Adam."[56] This idea comes through clearly in Freemasonry, as expressed by George Oliver:

> The principles of speculative Masonry, which had been communicated to Adam in Paradise, were never by him forsaken after having tasted the bitter fruit of the forbidden tree; and as his progeny increased, he communicated to them the divine precepts and injunctions which were enfolded in that pure and sublime science.[57]

Albert Pike describes how many of the symbols found in speculative Masonry came from alchemy: "By this and many other proofs we know that the symbols of Freemasonry were introduced into it by the Hermetic philosophers of England."[58] Manly P. Hall states that Hermes "was the author of the Masonic initiatory rituals" and that "nearly all of the Masonic symbols are Hermetic in character."[59]

Medieval alchemists experimented with turning lead to gold, but their more immediate preoccupation was in changing the base human materials into the divine. They employed symbols of metals, elements, the planets, and chemical processes to describe and understand the spiritual process of personal improvement. To Renaissance thinkers who followed in these footsteps, the natural world was a reflection of the divine. Through certain magical practices in this world a person could achieve true salvation in the next. This form of alchemy is comparable with that of treasure diggers in early New England who sought lost valuables. While these folks did actually dig for treasure, to many the allegory represented by treasure-seeking was the spiritual point of the exercise. Their activity "had more to do with obtaining experiential knowledge of God and the celestial hierarchies" than "digging for vulgar gold."[60] Smith's early involvement with treasure-seeking,

---

interpretation imparted by God to Adam and all worthy prophets after him. Joseph certainly was not using the knowledge of Hebrew imparted to him in Kirtland nine years earlier when he gave his exegesis of *Bereshith bara Elohim,* or plural interpretation of *Elohim.* Was then the 'old Bible' he used the *Zohar*? And was the 'learned man of God' he mentioned Simeon ben Yochai, the prophetic teacher attributed with these words in the *Zohar*? Joseph wove Hebrew into several of his discourses during the final year of his life. In these late Nauvoo discourses, however, he interpreted the Hebrew not as a linguist but as a Kabbalist—a reflection of his own predilections and of the fortuitous aid of his tutor, Alexander Neibaur."

56. Gershom Scholem, *Major Trends in Jewish Mysticism,* 21.

57. George Oliver, *The Antiquities of Freemasonry; Comprising Illustrations of the Five Grand Periods of Masonry from the Creation of the World to the Dedication of King Solomon's Temple,* 46.

58. Arturo de Hoyos, trans. and ed., *Albert Pike's Esoterika: The Symbolism of the Blue Degrees of Freemasonry,* 104.

59. Manly P. Hall, *A Encyclopedic Outline of Masonic, Hermetic, Qabbalistic and Rosicrucian Symbolical Philosophy, Being an Interpretation of the Secret Teachings concealed within the Rituals, Allegories, and Mysteries of all Ages,* 37.

60. Owens, "Joseph Smith and Kabbalah," 156.

as well as his later preoccupation with Kabbalistic and Masonic thought, seems to follow this type of motivation.

The Grand Council

In speaking of the "head one of the Gods,"[61] Joseph Smith also described a "Head Council" composed of these divine beings. In Willard Richards's account, Smith preached, "The head one called the Gods together in grand coun[c]il" where they "concoct[e]d a scheme to create this world."[62] This idea builds upon that found in the Book of Abraham, which depicts a divine Grand Council. Here, God, in the midst of an assembly of other divine beings, presided over the creation of the earth (Abr. 3:22–26). This conception resembles the Masonic idea of a Grand Council in Heaven, overseen by the Grand Master of the Universe. In particular, the Royal Arch Degree in Freemasonry contains a ritual celestial ascent into the presence of a Grand Council situated in the Holy of Holies, while passing veils and receiving tests of knowledge regarding the various names, signs, and tokens associated therewith. They recover "That Which Was Lost" and in the presence of the Grand Council are rewarded for their labors by being crowned and made Companions in what Royal Arch Masons call "The Rite of Exaltation." The prayer associated with this degree specifically states that the Grand Council represents that Grand Council in Heaven.

Masonic governing bodies are similarly known as Grand Councils and are patterned after the heavenly Grand Council. Moreover, Masons expect to be gathered into this august body after their mortal death:

> As the morning dew ascends to heaven, rich with the fragrance of the flowers it has refreshed and beautified, so may our good deeds, as Council Masons, continue to ascend to heaven, laden with the blessings of those upon whom they have shed a ray of warm and genial sunshine. And when the last sound of the Gavel shall be heard, . . . and the secret vault forever closed, may we be permitted to enter the Grand Council above, and with God and angels ever dwell.[63]

Creation from Disorder

In the King Follett discourse, Joseph Smith noted that theologians of the day—"doctors"—taught that God "created the earth out of nothing."[64] He, however, took a more Kabbalistic (and therefore Masonic) view. *Barau*, Smith

---

61. This phrase is used in all four of the accounts.

62. "Discourse, 7 April 1844, as Reported by Willard Richards," The Joseph Smith Papers, 68.

63. *Proceedings of the Most Puissant Grand Council of Royal and Select Masters of the State of New Jersey at the 13th and 14th Annual Assemblies, Held at Trenton, Jan. 17th, 1871 and Jan. 16th, 1872*, 63.

64. "Discourse, 7 April 1844, as Reported by Willard Richards," 68.

explained, meant to "organize the world out of chaotic matter."[65] In his view, elements were principles that could not be dissolved, although they could be organized and reorganized. Though traditional Christianity counted it blasphemy to say that elements had always existed, the idea went along with the motto of the thirty-third degree of the Scottish rite of Freemasonry: "Ordo ab Chao," or "order from disorder."

Dermott's *Ahiman Rezon*, a mid-eighteenth-century composition, contained a poem illustrating this Masonic conception of Creation:[66]

Progress of Masonry

As all in confusion the chaos yet lay,
E're evening and morning had made the first day;
The unform'd materials lay tumbling together,
Like so many Dutchmen in thick foggy weather.

When to this confusion no end there appear'd,
The sovereign mason's word sudden was heard;
Then teem'd mother chaos with maternal throes,
By which this great lodge of the world then arose.

Then earth and the heavens with Jubile[e] rung,
And all the creation of Masonry sung;
When lo! to compleat and adorn the gay ball,
Old *Adam* was made the grand-master of all.[66]

As discussed in Chapter 6, Smith had previously presented these ideas in the Doctrine and Covenants and in the Pearl of Great Price, a record he presented as containing the writings of Abraham. These books of scripture do not portray creation *ex nihilo* (out of nothing) but *ex materia* (from existing materials). In his discourse, Smith reiterated concepts he explained had been given to the Egyptians in antiquity and preserved by the Masons—albeit in a corrupted form and in need of restoration.

At the climax of the sermon, Smith combined two Masonic principles, *Ordo ab Chao* and the divine nature of man, to bring forth the idea of the immutability of the human spirit: "I might be bold to say that God never did have power to create the spirit of man at all. He could not create himself—Intelligence exists upon a selfexistent principle—is a spirit from age to age & no creation about it."[67] As God is a self-existing being, so is man. Neither the spirit nor the mind have a beginning or end. For Smith, these realities were calculated to exalt the human race.

---

65. Woodruff journal, April 7, 1844.

66. Laurence Dermott, *Ahiman Rezon, Or a Help to All that are (or Would Be) Free and Accepted Masons: Containing The Quintessence of All that Has Been Publish'd on the Subject of Free Masonry*, 144–45.

67. "Discourse, 7 April 1844, as Reported by William Clayton," 16.

A spirit model very similar to the one advocated by Smith was described in William Hutchinson's 1775 *The Spirit of Masonry*: "[T]he Supreme Being . . . was not the creator of the universe, nor the alone independent Being: for, according to them [the maintainers of the Egyptian philosophy], matter too was eternal."[68] Hutchinson's book was well known throughout America and continuously published for over a century. Smith thus likely was well acquainted with these concepts.

The Bright Fraternal Chain: Purpose of Masonic Ritual

One of the fundamental purposes of Masonic ritual is to link together both heaven and earth, the quick and the dead, into what Freemasons identify as "the bright fraternal chain"[69] that links every Masonic Brother and related family member together by virtuous action.[70] The eternal nature of this bond is signified by the Masonic motto *"virtus junxit mors non separabit,"* or "what virtue unites, death cannot separate"—a phrase that was printed in public newspapers in upstate New York as early as the late 1820s.[71] This motto was inscribed upon a plain gold band that was presented to each brother who had received the fourteenth degree of the Rite of Perfection Associated with Masonry since at least 1783; this ring ceremony was well known by Masons in the days of Joseph Smith.[72] During the ceremony of reception, the candidate was instructed:

> Receive this ring as a token of Alliance, and to shew that you have made a Contract with Virtue and with the Virtuous: Do promise me dear Brother never to part with this Ring, untill death, and that you never will give it to any, but your wife, your Eldest son, or your nearest friend.[73]

---

68. William Hutchinson, *The Spirit of Masonry: in Moral and Elucidatory Lectures*, 62.

69. An LDS version of the Mason's *Bright Fraternal Chain* has been called the "Great Chain of Belonging" by LDS writer Samuel Brown. See Samuel Morris Brown, "The Early Mormon Chain of Belonging," 3.

70. "Since ye are met upon the Square, / Bid love and friendship jointly reign: / Be peace and harmony your care, / They form an adamantine chain." Luke Eastman, *Masonick Melodies*, 119.

71. For example, see "Virtus Junxit, Mors Non Separabit," 1, where the motto appears in its Latin form (i.e., *virtus junxit mors non separabit*) on the first page. It is directly beneath a representation of the Divine Name in a triangle, surrounded by a glory, following the words UNITAS, CONCORDIA FRATRUM. Following the whole is an announcement of the next meeting of a Grand Council of the Princes of Jerusalem. The inclusion of the Latin version of the motto suggests that its meaning was well-known among Masons, as is true with the other Latin phrases appearing in the AMR. Thus, the phrase was not only well-known in the Fraternity in a general sense but was accessible in Joseph Smith's immediate environment.

72. Arturo de Hoyos, *Freemasonry's Royal Secret: The Jamaican "Francken Manuscript" of the High Degrees*, 94.

73. de Hoyos, 104.

To Masons, this ring was a token of the understanding that death could not break certain familial and fraternal ties, because those near and dear were united to them by virtue. It demonstrates a Masonic faith—related to their belief in the immortality of the soul—that the tenderest ties of kinship and fraternity extend beyond the grave. The golden band of the fourteenth degree was a reminder to the friends and loved ones of the departed that not even death had the power to divide those relationships that Virtue (which may be read as a metaphor for God) had joined. It is an indissoluble chain, forged by the hand of God, with each link bright and virtuous.

Smith deployed this understanding in the King Follett discourse, where he illustrated the principle using his very own ring. He preached that God was a self-existing being and that man exists upon the same principle:

> [Y]ou who mourn the loss of friends are ownly seperated for a moment. . . . [I]s it logic to say the spirit of man had a begin[n]ing & yet had no end[?] it does not have a begin[n]ing or end, my ring is like the exhistanc[e] of man it has no begin[n]ing or end, if cut into their would be a begin[n]ing & end, so with man if it had a beginning it will have an end.[74]

He continued,

> [I]f I am right, I mi[gh]t with boldness proclaim from the house top that God never had power to create the Sp[irit] of man at all. . . . God himself co[ul]d not create himself[.] [I]ntelligence is self existent it is a Sp[irit] from age to end & there is no creat[io]n ab[ou]t it.[75]

The Hidden Kingdom

William Law, former counselor in the First Presidency of the Church, wrote his impressions of the April 1844 general conference in his diary: "Conference is over, and some of the most blasphemous doctrines have been taught by J. Smith & others." Law summarized what Joseph Smith had taught: "a plurality of Gods, other gods as far above our God as he is above us. That he wrought out his salvation in the flesh with fear and trembling, the same as we do." Law continued with additional teachings given in the 1844 conference that applied to both Masonry and the newly formed Council of Fifty: "that secret meetings are all legal and right and that the Kingdom [of God] must be set up after the manner of a Kingdom (and of course have a King)."[76]

There is little doubt that Smith's King Follett Discourse is Masonic in character. It was given on behalf of a Masonic Brother, intended for a Masonic audience, and contains numerous Masonic allusions. While its content is purely

---

74. Woodruff journal, April 7, 1844.

75. "Discourse, 7 April 1844, as Reported by Thomas Bullock," 18.

76. William Law diary, April 15, 1844, cited in Andrew F. Ehat, "Joseph Smith's Introduction of Temple Ordinances and the 1844 Succession Question," 174.

Mormon, the framing—the staging—is undeniably Masonic in character. As he was encouraged to do as a Freemason, Smith demonstrated his facility for applying Masonic language to his own beliefs. In the King Follett Discourse, he elucidated for his followers the aim and purpose of human existence, using both analogies and language borrowed from Masonic ritual and discourse.

Freemasonry was an important influence in shaping Smith's theology of the "chain of belonging" and the conquest of death.[77] What Freemasons express in the Latin phrase *"Virtus junxit mors non separabit"* ("What virtue unites death cannot separate"), Smith reworded into the uniquely Mormon doctrine of eternal companionship. The "bright fraternal chain" of Masonry[78] became the endless priesthood chain of Mormonism.[79] Smith unveiled the relationship between the living and the dead, describing how death changes and transforms us. He spoke on the meaning of human perfectibility and connection with the gods. These concepts all appear to have come from his meditation on Masonic ideas and the fruit of his own revelations on these subjects. They were evidence of his claim to have recovered the Lost Master's Word. Presented just over two months before his death, the King Follett Discourse represented the apex of Masonic experience and the *summum bonum* of Joseph Smith's own work.

---

77. For a discussion of Joseph Smith's theology of "chain of belonging," see Brown, "The Early Mormon Chain of Belonging," 1–3.

78. In a brief 1814 address to the Duke of Sussex regarding the recent union of the Antient and Moderns Grand Lodges, HRH Prince Augustus Frederick, the Grand Master of the United Grand Lodge of Antient Free Masons of England, spoke of that "fraternal chain, which links us [Freemasons] to each other" in bonds "firm and indissoluble." See William Shadbolt, Robert L. Percy, and J. C. Burckhardt, "To His Royal Highness Prince Augustus Frederick," 203. See also Henry Clinton Atwood, *The Master Workman; Or, True Masonic Guide: Containing Elucidations of the Fundamental Principles of Freemasonry, Operative and Speculative—Morally and Beneficially*, 127: "the fraternal chain that binds us together; may we, who survive him, be more strongly cemented in the ties of union and friendship."

79. "It will be remembered what an unconquerable aversion Joseph manifested, even as a boy of fifteen, to receiving any particle of faith or authority from the churches of Christendom, and also that he was commanded by the personage in the first vision to join none of them. What then is the significance of his becoming a Free Mason? This: He understood that the chain of Masonry is the endless chain of brotherhood and priesthood, linking all the worlds,—the heavens and the earths,—but he believed that this earth had lost much of its purpose, its light, its keys, and its spirit,—its chief loss being the key of revelation. For instance, his concept might be expressed in the statement that the Masonic Church on earth ought to be in communion with the Masonic Church in the heavens, thus constituting a universal brotherhood indeed, notwithstanding its many nations, races, religions, civilizations, and lawgivers." Edward W. Tullidge, *The Life of Joseph Smith the Prophet*, 391–92.

CHAPTER 17

DEATH OF A BUILDER

"Do you meet an enemy in battle array? The token of a Mason instantly converts him into a guardian angel. . . . Is your life in jeopardy from any casualty of time, place or circumstance? a brother's arm is nerved for your assistance, and his own life jeopardized for your safety."
—Salem Town, *A System of Speculative Masonry*

It is written of Jesus of Nazareth that he both acted and was "acted upon" to fulfill prophecy. He, like other would-be messiahs, intentionally emulated scripture, such as when he rode a white donkey through the gate of Jerusalem, fulfilling a recognized prophecy.[1] Much later, his followers and biographers found additional instances in his ministry which they deemed to be the realization of Old Testament prophecies.[2] Similarly, Joseph Smith sought to fulfill prophecy and recover authentic Freemasonry as part of the restoration of true Christianity. On occasion, he consciously replicated Masonic stories and legends in his own life and ministry. At other times, unintentional parallels with the Masonic allegory of Hiram Abiff became evident. Never was this more startling than in the events surrounding his death.

The Work on the Trestleboard

In the allegorical play performed during the third degree of Freemasonry, Hiram Abiff, the chief architect of Solomon's Temple, safeguards the secrets of the Craft. Each day, he lays out on the trestleboard tasks for the workmen to complete. Once the temple is completed, they are to be given the secrets and earn the wages of a Master Mason. In a similar fashion, while overseeing the construction of the Nauvoo Temple, Joseph Smith sought to safeguard the secrets of the political and religious theocratic kingdom he was organizing, particularly through the Council of Fifty. During this time, the Mormon inner circle was conspiring to bring about a kingdom within the borders of the United States, sending ambassadors to other nations in an attempt to gain recognition. Though the Book of Mormon warned against a kingship (Mosiah 29:5–10), it also promoted the establishment of "just men to be . . . kings, who would establish the

---

1. See Zechariah 9:9 and Matthew 21:4–5.

2. Matthew was well known for writing about how Jesus fulfilled prophecy, as in Matthew 1:23, referencing Isaiah 7:14; Matthew 2:5–6, referencing Micah 5:2; Matthew 2:14–15, referencing Hosea 11:1; Matthew 2:16–18, referencing Jeremiah 31:15; Matthew 3:3, referencing Isaiah 40:3; and many others.

laws of God, and judge . . . according to his [God's] commandments" (v. 13). It is with this latter view that Smith sought to restore a purified Masonry and the divinely anointed throne of David.

Additional associations in Nauvoo labored to support the scheme of the Fifty, including the Anointed Quorum and the Masonic Lodge. After the successful dedication of their Hall on April 5, 1844, the Nauvoo Masons doggedly continued the work of making enough Masons for an independent Mormon Grand Lodge. Where other Masonic Lodges throughout the world met once a month, Nauvoo Lodge held "regular communications" twice a month, taking petitions and balloting for members. They also convened on almost a daily basis to initiate, pass, and raise Latter-day Saint men to the Masonic degrees. Visitors were welcomed from lodges such as Genessee Lodge in New York, St. John's Lodge in Boston, and Lodge No. 14 in Western Canada. Despite the scrutiny of visitors, Nauvoo Lodge ignored Masonic convention that no more than three men could be put through a particular degree at a time. Sometimes as many as five Masons were passed or raised at a single meeting,[3] and occasionally men would receive two degrees at the same meeting.[4]

Joseph Smith attended Nauvoo Lodge in 1844, as he had in previous years; however, April 12, two and a half months before his death, was the last time his attendance was recorded in the minutes. Smith seemed content that trusted officiators were going forward with the work of making many Masons. His brother Hyrum, Master of the Lodge, was often absent in the early months of 1844, but Lucius Scovil took up the reins of the Masonic work as Master *pro tempore*,[5] with William Clayton and occasionally Thomas Bullock writing the minutes as secretary and treasurer. Their minutes were terse, but they did mention that charges were preferred against Brothers Wilson Law and Robert D. Foster "for gross unmasonic conduct" on May 2, 1844.[6] This action against men who were endeavoring to expose what they saw as flaws in the Church points to the brewing discontent in Nauvoo and demonstrates conflation of the work of the Lodge with Mormonism.

In Masonic legend, Hiram Abiff is sequentially accosted at the East, South, and West gates of Solomon's Temple by three ruffians who have conspired to wrest from him the secrets of a Master Mason. The architect refuses to divulge

---

3. See "Nauvoo Masonic Lodge minutes, 1841–1846," May 17, 20, 1844; June 8, 1844.

4. See "Nauvoo Masonic Lodge minutes, 1841–1846," May 17, 22, 25, 28, 1844.

5. Scovil was accustomed to acting as Worshipful Master *pro tempore* even before the dedication of the Lodge, and sometimes on occasions when Hyrum Smith was actually present. See, for example, "Nauvoo Masonic Lodge minutes, 1841–1846," March 21, 1844.

6. "Nauvoo Masonic Lodge minutes, 1841–1846," May 2, 1844. It was resolved that Law and Foster should appear before the Lodge on Tuesday, May 7, to answer the charges, with Charles Allen and Austin Cowles to serve as witnesses. When the accused did not show up on that Tuesday, the charges were laid over until they could be called up by Hyrum Smith, the Master of the Lodge.

what he knows, explaining that the Grand Omnific Word can only be revealed in the presence of three: King Solomon, Hiram the King of Tyre, and himself. As each ruffian fails to get what he wants, he strikes Abiff with one of the working tools. The third ruffian strikes him on the head with a setting maul, killing him.

Like Hiram Abiff, Joseph Smith was killed prior to the completion of the Temple. Three distinct groups were complicit in the final attack at Carthage Jail where Smith was held prisoner: Mormon apostates,[7] high-ranking Masonic leaders, and combined military[8] and vigilante[9] forces. All three groups included Smith's Masonic brethren.

First Blow: Apostates

On New Year's Day 1877, Brigham Young spoke of King Solomon's Temple, saying, "It is true that Solomon built a Temple for the purpose of giving endowments, but . . . one of the high priests was murdered by wicked and corrupt men, who had already begun to apostatize, because he would not reveal those things appertaining to the Priesthood that were forbidden him to reveal until he came to the proper place."[10] This statement is clearly Masonic, rather than biblical, as it references both endowments and a high priest (Abiff) who was murdered because he would not disclose priesthood secrets. More importantly, Young was referencing the parallel that the Hiram Abiff story had to apostate members of the Church who were involved in Joseph Smith's death.

Several Mormon apostates who were also Freemasons began stirring things up in Nauvoo in the early spring of 1844. John C. Bennett, for example, was an intimate associate of Smith and was well acquainted with the framework the Prophet established to arrogate authority from the established state. This enabled him to expose Smith's plans, which constituted treason in the eyes of many of his countrymen. Having been instrumental in establishing the Lodge in Nauvoo, Bennett also accused the Mormons of clandestine Masonic activities.

William Law, previously a loyal and faithful member of the Church, became agitated over Smith's teaching of plural marriage. Together, William and Wilson Law, Robert and Charles Foster, Francis and Chauncey Higbee, and Charles Ivins published a newspaper, the *Nauvoo Expositor*, which accused Smith of adultery, teaching false doctrine, and establishing himself as a theocratic king.[11] This group of Mormon renegades struck the first blow against their former leader.

---

7. William Law, Robert D. Foster, Charles A. Foster, Joseph H. Jackson.

8. Carthage "Greys," the Hancock County militia unit assigned to guard the jail where Joseph Smith was incarcerated; Warsaw troops under Minor Deming, discharged at Golden's Point, but continuing on to Carthage on their own.

9. A mob of citizenry in blackface, coming from the west, represented by Mark Aldrich, Thomas Sharp, Levi Williams.

10. Brigham Young, January 1, 1877, *Journal of Discourses*, 18:303.

11. All Master Masons according to "Nauvoo Masonic Lodge minutes, 1841–1846."

Because it threatened to disrupt the order in the growing city, the Nauvoo City Council ruled the *Expositor* a public nuisance, and Smith, as mayor, directed the city marshal to destroy the press. Once the press was demolished on June 10, Smith and his brother Hyrum were in return charged with inciting riot and treason. After they were acquitted twice by sympathetic Nauvoo justices of the peace, protesters throughout Illinois, Iowa, and Missouri threatened violence. Illinois Governor Thomas Ford demanded that the Smiths come to Carthage and submit themselves to what he hoped would be a more impartial trial. Though few of the publishers of the *Expositor* were present at Carthage Jail when the Prophet was shot, they were all considered by early Church members to be complicit in his murder. [12]

A Lamb to the Slaughter

Fearing further turmoil, Joseph Smith instructed his closest followers to destroy the evidence of his politically subversive intentions, telling them to bury or burn their temple clothes and the Council of Fifty records. Then Smith, his brother Hyrum, and a small party of men left for Carthage on June 24, the day Freemasons traditionally commemorate the feast of the New Testament's first martyr, St. John the Baptist. Perhaps Hyrum had this in mind as he carried with him the Worshipful Master's Jewel of Nauvoo Lodge.[13]

The party left the city at 6:30 a.m., riding southeast for three and a half hours—and then returned to Nauvoo to fulfill an order by Governor Ford, who demanded that the Nauvoo Legion surrender all state arms in its possession.[14] The arms were kept in the lower floor of the Nauvoo Masonic Hall. From this place, Smith is reported to have stated, "Boys, if I don't come back, take care of yourselves; I am going like a lamb to the slaughter."[15]

In recapturing the image of Smith's exodus, Nauvoo Freemasons clearly attributed Masonic symbolism to the event. The official account of the Prophet's parting words states, "I am going like a lamb to the slaughter; but I am calm as

---

12. Francis M. Higbee appears on Jacob Backenstos's list of mob members involved in the Smiths' murder. None of the other Expositor publishers are included on that list. William Law's diary, for example, shows that though he had been present in Carthage earlier in the day, he was not there at the time of the murder. Despite this, the *History of the Church* appends to Backenstos's list another by Willard Richards that includes both Law brothers, Robert D. and Charles A. Foster, Francis M. and Chauncey L. Higbee, and ten others "aided and abetted by Charles Ivins and family." See "History, 1838–1856, volume F-1 [1 May 1844–8 August 1844]," The Joseph Smith Papers, 239; see also Joseph Smith Jr. et al., *History of the Church of Jesus Christ of Latter-day Saints*, 7:146.

13. "Mormons Owned Officers' Jewels of Herman Lodge," 3.

14. Robert S. Wicks and Fred R. Foister, *Junius and Joseph: Presidential Politics and the Assassination of the First Mormon Prophet*, 155.

15. "History, 1838–1856, volume F-1 [1 May 1844–8 August 1844]," 153. Contested in Wicks and Foister, *Junius and Joseph*, 156n34.

a summer's morning; I have a conscience void of offense towards God, and towards all men" (D&C 135:4). As much as it refers to Isaiah 53:7, this quotation also replicates the teachings of the Masonic Lodge. When Freemasons are first received into the Lodge, they receive a lambskin apron that has significance in both color and material. The apron must be made of unspotted white lambskin, an emblem of purity by which the Freemason is reminded of the cleanliness of life that is necessary to his gaining admission to the Celestial Lodge above. Freemasons of Smith's day, steeped in the Christian symbolism of the Lodge, were also reminded of Jesus Christ, the Lamb of God. Using language identical to Smith's reported concerns as he left Nauvoo, Masons are instructed that the "Masonic Apron is exhibited as a continual memento, both to himself and those around him, that he is under peculiar engagements to keep his conscience void of offense, both to God and man."[16]

Second Blow: High-Ranking Masonic Leaders

A celebration of St. John's Day had not been planned by Nauvoo Lodge, but Bodley Lodge No. 1, in nearby Quincy, kept the tradition in style. In Bodley's official minutes, a secretary preserved the names of the members and visitors who were celebrating that evening while Joseph and Hyrum Smith were riding to Carthage to surrender themselves. Among the many visitors from Illinois and Missouri, three men were particularly noteworthy: Stephen W. B. Carnegy, Priestly H. McBride, and Abraham Jonas.[17]

Carnegy was nationally prominent in Masonic circles, having served as a delegate at the 1843 Baltimore Convention, where he was lauded for his service as co-author of a standardized ritual for the proposed Grand Lodge of the United States.[18] Carnegy had served as Grand Master of Missouri from 1836 to 1838, during the height of anti-Mormon hostilities in that state. Priestly H. McBride was the sitting Grand Master of Missouri and a judge appointed to his current position on the Missouri Fourth Circuit Court by Governor Lilburn Boggs.[19] Residual tensions from the Mormons' sojourn in Missouri had already caused discord between the Nauvoo Lodge and these high-ranking Missouri Masonic officials.[20] Their decision to neglect their own jurisdiction and instead observe one of the most important Masonic celebrations of the year in nearby Quincy would have likely aroused suspicion among the Nauvoo Masons had it been known at such a critical juncture. Meanwhile, Past Grand Master Abraham Jonas

---

16. John Sherer, *The Masonic Ladder: Or the Nine Steps of Ancient Freemasonry*, 16–17.

17. Records of Bodley Lodge No. 1, June 24, 1844.

18. Charles W. Moore and S. W. B. Carnegy, *The Masonic Trestle-Board, Adapted to the National System of Work and Lectures, as Revised and Perfected by the United States Masonic Convention at Baltimore, Maryland, A. L. 5843*, 7.

19. *History of Audrain County, Missouri*, 231–32.

20. See McBride and Carnegy's rebuff by Nauvoo Lodge in Chapter 13.

of Illinois, who had earlier helped the Mormons establish their lodge in Nauvoo (see Chapter 11), had turned against the Mormons and recently sold his printing press to the men who would publish the *Nauvoo Expositor.*

Upon reaching Carthage near midnight, Joseph and Hyrum Smith rented their usual upstairs south room at the hotel of Artois Hamilton. The larger upstairs room on the north side of the hotel was used for various functions, including the meetings of Carthage's Hancock Lodge No. 20 and Warsaw Lodge No. 21.[21] Hancock Lodge's meetings were held "on the Monday preceding the full moon of each month."[22] With the full moon of June 1844 falling on Sunday, the thirtieth of the month, Hancock Lodge would have met just hours before the arrival of the Smiths, in the same hotel, on Monday, June 24.

On Tuesday morning, June 25, the Smith brothers were paraded before the gathered troops. The rest of the day found the brothers and their retinue in and out of court. A hearing was held at which the Smiths and thirteen other Latter-day Saints "entered into recognizances in the sum of five hundred dollars each."[23] Hours later, they were served with new writs that had been prepared the previous day in front of Justice Robert F. Smith. The writs charged Joseph and Hyrum with treason and served as justification to send the accused to Carthage Jail without bail to await an examination scheduled the next day.[24]

These legal manipulations could hardly have escaped the notice of those familiar with the William Morgan debacle. Accused of larceny for his failure to return a borrowed shirt and tie, Masonic exposer Morgan had been brought before the justice of the peace in Canandaigua, New York. After being released from this charge, he was immediately rearrested for an uncollected debt of $2.68 and thrown into the county jail. From there he was seized by Masonic activists and presumably murdered. Well aware of how Morgan had suffered, the Smiths spent the night of June 25 in the lower room of Carthage jail, guarded by Stephen Markham and other trusted friends while potential assailants peered through the windows.

The next day, before Joseph and Hyrum would face examination by Justice Smith, a secretive meeting convened in the upper lodge room of the Hamilton Hotel. Dr. Wall Southwick, who had spent the night in the jail with the Smiths, managed to infiltrate the meeting and abscond with the secretary's minutes. While those minutes have evidently not survived, they were summarized in a

---

21. William R. Hamilton et. al., "History," 10–11; "An Old Landmark Going," 5.

22. 1844 Return of Hancock Lodge No. 20, in *Reprint of the Proceedings of the Grand Lodge of Illinois, From its Organization in 1840 to 1880 Inclusive*, 153.

23. Wicks and Foister, *Junius and Joseph*, 158.

24. Wicks and Foister, 158; Thomas Ford, *A History of Illinois, from Its Commencement as a State in 1814 to 1847*, 336. Thomas Ford recorded: "all of them were discharged from custody except Joe and Hiram Smith, against whom the magistrate had issued a new writ, on a complaint of treason. They were immediately arrested by the constable on this charge, and retained in his custody to answer it" (p. 337).

letter written by Stephen Markham, who obtained them from Southwick the same day.[25]

Later commentators have often misinterpreted Markham's letter, assuming it to be a somewhat garbled description of a later militia meeting.[26] Markham, however, was writing to fellow Nauvoo Mason Wilford Woodruff, who would have immediately recognized the explicitly Masonic nature of the meeting described. Markham described the meeting as a "council," made up of "delegates," with a "sentinel." These seemingly ordinary structural terms signal the type of gathering that took place. Both "council" and "sentinel" are terms specifically used in higher degrees of Freemasonry, such as the Cryptic Rite. Markham's intentional use of "sentinel" to reference the person assigned to prevent unauthorized entry is highlighted by his frequent reference to guards throughout the rest of the letter. Further, Markham noted that along with Governor Ford and Captain Robert Smith of the Carthage Greys (the local militia charged with presiding over the Smith's court case and providing them with protection), there were delegates from every state in the union except three—coincidentally the number of states with organized grand lodges in 1844. Markham's reference to "delegates" is further important as a common reference to appointed representatives at large Masonic convocations, such as the 1843 Baltimore Convention, where Stephen W. B. Carnegy was the delegate from Missouri.[27]

The "purport of said meeting," wrote Markham,

> was to take into consideration the best way to stop Joseph & Hyrum Smith's career as his Views on Government was widely circulated & took like wild fire. He said that if he did not get in the Presidential chair this election he would be sure to next, & if Illinois & Missouri would join together to kill them they would not be brought to justice for them.[28]

Some authors, lacking an understanding of the Masonic context, have assumed that the unidentified speaker's reference to the "presidential chair" referred to Joseph Smith's quixotic political campaign.[29] This interpretation, however, is complicated by the inclusion of Hyrum Smith, who was not on any political ballot. In all probability, the delegates sought to ward off a very different concern. The phrase "presidential chair" was a common Masonic reference to the place of honor held by the Worshipful Master of a lodge or the Grand Master of a grand

---

25. Stephen Markham, letter to Wilford Woodruff, June 20, 1856.

26. Wicks and Foister, *Junius and Joseph*, 164–65.

27. See *Proceedings of the National Masonic Convention, Held at Baltimore, Maryland, May, A.L. 5843, A.D. 1843*, reprinted in Edward T. Schultz, *History of Freemasonry in Maryland, of All the Rites Introduced into Maryland, from the Earliest Time to the Present*, 3:78–100.

28. Markham to Woodruff, June 20, 1856.

29. Markham himself may have assumed this, as he was not physically present in the meeting and only read the minutes.

lodge.[30] The same phrase was used in reference to Emma Smith taking her place at the head of the Masonry-inspired Nauvoo Female Relief Society at its organizational meeting two years earlier.[31]

The presidential chair referred to in this council was that of the proposed National Grand Lodge of the United States, which would have made Joseph Smith the most powerful Freemason in the country if he were elected to that position. Action on the proposal for a National Grand Lodge had been set for 1846 at a triennial grand convocation. With the number of Mormon Freemasons already approaching a national majority and a public relations campaign driven by Smith's political pamphleteering, prominent Masons could foresee the very real possibility that Joseph Smith could soon become Grand Master of the United States. Hyrum Smith, as Worshipful Master of the premier Mormon Lodge at Nauvoo and likely Grand Master of a contemplated Mormon Grand Lodge, would himself gain significant power and influence. At a time when Freemasonry was finally recovering from the destruction of the Morgan affair, Masonic leaders were unwilling to countenance such a scenario.

Given their timely proximity to Carthage just two days earlier, it is likely that Priestly H. McBride, Stephen W. B. Carnegy, and Abraham Jonas attended this council. These Masonic officials would have been aware of both the irregularities in the Mormon lodges and Smith's doctrine of Masonic restoration. Had these transgressions been reported to the others, it would have caused further consternation and justification for the council's final decision to assassinate the Mormon prophet and his brother.

The words and actions of some Mormons at the time suggest that they were aware of active Masonic involvement in the murder of the Smiths. Dr. B. W. Richmond, a non-Mormon, arrived in Nauvoo on June 24, just before Joseph and Hyrum left for Carthage. Sometime between then and the murder of the Smiths, he visited with Lucinda Pendleton Morgan Harris, knowing of her history as the widow of William Morgan. He later wrote that she had a copy of *An Inquiry into the Nature and Tendency of Speculative Free-Masonry* by John G. Stearns laying out. Richmond's detailed description of the book, however, specifically noting its fine frontispiece engraving of William Morgan, indicates that he misidentified the book. In all likelihood, Lucinda was displaying the equally popular *Light on Masonry: A Collection of All the Most Important Documents on the Subject of Speculative Free Masonry* by Elder David Bernard. "She had taken it out," Richmond wrote, "and thought if the mob did come, and she was obliged to flee, or jump into the Mississippi, she would take it with her."[32] One might imagine

---

30. See, for example, "Address to Alexander Grant, Esq., Master of Lodge 93, and Past Grand Secretary of Bengal, etc.," 349–50; "Lodge of Fortitude No. 281, Lancaster Festival of St. John the Baptist and Presentation to Bro. Dr. Moore," 409; and "Installation Meeting Report, Humber Lodge No. 57," 4.

31. "Ladies' Relief Society," 743.

32. B. W. Richmond, "The Prophet's Death," 51–52.

her treasuring this volume in the days before photography with its rare image of her first husband, the father of her children. Now, as one of Joseph Smith's many wives, Lucinda seems to have drawn a direct parallel between the murder of her first husband and the feared impending murder of her prophetic husband.

Several Mormons would comment in the aftermath of the murders on the involvement of Freemasons in the mob storming the jail. Years later, Brigham Young made a seemingly direct accusation regarding the Masonic council of June 26, 1844, stating that "the people of the United States had sought our destruction and they had used every exertion to perfect it they have worked through the Masonic institution to perfect it." Young continued,

> Joseph & Hyrum Smith were Master Masons and they were put to death by masons or through their instigation and he gave the sign of distress & he was shot by masons while in the act and there were delegates from the various lodges in the union to see that he was put to death.[33]

Third Blow: Military and Vigilante Forces

When Governor Thomas Ford arrived in Carthage on June 21, he discovered a force of more than one thousand militia men had gathered and were threatening to attack Nauvoo.[34] Hundreds more were assembled at Warsaw. Joseph and Hyrum Smith planned to escape and left Nauvoo, crossing the river into Iowa on the evening of June 22, 1844.[35] The next morning a posse arrived in Nauvoo and word was sent to the Prophet that the governor intended to station troops in the city until he and Hyrum submitted to arrest. The Smith brothers decided to return to Nauvoo and then acquiesce to the governor's orders to stand trial in Carthage.

Emotions in Carthage, and indeed throughout Illinois and Missouri, had reached the boiling point. For many months, newspaper editor Thomas Sharp of the *Warsaw Signal* had stirred up political anti-Mormonism in the style of political anti-Masonry. "[W]e hold ourselves at all times in readiness to co-operate with our fellow citizens . . . to exterminate, utterly exterminate, the wicked and abominable Mormon leaders," he reported.[36] Sharp's comments on the destruction of the *Expositor* appeared in a June 12, 1844, *Signal* extra:

---

33. Wilford Woodruff journal, August 19, 1860.

34. Wicks and Foister, *Junius and Joseph*, 150, 152.

35. Editors of the Joseph Smith Papers project explain: "In a letter to his wife on 23 June, J[oseph] S[mith] wrote that he did not know where he would go or what he would do, but that 'if possible' he would 'endeavor to get to the city of Washington.' In an account based on reminiscent sources and clearly influenced by intervening events, compilers of JS's history later wrote that he left Nauvoo for 'the Great Basin in the Rocky Mountains.'" See Editorial Note, "Journal, December 1842–June 1844; Book 4, 1 March–22 June 1844," The Joseph Smith Papers, 170.

36. Thomas Sharp, "Address," 1.

War and extermination is inevitable! CITIZENS ARISE, ONE AND ALL!! Can you stand by, and suffer such INFERNAL DEVILS! to ROB men of their property rights, without avenging them. We have no time for comment! Every man will make his own. LET IT BE WITH POWDER AND BALL![37]

This threatening invective infected the minds of both common citizens and military troops.

The Carthage Greys' lieutenant, Samuel Williams, wrote of the spectacle on the morning of June 25 when Joseph and Hyrum Smith were paraded before the militia, describing the loud "hissing groaning and all kinds of discordant sounds" that the Greys made when the Smiths walked past. "I all the time tried my utmost to preserve silence but had no more command over them than I would have had over a pack of wild Indians. At this demonstration of feeling on the part of the Greys Jo actually fainted," Williams reported.[38]

Governor Ford, who encouraged the Smiths to surrender, was also disturbed by the behavior of the militia. He originally planned to march them all into Nauvoo in a show of force, but he soon decided to dismiss the majority of troops and retain a single company. Thus, hundreds of enraged and thwarted men were released to return to their homes or, in many cases, throng the countryside as swarms of buzzing vigilantes.

On the evening of June 26, sometime after the Masonic council meeting, a number of the "old citizens" of Hancock and surrounding counties had formed a secret tribunal known as "the Vigilance Committee of Safety" in the upstairs lodge room of Hamilton's Hotel. They were "joined by Illinois Whig Central Committee member George T. M. Davis." According to Davis, the committee, enraged with the Mormons' actions in Illinois, considered an organized attack to destroy the city of Nauvoo entirely. Ultimately, however, the committee determined to see that Joseph and Hyrum Smith were both put to death, with the remainder of the Mormons spared to leave the state.[39]

In Ford's January 1845 analysis of events, he spoke of "secret machinations" that were afoot, but he claimed that pains were taken to conceal the plot from him and the Brigadier General in command.[40] When asked about the conspiracy,

---

37. Thomas Sharp, "Unparalled Outrage at Nauvoo," 2; emphasis in original.

38. Samuel Williams to John Prickett, July 10, 1844, quoted in Roger D. Launius, "The Murders in Carthage: Non-Mormon Reports of the Assassination of the Smith Brothers," 23.

39. Wicks and Foister assume that Davis was present at the Hamilton Hotel during the meeting. They cite "his detailed remarks on the proceedings in his Autobiography" as evidence and add, "[S]worn to secrecy, he never admitted to being in attendance." Wicks and Foister, *Junius and Joseph*, 164n22. See also George T. M. Davis, *An Authentic Account of the Massacre of Joseph Smith, the Mormon Prophet, and Hyrum Smith, His Brother, Together with a Brief History of Rise and Progress of Mormonism, and All the Circumstances Which Led to Their Death*, 27–29.

40. Thomas Ford, "Message from the Governor, in Relation to the Disturbances in Hancock County," 2.

Davis exonerated Ford but would not reveal "facts within my personal knowledge" because "under the strictest injunctions of confidence," he was "precluded from disclosing" them.

The same evening that the Carthage Vigilance Committee of Safety held their council meeting, another group gathered in nearby Warsaw. On this occasion, three military leaders, Jacob C. Davis (captain of the Warsaw Rifle Company),[41] William N. Grover (captain of the Warsaw Cadets), and Major Mark Aldrich (commander of the Warsaw Independent Battalion), [42] reportedly chose twenty men from among their troops "to go and kill Joseph and Hiram Smith in the jail at Carthage."[43]

A scant group of eight men from the Carthage Greys were assigned to guard the prison where Smith and his company were kept. The rest of their troop was camped on the public square a quarter mile away. Another company of the Greys, under Levi Williams, patrolled the area about eight miles from Carthage.[44] Of these, several of the commanding officers were Freemasons, including Mark Aldrich and Robert F. Smith, Captain of the Greys.

It appears that the Mormons expected Joseph Smith's Masonic status to count for something among these men, as Dan Jones, who accompanied the brothers to Carthage Jail, was sent to Governor Ford to inform him that Frank Worrell, the officer of the guard of the Carthage Greys, had vowed that "old Joe" would never leave the jail alive and that another troop of men had threatened to "kill those men if we have to tear the jail down." When Jones reported this to Ford, he shrugged it off, saying that alarm was unnecessary and that "the people are not that cruel." Jones indignantly replied that the Smiths were American citizens and "they are also Master Masons, and as such I demand of you the protection of their lives." Ford's visage reportedly "turned pale" at these words.[45]

A Master Mason's Last Words

The conspirators converged upon the jail in the early evening of June 27, 1844. The Greys made a token attempt to halt the pack, then allowed them to

---

41. Twenty-five-year-old Jacob C. Davis, of Nauvoo, petitioned for membership in Nauvoo Lodge on March 17, 1842. This is the only time he appears in the Nauvoo Lodge minutes. He may have received his degrees in one of the other Mormon lodges. This person loosely fits the description of the Jacob Cunningham Davis who was captain of the Warsaw Rifle Company and who was indicted and tried for the murders of Joseph and Hyrum Smith. He served as clerk of Hancock County and circuit clerk in 1841.

42. Mark Aldrich was treasurer and co-founder of the Warsaw Lodge.

43. William Daniels, grand jury testimony, October 1844, 13n41, cited in Wicks and Foister, *Junius and Joseph*, 166.

44. Hubert Howe Bancroft, *History of Utah, 1540–1886*, 175–83.

45. "History, 1838–1856, volume F-1 [1 May 1844–8 August 1844]," 174.

surge through.[46] An intense scuffle then ensued, during which Hyrum Smith was shot and killed, and John Taylor was severely wounded and rolled under a bed. Finally, the prophet Joseph Smith was shot as he jumped from the second-story window. According to a list of participants in the mob compiled by Jacob B. Backenstos, clerk of Hancock County Circuit Court, some of the leading men in the fraternity of Freemasons were among those who murdered the Smith brothers in Carthage Jail.[47] Seven of these were members of Hancock Lodge No. 20 in Carthage. Five belonged to Warsaw Lodge No. 21. An additional three hailed from other lodges in the state.[48] Thus, at least a third of the members of the two lodges were directly involved in the murders. According to observers, just prior to plummeting from the window of the jail, the Prophet gave the Masonic signal of distress. Instead of receiving the aid and protection that the signal called for, the answer "was 'the roar of his murderers' muskets and the deadly balls that pierced his heart."[49] A report of the Smiths' deaths published in the *Times and Seasons*, July 15, 1844, and attributed to John Taylor states that the men were

> shot to death, while, with uplifted hands they gave such signs of distress as would have commanded the interposition and benevolence of Savages or Pagans. They were both Masons in good standing. Ye brethren of "the mystic tie" what think ye! Where is our good master Joseph and Hyrum? Is there a pagan, heathen, or savage nation on the globe that would not be moved on this great occasion, as the trees of the forest by a mighty wind? Joseph's last exclamation was "O Lord my God."[50]

---

46. Davis, *An Authentic Account*, 28–29. See also William M. Daniels, *A Correct Account of the Murder of Generals Joseph and Hyrum Smith at Carthage on the 27th day of June, 1844*, 9–10.

47. "History, 1838–1856, volume F-1 [1 May 1844–8 August 1844]," 236–38.

48. Returns of 1843 show 27 members of the two lodges combined, and returns of 1844 show 30 members. See *Reprint of the Proceedings of the Grand Lodge of Illinois*, 110, 153. Therefore, about 40 percent of the members of these two lodges were involved in the murders. These included: Worshipful Master Abraham Chittenden, Mark Aldrich, John Montague, James Moss, and Henry Stephens from Warsaw Lodge No. 21; Franklin J. Bartlett, Elam Shaw Freeman, Onias C. Skinner, Captain Robert F. Smith, Alexander Sympson, George W. Thatcher, and Eli Hughes Williams from Hancock Lodge No. 20; Francis M. Higbee who had been raised in Nauvoo Lodge U.D.; Edward Jones who belonged to Springfield Lodge No. 4; and W. B. Warren from Harmony Lodge No. 3 in Jacksonville.

49. Orson F. Whitney, *Life of Heber C. Kimball, An Apostle: The Father and Founder of the British Mission*, 27.

50. "The Murder," 585. John Taylor was editor of the *Times and Seasons* at this time and was likely the author of this report. See also "History, 1838–1856, volume F-1 [1 May 1844–8 August 1844]," 269. Nicholas S. Literski has observed, "Perhaps unwittingly, John Taylor here revealed the true masonic office of Joseph Smith, 'our Good Master,' distinct from Hyrum. Later, the passage would be amended for publication in the *History of the Church* and elsewhere, to read 'Where are our good masters Joseph and Hyrum?' . . . Ultimately, the brethren of Nauvoo Lodge best recognized just how influential Joseph Smith had been in Mormon Freemasonry. On February 20, 1845, George A. Smith moved that the members of Nauvoo Lodge: 'procure the portraits of the three W[orshipful]

Members of Warsaw Lodge, 1843, 1844	Members of Hancock Lodge, 1843, 1844
Leonard B. Adams 1843, 1844	Benjamin Avise 1843, 1844
*Mark Aldrich 1843, 1844	*Franklin J. Bartlett 1843, 1844
German Andrews 1843, 1844	David Baldwin 1843
William A. Bacon 1843, 1844	E.B. Baldwin 1843
*Abraham J. Chittenden W.M. 1843, 1844	Thomas Bennett/Burnett 1843, 1844
J. Cochran/Isham Cockran 1844	J. Berry 1843
William Y. Head 1844	George Buckman/Bailman 1843, 1844
Benjamin F. Marsh 1843, 1844	Samuel Comer 1843, 1844
Levin B. Mitchell 1843, 1844	William Darnall/Daniel 1843, 1844
*John Montague 1843, 1844	Lewis Evans 1843, 1844
*James Moss 1843, 1844	*Elam S. Freeman 1843, 1844
Harmon G. Reynolds 1843, 1844	Benjamin A. Gallop 1843, 1844
*Henry G. Stephens 1843, 1844	David E. Head 1844
	Ellis Hughes 1843
	Daniel Prentis 1843
	Chauncey Robison 1843, 1844
	*Onias C. Skinner 1844
	*Robert F. Smith 1844
	*Alexander Sympson 1844
	*George W. Thatcher 1844
	*Eli H. Williams
	Wesley Williams 1844
	William G. Yetter 1843, 1844
*Freemasons who participated in the Smith murders according to Backenstos	
5/13 = 38%	7/23= 30%

The Masonic Grand Hailing Sign of Distress was taught to nineteenth-century brethren of the Craft in the Master Mason Degree. The sign was given "by raising both hands and arms to the elbows, perpendicularly, one on each side of the head, the elbows forming a square." The words "O Lord, my God! is there no help for the widow's son?" were then spoken, as the hands were solemnly lowered. The phrase is reportedly what King Solomon said when he learned of Hiram Abiff's murder.[51] Freemasons of the day took an obligation that "should I

M[asters] of this lodge, to wit: George Miller, Hyrum Smith, and Lucius N. Scovil, from Bro. Wm. W. Major, Portrait Painter, all to be taken clothed as W[orshipful] M[asters], which were to be kept for the use of the lodge. Amasa Lyman, the J[unior] D[eacon] moved an amendment by adding the name of our late martyred and lamented brother, Joseph Smith!!! which was seconded and carried unanimously.' Thus Joseph Smith was recognized among the true leaders of Mormon Freemasonry." See Nicholas S. Literski, "Where is our Good Master Joseph?," 11–13.

51. William Morgan, *Illustrations of Masonry by One of the Fraternity Who has Devoted Thirty Years to the Subject*, 69.

ever see that sign given or the word accompanying it, and the person who gave it, appearing to be in distress, I will fly to his relief at the risk of my life."[52]

Smith's close associates clearly imputed Masonic intentions to his last spoken words. John D. Lee, secretary of the Council of Fifty, left an embellished later account which included the entire phrase from the ritual: "Joseph left the door, . . . and cried out, 'Oh, Lord my God, is there no help for the widow's son!' as he sprang from the window, pierced with several balls."[53] Likewise, Zina D. H. Young, a member of the Quorum of the Anointed, later president of the Relief Society, and one of Smith's plural wives, proclaimed:

> I am the daughter of a master mason! I am the widow of a master mason, who, when leaping from the window of Carthage jail pierced with bullets, made the masonic sign of distress; but, gentlemen (addressing the representatives of the press that were present), those signs were not heeded except by the God of heaven. That man, the Prophet of the Almighty, was massacred without mercy! Sisters, this is the first time in my life that I have dared to give utterance to this fact, but I thought I could trust my soul to say it on this occasion; and I say it now in the fear of Israel's God, and I say it in the presence of these gentlemen, and I wish my voice could be heard by the whole brotherhood of masons throughout our proud land.[54]

Thus, the men and women surrounding Smith were unanimous on this point. With apparent pride in his standing as a Freemason, they called the Masons in the crowd of assassins to task for failing to come to his aid.

Another possibility why Smith might have given the Masonic call is suggested by a closer look at the legend behind the distress call in William Morgan's 1826 exposé. There, the brother representing King Solomon is told at the grave of Hiram Abiff that his body has been searched carefully for the Master's word and nothing has been discovered but "a feint resemblance of the letter G on the left breast." King Solomon then begins a three-fold distress call by raising his arms and exclaiming, "Nothing but a feint resemblance of the letter G! that is not the Master's word nor a key to it. I fear the Master's word is forever lost!" He repeats this phrase three times, and upon the third repetition adds the words, "O Lord my God, is there no help for the widow's son?"[55] Perhaps Smith, in the final moments of his life, feared that the "Master's word was forever lost"—that the Temple ordinances in their unfinished state, and the Mormon lodges in their current clandestine condition, would not be sufficient to bring to pass the restoration he had envisioned.

As mentioned, some modern Latter-day Saints, uncomfortable with the Masonic associations of this phrase, construe Smith's exclamation as a prayer. This interpretation is not completely at odds with a Masonic view of the Grand

---

52. Morgan, 67.

53. John D. Lee, *Mormonism Unveiled; Or The Life and Confessions of the Late Mormon Bishop, John D. Lee; (Written by Himself)*, 153.

54. Zina D. H. Young, "Woman's Mass Meeting, Salt Lake Theater, Nov. 16, 1878," 98.

55. Morgan, *Illustrations of Masonry*, 75.

Hailing sign. Every Masonic obligation ends with a plea, "So help me God, and keep me steadfast in the due performance of the same." The Grand Hailing cry can thus be given as a way to alert God to a man's distress when no human ear is there to hear.

Inside the jail, Willard Richards, a Freemason himself, dragged John Taylor to safety in another room and concealed him under a mattress. Not completely sure that the Smith brothers were dead, he elevated his hands three times and exclaimed, "Oh Lord, my God, spare Thy servants!"[56] Both Richards and Smith, in their hour of extremity, turned to Masonically inspired ritual to express their deepest longings.

Grand Hailing Sign of Distress, from William Morgan, *Illustrations of Masonry*, 1827 ed.

Images of the Martyrdom

Several additional descriptions and pictures of the martyrdom possessed distinctive Masonic characteristics. Newly baptized Mormon convert William M. Daniels collaborated with Nauvoo Freemason Lyman Littlefield to produce a pamphlet titled *A Correct Account of the Murder of Generals Joseph and Hyrum Smith at Carthage on the 27th day of June, 1844*. In this controversial 1845 account, Joseph Smith is depicted hanging out of the window of Carthage Jail, repeating the words O Lord my God "two or three times." Daniels insisted as an eyewitness that Smith was not shot until after a young man propped him "agains[t] the South side of the well-curb." Following the shooting, a sudden and powerful light "burst from the heavens upon the bloody scene," dissuading the ruffian who was about to decapitate him.[57] Although this account was questioned by the court at the trial of Smith's accused assassins, Latter-day Saint leaders embraced and perpetuated the myth. For examples, claims that

---

56. B. H. Roberts, *The Life of John Taylor: Third President of the Church of Jesus Christ of Latter-day Saints*, 140.

57. Daniels, *A Correct Account*, 13–15. The account was reprinted in the *Nauvoo Neighbor* on May 7 and 14, 1845. When officially questioned by Thomas Bullock in April 1854, Edward A. Bedell, an aide-decamp to Illinois Governor Thomas Ford at the time of Joseph and Hyrum Smith's martyrdom, confirmed that "in the main Daniels statements are correct." LaJean Purcell Carruth and Mark Lyman Staker, "John Taylor's June 27, 1854, Account of the Martyrdom," 28.

"Fig.1, the Carthage Greys. Fig. 2, Col. Williams. Fig. 3, the four ruffians who shot Gen. Joseph Smith. Fig.4, the well-curb. Fig. 5, the flash of light. Fig. 6, Elder Richards at the window of the jail from which Gen. Smith fell. Fig. 7, Gen Smith, after he was shot. Fig. 8, the ruffian who was about to sever his head from his body. Fig. 9, the door leading into the entry, through which the murderers entered. Fig. 10, Capt. Smith. Fig. 11, the mob. Fig. 12, the point of wood which the mob entered when going to the jail." From William M. Daniels, *A Correct Account of the Murder of Generals Joseph and Hyrum Smith at Carthage on the 27th day of June, 1844*, 1845.

a "man with a bowie knife raised his hand to cut off Joseph's head" and that "a vivid flash of lightning caused his arm to fall powerless" were reprinted in an 1882 Deseret Sunday School manual printed by Elder George Q. Cannon's Juvenile Instructor office.[58]

Daniels's pamphlet contains an engraving depicting the Masonic elements of the scene. With Smith fallen on his face next to the well, a "ruffian" is "about to sever his [Joseph's] head from his body" while streams of miraculous light break through the clouds. Prominent in the foreground is Colonel Levi Williams, who gave the order to shoot and kill Smith.

A similar 1851 lithograph places Smith's body upon the well-curb, with a masked man brandishing a knife above him.[59] The scene is also flooded with

---

58. *Questions and Answers on the Life and Mission of the Prophet Joseph Smith*, 51. See also Parley Parker Pratt, Jr., ed., *Autobiography of Parley Parker Pratt, One of the Twelve Apostles of the Church of Jesus Christ of Latter-day Saints*, 477, and N. B. Lundwall, *Fate of the Persecutors of the Prophet Joseph Smith: Being a Compilation of Historical Data on the Personal Testimony of Joseph Smith [. . .]*, 231–33, for similarly embellished accounts.

59. Masks are mentioned in an account by then thirteen-year-old Grafton Owen. Sitting on the rail fence near the well looking toward the jail, he saw the mob coming over the prairie. "Some of these men had on horns; some wore masks, and other queer things." After observing that Joseph Smith, "riddled with bullets, jumped from an upper window," Owen fled the scene. See T. Grafton Owen, *Drippings from the Eaves*, 40–41.

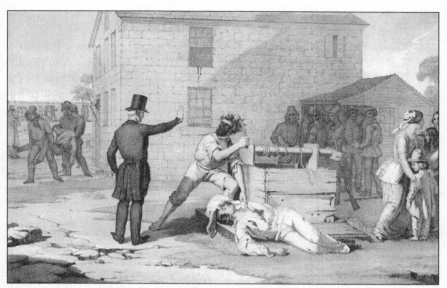

Martyrdom of Joseph and Hiram Smith in Carthage jail, June 27th, 1844. G.W. Fasel pinxit; on stone by C.G. Crehen; print by Nagel & Weingaertner, N.Y.

otherworldly light and the Carthage Greys skulking in the shadows. However, the commanding figure to the left of the well does not seem to represent Colonel Williams. Rather than instigating the murder, this fellow has his arm and hand raised in a halting gesture and seems almost to be an embodied heavenly messenger stopping the intended mutilation. Dressed in formal top hat and tails, he resembles nothing so much as a symbolic Freemason, dressed for a lodge meeting, and come to advocate for Smith in his final hour.[60]

While the attempted decapitation by the young ruffian was said to have been motivated by an offer of one thousand dollars for the head of Smith, it is notable that decapitation is also one of the penalties for a dishonored Mason. The elements of the well and the bright light are also found in Masonic legend. There, Hiram Abiff's spilled blood is traced "to a well in the north part of the Temple," where the searcher concludes that he "had been killed and thrown into this well." Seeing "a luminous meteor which stood over the well," he had it completely drained and therein found the Master's jewel. "It appears that Hiram Abiff, when attacked by the ruffians, must have plucked off this jewel, and thrown it into the well near the great staircase, rather than it should fall into the hands of such villains."[61] In other ritual portrayals of the story of Hiram Abiff, the jewel is found on his dead body, by which it is identified.

---

60. G. W. Fasel, "Martyrdom of Joseph and Hiram Smith in Carthage jail, June 27th, 1844."

61. "Description and catechism of the Degree of Perfect Master," in Richard Carlile, *Manual of Freemasonry: in Three Parts. With an Explanatory Introduction to the Science, and a Free Translation of some of the Sacred Scripture Names*, 3:35, 40. See also Michael W.

Jewels of the Lodge

When he went to Carthage, Hyrum Smith apparently carried on his person the Worshipful Master's jewel from Nauvoo Lodge. A Masonic jewel, in this usage, is a badge of office that a Masonic officer wears, often around his neck. The Nauvoo Masonic Lodge possessed a full set of such jewels, one for each officer in the Lodge. This set of jewels, missing one, was ultimately hidden in an old stable in Carthage. They were subsequently discovered in the 1920s and given to the Herman Lodge in Quincy. Later, the missing Worshipful Master's jewel was found hidden in the cell of the Carthage jail where Hyrum had been killed, and it was sent to the Herman Lodge to complete the set.[62] Their silver appearance and the similarity they possess to symbols used in early Mormon ceremonies suggest they were crafted by an early Mormon metalworker in Nauvoo.[63]

Another curious silver piece was said to have been found "in the Prophet's pocket at the time that he died," although it was not listed on an inventory of the deceased Smith's possessions.[64] This piece was a Jupiter talisman engraved according to instructions in occultist Francis Barrett's *The Magus* for making magic talismans.[65] On the piece were, among other symbols, the astrological sign for Jupiter and Hebrew letters representing the names of Deity. Charles Bidamon signed an affidavit saying that he received the amulet from his father, Lewis Bidamon, Freemason and second husband of Emma Smith. Charles Bidamon said that Emma Smith considered this talisman her husband's "intimate possession."[66] In

---

Homer, "'Similarity of Priesthood in Masonry': The Relationship Between Freemasonry and Mormonism," 96.

62. "Mormons Owned Officers' Jewels of Herman Lodge," 3.

63. Kent Walgren, "James Adams, Early Springfield Mormon and Freemason," 134.

64. Henry D. Moyle noted in his diary that during a 1902 trip to Illinois, Emma Smith's stepson Charles E. Bidamon told him that the Jupiter talisman was found in Joseph Smith's pocket when he died. Henry D. Moyle diary, 4 Sept 1902, quoted in D. Michael Quinn, *Early Mormonism and the Magic World View*, 82. An itemized list of the contents of Smith's pockets at his death was published in 1885 in the Ottumwa, Iowa, *Daily Democrat* by James W. Woods, Smith's lawyer, who collected the Prophet's personal effects after the martyrdom. "Received, Nauvoo, Illinois, July 2, 1844, of James W. Woods, $135.50 in gold and silver and receipt for shroud, one gold finger ring, one gold pen and pencil case, one pen knife and case, one pair of tweezers, one silk and one leather purse, one small pocket wallet containing a note of John P. Green for $50, and a receipt of Heber C. Kimball for a note of hand on Ellen M. Saunders for one thousand dollars, as the property of Joseph Smith. (Signed) Emma Smith." Woods's account was reprinted in Edward H. Stiles, *Recollections and Sketches of Notable Lawyers and Public Men of Early Iowa*, 271.

65. Quinn, *Early Mormonism and the Magic World View*, 82–85.

66. Affidavit of Charles Bidamon, January 5, 1938, cited in Richard Lloyd Anderson, "The Mature Joseph Smith and Treasure Searching," 541. Bidamon's claim that he obtained the piece through his father, Lewis Bidamon, is bolstered by documents proving the Masonic initiation of Lewis Bidamon in Reclamation Lodge No. 54, a lodge formed in Nauvoo after the Mormons departed.

Herman Lodge Jewels once belonging to the Nauvoo Lodge. Courtesy of Herman Lodge No. 39 in Quincy, Illinois.

1937, Bidamon sold the talisman to collector Wilford Wood, who displayed it in his museum for decades as "the Prophet's Masonic jewel." Although this is likely a conflation of Freemasonry with esoteric items relating to magic, a coincidence connects the talisman to Masonic ritual.

In the legend of Hiram Abiff, those who searched for his body were looking for something that may have preserved the Grand Omnific Word, the name of God. A Masonic jewel found on his body might serve as a key to distinguish him as the Master. In Joseph Smith's case, the amulet in his possession was engraved with the identifying astrological sign of Jupiter, under which planetary influence he had been born. It also contained names of God, with which the Lost Master's Word is often equated.

The Villains Escape Punishment

In the Master Mason ritual, the murderers of Hiram Abiff "flee into the interior parts of the country" to "avoid being taken as long as possible."[67] So, too, did several of those who were instrumental in the Smiths' deaths. Governor Ford returned to his residence in Springfield, and county officials removed important county records from Carthage to the town of Quincy. William Voorhease and Marcellus Black, two men who do not appear on Illinois Masonic returns but were identified as Freemasons, "sought safety from the law and Mormon vengeance by heading to the vicinity of El Dorado, Union County, Arkansas."[68] Voorhease had been wounded by Joseph Smith's pistol in the initial fray.

---

67. Malcolm C. Duncan, *Duncan's Masonic Ritual and Monitor or Guide to the Three Symbolic Degrees of the Ancient York Rite and to the Degrees of Mark Master, Past Master, Most Excellent Master, and the Royal Arch, Third Edition*, 109. See also Morgan, *Illustrations of Masonry*, 78–79.

68. Joseph D. Johnstun, "William Vorhease and the Murder of Joseph Smith," 52–56.

In October 1844, nine men were indicted for the murders, but four fled and were never arrested. Three of these were wounded by Smith and therefore most closely linked to the shootings—Voorhease, William Gallagher, and John Wills. Five remained to stand trial in Carthage in May 1845: Mark Aldrich (commander of the Warsaw Independent Battalion), Jacob C. Davis (state senator and commander of the Warsaw Cadets), Thomas C. Sharp (publisher of the *Warsaw Signal*), Levi Williams (colonel and commanding officer of the 59th Regiment of the Illinois militia), and William N. Grover (captain of the Warsaw Rifle Company).

Mark Aldrich had been a Freemason for over twenty years and was a founding member of Warsaw Lodge No. 21 in January 1843, serving as secretary that year. In October of 1843 he was elected as Steward. On December 19, 1844, Aldrich was elected Senior Deacon of the Lodge while under indictment for murder, despite Masonic prohibitions against elevating a member currently in conflict with the law. On June 24, 1845, shortly after his acquittal on May 30, he was elected Worshipful Master of the Lodge.[69]

Thomas Sharp and Levi Williams had crossed to the Missouri side of the Mississippi and negotiated with Illinois officials for several concessions. They agreed to return to Illinois and surrender only after Governor Ford promised reasonable bail and no state resistance to a motion for a change of venue. At their trial they were acquitted.[70] On September 23, 1844, Jacob C. Davis filed a petition with Warsaw Lodge No. 21 and by November 18 he was a Master Mason. On that day, Sharp and Williams followed suit, being passed on Jan. 9, 1845, and raised on March 17, 1845, respectively. This action was especially noteworthy for Sharp, who as a newspaper editor in western New York had been fiercely anti-Masonic. He was credited with inventing the term "'Jack Mason' for persons who refused to take part in the anti-Masonic movement of that day and neighborhood."[71] The timing of these petitions suggests that the men feared retaliation by the Mormons and hoped that association with the Lodge would protect them. They had good reason to expect a favorable result—their petitions were investigated by Mark Aldrich and Henry G. Stevens, both men who appeared on Backenstos's list of participants in the murder and who would not have thought this disqualified the petitioners from entering the Fraternity.

Warsaw Lodge was well aware of the pending indictments, having discussed them in their meetings prior to taking action.[72] Months later, when Bodley

---

69. John C. Reynolds, *History of the Most Worshipful Grand Lodge of Illinois, Ancient, Free, and Accepted Masons, From the Organization of the first Lodge within the present limits of the State, up to and including 1850*, 218–19, 254, 315.

70. Gregg Thomas, *History of Hancock County, Illinois, Together with an Outline History of the State, and a Digest of State Laws*, 752–56.

71. "Dear Sirs:—I Send You a Plate with an Engraved Likeness of T. C. Sharp," 2.

72. E. Cecil McGavin, *Mormonism and Masonry*, 23–24. A letter from Brother John Montague reports that "at the time said petitions were presented, the fact of these individuals being under indictment for the murder of Joseph and Hyram Smith, was

Lodge reported this irregularity to the Grand Lodge, a committee was appointed to examine the matter and "ascertain by any means in their power, whether said Lodge has conferred any of the degrees upon any person or persons while under indictment." Warsaw Lodge had not submitted their 1845 returns, perhaps in an effort to disguise their irregularities. Thus, the Grand Master, at his discretion, suspended their charter until the next annual communication of the Grand Lodge.[73] When the report of the committee was returned, they suggested that perhaps leniency should be extended to Warsaw Lodge: "Although the Lodge in question erred, and greatly erred, yet they conceive the error was an error of the head and not of the heart; that all the harm has been done in the case that can be done; the men have been since tried by the laws of their country and a jury of their peers, and acquitted."[74]

After hearing the report from his Committee on Warsaw Lodge, the Grand Master adopted the recommendation of the committee and deemed that "it would be well to let the Lodge off."[75] Notwithstanding that on October 5, 1846, the Grand Lodge voted to "receive said Lodge to their affectionate confidence," Warsaw Lodge did not reclaim their charter for almost five years.[76] Carthage Lodge was also closed just after the Grand Lodge made their decision.

A Curious Pattern of Burials

In the legend of Hiram Abiff presented during the Master Mason degree, after the three ruffians have murdered Abiff, they bury the body in temple rubble and plan to return at midnight to give the body a more secure interment. At the

---

referred to, and the question of the propriety of their admission fully discussed. . . . The standing of those individuals in the community had not been at all impaired by the indictment, but, on the contrary, they were regarded with greater consideration than before, from the fact that they had been particularly selected as the victims of Mormon vengeance." Quoted in Joseph E. Morcombe, *History of Grand Lodge of Iowa, A.F. and A.M.*, 166. From all this, historian Robin L. Carr concludes: "Retrospection makes it clear that the heat of the moment determined the attitude and actions of the citizens of Hancock County. Their political power had vanished as the political promise of Nauvoo had skyrocketed into prominence. They felt not only threatened politically, but physically, for the Nauvoo Legion, well-trained and well-armed, stood at the ready. Fear of the religious teachings of the strange people who now lived side-by-side with them and who practiced the dreadful sin of polygamy also stirred emotional turmoil. To the people of Hancock County, in such a light, the murderers of Joseph Smith became heroic instead of hideous, and the citizens of the county naturally tried to protect them. Unfortunately, one of the methods used included quickly initiating the accused into the Masonic Lodge at Warsaw." Robin L. Carr, *Freemasonry and Nauvoo 1839–1846*, 35.

73. *Reprint of the Proceedings of the Grand Lodge of Illinois*, 225.

74. *Reprint of the Proceedings of the Grand Lodge of Illinois*, 336–37.

75. *Reprint of the Proceedings of the Grand Lodge of Illinois*, 337.

76. When Warsaw Lodge began again in 1850 it became number 257.

appointed hour, they carry the body to a hill west of Mt. Moriah, where Abiff is reburied. The next day, the Fellowcrafts working in Solomon's Temple who did not go through with the conspiracy confess the plot. A search is conducted, and Abiff's body is found after it has been in the grave for fifteen days.[77]

Malcolm C. Duncan's *Masonic Ritual and Monitor* states:

> The body of our Grand Master [Hiram Abiff] was buried three times: first, in the rubbish of the Temple; secondly, on the brow of a hill west of Mount Moriah; and, thirdly and lastly, as near the "Sanctum Sanctorum, or Holy of Holies," of King Solomon's Temple, as Jewish law would permit.[78]

This story of Abiff's burial has several parallels to the curious pattern of burials that took place for Joseph and Hyrum Smith's bodies.

Perhaps wishing to imitate the legend, Joseph Smith had prepared a tomb on the grounds of the Nauvoo Temple patterned after the legendary Solomon's Vault as a place of interment for himself and his family. Joseph Johnstun has persuasively shown that "the Tomb of Joseph was located on the south side of the temple block, off the southeast corner of the temple, the same corner that William Clayton called 'Joseph's corner,' near Mulholland Street." It was a two-chambered structure, with one side meant for the family of Smith and the other for Sidney Rigdon.[79] Although these vaults were both completed, the Smith family was afraid that the bodies of Joseph and Hyrum would be desecrated if they were buried in the expected resting place. A complex subterfuge was required.

On the hot, sunny morning of Friday, June 28, 1844, two rough wooden boxes containing the bodies of the deceased brothers were conveyed to Nauvoo. With a protective covering of blankets, branches, and hay, they were escorted by their younger brother Samuel H. Smith, Willard Richards, and a guard of eight soldiers. After arriving around three in the afternoon, the bodies were laid out in coffins built by George Cannon and placed side by side beneath the south windows of the Mansion House dining room. This private viewing allowed the family to openly express their most profound grief. Captain Dan Jones later wrote:

> [M]y eyes beheld the blood of the two godly martyrs mingling in one pool in the middle of the floor, their elderly mother, godly and sorrowful, on her knees in the midst of the blood between the two, a hand on each one of her sons who lay in gore, her heart nearly broken by the excruciating agony and the indescribable grief.[80]

Mary Fielding Smith and Emma Smith entered the room to view the bodies of their respective husbands, each overwrought with their own painful sorrow. Perhaps

---

77. Duncan, *Duncan's Masonic Ritual and Monitor*, 124.

78. Duncan, 125.

79. Dr. B. W. Richmond, quoted in Joseph D. Johnstun, "'To Lie in Yonder Tomb': The Tomb and Burial of Joseph Smith," 170.

80. Dan Jones and Ronald D. Dennis, "The Martyrdom of Joseph Smith and his Brother Hyrum," 93.

most surprising, however, was the presence of another woman in what would seem to be a position of honored respect on the occasion. B. W. Richmond recalled:

> While the two wives were bewailing their loss, and prostrate on the floor with their eight children, I noticed a lady standing at the head of Joseph Smith's body, her face covered, and her whole frame convulsed with weeping. She was the widow of William Morgan, of Masonic memory, and twenty years before had stood over the body of her husband, found at the mouth of Oak Orchard Creek, on Lake Ontario. She was now the wife of a Mr. Harris, whom she married in Batavia, and who was a saint in the Mormon church, and a high Mason. [81]

Lucinda Pendleton Morgan Harris, whose first husband was most likely killed by vengeful Freemasons in New York, now mourned the murder of a second husband—albeit a secret one—at the hands of Freemasons in Illinois. For those few Masons present, her standing vigil no doubt evoked the image of the fabled monument atop Hiram Abiff's final resting place under the Holy of Holies of King Solomon's Temple, described as "a virgin weeping over a broken column, with a book open before her" representing the "unfinished state of the temple" and the fact that "one of the principal supports of Masonry had fallen."[82]

In Masonic lore, the ruffians who murdered Hiram Abiff immediately feared discovery and punishment. They quickly hid the body in the rubbish outside the west gate of the Temple, within the construction rubbish until "low twelve," or midnight, at which time they carried the body westward and buried it at the brow of a hill. Before making their escape, they marked the location with a small acacia tree.[83]

The morning following the family viewing, the Mansion House was opened to thousands of visitors for a public viewing of the Smith brothers' bodies. Once the crowds were cleared, the bodies were secretly hidden in a northeast corner closet adjoining the dining room where the viewing took place. The pine coffins, meanwhile, were filled with sandbags and rocks for weight, after which they were closed and carried in a large procession for public burial in the Nauvoo graveyard.[84]

At midnight, the bodies were removed from their hiding place by nine Freemasons: Dimick B. Huntington, Edward Hunter, William D. Huntington, William Marks, Jonathan H. Holmes, Gilbert Goldsmith, Alpheus Cutler,

81. Richmond, "The Prophet's Death," 51–52.

82. Morgan, *Illustrations of Masonry*, 89.

83. Arturo de Hoyos, *Light on Masonry: The History and Rituals of America's Most Important Masonic Expose*, 291–292 [71–72].

84. From the accounts of B. W. Richmond, Isaac Manning, and Elizabeth J. D. Roundy, Johnstun concludes: "It becomes clear that the place where the sand-filled coffins were deposited was the Nauvoo Cemetery situated east of Nauvoo on Parley Street, today known as the Old Nauvoo Burial Grounds, two miles east of Durphy Street (State Road 96). Regrettably, William D. Huntington, the sexton, did not record where the pine boxes were interred in the cemetery." Johnstun, "To Lie in Yonder Tomb," 176–77.

Lorenzo D. Wasson, and Philip B. Lewis.[85] While being guarded by James Emmet, member of both the Nauvoo Police and Council of Fifty, the men conveyed the coffins westward to the Nauvoo House, which was under construction nearby. There in the northwest corner of the foundation, two graves awaited, having been secretly prepared beforehand.[86] The bodies were buried, and the spot was covered with "chips of wood and stone and other rubbish"[87] to camouflage the site, secreting it until late fall or early winter.

These initial events corresponded with Hiram Abiff's first and second burials—in the rubbish of the temple and the brow of a hill westward of the temple. While the Mansion House was not a temple, the Smith brothers' bodies were briefly hidden from discovery there until midnight. Then, they were carried due westward, where their burial took place in the foundation of the Nauvoo House. A careful examination of the Nauvoo House reveals that the northwest corner burial was, in fact, on the brow of a hill, as the ground slopes from that point sharply down toward the Mississippi River.

The bodies remained in their temporary Nauvoo House graves until the fall of 1844 when Emma Smith and Mary Fielding Smith became concerned that renewed construction work on the building would inevitably reveal their hiding place.[88] Again at midnight, under Emma's direction, the bodies were moved by Dimick B. Huntington, William D. Huntington, Jonathan H. Holmes, and Gilbert Goldsmith, all Freemasons who had helped with the previous burial, to a location near the Smith Homestead where Emma resided. A small spring house or "bee house" marked and concealed the spot.[89] This seemed a fitting place of repose, bees being the Masonic symbol of regeneration and recovery from the grave.

In 1846, perhaps anticipating later claims that Brigham Young and the other apostles would have taken the bodies west with them, Emma again had the bodies secretly transported to a new location further from potential thieves. The new site, south of Nauvoo, lay within the wooded property of David Hibbard alongside the Mississippi River. According to a later account by Joseph F. Smith, this was the location referred to by the Prophet's son, David Hyrum Smith, in the hymn "The Unknown Grave." David was known to frequent the location so often that it remains known today as David's Chamber.[90] Many years later, with the assistance of a trusted Black servant by the name of Cleveland, Emma moved the bodies back to the Homestead, this time placing them beneath the exist-

---

85. All Master Masons according to "Nauvoo Masonic Lodge minutes, 1841–1846."

86. Richmond, "The Prophet's Death," 52.

87. "History, 1838–1856, volume F-1 [1 May 1844–8 August 1844]," 189.

88. Linda King Newell and Valeen Tippetts Avery, *Mormon Enigma: Emma Hale Smith*, 212–13.

89. Donna Hill, *Joseph Smith, the First Mormon*, 5; and Lachlan Mackay, "A Brief History of the Smith Family Nauvoo Cemetery," 242.

90. Joseph F. Smith, "Funeral of Isaac Manning," 2.

ing foundation of a spring house.[91] Over the years, other deceased Smith family members were reinterred in "Emma's garden." Emma herself was also buried there. It became a family plot, gathering together the Smith family according to Joseph's wishes, but the site gradually fell into decay, and the locations of Joseph and Hyrum's graves were forgotten.

The theme of a forgotten burial site was yet another correspondence to Masonic legend. Upon learning of Hiram Abiff's murder, King Solomon sent out Fellowcrafts in search of the body. One happened to rest himself on the hill where the body lay, and when rising, grasped hold of the acacia tree to help himself stand. The ease with which the tree gave way betrayed the recently disturbed soil, and soon the badly decayed body was discovered. King Solomon then directed that the body be reinterred beneath the Holy of Holies of the temple, the spot honored by a marble monument.[92]

By 1928, the Reorganized Church of Jesus Christ of Latter Day Saints (RLDS, now Community of Christ) had become the custodians of the Smith Homestead property. Driven by persistent rumors that Joseph's body was in Utah and new concerns that construction of the Keokuk Dam might cause the bodies to be lost in a flood of the Mississippi, RLDS Church president Frederick M. Smith directed a search for the bodies of Joseph, Hyrum, and Emma in the Nauvoo Smith Cemetery.[93] After six days, the bodies were rediscovered, carefully identified, raised, and finally reburied in a concrete tomb that would be safe from rising water. Beautiful new marble monuments and garden surroundings were added in a 1991 renovation under the joint direction of the LDS and then-RLDS churches.[94]

Where is Our Good Master?

The death of their prophet at the age of thirty-nine was a devastating blow to the Latter-day Saints, and they struggled mightily to make some sense of it. Connecting his death with the murder of Hiram Abiff—himself a symbol of Christ—was a way to give meaning to a horrific loss. The associations between this Masonic legend and the final chapter of Joseph Smith's life are remarkable. These were recognized and perpetuated by the Prophet's followers, their imaginations captured by the symbols they had learned from Masonry.

---

91. Barbara Hands Bernauer, "Still 'Side by Side': The Final Burial of Joseph and Hyrum Smith," 19.

92. de Hoyos, *Light on Masonry*, 301 [81].

93. "Officials of the Reorganized church say they have found it necessary to repudiate statements emanating from the Utah branch of the church that the bodies were in Utah." Taken from an article in the *Quincy Herald-Whig* (January 22, 1928) and quoted in Lundwall, *Fate of the Persecutors*, 248. Other concerns included rising water from a new dam at Keokuk.

94. Susan Easton Black, "The Tomb of Joseph," 36–46.

Hiram Abiff is one manifestation of the mystery school hero. This drama is foreshadowed in the biblical account of the Christian Messiah, but the formula is even more ancient. It is the concept of the sacred king, destined for sacrifice, who rises from death that the earth might become regenerated and uplifted by divine power.

The legend of Joseph Smith began with a young initiate experiencing a rite of passage that brought him into contact with the Divine. His "hero's journey" set him on a quest to bring forth sacred scripture and to restore the Lost Word. Along the way he struggled to build a holy city, and he almost succeeded in Nauvoo. He developed ritual ceremonies to usher his people into a state of initiation so that they could experience the same journey to become kings and priests, queens and priestesses. Finally thrust out of his kingdom, he entered the condition of lonely, persecuted hero. The addition of Masonic overtones added meaning to what was otherwise a futile, bloody death. God would hear the Prophet's cry of distress even if no one else did. His public martyrdom made him even more powerful in death than he was in life.

Though the Master Mason's Word was lost by three great knocks at the death of the Master Hiram, it becomes each Mason's duty to recover that symbolic Word. The Nauvoo Masons would not end their work with their prophet's passing. The funeral of Joseph and Hyrum included a procession of the various Mormon lodges,[95] which would continue to work tirelessly, bringing hundreds more Mormon men into the craft of Freemasonry. Though persecution and conflict continued for years, the Saints were no longer committed to work within the established political or social system. Brigham Young would pick up where his predecessor left off, presiding over the merging of Mormon lodges and dictating the rapidity of Masonic work and LDS temple work simultaneously from 1844 to 1846.[96] Then at last, they would leave Nauvoo and Freemasonry behind.

---

95. R. W. Mac, "Mormonism in Illinois. No. III," 533.

96. Hosea Stout diary, July 3, 1845; Stanley B. Kimball, ed., *On The Potter's Wheel: The Diaries and Journals of Heber C. Kimball*, 103.

CHAPTER 18

ALL MANNER OF "–ITES"

They're traced in lines on the Parthenon,
Inscribed by the subtle Greek;
And Roman legions have carved them on
Walls, roads and arch antique;
In Syria, Carthage and Pompeii,
Buried and strewn and stark,
The Mason craft in many a land
Has graven its Mason mark.

—Anonymous

ollowing the death of its core luminary in 1844, the Latter-day Saint movement exploded like a star into shards both great and small. Individual Saints, like dust, began to coalesce around larger personalities, eventually forming groups and constellations of groups. Each held within it sparks of that original genius from the mind and heart of the Prophet Joseph Smith; each sought to replicate the brilliance of that original star. Like Kepler's music of the spheres, these new bodies gave off their own unique sound, imbued with the truth of those principles brought from the original star, blended with the sounds and unique genius of their formative persona. The focus of these groups varied, but each retained remnants of the Masonic influence that Smith had brought to Mormonism.

Brigham Young: Proprietor of the Ritual

After Joseph Smith's death, the annual meeting of the Grand Lodge of Illinois was held on October 7, 1844, in Jacksonville, Illinois. The dispensations for Nauvoo, Helm, Nye, and Keokuk Lodges had been revoked and a messenger sent to Nauvoo to demand their dispensation. This communication "was treated with contempt, and not only a positive refusal given by said Lodge, but a determination expressed to continue their work."[1] Therefore, the Grand Lodge declared the Mormon lodges clandestine and all fellowship was withdrawn.

At the time of Smith's assassination there were approximately seven hundred Master Masons listed in the minute book of Nauvoo Lodge. By the end of 1845 over thirteen hundred Master Masons had been made in that lodge. Not only did lodge work continue after Smith's death, but the pace practically doubled.

---

1. George W. Warvelle, ed., *A Compendium of Freemasonry in Illinois, Embracing a Review of the Introduction, Development, and Present Condition of All Rites and Degrees*, 1:35.

The Nauvoo Temple opened for ordinances on December 10, 1845, and closed on February 7, 1846—the same date on the final existing document for a Nauvoo Lodge meeting. The shared closure date has been overlooked and demonstrates a connection of sorts between the rituals performed in each building, but clearly one sort of ritual did not replace the other. Some have supposed that after endowments became available, lodge work ceased; however, to the contrary, Nauvoo Lodge continued to initiate, pass, and raise Masons until just a few days before Brigham Young and the first company of Saints crossed the frozen Mississippi River. At the final meeting of Nauvoo Lodge, business was carried on as usual, with Hirum Jackson visiting from Montrose, Benjamin Meginnis initiated, and William W. Meguire and Robert

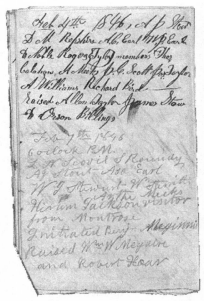

Page from Nauvoo Masonic Lodge minute book, final day of lodge work.

Hoar raised Master Masons.[2] Even under the direction of Brigham Young and the Twelve, neither reception of the endowment nor even the Second Anointing eliminated the value of receiving the Masonic Degrees.[3] Like Meginnis, some of the men who were raised in the final months of Lodge work had been endowed previously, demonstrating that Masonic degrees accompanied the LDS endowment and were not given solely as a precursor.

After the death of Smith, it was not the Worshipful Master of the Lodge who directed the Mormon Masonic work; it was instead the president of the Quorum of the Twelve, Brigham Young, who held no regular position in any Masonic body whatsoever. By virtue of his priesthood authority and as the keeper of Smith's own restored and purified ritual, Young regulated all ritual work taking place in Nauvoo. This infuriated non-Mormon Masons in Illinois. Latter-day Saint Masons, however, accustomed to the role of Smith in Masonic affairs, seemed to take it in stride.

For example, the officers of Nauvoo Lodge had routinely taken orders from Church leaders. On the pleasant spring day of April 10, 1845, the Twelve sequestered themselves in the upper room of Willard Richards's home to discuss Church business. During the afternoon, Lucius Scovil, then serving as Master of

---

2. Benjamin Meginnis was endowed in the Nauvoo Temple on February 5, 1846.

3. For information on the Second Anointing, see David John Buerger, "'The Fulness of the Priesthood': The Second Anointing in Latter-day Saint Theology and Practice," 11–44.

the Nauvoo Lodge, was called to the meeting. The brethren directed Scovil to "get
the Masonic Hall [set up] fore [a] Printing
office."[4] This directive was in response to a
Council of Fifty conversation on March 22
on the subject of upcoming printing projects. There had been difficulties in keeping
in print both the secular *Nauvoo Neighbor*
and the church-oriented *Times and Seasons*
to which "the saints look for religious matters, minutes of meetings, minutes of conferences, and items of doctrine."[5] Keeping
the journals in press was to take prece-
dence over the making of Masons, which
Scovil was asked to do "only as times shall
permit."[6] That a sitting Worshipful Master
would take instruction from an ecclesiastical body on the operation of the Lodge

Brigham Young pictured wearing his
Masonic pin, ca. 1853.

building and the frequency of Masonic work is unparalleled. Scovil acquiesced to
these instructions, but the Nauvoo Lodge would still raise at least 228 additional
Masons following this April mandate—more than twenty per month.

Young believed that Freemasons in Illinois and nationwide conspired to kill
Joseph and Hyrum Smith and that non-Mormon Freemasonry operated contrary
to the interests of the Church. After the exodus from Nauvoo, there were many
Mormon Freemasons who hoped for the formation of a Mormon-controlled
Grand Lodge within the State of Deseret. George A. Smith, though realizing that
the association of Mormon and non-Mormon lodges was like "mix[ing] hair and
wool," still proposed a trip to England to "obtain five Charters for lodges which
would give us a Grand Lodge which would make us independent of all other grand
lodges in the world."[7] While Scovil supported this idea, Young feared that non-
Mormon Masons moving into the territory planned to establish a lodge to "try to

---

4. Stanley B. Kimball, ed., *On the Potter's Wheel: The Diaries and Journals of Heber C.
Kimball*, 103.

5. "Council of Fifty, Minutes, March 1844–January 1846; Volume 2, 1 March–6 May
1845," The Joseph Smith Papers, 228.

6. Kimball, *On the Potter's Wheel*, 103. The complete wording used by Heber C. Kimball
is the following: "We cold [called] Lucious N. Scovil in to get the Masonic Hall fore
Printing office, and to stop making Masons, only as times shall permit." Some authors
have interpreted this statement to mean that "on April 10, 1845, Brigham Young advised
Scovil to suspend the work of the Masons in Nauvoo." This view is not warranted as Nauvoo
Lodge continued the work of making 228 Masons in the ten months after the directive.

7. This is a reference to Leviticus 19:19 and Deuteronomy 22:11, which prohibit the
mixing of materials and fibers that are of completely different characteristics.

get an influence with some here to lay a plan to try to murder me & the leaders of the Church." He considered the idea of bringing Masonry into Utah Mormonism but ultimately decided that "we have got to look to Lord God of Israel to sustain us & not to any institution or kingdom or people upon the earth except the kingdom of God." He thus told his followers that the establishment of such a Grand Lodge would in the end be used to destroy the Church and its work.[8]

Ironically, the Mormon lack of action was a self-fulfilling prophecy, for the Church's delay in this matter left the formation of a Grand Lodge to both "Gentiles" and LDS critics residing in Utah Territory. These non-Mormon lodges were supported by surrounding Grand Lodges that required as a part of their sponsorship the barring of active Latter-day Saints from membership.

Though he opposed establishing a Grand Lodge in Utah, Young continued to identify as a Mason by wearing his Masonic pin, and he used Masonic references in his speeches, indicating his continued belief in the literal nature of Masonic myth.[9] Furthermore, he "delig[h]t[ed] to speak of it [the endowment] as 'Celestial Masonry'"[10] and retained—and possibly even added to—overt Masonic elements of the ritual such as tokens, signs, and penalties, three knocks at the veil, Masonic markings on garments, and the five points of fellowship. However, after the tragedy at Mountain Meadows, Young removed his Masonic pin and never wore it again, aware that Freemasons from Arkansas, possibly including members of the Fancher party, were responsible for the murder of Parley P. Pratt.[11]

Sidney Rigdon, Freemason to the End

Sidney Rigdon was raised a Master Mason along with Joseph Smith at the installation of the Nauvoo Lodge in March 1842. Although he had a somewhat rocky ride in Church leadership, he was nevertheless the senior surviving member of the First Presidency of the Church following the tragic deaths of Joseph and Hyrum Smith in June 1844. (At that time, he was in Pittsburgh establishing residency there as Joseph Smith's vice presidential running mate for the 1844 campaign.) Rigdon arrived back in Nauvoo on Saturday, August 3, and the next day he preached a sermon to the grieving Saints. There, he related "a vision which the Lord had shown him concerning the situation of the Church" and the necessity of having "a Guardian appointed to build the Church up to Joseph as he has begun it."[12]

---

8. Wilford Woodruff journal, August 19, 1860.

9. Brigham Young, January 1, 1877, *Journal of Discourses*, 18:303.

10. Ann Eliza Young, *Wife No. 19: Or, The Story of a Life in Bondage*, 371.

11. For the Masonic involvement in the murder of Pratt, see "The Killing of Pratt—Letter from Mr. McLean," 2.

12. Quotes by Sidney Rigdon and perspective of the morning meeting taken from LaJean Purcell Carruth and Robin Scott Jensen, "Sidney Rigdon's Plea to the Saints: Transcription of Thomas Bullock's Shorthand Notes from the August 8, 1844, Morning Meeting," 123.

A large assembly was held in the Grove on the morning of Thursday, August 8, 1844, attended by the nine members of the Twelve Apostles who had been able to arrive in Nauvoo after the death of the Smiths. At the morning meeting, Rigdon made a claim to succeed Joseph Smith by asserting that he "should be a spokesman for our prophet who has been taken from us." Brigham Young opposed Rigdon's claim and called for a decision to be made in the afternoon meeting, instead of on August 13, as had been originally slated. Young's and Rigdon's speeches were carefully stated to be as unifying as possible. Young asked "Brother Rigdon [to] come and take his seat at our right hand . . . and we can do the business in 5 minutes."[13]

Sidney Rigdon, 1873.

In the more well-attested afternoon meeting, Young and several of the apostles advocated that the leadership of the Church be given to the Twelve. Rigdon "did not ask that his name be submitted for vote and committed himself to fully support the decision of the Church by following the Twelve."[14]

Despite this cautiously hopeful beginning, Rigdon and the Twelve would part ways less than a month later. Rigdon was cut off from the Church, and in return, he petulantly excommunicated the members of the Twelve. He then left Nauvoo in a huff of antagonism. Historians LaJean Carruth and Robin Jensen write that it was "due in part to these later activities" that "Rigdon became increasingly marginalized and vilified in the narrative surrounding the death of Smith and the Twelve's assumption of authority over the Church."[15]

Back in Pittsburg, Rigdon briefly led a faction of Latter-day Saints called the "Church of Christ" or the "Church of Jesus Christ of the Children of Zion." It was reorganized at a conference on April 6, 1845, with a First Presidency, Quorum of Twelve Apostles, High Council, Presiding Bishopric, and Presiding Patriarch. The organization did not last long, however, and was dissolved two years later. During its brief existence, the group retained many of the Masonic features evident in the Church under the direction of Smith. Rigdon's sect was directed by a "Grand Council" of seventy-three men. In an endowment ritual,

---

13. Carruth and Jensen, 129.
14. Carruth and Jensen, 126.
15. Carruth and Jensen, 126–27.

Rigdon pronounced initiates "kings over whom the Son of God shall reign as King of Kings and Lord of Lords."[16]

After the dissolution of Rigdon's Church of Christ in 1847, he retained his association with Freemasonry and continued to be strongly influenced by the Craft until the end of his life. Upon leaving Pennsylvania, he and his Mormon sons-in-law joined local Masons to petition for a Lodge in Friendship, New York, in the spring of 1851. Among the charter members were Rigdon, George W. Robinson, Jeremiah Hatch, and Edward B. Wingate.[17] All four of these men had been raised Master Masons in Nauvoo Lodge and deemed it important to continue to affiliate with Freemasonry. Allegany Lodge No. 225 received a dispensation on April 25, 1851, with Robinson as Worshipful Master and Hatch as Junior Warden.[18] The Lodge was given a warrant on June 18, 1851. Rigdon's son, John W., noted that his father was a "very devoted Mason and was a regular attendent [sic] at the Masonic Lodge." In addition, John maintained that his father was "frequently called upon to speak on public occasions of the order."[19] When Rigdon died on July 14, 1876, lodge members mourned "the loss of our brother as one of the oldest and most venerable members of our fraternity, whose counsel and advice always challenged our respect."[20] Rigdon was buried with Masonic honors, and the Lodge was draped in mourning for thirty days.[21]

Strangite Masonry and the Order of Illuminati[22]

James J. Strang, a New York Freemason, was a careful student and aspiring successor of Joseph Smith. As a young man, Strang kept a diary documenting the years 1832 to 1836. Portions of his diary he deemed too esoteric for common mortals were encoded in a slight variation of a cipher associated with Royal Arch Masonry, demonstrating an early familiarity with the Craft. Strang used the code to record such confessions as "I have spent the day in trying to contrive some plan of obtaining in marriage the heir to the English crown . . . my mind has allways [sic] been filled with dreams of royalty and power" and "I am a perfect atheist but

---

16. "Minutes of a Conference of the Church of Christ," 168.

17. "The History of Friendship," 31.

18. John Stearns Minard and Georgia Drew Merrill, eds., *Allegany County and its People: A Centennial Memorial History of Allegany County, New York, 1896*, 717; *Proceedings of the Grand Lodge of Free and Accepted Masons of the State of New York, One Hundred and Twenty-Ninth Annual Communication*, 185.

19. John W. Rigdon, "Life Story of Sidney Rigdon," 186–87.

20. E. J. Cannon, "Masonic."

21. See "Death of Hon. Sidney Rigdon." For more on Sidney Rigdon's religious activities after 1844, see Karl Keller, ed., "'I Never Knew a Time when I did not Know Joseph Smith': A Son's Record of the Life and Testimony of Sidney Rigdon," 15–42.

22. This section is adapted from Cheryl L. Bruno, "Strangite Masonry and the Order of Illuminati," 1–21.

do not confess it lest I bring my father grey hair with sorrow to the grave."[23]

Strang traveled to Nauvoo in February 1844 and was instructed by Joseph and Hyrum Smith and Sidney Rigdon. He was baptized and confirmed by the Prophet on February 25, 1844, and ordained an elder the next Sunday by Hyrum Smith.[24] During his short time in Nauvoo, Strang observed Joseph Smith closely. After the Prophet's death, Strang related that he had received two visions, one of them involving an angel who anointed his head. Additionally, he claimed that Smith had written him a letter of appointment shortly before his death calling him to gather the Saints to Wisconsin to establish a settlement named "Voree" and build there a house of God.[25]

James J. Strang, 1856.

On September 1, 1845, Strang claimed to have received a vision of records that, like Smith's golden plates, were written and buried in the ancient past. The details of the discovery of these records align with the coming forth of the Book of Mormon as well as the Masonic story of a golden plate engraved with the name

---

23. James J. Strang, *James Jesse Strang Diary, July 1831–Jan. 1836*.

24. "A Record of the establishment and doings of the Stake of Zion called Voree in Wisconsin, made by the Scribes appointed to that office" (or "Chronicles of Voree"), 591, quoted in Robin Scott Jensen, "Gleaning the Harvest: Strangite Missionary Work, 1846–1850," 4. Jensen explains, "The 'Chronicles of Voree' is apparently a contemporary manuscript dated journal of the Strangite Church of unknown authorship. A transcription of this manuscript has been compiled by John J. Hajieck (Burlington, Wisconsin: J. J. Hajicek, 1992)." In footnote 9, Jensen quotes from the manuscript that Joseph Smith "blessed him with many and great blessings and said I seal upon thy head against God's own good time the keys of the Melchisedec Priesthood and afterwards but in the same ordinance Thou shalt hold the keys of the Melchisedec Priesthood, shalt walk with Enoch, Moses and Elijah and shalt talk with God face to face." Jensen also notes, "A search of the elder's licenses granted at Nauvoo during these months in 1844 does not list Strang. When later asked to produce his license, it was said that he did not have a license because he had not received one."

25. "The Letter of Appointment, from Joseph Smith, appointing James J. Strang as his successor," in "The Revelations of James J. Strang," Church of Jesus Christ of Latter Day Saints. Robin Jensen notes, "Present-day tests and comparisons show that the postmark is genuine but that the writing is a forgery. According to one interpreter, Joseph Smith, or at least someone from Nauvoo, did indeed send a letter to Strang but when it reached him, someone—perhaps Strang—likely tampered with the letter, carefully keeping the postmark intact." See Jensen, "Gleaning the Harvest," 6n17.

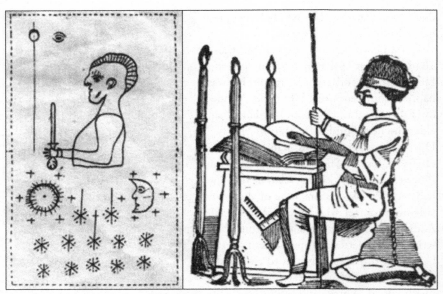

(Left) From an 1845 broadside of the Voree Plates. (Right) A candidate taking the Fellow Craft obligation from William Morgan, *Illustrations of Masonry*, 1827 ed.

of God being found in an underground cavern. Less than two weeks after his vision, on September 13, Strang directed four of his followers to go and dig up the plates he had envisioned. The Voree plates were found on a hill beneath a tree, and by September 18, Strang had provided a translation of the record.

The description of the Voree plates, as well as the printed depiction, have Masonic elements. The cut of the first of the Voree plates is composed of a surfeit of Masonic symbols: in the top left-hand corner is a plumb line, the Masonic emblem of uprightness; next to this is an all-seeing eye, in Masonic terms representing Divine omniscience or enlightenment, wisdom, and intelligence. The character in the center of the plate holds his arm to the square and grasps a sword, similar to a candidate taking the Fellow Craft obligation, as shown in William Morgan's *Illustrations of Masonry*. Below the figure are three marks that look like candlesticks, the "lesser lights" of Masonry that are placed in a triangular configuration around the altar, and surrounding these, on the bottom third of the plate, are the sun, moon, and stars, which are readily recognized by Masons as the "great lights."

The Voree plates were written in a sophisticated cipher, reminiscent of those used by Freemasons. More complicated than the code in Strang's early diary, the "Vorite" language still contained Masonic elements. For instance, one of the plates contains a representation of the Divine name, a preoccupation of Freemasons. Strang's goal then was the same as it was for Joseph Smith and for the Masons: to recover the lost name of Deity.

A revelation dated July 1, 1846, commanded the Voree Saints to build both a house for Strang and a house for the Lord in preparation for a holy endowment.[26] In this ritual, they were to be instructed in the principles and the mysteries of the kingdom of God. Strang began work on a temple in 1848 after moving his followers to Beaver Island in Lake Michigan. Here, he promised his followers an endowment and a restoration, carrying on Joseph Smith's vision of building a temple to restore that which was lost.

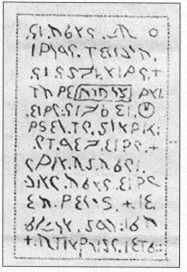

Cipher from an 1845 broadside of the Voree Plates.

Members of the Strangite movement were encouraged to make a covenant, also known as the Oath of the Illuminati, that replicated the obligations taken in Blue Lodge Masonry and used specific oaths and language from the Masonic ritual. The Strangite covenant professed faith in God, Jesus Christ, the Holy Spirit, and James J. Strang as "Prophet of God; Apostle of the Lord Jesus; and chief Pastor of the Flock." Adherents entered God's "oath and covenant" solemnly promising to "forever hail, ever conceal, and never reveal, any of the ceremonies, secrets and misteries [sic] of the order of the Illuminatti, which I may now or at any time hereafter be acquainted with, to any person in the world except it be an Illuminattus [sic]."[27] In addition, they "renounce[d] all allegiance to any and every other Potentate State and Nation," and they vowed to maintain the kingdom of God "in defiance" of any other kingdom, state, or nation. This was a revolution of the social order that clothed subversive oaths in the language of Masonry. The Oath placed Strangites in the same treasonous condition in which Joseph Smith was found. It even concluded with a lurid penalty.[28]

---

26. "The Revelations of James J. Strang."

27. Compare with the obligation of an Entered Apprentice Mason: "I . . . hereby and hereon most solemnly and sincerely promise and swear that I will always hail, ever conceal and never reveal any part or parts, art or arts, point or points of the secret arts and mysteries of ancient Freemasonry which I have received, am about to receive, or may hereafter be instructed in, to any person or persons in the, known world, except it be to a true and lawful brother Mason." William Morgan, *Illustrations of Masonry by One of the Fraternity Who has Devoted Thirty Years to the Subject*, 21.

28. "But should I be so corrupt treacherous and abominable as to despise cast off and violate the covenant I this day make with God and with his chosen ones: May the just judgments of God, due to all like apostates traitors and perjured villains be executed on my head: May all men know me perjured: and may they look on me as loathsome and wretched: May God the Eternal father execute judgment and justice on me without

Many influential Nauvoo Masons such as John C. Bennett, George Miller, George J. Adams, William Marks, William Smith, and John E. Page joined Strang's organization and contributed to the development of his rituals. The logical conclusion to those who had been involved in Smith's Council of Fifty was the crowning of their leader as King. Just as Joseph Smith, on April 11, 1844, had been "ordained a king, to reign over the house of Israel forever," so the Beaver Island Saints moved forward with the implications of Smith's theocratic ideas.[29] A royal procession of several hundred proceeded to the unfinished Beaver Island tabernacle on July 8, 1850, to witness the coronation of James Jesse Strang.

Thespian George J. Adams presided over the ritual. The emergent king was accompanied by his council and a grand procession of twelve Elders, the Seventy, and additional quorums as he marched into the tabernacle. Strang's robe was bright red, a color assigned in Freemasonry to the Royal Arch degree and symbolic of life and regeneration. It had been fashioned under Adams's direction to resemble the Masonic conception of a Jewish High Priest and was further ornamented with Masonic regalia.[30]

In a dramatic ceremony, Strang took his seat on a large chair on an elevated platform. Surrounding his makeshift throne were painted panels replicating pillars. He was invested with a wooden scepter and crowned with a thin metal circlet adorned with a projecting cluster of stars.[31] Strang chose a "grand council of 8" to serve with him as a ruling body.[32] This group totaling nine men numbered the same as the minimum number required to form a chapter of Royal Arch Masons. The same number formed Joseph Smith's first group inaugurated into the Anointed Quorum.

Filled with emotion at the religious display they had witnessed, Strang's followers took the Oath of the Illuminati as it had been given in Voree, and they covenanted with God to become "a nation of Kings and Priests to the nations of the earth."[33] They then signed a document entitled the "Record of the Organization of the Kingdom,"[34] in like manner to Masons, who do not become full members

---

mercy: And Jesus Christ the Redeemer turn from me and remember his loving kindness no more: Cast out from the society of the good on the earth: and cut off from hope in Heaven: may evil men and the worms destroy me always: May disease rot my bones within me: Parched and thirsty may I die without friends or succor: unloved of the good: cursed of evil doers: and the gates of Heaven closed against me: beholding bliss and feeling perdition evermore." See "Covenant, or Oath of the Illuminati."

29. William Marks, "Epistle," 53.

30. Roger Van Noord, *King of Beaver Island: The Life and Assassination of James Jesse Strang*, 106.

31. Van Noord, 106–7.

32. Stephen Post journal, July 8, 1850.

33. *Book of the Law of the Lord* 35:15.

34. *Record of the Organization of the Kingdom.* "As at Voree, the covenant usually was administered while the initiate's right hand touched or grasped a wooden cross resting on

of a lodge until they sign the lodge's bylaws. Thereafter, the commemoration of "King's Day" on July 8 would be marked with a "convocation and a feast,"[35] similar to the celebration of St. John's Day in Masonic lodges worldwide.[36]

One of Strang's plural wives, Elvira Field (who masqueraded for a time as his male assistant "Charles Douglas"), was supportive of the religion's Masonic ideals. While in Baltimore, she wrote an article published in the November 17, 1849, *Gospel Herald* touting the benefits of secret combinations. In this piece, Field elegantly synthesizes the secular and legendary history of secret societies and hinted at a new secret society (the Strangite Illuminati) founded on religious principles and containing all that is good in Masonry. The principles of elevation of the worker, a one-minded body, and support of government that would secure their ends were all expounded.[37]

In 1853, a letter signed by "Jas. J. Strang, Master Mason" and seven other men was sent from St. James, Beaver Island, to the Grand Lodge of Michigan requesting dispensation to form a Masonic lodge on the island and to engage in the ritual work of Freemasonry, with George Miller as proposed Master. Just over a decade earlier, half of the petitioners for this new lodge had been made Masons in Nauvoo Lodge, U.D., where George Miller had served as first Master. Even after providing the rite of illumination to his followers and being crowned king, Strang still wanted to create a local Masonic lodge under the jurisdiction of a recognized Grand Lodge.

It is not known if the Grand Lodge of Michigan ever officially responded to the request for a Beaver Island lodge. But long before this letter of petition, the Strangite organization had already succeeded in continuing and creatively expanding Joseph Smith's Mormon Masonry.

James J. Strang died six years and one day after he had been crowned king. Though he lived for weeks after being fatally wounded by an assassin, he refused to name a successor. Thus, the movement that was closest in numerical strength to challenging the claims of Brigham Young and the Twelve foundered. Students of Strang's legacy cannot help but be impressed by the similarities in Joseph Smith's and James Strang's utilization of Masonic forms in Mormonism's highest rituals.

---

a Bible, aptly, the King James version. Sometimes several persons touched the cross at the same time. The covenant was read sentence by sentence, and the initiate nodded his or her assent at the end of each sentence. After the oath was completed, the initiates signed their names in the covenant book." Van Noord, *King of Beaver Island*, 101.

35. *Book of the Law of the Lord*, 40:3; William Shepard, Donna Falk, and Thelma Lewis, eds., *James J. Strang, Teaching[s] of a Mormon Prophet*, 108–10.

36. The first Grand Lodge was formed on June 24, 1717. This was the feast day of John the Baptist, recognized as patron of stonemasons in continental Europe during the Middle Ages. St. John's Day has traditionally been celebrated in Masonic lodges with sumptuous repasts and commemorative events.

37. Charles Douglas [Elvira Field], "Secret Societies," 212–15.

Charles Thompson:
The Free and Accepted Order of Baneemy,
and Fraternity of the Sons of Zion[38]

Charles Thompson was born a Quaker in 1814 and was baptized into the Methodist Episcopal Church at age eighteen. However, within two years he became dissatisfied with his new faith's doctrine and desired to find something more rewarding. After closing up his tailor's shop and traveling about, he arrived in Kirtland, Ohio, where he was promptly baptized into the faith that would be his religious home for the next decade. Joseph Smith performed the ordinance of confirmation on February 10, 1835.

In Kirtland, Thompson was anointed in the House of the Lord in 1836. In March of that year, he received "the washing of feet at the Solemn Assembly held in the Temple."[39] He passed through the tribulations in Missouri, then served in New York state, organizing the Genesee Conference of the Church in Le Roy, Genesee County, New York. At the counsel of Smith, he moved to Hancock County, Illinois, in 1843.

Thompson remained in Nauvoo after the martyrdom of the Smith brothers, and he at first supported the Twelve. He was ordained a high priest and joined the Masonic Lodge there, an act with profound influence on his later religious workings.[40] On Christmas Eve, 1845, he was endowed in the Nauvoo Temple and was both remarried and sealed to his wife, as well as sealed to his first wife who died a few months after childbirth in 1839.[41] Despite being eternally sealed to both women, he was strongly opposed to polygamy and severed ties with Brigham Young over it.

In 1846 Thompson became a follower of James J. Strang. Eventually, however, Thompson criticized Strang for his ordination by an angel, his inability to translate without heavenly assistance, and for moving his headquarters to Beaver Island.[42] After breaking with Strang, Charles moved to St. Louis, Missouri, with his family. There, he formed the Congregation of Jehovah's Presbytery of Zion. In 1848 he issued his first "Proclamation," which he published in a newspaper he founded and called *Zion's Harbinger and Baneemy's Organ*.

Beginning in October 1852, Thompson published extracts of the Ethiopic Book of Enoch, which had been reintroduced into Europe by Freemason James Bruce in 1773. This work of pseudepigrapha, with themes of transformation, theosis, and communion with the Divine, significantly influenced American Royal

---

38. This section is adapted from Cheryl L. Bruno, "The Melodious Sounds of Baneemy's Organ," 151–76.

39. Charles B. Thompson, "Who is Charles B. Thompson?," 60.

40. Thompson was raised a Master Mason in Nauvoo Lodge on November 8, 1844.

41. Lisle G. Brown, *Nauvoo Sealings, Adoptions, and Anointings: A Comprehensive Register of Persons Receiving LDS Temple Ordinances, 1841–1846*, 311.

42. Charles B. Thompson, "Letter for the *Gospel Herald*," 22–24.

Arch Freemasonry.[43] Just as Joseph Smith
drew from the Enoch pseudepigrapha
through Freemasonry's Enoch legends to
produce his inspired version of the biblical
account now found in the Pearl of Great
Price (see Chapter 6), Thompson carried
on this tradition in monthly installments in
his *Zion's Harbinger and Baneemy's Organ.*
Thompson's publication of the Ethiopic
Book of Enoch was based on Richard
Lawrence's translation of 1821, but it was
"revised, corrected, and the missing parts
restored by Divine inspiration, through
Baneemy, Patriarch of Zion."[44] The result was Mormon and Masonic in flavor,
showing evidence of borrowing, expansion, recontextualization, and revelation
upon the ancient Enoch tradition. One
of Thompson's restored passages speaks of
Iame (the embodiment of all intelligence)
who created *Iada* (the place of light) out of
unorganized matter. *Iame* impregnated *Iada*
with "the seed of intelligence," and she brought forth many intelligences who were
clothed with refined matter and were called Spirits.

Charles Thompson, 1841.

> Iame, therefore, finding these Spirits imperfect as to the quantity of intelligence
> they possessed, by his wisdom concerted a plan to increase their intelligence and
> thereby make them perfect; and having completed the plan, he called them together
> to consult them in reference to their willingness to enter into his plan; and when he
> had made known his plan to them they were glad, and he organized them that they
> might accomplish his will and be made perfect.[45]

This passage is indebted both to Joseph Smith's conception of premortal
intelligences (Abr. 3:22) and the Masonic Grand Council. It continues with a
Masonic ordination of four grand quorums of Angels, twenty-four ministers,
and seven Chief Ones, with three of these presiding over the seven and an Elect,
Anointed, or "Concealed One" under the appellation of "Father."[46]

By 1854 Thompson's group had attracted between fifty and sixty families
who eventually moved to Monona County, Iowa. There they established a com-

---

43. See Cheryl L. Bruno, "Congruence and Concatenation in Jewish Mystical Literature,
American Freemasonry, and Mormon Enoch Writings," 5–6.

44. Charles B. Thompson, "The Book of Enoch," 73.

45. Thompson, 73.

46. Thompson, 73–74.

munal settlement they called Preparation. At its zenith in 1858, the settlement had swelled to over five hundred inhabitants.[47] In Preparation, Thompson carried on in the traditions of both Joseph Smith and James Strang, founding an organization that was overtly Masonic in nature. The full name of Thompson's group, "The Free and Accepted Order of Baneemy, and Fraternity of the Sons of Zion" (also known as the Presbytery of Zion), suggests this influence, patterned as it was after the fraternal organization known as the "Free and Accepted Order of Masons."

Thompson did not intend for the Presbytery of Zion to take the place of a church. Rather, he envisioned an extra-ecclesiastical body of the priesthood, organized for the purpose of completing the work of gathering preparatory to the Second Coming.[48] Like Masonry, Thompson's system could also be described as "a progressive science taught by degrees" through which God's grand design would eventually be revealed to the individual outside the context of a church organization. Thompson formulated his own innovative system of degrees within priesthood schools, utilizing, as do Masons, a catechism as a tool of instruction.

The covenant members took upon themselves when entering the Presbytery of Zion was remarkably similar to a Masonic obligation. For instance, initiates assumed an allegorical new name as in the Entered Apprentice degree.[49] Perhaps Thompson came closest to realizing his ritual ideal in a ceremony he instituted at the August Solemn Assembly in 1856. There, members were asked to give Thompson a paper bill of sale for everything they owned. As they came into a darkened room, he poured alcohol on the paper and burned it in token of their full and complete sacrifice. Two chiefs, Guy C. Barnum and Rowland Cobb, entered the room, surrendered their clothing, and were given a simple cotton smock that Thompson named the "Garment of Holiness."[50] Barnum and Cobb then seated themselves on either side of Thompson. After this, the rest of the members, men and women in turn, came into their presence and repeated the ritual enactment.[51] Mormon Masons would likely have been moved by this ceremony, as it contained elements of both the Masonic initiation rite and the temple endowment.

---

47. "Ecclesiastical Items," 91–92.

48. Charles B. Thompson, "The Word of the God of Abraham, of Isaac and of Jacob to his servants of the seed of the Church of Jesus Christ of Latter-day Saints, Having the testimony of Jesus Christ, Concerning their Organization, in preparation for the Endowments of the Priesthood, and their Regeneration in the Family of Israel," 2.

49. Charles B. Thompson, "Covenant, to be Taken upon Entering the Congregation of Jehovah's Presbytery of Zion," 9. The covenant to be taken upon entering the first department of the School of Faith begins, "I do now most solemnly and sincerely subscribe, with my hand unto Jehovah, and surname myself Israel, that I may be called after the name of Jacob, in Jehovah's Presbytery of Zion."

50. The garment was not worn permanently, but thereafter the member retained only enough clothing as was barely necessary.

51. C. R. Marks, "Monona County, Iowa, Mormons," 336.

Zion's Harbinger and Baneemy's Organ published its last issue under the date of December 1854. By then, Baneemyites were becoming disillusioned with the hardscrabble details of their communal lifestyle. Over the next few years, increased demands and poor decisions on Thompson's part would cause his disgruntled followers to dramatically eject him, signaling the collapse of the settlement in October 1858. Twice, Thompson endeavored to reestablish the congregation, but neither attempt was successful.

Despite an ignominious ending, Thompson left an important legacy. For a brief period, he provided a home for the religiously dispossessed. He kept alive the principle of gathering and of Mormon communitarianism. He introduced the idea of a priesthood group independent of a church—a uniquely Mormon variation of a Masonic idea. Charles B. Thompson thus included Freemasonry in his own distinctive and irreplaceable part of the broader Restoration movement.

Lyman Wight and the Community at Zodiac

A more dedicated Mormon could not be found than Lyman Wight, affectionately nicknamed the "Wild Ram of the Mountains." This stalwart advocate of Joseph Smith joined the Church in 1830 and was heavily involved in the spotlight events of early Mormonism. Wight had been a part of Isaac Morley's common-stock utopian society in Kirtland, and after his conversion he remained therein. He attended the School of the Prophets for two and a half months and received his washings and anointings prior to the dedication of the Kirtland Temple. Over the years he was a member of Zion's Camp, a Danite leader in Missouri, part of the stake presidency in Adam-ondi-Ahman, and in both the Quorum of the Twelve and the Council of Fifty. On April 28, 1842, Wight was raised a Master Mason in Nauvoo Lodge, just over a month after Smith. Two years later he became a member of the Anointed Quorum, receiving his endowment on May 14, 1844. Weeks before Smith's death, Wight, as a member of the Fifty, was appointed by the Prophet to lead a mission to form a Mormon colony in Texas. According to Wight, Smith ordained him to be like Moses, leading "the armys of Israel to Zion . . . [to] lead the children of Israel out of Egypt," and gave him "a white seer stone" to help him accomplish this task.[52]

Wight and George Miller were two of the mainstays of the lumbering effort in the Wisconsin pineries (see Chapter 13). At Black River, they led a group of families in a communal arrangement as they worked to send lumber down the Mississippi to Nauvoo for use in Church building projects. Wight initially supported Brigham Young in the succession crisis following the death of Joseph Smith, and Young reluctantly gave Wight and George Miller permission to lead the former "Pine Company" on an expedition to Texas to fulfill Smith's request.

---

52. Melvin C. Johnson, "Wightites in Wisconsin: The Formation of a Dissenting Latter Day Community (1842–1845)," 68.

Wight departed Nauvoo with a company of 160 on the riverboat *General Brooks* for Black River, Wisconsin, to prepare for departure to Texas in the spring. Many of these persons were Freemasons. A family history relates that Lavinia Hawley died on the boat and was taken ashore at Potosi, Wisconsin. Since the company could not stop long enough for a funeral, her son Pierce, an ardent Freemason, "gave his mother's body into the hands of the Masons of the town of Potosi with implicit confidence that it would be carefully, even tenderly buried."[53]

When the company reached what they called "the Valley of Loami," Wisconsin, they performed the ritual acts of rebaptism, partook of their own version of the Passover, ordained both a patriarch and a bishop, confirmed members, offered sustaining votes of the Twelve, held a ceremonial feast, and blessed children.[54]

In April 1845, the Wight group started their 1,400-mile journey to Texas, arriving at their destination nearly seven months later on November 10, where they spent the winter in the ruins of old Fort Johnson. The next spring, they passed several months in Austin before finally founding a small communitarian colony four miles down the Pedernales River from Fredricksburg. They named their town Zodiac.

In 1848, the twenty-six families were joined by George Miller and a few others. The settlement was constructing a large, two-story log building that would serve as a multi-purpose community center with room for a storehouse; an upstairs floor would serve as a functioning temple.[55] In December of 1848, Wight was disfellowshipped and later excommunicated by the Brighamites for refusing to join with the Saints in the West. He had never received his endowment in Nauvoo, but George Miller had.[56] From what is known about the Wightite temple rites, it seems likely that Miller contributed his Mormon and Masonic knowledge of ritual to the development of the ceremonies.

Temple ordinances at Zodiac were concise and crisp compared with the lengthy Utah version.[57] With their emphasis on foot washings and anointings, they seemed to be based more upon the earlier Mormon ritual that Wight had received in the Kirtland Temple. However, influence from the Nauvoo ritual

---

53. Helen Hawley Booker, *Life Story of John P. Hawley*, 18. Since other accounts mention that only one man and one little girl died on this journey, Melvin C. Johnson has suggested that the genealogical history confused young Lavinia Hawley with her mother. See Johnson, "Wightites in Wisconsin," 69. See also Asher Gressmen, letter to Levi Moffett, November 6, 1844, 1.

54. Gressmen to Moffett, November 6, 1844, 1.

55. Melvin C. Johnson, "'So We Built a Good Little Temple to Worship In': Mormonism on the Pedernales—Texas, 1847–1851," 91. The building was completed on February 17, 1849.

56. Miller was endowed in the Nauvoo temple on December 10, 1845.

57. John Hawley, the only known person to have experienced both the Wightite and the Brighamite temple rituals, described in several places how the ceremonies differed. See John Hawley, *Autobiography of John Hawley*, 28–29.

was also apparent. Celebrants wore a special garment and an apron during the ceremony, and they were ordained kings, queens, and priests, as in the Nauvoo Second Anointing. Covenants they made, such as submission to "the principle of all they have and being placed under the control of the Almighty God," were similar to those in the Nauvoo endowment. No less than the ceremonies in both Kirtland and Nauvoo, Zodiac's ritual carried the aroma of Freemasonry.[58]

In uniquely Mormon adaptations of Nauvoo ritual, baptisms for the dead were vital, and marriage and adoption sealings were performed both for monogamous and polygamous relationships. One of Wight's

Lyman Wight, date unknown.

followers, Gideon Carter Jr., affirmed, "Lyman Wight also said that Joseph Smith had given him othority [sic] to perform these plural marriage ceremonies in connection with other ceremonies of the Church."[59] The Zodiac temple functioned from 1849 to 1851.

Wight believed that the Prophet's youngest surviving brother, William, had patrilineal rights to the office of "Patriarch of the Most High God" with "the blessing of Prophet and Seer to rest upon Joseph's eldest son if he will receive it."[60] Therefore, Wight was in frequent communication with William. On October 3, 1849, every member of the Zodiac group, without exception, pledged to sustain William Smith as "prophet, seer, revelator, and translator" until someone of Joseph's posterity came forth to take his place.[61] In the spring of 1850, William

58. The Reorganized Church of Jesus Christ of Latter Day Saints, Complainant, Vs. the Church of Christ at Independence, Missouri, in *Abstract of Evidence Temple Lot Case. U.S.C.C*, 452–53, 457; Lyman Wight, "Revelation on Baptism for the Dead," February 10, 1851, cited in Johnson, "So We Built a Good Little Temple," 94–96.

59. Gideon Carter statement, February 27, 1894.

60. The Wightites committed to this idea at a Zodiac conference held in August 1849, pledging themselves to Joseph III when he became old enough to claim his father's role as church president, and that they would sell their property and return to Jackson County, Missouri. Thus, their settlement was considered a temporary situation. See Melvin C. Johnson, *Polygamy on the Pedernales: Lyman Wight's Mormon Villages in Antebellum Texas, 1845 to 1858*, 125–26.

61. Lois Cutler mentioned this phrase when describing the keys, powers, and authority of the Melchizedek Priesthood her husband Alpheus Cutler received when he was given the Second Anointing by Joseph Smith. See Sylvester J. Whiting's testimony cited in Christopher James Blythe, "'The Upper Room Work': Esotericism in the Church of Jesus Christ (Cutlerite), 1853–1912," 55.

Smith held a conference at Covington, Kentucky, which was attended by a delegation of four men from the Zodiac community. Otis Hobart, one of the delegates, died suddenly upon arrival. As in a Masonic or Mormon burial, Hobart was interred in his ceremonial clothing.[62]

According to the minutes of the 1850 Covington Conference published in Isaac Sheen's *Melchisedek & Aaronic Herald*, William Smith planned for his congregation to immigrate to Texas and unite with Lyman Wight's group. Here they were to receive endowments and ordinances in the Zodiac temple.[63] William accepted that temple as his own and also called for another to be built in Jackson County, Missouri.[64]

Flooding of the Zodiac mill dam caused the community to pick up stakes. As they moved from place to place over the next seven years, the colony was gradually reduced. In 1858, Lyman Wight and a small band of followers started for Jackson County, Missouri. However, before they left central Texas, Wight died of a seizure on March 31. His oldest son, Orange Lysander Wight, assisted in the last rites. These "consisted of washing and anointing the body from head to foot, then dressing it in holy garments—the cap, loose-frock robe, apron, and moccasins associated with the ritual of the Zodiac temple."[65]

Lyman Wight and his followers found justification for their mission to find a dwelling place for the Saints in Texas from Wight's appointment from the "Grand Council" of Mormonism—the theocratic Council of Fifty. Thanks to his experiences in Missouri and Nauvoo, Wight had learned much about living in peace with dissimilar and discontented neighbors. In his pursuit of his assignment and his duty, he focused on Christian principles such as millennialism and communitarianism. But the Mormon character and Masonic significance of his religion emerged from time to time, especially in his adaption of temple ritual.

Alpheus Cutler:
Chief Architect and Master Workman of God's Holy Houses

Remnants of the Masonic nature of Mormon temple ordinances were also seen in Alpheus Cutler's Church of Jesus Christ. Cutler was a stonemason by trade and was raised to Master Mason in Nauvoo Lodge on January 14, 1843. He was said to have a "natural parabolical, allegorical symbolical, mysterious, secretive way of telling things," which would have suited him well as a nineteenth-century Freemason.[66] In Kirtland, he attended the School of the Prophets

62. Johnson, *Polygamy on the Pedernales*, 127; Isaac Sheen, "The Greatest Annual Conference," 4.

63. Isaac Sheen, "A Revelation, given March 20, 1850," 1.

64. Isaac Sheen, "Special Conference," 4.

65. Johnson, *Polygamy on the Pedernales*, 206–7.

66. Orson Hyde, George A. Smith, and Ezra T. Benson, "A Report to Brigham Young, Heber C. Kimball, Willard Richards, and the Authorities of the Church of Jesus Christ of

and worked on the construction of the Kirtland Temple. In Missouri, he was named "chief architect and master workman of all God's holy houses" and laid the cornerstone for the Far West Temple.[67] In Nauvoo, he oversaw construction of the Nauvoo Temple and supervised workmen cutting logs for the building in the Wisconsin Pineries. As a member of the Anointed Quorum, Cutler received his endowment on October 12, 1843, and his Second Anointing on November 15 of that same year. He was brought into the Council of Fifty and directed by Joseph Smith to serve a mission to the Lamanites, taking this as seriously as Lyman Wight took his assignment to Texas.

Alpheus Cutler, ca. 1840s.

After Smith's martyrdom, Cutler sided with Brigham Young and the Twelve. As a member of the High Council, he participated in the excommunication trials of Sidney Rigdon, James Strang, and William Smith. He renewed his endowment in the Nauvoo Temple in December 1845 and then helped establish the launching communities of Cutler's Park and Winter Quarters, Nebraska, for the emigrating Saints. With the approval of Young, he began missionary work among the Native American tribes in the fall of 1847. He soon, however, ran afoul of Orson Hyde, who as a member of the Twelve attempted to regulate his efforts. Cutler broke with the Saints heading west in 1851 and brought a small group of followers with him to Manti, Iowa.

On September 19, 1853, Alpheus Cutler organized "the Church of Christ," a reorganization of Joseph Smith's church that he believed had become necessary because of the failure of the Saints to complete the Nauvoo Temple. Under Cutler's authority, all ordinances, including baptism and temple endowments, would need to be repeated, and the Law of Consecration would have to be established. A meetinghouse was constructed with a floor plan similar to that of the Nauvoo Temple. It served as a pattern for three future Cutlerite meetinghouses with a public assembly hall on the first floor, a private space on the upper floor, and a baptismal font in the basement.[68] In this edifice, work on the upper floor retained Masonic elements from the Nauvoo Temple ritual. According to Cutler biographer Danny Jorgensen, this "involved a secretive initiation, assignment of a sacred personal

---

Latter Day Saints in Zion," March 14–April 5, 1849, 12.

67. Rupert J. Fletcher and Daisy Whiting, *Alpheus Cutler and The Church of Jesus Christ*, 25; see also Danny L. Jorgensen, "Conflict in the Camps of Israel: The 1853 Cutlerite Schism," 29.

68. Blythe, "The 'Upper Room Work,'" 61.

identity, passwords to the celestial world, endowments (or blessings), ritual clean-
ing by water and anointings with oil, the receipt of a sacred undergarment, and
ritual reenactment of sacred myths." Other ordinances included baptism by proxy
for the salvation of the dead and monogamous marriage for eternity.[69]

Males progressed through three degrees of the priesthood: Aaronic,
Melchisedek, and High Priest. Though sermons from the Manti period "stressed
the essential nature of the office of high priest," Cutler disclosed in 1860 that
"there were 'two keys' remaining, an allusion to ordination as a king and priest
through the second anointing ceremony associated with the Holy Order and later
with the temple in Nauvoo." Cutler had received this ritual, providing him with
the fulness of the Priesthood and guaranteeing exaltation. According to historian
Christopher Blythe, "These final keys, along with the preliminary endowment
ceremony, pertained to entrance in the Kingdom of God."[70]

Blythe theorizes that "the strategy of the [Cutlerite] ritual system and its associated discourse was designed to produce a collective identity." This corresponds
with the effect of the ritual system in the fraternal structure of Freemasonry. In a
further parallel, Blythe adds that the progressive nature of the ritual system "was
intended to strengthen bonds within the community, as individuals advanced
through the series of rites and ordinances." In Cutler philosophy, advancement
by degrees was key to beginning the process of sanctification.[71]

After the death of Alpheus Cutler on June 10, 1864, the Cutlerites moved to
Clitherall, Minnesota. Here, the few remaining families established the "Order
of Enoch," a religiously based common-stock company similar to the Mormon
United Order, organized and directed by its church corporation. A two-story
log church was built and dedicated in 1867. In Masonic form, ordinances were
practiced on the second floor of the building. "Windows were covered with cur-
tains and space set aside for the secret temple ordinances they had learned in
Nauvoo." These included "blessings, sealings, baptisms for the dead, ordinations
and other secret rituals of Nauvoo Mormonism."[72] Hallie Gould, raised as a child
in Clitherall, described the upper room as a "secret chamber" where only those
men or women holding the priesthood were allowed to enter, "and we have heard
rumors of strange ceremonies, covenants, and endowments, the altar, the tree
of life, the ordinance of feet washing, and the peculiar though necessary and

---

69. Danny L. Jorgensen, "The Fiery Darts of the Adversary: An Interpretation of Early
Cutlerism," 75.

70. Christopher James Blythe, "Recreating Religion: The Response to Joseph Smith's
Innovations in the Second Prophetic Generation of Mormonism," 52.

71. Blythe, "The 'Upper Room Work,'" 61, 63.

72. Biloine Whiting Young, *Obscure Believers: The Mormon Schism of Alpheus Cutler*,
109, 177–78. See also Jorgensen, "The Fiery Darts of the Adversary," 75–76; and Blythe,
"'The Upper Room Work,'" 61.

significant grave-clothes which no one will explain."[73] Gould speculated "as to where the ideas executed there originated," adding that "some have wondered if masonry did not have an influence on them and affect their secret rites."[74]

Blythe has pointed out that F. Lewis Whiting, an endowed Cutlerite member, preached a conference sermon advocating the internal Masonic narrative "that Masonry had first been revealed in King Solomon's Temple." Blythe observes that the "Cutlerites, like others who placed their faith in the antiquity of fraternal rites, did not see a ceremony stemming from God or from Freemasons as mutually exclusive ideas."[75]

William Smith's Priest and Priestess Lodges

William Smith, brother of Joseph and Hyrum, was raised a Master Mason in the Nauvoo Lodge on April 13, 1842, during its first full month of operation. Though he and his brother had a rocky relationship, Joseph was supportive of William and was influential in securing his call as an inaugural member of the Council of Twelve Apostles.[76] Following his brother's lead, William associated the concept of a Masonic Lodge and its structure with confidential instruction and plural marriage. William was practicing unauthorized spiritual wifery as early as 1842 while serving a mission in the Eastern States. Elder John Hardy exposed "the base and Licentious Teachings and Practices" of Elder George J. Adams and William Smith while in New Bedford, Massachusetts. In return, Hardy was accused of slander, and at Hardy's trial, testimony was given that Adams brought Miss Susan Clark and another sister "into a room and swore them into the secrets of a lodge, which secrets were not to be revealed under the penalty of their lives." Additionally, a letter was cited "sent from Boston by Elder G. J. Adams, to an Elder in New York," reading, "I have just returned from New Bedford and sister Susan is with me. I was S. U. [sealed up] to her last night, go it!"[77]

According to historian Connell O'Donovan, while in the East, William "set up his own abolitionist and feminist oriented newspaper that also politically

---

73. Women were considered to hold priesthood in connection with their husbands and were not ordained to priesthood offices.

74. Hallie M. Gould, "Like Sheep that Went Astray: Concerning the Cutlerite Faction of the Church that Went North During the Dark and Cloudy Day," 53.

75. Blythe, "The 'Upper Room Work,'" 85, citing "Conference Minutes," April 10, 1892.

76. "At the time the Twelve were chosen in Kirtland, and I may say before, it had been manifested that brother Phineas [Young] was entitled to occupy the station as one of the number; but owing to brother Joseph's urgent request at the time, brother David and myself yielded to his wish, and consented for William to be selected, contrary to our . . . feelings and judgment, and to our deep mortification ever since." Oliver Cowdery, letter to Brigham Young, February 27, 1848, 2.

77. John Hardy, *The Trials of Elder John Hardy, Before the Church of Latter Day Saints in Boston, for Slander, in Saying that G. J. Adams, S. Brannan and Wm Smith were Licentious Characters*, 4.

stumped for unapproved political candidates" and "established several 'Penny & Sewing Societies'" that were almost identical to the Nauvoo Female Relief Society in structure and purpose.[78] William's involvement in clandestine spiritual wifery, however, casts an ominous light on these seemingly progressive activities.

William did not return to Nauvoo until May 4, 1845, almost a year after the death of his brothers. As next in line to his brother Hyrum, he seemed determined to stand in the station of "Patriarch over the whole Church,"[79] but Brigham Young's position that William must be subject to the control of the Twelve caused tension, and William was excommunicated on October 19, 1845.

William B. Smith, ca. 1860.

William followed James Strang until 1847, when he announced his leadership of the Latter Day Saint Church to gather in Lee County, Illinois. Lyman Wight put the support of his followers behind William's claims in 1849 and 1850.

In 1851 at Palestine Grove, Illinois, William established a recreation of the Masonically based Nauvoo Anointed Quorum and Relief Society, which he called the "Priests Lodge" for men, and the "Priestess Lodge" for women. Few records exist documenting what occurred in these lodges, but it is apparent that they were oath-bound societies in which William performed washings and anointings and plural sealings. In a letter dated July 18, 1851, a revelation by William stated:

> [C]oncerning those females who have received the priesthood by being sealed to my servants William Smith and Joseph W[oo]d, and have been washed and anointed and ordained under their hands having been received into the priestess lodge—having taken the covenant thereof; if they, or either of them, shall fall, or altogether turn therefrom, she or they shall be excluded therefrom and from my church also, and shall not come forth in the resurrection of the just.[80]

In a further Masonic amplification, men were to "exalt" their wives and make them their Queens by performing the Second Anointing ceremony.

---

78. O'Donovan, "William Smith, Isaach Sheen, and the *Melchisedek & Aaronic Herald*."

79. William Smith, "Patriarchal," 905.

80. William Smith letter of July 18, 1851, in "Slander Refuted," *Dixon Telegraph* (April 30, 1853); see also Kyle R. Walker, *William B. Smith: In the Shadow of a Prophet*, 396–97. Walker has identified William Smith, Aaron Hook, and Joseph Wood as members of the Priests Lodge; with Rosa Hook, other females in the Hook family, at least two members of the Waukesha, Wisconsin Branch, and several residents of Palestine Grove belonging to the Priestess Lodge. Other members of the sect may have been involved, but most of his followers remained unaware of William's secret lodge.

As he had in Boston, William used Masonically based, oath-bound societies to introduce the practice of polygamy to the members of his sect. Incorporating a lodge for females demonstrated his familiarity with his brother's brand of Masonry in Nauvoo. There, Joseph Smith played with male-transmitted authority, binding women to his doctrines and practices, yet attempting to provide them with opportunities not often available in Victorian society.

William proved unable to sustain the loyalty of his followers. One of his apostles, Jason Briggs, wrote about his discovery that plural marriage was still taught in William's organization. At a conference in October 1851, Briggs was initiated into the inner circle. Here, he wrote, "they threw off the mask, in a council called the Priests' Lodge, and confessed to the practice of polygamy in the name of the Lord." Briggs wrote that William's "true character was discovered by many of us," indicating that more than a few were introduced into the secret society.[81]

As members of William Smith's movement discovered his secrets, more and more of them defected. Many joined Briggs in a movement that would become the Reorganized Church of Jesus Christ of Latter Day Saints in 1860 under William's nephew, Joseph Smith III. The son of Joseph Smith Jr. commented on his uncle's system of polygamy, calling it "a sort of promiscuity of affinities under the guiss [guise] of a 'priestess lodge.'"[82]

The Smith Family and the Reorganization

After the death of her husband, Emma Hale Smith married Lewis Bidamon, a non-Mormon major in the Illinois militia. When, in 1848, a group of non-Mormon Masons formed a lodge in Nauvoo they named "Reclamation Lodge," Bidamon became a member. Though he was expelled from the Lodge in 1856, the Smith boys were raised in a home where Masonry was part of their experience.

Unlike other groups springing from Joseph Smith's original vision, the followers of his son Joseph Smith III were largely ambivalent toward what they saw as Nauvoo-era innovations such as polygamy and Freemasonry. Smith III resisted aligning himself with either Masonry or anti-Masonry, even though there was great pressure for him to do so. However, his son and the founding prophet's grandson, Frederick Madison Smith, was very involved with Fraternal organizations. He was raised a Master Mason in 1927 while he was the president of the Reorganized Church of Jesus Christ of Latter Day Saints and served vigorously in various officer positions, including Worshipful Master, in his lodge of over 600 men. F. M. Smith was also a Knight Templar, a Scottish Rite Mason, and a

---

81. J. W. Briggs, "J. W. Briggs Letters," 3.

82. Joseph Smith III, letter to Warren E. Peak, January 4, 1911, cited in Blythe, "Recreating Religion," 27.

Smith brothers with Lews Bidamon (seated bottom left); Joseph Smith III is
seated bottom right, ca. 1850.

Shriner.[83] His progression through the Masonic degrees affected his development
as a mystic and proponent of the social gospel.

Freemasonry's Legacy Among the Mormons

Masonry was a part of the calculus of many of the Restoration groups that
formed after the death of Joseph Smith. This widespread continuation of esoteric
and Masonic tendencies confirms their existence in the early Church. Those who
claimed the right to Mormon succession continued along the path laid out by
Joseph Smith. There is clear evidence that these groups intentionally retained
Masonic elements as part of their version of the temple endowment. Their followers, a large number of whom were Masons, knew these features were Masonic
and did not question their presence.

In several cases, successors took steps to continue their association with authorized Freemasonry. They understood that Masonry was an important part of the
restoration of Mormonism and made efforts to officially petition for lodges where
they did not already exist. It was not until the twentieth century that Masonry
would lose its significance in the collective memory of the Mormon diaspora.

83. James A. Marples, "Brother Frederick Madison Smith, Past Master; 32° Mason;
and an Ordained Minister."

CHAPTER 19

THAT WHICH WAS LOST

M. Most Perfect Senior Warden, what is the o'clock?'
SW. The moment when the vail of the temple was rent; when darkness and consternation covered the earth; when the stars disappeared, and the lamp of day was darkened; when the implements of Masonry were lost, and the cubic stone [sweat] blood and water; that was the moment when the great Masonic Word was lost.
M. Since Masonry, my brethren, has sustained so great a loss, let us employ ourselves, by new works, to recover the Word which was lost.
-Light on Masonry: The History and Rituals of
America's Most Important Masonic Exposé

As the founder and builder of one of the most American of religions, Joseph Smith chose stones from many quarries to create the institution of Mormonism. By itself, Freemasonry cannot stand as a suitable explanation for every aspect of the Mormon restoration, nor can it impart meaning to every important development within the faith. However, its explanatory power is significant and may be acknowledged as a substantial contributing factor to many of its aspects. Smith's involvement in Masonry was earlier and broader than modern historians have supposed. This book has highlighted some of the gems that the Prophet mined from Freemasonry to beautify his religious edifice. These include a recovered Book of the Law, bifurcated priesthoods, oath-bound organizations, and a temple in the tradition of King Solomon with a ritual-based ceremony to fill it. Smith's use of Masonic midrash in developing new scripture, as well as his aspirations to restore and eventually lead all American Freemasonry, were important structural elements in the construction of Mormonism. In the final analysis, the Mormon story can appropriately be seen as the story of "that which was lost"—a major theme of Freemasonry.

In Edward FitzGerald's adaptation of Omar Khayyám's *Rubáiyát*, the narrator laments:

> Ah Love! could you and I with Him conspire
> To grasp this sorry Scheme of Things entire,
> Would not we shatter it to bits—and then
> Re-mould it nearer to the Heart's Desire![1]

Such longing rests at the very core of Smith's religious experimentation. Throughout his life he sought to break social convention—that "sorry scheme of

---

1. Omar Khayyám, *Rubáiyát of Omar Khayyám: The Astronomer-Poet of Persia*, 49.

things" that ground the face of the poor, held no regard for the plight of widows and orphans, held back individual progress, and offered no salvation of any kind in this world or in the world to come. He and his associates worked to replace the existing system with a social, political, economic, and spiritual order "nearer to the heart's desire." Such an order would recognize our nature as children of God and reflect the interrelatedness and interdependence of all humanity. Whatever the weaknesses of the system they envisioned, these men desired a society with a soul and conscience that recognized the innate value of each individual and sought to lift and empower. This shared and Masonically inspired grand vision was a persistent thread running through early Mormonism: socially progressive but also inherently subversive, morally shocking, and politically treasonous.

Joseph Smith, like many Masons of his day, believed that an ancient, pristine form of Freemasonry had become apostate. He believed he had found "that which was lost," enabling him to restore both true religion and pure Masonry to the earth.[2] By starting work on the construction of a temple and bringing forth the ritual that would be therein enacted, he had done what King Solomon, Hiram Abiff, and Hiram of Tyre had not been able to do.[3] By building up Mormon Masonic lodges in Nauvoo and surrounding areas, his people were well placed to influence Freemasonry in Illinois and on a national scale. Smith's vision likely included a reconciliation of what he saw as "spurious" Freemasonry and the pure form he had restored. There is not enough evidence to know how Smith planned to merge the two. With his death, the Prophet's vision regarding how Freemasonry would work in tandem with the Church was abandoned.

Transition by Degrees

Brigham Young's decision not to pursue Masonry in Utah began an estrangement between Freemasonry and Mormonism of the Intermountain West.

---

2. "Joseph Smith out-masoned Solomon himself, and declared that God had revealed to him a great key-word, which had been lost, and that he would lead Masonry to far higher degrees, and not long after their charter was revoked by the Grand Lodge. How much of Masonry proper has survived in the Endowment, the writer will not pretend to say; but the Mormons are pleased to have the outside world connect the two, and convey the impression that this is 'Celestial Masonry.'" John H. Beadle, *Life in Utah; or, The Mysteries and Crimes of Mormonism, Being an Expose of the Secret Rites and Ceremonies of the Latter-Day Saints, With a Full and Authentic History of Polygamy and the Mormon Sect From Its Origin to the Present Time*, 499.

3. At the establishment of Nauvoo in 1841, the fulness of the priesthood was not available. A revelation stated: "For there is not a place found on earth that he may come to and restore again that which was lost unto you, or which he hath taken away, even the fulness of the priesthood" (D&C 124:28). Temple ordinances, including baptism for the dead, "belongeth to my house, and cannot be acceptable to me, only in the days of your poverty, wherein ye are not able to build a house unto me. But I command you, all ye my saints, to build a house unto me" (vv. 30–31).

Like their leader, the typical Mormon of Young's day distrusted the people they called their "gentile" neighbors. Latter-day Saints were forced to hide their polygamous lifestyle for fear of being thrown in jail, and they felt persecuted and ridiculed for dearly cherished beliefs. In addition, gentile lodges began prohibiting active Latter-day Saints from joining their fraternities, despite such a policy being a violation of Masonic principles of inclusiveness. On the other hand, non-Mormons in Utah struggled with exclusive economic policies encouraged by the Church. They felt Latter-day Saint loyalty to religious authority was obsessive and unhealthy and that allegiance to an institution that would ask their members to break the law was likewise inconsistent with Masonic principles.

By the late nineteenth century, Mormonism was in profound transition. As those fires that had driven its vision of revolution began to cool, the Church worked to reinvent itself, seeking both renewed theological and social relevance in a rapidly changing world. The cost for this was high: Mormon leaders understood they would be forced to abandon the fundamental theocratic system for which they had struggled and sacrificed. Concepts related to nineteenth-century Freemasonry had served as a model for early Mormon social transformation; these would be laid aside in favor of something friendlier to established American institutions the Church had once excoriated. What is often called the "modernization of Utah" was in some degree an assimilation, bringing it closer to those American mainstream values that made it an acceptable candidate for Statehood.

Despite transitioning into the new century and greater accommodation to American Christian mores and values, Latter-day Saints and Freemasons in Utah continued to harbor strong animosities. The divides of prejudice and culture would take nearly a century to find amicable resolution. One notable event was the publication of literature critical of the Church by Samuel Goodwin, Congregationalist minister and Past Grand Master of Masons in Utah. Widely circulated and compelling, his 1921 *Mormonism and Masonry: Origins, Connections and Coincidences between Mason and Mormon Temple/Templar Ritual* troubled many readers. Particularly worrisome to Latter-day Saints was his assertion that Mormon Temple rites were largely pilfered from Masonic ritual and that endowed Latter-day Saints were participating in what amounted to a form of clandestine Masonry. Freemasons were similarly galled by Goodwin's accusation that contemporary Mormons commonly believed Freemasonry was nothing more than a poor imitation of God's true ordinances—a secret combination handed down from Cain and authored by the evil one.

In response, LDS President Heber J. Grant formed a committee with Elder George F. Richards as the chairman. One of the tasks of this committee was to revise elements of LDS temple ritual that corresponded to Masonic rituals and had been exposed by Goodwin. For the first time, portions of the endowment were specifically modified or eliminated to remove overtly Masonic aspects.[4]

Allen Roberts and others have noted that the transformation within Mormonism sought to emulate a more "respectable" Christian tradition. As the Church came to adopt more Protestant Christian theological views, they also took in negative views of mainstream Christianity about Masonry. This resulted in Great Basin Mormons becoming further distanced from their mystical and hermetic roots and viewing Joseph Smith's and the early Latter-day Saints' experiences regarding Freemasonry with ambivalence. Masonic symbols that had been enthusiastically embraced by earlier generations of Saints were eventually the cause of "embarrassment, suspicion, and even disdain."[5] Gradually, they pulled away from doctrines, traditions, and organizations that were deeply rooted in the Craft.

A Loss of Understanding

Because the Masonic connection within many of the church organizations that Joseph Smith created has been lost, it is sometimes difficult to understand their meaning and purpose. Every institution set up by Smith may be seen as an experimentation with Masonic form. The Danite band in Missouri, for example, is difficult for the modern eye to comprehend. Without the Masonic connection, Danite looting and shooting appears brutal and unseemly. Its symbolic and ritual structure, fraternal zeal, and defensive intentions are obscured. Similarly, the Council of Fifty is best understood from a Masonic perspective. Once its radical, revolutionary nature had been subdued—once its purpose as a kingdom

---

4. George F. Richards suggested a change in the order of robing (formerly the robe was placed on the right shoulder, then on the left, then back to the right). His proposed change was "to place the robe first on the Left shoulder, . . . then to change it to the Right shoulder, . . . thus obviating one of the changes heretofore made, and more effectively indicating transition from the lower to the hig[h]er orders of the Priesthood." See George F. Richards memorandum, June 7 and October 5, 1922. Richards also suggested eighteen wording changes in the ceremony, including writing a script for previously unscripted portions dealing with the covenants and instructions for the prayer circle and veil. His changes were approved by the First Presidency and announced to Salt Lake City temple workers on August 14. Four years later, administrators at the St. George Temple were notified: "At request of President Grant we have already adopted some of the changes decided upon, and it will be in order for you to do the same. In sealing for the dead, whether one or both be dead, omit the kissing. Omit from the prayer in the circle all references to avenging the blood of the Prophets. Omit from the ordinance and lecture all reference to retribution. . . . This letter is written with the approval of the Presidency." See George F. Richards, "Letter to the President of the St. George Temple, February 15, 1927."

5. Allen D. Roberts, "Where Are the All-Seeing Eyes? The Origin, Use and Decline of Early Mormon Symbolism," 39–40.

Plaque on Spring City Endowment House, featuring square, compasses, and beehive. Courtesy of Utah State Historical Society.

with keys and power sustaining a prophet, priest, and king was removed—it had little reason for existence and was eliminated.[6]

Mormon material culture was once rich in iconography suggestive of that restored, celestialized Masonry that surrounded the early Saints and formed a part of their cultural experience. By the mid-1900s, the Latter-day Saint sense of the sacred had significantly evolved. Symbols such as the square and compasses, once prominently featured, became a little-understood aspect of the temple ceremony and inappropriate for public exposure. For example, the angel weathervane that had graced the Nauvoo temple was designed with a flaming heart, the intertwined square and compasses, and "Book of the Law." In 2002, when the temple was rebuilt, the angel was replaced with a modern, upright Moroni. Reproductions of the weathervane angels, sold as memorabilia, likewise lack the Masonic symbolism.

Similarly, the square and compasses were engraved on a plaque on a small brick edifice in Spring City, Utah, first constructed in 1876 as a Relief Society building and later used as a school.[7] When Elders Spencer W. Kimball and Ezra Taft Benson became aware of the symbols in the 1970s, they requested that they be effaced from the plaque, explaining that "sacred symbols openly displayed would

---

6. The Council of Fifty assisted in the Mormon migration to the Great Basin in 1846. It assisted in establishing civil government until September 1850 when Congress granted territorial status to Utah. Meetings were suspended in October 1851. The council met briefly in 1867 and 1868 to vote for the establishment of Zion's Co-operative Mercantile Institution (ZCMI), and during the administration of John Taylor, to combat federal involvement in overseeing Utah elections. Its last recorded meeting was in 1884.

7. The Relief Society building in Spring City was sold in 1878 to the Spring City School District and commonly called the Allred School. It has been called the "Endowment House" from a bit of folklore that says that Orson Hyde's office was located there and that he may have performed endowments in his office. Hyde's journal does mention the performance of an endowment but does not specify where exactly. There is no evidence that Hyde's office was located in this building.

only create confusion among the members."[8] When the Masonic significance of the square and compasses had been more widely known and understood, Latter-day Apostles and members would not have been confused at their presence outside of the temple. They would have recognized that the symbolism of "square," or ethical actions and circumspect or prudent living, was as appropriate for Relief Society or educational uses of the building as it was for secret temple rites.

Masonic icons with symbolism once meaningful to early Mormons also included the all-seeing eye, the inverted star, the fraternal handshake, the bee-hive, and representations of the celestial bodies. The Salt Lake City Endowment House, a temporary building where ordinances were performed while temples were being constructed, incorporated "representations of the square, compass, level, and plumb on the garden room walls, the depiction of sun, moon, and stars in the same room, and flaming swords over the door in the world room."[9] Public versions of these symbols also abounded. The all-seeing eye was a common feature on signs advertising Zion's Cooperative Mercantile Institution (ZCMI), America's first department store. With the Masonic import that God's searching eye watches everyone, it was meaningful to Mormons who valued honesty in their business dealings. Once placed on temples, tabernacles, business establishments, and even coins, the symbol has gradually lost favor in the Intermountain West. As well as disappearing from public view, the all-seeing eye was painted out of the walls in the St. George and other temples.

As Mormonism's profound and vital material culture has receded, so has its interior symbolism. Unlike the first generation of Mormons, contemporary Saints no longer understand the endowment in relation to Masonry. Masonic symbols or gestures used in Latter-day Saint temples have been reinterpreted by members with no Masonic background. Retaining little to no relevance to modern Mormons, it is not surprising to see such elements disappear. Under George F. Richards' purview, the Oath of Vengeance and Masonic significance of the symbolic penalties were removed. In 1936, hoping to generate greater reverence for the temple garment, it was recommended that "a definition be given in the temple of the symbolism and significance of the various marks in the garment." Similar but reinterpreted LDS meanings of these Masonic markings were given by President David O. McKay, who was not a Freemason:

> A. The square: Honor, integrity, loyalty, trustworthiness. B. The compass: An unde-
> viating course in relation to truth. Desires should be kept within proper bounds. C.

---

8. Allen D. Roberts, "The 'Other' Endowment House: Unraveling a Mystery," 9–10. The building was subsequently purchased by preservationists Craig Call and Allen Roberts, who restored an engraved version of the square and compasses to the plaque.

9. Lisle G. Brown, "'Temple Pro Tempore': The Salt Lake City Endowment House," 40–41, 67.

The navel: That spiritual life needs constant sustenance. D. The knees: Rever[e]nce for God, the source of divine guidance and inspiration.[10]

Continuing this trend, the lecture at the veil, what remained of the penalties, and the five points of fellowship were omitted from the endowment in 1990. The latter was a meaningful ritual to eighteenth- and nineteenth-century Masons, with each point of contact being a welcoming reminder of principles binding them together as companions. Times changed, and young Latter-day Saints with modern ideas of personal space found the symbolic embrace baffling and uncomfortable when they encountered it prior to serving a mission or getting married. The ritual no longer served the purpose for which it was originally adopted. Finally, the threefold "return and report" sequence modeled upon the ritual opening of a Lodge was gradually truncated until it was completely removed in 2019.

In recent decades, Mormon apologists have pointed to subtle similarities between the LDS temple endowment and ancient rituals in order to reject the Masonic context of many crucial elements.[11] As seen, when disconnected from traditional Masonic interpretations, many features of the endowment could not stand on their own and were eliminated from the ceremony, sometimes at the expense of what their Masonic origins might reveal to the thoughtful Latter-day Saint.

In addition to the loss of specific aspects of Mormonism's material culture and shared ritual elements, Latter-day Saints became increasingly disconnected from the nuances of their earlier shared history. Eventually, they could no longer recall the significant role Masonry played in shaping Mormon scripture, theology, and ritual practice. Concepts such as the chain of belonging,[12] the eternity of matter, eternal regression of divinity, the grand chain of masters and dispensation heads, the Grand Council in Heaven, and the earthly gathering of Adam and his posterity at Adam-ondi-Ahman came to be viewed as singular revelations to Joseph Smith without precedent. Likewise, following the loss of knowledge of important Masonic concepts, Book of Mormon scriptural passages lost the underlying contrast between Spurious and Authentic Masonry and were read as a carte blanche criticism of "secret combinations" like Freemasonry. For Saints of the last century,

---

10. George F. Richards, Joseph Fielding Smith, Stephen L. Richards, and Melvin J. Ballard, Committee Report to the First Presidency and Council of the Twelve Apostles, April 22, 1936. Originally, the markings on the Latter-day Saint temple garment represented the following Masonic symbolic tools: square, compass, level, and plumb. A simple interpretation of the square is a symbol of morality. The compasses symbolize "the strength to circumscribe our desires and keep our passions within due bounds." The level is a symbol of equality, and the plumb of integrity or upright character.

11. For example, see Jeffrey M. Bradshaw, "Freemasonry and the Origins of Modern Temple Ordinances," 159–237.

12. Described in Samuel Morris Brown, "The Early Mormon Chain of Belonging," 1–52, but better known to Freemasons via Rob Morris as the "Bright Fraternal Chain."

Masonry's connection with Mormonism has largely been diminished to a historical footnote and to a few remaining but obvious ritual borrowings.

This loss slowly and quietly continued over the course of time, from the
move to the Great Basin up to the present day. This is evidenced by an 1884 Paris,
Idaho, Stake Conference question and answer session, when Stake President
William Budge was asked if elders of the Church were justified in performing
the rites and ceremonies of the Freemasons. He answered, "No! All the good
that may be found in such societies are found in the Gospel of Christ and what
do we want more?"[13] Such a rejection of Masonic influence upon the Church
was also exemplified in Apostle Anthony W. Ivins's 1934 response to Samuel H.
Goodwin's *Mormonism and Masonry*. In his work, Goodwin devotes some time
to describing certain symbols of Mormonism and, according to Ivins, "infers
that they are taken from Freemasonry."[14] Rejecting this, Ivins indignantly affirms that "the Church of Jesus Christ of Latter-day Saints was not influenced by
Masonry, either in its doctrines, organization, or the bringing forth of the Book
of Mormon."[15] For example, he insists that the all-seeing eye and clasped hands
"were at no time in general use" among the Latter-day Saints, or, if they were in
use, "have long since become obsolete." Ivins continues:

> There are not in the Salt Lake Temple, or any other temple of the Church, a series of
> stones, "in emblematical and significant designs," as stated [by Goodwin] . . . the few
> astrological figures which are engraved on the outside of the temple . . . are without
> significance to Church members.[16]

It is astounding that such well-known symbols could be so easily discounted.

As noted in the Introduction to this volume, this forgetting of Mormonism's
Masonic past was well under way by the time Apostle Franklin D. Richards travelled back to Nauvoo in 1885 to witness the pillars Jachin and Boaz on the
woodpile waiting to be burned. Only Richards's sharp eye caught the significance
of what had been discarded in a jumble on the trash-heap—the items were meaningless for later builders who removed the lodge-room story when renovating
the home. To Richards, this was a poignant indication of a loss of the Mormon
collective memory.

Richards's fears have been realized. Sharing the name of a large multi-purpose
room in modern Latter-day Saint meetinghouses that accommodate anything
from proms to basketball games, Nauvoo's restored Masonic Hall is now identified as "The Cultural Hall" with barely a nod to its Masonic functions. The
third-floor room where Nauvoo Lodge met thrice daily for over four years, where
hundreds of Mormon men were made Masons, is an open space with no Masonic

13. Paris, Idaho, Stake Minutes, May 3, 1884.
14. Anthony W. Ivins, *The Relationship of "Mormonism" and Freemasonry*, 87.
15. Ivins, 89.
16. Ivins, 92–93; see also Samuel H. Goodwin, *Mormonism and Masonry: Origins, Connections and Coincidences between Mason and Mormon Temple/Templar Ritual*, ch. 7.

furnishings. Visitors are informed by guides that here in this room, banquets and balls were held. The modern revisioning gives no insight into the original form and function of the Lodge's ritual space. Activities like dances and dinners would have been impossible given the Nauvoo-era Lodge furnishings, including an altar prominently placed in the center of the room. Despite refinishing, faint marks in the floor still bear witness to hundreds of Latter-day Saint men who circumambulated and then knelt at that altar to promise God to be good men and true.

Human beings reshape all that we inherit from the past according to our current needs and understandings. Sometimes, strict historical truthfulness is sacrificed in order to create a narrative that is whole, consistent, and meaningful. Such reconstruction of the history and relationship between Mormons and Freemasons is an adjustment brought about by the quite natural dislocations of our current faith and belief on these points.

In his book *Understanding Freemasonry*, Roy Wells explains that in a Master Mason's lodge a substitute is given for "that which was lost." This secret is "declared to be sanctioned and confirmed until time or circumstances shall restore the genuine." Only "patience and industry" can entitle the worthy Freemason to recover what has been lost:

> We all accept that Freemasonry is a system of morality veiled in allegory and illustrated by symbols, and that alone calls for some effort to understand not only what the ritual says but what it sets out to do. It certainly provides the tools but the application rests entirely with ourselves. The building of a Temple within ourselves commences when we begin to understand exactly what is "veiled in allegory and illustrated by symbols". The search for "that which was lost" began after Adam fell from favour and bequeathed to mankind that everlasting quest, for in every age there is that fall from grace.[17]

Because of the concerns about Freemasonry that existed in the post-Morgan United States, Mormonism, which embodied many of its ideas, was feared and rejected throughout the greater society. Yet history is not without a sense of irony. In the modern age Freemasonry itself, as it existed in the first sesquicentennial of this country, declined sharply, both in numbers and in influence. In order to survive, it too underwent a great transformation. Stephen Bullock writes of the slow return of the Fraternity following the heyday of Antimasonry in the 1830s:

> Antimasonry's success cannot be measured simply by the number of brothers who left or who returned. The movement's victory lay, rather, in its humbling of Masonic pretensions. Antimasons decisively demystified the order, making its secrets available for a few cents in a bookstore or a tavern and allowing people to voice a distaste that would have been unbecoming when Masonry seemed a central emblem of religion or the Republic. The destruction of brothers' openly expressed dreams of splendor and grandeur and the end of American society's willingness to credit post-Revolutionary Masonry's high claims allowed the fraternity to return—but only in another incarna-

---

17. Roy A. Wells, *Understanding Freemasonry*, 117–19.

"Ruins of the Temple at Nauvoo," from Frederick Piercy, *Route from Liverpool to Great Salt Lake Valley*, 1855.

tion. Just as the post-Revolutionary swelling of Masonry's numbers and pretensions shaped and energized Antimasonry, so the fires of opposition molded a new fraternity.[18]

Mormonism experienced the same after the martyrdom of Joseph Smith in July of 1844. The Theocratic Kingdom did not move to Texas; rather, it moved West one final time, sputtered, and finally gave up its aspirations for a political kingdom of God. Over the years the Latter-day Saints moved toward a slightly unconventional form of Christianity. The Church no longer retains the undergirding of a literal understanding of kingdom-building nor the social institutions that support it, but only the remnants of the institutions that Joseph engendered. His hope was that the Mormon kingdom would shatter all things to pieces, as prophesied by Daniel. Instead, its own radical ideas and practices were broken and scattered. Today The Church of Jesus Christ of Latter-day Saints no longer embodies the most beautiful nor the most feared ideas of Masonry.

Seeing that Mormonism has sustained such an exceedingly great loss, we have here attempted to "employ ourselves, by new works, to recover" Mormonism's early connection with Freemasonry, providing a key with which to view the shared past of Mormonism and Freemasonry in a way that is true and square.

---

18. Steven C. Bullock, *Revolutionary Brotherhood: Freemasonry and the Transformation of the American Social Order, 1730–1840*, 315–16.

BIBLIOGRAPHY

Abstract of Evidence Temple Lot Case. U.S.C.C. Independence, MO: Herald Publishing House, 1893.

Adair, James. *History of the American Indians; Particularly those Nations Adjoining to the Mississippi, East and West Florida, Georgia, South and North Carolina, and Virginia.* London, 1775.

Adamson, Henry. *The Muses Threnodie; or Mirthfull Mournings on the Death of Master Gal.* Edinburgh: King James College, 1638.

Adamson, Jack. "The Treasure of the Widow's Son." In *Joseph Smith and Masonry: No Help for the Widow's Son: Two Papers on the Influence of the Masonic Movement on Joseph Smith and His Mormon Church*, edited by Jack Adamson and Reed C. Durham, 3–12. Nauvoo, IL: Martin Publishing Company, 1980.

Addis, William Edward, and Thomas Arnold. *A Catholic Dictionary Containing Some Account of the Doctrine, Discipline, Rites, Ceremonies, Councils, and Religious Orders of the Catholic Church.* Catholic Publication Society Company, 1885.

"Address to Alexander Grant, Esq., Master of Lodge 93, and Past Grand Secretary of Bengal, etc." *The Freemason's Quarterly Review* (September 30, 1844): 349–50.

Albanese, Catherine. "The Metaphysical Joseph Smith." In *Joseph Smith Jr.: Reappraisals after Two Centuries*, edited by Reid L. Neilson and Terryl L. Givens, 65–72. Oxford University Press, 2008.

"Alexander Neibaur, Journal, 24 May 1844, extract." The Joseph Smith Papers, accessed December 3, 2021, https://www.josephsmithpapers.org/paper-summary/alexander -neibaur-journal-24-may-1844-extract.

Alighieri, Dante. *Inferno: First Book of the Divine Comedy*, translated by Allen Mandelbaum. Oakland: University of California Press, 1980.

Allaman, John Lee. "Policing in Mormon Nauvoo." *Illinois Historical Journal* 89, no. 2 (Summer 1996): 85–98.

Allen, James B. "Nauvoo's Masonic Hall." *John Whitmer Historical Association Journal* 10 (1990): 39–49.

Allyn, Avery. *A Ritual of Freemasonry: Illustrated by Numerous Engravings.* New York: William Gowans, 1853.

An Abstract of the Proceedings of the Antimasonic State Convention of Massachusetts, Held in Faneuil Hall, Boston, May 19 & 20, 1831. Boston: Office of the Boston Press, for the Publishing Committee, 1831.

"An Old Landmark Going." *The Carthage Republican* (November 8, 1891): 5.

Anderson, Devery S. "The Anointed Quorum 1842–1845." *Journal of Mormon History* 29, no. 2 (2003): 137–57.

———, ed. *The Development of LDS Temple Worship, 1846–2000: A Documentary History.* Salt Lake City, Signature Books, 2011.

Anderson, Devery S., and Gary James Bergera, eds. *Joseph Smith's Quorum of the Anointed, 1842–1845: A Documentary History.* Salt Lake City: Signature Books, 2005.

————, eds. *The Nauvoo Endowment Companies, 1845–1846: A Documentary History.* Salt Lake City: Signature Books, 2005.

Anderson, James. *The Constitutions of the Free-Masons, Containing the History, Charges, Regulations, &c. of that Most Ancient and Right Worshipful Fraternity.* London: William Hunter, 1723.

————. *The New Book of Constitutions of the Antient and Honourable Fraternity of Free and Accepted Masons, Containing their History, Charges, Regulations, &c., Collected and Digested by Order of the Grand Lodge from their Old Records, faithful Traditions, and Lodge-Books, for the Use of the Lodges.* London: Brothers Caesar Ward and Richard Chandler, 1738.

Anderson, Lavina Fielding, ed. *Lucy's Book: A Critical Edition of Lucy Mack Smith's Family Memoir.* Salt Lake City: Signature Books, 2001.

Anderson, Richard Lloyd. "The Mature Joseph Smith and Treasure Searching." *BYU Studies Quarterly* 24, no. 4 (Fall 1984): 489–560.

Andrew, Laurel B. *The Early Temples of the Mormons: The Architecture of the Millennial Kingdom in the American West.* Albany: State University of New York Press, 1978.

Angell, Truman O. Autobiography, 1884. Church History Library, accessed December 3, 2021, https://catalog.churchofjesuschrist.org/assets/a1e047c4-3a98-4f00-b661 -036344b4edcb/0/0.

Ankrom, Reg. "Once Upon a Time in Quincy: Jonas Was Father of Freemasonry in Illinois." *Quincy Herald-Whig,* August 2, 2015, https://www.whig.com/archive/ article/once-upon-a-time-in-quincy-jonas-was-father-of-freemasonry-in-illinois/ article_e7f579cd-bff5-54d1-a27c-740aa1c8bd9d.html.

"Appendix 1: Missouri Extradition Attempt, 1842–1843, Selected Documents, Introduction." The Joseph Smith Papers, accessed December 3, 2021, http://www.josephsmithpapers .org/paper-summary/appendix-1-missouri-extradition-attempt-1842-1843-selected -documents-introduction/1.

"Appendix 2: Constitution of the Society of the Daughter of Zion, circa Late June 1838." The Joseph Smith Papers, accessed September 17, 2021, https://www .josephsmithpapers.org/paper-summary/appendix-2-constitution-of-the-society -of-the-daughter-of-zion-circa-late-june-1838/1.

"Appendix 2: William Clayton, Journal Excerpt, 1–4 April 1843." The Joseph Smith Papers, accessed December 3, 2021, https://www.josephsmithpapers.org/paper -summary/appendix-2-william-clayton-journal-excerpt-1-4-april-1843.

"Appendix 3: Discourse, circa 4 July 1838." The Joseph Smith Papers, accessed December 3, 2021, https://www.josephsmithpapers.org/paper-summary/appendix-3-discourse -circa-4-july-1838.

Appleby, William I. Autobiography and Journal, 1848–1856. Church History Library, accessed December 3, 2021, https://catalog.churchofjesuschrist.org/assets/2268fba0 -a47f-4ae1-b1c3-9560b357e2c9/0/36.

Arrington, Leonard J. "Oliver Cowdery's Kirtland, Ohio, 'Sketch Book,'" *BYU Studies Quarterly* 12, no. 4 (1972): 410–26.

Ashurst-McGee, Mark. "A Pathway to Prophethood: Joseph Smith Junior as Rodsman, Village Seer, and Judeo-Christian Prophet." Master's Thesis, Utah State University, 2000.

Atwood, Henry Clinton. *The Master Workman; Or, True Masonic Guide: Containing Elucidations of the Fundamental Principles of Free-masonry, Operative and Speculative— Morally and Beneficially.* New York: Simons & Macoy, 1850.

Avery, Valeen Tippetts. "Emma, Joseph, and the Female Relief Society of Nauvoo: Unsuspected Arena for a Power Struggle." Paper presented at Mormon History Association annual meeting, Rexburg, ID, May 2, 1981.

Baer, Klaus. "The Breathing Permit of Hôr: A Translation of the Apparent Source of the Book of Abraham." *Dialogue: A Journal of Mormon Thought* 3, no. 3 (Autumn 1968): 109–34.

Ballou, Hosea. *A Sermon, Delivered at Montpelier, Before the Aurora Lodge of Free and Accepted Masons, at their Celebration of the Festival of St. John, the Evangelist, December 27th, A.L. 5805.* Randolph, VT: Sereno Wright, 1807.

———. *A Sermon, Delivered at Wilmington, Before the Mount Moriah Lodge of Free and Accepted Masons, at their Celebration of the Festival of St. John, the Baptist, June 24th, A.L. 5805.* Randolph, VT: Sereno Wright, 1805.

Bancroft, Hubert Howe. *History of Utah, 1540–1886.* San Francisco: The History Company Publishers, 1889.

Barker-Cryer, Neville. "The De-Christianizing of the Craft." *Ars Quatuor Coronathrum* 97 (1984): 34–60.

Barlow, Philip. *Mormons and the Bible: The Place of the Latter-day Saints in American Religion.* New York: Oxford University Press, 1991.

Barnes, Michael. "Spoilt for Choice," *MQ Magazine,* July 2004, 61–62, http://www.mqmagazine.co.uk/issue-10/p-61.php.

Bartholomew, Clinton. "Cipher in the Kirtland Snow: The Royal Arch Cipher and Joseph Smith's Conception of Ancient Languages." Paper given at the Mormon History Association Conference, May 2011.

Bateman, Daniel R. Statement, Midvale, UT, June 20, 1932. MS 4106, Church History Library.

Baugh, Alexander L. *A Call to Arms: The 1838 Mormon Defense of Northern Missouri.* Provo, UT: Joseph Fielding Smith Institute for Latter-day Saint History, 2000.

Beadle, John H. *Life in Utah; Or, The Mysteries and Crimes of Mormonism.* Philadelphia: National Publishing Company, 1870.

Beecher, Maureen Ursenbach, ed. "All Things Move in Order in the City: the Nauvoo Diary of Zina Diantha Huntington Jacobs." *BYU Studies* 19, no. 3 (Spring 1979): 285–320.

"Becoming Like God." The Church of Jesus Christ of Latter-day Saints, accessed October 18, 2021, https://www.churchofjesuschrist.org/study/manual/gospel-topics-essays/becoming-like-god.

Bennett, John C. "Astounding Disclosures! Letters from Gen. Bennett: For the Sangamo Journal, June 27, 1842." *Sangamo Journal* 10, no. 46 (July 8, 1842): 2.

———. "Gen. Bennett's 4th Letter, July 15, 1842." *Sangamo Journal* 10, no. 48 (July 22, 1842): 2.

———. "General Bennett's Third Letter, July 4, 1842." *Sangamo Journal* 10, no. 47 (July 15, 1842): 2.

———. *History of the Saints, or, An Exposé of Joe Smith and Mormonism.* Boston: Leland and Whiting, 1842.

Bentley, A. P. *History of the Abduction of William Morgan, and the Anti-Masonic Excitement of 1826–30.* Mt. Pleasant, IA: Van Cise and Throop, Free Press Office, 1874.

Bernard, David. *Light on Masonry: A Collection of All the Most Important Documents on the Subject of Speculative Free Masonry: Embracing the Reports of the Western Committees in Relation to the Abduction of William Morgan, etc.* Utica, NY: William Williams, Printer, 1829.

Bernauer, Barbara Hands. "Still 'Side by Side': The Final Burial of Joseph and Hyrum Smith." *The John Whitmer Historical Association Journal* 11 (1991): 17–33.

Berry, Robert. *The Bright Mason: An American Mystery.* Trenton, GA: Booklocker, 2008.

Bierce, Lucius V. "Hiram." *The Portage County Democrat* 31, no. 12 (February 15, 1860): 1–2.

Black, Susan Easton. "The Tomb of Joseph." In *The Disciple as Witness: Essays on Latter-day Saint History and Doctrine in Honor of Richard Lloyd Anderson,* edited by Stephen D. Ricks, Donald W. Parry, and Andrew H. Hedges, 36–46. Provo, UT: Neal A. Maxwell Institute for Religious Scholarship, 2000.

Bleak, James G. "Dedication of St. George Temple Site." *Millennial Star* 36, no. 16 (April 21, 1874): 252–55.

Bloom, Harold. *The American Religion: The Emergence of the Post-Christian Nation.* New York: Simon & Shuster, 1992.

Blythe, Christopher James. "Recreating Religion: The Response to Joseph Smith's Innovations in the Second Prophetic Generation of Mormonism." MA Thesis, Utah State University, 2011.

———. "'The Upper Room Work': Esotericism in the Church of Jesus Christ (Cutlerite), 1853–1912." *Journal of Mormon History* 40, no. 3 (Summer 2014): 43–92.

"Book of Abraham and Facsimiles, 1 March–16 May 1842." The Joseph Smith Papers, accessed October 18, 2021, https://www.josephsmithpapers.org/paper-summary/book-of-abraham-and-facsimiles-1-march-16-may-1842.

"Book of Commandments, 1833." The Joseph Smith Papers, accessed December 3, 2021, https://www.josephsmithpapers.org/paper-summary/book-of-commandments-1833/.

Book of the Law of the Lord. Church of Jesus Christ of Latter Day Saints, accessed December 6, 2021, https://www.ldsstrangite.com/uploads/2/0/9/4/20947834/book_of_the_law_of_the_lord_1.pdf.

Book of the Scarlet Line: Heroines of Jericho. Richmond, VA: Macoy Publishing, 1948.

Booker, Helen Hawley. *Life Story of John P. Hawley.* Iowa Falls: General Publishing and Binding, 1972.

Bowen, Norman R., ed. *A Gentile Account of Life in Utah's Dixie: Elizabeth Kane's St. George Journal.* Salt Lake City: University of Utah Tanner Trust Fund, 1995.

Bradley, Don. "'The Grand Fundamental Principles of Mormonism': Joseph Smith's Unfinished Reformation." *Sunstone,* April 2006, 32–41.

———. *The Lost 116 Pages: Reconstructing the Book of Mormon's Missing Stories.* Salt Lake City: Greg Kofford Books, 2019.

Bradley, Don, and Mark Ashurst-McGee. "Joseph Smith and the Kinderhook Plates." In *A Reason for Faith: Navigating LDS Doctrine and Church History,* edited by Laura Harris Hales, 93–115. Salt Lake City and Provo, UT: Deseret Book and BYU Religious Studies Center, 2016.

Bradley, Joshua. *Some of the Beauties of Free-masonry.* Rutland, VT: Fay and Davison, 1816.

Bradshaw, Jeffrey M. "Freemasonry and the Origins of Modern Temple Ordinances." *Interpreter: A Journal of Latter-day Saint Faith and Scholarship* 15 (2015): 159–237.

Bradshaw, Jeffrey M., and David J. Larsen. "The Vision of Moses as a Heavenly Ascent." In Jeffrey M. Bradshaw, *Temple Themes in the Book of Moses*, 23–50. Salt Lake City: Eborn Publishing, 2010.

"Brethren Are Hereby Notified, The." *Times and Seasons* 3, no. 1 (November 1, 1841): 585.

Brewster, James Colin. *Very Important! To the Mormon Money Diggers*. Springfield, IL: 1843.

Briggs, J. W. "J. W. Briggs Letters." *The Return* 4, no. 21 (December 1895): 2–3.

Brodie, Fawn McKay. *No Man Knows My History: The Life of Joseph Smith*. New York: Vintage Books, 1995.

Brodsky, Michael L. "Why was the Craft De-Christianized?" *Ars Quatuor Coronaturum* 99 (1986).

Brooke, John L. *The Refiner's Fire: The Making of Mormon Cosmology, 1644–1844*. New York: Cambridge University Press, 1994.

Brown, Lisle G. *Nauvoo Sealings, Adoptions, and Anointings: A Comprehensive Register of Persons Receiving LDS Temple Ordinances, 1841–1846*. Salt Lake City: The Smith-Pettit Foundation, 2006.

———. "'Temple Pro Tempore': The Salt Lake City Endowment House." *Journal of Mormon History* 34, no. 4 (2008): 1–68.

Brown, Matthew B. *Exploring the Connection between Mormons and Masons*. American Fork, UT: Covenant Communications, 2009.

———. "Of Your Own Selves Shall Men Arise." *FARMS Review of Books* 10, no. 1 (1998): 97–131.

Brown, Samuel Morris. "The Early Mormon Chain of Belonging." *Dialogue: A Journal of Mormon Thought* 44, no. 1 (Spring 2011): 1–52.

———. *In Heaven as It Is on Earth: Joseph Smith and the Early Mormon Conquest of Death*. New York: Oxford University Press, 2012.

Browne, George Waldo, ed. *Early Records of the Town of Derryfield, now Manchester, N.H.*, 2 vols. Manchester, NH: John B. Clarke Co., 1905.

Browne, John. *Browne's Masonic Master-Key through the Three Degrees, by Way of Polyglot. Under the Sanction of the Craft in General*, 2nd ed. London, 1802.

Bruno, Cheryl L. "Congruence and Concatenation in Jewish Mystical Literature, American Freemasonry, and Mormon Enoch Writings." *Journal of Religion and Society* 16 (September 2014): 1–19.

———. "Keeping a Secret: Freemasonry, Polygamy, and the Nauvoo Relief Society, 1842–44." *Journal of Mormon History* 39, no. 4 (Fall 2013): 158–81.

———. "The Melodious Sounds of Baneemy's Organ." *John Whitmer Historical Association Journal* 34, no. 1 (Spring/Summer 2014): 151–76.

———. "Strangite Masonry and the Order of Illuminati." *Journal of Mormon History* 47, no. 3 (July 2021): 1–21.

Buerger, David John. "'The Fullness of the Priesthood': The Second Anointing in Latter-day Saint Theology and Practice." *Dialogue: A Journal of Mormon Thought* 16 (1983): 10–44.

———. *The Mysteries of Godliness: A History of Mormon Temple Worship*. San Francisco: Smith Research Associates, 1994.

Bullamore, George W. "The Beehive and Freemasonry." *Ars Quatuor Coronatorum* 36 (1923): 219–46.

Bullock, Steven C. *Revolutionary Brotherhood: Freemasonry and the Transformation of the American Social Order, 1730–1840*. Chapel Hill: University of North Carolina Press, 1996.

Bunyan, John. *Solomon's Temple Spiritualized, or, Gospel-light Brought out of the Temple at Jerusalem, to Let Us More Easily into the Glory of New-Testament Truths*. London, 1688.

Burton, Richard F. *The City of the Saints, and Across the Rocky Mountains to California*. New York: Harper & Brothers, 1862.

Bushman, Richard L. *Joseph Smith and the Beginnings of Mormonism*. Chicago: University of Illinois Press, 1984.

———. *Joseph Smith—Rough Stone Rolling: A Cultural Biography of Mormonism's Founder*. New York: Alfred A. Knopf, 2005.

Butterfield, Kevin. "The Right to Be a Freemason: Secret Societies and the Power of the Law in the Early Republic." *Common-Place: The Journal of Early American Life* 12, no. 1 (October 2011), http://commonplace.online/article/the-right-to-be-a-freemason/.

Calcott, Wellins. *A Candid Disquisition of the Principles and Practices of the Most Ancient and Honorable Society of Free and Accepted Masons*. London: James Dixwell, 1769.

Caldwell, Michael R. *The John Johnson Family of Hiram, Ohio: For He Is a Descendant of Joseph*. Denver, Co: Outskirts Press, 2016.

Campbell, Alexander. "Delusions." *Millennial Harbinger* 2, no. 2 (February 7, 1831): 85–96.

Cannon, Donald Q. "The King Follett Discourse: Joseph Smith's Greatest Sermon in Historical Perspective." *BYU Studies* 18, no. 2 (1978): 179–92.

———. "Spokes on the Wheel: Early Latter-day Saint Settlements in Hancock County." *Ensign*, February 1986, 62–68.

Cannon, E. J. "Masonic." *Friendship Register* (July 18, 1876). Typescript at Uncle Dale's Readings in Early Mormon History, accessed December 6, 2021, http://www.sidneyrigdon.com/dbroadhu/NY/miscNYS5.htm.

Carlile, Richard. *Manual of Freemasonry: In Three Parts. With an Explanatory Introduction to the Science, and a Free Translation of some of the Sacred Scripture Names*. London: Andrew Vickers, 1855.

———. "To William Williams, Esq., M. P. Provincial Grand Master for the County of Dorset of the Association of Freemasons. Letter II." *The Republican* 12, no. 4 (July 15, 1825): 33–51.

———. "To William Williams, Esq., M. P. Provincial Grand Master of the Association of Freemasons for the Country of Dorset. Letter IV." *The Republican* 12, no. 4 (July 29, 1825): 105–27.

Carnes, Mark C. *Secret Ritual and Manhood in Victorian America*. New Haven, CT: Yale University Press, 1989.

Carr, Harry, ed. *The Early Masonic Catechisms*, 2nd ed. London: Quatuor Coronati Lodge, 1975.

———. *The Freemason at Work*, 7th and rev ed. Runnymede, Eng.: Ian Allan Printing, 1992.

———, ed. *Le Parfait Maçon or The Genuine Secrets of the four Grades of Apprentices, Fellows, ordinary & Ecossois Masters of Freemasonry*. Pub. 1744, reprinted in *The Early French Exposures*, edited by Harry Carr. London: The Quatuor Coronati Lodge No. 2076, 1971.

Carr, Robin L. *Freemasonry and Nauvoo 1839–1846*. Normal, IL: Masonic Book Club, 1989.

Carruth, LaJean Purcell, and Mark Lyman Staker. "John Taylor's June 27, 1854, Account of the Martyrdom." *BYU Studies* 50, no. 3 (2011): 25–62.

Carruth, LaJean Purcell, and Robin Scott Jensen. "Sidney Rigdon's Plea to the Saints: Transcription of Thomas Bullock's Shorthand Notes from the August 8, 1844, Morning Meeting." *BYU Studies Quarterly* 53, no. 2 (2014): 121–39.

Carter, Gideon. Statement, February 27, 1894. Church History Library, accessed December 6, 2021, https://catalog.churchofjesuschrist.org/assets/d75f9b0a-0165 -43c3-b52d-6e6fe2c76eb0/0/0.

Carter, James Davis. *Masonry in US History—through 1846.* Waco, TX: Grand Lodge of Texas A.F. & A.M, 1955.

Cartwright, Peter. *Autobiography of Peter Cartwright: The Backwoods Preacher.* Cincinnati: L. Swormstedt and A. Poe, 1859.

Castells, F. de P. *Antiquity of the Holy Royal Arch: The Supreme Degree in Freemasonry.* London: A. Lewis, 1960.

———. *Genuine Secrets in Freemasonry Prior to AD 1717.* London: A. Lewis, 1930.

———. *Historical Analysis of the Holy Royal Arch Ritual.* London: A. Lewis, 1929.

"Celebration of the 4th of July." *Elders' Journal* 1, no. 4 (August 1838): 60.

Census for 1820. Washington, DC: Gales & Seaton, 1821.

Ceremonials Compiled for use of Lodges Working under Jurisdiction of the M.W. Grand Lodge of Free and Accepted Masons of the State of Illinois. Freeport, IL: Journal Power Press and Bindery, 1893.

"Charles C. Rich biographical information, circa 1906." Church History Library, accessed June 25, 2021, https://catalog.churchofjesuschrist.org/assets/4932cbc0 -519c-4c2d-b23c-d03b7e61a614/0/0.

Church of Jesus Christ of Latter-day Saints, The. *Saints: The Story of the Church of Jesus Christ in the Latter Days, Volume 1: The Standard of Truth 1815–1846.* Salt Lake City: The Church of Jesus Christ of Latter-day Saints, 2018.

"'Church History,' 1 March 1842." The Joseph Smith Papers, accessed December 3, 2021, https://www.josephsmithpapers.org/paper-summary/church-history-1-march -1842/1.

Citizen of Massachusetts, A. *Free Masonry: A Poem. In Three Cantos.* Leicester: Samuel A. Whittemore, 1830.

Claret, George. *The Whole Craft of Free-Masonry,* 2nd ed. London: G. Claret, 1841.

Clarke, Adam. *The Holy Bible, Containing the Old and New Testaments. A Commentary and Critical Notes Designed as a Help to a Better Understanding of the Sacred Writings. Volume 1: Genesis to Deuteronomy.* Baltimore: John J. Harrod, 1834.

Claudy, Carl H. *Introduction to Freemasonry.* 3 vols. Washington, DC: The Temple Publishers, 1963. First published in 1931.

Clegg, Robert Ingham. *Mackey's History of Freemasonry,* vol. 2. Chicago: The Masonic History Co., 1921.

Coil, Henry Wilson. *Coil's Masonic Encyclopedia,* revised by Allen E. Roberts. Richmond, VA: Macoy Publishing and Masonic Supply Co., Inc., 1996.

Cole, Samuel. *The Freemasons' Library and General Ahiman Rezon: Containing a Delineation of the True Principles of Freemasonry, Speculative and Operative, Religious and Moral.* Baltimore: Benjamin Eder, 1817.

Collier, Fred C. *The Teachings of President Brigham Young, Vol. 3, 1852–1854.* Salt Lake City: Collier's Publishing Co., 1987.

Compton, Todd. *In Sacred Loneliness: The Plural Wives of Joseph Smith.* Salt Lake City: Signature Books, 1997.

"Conference Minutes: Continuation of Last April's Conference." *Times and Seasons* 5, no. 15 (August 15, 1844): 612–17.

Cooke, Matthew, ed. *The History and Articles of Masonry*. London, 1861.

Corrill, John. *A Brief History of the Church of Christ of Latter Day Saints (Commonly Called Mormons) Including an Account of Their Doctrine and Discipline, with the Reasons of the Author for Leaving the Church*. St. Louis, 1839.

"Council of Fifty, Minutes, March 1844–January 1846; Volume 1, 10 March 1844–1 March 1845." The Joseph Smith Papers, accessed December 3, 2021, https://www.josephsmithpapers.org/paper-summary/council-of-fifty-minutes-march-1844-january-1846-volume-1-10-march-1844-1-march-1845/1.

"Council of Fifty, Minutes, March 1844–January 1846; Volume 2, 1 March–6 May 1845." The Joseph Smith Papers, accessed December 3, 2021, https://www.josephsmithpapers.org/paper-summary/council-of-fifty-minutes-march-1844-january-1846-volume-2-1-march-6-may-1845/1.

"Covenant, or Oath of the Illuminati." Beinecke Library, Yale University, New Haven, CT.

Cowdery, Oliver. Diary, January-March 1836. Church History Library, accessed December 6, 2021, https://catalog.churchofjesuschrist.org/assets/d11962ee-4618-4177-90aa-aa72cedc0f98/0/26.

Cowdery, Oliver. "Egyptian Mummies—Ancient Records." *The Latter Day Saints' Messenger and Advocate* II, no. 3 (December 1835): 233–37.

———. Letter to Brigham Young, February 27, 1848. Church History Library, accessed December 6, 2021, https://catalog.churchofjesuschrist.org/assets/4db552ae-c90c-411e-8b15-11792500395d/0/0.

———. Letter to Lyman Cowdery, January 13, 1834. Book of Abraham Project—Oliver Cowdery Letters, accessed September 1, 2021, http://www.boap.org/LDS/Early-Saints/Letters-cowdery.html.

———. "Letter to W. W. Phelps." *Latter Day Saints' Messenger and Advocate* 2, no. 1 (October 1835): 195–202.

Crocheron, Augusta Joyce. *Representative Women of Deseret: A Book of Biographical Sketches to Accompany the Picture Bearing the Same Title*. Salt Lake City: J.C. Graham and Co., 1884.

Cross, Jeremy L. *The True Masonic Chart, or Hieroglyphic Monitor*, 4th ed. New Haven, CT: T. G. Woodward and Co., 1826.

Cross, Whitney R. *The Burned-Over District: The Social and Intellectual History of Enthusiastic Religion in Western New York, 1800–1850*. New York: Cornell University Press, 1982.

Crossee, Philip. "The Baal's Bridge Square." *The Builder Magazine* 15, no. 12 (December 1929). Typescript at The Phoenixmasonry Masonic Museum and Library, accessed December 6, 2021, http://www.phoenixmasonry.org/the_builder_1929_december.htm.

Cryer, Neville Barker. *The Royal Arch Journey*. Hersham, Surrey: Ian Allan Publishing, Ltd., 2009.

Cummings, Horace H. "True Stories from My Journal." *Juvenile Instructor* 64, no. 8 (August 1929): 440–41.

D'Olivet, Fabret. *The Hebraic Tongue Restored: And the True Meaning of the Hebrew Words Re-established and Proved by their Radical Analysis*, trans. Nayan Louise Redfield. New York: G. P. Putnam's Sons, 1921.

Dafoe, Stephen, ed. The Masonic Dictionary Project, accessed September 16, 2021, http://www.masonicdictionary.com/.

———. *Morgan: The Scandal that Shook Freemasonry.* New Orleans: Cornerstone Publishing, 2009.

Daniels, William M. *A Correct Account of the Murder of Generals Joseph and Hyrum Smith at Carthage on the 27th day of June, 1844.* Nauvoo, IL: John Taylor, 1845.

Darowski, Joseph F. "Schools of the Prophets: An Early American Tradition." *Mormon Historical Studies* 9, no. 1 (Spring 2008): 1–13.

Davis, George T. M. *An Authentic Account of the Massacre of Joseph Smith, the Mormon Prophet, and Hyrum Smith, His Brother, Together with a Brief History of Rise and Progress of Mormonism, and All the Circumstances Which Led to Their Death.* St. Louis, MO: Chambers and Knapp, 1844.

Davis, Robert G. *The Mason's Words: The History and Evolution of the American Masonic Ritual.* Guthrie, OK: Building Stone Publishing, 2013.

de Hoyos, Arturo, trans. and ed. *Albert Pike's Esoterika: The Symbolism of the Blue Degrees of Freemasonry.* Washington, DC: Scottish Rite Research Society, 2014.

———. *Albert Pike's Morals and Dogma of the Ancient and Accepted Scottish Rite of Freemasonry, Annotated Edition.* Washington, DC: Supreme Council, 33°, S.J., 2011.

———. *Freemasonry's Royal Secret: The Jamaican "Francken Manuscript" of the High Degrees.* Washington, DC: Scottish Rite Research Society, 2005.

———. *Light on Masonry: The History and Rituals of America's Most Important Masonic Exposé.* Washington, DC: Scottish Rite Research Society, 2008.

———. "The Mistery of the Royal Arch Word." *Pietre-Stones Review of Freemasonry* 2 (1993): http://www.freemasons-freemasonry.com/royal_arch_word.html.

de Hoyos, Arturo, and S. Brent Morris, trans. and ed. *The Most Secret Mysteries of the High Degrees of Masonry Unveiled, or The True Rose-Croix, Translated from the English, Followed by Noachite, Translated from the German. From the First Edition of 1766.* Originally edited by M. de Berage. Washington, D.C.: The Scottish Rite Research Society, 2005.

"Dear Sirs:—I Send You a Plate with an Engraved Likeness of T. C. Sharp." *Nauvoo Neighbor* 2, no. 29 (November 13, 1844): 2.

"Death of Hon. Sidney Rigdon." *Jamestown Journal* 51, no. 112 (July 21, 1876). Typescript at Uncle Dale's Readings in Early Mormon History, accessed December 6, 2021, http://www.sidneyrigdon.com/dbroadhu/NY/miscNYS5.htm#072176.

"Death of our Beloved Brother Willard Richards." *Deseret News* 4, no. 9 (March 16, 1854): 2.

Deci, Ted. "The Short But Eventful Story of Mt. Moriah Lodge No. 112 F.A.M." Unpublished paper in authors' possession, 1975.

Dennis, Geoffrey. "Tzohar: Gem of Noah, Light of Heaven." Jewish Myth, Magic and Mysticism, official blog for *The Encyclopedia of Jewish Myth, Magic, and Mysticism*, April 2, 2014, http://ejmmm2007.blogspot.com/2008/10/tzohar-miraculous -light-of-noah-window.html.

Denslow, William R. *10,000 Famous Freemasons*, 4 vols. Richmond, VA: Macoy Publishing & Masonic Supply Co., 1957.

Dermott, Laurence. *Ahiman Rezon, Or a Help to All that Are (or Would Be) Free and Accepted Masons: Containing The Quintessence of All that Has Been Publish'd on the Subject of Free Masonry*, 2nd ed. London: Robert Black, 1764.

Dickson, Moses. *Revised Landmarks and Ceremonies of Courts of Heroines of Jericho*. Cairo: IL: E. A. Burnett, 1884.

Dinger, John S., ed. *The Nauvoo City and High Council Minutes*. Salt Lake City: Signature Books, 2011.

"Difficulties at Nauvoo—the Other Side of the Story—John C. Bennett—'Spiritual Wives,' &c. &c., The." *Quincy Whig* 5, no. 12 (July 16, 1842): 2.

"Discourse, 1 May 1842, as Reported by Willard Richards." The Joseph Smith Papers, accessed December 3, 2021, http://www.josephsmithpapers.org/paper-summary/discourse-1-may-1842-as-reported-by-willard-richards.

"Discourse, 11 June 1843–A, as Reported by Franklin D. Richards." The Joseph Smith Papers, accessed December 3, 2021, http://www.josephsmithpapers.org/paper-summary/discourse-11-june-1843-a-as-reported-by-franklin-d-richards.

"Discourse, 27 August 1843, as Reported by Franklin D. Richards." The Joseph Smith Papers, accessed December 3, 2021, https://www.josephsmithpapers.org/paper-summary/discourse-27-august-1843-as-reported-by-franklin-d-richards.

"Discourse, 27 June 1839, as Reported by Willard Richards." The Joseph Smith Papers, accessed December 3, 2021, http://www.josephsmithpapers.org/paper-summary/discourse-27-june-1839-as-reported-by-willard-richards.

"Discourse, 7 April 1844, as Reported by Thomas Bullock." The Joseph Smith Papers, accessed December 3, 2021, https://www.josephsmithpapers.org/paper-summary/discourse-7-april-1844-as-reported-by-thomas-bullock.

"Discourse, 7 April 1844, as Reported by Willard Richards." The Joseph Smith Papers, accessed December 3, 2021, https://www.josephsmithpapers.org/paper-summary/discourse-7-april-1844-as-reported-by-willard-richards.

"Discourse, 7 April 1844, as Reported by William Clayton." The Joseph Smith Papers, accessed December 3, 2021, http://www.josephsmithpapers.org/paper-summary/discourse-7-april-1844-as-reported-by-william-clayton.

"Discourse, between circa 26 June and circa 4 August 1839–A, as Reported by Unknown Scribe." The Joseph Smith Papers, accessed December 3, 2021, https://www.josephsmithpapers.org/paper-summary/discourse-between-circa-26-june-and-circa-4-august-1839-a-as-reported-by-unknown-scribe/.

"Discourse, between circa 26 June and circa 4 August 1839–A, as Reported by Willard Richards." The Joseph Smith Papers, accessed Jun 27, 2021, https://www.josephsmithpapers.org/paper-summary/discourse-between-circa-26-june-and-circa-4-august-1839-a-as-reported-by-willard-richards.

"Dismissal of Dr. Oliver." *The Freemason's Quarterly Review* 9, no. 2 (June 30, 1842): 119–20.

"Doctrine and Covenants, 1835." The Joseph Smith Papers, accessed December 3, 2021, https://www.josephsmithpapers.org/paper-summary/doctrine-and-covenants-1835.

"Doctrine and Covenants, 1844." The Joseph Smith Papers, accessed December 3, 2021, https://www.josephsmithpapers.org/paper-summary/doctrine-and-covenants-1844.

Document Containing the Correspondence, Orders, &c. in Relation to the Disturbances With the Mormons; and the Evidence Given Before the Hon. Austin A. King, Judge of the Fifth Judicial Circuit of the State of Missouri, at the Court-House in Richmond, in a Criminal Court of Inquiry Begun November 12, 1838, on the Trial of Joseph Smith, Jr., and Others, for High Treason and Other Crimes Against the State. Fayette, MO: Office of the Boon's Lick Democrat, 1841.

Doesburg, Jacob O. *Freemasonry Illustrated. The Complete Ritual of the First Seven Masonic Degree*. Chicago: Ezra A. Cook, 1916.

Dorchester, Daniel. "St. John's Rod." *The Christian Standard* 14 (July 26, 1879): 235.

Douglas, Charles [Elvira Field]. "Secret Societies." *Gospel Herald* (Baltimore) 6, no. 39 (December 13, 1849): 212–15.

Driver, Tom F. *Liberating Rites: Understanding the Transformative Power of Ritual*. Boulder, CO: Westview Press, 1998.

Duncan, Malcolm C. *Duncan's Masonic Ritual and Monitor or Guide to the Three Symbolic Degrees of the Ancient York Rite and to the Degrees of Mark Master, Past Master, Most Excellent Master, and the Royal Arch*. 3rd ed. New York: Dick & Fitzgerald, 1866.

Durham, Reed C. Jr. "Is There No Help for the Widow's Son?" Presidential Address presented at the Mormon History Association Annual Conference, Nauvoo, IL, April 20, 1974.

Dyer, Colin. *Symbolism in Craft Freemasonry*. Hersham, Surrey: Lewis Masonic, 2006.

Early Records of the Grand Chapter of the State of Vermont—1804 to 1850 Inclusive. Burlington: Free Press, 1878.

Early Records of the Grand Lodge of Vermont, F. & A. M., From 1794 to 1846 Inclusive. Burlington: The Free Press Association, 1879.

Eastman, Luke. *Masonick Melodies*. Boston: Ev T. Rowe, 1818.

"Ecclesiastical Items." *The United Presbyterian Magazine* (February 1859): 91–92.

Ehat, Andrew F. "'It Seems Like Heaven Began on Earth': Joseph Smith and the Constitution of the Kingdom of God." *BYU Studies Quarterly* 20, no. 3 (Spring 1980): 253–80.

———. "Joseph Smith's Introduction of Temple Ordinances and the 1844 Succession Question." MA Thesis, Brigham Young University, 1981.

———. "'They Might Have Known That He Was Not a Fallen Prophet'—The Nauvoo Journal of Joseph Fielding." *BYU Studies Quarterly* 19, no. 2 (Winter 1979): 133–66.

Eitel, Gustav A. "The Baltimore Convention." *The Builder Magazine* 2, no. 11 (November 1916). Typescript at The Phoenixmasonry Masonic Museum and Library, accessed December 6, 2021, http://www.phoenixmasonry.org/the_builder_1916_november .htm.

Eliade, Mircea. *Myth and Reality*. New York: Harper Colophon Books, 1963.

Emeline. "Mormon Endowments." *Warsaw Signal* 3, no. 3 (April 15, 1846): 2.

Emerson, Edgar C., ed. *Our County and Its People: A Descriptive Work on Jefferson County New York*. New York: The Boston History Company, 1898.

England, Eugene, ed. "George Laub's Nauvoo Journal." *BYU Studies Quarterly* 18, no. 2 (1978): 151–78.

Esplin, Ronald K. "Life in Nauvoo, June 1844: Vilate Kimball's Martyrdom Letters." *BYU Studies Quarterly* 19, no. 2 (1979): 231–40.

Evans, Henry R. *Cagliostro and His Egyptian Rite of Freemasonry*. Lafayette, LA: Cornerstone Book Publishers, 2003.

"Explanation of Facsimile 2, circa 15 March 1842." The Joseph Smith Papers, accessed December 3, 2021, https://www.josephsmithpapers.org/paper-summary/explanation -to-accompany-facsimile-2-circa-15-march-1842/1.

Finney, Charles G. *The Character, Claims, and Practical Workings of Freemasonry*. Cincinnati: Western Tract and Book Society, 1869.

Flatow, Alisa M., and Adina Anflick. "Guide to the Papers of the Seixas Family, undated, 1746–1911, 1926, 1939." Center for Jewish History, American Jewish Historical Society, accessed June 3, 2021, https://archives.cjh.org//repositories/3/resources/13255.

Fletcher, Rupert J. and Daisy Whiting Fletcher. *Alpheus Cutler and the Church of Jesus Christ.* Independence, MO: The Church of Jesus Christ, 1974.

Ford, Thomas. *A History of Illinois, from Its Commencement as a State in 1814 to 1847.* Chicago: S. C. Griggs & Co., 1854.

———. "Message from the Governor, in Relation to the Disturbances in Hancock County." *Nauvoo Neighbor* 2, no. 35 (January 1, 1845): 1–2.

Forsberg, Clyde R., Jr. *Divine Rite of Kings: Land, Same Sex and Empire in Mormonism and the Esoteric Tradition.* Newcastle upon Tyne, UK: Cambridge Scholars Publishing, 2016.

———. *Equal Rites: The Book of Mormon, Masonry, Gender, and American Culture.* New York: Columbia University Press, 2004.

Fort, George F. *The Early History and Antiquities of Freemasonry, as Connected with Ancient Norse Guilds, and the Oriental and Medieval Building Fraternities.* Rev. ed. Philadelphia: Bradley & Company, 1881.

Friend to the Mormons. "Mr. Editor." *Times and Seasons* 5, no. 6 (March 15, 1844): 476–77.

Frisbie, Barnes. *The History of Middletown, Vermont, In Three Discourses Delivered Before the Citizens of That Town, February 7 and 21, and March 30, 1867.* Rutland, VT: Tuttle and Co., 1867.

G. S. R. "Lifting the Vail." *Salt Lake Daily Tribune* 17, no. 139 (September 28, 1879): 4.

Gardner, A. "Mummies." *Painesville Telegraph* 6, no. 40 (March 27, 1835). Typescript at Uncle Dale's Readings in Early Mormon History, accessed December 6, 2021, http://www.sidneyrigdon.com/dbroadhu/OH/paintel4.htm#032735.

Gardner, Gerald B. "Drawing Down the Moon." Internet Sacred Text Archive—Gardnerian Book of Shadows, accessed September 22, 2021, https://www.sacred-texts.com/pag/gbos/gbos01.htm.

Gates, Susa Young. "The Open Door for Woman." *Young Women's Journal* 16 (1905): 117.

Gee, John. *An Introduction to the Book of Abraham.* Salt Lake City and Provo, UT: Deseret Book and BYU Religious Studies Center, 2017.

Gentry, Leland H. "The Danite Band of 1838." *BYU Studies Quarterly* 14, no. 4 (Summer 1974): 421–50.

Gentry, Leland H., and Todd M. Compton. *Fire and Sword: A History of the Latter-day Saints in Northern Missouri, 1836–39.* Salt Lake City: Greg Kofford Books, 2011.

"George Oliver, Early Masonic Writer." *The New Age* 63, no. 4 (April 1955): 245.

Giddins, Edward. *Anti Masonic Almanac for the year 1831.* Utica, NY: William Williams, 1831.

Givens, Terryl L., and Brian M. Hauglid. *The Pearl of Greatest Price: Mormonism's Most Controversial Scripture.* New York: Oxford University Press, 2019.

Givens, Terryl L., and Matthew J. Grow. *Parley P. Pratt: The Apostle Paul of Mormonism.* New York: Oxford University Press, 2011.

Goddard, M. E., and Henry V. Partridge. *A History of Norwich Vermont.* Hanover: The Dartmouth Press, 1905.

Godfrey, Kenneth W. "Causes of Mormon Non-Mormon Conflict in Hancock County, Illinois, 1839–1846." Ph.D. diss., Brigham Young University, 1967.

———. "Freemasonry in Nauvoo." In *Encyclopedia of Mormonism,* 4 vols., edited by Daniel H. Ludlow. New York: MacMillan, 1992, 2:527–28.

"Gold Bible, No. 4." *Palmyra Reflector* 2, no. 13 (February 14, 1831): 100–101.

Goodwin, Samuel H. *Mormonism and Masonry: Origins, Connections and Coincidences between Mason and Mormon Temple/Templar Ritual.* Salt Lake City: Grand Lodge F&M of Utah, 1920.

Gould, Hallie M. "Like Sheep that Went Astray: Concerning the Cutlerite Faction of the Church that Went North During the Dark and Cloudy Day." *Autumn Leaves* 34, no. 2 (Feb 1921): 49–55.

"Grammar and Alphabet of the Egyptian Language, circa July–circa November 1835." The Joseph Smith Papers. https://www.josephsmithpapers.org/paper-summary/grammar-and-alphabet-of-the-egyptian-language-circa-july-circa-november-1835.

Grand Lodge of the Most Ancient and Honorable Fraternity of Free and Accepted Masons of the State of Ohio at its Several Grand Communications from 1808 to 1847, Inclusive, The. Columbus: Follett, Foster and Company, 1857.

Green, Henry, ed. *Whitney's "Choice of Emblemes," A Fac-simile Reprint.* London: Lovell, Reeve & Co., 1866.

Green, Nelson Winch. *Fifteen Years among the Mormons; Being the Narrative of Mrs. Mary Ettie V. Smith, Late of Great Salt Lake City.* New York: H. Dayton, 1859.

Greene, Samuel D. *The Broken Seal: or, Personal Reminisces of the Morgan Abduction and Murder.* Chicago: Ezra Cook and Co., 1878.

Gressmen, Asher. Letter to Levi Moffett, November 6, 1844. Church History Library, accessed December 6, 2021, https://catalog.churchofjesuschrist.org/assets/8cf459d2-c43d-4dc3-8158-c0cbf51ce272/0/0.

Groat, Joel B. "Occultic and Masonic Influence in Early Mormonism." Institute for Religious Research, August 3, 2011, http://mit.irr.org/occultic-and-masonic-influence-in-early-mormonism.

Grunder, Rick. *Mormon Parallels: A Bibliographic Source.* Lafayette, NY: Rick Grunder Books, 2014.

Guthrie, Charles Snow. *Kentucky Freemasonry, 1788–1978: The Grand Lodge and the Men Who Made It.* Grand Lodge of Kentucky, F&AM, 1981.

Hackett, David G. *That Religion in Which All Men Agree: Freemasonry in American Culture.* Berkeley: University of California Press, 2014.

Hales, Brian C. *Joseph Smith's Polygamy.* 3 vols. Salt Lake City: Greg Kofford Books, 2013.

Hall, Manly P. *A Encyclopedic Outline of Masonic, Hermetic, Qabbalistic and Rosicrucian Symbolical Philosophy, Being an Interpretation of the Secret Teachings Concealed within the Rituals, Allegories, and Mysteries of all Ages.* 7th ed. Los Angeles: Philosophical Research Society, 1945.

———. *Freemasonry of the Ancient Egyptians, to which is added an Interpretation of the Crata Repoa Initiation Rite.* Los Angeles: Philosophical Research Society, 1965.

———. *The Lost Keys of Freemasonry: The Legend of Hiram Abiff.* 2nd ed. Los Angeles: Hall Publishing Co., 1924.

Halliwell, James Orchard. *The Early History of Freemasonry in England.* London: Thomas Rodd, 1840.

Hamblin, William J., and David Rolph Seely. *Solomon's Temple: Myth and History.* London: Thames and Hudson Ltd., 2007.

Hamilton, William R., et. al. "History." In *By-Laws of Hancock Lodge #20, Free and Accepted Masons.* Carthage, Illinois: n.p., 1890.

Hansen, Klaus J. "The Metamorphosis of the Kingdom of God: Toward a Reinterpretation of Mormon History." In *The New Mormon History: Revisionist Essays on the Mormon Past*, edited by D. Michael Quinn, 221–46. Salt Lake City: Signature Books, 1992.

Hardie, James. *The New Free-Mason's Monitor; or, Masonic Guide. For the Direction of Members of that Ancient and Honourable Fraternity, as well as for the Information of Those, who may be Desirous of Becoming Acquainted with its Principles.* New York: George Long, 1818.

Hardy, John. *The Trials of Elder John Hardy, before the Church of Latter Day Saints in Boston, for Slander, in Saying that G. J. Adams, S. Brannan and Wm Smith were Licentious Characters.* Boston: Conway & Company, 1844.

Harris, Earl D. "An Outline of Rules of Order (Parliamentary Procedure) for use in Georgia Masonic Lodges." MELD: The Grand Lodge of Georgia Free and Accepted Masons, revised 1990, http://mason33.org/content/us/glofga/images/MELD-StudyGuides/RulesofOrder.pdf.

Harris, James R. *The Facsimiles of the Book of Abraham: A Study of the Joseph Smith Egyptian Papyri.* Payson, UT: Harris House, 1990.

Harrison, David. *The Genesis of Freemasonry.* London: Lewis Masonic, 2014.

Hartley, William G. "Mormons and Early Iowa History (1838 to 1858): Eight Distinct Connections." *The Annals of Iowa* 59, no. 3 (Summer 2000): 217–60.

Hatch, John P., ed. *Danish Apostle: The Diaries of Anthon H. Lund, 1890–1921.* Salt Lake City: Signature Books, 2006.

Hauglid, Brian M. "The Book of Abraham and the Egyptian Project: 'A Knowledge of Hidden Languages.'" In *Approaching Antiquity: Joseph Smith and the Ancient World*, edited by Lincoln H. Blumell, Matthew J. Grey, and Andrew H. Hedges, 474–511. Provo, UT: Religious Studies Center, 2015.

Hawley, John. *Autobiography of John Hawley.* Miscellaneous Letters and Papers, P13, f317, Community of Christ Archives, Independence, MO.

Hayden, A. S. *Early History of the Disciples in the Western Reserve, Ohio.* Cincinnati: Chase & Hall, 1875.

Haywood, Harry L. "How Operative Masonry Changed to Speculative Masonry: The Period of Transition." *The Builder Magazine* 10, no. 2 (February 1924). Typescript at The Phoenixmasonry Masonic Museum and Library, accessed December 6, 2021, http://www.phoenixmasonry.org/the_builder_1924_february.htm.

———. *Symbolical Masonry: An Interpretation of the Three Degrees.* Kingsport, TN: Southern Publishers, Inc., 1923.

Heath, Steven H. "The Sacred Shout." *Dialogue: A Journal of Mormon Thought* 19, no. 3 (Fall 1986): 115–23.

"Henry G. Sherwood statements, circa 1854." Church History Library, accessed December 3, 2021, https://catalog.churchofjesuschrist.org/assets/7d357a6c-30e1-4658-ae18-d9bb0daa5241/0/0.

Henry, Matthew, and Thomas Scott. *A Commentary upon the Holy Bible from Henry and Scott: Genesis to Deuteronomy.* London: The Religious Tract Society, 1836.

Hill, Donna. *Joseph Smith, the First Mormon.* New York: Doubleday, 1977.

Hill, Marvin S. *Quest for Refuge: The Mormon Flight from American Pluralism.* Salt Lake City: Signature Books, 1989.

Hill, Marvin C., Keith Rooker, and Larry T. Wimmer. "The Kirtland Economy Revisited: A Market Critique of Sectarian Economics." *BYU Studies Quarterly* 17, no. 4 (Summer 1977): 391–476.

Hills, Gustavus. "Minutes of a Special Conference." *Times and Seasons* 4, no. 21 (September 15, 1843): 329–32.

———. "Nauvoo Lyceum," *Nauvoo Neighbor* 1, no. 31 (November 29, 1843): 2.

"History, 1834–1836." The Joseph Smith Papers, accessed December 3, 2021, http://www.josephsmithpapers.org/paper-summary/history-1834-1836.

"History, 1838–1856, volume A-1 [23 December 1805–30 August 1834]." The Joseph Smith Papers, accessed December 3, 2021, http://josephsmithpapers.org/paperSummary/history-1838-1856-volume-a-1-23-december-1805-30-august-1834.

"History, 1838–1856, volume B-1 [1 September 1834–2 November 1838]." The Joseph Smith Papers, accessed December 3, 2021, https://www.josephsmithpapers.org/paper-summary/history-1838-1856-volume-b-1-1-september-1834-2-november-1838.

"History, 1838–1856, volume C-1 [2 November 1838–31 July 1842]." The Joseph Smith Papers, accessed December 3, 2021, http://josephsmithpapers.org/paperSummary/history-1838-1856-volume-c-1-2-november-1838-31-july-1842.

"History, 1838–1856, volume C-1 Addenda." The Joseph Smith Papers, accessed December 3, 2021, http://www.josephsmithpapers.org/paper-summary/history-1838-1856-volume-c-1-addenda.

"History, 1838–1856, volume D-1 [1 August 1842–1 July 1843]." The Joseph Smith Papers, accessed December 3, 2021, http://www.josephsmithpapers.org/paper-summary/history-1838-1856-volume-d-1-1-august-1842-1-july-1843.

"History, 1838–1856, volume E-1 [1 July 1843–30 April 1844]." The Joseph Smith Papers, accessed December 3, 2021, http://www.josephsmithpapers.org/paper-summary/history-1838-1856-volume-e-1-1-july-1843-30-april-1844.

"History, 1838–1856, volume F-1 [1 May 1844–8 August 1844]." The Joseph Smith Papers, accessed December 3, 2021, https://www.josephsmithpapers.org/paper-summary/history-1838-1856-volume-f-1-1-may-1844-8-august-1844.

"History, circa June 1839–circa 1841 [Draft 2]." The Joseph Smith Papers, accessed December 3, 2021, https://www.josephsmithpapers.org/paper-summary/history-circa-june-1839-circa-1841-draft-2.

History of Audrain County, Missouri. St. Louis: National Historical Company, 1884.

"History of Brigham Young." *The Latter-Day Saints' Millennial Star* 30, no. 26 (July 23, 1864): 470–72.

"History of Friendship, The." Copy located in Arlene Hess, "Collected Materials Relative to Sidney Rigdon and his Descendants and Other Subjects Used in Preparation for the History of Friendship, New York." Harold B. Lee Library, Brigham Young University, Provo, Utah.

"History of Joseph Smith. Tuesday, 10th." *The Latter-Day Saints' Millennial Star* 15, no. 27 (July 2, 1853): 423–24.

History of Pickaway Lodge No. 23 Free and Accepted Masons. Circleville, OH: n.p., Sept. 2, 1975.

Hogan, Mervin B. *The Dedication of the Nauvoo Masonic Temple and the Strange Question of Dr. Goforth.* Salt Lake City: n.p., 1983.

———. *The Founding Minutes of Nauvoo Lodge U.D.* Des Moines, IA: Research Lodge No. 2, 1971.

———. "John Cook Bennett and Pickaway Lodge No. 23." Mervin B. Hogan Papers, J. Willard Marriot Library, University of Utah.

———. "Nauvoo Lodge at Work." Mervin B. Hogan Papers, University of Utah Library.

———. *The Official Minutes of Nauvoo Lodge, U.D.* Des Moines, IA: Research Lodge No. 2, 1974.

Holbrook, Josiah. *American Lyceum, or Society for the Improvement of Schools and Diffusion of Useful Knowledge.* Boston: Perkins and Marvin, 1829.

Holley, Orville Luther. *An Address Delivered at the Request of the Mount Moriah Lodge at Palmyra.* Palmyra: T. C. Strong, 1822.

Holm, James B., ed. *Portage Heritage.* Ravenna, OH: Portage Co. Historical Society, 1957.

Homer, Michael W. *Joseph's Temples: The Dynamic Relationship between Freemasonry and Mormonism.* Salt Lake City: The University of Utah Press, 2014.

———. "'Similarity of Priesthood in Masonry': The Relationship between Freemasonry and Mormonism." *Dialogue: A Journal of Mormon Thought* 27, no. 3 (Fall 1994): 1–116.

Horne, Alex. *Sources of Masonic Symbolism.* Richmond, VA: Macoy Publishing and Masonic Supply Co., 1981.

Hornung, Erik. *The Secret Lore of Egypt: Its Impact on the West.* Translated by David Lorton. Ithaca and London: Cornell University Press, 2001.

Howe, Eber D., *Mormonism Unvailed: Or, a Faithful Account of that Singular Imposition and Delusion, from Its Rise to the Present Time.* Painesville, OH: Howe, 1834.

———. "Our Neighbor-in-law." *Painesville Telegraph* 2, no. 40 (March 22, 1831): 2.

Hullinger, Robert N. *Joseph Smith's Response to Skepticism.* Salt Lake City: Signature Books, 1992.

Hulse, Rocky. *When Salt Lake City Calls: Is There a Conflict between Mormonism and the Public Trust?* Maitland, FL: Xulon Press, 2007.

Huntington, Dimick B. "Statement of Dimick B. Huntington, December 12, 1878, Salt Lake City." Zina Y. Card Papers, Archives and Manuscripts, Harold B. Lee Library, Brigham Young University, Provo, Utah.

Huntington, Oliver. "History of the Life of Oliver B. Huntington, Also His Travels & Troubles / Written by Himself, 1843–1844." Harold B. Lee Library, accessed December 6, 2021, https://contentdm.lib.byu.edu/digital/collection/SCMisc/id/25593.

———. Journal, Volume 2, 1845–1846. Harold B. Lee Library, accessed December 6, 2021, https://contentdm.lib.byu.edu/digital/collection/SCMisc/id/27903.

———. Journal, Volume 13, 1858–1880. Harold B. Lee Library, accessed December 6, 2021, https://contentdm.lib.byu.edu/digital/collection/SCMisc/id/26292.

Hutchens, Rex R. *A Bridge to Light.* Washington, DC: Supreme Council, 33°, 1988.

Hutchinson, Anthony A. "A Mormon Midrash? LDS Creation Narratives Reconsidered." *Dialogue: A Journal of Mormon Thought* 21, no. 4 (Winter 1988): 11–74.

Hutchinson, William. *The Spirit of Masonry: In Moral and Elucidatory Lectures.* London, 1775.

Hyde, Orson, *Ein Ruf aus der Wüste (A Cry out of the Wilderness).* Frankfurt: Im Selbsverlage des Verfassers, 1842. English translation extract by Marvin H. Folson at The Joseph Smith Papers, accessed December 6, 2021, https://www.josephsmithpapers.org/paper-summary/orson-hyde-ein-ruf-aus-der-wste-a-cry-out-of-the-wilderness-1842-extract-english-translation.

Hyde, Orson, George A. Smith, and Ezra T. Benson. "A Report to Brigham Young, Heber C. Kimball, Willard Richards, and the Authorities of the Church of Jesus Christ of Latter Day Saints in Zion." March 14–April 5, 1849. Church History Library, accessed December 6, 2021, https://catalog.churchofjesuschrist.org/assets/3aad7abf-bf52-4480-99c9-b7594c06a805/0/0.

Hymns of The Church of Jesus Christ of Latter-day Saints. Salt Lake City: The Church of Jesus Christ of Latter-day Saints, 1985.

"In the Ante-Room." *The American Tyler* 18, no. 20 (April 15, 1904): 452–53.

"Installation Meetings, etc: Humber Lodge No. 57." *The Freemason's Chronicle: A Weekly Record of Masonic Intelligence* 27, no. 678 (January 7, 1888): 4.

"Interview, 29 August 1843, Extract." The Joseph Smith Papers, accessed August 16, 2021, https://www.josephsmithpapers.org/paper-summary/interview-29-august-1843 -extract/1.

Introvigne, Massimo. "Arcana Arcanorum: Cagliostro's Legacy in Contemporary Magical Movements." *Journal of Alternative Religion and Culture* 1, no. 2 (1992): 117–35.

Ivins, Anthony W. *The Relationship of "Mormonism" and Freemasonry.* Salt Lake City: The Deseret News Press, 1934.

Jachin and Boaz; or, An Authentic Key to the Door of Free-Masonry. London: St. Paul's Church-Yard, 1762.

Jackman, Levi. *A Short Sketch of the Life of Levi Jackman.* Huntington Library, accessed on December 7, 2021, https://hdl.huntington.org/digital/collection/p16003coll15/id/1591. Typescript at Book of Abraham Project, accessed December 7, 2021, http://www.boap.org/LDS/Early-Saints/LJackman.html.

Jacob, Margaret C. *Living the Enlightenment: Freemasonry and Politics in Eighteenth-Century Europe.* New York: Oxford University Press, 1991.

Jacob, Norton. Journal, 1844 May–1852 January. Church History Library, accessed December 7, 2021, https://catalog.churchofjesuschrist.org/assets/267ee8cd-06d9 -4265-b057-ba35027a7274/0/0.

Jensen, Anthony K. "Philosophy of History." Internet Encyclopedia of Philosophy, accessed June 22, 2021, http://www.iep.utm.edu/history/.

Jensen, Robin Scott. "Gleaning the Harvest: Strangite Missionary Work, 1846–1850." MA Thesis, Brigham Young University, 2005.

Jenson, Andrew. *Latter-day Saint Biographical Encyclopedia.* 4 vols. Salt Lake City, 1901–1936. Reprint Salt Lake City, Greg Kofford Books, 2012.

———. "Plural Marriage." *Historical Record* 6 (July 1887): 232–33.

Jessee, Dean C., ed. "Joseph Knight's Recollection of Early Mormon History." *BYU Studies Quarterly* 17, no. 1 (Autumn 1976): 29–39.

Jessee, Dean C. and David J. Whittaker, eds. "The Last Months of Mormonism in Missouri: The Albert Perry Rockwood Journal Edited." *BYU Studies Quarterly* 28, no. 1 (Winter 1988): 5–34.

"John Whitmer, History, 1831–circa 1847." The Joseph Smith Papers, accessed December 3, 2021, https://www.josephsmithpapers.org/paper-summary/john-whitmer-history -1831-circa-1847.

Johnson, Benjamin F. *My Life's Review: The Autobiography of Benjamin F. Johnson.* Provo: Grandin Book Company, 1997.

Johnson, Charles W. *The Nature of Vermont: Introduction and Guide to a New England Environment.* Hanover, NH: University Press of New England, 1980.

Johnson, Melvin C. *Polygamy on the Pedernales: Lyman Wight's Mormon Villages in Antebellum Texas, 1845 to 1858*. Logan, UT: Utah State University Press, 2006.

———. "'So We Built a Good Little Temple to Worship In': Mormonism on the Pedernales—Texas, 1847–1851." *The John Whitmer Historical Association Journal* 22 (2002): 89–98.

———. "Wightites in Wisconsin: The Formation of a Dissenting Latter Day Community (1842–1845)." *John Whitmer Historical Association Journal* 32, no. 1 (Spring/Summer 2012): 63–78.

Johnstun, Joseph D. "'To Lie in Yonder Tomb': The Tomb and Burial of Joseph Smith." *Mormon Historical Studies* 6, no. 2 (Fall 2005): 163–80.

———. "William Vorhease and the Murder of Joseph Smith." *The John Whitmer Historical Association Journal* 35, no. 1 (Spring/Summer 2015): 38–61.

Jonas, Abraham. Letter to George Miller, May 4, 1842. Letters Pertaining to Freemasonry in Nauvoo, 1842, Church History Library, accessed December 7, 2021, https://catalog.churchofjesuschrist.org/assets/ea8928d0-d2ae-4373-9410-083cc11689a7/0/0.

Jones, Bernard E. *Freemason's Book of the Royal Arch*. 2nd ed. Revised by Harry Carr and A. R. Hewett. London: Harrap, 1969.

Jones, Dan, and Ronald D. Dennis. "The Martyrdom of Joseph Smith and his Brother Hyrum." *BYU Studies* 24, no. 1 (Winter 1984): 78–109.

Jorgensen, Danny L. "Conflict in the Camps of Israel: The 1853 Cutlerite Schism." *Journal of Mormon History* 21, no. 1 (1995): 25–64.

———. "The Fiery Darts of the Adversary: An Interpretation of Early Cutlerism." *John Whitmer Historical Association Journal* 10 (1990): 67–83.

———. "The Morley Settlement in Illinois, 1839–1846." *The John Whitmer Historical Association Journal* 32, no. 2 (Fall/Winter 2012): 149–70.

"Joseph Smith History, circa Summer 1832." The Joseph Smith Papers, accessed December 3, 2021, http://josephsmithpapers.org/paperSummary/history-circa-summer-1832.

Josephus, Flavius. *Antiquities of the Jews*. Early Jewish Writings, accessed September 1, 2021, http://www.earlyjewishwritings.com/josephus.html.

Joslin, Gary James. *Saint Masons: The Divine Restoration and Freemasonry*. San Diego: Washington Institute for Graduate Studies, 1994.

"Journal, 1835–1836." The Joseph Smith Papers, accessed December 3, 2021, https://www.josephsmithpapers.org/paper-summary/journal-1835-1836.

"Journal, December 1841–December 1842." The Joseph Smith Papers, accessed December 3, 2021, http://www.josephsmithpapers.org/paper-summary/journal-december-1841-december-1842.

"Journal, December 1842–June 1844; Book 1, 21 December 1842–10 March 1843." The Joseph Smith Papers, accessed December 3, 2021, http://www.josephsmithpapers.org/paper-summary/journal-december-1842-june-1844-book-1-21-december-1842-10-march-1843.

"Journal, December 1842–June 1844; Book 2, 10 March 1843–14 July 1843." The Joseph Smith Papers, accessed August 31, 2021, https://www.josephsmithpapers.org/paper-summary/journal-december-1842-june-1844-book-2-10-march-1843-14-july-1843.

"Journal, December 1842–June 1844; Book 3, 15 July 1843–29 February 1844." The Joseph Smith Papers, accessed December 3, 2021, http://www.josephsmithpapers.org/paper-summary/journal-december-1842-june-1844-book-3-15-july-1843-29-february-1844.

"Journal, December 1842–June 1844; Book 4, 1 March–22 June 1844." The Joseph Smith Papers, accessed December 3, 2021, http://www.josephsmithpapers.org/paper-summary/journal-december-1842-june-1844-book-4-1-march-22-june-1844.

"Journal, March–September 1838." The Joseph Smith Papers, accessed December 3, 2021, https://www.josephsmithpapers.org/paper-summary/journal-march-september-1838.

Journal of Discourses. 26 vols. London and Liverpool: LDS Booksellers Depot, 1854–86.

Keller, Karl, ed. "'I Never Knew a Time when I did not Know Joseph Smith': A Son's Record of the Life and Testimony of Sidney Rigdon." *Dialogue: A Journal of Mormon Thought* 1, no. 4 (1966): 15–42.

Kelley, William H. "The Hill Cumorah, and the Book of Mormon." *The Saints' Herald* 28, no. 11 (June 1, 1881): 161–68.

Khayyám, Omar. *The Rubáiyát of Omar Khayyám, the Astronomer-Poet of Persia*. Translated by Edward FitzGerald. Springfield, MA: Will Bradley, 1897.

"Killing of Pratt—Letter from Mr. McLean, The." *Daily Alta California* 9, no. 179 (July 9, 1857): 2.

Kimball, Heber C. "History of Brigham Young." *The Latter-Day Saints' Millennial Star* 26 (August 6, 1864): 503–4.

———. Journal, 1842 September, 1844 May – 1845 May. Church History Library, accessed December 7, 2021, https://catalog.churchofjesuschrist.org/assets/1c66d65a-8781-4476-b3dc-a12c6db39174/0/0.

———. Letter to Parley P. Pratt, June 17, 1842. Church History Library, accessed June 22, 2021, https://catalog.churchofjesuschrist.org/assets/707c7146-38a5-41e6-98d8-1cad8d89bcc5/0/1.

Kimball, James L., Jr. "The Nauvoo Charter: A Reinterpretation." In *Kingdom on the Mississippi Revisited: Nauvoo in Mormon History*, edited by Roger D. Launius and John E. Hallwas, 39–47. Chicago: University of Illinois Press, 1996.

Kimball, Stanley B. *Heber C. Kimball: Mormon Patriarch and Pioneer*. Chicago: University of Illinois Press, 1981.

———. "Nauvoo West: The Mormons of the Iowa Shore." *BYU Studies Quarterly* 18, no. 2 (Winter 1978): 132–42.

———, ed. *On the Potter's Wheel: The Diaries and Journals of Heber C. Kimball*. Salt Lake City: Signature Books, 1987.

King, Thomas Starr. "Oration by Rev. Thos. Starr King. Delivered before the Grand Lodge of Free and Accepted Masons of California, at its Annual Communication, May, A. L. 5863." In *Representative and Leading Men of the Pacific*, edited by Oscar Tully Shuck, 211–18. San Francisco: Bacon and Company, 1870.

Kline, Julius Reynolds. "Some Things an Entered Apprentice Should Know." *Masonic Voice-Review* 16, no. 3 (March 1914): 72–73.

Kozak, Gayle. Email to Joe Steve Swick III. December 18, 2017.

Kraut, Ogden, ed. *L. John Nuttall: Diary Excerpts*. Salt Lake City: Pioneer Press, 1994.

Kuruvilla, T. T. "The Excellent Masters' Degree (Passing The Veils)—A Link Between The Craft And The Holy Royal Arch." Masonicpaedia.org, July 15, 2006, http://masonicpaedia.org/showarticle.asp?id=219.

"Ladies' Relief Society." *Times and Seasons* 3, no. 11 (April 1, 1842): 743.

Larson, A. Karl, and Katharine Miles Larson, eds. *Diary of Charles Lowell Walker*. 3 vols. Logan: Utah State University Press, 1980.

Larson, Stan, ed. *A Ministry of Meetings: The Apostolic Diaries of Rudger Clawson*. Salt Lake City: Signature Books in association with Smith Research Associates, 1993.

Launius, Roger D. "The Murders in Carthage: Non-Mormon Reports of the Assassination of the Smith Brothers." *John Whitmer Historical Association Journal* 15 (1995): 17–34.

Launius, Roger D., and John E. Hallwas. *Kingdom on the Mississippi Revisited: Nauvoo in Mormon History*. Chicago: University of Illinois Press, 1996.

Lectures of the Three Degrees in Craft Masonry, The. Rev. ed. London: A. Lewis, 1874.

Lee, John D. Journals, May 1844–November 1846. Church History Library, accessed September 21, 2021, https://catalog.churchofjesuschrist.org/assets/0ffa29ec-9981-4230-8252-29af13e59726/0/0.

———. *Mormonism Unveiled; Or The Life and Confessions of the Late Mormon Bishop, John D. Lee; (Written by Himself)*. Edited by W. W. Bishop. St. Louis: Bryan, Brand & Company, 1877.

Lee, Samuel. *Orbis Miraculum, or, The Temple of Solomon Pourtrayed by Scripture-light Wherein All Its Famous Buildings, the Pompous Worship of the Jewes, with Its Attending Rites and Ceremonies, the Several Officers Employed in that Work, with Their Ample Revenues, and the Spiritual Mysteries of the Gospel Vailed Under All, Are Treated at Large*. Ann Arbor: University of Michigan Digital Library Production Service, 2011. Typescript of the 1659 original.

Leigh, William. *The Ladies' Masonry: Or, Hieroglyphic Monitor*. Louisville, KY, 1851.

LeSueur, Stephen C. *The 1838 Mormon War in Missouri*. Columbia, University of Missouri Press, 1987.

———. "The Danites Reconsidered: Were They Vigilantes or Just the Mormons' Version of the Elks Club?" *The John Whitmer Historical Association Journal* 14 (1994): 35–51.

"Letter from Alanson Ripley, 10 April 1839." The Joseph Smith Papers, accessed December 3, 2021, https://www.josephsmithpapers.org/paper-summary/letter-from-alanson-ripley-10-april-1839.

"Letter from Don Carlos Smith, circa Late May 1838." The Joseph Smith Papers, accessed December 3, 2021, https://www.josephsmithpapers.org/paper-summary/letter-from-don-carlos-smith-circa-late-may-1838/1.

"Letter to Israel Daniel Rupp, 5 June 1844." The Joseph Smith Papers, accessed December 3, 2021, https://www.josephsmithpapers.org/paper-summary/letter-to-israel-daniel-rupp-5-june-1844.

"Letter to the Church and Edward Partridge, 20 March 1839." The Joseph Smith Papers, accessed December 3, 2021, http://www.josephsmithpapers.org/paper-summary/letter-to-the-church-and-edward-partridge-20-march-1839/.

"Letter to the Saints Abroad, 24 May 1841." The Joseph Smith Papers, accessed December 3, 2021, https://www.josephsmithpapers.org/paper-summary/letter-to-the-saints-abroad-24may-1841.

"Letter to William W. Phelps, 11 January 1833." The Joseph Smith Papers, accessed December 3, 2021, https://www.josephsmithpapers.org/paper-summary/letter-to-william-w-phelps-11-january-1833.

"Letterbook 1." The Joseph Smith Papers, accessed June 27, 2021, https://www.josephsmithpapers.org/paper-summary/letterbook-1.

"Levi Richards, Journal, 11 June 1843, Extract." The Joseph Smith Papers, accessed December 3, 2021, https://www.josephsmithpapers.org/paper-summary/levi-richards-journal-11-june-1843-extract.

Lewis, Joseph, and Hiel Lewis. "Mormon History: A New Chapter, About to be Published." *Amboy Journal* 24, no. 5 (Apr. 30, 1879): 1. Typescript at Uncle Dale's Readings in Early Mormon History, accessed December 6, 2021, http://www.sidneyrigdon.com/dbroadhu/IL/miscill3.htm#043079.

Lewiston Committee. *A Narrative of the Facts and Circumstances Related to the Kidnapping and Murder of William Morgan.* Chicago: Ezra A. Cook & Co., 1827.

Lindsay, Jeff. "An Overview of the Danites and the Church in Missouri." LDS FAQ: Mormon Answers, last updated June 13, 2008, http://www.jefflindsay.com/LDSFAQ/FQ_Missouri.shtml.

Lisonbee, Dan A. *Far West Missouri: It Shall Be Called Most Holy.* Springville, UT: Cedar Fort, 2010.

Literski, Nicholas S. "Joseph Smith's Masonic Tutors." Unpublished paper presented at the Mormon History Association Conference, 2004, in Provo, UT.

———. "Where is our Good Master Joseph?" Paper presented at John Whitmer Historical Association Conference, September 29–August 2, 2005, Springfield, IL.

Littlefield, Lyman O. "Communicated." *Nauvoo Neighbor* 1, no. 47 (March 20, 1844): 2.

"Lodge of Fortitude No. 281, Lancaster. Festival of St. John the Baptist and Presentation to Bro. Dr. Moore." *The Freemason* (July 6, 1872): 409.

Lucinda Morgan Harris Patriarchal Blessing. Copy in authors' possession.

"Lucius N. Scovil statement, circa 1854–1856." Church History Library, accessed December 3, 2021, https://catalog.churchofjesuschrist.org/assets/2175562f-7a0b-4e19-a85c-70ade680b018/0/0.

Lundwall, N. B. *Fate of the Persecutors of the Prophet Joseph Smith: Being a Compilation of Historical Data on the Personal Testimony of Joseph Smith [. . .].* Salt Lake City: Bookcraft, 1952.

M. A. "A Swindling Saint." *The Daily Inter Ocean* 4, no. 127 (August 20, 1875): 5.

Mac, R. W. "Mormonism in Illinois. No. III." *The American Whig Review* 9, No. 6 (June 1852): 524–34.

MacBride, Andrew Sommerville. *Speculative Masonry: Its Mission, Its Evolution, and Its Landmarks.* New York: George H. Doran Co, 1924.

Mace, Wandle. *Autobiography of Wandle Mace.* Typescript. Harold B. Lee Library, Brigham Young University, Provo, UT.

Mackay, Lachlan. "A Brief History of the Smith Family Nauvoo Cemetery." *Mormon Historical Studies* 3, no. 2 (Fall 2002): 241–52.

Mackenzie, Kenneth, ed. *The Royal Masonic Cyclopaedia of History, Rites, Symbolism, and Biography.* London: John Hogg, Paternoster Row, 1877.

Mackey, Albert Gallatin. *The History of Freemasonry: Its Legendary Origins.* New York: Dover Publications, 2008. Reprint of an 1898 edition.

———. *A Lexicon of Freemasonry; Containing a Definition of all its Communicable Terms, Notices of its History, Traditions, and Antiquities, and an Account of all the Rites and Mysteries of the Ancient World.* London and Glasgow: Richard Griffin and Company, 1860.

———. *The Symbolism of Freemasonry: Illustrating and Explaining its Science and Philosophy, its Legends, Myths, and Symbols.* New York: Clark and Maynard, 1869.

———. *A Text Book of Masonic Jurisprudence; Illustrating the Written and Unwritten Laws of Freemasonry.* New York: Clark & Maynard, Publishers, 1872.

———. *A Text-Book Illustrating the Written and Unwritten Laws of Freemasonry.* 7th ed. Chicago: Masonic History Company, 1857.

Mackey, Albert G., William J. Hughan, and Edward L. Hawkins. *An Encyclopedia of Freemasonry and Its Kindred Sciences, Comprising the Whole Range of Arts, Sciences and Literature as Connected with the Institution.* New and rev. ed. 2 vols. New York: The Masonic History Company, 1913.

MacNulty, W. Kirk. *Freemasonry: Symbols, Secrets, Significance.* London: Thames & Hudson Ltd., 2006.

———. *The Way of the Craftsman: A Search for the Spiritual Essence of Craft Freemasonry.* London: Central Regalia Ltd., 2002.

Macoy, Robert. *Adoptive Rite Ritual: A Book of Instruction in the Organization, Government and Ceremonies of Chapters of the Order of the Eastern Star.* Rev. ed. New York: Masonic Publishing Co. 1897.

———. *Adoptive Rite Ritual: Instruction, Organization, Government and Ceremonies of Order of the Eastern Star, Queen of the South, Administrative Degree, Installation, Dedication of Hall, Chapter of Sorrow, Burial Service.* Rev. ed. Richmond, VA: Macoy Publishing & Masonic Supply Co., 1998.

———, comp. *The Masonic Vocal Manual.* New York: Robt Macoy, 1859.

Markham, Stephen. Letter to Wilford Woodruff, June 20, 1856. Church History Library, accessed December 7, 2021, https://catalog.churchofjesuschrist.org/assets/67261bd7-29dc-44d0-b2b6-9d4b0148ceb3/0/0.

Marks, C. R. "Monona County, Iowa, Mormons." *Annals of Iowa* 7, no. 5 (April 1906): 321–46.

Marks, William. "Epistle." *Zion's Harbinger and Baneemy's Organ* 3, no. 7 (July 1853): 53.

Marples, James A. "Brother Fredersigk Madison Smith, Past Master; 32° Mason; and an Ordained Minister." Societas Rosicruciana In Civitatibus Foederatis, accessed December 7, 2021, http://www.masonic.benemerito.net/msricf/papers/marples/marples-frederick.madison.smith.pdf.

Marquardt, H. Michael. "Ezra Booth on Early Mormonism: A Look at his 1831 Letters." *John Whitmer Historical Association Journal* 28 (2008): 65–87.

———. *The Rise of Mormonism: 1816–1844.* Longwood, FL: Xulon Press, 2005.

Marshall, George L., Jr. "Reverend Jonathan Nye, 2nd Grand Master of the Grand Encampment 1829–1835." Knight Templar, September 29, 2014, https://www.knightstemplar.org/pgeo/mepgm/2.html.

"Masonic Hall." *Loraine County News* 7, no. 368 (March 20, 1867): 3.

Masonic Information Center, "Statement on Freemasonry and Religion." Masonic Service Association of North America, accessed November 12, 2020, http://www.msana.com/religion.asp.

"Masonic Notice." *Warsaw Message* 1, no. 2 (January 14, 1843): 2.

Masonic Services Association of North America. "What is Freemasonry?" 11th District of New Jersey, last revised July 7, 2016, http://www.mastermason.com/11th-district -of-nj/What%20is%20Freemasonry.htm.

"Masonry." Church History Topics, The Church of Jesus Christ of Latter-day Saints, accessed December 3, 2021, https://www.churchofjesuschrist.org/study/history/ topics/masonry.

"Masonry in the Great Light." *Short Talk Bulletin* 12, no. 6 (June 1934), online at http:// www.themasonictrowel.com/masonic_talk/stb/stbs/34-06.htm.

Mataraly, F. V. "The Spiritual Significance of Some of Our Symbols." The Skirret, accessed September 20, 2020, https://skirret.com/archive/dormer/spiritual_significance_ of_some_of_our_symbols.html.

Matthews, Robert J. "Joseph Smith Translation of the Bible (JST)." In *Encyclopedia of Mormonism*, 4 vols., edited by Daniel H. Ludlow, 2:765. New York: Macmillan Publishing Company, 1991.

May, Dean. "A Demographic Portrait of the Mormons, 1830–1980." In *The New Mormon History: Revisionist Essays on the Mormon Past*, edited by D. Michael Quinn, 121– 35. Salt Lake City: Signature Books, 1992.

May, Gerhard. *Creatio Ex Nihilo: The Doctrine of 'Creation out of Nothing' in Early Christian Though*. Translated by A. S. Worrall. London: T&T Clark International, 2004.

McCain, Nancy. "Recollections of Nancy McCain." Unpublished manuscript. Ontario County Historical Society, Canandaigua, NY.

McCarthy, Charles. *The Antimasonic Party: A Study of Political Antimasonry in the United States, 1827–1840*. Madison: University of Wisconsin, 1902.

McClellan, Richard. "Sidney Rigdon's 1820 Ministry: Preparing the Way for Mormonism in Ohio." *Dialogue: A Journal of Mormon Thought* 36, no. 4 (Winter 2003): 151–59.

McClenachan, Charles T. *The Book of the Ancient and Accepted Scottish Rite of Freemasonry: Containing Instructions in All the Degrees from the Third to the Thirty-third, and Last Degree of the Rite*. New York: Masonic Publishing and Manufacturing Co, 1868.

McCoy, Robert. *The Masonic Manual, A Pocket Companion for the Initiated: Containing the Rituals of Freemasonry Embraced in the Degrees of the Lodge Chapter and Encampment*. New York: Clark and Maynard, 1867.

McGavin, E. Cecil. *Historical Background of the Doctrine and Covenants*. Salt Lake City: Paragon Printing Company, 1949.

———. *Mormonism and Masonry*. Salt Lake City: Bookcraft, 1949.

McLeod, Wallace, ed. *The Old Gothic Constitutions*. Bloomington, IL: The Masonic Book Club, 1985.

McNamara, Robert. "American Lyceum Movement." ThoughtCo, updated October 31, 2018, https://www.thoughtco.com/american-lyceum-movement-1773297.

Metcalfe, Brent Lee. Correspondence with Authors, December 29, 2013. In authors' possession.

———. "Whence and Whither the Five Points of Fellowship? Being a Treatise on the Evolution of the Embrace from 1696 to 1990." Mormon Scripture Studies, accessed March 5, 2016, http://www.mormonscripturestudies.com/tem/blm/fpof.asp.

Miller, George. Letter to Abraham Jonas, September 29, 1842. Letters Pertaining to Freemasonry in Nauvoo, 1842, Church History Library, accessed December 7, 2021, https://catalog.churchofjesuschrist.org/assets/ea8928d0-d2ae-4373-9410 -083cc11689a7/0/20.

Mills, H. W. "De Tal Palo Tal Astilla." *Annual Publication of the Historical Society of Southern California* 10, no. 3 (1917): 86–174.

Minard, John Stearns, and Georgia Drew Merrill, eds. *Allegany County and its People: A Centennial Memorial History of Allegany County, New York, 1896*. Allegany County, NY: W. A. Fergusson & Company, 1896.

Miner, Ovid. "The Rodsmen." *Vermont American* (May 7, 1828): 2. Typescript at Uncle Dale's Readings in Early Mormon History, accessed June 5, 20201, http://www .sidneyrigdon.com/dbroadhu/NE/miscne00.htm#050728.

"Minute Book 1." The Joseph Smith Papers, accessed December 3, 2021, https://www .josephsmithpapers.org/paper-summary/minute-book-1.

"Minute Book 2." The Joseph Smith Papers, accessed December 3, 2021, http:// josephsmithpapers.org/paperSummary/minute-book-2.

"Minutes and Blessings, 28 February–1 March 1835." The Joseph Smith Papers, accessed December 3, 2021, https://www.josephsmithpapers.org/paper-summary/minutes -and-blessings-28-february-1-march-1835.

"Minutes of a Conference of the Church of Christ." *Messenger and Advocate of the Church of Christ* 1, no. 11 (April 15, 1845): 168–76.

Minutes of Bodley Lodge No. 1, A.F. & A.M. of Illinois. Located at Bodley Lodge No. 1, Quincy, Illinois. Photographic reproductions in possession of the authors.

Minutes of Pickaway Lodge No. 23 Free and Accepted Masons, Circleville, Ohio. Privately published, 1975.

Moore, Charles W., and S. W. B. Carnegy. *The Masonic Trestle-Board, Adapted to the National System of Work and Lectures, as Revised and Perfected by the United States Masonic Convention at Baltimore, MD, A.L. 5843*. Boston: Charles W. Moore, 1846.

Moore, Cornelius. *The Craftsman, and Freemason's Guide; Containing a Delineation of the Rituals of Freemasonry*. 8th ed. Cincinnati: Jacob Ernst, 1854.

Moore, Duncan. *In Search of That Which Was Lost: True Symbolism of the Royal Arch*. Surrey: Ian Allan Publishing Ltd, 2013.

Moore, Richard G., ed. *The Writings of Oliver H. Olney: April 1842 to February 1843— Nauvoo, Illinois*. Salt Lake City: Greg Kofford Books, 2019.

Morcombe, Joseph E. *History of Grand Lodge of Iowa, A.F. and A.M. Volume 1*. Cedar Rapids: Grand Lodge of Iowa, 1910.

Morgan, Lucinda. "Letter from the Bereaved Widow." *Anti-Masonic Telegraph* 1, no. 47 (February 24, 1830): 1.

Morgan, William. *Illustrations of Masonry by One of the Fraternity Who has Devoted Thirty Years to the Subject*. Batavia, NY: 1826.

"Mormonism on the Wing." *Painesville Telegraph* 2, no. 52 (June 14, 1831). Typescript at Uncle Dale's Readings in Early Mormon History, accessed December 6, 2021, http://www.sidneyrigdon.com/dbroadhu/oh/paintel2.htm#061431.

"Mormons Owned Officers' Jewels of Herman Lodge." *The Quincy Herald-Whig* (January 22, 1928): 3.

Morris, Larry E. "Oliver Cowdery's Vermont Years and the Origins of Mormonism." *BYU Studies Quarterly* 39, no. 1 (January 2000): 107–29.

Morris, Rob. *History of Freemasonry in Kentucky: In Its Relations to the Symbolic Degrees*. Louisville, KY: Rob Morris, 1859.

————. *The Masonic Martyr: The Biography of Eli Bruce, Sheriff of Niagara County, New York, Who, For His Attachment to the Principles of Masonry, and his Fidelity to His Trust, was Imprisoned Twenty-Eight Months in the Canandaigua Jail.* Louisville: Morris & Monsarrat, 1861.

————. *Masonic Odes and Poems.* New York: Macoy and Sickels, 1864.

————. "The Mason's Vows." *Masonic Voice-Review* 3 no. 1 (January 1901): 57.

————. *The Poetry of Freemasonry.* Chicago: Knight and Leonard, 1884.

————. *William Morgan; Or, Political Anti-Masonry, Its Rise, Growth and Decadence.* New York: Robert Macoy, Masonic Publisher, 1883.

Morris, S. Brent. "The High Degrees in the United States: 1730–1830." Pietre-Stones Review of Freemasonry, last updated April 1, 2008, http://www.freemasons-freemasonry.com/brentmorris3.html.

Morrison, Larry R. "The Religious Defense of American Slavery before 1830." *The Journal of Religious Thought* 37, no. 2 (September 1981): 16–29.

Mortensen, Joann Follett. *The Man behind the Discourse: A Biography of King Follett.* Salt Lake City: Greg Kofford Books, 2011.

"Murder, The." *Times and Seasons* 5, no. 13 (July 15, 1844): 585.

Myrick, Osborne. "A Historical Discourse delivered at the Centennial Celebration of the Congregational Church in Middletown, Vt., June 22, 1881." Rutland Historical Society, Rutland, VT.

Narrative of the Facts and Circumstances Relating to the Kidnapping and Presumed Murder of William Morgan, A, 3rd ed. Rochester, NY: Edwin Scranton, 1828.

"Nauvoo City Council Rough Minute Book, November 1842–January 1844." The Joseph Smith Papers, accessed December 3, 2021, https://www.josephsmithpapers.org/paper-summary/nauvoo-city-council-rough-minute-book-november-1842-january-1844.

"Nauvoo Masonic Lodge minutes 1841–1842." Church History Library, accessed December 3, 2021, https://catalog.churchofjesuschrist.org/assets/67a0bf8a-a1d2-4099-a3f7-e8f51b644b2d/0/0.

"Nauvoo Masonic Lodge minutes, 1841–1846." Special Collections, Marriott Library, University of Utah, Salt Lake City.

"Nauvoo Relief Society Minute Book." The Joseph Smith Papers, accessed December 3, 2021, http://josephsmithpapers.org/paperSummary/nauvoo-relief-society-minute-book.

Nelson, Russell M. "Hosanna Shout." Presented at the general conference of The Church of Jesus Christ of Latter-day Saints on April 5, 2020, https://abn.churchofjesuschrist.org/study/general-conference/2020/04/46nelson.

Nevins, Calvin A. "Centennial History of Springfield Lodge No. 4 A.F. & A.M." Unpublished draft document in possession of Springfield Lodge No. 4, 1939.

Newell, Linda King, and Valeen Tippets Avery. *Mormon Enigma: Emma Hale Smith.* 2nd ed. Champaign: University of Illinois Press, 1994.

Nibley, Hugh. *Ancient Documents and the Pearl of Great Price.* Provo, Utah: FARMS, 1994.

————. *An Approach to the Book of Mormon.* 3rd ed. Salt Lake City: Deseret Book, 1988.

Nuttall, L. John. *Diary of L. John Nuttall, Dec. 1876–Mar. 1884.* Typescript copied by Brigham Young University, 1948.

Nye, Jonathan. "For a General Grand Lodge!" *The Builder Magazine* 11, no. 6 (June 1925). Typescript at The Phoenixmasonry Masonic Museum and Library, http://www.phoenixmasonry.org/the_builder_1925_june.htm.

O'Donovan, Connell. "William Smith, Isaac Sheen, and the *Melchisedek & Aaronic Herald*." Website of Connell O'Donovan, accessed December 7, 2021, http://www.connellodonovan.com/smith_sheen.pdf.

O'Driscoll, Jeffrey W. Email to Nicholas S. Literski, October 23, 2005. In authors' possession.

———. *Hyrum Smith: A Life of Integrity*. Salt Lake City: Deseret Book, 2003.

O'Neill, Timothy. "The Grand Copt." *Gnosis: A Journal of the Western Inner Traditions* 24 (Summer 1992): 23–29.

Oliver, George. *The Antiquities of Freemasonry; Comprising Illustrations of the Five Grand Periods of Masonry from the Creation of the World to the Dedication of King Solomon's Temple*. London: G and W. B. Whittaker, 1823.

———. *A Dictionary of Symbolical Masonry, Including the Royal Arch Degree; According to the System Prescribed by the Grand Lodge and Supreme Grand Chapter of England*. London: Richard Spencer, 1853.

———. *Historical Landmarks and Other Evidences of Freemasonry, Explained; a Series of Practical Lectures, with Copious Notes*. 2 vols. London: Richard Spencer, 1846.

———. *The History of Initiation, in Twelve Lectures; Comprising a Detailed Account of the Rites and Ceremonies, Doctrines and Discipline, of all the Secret and Mysterious Institutions of the Ancient World*. New York: Jno. W. Leonard & Co., American Masonic Agency, 1855.

———. "On Freemasonry. The Number Three." *The Freemason's Quarterly Review* 1, no. 3 (September 30, 1843): 353–63.

———. *The Origin of the Royal Arch Order of Masonry, Historically Considered*. New ed. London: Brother Richard Spencer, 1867.

———. *Signs and Symbols: Illustrated and Explained in a Course of Twelve Lectures on Freemasonry*. Grimsby, Eng.: Skelton, 1826.

Olmstead, Jacob W. "From Pentecost to Administration: A Reappraisal of the History of the Hosanna Shout." *Mormon Historical Studies* 2, no. 2 (Fall 2001): 7–37.

Olney, Oliver H. *The Absurdities of Mormonism Portrayed: A Brief Sketch*. Hancock Co., Illinois, 1843.

Oman, Nathan. "'Secret Combinations': A Legal Analysis." *The FARMS Review* 16, no. 1 (2004): 49–73.

Oman, Richard G. "Beehive Symbol." In *Encyclopedia of Mormonism*, 4 vols., 1:99. New York: Macmillan Publishing Company, 1991.

Osgood, Emory. "Masonic Sermon." *Palmyra Register* 2, no. 16 (March 10, 1819): 1.

"Outrages at Batavia." *The Geneva Gazette and General Advertiser* 18, no. 21 (November 1, 1826): 1.

Owen, T. Grafton. *Drippings from the Eaves*. Seattle: Lowman and Hanford Company, 1911.

Owens, Lance S. "Joseph Smith and Kabbalah: The Occult Connection." *Dialogue: A Journal of Mormon Thought* 27, no. 3 (Fall 1994): 117–94.

Palmer, John C. *The Morgan Affair and Anti-Masonry*. Washington, DC: The Masonic Service Association of the United States, 1924.

Paris, Idaho Stake Minutes, May 3, 1884. Church History Library, Salt Lake City, UT.

Parker, Van Dyke. "Freemasonry and Communism." Speech given at the 9th Inter-Provincial Conference of the Officers of the Four Western Masonic Jurisdictions of Canada, Banff, Alberta, 1949.

Partridge, Edward. Diary, January 27, 1835–July 8, 1836. Church History Library, accessed December 7, 2021, https://catalog.churchofjesuschrist.org/assets/700076c7-2725 -4672-9f6b-9613235b86ad/0/0.

Paul, Robert. "Joseph Smith and the Manchester (New York) Library." *BYU Studies Quarterly* 22, no. 3 (1982): 333–56.

Pease, Theodore Calvin, ed. *Illinois Election Returns 1818–1848*. Springfield: Illinois State Historical Society, 1923.

Peck, Reed. *The Reed Peck Manuscript*. Quincy Adams City, IL: 1839.

Perkins, William. "Antimasonic Religion." *The Geauga Gazette* 3, no. 7 (March 15, 1831): 1.

"Persecution." *Times and Seasons* 3, no. 20 (August 15, 1842): 887–88.

"Persons Who Have Been Initiated, Passed, Raised, or Admitted as Adjoining Members of Ontario Lodge No. 23, held at Canandaigua, Ontario County, State of New York, From December 27, 1817, to December 27, 1818." The Chancellor Robert R. Livingston Masonic Library, New York City, NY.

Peterson, H. Donl. "The History and Significance of the Book of Abraham." In *Studies in Scripture*, vol. 2, *The Pearl of Great Price*, edited by Robert L. Millett and Kent P. Jackson, 161–81. Salt Lake City: Randall Book Company, 1985.

Peterson, J. W. "Another Testimony." *Deseret Evening News* 27, no. 11 (January 20, 1894): 11.

Phelps, W. W. "Despise not Prophesyings." *Times and Seasons* 2, no. 7 (Feb 1, 1841): 297–99.

———. "God is Love." *Latter Day Saints' Messenger and Advocate* 1, no. 9 (June 1835): 144.

———. "Renunciation." *The Seneca Farmer and Waterloo Advertiser* 5, no. 28 (February 6, 1828). Typescript at Oliver Cowdery Memorial Home Page, accessed December 7, 2021, http://www.olivercowdery.com/smithhome/Phelps/PhelpsSources1.htm #020628.

———. "This Earth Was Once a Garden Place." In *Hymns of The Church of Jesus Christ of Latter-day Saints*, 49. Salt Lake City: The Church of Jesus Christ of Latter-day Saints, 1985.

———. Witness statement, November 12, 1838. *Mormon War Papers, 1837–1841*. Missouri State Archives, accessed December 7, 2021, https://www.sos.mo.gov/ archives/resources/findingaids/rg005-01.

Philalethes, Eugenius [Thomas Vaughan]. *Long Livers, a Curious History of Such Persons of Both Sexes who Have Liv'd Several Ages, and Grown Young Again*. London, 1722.

Pierce, Simon. "Master Mason Apron." Masonic Lodge of Education: Understanding Freemasonry, accessed July 8, 2021, https://www.masonic-lodge-of-education .com/master-mason-apron.html.

Pike, Albert. *Morals and Dogma of the Ancient and Accepted Scottish Rite of Freemasonry*. Charleston: A. M., 1871.

Platt, Lyman D. "Early Branches of the Church of Jesus Christ of Latter-day Saints, 1830–1850." *Nauvoo Journal* 3 (1991): 3–50.

Porter, Larry C. "Reverend George Lane—Good 'Gifts,' Much 'Grace,' and Marked 'Usefulness.'" *BYU Studies Quarterly* 9, no. 3 (Spring 1969): 321–40.

———. "A Study of the Origins of the Church of Jesus Christ of Latter-day Saints in the States of New York and Pennsylvania, 1816–1831." PhD diss., Brigham Young University, 1971.

Post, Stephen. Journal, January 1849–March 1859. Church History Library, accessed December 7, 2021, https://catalog.churchofjesuschrist.org/assets/d54a548b-0ad4 -4b09-8f03-0bc086ed3f4d/0/0.

Pratt, Milando. "The Life and Labors of Orson Pratt," *The Contributor* 12, no. 3 (January 1891): 81–86.

Pratt, Orson. [Eight Pamphlets on the First Principles of the Gospel.] Liverpool, Eng.: 1856.

———. *A[n] Interesting Account of Several Remarkable Visions, and of the Late Discovery of Ancient American Records.* Edinburgh: Ballantyne and Hughes, 1840.

Pratt, Parley P. *The Angel of the Prairies; A Dream of the Future.* Salt Lake City: A. Pratt, 1880.

———. *History of the Late Persecution Inflicted by the State of Missouri upon the Mormons.* Detroit: Dawson and Bates, 1839.

———. "Proclamation to the Church of Jesus Christ of Latter-day Saints: Greeting." *The Latter-Day Saints' Millennial Star* 5, no. 10 (March 1845): 149–53.

———. "Regeneration and the Eternal Duration of Matter." In *The Millennium, and Other Poems: To which is Annexed a Treatise on the Regeneration and Eternal Duration of Matter,* 105–48. New York: W. Molineux, 1840.

———. *A Voice of Warning and Instruction to All People, or, An Introduction to the Faith and Doctrine of the Church of Jesus Christ of Latter-day Saints.* 11th ed. Salt Lake City: Deseret News Company, Printers and Publishers, 1881.

Pratt, Parley P., Jr., ed. *The Autobiography of Parley Parker Pratt, One of the Twelve Apostles of the Church of Jesus Christ of Latter-day Saints: Embracing His Life, Ministry and Travels, with Extracts, in Prose and Verse, from His Miscellaneous Writings.* New York: Russell Brothers, 1874.

"President Woodruff Speaks." *Deseret News* 39, no. 24 (December 7, 1889): 1–2.

Preston, William. *Illustrations of Masonry.* 9th ed. London: G and T Wilkie, 1796.

Prichard, Samuel. *Masonry Dissected: Being a Universal and Genuine Description of All Its Branches from the Original to this Present Time.* 2nd ed. London, 1730.

Proceedings of the Grand Chapter of Royal Arch Masons of the State of California. San Francisco: Frank Eastman, Printer, 1876.

Proceedings of the Grand Chapter of Royal Arch Masons of the State of New York, at its Eighty-Fifth Annual Convention, Held at the City of Albany. Buffalo: Young, Lockwood, and Co.'s Steam Press, 1882.

Proceedings of the Grand Lodge of Free and Accepted Masons of the State of New York, One Hundred and Twenty-Ninth Annual Communication. New York, J.J. Little & Ives Co., 1910.

Proceedings of the Grand Lodge of the State of Missouri, at their Grand Annual Convocation, Held at the City of Saint Louis, on Monday, the 9th of October, A.D. 1843, A.L. 5843. Chambers & Knapp, 1843.

Proceedings of the Most Puissant Grand Council of Royal and Select Masters of the State of New Jersey at the 13th and 14th Annual Assemblies, Held at Trenton, Jan. 17th, 1871 and Jan. 16th, 1872. Trenton, NJ: Murphy & Bechtel, Printers, 1872.

Proceedings of the National Masonic Convention, Held at Baltimore, Maryland, May, A.L. 5843, A.D. 1843. Baltimore: J. Robinson, 1843.

Public Documents Printed by Order of the Senate of the United States, During the Second Session of the Twenty-Sixth Congress, Begun and Held at the City of Washington, December 7, 1840, and in the Sixty-Fifth Year of the Independence of the United States, 5 vols. Washington, DC: Blair and Rives, 1841.

Purple, William D. *Historical Reminiscences of Eastern Light Lodge, No. 126, F. & A. M., of Greene, Chenango County, N.Y., From 5811 [1811] To 5897 [1897], with Biographical Sketches, revised and published by the Lodge, 1897.* Greene, NY: Hall's Steam Print, 1897.

Questions and Answers on the Life and Mission of the Prophet Joseph Smith. Salt Lake City: Juvenile Instructor's Office, 1882.

"Questions Proposed to the Mormonite Preachers and Their Answers Obtained before the Whole Assembly at Julian Hall, Sunday Evening, August 5, 1832." *Boston Investigator* 2, no. 20 (August 10, 1832): 2.

Quincy, Josiah. *Figures of the Past from the Leaves of Old Journals.* Boston: Roberts Brothers, 1883.

Quinn, D. Michael. "The Council of Fifty and Its Members, 1844–1945." *BYU Studies Quarterly* 20, no. 2 (Winter 1980): 163–97.

———. "The Culture of Violence in Joseph Smith's Mormonism." *Sunstone Magazine* 164 (October 2011): 16–28.

———. *Early Mormonism and the Magic World View.* Rev. ed. Salt Lake City: Signature Books, 1998.

———. "Latter-day Saint Prayer Circles." *BYU Studies Quarterly* 18, no. 1 (1979): 79–105.

———. *The Mormon Hierarchy: Origins of Power.* Salt Lake City: Signature Books, 1994.

"R. S. Reports." *Woman's Exponent* 9, no. 7 (September 1, 1880): 53–54.

Ramsay, Chevalier Andrew Michael. *Ramsay's Oration of 1737.* In Robert Freke Gould, *Gould's History of Freemasonry throughout the World,* revised by Dudley Wright, 3:10–15. New York: Charles Scribner's Sons, 1936.

Ramsay, Robert. "Rambling Jottings." *Masonic Review* 57, no. 1 (February 1882): 8–11.

Record of the Organization of the Kingdom. James Jesse Strang Papers, Beinecke Rare Book and Manuscripts Library, Yale University, New Haven, CT.

Records of Bodley Lodge No. 1. Quincy, Illinois. Photographic reproductions in possession of the authors.

Records of Manchester Lodge No. 269. The Chancellor Robert R. Livingston Masonic Library, New York City, NY.

Records of Mount Moriah Lodge No. 112. The Chancellor Robert R. Livingston Masonic Library, New York City, NY.

Records of the Grand Chapter of the State of Vermont, 1804–1850, Inclusive. Burlington: Free Press and Times Printing, 1878.

Records of the Grand Lodge of Free and Accepted Masons of the State of Vermont from 1794 to 1846 Inclusive. Burlington, VT: The Free Press Association, 1879.

Register of the Grand Lodge of Vermont, 1794 to 1846. Located at Grand Lodge of Vermont, Barre, VT.

Reid, J. M. *Sketches and Anecdotes of the Old Settlers and New Comers, the Mormon Bandits and Danite Band.* Keokuk, IA: R. B. Ogden, 1877.

Relief Society Record, 1880–1892. Church History Library, accessed December 7, 2021, https://catalog.churchofjesuschrist.org/assets/224063d5-1ed1-498c-95e8 -0ec36f7603a2/0/0.

Reprint of the Proceedings of the Grand Lodge of Illinois, From its Organization in 1840 to 1880 Inclusive. Freeport: Grand Lodge of Illinois, 1891.

Retired Member of the Craft, A. *The Text Book of Freemasonry: A Complete Handbook of Instruction to All the Workings in the Various Mysteries and Ceremonies of Craft Masonry.* London: Reeves and Turner, 1870.

Return of Mount Moriah Lodge No. 112 held at Palmyra in the County of Ontario and State of New York from Dec. 26th 1811 to Jun 24th 1814. The Chancellor Robert R. Livingston Masonic Library, New York City, NY.

Returns of Friendship Lodge No. 129, 1 June 1827–1 June 1829. The Chancellor Robert R. Livingston Masonic Library, New York City, NY.

"Revelation Book 1." The Joseph Smith Papers, accessed December 3, 2021, http://josephsmithpapers.org/paperSummary/revelation-book-1.

"Revelations of James Strang, The." Church of Jesus Christ of Latter Day Saints, last updated August 2018, http://www.strangite.org/Reveal.htm.

Reynolds, John C. *History of the Most Worshipful Grand Lodge of Illinois, Ancient, Free, and Accepted Masons, From the Organization of the First Lodge within the Present Limits of the State, Up to and Including 1850.* Springfield: Masonic Trowel Office, 1869.

Richards, Franklin D. Journals, 1844–1899. Church History Library, accessed December 2, 2021, https://catalog.churchofjesuschrist.org/record/23574933-c40b-4860-99ab-3ca67cacd933/739c0a48-6265-49a9-adff-16c031a2ac34.

———. "A Visit to Pueblo, Independence, Carthage, Nauvoo, Richmond, etc." *The Latter-day Saints' Millennial Star* 47, no. 30 (July 27, 1885): 465–73.

Richards, George F. Letter to the President of the St. George Temple, February 15, 1927. Saint George Temple president's correspondence, 1882–1954. Church History Library, Salt Lake City, UT.

———. Memorandum, June 7, 1922, October 5, 1922. Saint George Temple President's Correspondence, 1882–1954. Church History Library, Salt Lake City, UT.

Richards, George F., Joseph Fielding Smith, Stephen L. Richards, and Melvin J. Ballard. Committee Report to the First Presidency and Council of the Twelve Apostles, April 22, 1936.

Richards, Willard, "Special Conference." *Times and Seasons* 5, no. 8 (April 15, 1844): 504–6.

Richardson, Jabez. *Richardson's Monitor of Free-Masonry.* New York: Fitzgerald, 1860.

Richmond, B. W. "The Prophet's Death." *The Latter-day Saints' Millennial Star* 38, no. 4 (January 24, 1876): 51–52.

Rigdon, John W. "Life Story of Sidney Rigdon." Church History Library, accessed December 7, 2021, https://catalog.churchofjesuschrist.org/assets/a4629ae5-a0a6-445f-bdf4-dda30a7e743a/0/0.

Ripley, Alanson. "To the Elders Abroad." *Elders' Journal* 1, no. 3 (July 1838): 39.

Ritner, Robert K. *The Joseph Smith Egyptian Papyri: A Complete Edition, P. JS 1–4 and the Hypocephalus of Sheshonq.* Salt Lake City: The Smith-Pettit Foundation, 2011.

Roberts, Allen D. "The 'Other' Endowment House: Unraveling a Mystery." *Sunstone Magazine* 3, no. 5 (July/August 1978): 9–10.

———. "Where Are the All-Seeing Eyes? The Origin, Use and Decline of Early Mormon Symbolism." *Sunstone Magazine* 10, no. 5 (May 1985): 36–48.

Roberts, B. H., ed., *History of the Church of Jesus Christ of Latter-day Saints.* 7 vols. Salt Lake City: Deseret News, 1902–1932.

———. *The Life of John Taylor: Third President of the Church of Jesus Christ of Latter-day Saints.* Salt Lake City: George Q. Cannon & Sons Co., 1892.

———. *The Rise and Fall of Nauvoo.* Salt Lake City: Deseret News, 1900.

Robertson, James Burton. *Lectures on Some Subjects of Modern History and Biography.* Dublin: William Bernard Kelly, 1864.

Robinson, Ebenezer. "Items of Personal History of the Editor, No. 6, Including Some Items of Church History Not Generally Known." *The Return* 1, no. 10 (Oct. 1889): 145–51.

———. "Items of Personal History of the Editor, No. 7, Including Some Items of Church History Not Generally Known." *The Return* 1, no. 11 (Nov. 1889): 169–74.

Romig, Ronald E. *Eighth Witness: The Biography of John Whitmer.* Independence, Missouri: John Whitmer Books, 2014.

"Royal Arch." *Weekly Wanderer* (June 25, 1804): 4.

Ryder, Charles H. "A Hill of Zion: Reminiscences of the Early Days of Mormonism in Ohio." *The New York Herald* (September 10, 1877): 9.

"Sample of Pure Language, between circa 4 and circa 20 March 1832." The Joseph Smith Papers, accessed December 3, 2021, https://www.josephsmithpapers.org/paper-summary/sample-of-pure-language-between-circa-4-and-circa-20-march-1832.

Sargant, Thomas. *The Royal Arch Companion: A Manual of Royal Arch Masonry.* Toronto: Masonic Publishing Co., 1880.

Saunders, Richard L., ed. *Dale Morgan on the Mormons: Collected Works, Part I, 1939–1951.* Norman, OK: The Arthur H. Clark Co., 2012.

Savini, Tom. Correspondence to Nicholas S. Literski, May 30, 2003. In authors' possession.

Schindler, Harold. *Orrin Porter Rockwell: Man of God, Son of Thunder.* Salt Lake City, University of Utah Press, 1966.

Scholem, Gershom. *Major Trends in Jewish Mysticism.* New York: Schocken Books, 1974.

"School of the Prophets Salt Lake City Meeting Minutes, 1883, August–December." Church History Library, accessed December 7, 2021, https://catalog.churchofjesuschrist.org/assets/94111455-7896-451c-8cff-311dfd48c6c6/0/0.

Schryver, William, "The Meaning and Purpose of the Kirtland Egyptian Papers." Address delivered at the 2010 Conference of the Foundation for Apologetic Information and Research. Typescript at FAIR, accessed December 7, 2021, https://www.fairlatterdaysaints.org/conference/august-2010/the-meaning-of-the-kirtland-egyptian-papers-part-i. Video at https://vimeo.com/16276910.

Schultz, Edward T. *History of Freemasonry in Maryland, of All the Rites Introduced into Maryland, from the Earliest Time to the Present.* 4 vols. Baltimore: J. H. Medairy & Co., 1884–88.

Scovil, Lucius N. Letter to the Editor, *Deseret News* (February 20, 1884): 2.

Seaver, David. *Freemasonry at Batavia, N. Y., 1811–1891.* Batavia: J. F. Hall & Co., 1891.

Shadbolt, William, Robert L. Percy, and J. C. Burckhardt. "To His Royal Highness Prince Augustus Frederick." *The European Magazine, and London Review* 66 (September 1814): 203.

Sharp, Thomas. "Address." *Warsaw Signal* 19 (June 19, 1844): 1.

———. "Unparalled Outrage at Nauvoo." *Warsaw Signal* 18 (June 12, 1844): 2.

Sheen, Isaac. "The Greatest Annual Conference." *Melchisedek & Aaronic Herald* 1, no. 9 (April 1850): 2–4.

———. "A Revelation, given March 20, 1850." *Melchisedek & Aaronic Herald* 1, no. 9 (April 1850): 1.

———. "Special Conference." *Melchisedek & Aaronic Herald* 1, no. 4 (June 1849): 4.

Sheldon, Henry. "Rupert." In *Vermont Historical Gazeteer, a Magazine Embracing a History of Each Town*, vol. 1, edited by Abby Maria Hemenway, 220–27. Burlington, VT: Miss A. M. Hemenway, 1867.

Shepard, William, and H. Michael Marquardt. *Lost Apostles: Forgotten Members of Mormonism's Original Quorum of Twelve*. Salt Lake City: Signature Books, 2014.

Shepard, William, Donna Falk, and Thelma Lewis, eds. *James J. Strang. Teaching[s] of a Mormon Prophet*. Michigan: Church of Jesus Christ of Latter Day Saints, 1977.

Sherer, John. *The Masonic Ladder: Or the Nine Steps of Ancient Freemasonry*. Cincinnati: R.W. Carroll & Co., Publishers, 1876.

Sheville, John, and James L. Gould. *Guide to the Royal Arch Chapter: A Complete Monitor for Royal Arch Masonry*. New York: Macoy Publishing and Masonic Supply Co., 1897.

Shurtliff, Luman Andros. "Autobiography (1807–1847)." Typescript at Book of Abraham Project, accessed September 17, 2021, http://www.boap.org/LDS/Early-Saints/LShurtliff.html.

Sickels, Daniel. *The General Ahiman Rezon and Freemason's Guide*. New York: Masonic Publishing and Manufacturing Co., 1868.

"Slander Refuted." *Dixon Telegraph* 2, no. 51 (April 30, 1853). Typescript at Uncle Dale's Readings in Early Mormon History, accessed December 6, 2021, http://www.sidneyrigdon.com/dbroadhu/IL/miscill3.htm#043053.

Smith, Andrew F. *The Saintly Scoundrel: The Life and Times of Dr. John Cook Bennett*. Urbana, University of Illinois, 1987.

Smith, Bathsheba. "Recollections of Joseph Smith." *Juvenile Instructor* 27, no. 11 (1 June 1892): 344–45.

Smith, Eldred. Presentation given at the Joseph Smith Academy in Nauvoo, Illinois, December 31, 2003.

Smith, Emma. *A Collection of Sacred Hymns for the Church of the Latter Day Saints*. Kirtland, OH: F. G. Williams & Co., 1835.

———. "Virtue Will Triumph." *Nauvoo Neighbor* 1, no. 47 (20 Mar. 1844): 2.

Smith, George D., ed. *An Intimate Chronicle: The Journals of William Clayton*. Salt Lake City: Signature Books, 1991.

Smith, Gregory L. "Cracking the Book of Mormon's 'Secret Combinations'?" *Interpreter: A Journal of Mormon Scripture* 13 (2015): 63–109.

Smith, Hyrum. "Missouri vs Joseph Smith." *Times and Seasons* 4, no. 16 (July 1, 1843): 255.

———. Patriarchal Blessing to Leonora Cannon Taylor, July 28, 1843. George L. Taylor Papers, 1832–1909. Church History Library, Salt Lake City, UT.

Smith, John. Journal, 1781–1854. Typescript, Church History Library, accessed September 17, 2021, https://catalog.churchofjesuschrist.org/assets/4887b2b8-2d2a-4fcf-8a17-72c96710e0f3/0/138.

Smith, Joseph, Jr. "Extract of a Letter to Bishop Partridge." *Millennial Star* 5, no. 5 (Oct. 1844): 69–72.

———. "The Globe." *Times and Seasons* 5, no. 8 (April 15, 1844): 508–10.

———. "The Government of God." *Times and Seasons* 3, no. 18 (15 July 1842): 855–58.

———. "In Obedience to Our Promise." *Elders' Journal* (July 1838): 42–44.

Smith, Joseph, Jr., et al. *History of the Church of Jesus Christ of Latter-day Saints*. Edited by B. H. Roberts. 7 vols. 2nd ed. rev. Salt Lake City: Deseret Book, 1948 printing.

Smith, Joseph F. "Correction." *Deseret Evening News* (Feb. 18, 1882): 2.

———. "Funeral of Isaac Manning." April 20, 1911. Journal History of the Church, 1830–2008, Church History Library, Salt Lake City, UT.

Smith, Joseph Fielding. "Restoration of the Melchizedek Priesthood." *Improvement Era* 7, no. 12 (October 1904): 938–43.

———. *The Way to Perfection*. Salt Lake City: Deseret Book, 1984.

Smith, William. *The Book M: or, Masonry Triumphant*. Newcastle upon Tyne: Leonard Umfreville and Co., 1736.

Smith, William. "Mormonism. A Letter from William Smith, Brother of Joseph, the Prophet." *New York Tribune* 17, no. 5025 (May 28, 1857): 5.

———. "Patriarchal." *Times and Seasons* 6, no. 9 (May 15, 1845): 904–5.

Smith, William V. "The Parallel Joseph." Book of Abraham Project, accessed June 22, 2021, http://www.boap.org/LDS/Parallel/1841.

Smyth, Thomas Cartwright. *Free Masonry; in It's Claims to the Regard of Men of Intelligence, Honor, and Christian Principle*. Agra: Secundra Orphan Press, 1855.

Snow, Eliza R. "The Female Relief Society: A Brief Sketch of Its Organization and Workings in the City of Nauvoo, Hancock, Co., Ill." *Woman's Exponent* 1, no. 2 (June 15, 1872): 10.

"Song of the Vermonters; the Ode Attributed to Ethan Allen." *The New York Times* 26, no. 8080 (August 6, 1877): 2.

Stafford, John. *A Discourse on the Urim and Thummim, Delivered Before Hiram Lodge, No. 72, at Mount Pleasant, Westchester County, on St. John's Day, Dec. 27, 1800*. 2nd ed. New York, E. Conrad, 1820.

Staker, Mark Lyman. *Hearken, O Ye People: The Historical Setting of Joseph Smith's Ohio Revelations*. Salt Lake City: Greg Kofford Books, 2010.

Stavish, Mark. *Freemasonry: Rituals, Symbols & History of the Secret Society*. Woodbury, MN: Llewelleyn Publications, 2007.

Stearns, John G. *An Inquiry into the Nature and Tendency of Speculative Free-Masonry*. Utica, NY: Northway & Porter, Printers, 1829.

———. *Letters on Freemasonry: Addressed Chiefly to the Fraternity*. Utica, NY: T.W. Seward, 1860.

Stelter, John H. "History of Freemasonry in Ontario County, New York." *Transactions* 8, no. 3, New York: The American Lodge of Research, Free and Accepted Masons, 1962.

Stevens, Albert Clark, comp. *The Cyclopaedia of Fraternities, A Compilation of Existing Authentic Information and the Results of Original Investigation as to the Origin, Derivation, Founders, Development, Aims, Emblems, Character, and Personnel of More than Six Hundred Secret Societies in the United States*. 2nd ed. New York: E.B. Treat and Company, 1907.

Stichting, Argus. "Ritual for the Royal Arch Degree, Indiana." Freemasonry and Fraternal Organizations, accessed June 20, 2001, http://www.stichtingargus.nl/vrijmetselarij/r/indianara_r.html.

Stiles, Edward H. *Recollections and Sketches of Notable Lawyers and Public Men of Early Iowa*. Des Moines: Homestead Publishing, 1916.

Still, William T. *New World Order: The Ancient Plan of Secret Societies*. Lafayette, LA: Huntington House Publishers, 1990.

Stillson, Henry Leonard, and William James Hughan, eds. *History of the Ancient and Honorable Fraternity of Free and Accepted Masons and Concordant Orders*. Boston and New York: The Fraternity Publishing Co., 1891.

Stout, Allen. *Allen Stout Journal.* Typescript, Harold B. Lee Library, Brigham Young University, Provo, UT.

———. Letter to Hosea Stout, September 10, 1843. Allen J. Stout Letters, Church History Library, accessed December 7, 2021, https://catalog.churchofjesuschrist .org/assets/7bc69e67-56d9-4fff-8c95-a2c1d452fa08/0/0.

———. Letter to Hosea Stout, September 13, 1843. Allen J. Stout Letters, Church History Library, accessed December 7, 2021, https://catalog.churchofjesuschrist .org/assets/7bc69e67-56d9-4fff-8c95-a2c1d452fa08/0/2.

———. Reminiscence and Journal, 1845–1850, 1865–1889. Church History Library, accessed December 7, 2021, https://catalog.churchofjesuschrist.org/assets/2f9886f6 -7a7b-4b26-a038-f402586a9087/0/0.

Stout, Hosea. Diary. Typescript at Book of Abraham Project, accessed Jun 27, 2020, http://boap.org/LDS/Early-Saints/HStout.html.

Strang, James J. *James Jesse Strang Diary.* July 1831–January 1836. Typescript, Beinecke Library, Yale University, New Haven, CT.

Strong, James. *A Concise Dictionary of the Words in the Hebrew Bible with Their Renderings in the Authorized English Version.* Nashville, Abingdon Press, 1890.

Swartzell, William. *Mormonism Exposed, Being a Journal of a Residence in Missouri From the 28th of May to the 20th of August, 1838.* Pekin, OH: 1840.

Swift, Jonathon. "Letter from the Grand Mistress of the Female Freemasons to Mr. Harding the Printer." In *The Works of Jonathan Swift, D. D.*, 12:328–48. Dublin: London, 1755.

"Symbolic Ancient Craft Masonry." King Solomon's Lodge, accessed June 22, 2021, http:// www.kingsolomonslodge.org/freemasonry/blue-lodge.php.

Talmage, James E. *Articles of Faith, A Series of Lectures on the Principal Doctrines of the Church of Jesus Christ of Latter-Day Saints.* Salt Lake City: The Deseret News, 1901.

Taylor, Alan. "Rediscovering the Context of Joseph Smith's Treasure Seeking." *Dialogue: A Journal of Mormon Thought* 19, no. 4 (Winter 1986): 18–28.

Taylor, Bruce T. "Book of Moses." In *Encyclopedia of Mormonism*, 4 vols., edited by Daniel H. Ludlow, 1:216–17. New York: Macmillan Publishing Company, 1991.

Taylor, John. "Conference Minutes." *Times and Seasons* 5, no. 15 (August 15, 1844): 612–17.

Teachings of Presidents of the Church: John Taylor. Salt Lake City: The Church of Jesus Christ of Latter-day Saints, 2001.

Temple, Wayne C. "An Aftermath of 'Sampson's Ghost': A New Lincoln Document." Unpublished manuscript in possession of Springfield Lodge No. 4, Ancient Free & Accepted Masons of Illinois.

Thomas, Gregg. *History of Hancock County, Illinois, Together with an Outline History of the State, and a Digest of State Laws.* Chicago: Charles C. Chapman, 1880.

Thompson, Charles B. "The Book of Enoch." *Zion's Harbinger and Baneemy's Organ* 2, no. 10 (Oct 1852): 73–78.

———. "Covenant, to be Taken upon Entering the Congregation of Jehovah's Presbytery of Zion." *Zion's Harbinger and Baneemy's Organ* 4, no. 1 (January 1854): 9.

———. "Letter for the *Gospel Herald.*" *Zion's Harbinger and Baneemy's Organ* 2, no. 3 (March 1852): 22–24.

———. "Who is Charles B. Thompson?" *Zion's Harbinger & Baneemy's Organ* 2, no. 8 (Aug. 1852): 59–61.

———. "The Word of the God of Abraham, of Isaac and of Jacob to his servants of the seed of the Church of Jesus Christ of Latter-day Saints, Having the testimony of Jesus Christ, Concerning their Organization, in preparation for the Endowments of the Priesthood, and their Regeneration in the Family of Israel." *Zion's Harbinger and Baneemy's Organ* 1, no. 2 (April 1850): 2.

Thompson, John E. *The Masons, the Mormons and the Morgan Incident*. Ames, IA: Iowa Research Lodge No. 2 A.F. & A.M., 1985.

Thornton, Joseph. "The Compass and Square." In *Masonic Songs, Old and New: Including those Published in The Free-Masons' Melody*, edited by W. S. Barlow, 149–50. Bury, Eng.: W. S Barlow at the Caxton Works, Fleet Street, 1885.

"Three Degrees of Masonry, The." North Raleigh Masonic Lodge, accessed September 20, 2021, http://www.jjcrowder743.com/threedegrees.html.

Throckmorton, Tom B. "Morgan, Mormons, and Masonry, a New Approach." In *Grand Lodge Bulletin*, Grand Lodge of Iowa 47, no. 2 (February 1947): 38.

Tillotson, Lee S. *Ancient Craft Masonry in Vermont*. Montpelier: Capital City Press, 1920.

"To the Public." *Sangamo Journal* 7, no. 4 (November 25, 1837): 2.

Toscano, Paul. *The Serpent and the Dove: Messianic Mysteries of the Mormon Temple*. 2nd ed. San Bernadino, CA: Merrill & Toscano Inc., 2015.

Town, Salem. *A System of Speculative Masonry in its Origin, Patronage, Dissemination, Principles, Duties, and Ultimate Designs, Laid Open for the Examination of the Serious and Candid*. Salem, NY: Dodd and Stevenson, 1818.

Townsend, Colby. "Revisiting Joseph Smith and the Availability of the Book of Enoch." *Dialogue: A Journal of Mormon Thought* 53, no. 3 (Fall 2020): 41–71.

"Translation, A." *Times and Seasons* 3, no. 6 (March 1, 1842): 704–6.

Trento, Salvatore Michael. *Field Guide to Mysterious Places of Eastern North America*. New York: Henry Holt & Co., 1997.

Tucker, Pomeroy. *Origin, Rise, and Progress of Mormonism: Biography of its Founders and History of its Church*. New York: Appleton & Co., 1867.

Tullidge, Edward W. *The Life of Joseph Smith the Prophet*. New York: Tullidge & Crandall, 1878.

———. *The Women of Mormondom*. New York: Tullidge & Crandall, 1877.

Turnbull, Everett R. *The Rise and Progress of Freemasonry in Illinois 1783–1952*. Springfield: Most Worshipful Grand Lodge of A. F. and A. M. of the State of Illinois, 1952.

Turner, John G. *Brigham Young: Pioneer Prophet*. Cambridge, MA: The Belknap Press of Harvard University Press, 2012.

Tuveson, Ernest Lee. *Redeemer Nation: The Idea of America's Millennial Role*. Vol. 2. Chicago: University of Chicago Press, 1968.

Tvedtnes, John A. "The Use of Mnemonic Devices in Oral Traditions, as Exemplified by the Book of Abraham and the Hor Sensen Papyrus." *Newsletter and Proceedings of the SEHA* 120 (April 1970): 2–10.

Udall, Alvah. "Early History of Hiram: A Few Anecdotes Will Serve." *The Journal* (July 8, 1880). Typescript at Uncle Dale's Readings in Early Mormon History, accessed December 6, 2021, http://sidneyrigdon.com/RigdonO3.htm#1880-0708.

Ulrich, Laurel Thatcher. *A House Full of Females: Plural Marriage and Women's Rights in Early Mormonism, 1835–1870*. New York: Knopf, 2017.

Van Dusen, Increase McGee. *Positively True: A Dialogue between Adam and Eve, the Lord and the Devil, Called the Endowment*, expanded version. Albany, NY: C. Killmer, 1847.

Van Noord, Roger. *King of Beaver Island: The Life and Assassination of James Jesse Strang.* University of Illinois Press, 1988.

Van Wagenen, Michael Scott. *The Texas Republic and the Mormon Kingdom of God.* College Station: Texas A&M University Press, 2002.

"Veil, The." The LDS Endowment, accessed September 22, 2021, http://www.ldsendowment .org/veil.html.

Vermont Vital Records through 1870, Index. New England Historic Genealogical Society, Boston, MA.

"Virtus Junxit, Mors Non Separabit." *American Masonic Record and Albany Saturday Magazine* 1, no. 50 (January 12, 1828): 1.

"Visions, 3 April 1836 [D&C 110]." The Joseph Smith Papers, accessed December 3, 2021, http://www.josephsmithpapers.org/paper-summary/visions-3-april-1836-dc-110.

Vogel, Dan. *Book of Abraham Apologetics: A Review and Critique.* Salt Lake City: Signature Books, 2021.

———, ed. *Early Mormon Documents.* 5 vols. Salt Lake City: Signature Books, 1996–2003.

———. "Echoes of Anti-Masonry: A Rejoinder to the Critics of the Anti-Masonic Thesis." In *American Apocrypha*, edited by Dan Vogel and Brent Lee Metcalfe, 275–320. Salt Lake City: Signature Books, 2002.

———. *Indian Origins and the Book of Mormon: Religious Solutions from Columbus to Joseph Smith.* Salt Lake City, Signature Books, 1986.

———. *Joseph Smith: The Making of a Prophet.* Salt Lake City: Signature Books, 2004.

———. "The Locations of Joseph Smith's Early Treasure Quests." *Dialogue: A Journal of Mormon Thought* 27, no. 3 (Fall 1994): 209–13.

———. "Mormonism's Anti-Masonick Bible." *The John Whitmer Historical Association Journal* 9 (1989): 17–30.

Voorhis, Harold Van Buren. "What Really Happened to William Morgan? A Plausible 'Story.'" Reprinted in *Little Masonic Library*, vol. 2, edited by Silas H. Shepherd, Lionel Vibert, and Roscoe Pound, 249–66. Richmond: Macoy Publishing & Masonic Supply Co., Inc., 1977.

W. O. Vn. *The Three Distinct Knocks, Or the Door of the Most Antient Free-Masonry, Opening to all Men, Neither Naked nor Cloath'd, Bare-foot nor Shod, &c.* Dublin, 1795.

Wagner, Martin L. *Freemasonry: An Interpretation.* Grosse Pointe, MI: Seminar Tapes and Books, 2014.

Waite, Arthur Edward. *A New Encyclopaedia of Freemasonry (Ars Magna Latomorum) And of Cognate Instituted Mysteries: Their Rites, Literature and History.* 2 vols. London: W. Rider and Son, 1921.

———. *Strange Houses of Sleep.* London: Philip, Sinclair, and Wellby, 1906.

Walgren, Kent L. "Fast and Loose Masonry." *Dialogue: A Journal of Mormon Thought* 18, no. 3 (Fall 1995): 172–76.

———. *Freemasonry, Anti-Masonry and Illuminism in the United States, 1734–1850: A Bibliography.* Worcester, MA: American Antiquarian Society, 2003.

———. "James Adams, Early Springfield Mormon and Freemason." *Journal of the Illinois State Historical Society* 75, no. 2 (Summer 1982): 121–36.

Walker, Kyle R. *William B. Smith: In the Shadow of a Prophet.* Salt Lake City: Greg Kofford Books, 2015.

Walker, Ronald W. "Joseph Smith, the Palmyra Seer." *BYU Studies* 24, no. 4 (Fall 1984): 429–59.

Ward, Henry Dana. *Free Masonry: Its Pretensions Exposed in Faithful Extracts of Its Standard Authors.* New York, 1828.

Ward, Maurine Carr. "The Maverick Historian: A Conversation with Stanley B. Kimball." *Mormon Historical Studies* 3, no. 1 (2002): 99–129.

Warvelle, George W., ed. *A Compendium of Freemasonry in Illinois, Embracing a Review of the Introduction, Development, and Present Condition of All Rites and Degrees.* 2 vols. Chicago: The Lewis Publishing Company, 1897.

Wayment, Thomas A., and Haley Wilson-Lemmon. "A Recovered Resource: The Use of Adam Clarke's Bible Commentary in Joseph Smith's Translation." In *Producing Ancient Scripture: Joseph Smith's Translation Projects in the Development of Mormon Christianity,* edited by Michael Hubbard MacKay, Mark Ashurst-McGee, and Brian M. Hauglid, 262–84. Salt Lake City: University of Utah Press, 2020.

"We Want Our Mystic Brethren." *Republican Farmer's Free Press* 19, no. 53 (December 31, 1830): 2.

"We Were Not the Aggressors." *Wasp* 1, no. 6 (May 21, 1842): 22.

Webb, Thomas Smith. *The Freemason's Monitor.* Salem, MA: Cushing and Appleton, 1808.

Webster, Noah. *An American Dictionary of the English Language.* 2 vols. New Haven, CT: 1828.

Weed, Thurlow. *Life of Thurlow Weed Including His Autobiography and a Memoir.* 2 vols. Edited by Harriet A. Weed. Boston: Houghton, Mifflin, and Co., 1884.

Wells, Roy A. *Understanding Freemasonry.* London: Lewis, 1991.

West, Aaron L. "Sustaining a New First Presidency in 1847." Church History, March 18, 2019, https://history.churchofjesuschrist.org/content/historic-sites/iowa/kanesville/why-we-remember-the-kanesville-tabernacle.

West, William S. *A Few Interesting Facts Respecting the Mormons.* Ohio, 1837.

Westergren, Bruce N., ed. *From Historian to Dissident: The Book of John Whitmer.* Salt Lake City: Signature Books, 1995.

"What is Royal Arch Masonry?" Supreme Grand Chapter of Royal Arch Masons of England, accessed May 9, 2021, https://www.supremegrandchapter.org.uk/about-royal-arch-masonry/what-is-royal-arch-masonry.

White, Jean Bickmore, ed. *Church, State, and Politics: The Diaries of John Henry Smith.* Salt Lake City: Signature Books, 1990.

Whitney, Helen Mar Kimball. "Life Incidents: No. II." *Woman's Exponent* 9, no. 4 (July 15, 1880): 25–26.

———. "Scenes and Incidents in Nauvoo. The Next Important Event." *Woman's Exponent* 11, no. 4 (15 July 1882): 26.

Whitney, Elizabeth Ann. "A Leaf from an Autobiography: My husband traveled." *Woman's Exponent* 7, no. 9 (October 1, 1878): 71.

Whitney, Newel K. Letter to Painesville, Ohio Masonic Chapter, March 27, 1827. Harold B. Lee Library, accessed December 7, 2021, http://archives.lib.byu.edu/repositories/14/archival_objects/62231.

Whitney, Orson. *Life of Heber C. Kimball, An Apostle; The Father and Founder of the British Mission.* Salt Lake City: Juvenile Instructor Office, 1888.

Wicks, Robert S. and Fred R. Foister. *Junius and Joseph: Presidential Politics and the Assassination of the First Mormon Prophet.* Logan: Utah State University Press, 2005.

"William A. Weston, et. al., to The Most Worshipful Grand Lodge of the Territory of Iowa." April 1, 1844, in Lodge Petition Files, Archives, Grand Lodge of Iowa, Cedar Rapids, Iowa.

Williams, J. D. "The Separation of Church and State in Mormon Theory and Practice." *Dialogue: A Journal of Mormon Thought* 1, no. 2 (1966): 30–54.

Wilmshurst, Walter L. *The Meaning of Masonry.* 2nd ed. New York: E. P. Dutton & Co., 1922.

Wilson, Haley, and Thomas Wayment. "A Recently Recovered Source: Rethinking Joseph Smith's Bible Translation." *Journal of Undergraduate Research* (March 2017): http://jur.byu.edu/?p=21296.

"Wilson Law and Others, Affidavit, 4 January 1843, Willard Richards Copy [*Extradition of JS for Accessory to Assault*]." The Joseph Smith Papers, accessed January 7, 2022, https://www.josephsmithpapers.org/paper-summary/wilson-law-and-others-affidavit-4-january-1843-willard-richards-copy-extradition-of-js-for-accessory-to-assault/1.

Winslow, Brady. "Irregularities in the Work of Nauvoo Lodge: Mormonism, Freemasonry, and Conflicting Interests on the Illinois Frontier." *John Whitmer Historical Association Journal* 34, no. 2 (Fall/Winter 2014): 58–79.

Woman's Society of the Western Presbyterian Church, The, comp. *Palmyra, Wayne County, New York.* Rochester: The Herald Press, 1907.

Woodley, Thomas Frederick. *The Great Leveler: The Life of Thaddeus Stevens.* North Stratford, NH: Ayer Publishing, 1937.

Woodruff, Wilford. Journals, 1833–1898. Church History Library, accessed December 7, 2021, https://catalog.churchofjesuschrist.org/record/400c3266-ede2-43cf-9a24-50153adebbeb/0.

Wyl, William. *Mormon Portraits of the Truth about the Mormon Leaders from 1830 to 1886.* Salt Lake City: Tribune Printing and Publishing Company, 1886.

Yates, John V. N. and Joseph W. Moulton. *History of the State of New-York, Including its Aboriginal and Colonial Annals.* 2 vols. New York: A.T. Goodrich, 1824–1826.

Young, Ann Eliza Webb. *Wife No. 19: Or, the Story of a Life in Bondage.* Hartford, CT: Dustin, Gilman and Co., 1876.

Young, Biloine Whiting. *Obscure Believers: The Mormon Schism of Alpheus Cutler.* Kansas City: Pogo Press, 2002.

Young, Emily D. P. "Autobiography of Emily D. P. Young." *Woman's Exponent* 14, no. 3 (July 1, 1885): 17–18.

Young, Frances. "'Creatio Ex Nihilo': A Context for the Emergence of the Christian Doctrine of Creation." *Scottish Journal of Theology* 44, no. 2 (1991): 139–52.

Young, Zina D. H. "Woman's Mass Meeting, Salt Lake Theater, Nov. 16, 1878." *Woman's Exponent* 7, no. 13 (Dec. 1, 1878): 97–103.

Zucker, Louis C. "Joseph Smith as a Student of Hebrew." *Dialogue: A Journal of Mormon Thought* 3, no. 2 (Summer 1968): 41–55.

INDEX

Also available from
GREG KOFFORD BOOKS

Hearken, O Ye People:
The Historical Setting of Joseph Smith's Ohio Revelations

Mark Lyman Staker

Hardcover, ISBN: 978-1-58958-113-5

2010 Best Book Award - John Whitmer Historical Association

2011 Best Book Award - Mormon History Association

More of Mormonism's canonized revelations originated in or near Kirtland than any other place. Yet many of the events connected with those revelations and their 1830s historical context have faded over time. Mark Staker reconstructs the cultural experiences by which Kirtland's Latter-day Saints made sense of the revelations Joseph Smith pronounced. This volume rebuilds that exciting decade using clues from numerous archives, privately held records, museum collections, and even the soil where early members planted corn and homes. From this vast array of sources he shapes a detailed narrative of weather, religious backgrounds, dialect differences, race relations, theological discussions, food preparation, frontier violence, astronomical phenomena, and myriad daily customs of nineteenth-century life. The result is a "from the ground up" experience that today's Latter-day Saints can all but walk into and touch.

Praise for *Hearken O Ye People*:

"I am not aware of a more deeply researched and richly contextualized study of any period of Mormon church history than Mark Staker's study of Mormons in Ohio. We learn about everything from the details of Alexander Campbell's views on priesthood authority to the road conditions and weather on the four Lamanite missionaries' journey from New York to Ohio. All the Ohio revelations and even the First Vision are made to pulse with new meaning. This book sets a new standard of in-depth research in Latter-day Saint history."

-Richard Bushman, author of *Joseph Smith: Rough Stone Rolling*

"To be well-informed, any student of Latter-day Saint history and doctrine must now be acquainted with the remarkable research of Mark Staker on the important history of the church in the Kirtland, Ohio, area."

-Neal A. Maxwell Institute, Brigham Young University

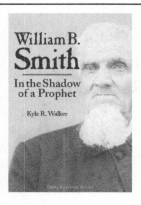

William B. Smith:
In the Shadow of a Prophet

Kyle R. Walker

Paperback, ISBN: 978-1-58958-503-4

Younger brother of Joseph Smith, a member of the Quorum of the Twelve Apostles, and Church Patriarch for a time, William Smith had tumultuous yet devoted relationships with Joseph, his fellow members of the Twelve, and the LDS and RLDS (Community of Christ) churches. Walker's imposing biography examines not only William's complex life in detail, but also sheds additional light on the family dynamics of Joseph and Lucy Mack Smith, as well as the turbulent intersections between the LDS and RLDS churches. *William B. Smith: In the Shadow of a Prophet* is a vital contribution to Mormon history in both the LDS and RLDS traditions.

Praise for *William B. Smith*:

"Bullseye! Kyle Walker's biography of Joseph Smith Jr.'s lesser known younger brother William is right on target. It weaves a narrative that is searching, balanced, and comprehensive. Walker puts this former Mormon apostle solidly within a Smith family setting, and he hits the mark for anyone interested in Joseph Smith and his family. Walker's biography will become essential reading on leadership dynamics within Mormonism after Joseph Smith's death." — Mark Staker, author *Hearken, O Ye People: The Historical Setting of Joseph Smith's Ohio Revelations*

"This perceptive biography on William, the last remaining Smith brother, provides a thorough timeline of his life's journey and elucidates how his insatiable discontent eventually tempered the once irascible young man into a seasoned patriarch loved by those who knew him." — Erin B. Metcalfe, president (2014–15) John Whitmer Historical Association

"I suspect that this comprehensive treatment will serve as the definitive biography for years to come; it will certainly be difficult to improve upon." — Joe Steve Swick III, Association for Mormon Letters

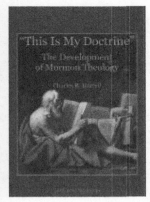

"This is My Doctrine":
The Development of Mormon Theology

Charles R. Harrell

Hardcover, ISBN: 978-1-58958-103-6

The principal doctrines defining Mormonism today often bear little resemblance to those it started out with in the early 1830s. This book shows that these doctrines did not originate in a vacuum but were rather prompted and informed by the religious culture from which Mormonism arose. Early Mormons, like their early Christian and even earlier Israelite predecessors, brought with them their own varied culturally conditioned theological presuppositions (a process of convergence) and only later acquired a more distinctive theological outlook (a process of differentiation).

In this first-of-its-kind comprehensive treatment of the development of Mormon theology, Charles Harrell traces the history of Latter-day Saint doctrines from the times of the Old Testament to the present. He describes how Mormonism has carried on the tradition of the biblical authors, early Christians, and later Protestants in reinterpreting scripture to accommodate new theological ideas while attempting to uphold the integrity and authority of the scriptures. In the process, he probes three questions: How did Mormon doctrines develop? What are the scriptural underpinnings of these doctrines? And what do critical scholars make of these same scriptures? In this enlightening study, Harrell systematically peels back the doctrinal accretions of time to provide a fresh new look at Mormon theology.

"*This Is My Doctrine*" will provide those already versed in Mormonism's theological tradition with a new and richer perspective of Mormon theology. Those unacquainted with Mormonism will gain an appreciation for how Mormon theology fits into the larger Jewish and Christian theological traditions.

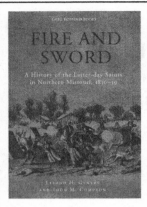

Fire and Sword: A History of the Latter-day Saints in Northern Missouri, 1836-39

Leland Homer Gentry and Todd M. Compton

Hardcover, ISBN: 978-1-58958-103-6

Many Mormon dreams flourished in Missouri. So did many Mormon nightmares.

The Missouri period—especially from the summer of 1838 when Joseph took over vigorous, personal direction of this new Zion until the spring of 1839 when he escaped after five months of imprisonment—represents a moment of intense crisis in Mormon history. Representing the greatest extremes of devotion and violence, commitment and intolerance, physical suffering and terror—mobbings, battles, massacres, and political "knockdowns"—it shadowed the Mormon psyche for a century.

Leland Gentry was the first to step beyond this disturbing period as a one-sided symbol of religious persecution and move toward understanding it with careful documentation and evenhanded analysis. In Fire and Sword, Todd Compton collaborates with Gentry to update this foundational work with four decades of new scholarship, more insightful critical theory, and the wealth of resources that have become electronically available in the last few years.

Compton gives full credit to Leland Gentry's extraordinary achievement, particularly in documenting the existence of Danites and in attempting to tell the Missourians' side of the story; but he also goes far beyond it, gracefully drawing into the dialogue signal interpretations written since Gentry and introducing the raw urgency of personal writings, eyewitness journalists, and bemused politicians seesawing between human compassion and partisan harshness. In the lush Missouri landscape of the Mormon imagination where Adam and Eve had walked out of the garden and where Adam would return to preside over his posterity, the towering religious creativity of Joseph Smith and clash of religious stereotypes created a swift and traumatic frontier drama that changed the Church.

The Lost 116 Pages: Reconstructing the Book of Mormon's Missing Stories

Don Bradley

Paperback, ISBN: 978-1-58958-760-1
Hardcover, ISBN: 978-1-58958-040-4

On a summer day in 1828, Book of Mormon scribe and witness Martin Harris was emptying drawers, upending furniture, and ripping apart mattresses as he desperately looked for a stack of papers he had sworn to God to protect. Those pages containing the only copy of the first three months of Joseph Smith's translation of the golden plates were forever lost, and the detailed stories they held forgotten over the ensuing years—until now.

In this highly anticipated work, author Don Bradley presents over a decade of historical and scriptural research to not only tell the story of the lost pages but to reconstruct many of the detailed stories written on them. Questions explored and answered include:

+ Was the lost manuscript actually 116 pages?
+ How did Mormon's abridgment of this period differ from the accounts in Nephi's small plates?
+ Where did the brass plates and Laban's sword come from?
+ How did Lehi's family and their descendants live the Law of Moses without the temple and Aaronic priesthood?
+ How did the Liahona operate?
+ Why is Joseph of Egypt emphasized so much in the Book of Mormon?
+ How were the first Nephites similar to the very last?
+ What message did God write on the temple wall for Aminadi to translate?
+ How did the Jaredite interpreters come into the hands of the Nephite kings?
+ Why was King Benjamin so beloved by his people?

Despite the likely demise of those pages to the sands of time, the answers to these questions and many more are now available for the first time in nearly two centuries in *The Lost 116 Pages: Reconstructing the Book of Mormon's Missing Stories.*

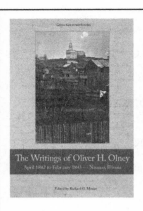

The Writings of Oliver Olney: April 1842 to February 1843 — Nauvoo, Illinois

Edited by Richard G. Moore

Hardcover, ISBN: 978-1-58958-762-5

Oliver H. Olney, an early convert to The Church of Jesus Christ of Latter-day Saints, fled to Nauvoo, Illinois, following persecution in Missouri. In Nauvoo, Olney became disgruntled with church leadership and viewed Joseph Smith as a fallen prophet. His writings, consisting of journal entries, letters, and booklets, express his concerns about what he viewed as serious iniquity within the Church. Despite his opposition to church leadership resulting in his excommunication, Olney remained in Nauvoo and wrote about the things he witnessed.

The handwritten papers of Oliver Olney are housed in the Beinecke Rare Book and Manuscript Library at Yale University and are made available in published form for the first time. They offer historical researchers and interested readers of the early Latter-day Saint movement a unique glimpse from the margins of religious society in Nauvoo. Olney's writings add light to key events in early Mormonism such as rumors of polygamy, the influence of Free Masonry in Nauvoo, plans to migrate westward to the Rocky Mountains, as well as growing tensions with disaffected church members and rising conflict with Nauvoo's non-Mormon neighbors.

Praise for *The Writings of Oliver Olney*:

"Provides historians a chance to view the unprecedented extent of social upheaval, revelatory innovation, and deep confusion present in this important moment in Mormon history" — Benjamin E. Park, author, *Kingdom of Nauvoo: The Rise and Fall of a Religious Empire on the American Frontier*

"Such a rare collection of documents . . . is crucial to gain an understanding of Nauvoo during the time of Joseph Smith." — Steven L. Shields, author, *Divergent Paths of the Restoration*

The Annals of the Southern Mission:
A Record of the History of
the Settlement of Southern Utah

James Godson Bleak
Edited by Aaron McArthur and Reid L. Neilson

Hardcover, ISBN: 978-1-58958-652-9

James G. Bleak's *Annals of the Southern Mission* (1900–1907) number 2,266 loose and lined pages and represent the finest early history of Southern Utah stretching from its initial Mormon settlement in 1849 into the early years of the twentieth century.

Bleak submitted the first portion of the history, numbering over 500 pages, to the Church Historian's Office in April 1903. He submitted additional increments of the manuscript when he visited Salt Lake City, usually for general conferences. He delivered the final installment of his Annals to the Historian's Office in October 1907. The complete holograph manuscript has been in the continuous custody of the Church History Department (formerly the Church Historian's Office) ever since.

Carefully transcribed and annotated by Aaron McArthur and Reid L. Neilson, this important work provides a detailed historical, ecclesiastical, agricultural, governmental, and cultural record of Southern Utah in the latter half of the nineteenth century.

Praise for *The Annals of the Southern Mission*:

"Professional historians and lay readers will be inspired by this vivid account of the pioneer experiences mostly before statehood or modernization. Developing water systems, establishing schools, creating courts and laws, constructing civic and commercial building and homes, raising food and animals promoting the arts, and generating faith and community harmony in some forty villages in Southern Utah and nearby Nevada and Arizona are all captured by James G.. Bleak. We will all be indebted to Brandon Metcalf for the fine Introduction and to Aaron McArthur and Reid Nielson for their brilliant editing of this important and extensive document." —Douglas Alder, Professor Emeritus and Former President of Dixie College

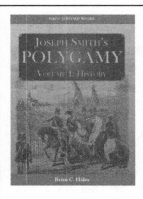

Joseph Smith's Polygamy, 3 Vols.

Brian Hales

Hardcover
Volume 1: History 978-1-58958-189-0
Volume 2: History 978-1-58958-548-5
Volume 3: Theology 978-1-58958-190-6

Perhaps the least understood part of Joseph Smith's life and teachings is his introduction of polygamy to the Saints in Nauvoo. Because of the persecution he knew it would bring, Joseph said little about it publicly and only taught it to his closest and most trusted friends and associates before his martyrdom.

In this three-volume work, Brian C. Hales provides the most comprehensive faithful examination of this much misunderstood period in LDS Church history. Drawing for the first time on every known account, Hales helps us understand the history and teachings surrounding this secretive practice and also addresses and corrects many of the numerous allegations and misrepresentations concerning it. Hales further discusses how polygamy was practiced during this time and why so many of the early Saints were willing to participate in it.

Joseph Smith's Polygamy is an essential resource in understanding this challenging and misunderstood practice of early Mormonism.

Praise for *Joseph Smith's Polygamy*:

"Brian Hales wants to face up to every question, every problem, every fear about plural marriage. His answers may not satisfy everyone, but he gives readers the relevant sources where answers, if they exist, are to be found. There has never been a more thorough examination of the polygamy idea." —Richard L. Bushman, author of *Joseph Smith: Rough Stone Rolling*

"Hales's massive and well documented three volume examination of the history and theology of Mormon plural marriage, as introduced and practiced during the life of Joseph Smith, will now be the standard against which all other treatments of this important subject will be measured." —Danel W. Bachman, author of "A Study of the Mormon Practice of Plural Marriage before the Death of Joseph Smith"

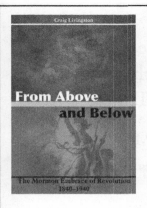

From Above and Below: The Mormon Embrace of Revolution, 1840–1940

Craig Livingston

Paperback, ISBN: 978-1-58958-621-5

**2014 Best International Book Award,
Mormon History Association**

Praise for *From Above and Below*:

"In this engaging study, Craig Livingston examines Mormon responses to political revolutions across the globe from the 1840s to the 1930s. Latter-day Saints saw utopian possibilities in revolutions from the European tumults of 1848 to the Mexican Revolution. Highlighting the often radical anti-capitalist and anti-imperialist rhetoric of Mormon leaders, Livingston demonstrates how Latter-day Saints interpreted revolutions through their unique theology and millennialism."
--Matthew J. Grow, author of *Liberty to the Downtrodden: Thomas L. Kane, Romantic Reformer*

"Craig Livingston's landmark book demonstrates how 21st-century Mormonism's arch-conservatism was preceded by its pro-revolutionary worldview that was dominant from the 1830s to the 1930s. Shown by current opinion-polling to be the most politically conservative religious group in the United States, contemporary Mormons are unaware that leaders of the LDS Church once praised radical liberalism and violent revolutionaries. By this pre-1936 Mormon view, 'The people would reduce privilege and exploitation in the crucible of revolution, then reforge society in a spiritual union of peace' before the Coming of Christ and His Millennium. With profound research in Mormon sources and in academic studies about various social revolutions and political upheavals, Livingston provides a nuanced examination of this little-known dimension of LDS thought which tenuously balanced pro-revolutionary enthusiasms with anti-mob sentiments."
--D. Michael Quinn, author of *Elder Statesman: A Biography of J. Reuben Clark*

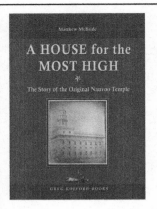

A House for the Most High: The Story of the Original Nauvoo Temple

Matthew McBride

Hardcover, ISBN: 978-1-58958-016-9

This awe-inspiring book is a tribute to the perseverance of the human spirit. *A House for the Most High* is a groundbreaking work from beginning to end with its faithful and comprehensive documentation of the Nauvoo Temple's conception. The behind-the-scenes stories of those determined Saints involved in the great struggle to raise the sacred edifice bring a new appreciation to all readers. McBride's painstaking research now gives us access to valuable first-hand accounts that are drawn straight from the newspaper articles, private diaries, journals, and letters of the steadfast participants.

The opening of this volume gives the reader an extraordinary window into the early temple-building labors of the besieged Church of Jesus Christ of Latter-day Saints, the development of what would become temple-related doctrines in the decade prior to the Nauvoo era, and the 1839 advent of the Saints in Illinois. The main body of this fascinating history covers the significant years, starting from 1840, when this temple was first considered, to the temple's early destruction by a devastating natural disaster. A well-thought-out conclusion completes the epic by telling of the repurchase of the temple lot by the Church in 1937, the lot's excavation in 1962, and the grand announcement in 1999 that the temple would indeed be rebuilt. Also included are an astonishing appendix containing rare and fascinating eyewitness descriptions of the temple and a bibliography of all major source materials. Mormons and non-Mormons alike will discover, within the pages of this book, a true sense of wonder and gratitude for a determined people whose sole desire was to build a sacred and holy temple for the worship of their God.

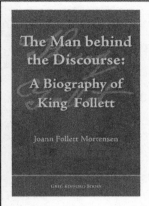

The Man behind the Discourse: A Biography of King Follett

Joann Follett Mortensen

ISBN: 978-1-58958-036-7

Who was King Follett? When he was fatally injured digging a well in Nauvoo in March 1844, why did Joseph Smith use his death to deliver the monumental doctrinal sermon now known as the King Follett Discourse? Much has been written about the sermon, but little about King.

Although King left no personal writings, Joann Follett Mortensen, King's third great-granddaughter, draws on more than thirty years of research in civic and Church records and in the journals and letters of King's peers to piece together King's story from his birth in New Hampshire and moves westward where, in Ohio, he and his wife, Louisa, made the life-shifting decision to accept the new Mormon religion.

From that point, this humble, hospitable, and hardworking family followed the Church into Missouri where their devotion to Joseph Smith was refined and burnished. King was the last Mormon prisoner in Missouri to be released from jail. According to family lore, King was one of the Prophet's bodyguards. He was also a Danite, a Mason, and an officer in the Nauvoo Legion. After his death, Louisa and their children settled in Iowa where some associated with the Cutlerities and the RLDS Church; others moved on to California. One son joined the Mormon Battalion and helped found Mormon communities in Utah, Idaho, and Arizona.

While King would have died virtually unknown had his name not been attached to the discourse, his life story reflects the reality of all those whose faith became the foundation for a new religion. His biography is more than one man's life story. It is the history of the early Restoration itself.

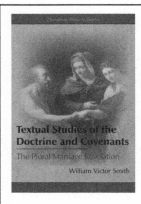

Textual Studies of the Doctrine and Covenants: The Plural Marriage Revelation

William Victor Smith

Paperback, ISBN: 978-1-58958-690-1
Hardcover, ISBN: 978-1-58958-691-8

Joseph Smith's July 12, 1843, revelation on plural marriage was the last of his formal written revelations and a transformational moment in Mormonism. While acting today as the basis for the doctrine of eternal nuclear families, the revelation came forth during a period of theological expansion as Smith was in the midst of introducing new temple rituals, radical doctrines on God and humanity, a restructured priesthood and ecclesiastical hierarchy, and, of course, the practice of plural marriage.

In this volume, author William V. Smith examines the text of this complicated and rough revelation to explore the motivation for its existence, how it reflects this dynamic theology of the Nauvoo period, and how the revelation was utilized and reinterpreted as Mormonism fully embraced and later abandoned polygamy.

Praise for *Textual Studies*:

"No Mormon text is as ritually important and as fundamentally mysterious as Doctrine and Covenants 132. William V. Smith's work is a fine example of what a serious-minded and meticulous blend of source and redaction critical methods can tell us about the revelations produced by Joseph Smith. This is a model of what the future of Mormon scriptural studies should be." — Stephen C. Taysom, author of *Shakers, Mormons, and Religious Worlds: Conflicting Visions, Contested Boundaries*

Made in the USA
Las Vegas, NV
01 February 2024

85162997R00319